Auditing and GRC Automation in SAP

Maxim Chuprunov

Auditing and
GRC Automation
in SAP

 Springer

Maxim Chuprunov
Riscomp GmbH
Rothenthurm, Switzerland

ISBN 978-3-642-43452-5   ISBN 978-3-642-35302-4 (eBook)
DOI 10.1007/978-3-642-35302-4

©2011 by Galileo Press, Bonn, Germany.
Title of the German original: Handbuch SAP-Revision
ISBN: 978-3-8362-1603-6

ACM Computing Classification (1998): J.1, K.4, K.5, K.6

Springer
© Springer-Verlag Berlin Heidelberg 2013
Softcover re-print of the Hardcover 1st edition 2013

Printed on acid-free paper.

Springer is part of Springer Science+Business Media
www.springer.com

Foreword

Over the last few years, financial statement scandals, cases of fraud and corruption, data protection violations, and other legal violations have led to numerous liability cases, damages claims, and loss of reputations. As a reaction to these developments, numerous regulations have been issued: Corporate Governance, Sarbanes-Oxley Act, IFRS, Basel II and III, Solvency II, BilMoG, to name just a few. The requirements behind these regulations are complex and no longer affect only internationally active listed companies – the topic of "compliance" has also found its way into management levels and monitoring bodies (such as supervisory boards, internal audit teams, auditing).

Under the term *compliance*, we generally understand the observance of legislation, guidelines, and voluntary codes within an organization. There are generally recognized framework concepts for setting up a compliance management system (for example, COSO, OECD principles of corporate governance), along with framework concepts that emphasize the specific details of individual industries or compliance-relevant areas (for example, FDA compliance).

The first step has been taken in many ways: organizations have reacted to the flood of national and international compliance laws and directives and have taken measures to ensure compliance. The task now is to integrate the individual activities, such as the internal control system, the risk management system, contract management, internal audit, etc. in a compliance management system and – as far as possible – to automate it in order to achieve a balance between compliance and performance. The observance of compliance alone represents an additional cost factor for organizations; it is only with the balance between compliance and performance that the opportunities offered by the implementation of the regulatory requirements can be used. Therefore, the improvements in the processes, combined with efficiency increases, can and should be implemented within the scope of observance of the regulatory requirements. In general, an improvement in and standardization of the processes, under consideration of regulatory requirements, requires the inclusion of the IT systems; here, the SAP solutions for GRC are an option.

The literature currently available restricts itself primarily to mapping controls in SAP ERP and auditing SAP systems. This book also provides help in this respect, but goes far beyond this content. Starting with the requirements for compliance (Part I), it not only addresses and answers compliance-relevant questions in the form of an audit guide for an SAP ERP system (Part II), but also shows how to map an (automated) compliance management system in an SAP ERP system (Part III). This book thus addresses the current need for solutions for implementing compliance management systems in an organization. Furthermore, the book shows which risks and controls internal and external audit should focus on when auditing an internal control system mapped in SAP or a compliance management system.

The implementation of a compliance management system in SAP ERP requires knowledge of both the underlying legislation and legal standards and the technical options for implementation. In this book, Maxim Chuprunov has applied his extensive experience from both areas. This experience comes from his professional career to date, during which he has been involved on one hand with auditing IT systems in general, and SAP systems in particular, and on the other hand with the implementation of SAP ERP systems and the SAP solutions for GRC.

I am convinced that it is precisely this combination of theoretical and practical knowledge that make this book so special. Both those who decide on and those who implement compliance and compliance management systems in an organization, as well as internal and external auditors and monitoring bodies, will benefit from this book in their respective fields of activities.

Annett Nowatzki, member of the board of directors at DSJ Revision und Treuhand AG, Berlin.

Trust Is Good, Control Is Cheaper: Introduction

The necessity of overcoming risks and establishing an internal control system (ICS) is at the very top of the agenda for top management in organizations and has brought audit and consultancy companies good business for many years.

Can the implementation of legal requirements have a deeper meaning and benefit beyond simply complying with legislation? Of course it can – if you do it correctly. Experience from practice shows the following:

Why compliance?

- One aspect that is often neglected is the fact that due to its traditional orientation on compliance, an ICS can also include the monitoring of business processes with regard to efficiency, profitability, and performance. Therefore, an ICS is not just about legislation.
- Even if the compliance is only in the sense of legislative compliance, this is generally more cost-effective as non-compliance can be expensive (as shown, for example, by the bribery scandal at SIEMENS in 2006, which was covered extensively in the press).
- As a set of rules issued by the state in the exercise of its regulatory role, compliance protects the general public from many evils. You may remember the spectacular bankruptcies of ENRON, FLOWTEX, etc. Amongst other things, they were caused by manipulation of external financial reporting.
- Various compliance initiatives require that complex processes in an organization are described cleanly (often for the first time). It is easier to control transparent processes, and the controls identified also benefit business operation.
- An inefficient compliance management process uses up a lot of resources. Automating this process can ease the workload for the organization's management considerably.
- And last but not least: compliance can have direct financial advantages, such as lower capital lockup as a result of more precise or risk-specific equity definition, or cheaper credit due to an improved rating by rating agencies.

Thus, there are numerous reasons for considering compliance requirements as something other than just a necessary evil. However, efficient implementation of these requirements and setting up an effective ICS were, and still are, not easy:

Why is compliance a challenge?

- The complex ERP environment requires specific know-how, and in the case of IT-supported business processes, it is not always clear what risks they bear and what control mechanisms are in place.
- Neglecting compliance requirements during the implementation of an SAP system can have serious consequences. Hindsight is always a great thing – but not considering compliance requirements when implementing SAP generally makes you poorer. Implementing SAP is a costly undertaking and a subsequent redesign is time-consuming and expensive.
- Controls must be lived: it is not the controls that are correctly documented and tested that are effective, but those that are actually executed. However, without a check, compliance is unimaginable – but the automation that is often missing

in practice causes a great deal of administrative effort. Microsoft Excel sheets, e-mails, and manual system evaluations often dominate the audit and ICS world, and real-time reporting is frequently not possible.

- The automation of an ICS could provide answers to many of the questions that currently occupy the world of compliance:
    - How can you bring operative and audit-specific views of control mechanisms together?
    - Is real-time reporting of the status of compliance available at the push of a button?
    - How can you map the ICS so that the different requirements of risk management, internal audit, external financial statement audit, and industry-specific control are fulfilled efficiently?

How to do it correctly   In order to implement an ICS correctly, you have to bring together many parts of the puzzle:

- Internal ICS and compliance objectives with regard to efficiency, profitability, and performance
- Legal requirements and their effect on today's world of ERP-supported processes
- "Translation" of the compliance requirements into the language of a respective ERP system – for example, SAP ERP
- Design and structure of an ICS model in the IT environment
- Automation of an ICS compliance process
- Automation of test and monitoring scenarios through integration
- Handling of internal and external audit as well as risk management integration.

The highly topical and exciting overview and the vision of the automated ICS and compliance processes in the SAP ERP environment of a well-managed organization, in which the individual pieces of the puzzle come together, motivated me to write this book.

Subject, Structure, and Content of the Book

Ever-increasing requirements   The big wave of legislation-driven ICS projects was triggered by the Sarbanes-Oxley Act in 2002. It also affected all European companies listed on the US stock exchange. Gradually, the requirements and risks etc. to be made transparent and minimized by the ICS encroached on other organizations in Europe through EU directives and other local legal initiatives. Overall, the worldwide trend, regardless of whether we consider the impending introduction of China SOX or developments in other emerging markets, shows that a functioning ICS, as a compliance requirement demanded by the state, is establishing itself quickly.

Compliance as part of GRC   The topic of governance, risk, and compliance as a single concept (referred to as an integrated GRC approach) appeared on the market only recently, and the merging of GRC with the topics of strategy and performance is a very new trend. It is reflected in relevant software solutions as well as recognized reference models. Thus, it is no longer appropriate to consider compliance in isolation.

In this book, compliance is understood as the process, mapped in an ICS, that is intended to guarantee conformity with legal requirements and internal policies and objectives (in particular, efficiency and profitability). An ICS was already known before the age of the computer, but new special features have arisen with the progress of information technology: the transaction audit as an audit approach, and in particular, the consideration of the ICS and the software-specific application controls within the framework of external audit have become established as mandatory. The answer to the question of what that all means for organizations whose processes run with ERP support must be clearly structured and described.

ICS in the IT environment

The last few years have seen an increase in the number of software products on the market that allow you to design the ICS process efficiently – where applicable, in interaction with risk management. However, the basic understanding of the processes in an IT-supported compliance management process is not delivered with the software.

Compliance at the push of a button

As you have seen, there are numerous puzzle pieces around the highly topical issues of ICS and compliance. You have to bring them together to get a good overview. This book considers the connection of compliance with the other parts of GRC (corporate governance and risk management), insofar as this is required by the integration view, in order to indicate the possible synergies and to explain the integrated GRC approach. This book, however, focuses on ICS compliance itself. It looks at this topic from the view of an SAP ERP-dominated IT environment, and develops it, from a design perspective, in three stages:

Concept of this book

1. From legislation to concept
2. From concept to content
3. From concept and content to automation

Figure 1 summarizes the idea and structure of this book.

PART I – From Legislation to Concept: ICS and Compliance in the ERP Environment

ICS compliance in the SAP ERP environment – these words trigger many questions, even for experts: Which view of compliance is meant? Which legal and internal requirements are in focus? What does an integrated GRC approach based on SAP software look like? The first part of the book provides answers to these fundamental questions.

In **Chap. 1**, "Legal Requirements in ICS Compliance," you will learn what is understood under the term ICS, and what the relevant legal compliance requirements are in an international and cross-industry comparison.

Chapter 2, "The Auditor Is Coming: When, Why, and How to Cope," explains the special conditions that the audit in the IT environment is subject to and summarizes the most important facts and recommendations from audit practice.

In **Chap. 3**, "ICS Requirements and ERP Systems: Basic Principles, Frameworks, Structure," we show you the basic principles for defining the content of an ICS in the SAP ERP environment and the internationally recognized studies and reference models that can help you to do this. The chapter highlights the importance of the continuous

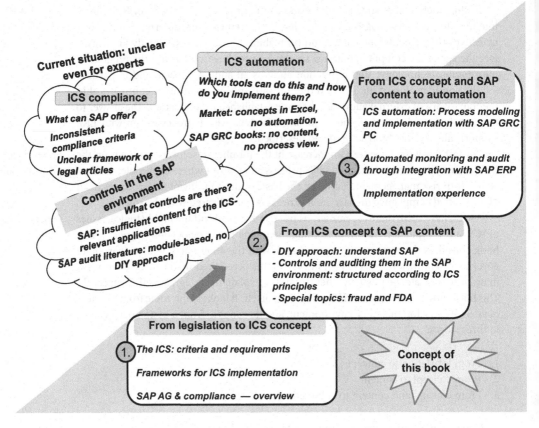

Figure 1 Concept of this book

monitoring approach. A new feature in this edition is the description of how to set up an efficiency-oriented and profitability-oriented ICS framework.

Chapter 4, "How Does SAP Deal with Risk- and Compliance-Related Topics?" summarizes the most important facts for making your compliance-relevant processes more efficient. These facts range from certification of SAP software solutions to sources of documentation for control mechanisms in SAP and an itemization of the software products. This chapter also describes the integrated GRC approach that is based on the components of the SAP solutions for GRC Release 10.0.

PART II – From Concept to Content: Audit Guide for SAP ERP

How do you translate the ICS compliance requirements into the language of SAP? What risks and controls are there in SAP ERP-supported processes? And how can you implement and monitor the efficiency of the SAP ERP-supported processes? You will find the answers to these questions in the second part of the book.

In **Chap. 5**, "Audit-Relevant SAP Basics," we explain the basic connections in the SAP system and provide you with a tool for an independent search for control- and audit-relevant information in SAP ERP.

Chapter 6, "IT General Controls in SAP ERP," looks at both general organizational controls and topics around change management, critical authorizations, and the basic system security.

In **Chap. 7**, "General Application Controls in SAP ERP," you will learn how to ensure the general observance of the principles of traceability and completeness during processing in SAP ERP.

The titles of **Chap. 8**, "Controls in Financial Accounting," **Chap. 9**, "Control Mechanisms in the SAP ERP-Supported Procure to Pay Process," and **Chap. 10**, "Control Mechanisms in the SAP ERP-Supported Order to Cash Process" speak for themselves: these SAP-supported processes bear risks that directly endanger observance of compliance. The related control mechanisms are vital for survival and are described in the respective chapters.

In **Chap. 11**, "Data Protection Compliance in SAP ERP Human Capital Management," you will learn which legal requirements regulate the treatment of personal data and how to implement these requirements in SAP ERP.

Chapter 12, "Fraud in an SAP System," is dedicated to the topic of fraud. There is always a risk of fraudulent activities wherever material values and money are dealt with using SAP. In this chapter we use examples to show how you can handle this risk.

Chapter 13, "Excursion: FDA Compliance and Controls in SAP," affects every reader of this book either directly or indirectly: the control mechanisms required by law in the pharmaceuticals and food industries, which focus primarily on the quality of the products manufactured, must be mapped in the SAP processes. We address the most important of these controls here.

Chapter 14, "Examples of Efficiency-Oriented and Profitability-Oriented Analysis Scenarios in SAP ERP," gives detailed examples for each of the four elements of an efficiency-oriented ICS framework: process-oriented analyses, quality of master data, master data changes and user input, and supplementing reports. The aim of the high level of detail presented is to provide you with "do-it-yourself" instructions for setting up various analysis scenarios. It is also intended to give you an impression of the work involved in implementing continuous monitoring scenarios.

PART III – From Concept and Content to Implementation: Automation of an Internal Control System

Compliance at the push of a button is a realistic scenario. Software products that help you to automate an ICS are now available on the market. What is not widely available on the market, however, is a range of ICS processes and ICS content, together with their software-based implementation, from one source. On one hand, the Big Four auditing companies, as well as various compliance consultancy agencies, offer ICS content and concepts often based on Microsoft Excel; on the other hand, the conceptual compliance view is missing in both existing literature about ICS and GRC software and from consultants from software companies. The aim of this part of the book is to give you both conceptual and technical instructions for implementing ICS and compliance management processes (based on the SAP solutions for GRC Release 10.0).

In **Chap. 15**, "ICS Automation: How to Set the COSO Cube in Motion," we address the conceptual importance of ICS automation and explain the individual building blocks that you can use to model the automation of ICS processes. You do this in the form of an ICS implementation matrix.

In **Chap. 16**, "ICS Automation Using SAP Process Control," we show you how to implement the compliance and ICS management process using SAP GRC Process Control. You will also learn why, and using which integration scenarios, Process Control can be seen as part of an integrated GRC concept and strategy and performance management concept.

In **Chap. 17**, "Implementation of Automated Test and Monitoring Scenarios in the SAP ERP Environment," we explain which options – including the integration of SAP Process Control with your SAP ERP systems – make the great vision of a "test at the push of a button" possible. We will take you step-by-step through the setup of the continuous monitoring approach in SAP GRC Process Control 10.0.

Chapter 18, "Experiences from Practice and Projects," presents numerous project experiences that show how organizations from various industries have automated their compliance processes. The chapter summarizes the most important facts about project setup for implementing SAP GRC Process Control and gives some examples of implementation projects at SAP customers.

Target Audience for this Book

As a reader, what existing knowledge do you have? Although only healthy common sense and some basic business knowledge is required for Part I of this book, overall, and particularly for the remaining parts, SAP ERP experience would be an advantage. A compliance and ICS consultancy background is ideal for this book.

Who is the target audience for this book?

- **ICS owners, internal audit employees, external auditors, IT auditors, compliance experts**
  This is the book for you – from the first to the last chapter!
- **Managers of SAP competence centers, project managers, data governance experts, business analysts, and consultants for SAP ERP implementations**
  It is not easy to consider the compliance requirements when implementing SAP ERP. Therefore, Part I and Part II in particular provide you with important information for designing your implementation projects so that they are audit-compliant and ICS-compliant, and for daily operation of the SAP ERP applications.
- **SAP consultants for SAP GRC Products**
  Part III should be mandatory reading for you. In your implementation projects, where the focus is on the process view of the ICS, you should never lose the reference to the ICS content: therefore, Part II is also important for you. And last but not least: it is essential that you understand the complex connections between legal requirements and the implementation of these requirements in the IT environment in order to find a common compliance language with customers. Therefore, Part I would also be relevant for you.
- **MBA, business, and information management students**
  Part I and Part II of this book are particularly interesting for you: Part I looks in detail at the legal requirements in an international comparison, as well as the business

design of the ICS in the IT environment. The overview of internationally recognized GRC reference models could also be interesting for you. Part III explains what the automation of an ICS means from a concept perspective.

- **Senior management**
Regardless of whether you are the CFO, CEO, or CIO in your organization, or are fulfilling your duties in the executive board or audit committee, you will not have been able to escape compliance issues. Even if you do not use SAP for processes in your organization, and a correct definition of the SAP-specific content of your ICS is irrelevant for you, you will certainly have thought about designing the ICS efficiently: the experiences of other organizations in handling ICS and compliance topics as described in Part II will provide you with good points of reference. Furthermore, the legal and other compliance requirements, recommendations for dealing with the external audit, and the overview of the GRC framework concepts from Part I of this book will be of interest to you. You should also not miss out on the visionary and conceptual explanations on the topic of "compliance at the push of a button" in Part III.

Notes for Reading this Book

This book contains various orientation aids that will help you to read it.

Gray information boxes provide information that is helpful and good to know, but that stands apart somewhat from the actual explanation text. To enable you to categorize the information in the boxes immediately, we have assigned symbols to the boxes:

Information boxes

Tip Start	❶

- The *Tips* and *Notes* identified by this symbol provide recommendations that will make your work easier. These boxes also contain information on further topics or important content that you should note.

 **Important Start**
- The *Caution* symbol draws your attention to topics or areas where you should exercise particular caution.

Example Start	[e.g.]

- *Examples*, indicated by this symbol, indicate scenarios from practice and illustrate the functions presented.

Marginal notes enable you to search the book for topics you are particularly interested in or to find parts that you have already read. The marginal notes are adjacent to the respective section that contains the corresponding information.

Marginal notes

The audit procedures that are integrated in the presentation, for example, are indicated throughout the book with the marginal note "Check:" (followed in each case by key words reflecting the content).

Acknowledgments

Now it is time to thank everyone without whose support I would not have been able to complete this book project.

The English edition of the book, which you are currently holding, would not have been possible without the highly professional translation by Tracey Duffy (TSD Translations). In addition to, in my opinion, a very successful translation, Tracey Duffy also contributed to the quality of this book with her comments regarding content and with her great attention to detail. Many thanks also to Ralf Gerstner (Springer) for his expert advice and support in this project.

During the time in which I wrote this book, in addition to my main task as managing director and consultant at Riscomp GmbH, and parallel to many exciting projects, my friends and family often had to do without me. I would firstly like to thank them for their understanding and support.

Many people gave me comments, ideas, and information on various questions: many thanks to the SAP experts Jürgen Möller, Dominik Yow-Sin-Cheung, Daniel Welzbacher, Jan Gardiner, David Ramsay, and Atul Sudhalkar – for support in tricky questions surrounding the SAP GRC suite. Heartfelt thanks also to Dr. Karol Bliznak (SAP AG) for input regarding mapping the "risk-intelligent strategic execution" approach with SAP products. I would also like to thank Jürg Kasper (Canton Zürich) for his creative input regarding the automation of test and monitoring scenarios.

Esteemed colleagues have also written contributions to this book: with his highly competent and proven in practice description of the control mechanisms in the SAP ERP-supported Procure to Pay and Order to Cash processes, Gerhard Wasnick relieved me of a great deal of work. Günther Emmenegger (SAP Schweiz AG) wrote the chapter on mapping FDA-requirements in the SAP environment. Volker Lehnert wrote the majority of the chapter on data-protection relevant controls in SAP ERP HCM. Marc Michely (PricewaterhouseCoopers) contributed the section on fraud scenarios in SAP. The practical reports on mapping compliance requirements arose in close cooperation with Jan Laurisjen (Ericsson) and Michele Poffo (Tecan). Reto Bachmann provided input for the contribution on efficiency-oriented scenarios. Andreas Wiegenstein (Virtualforge) has contributed to the Sect. 6.4.2 describing key elements of the ABAP code security.

For various support, information, and help, I would also like to thank Dr. Michael Adam (SAP AG), Dr. Gero Mäder, Thomas Schmale (SAP AG), Evelyn Salie (SAP Schweiz AG), Arnold Babel (SAP Schweiz AG), Peter Heidkamp (KPMG), Florian Köller (SAP AG), Walter Harrer (SAP Schweiz AG), and Christian Brunner (SAP Schweiz AG).

Two, three, or four heads are better than one: Annett Nowatzki (DSJ Revision und Treuhand AG) and Patricia Sprenger at Galileo Press read first drafts, preliminary versions, and raw versions, as well as the finished text of the German edition of the book and improved it with their comments.

Despite the support that I have received from many quarters, I alone am responsible for any errors that remain.

I hope that this book will help you to solve your tasks concerning compliance, audit, and ICS automation with SAP, and wish you every success and enjoyment with your reading.

Maxim Chuprunov

Contents

II From Concept to Content: Audit Guide for SAP ERP

III   From Concept and Content to Implementation: Automation of an Internal Control System

List of Abbreviations

AAF	Audit and Assurance Faculty Standard
AASB	Auditing and Assurance Standards Board
ACF	Automated Controls Framework
ACP	Acquisition and production costs
ADA	Asset database
AICPA	American Institute of Certified Public Accountants
AIS	Audit Information System
AktG	Aktiengesetz [Stock Corporation Act] (Germany)
AM	SAP Audit Management
AMF	Autorité des marchés financiers (France)
AMF	Automated Monitoring Framework
AMS	Application Management Services
ARF	Automated Rules Framework
ARM	Access Risk Management
AS	SAP NetWeaver Application Server
ASAP	Accelerated SAP
BaFin	Bundesanstalt für Finanzdienstleistungsaufsicht [Federal Financial Supervisory Authority] (Germany)
BC Set	Business Configuration Set
BDSG	Bundesdatenschutzgesetz [Data Protection Act] (Germany)
BetrVG	Betriebsverfassungsgesetz [Works Council Constitution Act] (Germany)
BMGS	Bundesministerium für Gesundheit und soziale Sicherung [Federal Ministry for Health and Social Affairs] (Germany)
BPP	Business Process Procedure
BRF	Business Rules Framework
BRG	Business Role Governance
BS	British Standard
BSI	Bundesamt für Sicherheit in der Informationstechnik [Federal Office for Information Security] (Germany)
CAAT	Computer Assisted Auditing Techniques
CAPA	Corrective And Preventive Actions
CATT	Computer Aided Test Tool
CCM	Continuous Control Monitoring
CCMS	Computer Center Management System
CEA	Centralized Emergency Access
CFR	Code of Federal Regulations (USA)
CHMP	Committee for Medicinal Products for Human Use
CICA	Canadian Institute of Chartered Accountants
CMF	Continuous Monitoring Framework
CMS	Compliance management software
CobiT	Control Objectives for Information and Related Technologies
COE	Council of Europe
COSO	Committee of Sponsoring Organizations of the Treadway Commission

CTS	Change and Transport Management System
CUP	Compliant User Provisioning
DART Tool	Data Retention Tool
DCGK	Deutscher Corporate Governance Kodex [Corporate Governance Code] (Germany)
DI	SAP NetWeaver Development Infrastructure
DMS	Documentation management system
eCATT	Extended CATT
ECN	Ericsson Corporate Network
ELC	Entity level controls
EMA	European Medicines Agency
EMEA	Economic zone Europe, Middle East, and Africa (Europe, Middle East, and Africa)
ERM	Enterprise Role Management
FDA	Food and Drug Administration (USA)
FEFO	First expired, first out
FIFO	First in, first out
FM	SAP Fraud Management
FOEN	Federal Office of the Environment (Switzerland)
FOPH	Federal Office of Public Health (Switzerland)
FPM	Financial Performance Management
FSA	Financial Services Agency
GAAP	Generally Accepted Accounting Principles
GAIT	Guide to the Assessment of IT Risk
GAMP	Good Automated Manufacturing Practice
GDPdU	Grundsätze zum Datenzugriff und zur Prüfbarkeit digitaler Unterlagen [Principles for data access and verifiability of digital documents] (Germany)
GLP	Good Laboratory Practice
GMP	Good Manufacturing Practice
GRC	Governance, risk, and compliance
GS	Guidance Statement
HCM	SAP ERP Human Capital Management
HIPAA	Health Insurance Portability and Accountability Act (USA)
HPFB	Health Products and Food Branch (Canada)
ICH	International Conference on Harmonization
IdM	SAP NetWeaver Identity Management
IDoc	Intermediate document
IDW	Institut der Wirtschaftsprüfer [Institute of Public Auditors] (Germany)
IFAC	International Federation of Accountants
IFRS	International Financial Reporting Standards
IIA	Institute of Internal Auditors
IMG	Implementation Guide
ISA	International Standards on Auditing
ISAE	International Standard on Assurance Engagements
ISPE	International Society for Pharmaceutical Engineering
ISS	Issue
ITAF	Information Technology Assurance Framework

ITIL	Information Technology Infrastructure Library
ITSEC	Information Technology Security Evaluation Criteria
ITSEM	IT Security Evaluation Manual
J-SOX	Japanese SOX
KDF	Vendor database
KonTraG	Gesetz zur Kontrolle und Transparenz im Unternehmensbereich [Control and Transparency in Business Act] (Germany)
KRI	Key Risk Indicator
LIFO	Last in, first out
LVA	Low value assets
MaRisk (VA)	Minimum Requirements for Risk Management (Germany, binding guideline)
MCF	Multiple Compliance Framework
MDEC	Medical Device Evaluation Committee (Australia)
MHLW	Ministry for Health, Labour and Welfare (Japan)
MOF	Microsoft Operations Framework
MQT	Multi Application Query Tool
MRC	Management Risk Controlling
NI	National Instrument
NPCB	National Pharmaceutical Control Bureau (Malaysia)
NWBC	SAP NetWeaver Business Client
OR	Correct reporting
P&L	Profit and loss statement
PC	SAP Process Control
PCI-DSS	Payment Card Industry Data Security Standard
PIC/S	Pharmaceutical Inspection Cooperation Scheme
PKI	Public Key Infrastructure
PMSB	Pharmaceutical and Medical Safety Bureau (Japan)
PublG	Publizitätsgesetz [Public Disclosure Act] (Germany)
RAR	Risk Analysis & Remediation
RBE	Reversed Business Engineering
REV	Review
RFC	Remote function call
RM	SAP Risk Management
RPL	Remediation plan
RTA	Real Time Agents
SAL	Security Audit Log
SAS	Self-assessment
SDF	G/L account database
SDM	Software Deployment Manager
SEC	Securities and Exchange Commission (USA)
SGB	Sozialgesetzbücher [Social Welfare Code] (Germany)
SHI	Swiss Agency for Therapeutic Products
SLA	Service Level Agreement
SoD	Segregation of duties
SOP	Standard Operation Procedure
SOS	Security Optimization Service
SOX	Sarbanes-Oxley Act

SPM	Superuser Privilege Management
SSO	Single sign-on
TGA	Therapeutic Goods Administration (Australia)
TMS	Transport Management System
UAM	User Access Management
UAR	User Access Review
UME	User Management Engine
VMP	Validation Master Plan
VRV	Invoice verification database: invoices
WIP	Work in progress

Part I   From Legislation to Concept: ICS and Compliance in the ERP Environment

Many readers will know this situation: the auditor is coming. Backed up by the power of the law, and juggling specialist terms such as compliance and internal control system, the auditor's (impending) presence in an organization often causes a tense atmosphere. Something that is often neglected is that the auditor can be helpful for your organization, and an ICS can certainly bring measurable benefits.

But before you can take any benefit from the auditor's visit, you have to understand why the auditor is coming and how you can satisfy his requirements. However, it is even more important to understand why it is primarily your organization itself, and not the auditor, that needs an ICS: it's not just about complying with legislation – it's also about profitability and efficiency.

This part of the book will give you an insight into the legal requirements that organizations have to consider and the observance of which the auditor has to check. You will also learn which rules organizations and auditors have to obey. We will also show you how an ICS is structured in the SAP environment, and which internationally recognized reference models can help you set up the GRC processes. After reading this part of the book, you will also know which products SAP offers for satisfying the compliance requirements as part of an integrated GRC approach.

Legal Requirements in ICS Compliance

On one hand there are laws to ensure compliance with various regulations; on the other hand there are other requirements that arise in an organization's own interests. In this chapter you will learn about the legal requirements in the area of ICS compliance and why, in contrast to widespread opinion, efficiency topics are also very much part of an ICS.

An internal control system (ICS) is a must for every organization. In contrast to profitability and efficiency, which are clearly in an organization's own interests, the legal framework that requires compliance with certain issues often appears unclear. In this chapter we summarize the most important legal provisions for you in an international comparison.

1.1 Definition of Terms and Differentiation

Before we look at the legal compliance requirements in depth, we must define two fundamental terms in this book more precisely: *compliance* and *internal control system*.

1.1.1 Compliance

What does *compliance* mean? If we were to put this question to a doctor, we would learn that the term refers to observing prescribed treatment of patients. The world of business processes, to which most readers of this book belong, can only relate to this in as much as some legal requirements that organizations have to comply with are perceived as a bitter (and quite expensive) pill to swallow.

    In this book, compliance means both legal conformity and harmony with the profitability-oriented and efficiency-oriented own interests of an organization. In detail, to comply with law, legal requirements connected to financial reporting and the associated risk management are important, as are ICS regulations, as shown by Fig. 1.1.

    Fraud or fraud-related issues are directly connected to the ICS topic. However, from the point of view of legislative authorities, penal law is applied directly in these cases and thus we will look at these issues separately (see Part II, in particular Chap. 12, "Fraud in an SAP System").

    In this book, when we describe important SAP application controls, we address industry-specific requirements of the US Food and Drug Administration (FDA, see Chap. 13, "Excursion: FDA Compliance and Controls in SAP") as well as similar European regulations and controls relevant for profitability and efficiency. We also address the important issue of data protection (see Chap. 11, "Data Protection Compliance in SAP ERP Human Capital Management").

Compliance with legal requirements

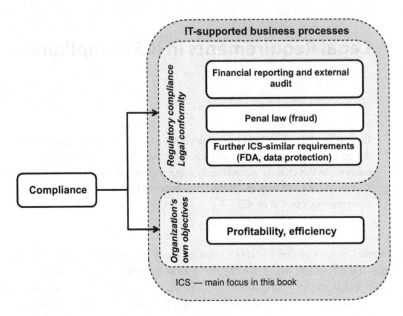

Figure 1.1   Use of the term "compliance" in this book

For the first time in literature known to the author, this book looks at the structure of the profitability-oriented and efficiency-oriented framework in the ERP environment systematically (see Sect. 3.1.5, "Structure of Efficiency-Oriented and Profitability-Oriented Controls in the ERP Environment"). It also gives appropriate examples from SAP ERP (Chap. 14, "Examples of Efficiency-Oriented and Profitability-Oriented Analysis Scenarios in SAP ERP").

Before looking at these topics, the first part of this book concentrates on the legal compliance requirements associated with external reporting and external audit.

1.1.2   Internal Control System (ICS)

We use controls to ensure that objectives are achieved and risks minimized. The ICS comprises all controls within an organization. One of its purposes is to ensure compliance with legal requirements.

Definition of an ICS   An ICS comprises the basic principles, procedures, and measures (regulations) introduced by the management of an organization and issued for the purposes of organizational implementation of the decisions taken by management. These decisions include, for example:

1. Decisions to safeguard the effectiveness and profitability of the business activity
2. Decisions to ensure correct and reliable internal and external reporting
3. Decisions to ensure compliance with the material legal regulations for the organization

It is generally easy to differentiate between the individual objectives of the ICS: while the first objective, profitability, focuses on profit, the second, correctness, is based on legal provisions. The aim of these provisions is to ensure that the annual financial statements communicated by the organization externally, including the details in the notes, are correct, and that the financial statements reflect the actual asset, finance, and revenue situation observing generally accepted accounting principles (GAAP). **Profitability vs. correctness**

If, for example, you use a control to address the risk of incorrect valuation or incorrect display of a specific financial statement item, then you are addressing the ICS objective of *correctness*.

Payment, Consideration of Cash Discount			**[e.g.]**

The difference between compliance-driven and profitability-driven controls becomes clear in the following example:

An organization can choose to pay invoices quickly and thus take advantage of cash discount, or to delay payment and thus the debit to the account.

- **Risk**
  If an organization does not take advantage of cash discount and pays invoices later, it loses the potential saving.
- **Control**
  The application controls in the payment functions in SAP can take terms of payment into account.
- **Relevance**
  Profitability: This control focuses on the principle of profitability. The law does not prohibit losses due to inefficient business processes, i. e., there is no direct reference to compliance.

To summarize: even if we can differentiate between the ICS objectives of compliance and profitability, they are not mutually exclusive. Generally, organizations follow both objectives in parallel.

1.2 Legal ICS Requirements Around the World – the Many Faces of SOX

There are a number of legal provisions and requirements from different authorities that organizations have to comply with and that address the necessity for a control system *directly*. The following pages give an overview of the most important direct ICS requirements in an international comparison.

The long-established *Sarbanes-Oxley Act* (SOX) originates from the USA. However, it is now used in other countries to describe local legal ICS requirements.

1.2.1 SOX in the USA

The Sarbanes-Oxley Act is the most well-known law originating in the USA and applicable for all organizations whose shares are traded on the US stock market. The law, **Origin of the term in the USA** passed on July 30, 2002 with the official name *Public Company Accounting Reform and Investor Protection Act*, has been renamed the Sarbanes-Oxley Act in practice after Senator Paul Sarbanes and the US Representative Michael G. Oxley, the people responsible for the legal initiative.

There are two main sections of US SOX:

SOX 302 – ICS   Section 302 directly requires an ICS that guarantees reliable financial reporting. According to this section, the management of an organization must confirm, in writing, their responsibility for setting up and maintaining such an ICS. Confirmation is also required that the ICS can ensure that the relevant information from other consolidated subsidiaries is also made available. Management must also publish statements about the effectiveness of the controls and disclose any weaknesses of the ICS to the auditor and the audit committee.

SOX 404 – ICS assessment   To comply with Section 404, the management of an organization must disclose the scope and effectiveness of the internal controls for financial reporting in an ICS report. An external auditor must also submit a confirmation. This regulation goes considerably further than the requirements in Section 302.

Scoping   In connection with US SOX, instructions are available on how to implement ICS requirements (for example, PCAOB Standard AS 5 and the interpretive instructions of the Securities and Exchange Commission, SEC – to a large extent identical to the auditing standard). These instructions give management some leeway when selecting relevant control mechanisms. They prescribe a top-down, risk-based selection of controls (the term *scoping* is often used here).

❶   Top-Down, Risk-Based Selection of Controls/Scoping

The top-down, risk-based selection of controls consists of the following steps:
- Identification of significant elements in financial reporting (G/L accounts or other details in the financial statements)
- Identification of material risks associated with these accounts or details
- Identification of controls across the organization (entity level controls, (ELC)) that address these risks with sufficient precision
- Identification of business process-related and transaction-related controls that address the remaining risks
- Identification of the type, scope, and period for which evidence must be provided and for the assessment of the selected controls

Penal consequences   Section 802 in US SOX allows for up to 20 years imprisonment in the event of evidence relevant for SOX in financial reporting being intentionally changed, falsified, destroyed, or concealed.

According to Section 1107, retaliation against persons who inform relevant authorities of violations of SOX provisions (known as *whistle blowers*) is punishable with up to 10 years imprisonment.

1.2.2 SOX in Canada (NI 52-109)

In NI 52-109 (*National Instrument*), also called *Canadian SOX*, the Canadian legislative authority requires to a large extent the same compliance with ICS requirements as US SOX. The main difference to US SOX is that according to Canadian law, no statement from the organization's management or external auditors is required with regard to the ICS. A further difference is that the Canadian legislative authority does not grant any relief for small organizations with regard to the time from which the requirements must be complied with.

No attestation by auditors

1.2.3 SOX in Japan

The *Financial Instruments and Exchange* law passed in June 2006 in Japan was quickly renamed *Japanese SOX* (J-SOX). The main differences in comparison to US SOX are as follows:

ICS framework of FSA in Japan

- Whilst US SOX does not prescribe a specific framework for the ICS implementation, the Japanese law stipulates that an ICS must be assessed according to the framework developed by the *Financial Services Agency* (FSA) in Japan. This framework is based on the COSO (Committee of Sponsoring Organizations) study, but contains additional control objectives such as *Safeguarding of Assets* and *Response to IT*.
- Whilst the US legislative body expects direct reporting from an auditor, in which the auditor assesses the effectiveness of controls for financial reporting and must present sufficient audit evidence for this, J-SOX limits itself to the assessment by an auditor of the extent to which the ICS reporting produced by the management of an organization is fairly stated.

Further differences relate to various fine details in the external audit of an ICS:

Differences in the external audit

- **Using work of others, USA vs. Japan**
  Whilst an auditor in the USA can use the ICS assessment results, for example, the internal audit, in his own work directly, an auditor in Japan is not permitted to do this (exception: use of such results as evidence for the ICS management assessment). The auditor must acquire a view of the independence and professional competence of the internal audit.
- **Audit methods, USA vs. Japan**
  With regard to audit methods, the corresponding auditing standards in Japan stipulate, in addition to the usual methods (for example, survey, observation, inspection, and repetition), a further method that can be used to assess the operational effectiveness of controls: the repetition of controls by management, which must take place under observation of an auditor.
- **Categorization of issues, USA vs. Japan**
  A further difference is in the categorization of issues documented by the auditor: in Japan there are only two categories (*deficiency* and *material weakness*). In the USA, however, there are three categories: *deficiency*, *significant deficiency*, and *material weakness*.

1.2.4 SOX in China

Basic Standard for Enterprise Internal Controll is a new corporate governance initiative in China that is frequently referred to as a country-specific version of SOX. The provisions approved by the Chinese government had to be fulfilled from July 1, 2009, and generally require the assessment of the effectiveness of the ICS and an annual publication of the respective assessment results. China SOX also requires the audit of the ICS by an independent expert or auditor.

IT-supported ICS automation

The introduction of a *business management IT system* addressed in Chapter 1, Article 7 of China SOX is particularly interesting: amongst other things, this system must contain internal control mechanisms. In this book, the following chapters are dedicated to this topic:

- Chapter 14: Examples of Efficiency-Oriented and Profitability-Oriented Analysis Scenarios in SAP ERP
- Chapter 15: ICS Automation: How to Set the COSO Cube in Motion
- Chapter 16: ICS Automation Using SAP Process Control

The laws valid in China that require an ICS are applicable not only, as is usually the case, to organizations whose shares are traded on the stock market (*public companies*), but also to private organizations.

1.3   ICS Requirements in Europe

Using a *corporate governance code*, most European countries require that a monitoring system is set up in companies listed on the stock exchange, with the audit committee being responsible for the monitoring. In this section, we address this topic and other country-specific and local legal requirements.

1.3.1 Eighth EU Directive

Audit Directive

The *Eighth EU Directive*, also called the Audit Directive, is a directive from EU company law. It is binding for every member state to which it is directed with regard to the objective to be achieved, but allows national bodies to select the form and means. All EU member states were required to implement the requirements in national law by June 29, 2008.

Objectives of the Eighth EU Directive

The Audit Directive regulates the audit of the year-end closing and the consolidated financial statements. It deals with public oversight, external quality assurance for the audit, the duties of the auditor, the application of international standards, and the independence of the auditor. Its objective is to strengthen and harmonize the function of financial statement audits in the member states of the European Union (EU). It applies for *organizations of public interest*, meaning any organization that issues transferable securities for trade on a regulated market.

Chapter X Article 41 of the Eighth EU Directive

The points of the directive comparable with the SOX regulations are contained mostly in Chapter X (Article 39 through 41) of the Eighth EU Directive. The most important points relevant particularly for organizations and their control and risk management systems are listed here:

- Article 41: regulations regarding the audit committee: the organizations that correspond to the directive must introduce an audit committee.
- Article 41 (2) describes the tasks of this audit committee. These include checking the effectiveness of the ICS and, where applicable, the internal audit system or risk management system.
- Article 41 (4) defines that the auditor/auditing company shall report to the audit committee on key matters arising from the statutory audit, and in particular on weaknesses in the internal control system of the respective organization and the financial reporting process.

Comparing the specifications of the Eighth EU Directive, also known as Euro SOX, with those of US SOX shows the following main differences: | Differences in content to US SOX

- Whilst the topic of strategic risks/risk management has been suppressed in US SOX, in the Eighth EU Directive it has been added to the topics to be monitored by the audit committee.
- The EU Directive also addresses the function of the internal audit, which is not the case for US SOX.
- Overall, the directive describes the aspects that the auditor has to assess with regard to ICS effectiveness in less detail.

1.3.2 Germany

Section 91 (2) of the German Stock Corporation Act (AktG) requires a monitoring system that can detect developments that endanger an organization at an early stage, and that the executive board must ensure that this monitoring system is set up. The AktG thus requires that corporations set up an ICS. | Stock Corporation Act

The above-mentioned provisions (as well as Section 317 (4) of the German Commercial Code (HGB), see below) were introduced by the *Control and Transparency in Business Act* (KonTraG), passed by the German Bundestag on March 5, 1998. One of the requirements of KonTraG is that the executive board has to take appropriate measures, in particular, set up a monitoring system, so that developments that endanger the progress of the company are detected early. The Act also states that an auditor must address, in a specific part of the audit report, whether measures are required to improve the internal monitoring system. | Internal monitoring system in KonTraG

There are similar provisions in Section 317 (4) HGB (see http://www.ecgi.org/codes/code.php?code_id=49): during the financial statement audit for listed companies, the auditor must also assess whether the executive board has set up a monitoring or risk early warning system as part of risk management, and whether this risk early warning system can fulfill its tasks. In brief: an ICS is mandatory for all corporations; for listed corporations, the ICS must also be checked. | Risk early warning system in HGB

The *German Corporate Governance Code* (DCGK) was published by the German Ministry of Justice and contains recommendations from the government commission that have assumed legal character with Article 161 AktG. As the contents of this document were influenced considerably by Dr. Gerhard Cromme, chairman of the *Government Commission, German Corporate Governance Code* until June 30, 2008, the term *Cromme Code* is often used as a synonym. | Cromme Code

The above-mentioned KonTraG can be seen as a predecessor of the DCGK, as its objective is also to improve corporate governance in German organizations.

ICS-relevant tasks of the audit committee

The DCGK (the last version is dated June 18, 2009) requires that the supervisory board appoints an *audit committee* that deals in particular with questions on the following issues:

- Reporting
- Risk management
- Compliance
- Auditor independence
- Granting of an audit assignment to the auditor
- Determination of the focuses of the audit
- Agreement of remuneration

According to DCGK, the head of the audit committee should have particular knowledge and experience in the application of reporting principles and internal control procedures.

BilMoG

Another law that should be mentioned here is the German Accounting Law Modernization Act (BilMoG), intended to reform accounting law. Its purpose is to implement the auditor directives (Directive 2006/43/EC as supplement to Directive 2006/30/EC) and the amending directive (Directive 2006/46/EC). In this context, Section 289a HGB (new form) and Section 289 (5), as well as Section 315 (2) no. 5 HGB are relevant: in accordance with these provisions, the executive board must present a written report to the annual meeting of stockholders. This report must include the new mandatory specifications added to the annual report or the group annual report on the ICS and risk management system with regard to the reporting process.

In Sect. 2.1, "ICS in the IT Environment from the View of Auditing," you will learn that one of the main features of an ICS is that it is oriented around risk. In the same way that, by definition, controls and risks are closely linked, this should also apply for processes in risk management and an ICS, meaning that they can be considered under the term *internal monitoring system* or as part of a uniform GRC concept (GRC = governance, risk, and compliance).

Orientation

We will look at the integrative aspects between an ICS and the risk management processes in Sects. 2.1 and 4.3. The practical implementation of the relevant approaches will be explained in Sects. 15.3.7, 16.4.2, 16.4.3 and 16.6.3.

We will discuss the further ICS-relevant legal provisions and statements that deal with ICS requirements from the specific aspects of IT and auditing (for example, GAP-CAS) separately in Sect. 3.1.1, "ICS Principles in the ERP Environment: From GAAP to GAPCAS."

1.3.3 Switzerland

Swiss SOX Light

In Switzerland, the phrase *SOX Light* is used in connection with the legal changes that came into force in 2007. The suffix "Light" refers to the fact that, in accordance with the new regulations in the Swiss Obligations Code (OR), the very existence of an ICS (and not the effectiveness or efficiency) must be checked by the audit.

The direct requirements have changed little: for all organizations entered in the trade register, as before, the principles of commercial bookkeeping in accordance with Art. 957 ff. OR (correct reporting) and for listed companies, in accordance with Art. 662a OR, apply. However, it is not only listed companies that are subject to the requirements for correct reporting but all organizations that – regardless of their legal form – are subject to proper audit. The provisions regarding the audit requirement apply for listed companies, limited liability companies, co-operatives, limited partnerships, associations, and foundations. In accordance with the unchanged Art. 716a (3) OR, the executive board of a listed company has the non-transferable task of setting up accounting and financial control systems. From this, we can derive the obligation to create an ICS.

The new aspects of the legislation affect primarily the object of the audit for the auditor or auditing body:

- According to Art. 728a (1) OR, the auditor checks whether an ICS exists.
- According to Art. 728a (2) OR, the auditor must take the internal control system into account when carrying out the audit and in determining the extent of the audit.
- According to Art. 728b (1) OR, the auditor provides the board of directors with a comprehensive report with conclusions on the reporting, the internal control system, as well as the execution and the result of the audit.

The Swiss auditing standard AS 890, *Verifying the Existence of the Internal Control System*, makes the provisions more specific from the auditor's point of view and describes the procedure for achieving an audit assessment about the existence of an ICS.

1.3.4 Austria

If you are applying Austrian law, Section 82 of the Austrian Stock Corporation Act (AktG), Section 22 of the Limited Liability Companies Act (GmbHG), and Art. 1 Section 39 of the *Statute for a European Company* contain requirements for setting up an appropriate ICS. The laws contain no further notes on the design of the ICS. Indirectly, the standard for professional practice of internal auditing, "2600 – Resolution of Senior Management's Acceptance of Risks," describes part of the control system.

One of the requirements of the *Austrian Corporate Governance Code*, issued by the Austrian Working Group for Corporate Governance, is that the audit committee must monitor the effectiveness of the ICS.

1.3.5 United Kingdom of Great Britain and Northern Ireland

For the United Kingdom, there are two documents that call for an ICS:

- **Combined Code**
  In the *Combined Code on Corporate Governance*, issued by the Financial Reporting Council (latest version June 2008), the *board* of an organization is referred to as the body that, amongst other things, ensures a fully functioning ICS, the effectiveness

of which is assessed at least once each year. The results of this assessment must be disclosed to the shareholders.

Turnbull Guidance

Turnbull Guidance is how the document *Internal Control: Guidance for Directors on the Combined Code* is referred to. It was initially published by the Financial Reporting Council in 1999 (latest version October 2005). This document address the topic of ICS in detail: it describes the elements of an ICS as well as the process for assessing the effectiveness of the controls (including the roles of individual parties involved).

1.3.6 France

The main relevant document in France is the publication "Corporate Governance and Internal Control – Disclosure and Publication Requirements for Securities Issuers." It was published on January 23, 2004 by the *Autorité des Marchés Financiers* (AMF). AMF is an independent public organization set up as a result of the *Loi de Sécurité Financière* (law regarding financial security) of August 1, 2003. The organization's primary objective is to protect the interests of investors. The afore-mentioned document states that the implementation of an ICS is mandatory for a listed company and that the results of the assessment of the effectiveness of controls must be disclosed by both the executive board and by the auditor within an annual report.

1.3.7 Denmark

Financial Statements Act

The relevant Danish legal provisions are documented in the *Financial Statements Act*, Section 107B(1)(vi) and 128(2). According to this act, an annual report must contain a description of the main elements of an ICS designed to focus primarily on the processes as part of financial reporting in order to prevent, detect, and correct major errors in the annual financial statements.

Auditors' Act

The Danish *Auditors' Act* mentions the necessity for an *audit committee* whose tasks include monitoring the effectiveness of the ICS.

1.3.8 Italy

Preda Code

The Italian corporate governance code, known as the *Preda Code*, (after Stefano Preda, the main author of the document), was published by the Italian stock exchange in 1999.

The code was added to in 2002 and 2006 after the money laundering scandal with Cirio and the financial fraud at Parmalat. The central points of the code are listed below:

- Management is responsible for ensuring the adequacy and effectiveness of the ICS; the persons responsible (at least one) must be appointed and they must be provided with sufficient resources.
- The internal control system is charged with the task of ensuring compliance with operational and administrative internal procedures to identify, prevent, and limit financial and operational risks and fraud.
- Persons responsible for the ICS must not be subject to instructions from management responsible for operative business processes in the hierarchy. Those responsible for the ICS must report on their work to the directors, the ICS committee, and the audit committee.
- An ICS committee must be established. This body has an advisory task in the ICS environment.

ICS tasks are more than just compliance

Segregation of duties in the ICS environment

Despite the fact that the provisions of the Preda Code are not binding, the code requires that all listed companies disclose whether the code has been complied with or not as part of the annual report. This *comply or explain principle* gives organizations the flexibility of following principles of corporate governance in accordance with their own special features.

Comply or explain principle

1.3.9 Spain

In Spain, a special working group was set up with the objective of supporting the Spanish *Securities Markets Commission* in an advisory capacity – in particular, with regard to harmonizing reporting requirements for listed companies. On May 19, 2006, this working group published the document "Good Governance of Listed Companies." Amongst other things, this document indicates options for strengthening corporate governance committees, for example, by setting up an *Audit and Compliance Committee*.

Good Governance

Similarly to Italy, Spain has opted for the comply or explain approach. The *Good Governance document,* however, generally focuses more on risk management. The ICS is seen as a means for managing risks efficiently: according to the document, the recommended *Control and Risk Management Policy* must, as a minimum requirement, describe risks that the organization is subject to. Internal reporting and the ICS should describe how the risks specified are to be dealt with. The audit committee is responsible for monitoring control and risk management systems and for the internal audit function.

Minimizing risks as an ICS objective

1.4 ICS Requirements in the Financial Sector

In this section we will look at the ICS-relevant legal requirements in the financial sector. Further industry-specific requirements for the manufacturers of foodstuffs, medicinal products, and manufacturing plants are described in Chap. 13, "Excursion: FDA Compliance and Controls in SAP."

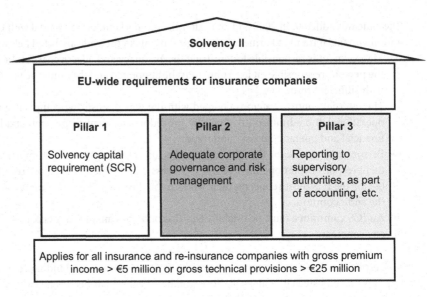

■ **Figure 1.2**   Solvency II – requirements in the insurance industry

1.4.1 Solvency II in the Insurance Industry

Solvency II is a European Commission project aimed at reforming insurance supervisory law. In April 2009, the negotiators of the 27 member states and of the European Parliament agreed on the new supervisory and equity capital rules Solvency II after the European Commission presented a proposal for a Solvency II framework directive to the European Parliament and the European Council. Solvency II was approved by the European Parliament on April 22, 2009, and by the European finance ministers on November 10, 2009. After the decree of the corresponding implementing rules, Solvency II will probably be implemented nationally from 2012.

Three pillars of Solvency II   As you can see in Fig. 1.2, there are three main components of Solvency II, also called *pillars*.

1. The *first pillar* deals with the amount of minimum solvency capital and the target solvency capital to be provided in proportion to the allowable own resources.
2. The *second pillar* concerns the risk management system and contains above all qualitative requirements.
3. The *third pillar* regulates the reporting requirements for insurance companies. These are the requirements to report to supervisory authorities and they cover details that must be published as part of the annual financial statements. In this context, the aim is also to achieve close integration with other legal reporting obligations (for example, in reporting, in particular the *International Financial Reporting Standards*, IFRS).

From an ICS perspective, the second and third pillars are interesting. With the publication of the *Minimum Requirements for Risk Management* (MaRisk, VA) as a binding guideline in January 2009, the German Federal Financial Supervisory Authority (BaFin) anticipated the requirements of the second pillar of Solvency II. The MaRisk (VA) guideline gives more specific information about Section 64a and Section 104 s of the German Insurance Supervision Act. The main effect of MaRisk (VA) within the scope of this book is the fact that, as a result of this legal initiative, efficient *monitoring and control mechanisms for business processes* – that is, an ICS – are required as an important component of risk management. The guideline also contains increased documentation requirements and the formalization of the function of the internal audit.

Example: implementation in Germany

It is to be expected that ICS will also be an increasingly important topic in the implementation of the requirements within the scope of the third pillar of Solvency II: the causal chain from external financial reporting to the ICS requirements is covered in Sect. 2.1, "ICS in the IT Environment from the View of Auditing."

Reporting obligations

1.4.2 Basel II and III in Banking

The term *Basel II* refers to the entirety of rules proposed by the Basel Committee on Banking Supervision in the last few years. In accordance with EU directives 2006/48/EC and 2006/49/EC, the rules had to be applied in the member states of the European Union for all financial institutions and financial service institutions with effect from January 1, 2007. The main objective of Basel II is to align the nationally required regulatory equity capital requirements more strongly with the actual risk.

As you can see from Fig. 1.3, Basel II consists of three complementary pillars:

- Minimum capital requirements
- Bank supervisory review process
- Extended disclosure (and market discipline)

The objective of the first pillar is to ensure that banks consider risks more precisely and appropriately when assessing whether they have sufficient equity capital. In summary: businesses that are subject to higher risk should hold more own capital than businesses with low risk potential. Bank-specific *credit default risks*, *market risks*, and *operational risks* are considered.

New: consideration of operational risks

Operational Risks: Definition

Operational risks are all operating risks that can cause damage in an organization.

The monitoring of operational risks is directly connected to the ICS. Thus, in the Basel II environment, an efficient ICS has a *direct financial benefit*: the better the ICS, the more precisely the equity capital adequacy can be calculated and the lower the capital that has to be tied in.

The second pillar requires the establishment of adequate risk management systems, for example, *Management Risk Controlling* (MRC), for banks and investment companies as well as monitoring of these systems by a supervisory body.

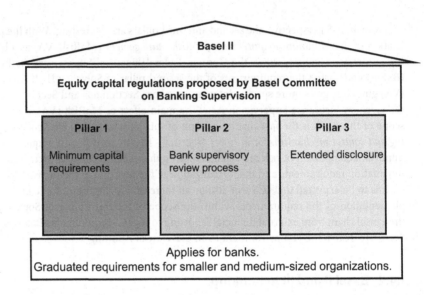

Figure 1.3   Basel II – requirements in banking

The objective of the third pillar is to strengthen *market discipline* through the multiple disclosure of information as part of external reporting by banks (for example, in annual financial statements, in quarterly reports, or in annual reports).

Basel III is coming

As a result of the financial and economic crisis, and based on experiences gathered with Basel II, in December 2010, the preliminary version of *Basel III* was defined. In these provisions, the heads of central banks and financial supervisory bodies from 27 countries defined the new rules for equity capital. The most important message: in future, financial institutions will need considerably higher equity capital. However, thanks to generous transition deadlines, they have time to build up this capital. The common equity (*Tier 1*) should increase from four to six percent of the "risk-weighted assets" by 2015; this is the assigned loans and securities that can default and that represent the future risk for the bank.

The implementation of the Basel III requirements in the European Union will take place via changes to the Capital Requirements Directive (CRD) and should come into force in stages from 2013.

1.5   ICS as Contributing Factor to Business Success?

In practice, the achievement of an organization's objectives is rarely associated directly with the ICS – and unjustly so. Which mechanisms do organizations usually employ otherwise to measure and control their own success? Let us look at the most widespread systems first.

Balanced Scorecard for financial and non-financial indicators

Balanced Scorecard (BSC) is a concept for measuring, documenting, and controlling the activities of a company or an organization with regard to its vision and strategy. (See Kaplan, Norton, Hilgner: *The Execution Premium: Linking Strategy to Operations for Competitive Advantage*).

Due to its extensive design options, you can use the Balanced Scorecard to set up an integrated management system. Using reference numbers for the functions and attributes of the objects in question in the BSC, you can follow the development of the business vision. You define *critical success factors* and use them, together with *key performance indicators* (KPI), to create a *performance measurement system* (scorecard). The measurement categories represent the degree of fulfillment of the *strategic* objectives. In a continuous process, you check objectives and objective achievement and control both with corrective measures.

In contrast to BSC, classic *performance measurement system* (such as the DuPont model) generally use financial indicators to assign various cause-effect relationships. The most well known performance measurement system is based on the calculation of the return on investment (ROI). The ROI is determined from the product of the key figures *sales profitability* and *capital turnover*.

Performance measurement systems

We have no intention of reinventing the wheel in this book; we merely wish to show that there are several existing terms and models that represent the basic concept that you can monitor business performance as part of an integrated approach and detect "unfavorable" developments early. This basic concept is also found in modern ICS approaches:

- On one hand, the ICS is considered as a component of an integrated GRC approach.
- On the other hand, the ICS is integrated with the existing ERP landscape in an organization.

Thus, as described in Sect. 1.1.1, "Compliance," the ICS can focus not only on the observance of legal requirements, but also on the achievement of an organization's objectives.

Viewed simply, we can establish the following difference between ICS (or GRC) and the known BSC and performance measurement models: BSC and performance measurement models are targeted at strategic levels that, from a content perspective, require aggregation of the data from individual business transactions; in contrast, the ICS/GRC approach also focuses on the non-aggregated operations, i. e., the individual transactions or business transactions. Therefore, BSC or performance measurement models are unlikely to produce, for example, statements such as "the moving average price was calculated incorrectly in the following good receipts document Numbers due to incorrect manual entries: the valuation of the following stocks must therefore be corrected accordingly."

ICS/GRC vs. Balanced Scorecard and performance measurement systems

We can already predict that this difference might disappear as a result of increasing automation and direct integration of BSC dashboards with ERP systems thanks to analysis performance that is increasing at an exponential rate. For example, drilling down from a KPI to the level of individual transactions, even with large volumes of data, could no longer be a problem thanks to in-memory technology (e.g., SAP HANA).

1.6 Summary

In this chapter, we have provided an overview of the objectives that you can achieve with an ICS. We focused on the objectives "correct reporting" and "compliance with legal regulations" (the ICS term and these objectives were explained in Sect. 1.1.2, "Internal Control System (ICS)") as well as on the efficiency of business processes.

Efficiency or profitability may not necessarily be connected to the term ICS in a "traditional" consideration, but in our opinion that is unjust. Therefore, in Sect. 3.1.5, we present a possible structure of an efficiency-oriented ICS framework in the ERP environment.

We have explained the most important legal requirements of an ICS in more detail. Specific legal requirements that can vary strongly from organization to organization depending on the industry, country, and other special features were addressed only briefly by example of the financial services industry. In Chaps. 11, "Data Protection Compliance in SAP ERP Human Capital Management," and 13, "Excursion: FDA Compliance and Controls in SAP," we describe further legal provisions: on one hand the requirements for handling personal data, and on the other hand, requirements that organizations are subject to in the field of food and medicinal products.

In every organization, business processes are almost as individual as human fingerprints. In spite of this, the use of standard software enables us to identify certain "typical" basic scenarios. In Chap. 14, "Examples of Efficiency-Oriented and Profitability-Oriented Analysis Scenarios in SAP ERP," you will find examples for efficiency-oriented scenarios in the SAP ERP environment.

You have seen that the ICS is gaining great importance as a means for ensuring compliance. This is the first step: you know which legal articles require an ICS.

Before we explain the special features of an ICS in an IT environment, we will first provide you with information about the many facets of the work of an auditor, whose tasks include investigating the ICS.

The Auditor Is Coming:
When, Why, and How to Cope

> The visit to the dentist, the appointment with the authorities, or a visit to the mother-in-law – sometimes you just can't avoid uncomfortable encounters. Afterwards they're usually nowhere near as bad as you expected, and you can even benefit from them.

In a survey by the magazine *Fast Company* (www.fastcompany.com), 82 % of all executives questioned admitted that they sometimes did not observe the rules of fair play when playing golf. Whilst this mostly goes unnoticed on the golf course and has no serious consequences, in financial reporting, not observing the rules is quite a different matter. Room for interpretation stretched beyond limits, accounting creativity bordering on criminality, or even falsified financial statements can (justifiably, of course) have serious consequences: an adverse opinion from the auditor, the negative effects on the granting of credit to or the creditworthiness of the organization, or penal consequences.

In order to prevent both intentional falsifications and unintentional errors, you need an internal control system (ICS). From Chap. 1, "Legal Requirements in ICS Compliance," you already know which legal provisions require an ICS and why.

To ensure compliance with legal requirements, internal audit and other in-house control instances, as well as independent auditors, take on the important *ICS assurance role*. It is essential to understand the corresponding rules, background, and procedures for executing this role in the environment of IT-supported business processes – not only to provide efficient support for an audit, but above all to take some benefit from it. The pages that follow will explain everything you need.

2.1 ICS in the IT Environment from the View of Auditing

In this chapter you will learn how IT influences the external audit procedure, why the necessity for an ICS audit goes hand in hand with the necessity for external financial reporting, and which guidelines and statements determine the audit work in the ERP environment.

In Germany, for example, auditors must check the annual financial statements in accordance with Section 316 of the German Commercial Code (HGB) and the accounting in accordance with Section 317 HGB. In the audit certificate, according to Section 322 HGB, they must also declare whether the accounting and the annual financial statements comply with generally accepted accounting principles and legal regulations. These regulations apply to both medium-sized and large corporations. The requirement for an audit also results from other regulations (for example, the German Public Disclosure Act (PublG) or from national and state regulations).

Necessity for external audit

There are similar legal provisions around the world and they all have one objective: providing the various interested parties – above all creditors and investors – with a true and clear picture of the asset and revenue position of an organization in order to protect their interests.

This is guaranteed by an independent specialist checking the contents of the external financial reporting of an organization and, where applicable, confirming the organization's credibility.

External financial reporting

The components of the external financial reporting relevant for audit purposes are generally the following:

- Balance sheet
- Profit and loss statement
- Appendix with year-end closing plus annual report; for corporations trading in a capital market, also the funds flow statement and the statement of shareholders' equity.

In the present situation, in which financial reporting takes place based on IT systems (or at least to a great extent) and the accounting-relevant figures arise in complex, interconnected IT-supported business processes, the challenge for an auditor is in having to test a "Hauch von Magnetismus [touch of magnetism]," in other words, the "magnetic" data recorded on hard drives (see Schuppenhauer, R.: Grundsätze für eine ordnungsmäßige Datenverarbeitung (GoDV), Düsseldorf 2005, p. 33, 378).

2.1.1 The Challenge Presented by Information Technology

Auditor's focus on IT systems

Since the beginning of the 1980s, IT systems have been increasingly influencing the tasks of external audit. At that time, specialist literature made the following findings on an increasingly frequent basis:

- Electronic data processing is changing the object of the audit – accounting – fundamentally: whilst the manual ledger was an image of document submission, in the automatic systems, data is broken down, changed, and reassigned. These activities cannot be recognized from the accounting alone (see, for example, Leffson, U.: Wirtschaftsprüfung, Wiesbaden 1980, p. 231).
- According to one source, as a result of their high level of integration and paperless processing, many systems lead to a loss of the classic audit trail. For example, audit-relevant intercompany profit and loss is only available in an incomplete form or in a form that can be read by machine, etc. (see Horwath, P.; Schäfer, H-Th.: Prüfung bei automatisierter Datenverarbeitung, Berlin 1983, p. 24; similar statements have been made by the following authors: Minz, G.; Zepf, G.: Computergestützte Jahresabschlussprüfung. Erfordernis, Möglichkeiten und Voraussetzungen, in: Betriebswirtschaftliche Forschung und Praxis (specialist journal), 1984, 36th year, Book 5, p. 398.)

These new conditions have changed auditing dramatically.

2.1.2 Transaction Audit as Audit Approach in the IT Environment

The new environment of audit-specific activities has also had a considerable influence on the approaches within the annual audit. The principle approaches for executing an annual audit are the *balance sheet audit* and the *transaction audit*. The difference between the two audit approaches is clear above all when we compare the objects of the audit.

Balance sheet audit and transaction audit

— **Balance sheet audit**

The *balance sheet audit* is based on auditing the preparation, evaluation, and display of the individual annual financial statement items, in particular, those that cannot be portrayed with system support (for example, some types of provisions). Therefore, it is a *time-based* audit that uses only result-oriented audit procedures. Balance sheet audits in the form of analytical audit procedures are essential in audit planning.

> **Results-Oriented Audit Procedures**   ❗
>
> *Results-oriented audit procedures* are all audit procedures that are based on an imme-
> diate assessment of proper treatment of the assets and liabilities, as well as expenses
> and revenues, displayed in the accounts and annual financial statement items. Results-
> oriented audit procedures can be categorized into *detailed auditing of results* (audit of
> the business transactions and balances) and *global* or *analytical audit procedures* (plau-
> sibility assessments).
>
> In American audit literature, these audit procedures are referred to as "substantive
> tests of details" and "analytical reviews."

— **Transaction audit**

In contrast to the balance sheet audit, the *transaction audit* is based on auditing the processing and control system of the organization that is responsible for the processing results portrayed in the annual financial statements. This *period-based* audit strategy is based on the knowledge that the processing results, and thus the facts portrayed in the annual financial statements, have passed through the ICS. If this system is working reliably, then it is safe to assume that the processing results are reliable (i.e., do not have errors).

Both approaches existed long before IT came along. The focus on the ICS for the purposes of reducing the audit scope is the main feature of the auditing of procedures that appeared in specialist literature at the beginning of the twentieth century: "Where there is a satisfactory system of internal check, the auditor is not expected, and shall not attempt, to make a detailed audit." (Montgomery: Auditing Theory and Practice, New York 1912, p. 82).

However, it was the fast progress of IT that made the auditing of procedures indispensable, as already noted in specialist literature at the beginning of the 1980s: according to one source, the concept of ignoring the computer during auditing had become no longer justifiable; auditing of procedures was necessary, on a more or less large scale depending on the organization of the data processing areas (see Minz, G.: Ansätze einer Prüfungstheorie für Computergestützte Buchführungssysteme, in: Wirtschaftsprüfung

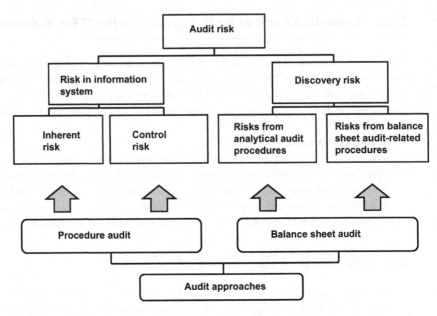

□ **Figure 2.1**   Covering audit risk with audit approaches

(specialist journal published by the German Institute of Public Auditors), 36th year, 1983, No. 18, p. 522).

2.1.3   Approaches for a Transaction Audit: Focus on ICS

Seen from the perspective of auditing theory, auditing of procedures, or the transaction audit, was triggered as a result of the appearance of new audit risks.

Audit risk, error risk, discovery risk   According to audit theory, the audit risk, consisting of the error risk and the discovery risk, must be reduced to a minimum. Viewed simply, when annual financial statements are, to a great extent, the result of IT-supported processes, an error in the financial statements would be the result of an error in the information system. Accordingly, the error risk could generally be equated with a risk in the information system.

As shown by Fig. 2.1, auditing of procedures is based on addressing the components of such a risk.

❗ Inherent Risk and Control Risk – Definition

The following definitions come from the international auditing standard ISA 400. The International Standards on Auditing (ISA) are defined by the International Federation of Accountants (IFAC):
- The *inherent risk* is the susceptibility of an account balance or class of transactions to misstatement that could be material – individually or when aggregated with misstatements in other balances or classes – assuming that there were no related internal controls.

> ■ The *control risk* is the risk that a misstatement that could occur in an account balance or class of transactions and that could be material individually or when aggregated with misstatements in other balances or classes, will not be prevented or detected and corrected on a timely basis by the accounting and internal control systems.

It goes without saying that the stronger the control mechanisms, the lower the audit risk associated with an information system. The auditor can rely more on the control mechanisms in an organization and can restrict other audit procedures. Therefore, orientation on the control system is the most important approach in a transaction audit.

ICS approach for
a transaction audit

Within the scope of the transaction or procedure audit, the ICS-oriented and risk-oriented approaches overlap. If the focus is on understanding the procedures and processes rather than on auditing balance sheet items, this equates to a *risk orientation* as the audit is restricted to the relevant (i. e., higher risk) processes. Provided *internal controls* are set up in the organization to ensure that the accounting-relevant information in the individual transaction cycles is entered completely and correctly, from the view of the auditor this represents a reduction in the risk (see Buchner, R.: Wirtschaftliches Prüfungswesen, Munich 1997, p. 159).

Risk approach for
a transaction audit

The primary objective of the analysis of IT processes in the transaction audit is the identification of the main IT risks and the assessment of the effects on the annual financial statements and the annual report. As these IT risks represent a considerable factor for the audit risk in the use of IT-supported accounting systems, *risk orientation* is the necessary prerequisite for the transaction audit (see also Sect. 3.1.3, "Control Identification Process" in connection with risk orientation). Note that in the last few years, the risk-oriented and control-oriented approaches have been required legally worldwide – specifically as a direct requirement for organizations in contrast to the "indirect" requirements resulting from the necessity for an independent attestation of annual financial statements by external auditors.

To delineate the object of the transaction audit and thus the possible investigation areas for controls and risks completely, we can identify the following focus areas within a transaction audit:

Object of the
transaction audit

- The IT application itself, in particular application controls
- Organizational structures within the organization
- Processes and procedures for IT systems, such as development and support of applications

In the second part of this book, Chap. 5 through 13, we will explain the ICS content in an SAP system – with regard to the different SAP applications and the relevant processes (for example, change management) and connections.

2.1.4 ICS and Mandatory Transaction Audit

The necessity for an ICS audit and in particular, the ICS approach for the transaction audit mentioned in Sect. 2.1.2, "Transaction Audit as Audit Approach in the IT Environ-

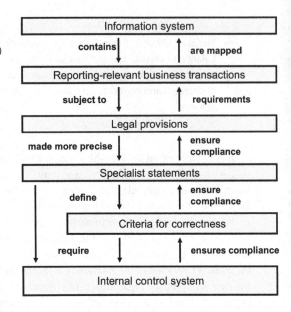

□ Figure 2.2 Necessity for an ICS from the view of external accounting (source: Peter Heidkamp, KPMG)

ment," are derived not only from auditing theory but have also become institutionalized in various ways.

As shown in Fig. 2.2, the IT-supported recording of accounting-relevant business transactions is subject to the following:

- **Relevant legal provisions**

This relates primarily to provisions in commercial and tax law that require both proper accounting and independent auditing of the same. Numerous legal provisions refer explicitly to the *Generally Accepted Accounting Principles* (GAAP) (for example, Section 238 (1) HGB or Section 243 (1) HGB). These principles define, for example, general criteria for correctness such as completeness, accuracy, timeliness, orderliness, traceability, and unalterability (Section 239 (1), (2), and (3) HGB).

From a legal perspective, GAAP is an indeterminate legal concept designed to close legal loopholes. This legal concept has been filled out with practical examples and by the actions of prudent business people, as well as through the legal system, decrees, recommendations, and expertise of authorities and associations and through scientific discussion.

In an international comparison, similar references to GAAP (Generally Accepted Accounting Principles) are found: in American law (US GAAP), in the IFRS environment (IFRS = International Financial Reporting Standards), and in the International Accounting Standards (IAS).

- **Specialist statements**

The legal provisions are dealt with, amongst other things, in various specialist *statements*, for example, in publications of the German Institute of Public Auditors (IDW). There are statements that specifically require an ICS and statements that regulate the work of auditors in relation to the ICS. There are also statements in which GAAP are adapted to IT concerns, and the topic of the internal control system is dealt with in particular in the environment of IT-supported accounting (see IDW RS FAIT 1; Sect. 3.1.1 "ICS Principles in the ERP Environment: From GAAP to GAPCAS"). In an international comparison numerous similarities are observed, for example, some IDW publications consider the *International Standards of Auditing* (ISA), issued by the *International Federation of Accountants* (IFAC). These standards are highly accepted worldwide.

In Germany, an obligation to audit the ICS was introduced by the IDW expert report 1/1988. Here, for the first time, the transaction and function audit of the ICS was defined as a binding mandatory component of the annual financial statement audit in addition to result-oriented audit procedures.

For the first time in Germany in 1988: ICS as obligation

Of the current auditing standards issued by the IDW, the following are important in this book:

Auditing standards: transaction audit

— **Year-end audit**
The auditing standard *IDW PS 330*, "Abschlussprüfung bei Einsatz von IT," relating to auditing financial statements when IT is used, corresponds to *ISA 401*, "Auditing in a Computer Information Systems Environment." It prescribes that IT-supported accounting systems must be assessed to determine whether they comply with legal requirements – in particular the requirements for security and proper accounting presented in IDW RS FAIT 1 (see Sect. 3.1.1). The legally required audit statements regarding the appropriateness of the accounting should be made on this basis.

— **Software certification**
Provided software products must be checked at the software manufacturer or software user before the implementation in the respective organizational environment of the software user, auditing standards such as *IDW PS 880*, "Die Prüfung von Softwareprodukten" (regarding the testing of software products) apply. The object of the software check is to assess GAAP in the procedure prescribed by the software. In practice, these certificates issued by auditors are often referred to as software attestation.

— **Transaction audit in the event of outsourcing**
The special features of the transaction audit in today's IT environment, often marked by outsourcing and shared services, are dealt with in the new *International Standard on Assurance Engagements 3402* (ISAE) (see Sect. 6.1.2, "IT Outsourcing: Who Is Responsible for the Controls?"). The auditing standards *IDW PS 951* (on auditing the ICS at service provider organizations for functions outsourced to the service provider organization) and *IDW PS 331* (on the annual audit for accounting functions partially outsourced to service provider organizations) should also be mentioned here.

— **ICS and risk approaches**
Auditing standard *IDW PS 261*, on detecting and assessing error risks and auditors' reactions to assessed error risks, replaces *IDW PS 260*, on internal control systems within the scope of annual financial statement audits. This standard reflects *ISA 315*, "Understanding the Entity and its Environment and Assessing the Risks of Material Misstatement," and *ISA 330*, "The Auditor's Procedures in Response to Assessed Risks." One particularly interesting aspect is the duty of the auditor, detailed in the standard, to assess at least the setup and the implementation of the relevant ICS for significant risks.

To highlight the international comparability of auditing standards, note the Swiss auditing standard *AS 890*, "Verifying the Existence of the Internal Control System."

2.2   ICS Assurance in Practice

Enough about the theory: in practice, the exercising of the ICS assurance role by an independent auditor has many facets. In the pages that follow you will learn:
- Which types of auditors exist
- Which rules the auditors have to comply with
- Which types of ICS-relevant audits exist in the SAP environment

We will also provide tips on how to make cooperation with the auditor easier, and on how to get the optimum benefits from the audit results.

2.2.1 The Auditor's Focus

To understand the objectives of the auditor, it is important to know which auditor you are working with. In practice, you can be working with various types of auditors:
- **External auditors**
  These auditors are primarily associated with the external audit of the annual financial statements. We generally think of the "Big Four" here (that is, PricewaterhouseCoopers, Ernst & Young, Deloitte, and KPMG), but there are numerous other medium-sized and smaller auditing companies. The main objective of the work of an external auditor is to certify in the audit report for the annual financial statements that the accounting and the annual financial statements comply with legal regulations. The purpose of this is to protect the shareholders and other interested parties.

> **❶ Example: Extract from a German Audit Report**
>
> After a successful audit, the annual financial statements of the respective company receive the following audit report.
> "We are of the opinion, based on our audit, that the end of year financial statement fulfills the legal requirements (and the supplementary provisions contained within the Memorandum and Articles of Incorporation of the company) and provides a realistic and accurate representation of the actual situation relating to the assets and complete financial situation of the company, with due reference to the principles of sound accounting.
> The report on the situation of the company agrees with the end of year financial statement and presents the opportunities and risks associated with future developments in an appropriate way."

- **Industry-specific external auditors**
  Depending on the industry, for example, for the financial sector or the pharmaceuticals industry, there are auditors whose task is to monitor compliance with industry-specific rules.
- **Specialist external auditors**
  Within a specific audit objective (such as reporting and the annual financial statements audit), there are specialists who can concentrate on a specific area. For ex-

ample, there are specialists who deal with tax reporting, determination of fraud, etc. In the field of technology, there are auditors who specialize in IT management, security, or applications (e. g., SAP ERP) and modules. The appointed external auditors engage specialized auditors to cover specific areas (for example, SAP-supported processes and evaluations, segregation of duties, etc.).

▬ **Tax audit**
Arranged and performed by tax authorities, the objective of this audit is to determine, check, and assess the dealings of a person or organization subject to tax. The authority requiring the audit is, for example, the Internal Revenue Service (IRS) in the USA, or the "Finanzamt" (tax office) in Germany. Audits in the field of customs duties and foreign trade also fall into this category.

▬ **Internal audit**
The primary task of internal audit is to support the management of an organization in their control function. From an audit perspective, an internal audit group performs audits that check content not only for compliance objectives, but also for other objectives such as profitability and quality. These audits can be performed periodically or for specific reasons. In order to fulfill their trusted, prevention, and information functions, internal auditors are generally independent and report to the audit committee of the organization. In practice, however, there can be an indirect organizational assignment to the CFO, for example, through the reporting of audit results. However, external independent auditors are frequently engaged to exercise the role of internal audit.

2.2.2 Selected Auditing Principles

In practice, there are numerous incorrect impressions of the role and tasks of an auditor as well as the rules that an auditor has to comply with. We address the most important aspects below.

Regardless of the type of auditor or the audit objective concerned, an auditor has to comply with certain basic rules in the exercise of his profession. Apart from official legislation, such as the German Professional Accountant Act, these basic rules consist of principles and ethical standards defined by country-specific professional associations, such as the American Institute of Certified Public Accountants (AICPA), the Institute of Internal Auditors (IIA), the German IDW, etc., and documented, for example, as a *Code of Professional Conduct*. Compared internationally, these standards and principles are very similar.

Who audits the auditor?

The task of the respective institute consists in monitoring observance of the principles and the quality of the work and further education of auditors.

▬ **Expert third party**
The auditor must be a master of his trade; this includes not only having the required technical knowledge, but also audit-specific expertise. This knowledge must be confirmed by certifications and professional examinations (in particular, for auditors of annual financial statements) that, besides the examination itself, also require a certain study focus or at least a minimum number of years of professional experience. For financial auditors, there are country-specific professional examinations targeted towards the special legal features and basic principles of accounting in the respective country: for example, Certified Public Accountants (CPA) in the USA. Some

professional examinations have a cross-country relevance because the underlying accounting standards are important across borders (CPA for US GAAP or Chartered Accountant for IFRS accounting).

However, there are also professional examinations for auditors that are not specific to the local legal special features and that therefore apply internationally: for example, the Certified Information System Auditor (CISA) in the field of IT audit, or the Certified Internal Auditor (CIA) for internal audit. Even if you are dealing with an audit assistant who has not yet taken any professional exams, the assistant's superior (audit manager, or higher – for example, partner) will certainly be appropriately qualified.

Independence

This important requirement has an effect on many aspects of the collaboration with an auditor. The independence restrictions are functional and organizational in nature.

A CIO may propose a period or a system to the auditor, for example, because this matches utilization or availability of the contact persons. However, it is up to the auditor whether he actually performs his evaluations in this system in this period. In general, the audit process must not be influenced – the auditor acts independently. The independence requirement influences, for example, the managerial authority and structures within the organization if the audit is an internal audit. Therefore, internal audit groups are generally only answerable to the audit committee.

Objectivity within the scope of independence — With regard to functional and organizational independence, the objectivity requirements refer to each individual auditor. For example, it is not permissible for a close relative of the CFO to audit the organization, or for an auditor to hold a large number of shares in the organization. It goes without saying that an auditor may not accept gifts that exceed a certain value. With regard to the content of the work performed by the auditor, an IT auditor may not, for example, audit an SAP system for which he has actively participated in the design or functional configuration.

Professional skepticism

The auditor's work requires professional skepticism. This means that year after year, you will be asked the same questions or asked to provide supporting documents that did not have to be made available in the past. The auditor has to find the correct balance between trust and mistrust to bring the audit risk to acceptable dimensions.

Audit trail

Someone who is dealing with an auditor for the first time may find it strange for the auditor to want to take away copies of various documents and fill thick folders with them. The reason for this "passion for collecting" however, is that the supporting documents filed, or stored by the auditors in electronic form, must be sufficient for another auditor to be able to come to the same conclusion regarding the audit result based on these documents (or rather, based on the *working papers*).

The principle "if I cannot prove a control step in the process, it did not take place," has annoyed many clients of auditing companies, in particular during SOX audits. The often negative attitude towards the apparently excessive verification requirements however, must be seen in relation to the responsibility that the auditor bears. Furthermore, the management of an organization should also be interested in having auditable proof that the business transactions work as planned or prescribed.

> **Evidence in Electronic Form**
>
> In the ERP environment, a series of prerequisites must be fulfilled for an auditor to be able to rely on evidence in electronic form. Checking these prerequisites (for example, unalterability, traceability of the origin and the recording, etc.) is one of the most important focuses of an ERP audit. The corresponding controls in SAP ERP are described in Sect. 7.1, "The Principle of Unalterability," and Sect. 7.2, "Controls for Data-Related Traceability."

[e.g.]

> **Sanctity of Basic Auditing Principles**
>
> Until a few years ago, the auditing company Arthur Anderson was named alongside the Big Four (in those days, the Big Five). In the meantime, this company has disappeared from view as a result of the Enron scandal and we now talk about the Big Four. The reason for the demise was that the basic principles presented above were not taken to heart by some employees in the company.

2.2.3 Types of External Audit in the ERP Environment

In addition to the numerous types of audits, there are many audit objectives that auditors follow in exercising their profession. The internationally recognized ICS framework of COSO (based on the study of the Committee of Sponsoring Organizations of the Treadway Committee of 1992) differentiates between four categories of audit objectives:

Four categories of audit objectives

- **Strategic objectives**
  High-level objectives associated with and supporting the mission of an organization
- **Operational objectives**
  Here the focus is on profitability and efficiency – including protecting the assets of an organization
- **Reporting**
  Reliability of external reporting, for example, presentation of the asset and revenue situation
- **Compliance**
  Compliance with relevant legal specifications, regulations, and guidelines

Up to this point, we have looked at IT processes and system audit in general. In the further course of this book, we will concentrate on SAP-supported processes, considering SAP for various types of audit. The most common cases in which the focus is on SAP are summarized in Table 2.1.

For the sake of simplicity, we have not addressed the difference between *review* and *audit* in this overview.

It is not always possible to clearly delineate the boundaries between the individual types of audit. From a content perspective, an SAP audit can look at many topics or can focus on one area (module-related or business process-related):

◻ Table 2.1 Overview of types of audit with SAP reference

Type of audit	Trigger	Details	Audit objective
Annual financial statements	Periodic	Assessment of the reliability of the data in SAP on which the financial reporting is based	Reporting
Tax audits	Periodic, event-driven	Assessment of the reliability of the tax calculations in SAP (for example, as part of the SAP program "advance return for tax on sales/purchases"), audits of the principles for data access and verifiability of digital documents	
ICS-related audits, (SOX, GAPCAS, etc.)	Periodic, initiative	Assessment of the accuracy of the design of the application controls in SAP and the configuration settings relevant to the ICS	Compliance
Data protection, HIPAA audits	Periodic, initiative	Check for compliance with the legally prescribed restrictions of access to specific data and transactions	
Security audit	Initiative	Check of the authorization concept and the security-relevant configurations in SAP (application as well as database) or on the interaction with SAP via networks (for example, RFC, gateways)	Operational
Fraud audit	Event-driven	Detective audit procedures for uncovering cases of fraud	
SAP implementation audit	Initiative	Monitoring of the SAP implementation processes, for example, in relation to project risks, status reports, etc.	
Change management audit	Initiative	Assessment of the process in which the results of the configuration and development in SAP are documented, performed, tested, and transported into the live environment	
SAP operations audit	Initiative	SLA-related (Service Level Agreement) assessment of the operational processes and administration in the SAP environment	
Audit of the organization and planning	Initiative	Assessment of SAP management: for example, alignment of SAP AG roadmaps for SAP applications with the planning and strategy in IT and business	Strategy
Software selection	Initiative	Check for the existence and observance of the rules for selecting software products	

■ As part of an *integrated audit approach* for an organization subject to SOX, in addition to the audit of the *annual financial statements*, the *effectiveness of the ICS* is also examined and a separate audit statement is given. Even for organizations that are not subject to SOX compliance regulations, the SAP systems used are examined during the audit of the annual financial statements: as already shown in Sect. 2.1.2, "Transaction Audit as Audit Approach in the IT Environment," a transaction audit is indispensable, and as you know from Sect. 2.1.3, "Approaches for a Transaction Audit: Focus on ICS," the focus of a transaction audit is on the assessment of the control mechanisms within an ERP application.

■ SAP audits that are somewhat more restricted focus on specific processes or questions: SAP-supported processes are complex enough, and thus every process can be an independent topic.

One Item – Several Topics   **[e.g.]**

For just one single financial statement item, such as *stock value,* the following topics in SAP ERP can be important, for example:

- Periodic valuation runs in the material ledger
- Material pricing (standard price control)
- Determination of lowest value according to movement rate, range of coverage, or market price
- Analysis of the fluctuations in the moving average price due to entry errors in the goods warehouse
- Clearing the GR/IR account

2.2.4 Recommendations for Working with the Auditor

Organizations that use SAP are well-acquainted with the following situation: an SAP audit is announced, and panic breaks out.

The first step is the request for access authorizations. Even in the initial phase, the following question arises: What is the auditor allowed to see and what is he not allowed to see? This question is easy to answer: In order to guarantee fulfillment of the "selected auditing principles" described in Sect. 2.2.2, an auditor may see everything in the system that he wants to see.

Recommendation No. 1 – Display Authorizations   ❶

Give the auditor extensive display authorizations (exception: HCM authorizations if there is no focus on this module – see Chap. 11, "Data Protection Compliance in SAP ERP Human Capital Management" on the topic of data protection). Authorization roles specially created for the audit are recommended.

Display
authorizations
There are a number of standard profiles in SAP that contain display authorizations (for example, S_A.SHOW); however, we advise against using these: *standard profiles often contain uncomfortable "surprises,"* and you almost certainly do not want an inexperienced auditor to immortalize themselves in an SAP document or other change log. A separate role set up for the auditor, with display authorizations, is better.

Recommendation No. 2 – Do Not Conceal Anything!

Do not attempt to conceal anything from the auditor. The truth is the most important prerequisite for trust.

Truth lasts longest
Hastily removing the generously distributed SAP_ALL authorizations or resetting the client settings to "conform" just before an audit is not practical: the auditor can track the assignment of the authorization profiles and the configuration changes back via the change history. Save yourself time and uncomfortable questions – due to the extensive logging in SAP, you cannot hide last-minute cosmetic repairs (see Sects. 7.2, "Controls for Data-Related Traceability," and 7.3, "Traceability of User Activities in SAP").

Recommendation No. 3 – Cooperation

Work with the auditor and not against him.

Benefit from the
auditor
Unfortunately, some organizations have an extremely reserved attitude towards SAP auditors. Cooperation is often restricted to handing over the (hopefully) available documentation (blueprints, process descriptions, etc.); for the rest of the time, there is no time for discussion with the auditor. This is quite wrong, because organizations can benefit from the auditor! You may know your processes inside out, but the auditor brings rare expertise regarding ICS setup in the SAP environment into the operative business – including a "fresh" and unbiased view of your processes.

Recommendation No. 4 – Ensure Resources

Retain a good SAP auditor!

SAP ERP knowledge
is a rare commodity
You will not find many auditors who bring well-founded SAP ERP expertise with them. For various reasons (few auditors with professional experience, fluctuation, etc.), such auditors were and still are a rare commodity. If an auditor has impressed you with his SAP and process knowledge, give the management of the audit team positive feedback. An SAP auditor can generally choose whether to be involved in the periodic audit of your organization in the next year, for example.

Recommendation No. 5 – Ask for Recommendations   ❶

Auditors bring with them accumulated expertise that they have acquired in many projects at many customers and that can be very useful for you.

Despite the lack of ERP expertise mentioned, even standard checklists that numerous auditors use according to a "one size fits all" principle represent the valuable cumulative knowledge of numerous auditors from various projects. They contain notes on typical errors and risks in the SAP environment and on common control mechanisms that counteract these errors and risks. A good auditor can show you which options exist for dealing with certain risks in SAP ERP and can tell you about his experiences of how "other customers have done it."

However, the auditor may also advise you of restrictions associated with his role as auditor and that "prohibit" him from performing consulting. And indeed, in order to comply with the principle of objectivity, the auditor must not proactively design the ICS that he is auditing. However, there is still sufficient leeway for benefiting from the auditors knowledge.

Audit vs. consulting

"The internal auditor's objectivity is *not* adversely affected when the auditor recommends standards of control for systems or reviews procedures before they are implemented. The auditor's objectivity *is* considered to be impaired if the auditor designs, installs, drafts procedures for, or operates such systems." (Source: Practice Advisory 1120-1 of the IIA.)

Similar provisions are found in the field of *external* audit: therefore, there are sufficient opportunities for getting good advice from an auditor. In practice, it is even usual for recommendations to be explicitly described in the communication of the audit findings, for example, in the form of a *management letter* – even if sometimes these recommendations are kept quite general. You can take this as an opportunity to ask the auditor for details.

One of the critical points of the cooperation with the auditor is the agreement of the audit results. Proper handling of this topic can save you a lot of annoyance.

Recommendation No. 6 – Agree Results   ❶

Agree the audit findings with your auditor in good time.

Dissatisfaction or even conflicts often arise when results are presented to the management of an organization being audited and are then questioned because, for example, the auditor has not assessed certain issues as fully free of defects. Sometimes, diplomacy in advance can be sufficient. Difficult repercussions can often be avoided with good communication at the level of the audit lead or the manager of the audit team, ensuring that findings are discussed and misunderstandings clarified.

2.3   Summary

Today, business processes run almost exclusively with IT support – in particular those that influence external financial reporting. You now know how diverse and complex the working environment of the auditor is because of this. You have also learned what a transaction audit is, in which cases IT systems are examined in more detail, and which rules the auditor has to comply with. We have also looked at the options you have for ensuring optimal cooperation with an auditor.

You are now faced with the exciting task of translating the legal requirements of an ICS, whose observance is assessed by auditors, into the language of information technology.

ICS Requirements and ERP Systems: Basic Principles, Frameworks, Structure

> Drinking tea and waiting or burying your head in the sand — these strategies are not particularly helpful in making your organization ready for an audit. You have to actively make sure that you establish an IT-capable ICS because these days, nothing works without IT.

The law prescribes and the auditor audits. And everything revolves around the internal control system. How can you make ICS requirements formulated in general terms more specific for IT-supported business processes? Where does the ICS content in the ERP environment come from? And how can you structure profitability and efficiency objectives in an ICS framework – above and beyond what is required by legislation? This chapter is dedicated to these questions. You will learn:

- How and which ERP-specific requirements are demanded of an ICS and how these requirements can be derived from generally accepted accounting principles
- Who defines the rules for compliance in the ERP environment
- How to find and structure the correct controls in the SAP environment
- Which internationally recognized studies, standards, and reference models are available for an ICS, particularly in the ERP environment

3.1 Defining ICS Content in the SAP ERP Environment

Who determines which risks are relevant in ERP-supported business processes and which controls cover these risks? How do we translate accounting-relevant compliance requirements into the language of the IT systems? The following explanations will help you to answer the most important questions regarding ICS content in the SAP ERP environment.

3.1.1 ICS Basic Principles in the ERP Environment: From GAAP to GAPCAS

From Chap. 1, "Legal Requirements in ICS Compliance," you already know which legal and internal requirements an ICS has to satisfy. There are further provisions that define how the requirements are to be understood with reference to the IT of an organization.

In this area, Germany has taken a leading role: almost no other country has compliance-based regulations that demonstrate ICS basic principles in the IT environment in any comparable form.

Requirements in Germany

In addition to the statements, standards, and guidelines specified in Chap. 1, in Germany the following IT-specific requirements are relevant. They are only recommendations, but have become firmly established in practice:

- The FAMA statement (FAMA = Technical Committee for Modern Accounting Systems at the Institut der Wirtschaftsprüfer Deutschland e.V. [Institute of Public Auditors in Germany, Incorporated Association] (IDW)) from 1987
- The IDW AcP FAIT 1 statement "Principles of Proper Accounting When Using Information Technology," which partly replaces the FAMA statement
- The IDW AcP FAIT 2 statement "Principles of Proper Accounting for Electronic Commerce"
- The IDW AcP FAIT 3 statement "Principles of Proper Accounting using Electronic Archiving Procedures"
- The Generally Accepted Principles of Computer-assisted Accounting Systems (GAPCAS) from 11/7/1995 (letter from the German Federal Finance Ministry from 11/7/1995 – IVA8 – S0316 – 52/95, Federal Tax Gazette I p. 738)

If we consider the content of the statements and GAPCAS, the following overview of requirements for correctness that an accounting-relevant IT system has to fulfill stands out.

GAPCAS as basis for ICS

As you can see in Fig. 3.1, most requirements for correctness are derived directly from *Generally Accepted Accounting Principles* (GAAP). However, there are also requirements that are only relevant in an IT environment (IT-specific requirements). The fulfillment of these two groups of requirements can be seen as the primary task of control mechanisms established in (and around) IT systems relevant for accounting purposes.

Formal requirements

In Germany, most *formal* correctness requirements (for example, security, archiving, traceability, unalterability) are derived directly from Sections 238 and 239 of the German Commercial Code (HGB). Requirements such as the document function, the account function, or the journal function represent a "translation" of Sections 238 and 239 into IT language.

Material requirements

The *material correctness requirements* define the logic of the calculation, evaluation, and reporting of certain financial statement items within external reporting. The implementation of these requirements in the form of IT-supported processes requires various application controls that guarantee the fulfillment of specific audit-relevant criteria in the production of the figures.

In the professional world, these criteria have become established as *assertions* and are summarized under the abbreviation CEAVOP. The individual criteria are:

- Completeness
- Existence
- Accuracy
- Valuation
- Ownership
- Presentation

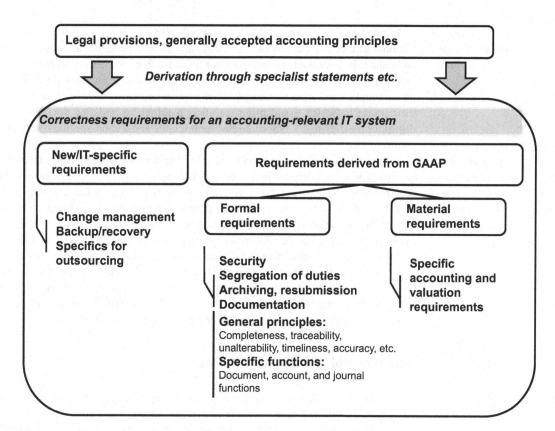

▣ **Figure 3.1** Correctness criteria for an accounting-relevant IT system

3.1.2   Who Defines the Rules in the SAP Environment?

The formal and material GAAP-driven requirements that an ICS has to satisfy have to be "translated" into the language of an IT application that maps the accounting-relevant processes.

Unalterability of Documents in SAP ERP	[e.g.]

The principle of unalterability of accounting documents can be negatively impacted if, in the SAP ERP system, authorizations that allow direct table changes are assigned for executing debugging activities. At this point, effective control mechanisms must be established, for example:

- Preventive: restrictive authorization assignment
- Preventive: emergency user concept
- Detective: review of system log

No national
application-specific
provisions

In practice, who performs this "translation" task? The state as legislator and professional auditor associations have to maintain their independence as issuers of various standards and guidelines and must not influence free competition on the software provider market. For this reason, and because of the simple fact that there are numerous applications from various providers who are constantly improving or changing their products (which would make the effort required for updating documentation disproportionately high), official bodies cannot issue application-specific compliance requirements.

Organizations and
auditors assume
the role of
translator

It is primarily organizations and companies themselves – as well as software manufacturers – who are interested in converting legal requirements into application-specific requirements. Various organizations, such as the *German-speaking SAP user group* (DSAG), represent these interests for the purposes of information exchange, networking, and the opportunity to exert influence. They publish guidelines that are helpful for implementing an ICS in the SAP environment. Amongst other things, these guidelines contain the experiences of many SAP users in dealing with *auditing companies*. As independent experts, auditors must be able to form their own opinion about the control mechanisms required in an ERP application. As the audit of legal compliance relevant to financial reporting is one of the primary tasks of the auditing companies, these companies predominate when it comes to defining application-specific ICS rules.

3.1.3   Control Identification Process

An ICS is used to address compliance as well as effectiveness and profitability. Section 3.1.1, "ICS Basic Principles in the ERP Environment: From GAAP to GAPCAS," describes the structure of financial reporting-driven compliance requirements in the IT environment. But how do we get from requirements or a conceptual ICS framework to the ICS content? This process for designing the ICS is presented below (see Fig. 3.2).

Finding risks

We also use the controls to minimize the relevant *risks*. This means that we first have to identify relevant risks. Figure 3.2 shows a simplified illustration of the three compliance areas as separate *ICS domains*. The domains are: financially-driven 1, industry-specific (for example, FDA) 2, and organization-specific 3.

Even though in the example in Fig. 3.2 three domains are relevant (assuming the organization concerned manufactures medicinal products), the domains all refer to *business processes*. The question is how to find the relevant risks in these business processes. The decisive factor is the application of ICS domain-specific criteria to the relevant processes.

Domain 1: External Financial Reporting

The main criteria here are the *assertions* referred to in Sect. 3.1.1, "ICS Basic Principles in the ERP Environment: From GAAP to GAPCAS."

[e.g.]   Main Criteria in Domain 1

If we look at the SAP-supported sales process, in the subprocess billing, for example, we would recognize the following causal chain in the determination of controls:

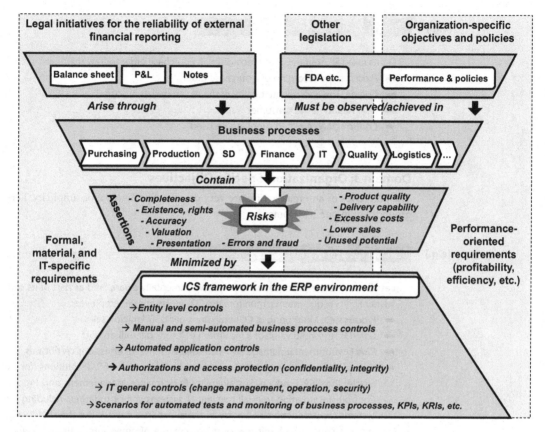

Figure 3.2 Process for identifying controls in an organization

- *Process step*: Billing (invoicing)
- *Criteria*: Completeness and valuation of receivables and sales revenue
- *Risk*: Some documents with incorrect status get "stuck" in the interface between the SAP components SD and FI
- *Control*: Contents of the SAP table VBRK are regularly monitored for incorrect billing documents

Domain 2: Requirements of Medicinal Products Manufacturers

You will learn about the main criteria for this domain in more detail in Chap. 13, "Excursion: FDA Compliance and Controls in SAP."

[e.g.]   Main Criteria in Domain 2

Let us take the example of the recording of a purchase order for raw materials:
- *Process step:* Recording of a purchase order
- *Criteria:* The appropriate quality of the raw materials procured
- *Risk:* Health of the consumer
- *Control:* Only qualified suppliers are used

Domain 3: Organization-Specific Objectives

The objectives of an organization are very diverse. For the sake of simplicity, here we group them in one ICS domain.

[e.g.]   Main Criteria in Domain 3

Let us assume the organization is very environmentally-aware, and as part of its own sustainability requirements, monitors the CO_2 emissions per employee:
- *Process step:* Monitoring of CO_2 emissions per USD 1 million sales
- *Criteria:* Threshold value of a maximum of X tons per million USD
- *Risk:* Environmental damage and increased expense for emissions certificates
- *Control:* An automated control based on the interaction of SAP solutions (for example, the SAP products Sustainability Performance Management and Process Control). Information from all relevant IT systems comes together, including the systems for production and entry of travel expense data: if the threshold value exceeds a predefined limit, the control owners are informed automatically via workflow – using special dashboards, they can analyze the causes (proportion of flights and company cars for business trips)

ICS framework   *ICS framework* is the term used for the set of derived control mechanisms as a whole. It is obvious that some controls can be relevant for more than one ICS domain simultaneously. The three ICS domains shown in Fig. 3.2 unfortunately often only form a single, standardized framework in theory; in practice, the ICS domains are primarily considered as self-contained silos.

For example, the control identified for domain 1 is also relevant for domain 3, as achieving higher sales is one of the fundamental interests of a company or organization. In the second part of this book, we will address the possibility of organizing individual ICS domains efficiently when automating the ICS in order to avoid the costly silo principle.

3.1.4 Structure of a Classic ICS Framework in the ERP Environment

What is the typical structure for an ICS framework in the ERP environment? To understand this structure, let us begin with a concrete example in SAP ERP. In the following explanation, we will focus on the "classic" consideration – compliance in the sense of

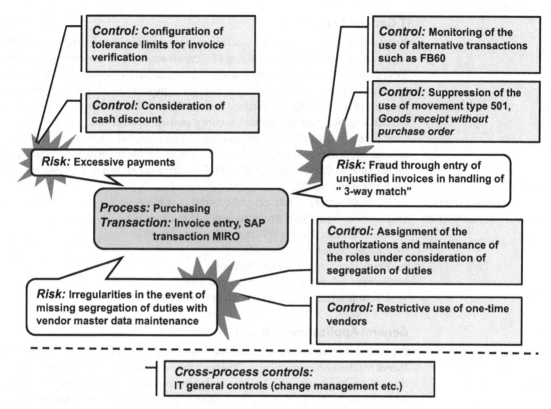

□ **Figure 3.3** Risks involved in invoice entry in SAP

legal compliance, thus, primarily the accuracy of the external financial reporting (see Sect. 1.1.1, "Compliance").

Let us take the SAP ERP-supported purchasing process (Procure to Pay) as an example. One of the process steps is invoice verification and entry. In SAP ERP, one of the ways to do this is using transaction MIRO. What risks does this transaction present and which controls are required? Figure 3.3 shows this example in a complete overview. The individual risks are as follows:

Example:
purchasing process

- Excessive payments
  This risk covers both compliance and profitability aspects: on one hand, excessive payments mean a direct loss and therefore economic damage, but no "violation" in the sense of compliance. On the other hand, the excessive payments affect the accuracy of the liabilities and therefore also affect compliance.
- Fraudulent activities through the bypassing of 3-way match controls
- Fraudulent activities due to missing segregation of duties between master data maintenance and posting authorizations
- General reliability, accuracy, and completeness of the relevant ERP processes

Let us begin by looking at the "foundation" that in Fig. 3.3 consists of the IT general controls and the general application controls.

Foundation

IT General Controls

In order to be able to rely on the accuracy of the processing logic for transaction MIRO, you have to ensure that the underlying IT controls are effective. For example, changes in the system (modifications, developments, configuration changes) must be documented, agreed, tested, free of errors, and released before they can be adopted in the live environment of an SAP ERP application. You also have to ensure that the general security standards (application and network security, password protection, general settings that affect the treatment of SAP authorization roles) are observed. Every organization has its own special features. In practice, however, and under the influence of recognized ICS studies such as CobiT, a group of control mechanisms known as *IT General Controls* has become established.

IT general controls: structure

The usual structure of IT general controls is as follows:
- Logical access to infrastructure, applications, and data
- Controls related to the system development life cycle
- Change management controls
- Physical security of computer centers
- Backup and recovery for systems and data
- Controls related to system operation (SLAs, basis support, etc.)

General Application Controls

In practice, it is not usual to consider the general application controls for covering some *formal requirements* separately, such as traceability, journal function, and account function, etc., unless the situation in question relates to a software certification. However, we do recommend this form of structure. With reference to transaction MIRO, for example, the general application controls would be part of the document number assignment that is supposed to satisfy the requirements for traceability.

These are controls for ensuring the following general basic principles:
- Traceability
- Unalterability
- Timeliness
- Document function

Process Controls

Based on business processes

Now let us look at the *process controls*: as the name suggests, their structure is based on the structure of the business processes in the respective organization. The process of entering incoming invoices bears risks such as incorrect consideration of cash discount, excessive payments, but also fraud risks. As you can see in Fig. 3.3, if there is no segregation of duties, for example, between the authorization for transaction MIRO and maintenance of the vendor master data, and there are no alternative controls that could compensate for the segregation of duties deficiency, there is a risk of intentional fraudulent activities (such as payment to someone's personal account).

Authorization roles according to segregation of duties

You can prevent this risk by designing and assigning SAP authorization roles compliant with segregation of duties. In practice, there are differing opinions about the assignment of segregation of duties in the ICS framework: often, segregation of duties is considered as belonging to the corresponding controls, such as IT general controls, because the topic of authorizations sounds very "technical." However, from the view of handling controls and as part of compliance management, as well as from a methodological perspective (for example, according to the CobiT study, see Sect. 3.2.2), segregation of duties is part of process controls.

Further process controls are:

- **Application controls**

  Configurative settings for the tolerance limits for invoice verification ensure that, for example, an invoice is automatically blocked if the invoice amount exceeds the purchase order amount by a specific threshold value. If the use of *movement type 501* (see Sect. 9.2.1, "Goods Receipts: Critical Movement Types") has been suppressed (for example, by the deletion of the accounts in account determination), no goods receipts can be entered without a purchase order reference.

- **Semi-automated controls**

  The consideration of cash discount is a typical example of this type of control because it can require manual steps. Another example is the calculation of taxes during invoice entry: depending on the configuration in SAP ERP, a tax key can "force" the correct amount; alternatively, the correct amount can be entered manually as a deviation to the default value.

- **Automated monitoring**

  These controls include steps that assume an auxiliary function and are not a direct part of the business processes; they are various evaluation options. For the MIRO-supported process of invoice verification presented, they are the following, for example:

  - Reports for monitoring invoices with a suspicion of duplicate entry (based on the same reference number, amount, and due date)
  - Reports for monitoring the other transactions (there are other transactions in addition to MIRO for entering an invoice without reference to a purchase order)

- **Manual controls**

  The observance of administrative regulations concerning one-time vendors or manual scanning and filing of original invoices can be classified as a manual control.

Thus we can note the following composition of process controls in SAP ERP.

Process Controls

Control mechanisms in business processes:
- Segregation of duties using authorizations
- Application controls (logic, configuration, master data)
- Semi-automated controls with a manual aspect
- Automated monitoring
- Manual controls

The structure of the processes is specific for each organization and, by definition, based on the organization's business processes. Where applicable, IT components are used. The following is a typical example of a division of processes in an industrial organization:

Further process controls

Division of processes

Table 3.1 Structure of an ICS framework for ensuring the reliability of external financial reporting

Control area	Control contents	SAP ERP reference
IT general controls	Logical access to infrastructure, applications, and data	Direct
	Controls related to the system development life cycle	Indirect
	Change management controls	Direct
	Physical security of computer centers	Indirect
	Backup and recovery for systems and data	Indirect
	Controls related to system operation	Direct
General application controls	Controls for ensuring the traceability, unalterability, and completeness of processing	Direct
Process controls	Segregation of duties using authorizations	Direct
	Application controls (logic, configuration, master data)	Direct
	Automated monitoring	Direct
	Semi-automated controls with a manual aspect	Direct
	Manual or organizational controls	Indirect
Entity level controls	General controls outside a direct value-added chain	None

— **Financial accounting processes**
Divided into accounts payable, accounts receivable, asset accounting, general ledger, period-end closing, and, where applicable, consolidation and consolidated financial statements

— **Procure to Pay (P2P)**
Determination of requirements, ordering, vendor selection, invoice verification, payments, bank-related accounting, etc.

— **Order to Cash (O2C)**
Order entry and verification, credit limit management, production, project management and valuation, warehouse management, material valuation, etc.

Entity level controls   *Entity level controls* (ELC) were named explicitly as such by *Auditing Standard No. 5* in the USA and cover that part of the ICS that is not directly part of the value-added chain. For example, these controls are the functions of the audit committee, internal audit, risk management, and the management of guidelines and regulations, etc. ELCs have no relevant reference to SAP and in this book, we consider them only marginally.

Table 3.1 summarizes the structure of an ICS framework.

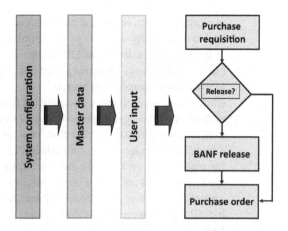

◻ Figure 3.4 Steps in a purchase order process

3.1.5 Structure of Efficiency-Oriented and Profitability-Oriented Controls in the ERP Environment

In Sect. 1.1.1, "Compliance," we stated that an ICS can focus on profitability and efficiency. Whilst the control areas of IT general controls and general application controls, as described in Sect. 3.1.4, "Structure of a Classic ICS Framework in the ERP Environment," form the standardized foundation for all ICS reference models, the main difference in the various ICS reference models lies in the contents of the process controls.

The objective of efficiency-oriented and profitability-oriented controls in the sense of this book is to address, at the deepest process or transaction level, risks that could endanger the economic success of an organization. In this book, we address primarily IT-supported or ERP-supported transactions. This means that the control mechanisms are data evaluations. The basic concept is to use the data present in an IT or ERP system to detect undesired changes in order to be able to introduce corrective measures. *Ensuring economic success*

Figure 3.4 shows a schematic illustration of a purchase order process.

Let us assume that the purchase order process is mapped in an ERP system. Which evaluations would help you to determine the optimization potential in this process? *Useful analyses*

1. **Analyses aimed at process efficiency**
   Time is money – this applies for example to manufacturing process as well: in order to satisfy customer wishes on time and deliver specific goods, these goods must first be manufactured or procured. Procurement definitely takes place – regardless of whether it is manufacturing materials or finished goods that are procured. In our case, the delay between a purchase requisition, its potential release, and conversion into a purchase order would have a negative effect on the purchasing process. In order to determine the improvement potential here, you have to perform date-related mass evaluations of individual purchase order transactions. Section 14.1, "Process-Related Data Analyses," contains further examples of analyses aimed at process efficiency.

2. **Quality of master data**
   To avoid processes stalling, the quality of the master data must be correct. If, for example, certain fields in the vendor, customer, material, or other master data are

missing, incorrect, or inconsistent, in some circumstances in our example this can lead to the inability to enter a purchase order; in that case, you would have to create or correct certain data in an ERP system manually. Section 14.2 contains further examples of analyses concerning master data quality.

3. **Manual data changes, user entries**

   Under some circumstances, uncontrolled data changes in a process (purchase requisitions, purchasing documents) can be the cause of process inefficiencies and also indicate poor data quality. Note that for some types of data, it is absolutely normal or part of daily operation that this data is changed. In any case, a mass analysis of the manual interventions, for example, in the purchase order process, can help to clarify the causes and, where applicable, introduce measures for reducing such interventions. Section 14.3, "Manual Data Changes," contains examples for analyses in SAP that focus on manual data changes.

4. **Enhancing reports**

   Standard reports available in an ERP system for monitoring specific processes (for example, in purchasing) are insufficient in some cases to cover the information requirements. In such cases, the results from data analyses whose results lists, for example, contain fields that standard reports do not have, can be used complementary to the standard reports. Section 14.4, "Supplementing SAP ERP Standard Reports," contains further SAP-specific examples on the topic of reports.

Figure 3.5 shows a simplified illustration of the process described that can help to increase the profitability and efficiency of the business processes.

Detective orientation

Finally, let us highlight a special feature of the efficiency-oriented and profitability-oriented approach in an ICS: whilst the "classic" compliance-oriented view differentiates between preventive and detective controls (primarily to reduce the audit effort by enabling reliance on preventive controls), in data analyses, mainly detective scenarios are used. Why is this so?

This is due to the nature of ERP systems: it is often extremely difficult or even impossible to design preventive controls in IT-supported processes so that they are watertight without simultaneously paying attention to IT general controls (particularly in change management) or general application controls (see Sect. 3.1.4). Preventive controls are based on the logic in the code or configuration settings. The controls can be performed on a key date, but do not provide information about whether the control has been active permanently or perhaps can still be circumvented. In practice, for example, it is not unusual in ERP implementation projects to use transaction data to check the accuracy of the business processes configured rather than simply inspecting configuration settings.

However, the main reason for the detective orientation of efficiency-oriented and profitability-oriented analyses is in the nature of such an orientation: in the same way that, when assessing the cholesterol level of a patient, a doctor will prefer to rely on the actual blood analyses rather than the contents of the patient's refrigerator, the individual events and transactions executed and documented in an ERP system must be examined to obtain a reliable statement about the efficiency and profitability in the business process. Thus there is less scope here for assumptions or for assessing the hypothetical potential than with a pure compliance focus in an ICS.

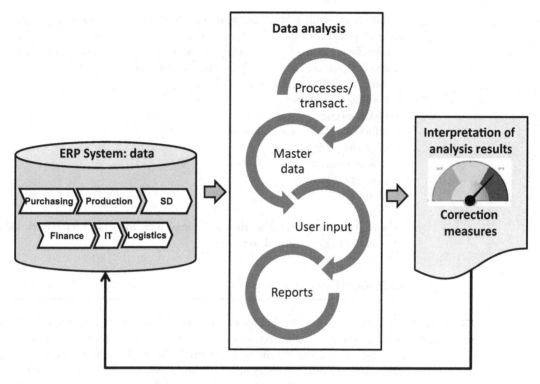

■ **Figure 3.5** Schematic illustration of the process for optimizing the efficiency and profitability of business processes

3.2 ICS-Relevant Reference Models and Standards

There are numerous theoretical approaches to designing an ICS. The range extends from in-house developments that can be purchased from the large auditing companies, to globally recognized studies and frameworks that are freely available. The frameworks or reference models are explained below: they each contain a brief overview and notes on their practical use.

3.2.1 COSO

The COSO cube is often the first framework you will think of when discussing GRC or   ICS classic
ICS frameworks. The acronym COSO is derived from *Committee of Sponsoring Organizations of the Treadway Commission.* James C. Treadway Jr., who gave COSO its name, was originally a member of the US Securities and Exchange Commission (SEC) and the first Chief Executive of this authority.

COSO has published studies that are ICS-relevant (including studies on the topic of fraud). The most well-known are:

- "Internal Control – An Integrated Framework" (1992, often referred to as a COSO classic)
- The Enterprise Risk Management study (COSO ERM 2004)

This second study is based on the original COSO framework and focuses more on risk management – a topic closely related to the ICS topic. The study describes approaches for achieving strategic and operative objectives as well as objectives in reporting and compliance. The COSO framework has eight main elements:

- Internal control environment
- Event identification
- Risk response
- Information and communication
- Objective setting
- Risk assessment
- Control activities
- Monitoring

With regard to governance, risk, and compliance, the COSO framework focuses more on the areas of risk and compliance.

3.2.2 CobiT

ICS in the IT environment

The CobiT framework (CobiT = Control Objectives for Information and Related Technologies, www.isaca.org/cobit) was developed by the IT Governance Institute (ITGI, *www.itgi.org*) and the Information Systems Audit and Control Association (ISACA, www.isaca.org) and is freely available. To some extent, CobiT can be seen as a more concrete form of COSO for IT concerns and it offers approaches for ICS and governance in the IT area.

Control objectives

The CobiT framework groups control objectives in four categories:

- Plan & Organize
- Acquire & Implement
- Deliver & Support
- Monitor & Evaluate

Each of these categories consists of 13 processes and these processes are designed to achieve a total of more than 200 illustrative control objectives (see Table 3.2). CobiT can be seen not only as an ICS, but also as an IT governance instrument.

ITGI document

The IT Governance Institute has published a helpful document – "IT Control Objectives for Sarbanes-Oxley." This document focuses on control mechanisms that have a direct reference to financial reporting and the associated compliance requirements. Illustrative business process-specific application controls in the appendix to this document represent a good basis for defining an ICS framework.

3.2.3 ITIL

IT service management in five books

The *Information Technology Infrastructure Library* (ITIL, www.itil-officialsite.com), published for the first time in the 1980s by the British Office of Government Commerce, cannot be referred to as an ICS framework in the classic sense. Instead, concentrating on IT governance, ITIL covers the area of governance in the GRC concept. The ITIL framework is designed for IT service management and offers procedures for identi-

◘ Table 3.2 Overview of CobiT properties (source: ISACA online conference)

Strengths	Appropriate for
Broad use and acceptance Good for industry Good for SOX compliance Can be integrated with ISO 2700*	Any organization with a large IT department Formalized processes Any company subject to SOX
Weaknesses	**Other notes**
Requires substantial time and effort Poor coverage for security A lot of information about "what to do" but little information on "how" to do it	ISACA provides mappings to other frameworks Can be mapped to COSO

◘ Table 3.3 Overview of ITIL properties (source: ISACA online conference)

Strengths	Appropriate for
Good for service-related IT topics Provides for a certification process Good for the availability aspects of IT governance ITIL "small scale implementation" version for smaller organizations	Mid-sized to large companies with large IT departments Organizations with formalized IT processes Particularly useful where availability of IT services is critical (e.g., banks, healthcare, etc.)
Weaknesses	**Other notes**
Not an ICS framework in the sense of this book	Five books for approx. $1,000 Training for approx. $10,000 Additional costs for ITIL software

fying, planning, processing, and supporting IT services for organizations. The ITIL consists of five books:
- Service Strategy
- Service Design
- Service Transition
- Service Operation
- Continual Service Improvement

Despite this, the ITIL structure can provide good points of reference for the structure of an ICS framework as it is designed for operative objectives (see Table 3.3).

3.2.4 GAIT

The *Guide to the Assessment of IT Risk*, published in 2007 by the US Institute of Internal Auditors, is one of the latest frameworks to address IT audit directly. Instead of a list of IT-specific control objectives, GAIT offers a risk-based method for prioritizing these controls.

IT general controls: checks

❏ **Table 3.4** Overview of GAIT properties (source: ISACA online conference)

Strengths	Appropriate for
Good for IT general controls IT not as a "science itself" but as a business service provider	Auditing Scoping
Weaknesses	**Other notes**
The IIA and ISACA approaches are sometimes different	Freely available

❏ **Table 3.5** Overview of ITAF properties (source: ISACA online conference)

Strengths	Appropriate for
Conveys an understanding of the IT audit process	IT auditors and their customers
Weaknesses	**Other notes**
The IIA and ISACA approaches are sometimes different No input for ICS content	Freely available

The first version of GAIT was intended to support the scoping process in SOX audits. The latest edition of GAIT extends this focus by enabling the general interaction of business and IT risks. In addition to compliance aspects, GAIT addresses efficiency and effectiveness topics. GAIT is based on the belief that not all IT risks can be monitored successfully within IT and that requirements from the main business processes of an organization should play a central role. This is a great plus point for GAIT because during the SOX wave, the impression arose that IT general controls are a science in themselves and that business is driven by IT and not vice versa.

Table 3.4 shows an overview of the GAIT properties.

3.2.5 ITAF

Reference model for IT audits

As already stated, ISACA offers reference models that follow a similar objective to GAIT. These reference models are ITAF and Risk IT.

The acronym ITAF stands for *Information Technology Assurance Framework*. This reference model is aimed at users who deal with topics in the area of IT applications, systems, and infrastructure, presented simply for IT auditors. The standards, guidelines, and audit procedures that ITAF contains can be useful not only for auditors, but also for the "consumers" of the audit results or reports. In detail, ITAF does the following:

- It offers good practice models for design, implementation, and reporting as part of IT audits
- It explains IT audit-specific concepts and standard roles for people involved in an IT audit
- It describes requirements for the expertise, experience, and code of conduct of an auditor, as well as typical processes for reporting

◻ Table 3.6 Overview of Risk IT properties (source: ISACA online conference)

Strengths	Appropriate for
Link between IT and business Content and concrete examples for risk management	Risk management in the IT domain
Weaknesses	**Other notes**
Little input for ICS content	Link to CobiT and Val IT

3.2.6 Risk IT

The Risk IT reference model from ISACA deals with risks in the IT field and supplements CobiT: whilst CobiT gives examples of controls that minimize IT risks, Risk IT provides a framework concept for identifying and managing IT-related risks.

Risk IT claims to link business risks with IT risks by establishing a connection to the business objectives in all areas (including in an example list of typical risk scenarios) and viewing the management of IT risks as part of the overall risk management process in an organization. It also considers a cost/benefit ratio in risk management.

IT risks as part of business risks

The overall model is divided into three large domains, and each of these domains consists of three processes:
- **Risk governance**
  Development of the risk content, integration of this content in the Enterprise Risk Management process, risk-conscious decisions in business processes
- **Risk evaluation**
  Information procurement, risk analysis, maintenance of the risk profile
- **Risk response**
  Communication of risks, task plans, reaction to events

The document "Risk IT Practitioner Guide" supports the Risk IT reference model with examples of the IT-specific key risk indicators (KRI), impact criteria for business, description of links to CobiT and Val IT, etc.

Risk IT fills the gap between *generic* reference models such as COSO ERM and *detailed* (primarily security-related) IT risk management reference models.

Table 3.6 shows an overview of the Risk IT properties.

3.2.7 Val IT

Val IT is a reference model for the management of investments in the IT domain. It consists of several documents. The objective of this reference model is to measure and control the benefits of IT investments from the view of the main business of an organization and to support organizations in achieving an optimal value contribution from their IT investments. Val IT consists of a series of principles and processes. In Version 2.0 (available since 2008), Val IT is based to a large extent on the structure and setup of CobiT. Val IT consists of three domains, and the following three processes are assigned to each of the domains:

◻ **Table 3.7** Overview of Val IT properties (source: ISACA online conference)

Strength	Appropriate for
Supplements CobiT Optimization of the value contribution from IT investments	Offers approaches for value engineering in IT
Weakness	**Other notes**
Provides more detailed reference models than Val IT	From a structural perspective, is oriented on CobiT Three domains, each with three processes

- Value governance
- Portfolio management
- Investment management

Relationship to CobiT

The description of the processes follows the approach in CobiT. The following are defined for each process:

- Key management practices
- Management guidelines
- RACI chart
- Goals and metrics

Val IT is intended to supplement or complete CobiT in the financial management domains in particular and to give information to those persons hoping for information on the value contribution of their IT. CobiT also contains governance elements from these domains, which means that certain overlaps are possible. However, Val IT also contains new perspectives that are missing in CobiT.

Relationship to VMM

From a content perspective, Val IT is related to a further reference model, Value Measuring Methodology (VMM). This reference model offers more detailed instructions than Val IT on the different types of added value. In particular, VMM differentiates between a tangible and measurable added value and an intangible added value. VMM also offers comparison models and examples for calculating the added value for various projects.

Table 3.7 shows an overview of the Val IT properties.

We can assume that the topic of "sustainability/success of IT investments" will continue to grow in importance. In this regard, Val IT makes a good contribution to the topic of "value management."

3.2.8 CMMI

Five degrees of maturity in software development

Capability Maturity Model Integration (CMMI) is a collection of reference models for various application areas. It is primarily a model for assessing the quality ("degree of maturity model") of the software process (development, maintenance, configuration, etc.) of organizations as well as for determining improvement measures for the process. At the end of 2003, CMMI replaced the older CM model in order to consolidate various CM models available at the time (every development discipline had a separate model)

◻ **Table 3.8** Overview of CMMI properties (source: ISACA online conference)

Strengths	Appropriate for
Optimization of the processes for software development in an organization Could be used as a source for ICS content in software development processes	Improving the organization in the area of software development Certification or assessment recognized in practice
Weaknesses	**Other notes**
Focus on software development, but not enough detail for large software companies	Official check of the degree of maturity is offered Parallels to ITIL with regard to determination of the degree of maturity

◻ **Table 3.9** Overview of MOF properties (source: ISACA online conference)

Strengths	Appropriate for
Available free of charge Logical and clear structure	Smaller companies that choose not to implement a larger framework
Weaknesses	**Other notes**
Not detailed enough for complex organizations Focuses on Microsoft Windows customers Does not address risk assessment	Closely related to ITIL V3 Attempts to be an IT governance framework, may have good prospects in future versions

and to create a new, standardized model. A CMMI model is a systematic representation of tested practices to support organizational improvement. At the center of CMMI are five levels between different degrees of maturity of the software development processes. For example, a CMMI model can be used for the following:

- To get an overview of the most common procedures (for example, in project planning)
- To analyze the strengths and weaknesses of an organization
- To determine improvement measures and bring them into a useful sequence

ITIL can be seen as partially related to CMMI as both models offer assessments based on degrees of maturity. However, the focus of the assessment in ITIL is on the IT infrastructure and on services. Table 3.8 shows an overview of the CMMI properties.

ITIL and CMMI

3.2.9 MOF

Microsoft Operations Framework (MOF) is a reference model from the software manufacturer Microsoft. It is not very well known in Europe, but is closely related to ITIL V3 and focuses on IT services. For the details of this model, see http://technet.microsoft.com/en-us/library/cc506049.aspx. From a content perspective, MOF represents an attempt to offer an integrated reference model between the areas of governance, risk, and compliance across the entire IT life cycle.

Table 3.9 shows the properties of Microsoft Operations Framework.

▣ Table 3.10 Overview of the properties of ISO 27k (source: ISACA online conference)

Strengths	Appropriate for
Focus on security policy Risk-based approach Strong standard with good data protection strategies	Generally for all organizations that use IT Used by IT auditors as a benchmark for security topics
Weaknesses	**Other notes**
Very technology-centric, requires a larger governance framework Addition of availability and integrity but these elements are part of data governance, which belongs to the security topic	Standards, not a framework Approx. $200 for ISO 27002 and $300 for ISO 27001 and 27002 Self-assessment and certification are possible (extra charge)

3.2.10 ISO 27k

Standards for security

ISO 27k (http://webstore.ansi.org) groups standards – therefore it is not a reference model. These standards arose in 2000 (British Standard BS 7799, subsequently ISO 17799) and were updated in 2005 and 2007. Basically, ISO 27k represents a checklist for controls in the field of information security. From a content perspective, ISO 27k is structured in three pillars:

- Confidentiality
- Availability
- Integrity

Table 3.10 shows the properties of ISO 27k.

3.2.11 PCI-DSS

Data security for plastic money

In connection with the scandals surrounding stolen credit card data, the PCI-DSS standard (PCI-DSS = Payment Card Industry Data Security Standard, www.pcisecuritystandards.org) is very interesting. Just like the ISO standards, PCI-DSS is a standard and not a reference model. It has been developed to supplement other standards, providing specific details in the field of "plastic money." From a content perspective, this standard could be projected onto another security environment that focuses on the protection of data (see Table 3.11).

3.2.12 Summary View of Reference Models

Four dimensions

As you can see, existing frameworks and reference models have content orientations and objects that are settled across four main dimensions with different degrees of cover:

- Strategy
- Performance
- Risk
- Compliance

Table 3.11 Overview of the properties of PCI-DSS (source: ISACA online conference)

Strengths	Appropriate for
Available free of charge Good data protection strategies Provides a self-assessment, although this is very generic	All organizations that produce, collect, store, or transfer cardholder data
Weaknesses	**Other notes**
Not a governance-based concept Very high-level, little specific information	Checklist approach rather than an established governance model

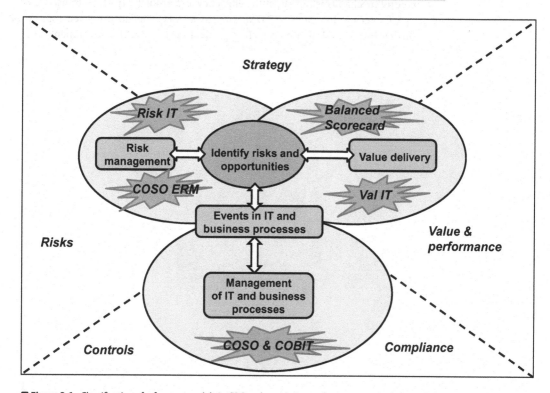

Figure 3.6 Classification of reference models in GRC and enterprise performance topics (source: Risk IT Overview)

Figure 3.6 shows the classification of some reference models into these four dimensions.

Whilst GRC, strategy, and business performance management concepts independent of one another is nothing new, their coming together is a trend that is still quite new (see Sect. 16.6.4, "Merging GRC, Strategy, and Performance Topics"). Of the four dimensions mentioned, in which C-level management is active (C = Chief, as in CFO, CEO, CIO), two are relevant in this book: *risk* and *compliance*. Therefore, in the following chapters, we will consider COSO and CobiT as reference models, particularly for the topic of ICS content and automation in the SAP environment.

3.3   Summary

In this chapter we have created a bridge between the legal requirements of an ICS and the practical structure of an ICS in the IT environment. We have classified and described ICS basic principles in the IT environment and presented the process for identifying the ICS content schematically. We have also provided a good overview of internationally recognized studies, reference models, and standards that can provide a lot of useful information with regard to the process and content in the design of an ICS.

From this chapter you also know that for IT-supported business processes, some control mechanisms can target the efficiency and profitability of the transactions.

Chapter 4, "How Does SAP Deal with Risk- and Compliance-Related Topics?" offers further help with designing your ICS, particularly in the SAP environment.

How Does SAP Deal with Risk- and Compliance-Related Topics?

> Regardless of how unique requirements may be, there are usually various ways of implementing them. In this chapter, you will learn about the solutions and products that SAP offers to enable organizations to meet compliance requirements and establish integrated governance, risk, and compliance processes.

In the ERP environment, compliance is naturally reflected at SAP in its capacity as a software manufacturer. In this chapter you will learn:

- How SAP handles certification of its own products
- Which relevant guides and instructions exist for implementing and checking compliance requirements
- Which SAP products support an integrated GRC (governance, risk, and compliance) process and what the key elements of this approach are
- Which sources are available to customers to enable them to get an overview of the control mechanisms in SAP-supported business processes

4.1 Software Certification

One of the compliance aspects in the SAP environment is the certification of SAP products – that is, confirmation by an independent expert of the general compliance of software with specific legal or other standards. In the pages that follow, you will learn which compliance certifications based on official sources SAP is required to have.

> ❯ **Differentiation – Software Certification and ICS Attestation** Before we look at software certification in more detail, let us address a common misunderstanding in practice: software certification and organization-specific ICS attestation are two different things.
> - **Software certification**
>   If an ERP system is "compliant," this does not mean that this system is also compliant when used in an organization. The certification refers to the basic nature of the software product.
> - **Attestation with reference to an organization-specific ICS**
>   This is a statement regarding whether an ERP system is used compliantly in an organization. It refers to controls in the organization.

4.1.1   SAP Note 671016

SAP Note for software certification

The SAP Notes that customers can access online via SAP Service Marketplace not only offer solutions for various technical problems, but also provide answers to frequently asked questions. SAP Note 671016, "Software Certifications," describes how SAP handles certification of its own products. The last change to the note is dated October 15, 2003, but its basic statements were still correct at the time of printing of this book.

Why does SAP certify its own software?

The note states that a software manufacturer is not obliged in principle to "have his standard software checked for correct processing by an authorized body." It also explains that SAP ensures that selected areas of its software modules are checked and attested sporadically (after weighing up new features in a release) to increase the quality of the software and customer satisfaction. SAP can make the existing test reports accessible to customers.

Criteria for software certification

With regard to the criteria for assessing the correctness of the software, this note refers to German standards (see Sect. 3.1.1, "ICS Basic Principles in the ERP Environment: From GAAP to GAPCAS"). In particular:

- Legal trade regulations (German Commercial Code (HGB))
- Tax regulations (German Fiscal Code (AO), Generally Accepted Principles of Computer-assisted Accounting Systems (GAPCAS))
- Statements from the German Institute of Public Auditors (IDW PS 330, RS FAIT 1, RS FAIT 2)

Auditors (generally one of the Big Four auditing companies) or authorities such as BSI (German Federal Office for Information Security) assess the software based on the above-mentioned regulations.

The SAP Note also comments that this form of assessment is only possible in Germany due to the professional requirements that exist there.

Nevertheless, an attestation given in Germany also has international importance, particularly as the underlying principles of assessment mainly arise from generally accepted accounting principles, the contents of which are often identical worldwide.

4.1.2   Certification Reports

SAP Note 671016 states where the current attestations are located. Customers and partners can access them via http://service.sap.com/certificates.

There are several areas in SAP Service Marketplace that contain certification reports. The certification attestations are located in the section on LEGAL REQUIREMENTS, see Fig. 4.1.

USA: Core Financial System Requirements

One of the certifications not created according to German regulations is the *Certificate of Compliance* awarded for mySAP ERP 2005. According to this certificate, the product corresponds with the principles of Core Financial Systems. The certification was performed by the *Financial Systems Integration Office*, a government agency in the USA. This agency is responsible for attesting software products in the financial environment. The attested products receive permission for use in the USA at government facilities, agencies, and for the government itself.

Certificate for mySAP ERP 2004

The majority of software certificates in the LEGAL REQUIREMENTS area of SAP Service Marketplace are created based on the German auditing standard IDW PS 880. The

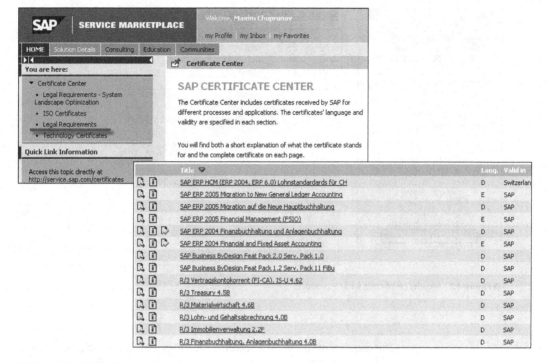

◘ Figure 4.1 SAP certification reports

current inspection report relates to mySAP ERP 2004 (SP 6). It refers to the correctness of the modules FI-GL, FI-AP, FI-AR, FI-AA with use of New General Ledger. The assessment criteria concerned two areas: GAPCAS and GdPDU (law regarding the verifiability of digital documents, the German legal standard that represents the interests of the tax authorities). The coverage of accounting-relevant valuation requirements referred exclusively to German commercial and tax law service.sap.com/security – in detail, the following:

- Commercial law regulations, in particular Section 238 ff. HGB
- Tax law regulations, in particular Section 140 ff. AO
- IDW statement on accounting, "Principles of Proper Accounting When Using Information Technology" (IDW RS FAIT 1, September 24, 2002)
- IDW statement on accounting "Generally Accepted Principles of Computer-assisted Accounting Systems (GAPCAS)" (letter from the German Federal Finance Ministry, November 7, 1995)

For the details, particularly with regard to the exclusion of certain functions from the scope of the audit or certification, see the original inspection report. The overall statement of the attestation confirms that the software product complies with the requirements specified – provided this software product is used properly. This means that we can assume that the generally valid processes within a software, which are to a large extent not release-specific, are consistent.

Compliance with proper use

□ **Figure 4.2**   Security certificates for SAP products

The mention of "proper use" confirms the importance of configurative application controls in SAP ERP. As a table-controlled application, SAP offers a wide range of design opportunities and options that take on important control functions. One of the main objectives of this book is to present the most important compliance-relevant application controls in SAP (see Part II, "From Concept to Content: Audit Guide for SAP ERP").

Security-related certification of SAP products   In addition to the certificates already mentioned, which cover the functional side of SAP products (focus: application controls), there are certifications that relate exclusively to the security of SAP applications. SAP customers and partners can access them online via SAP Service Marketplace at they include the security certificate issued by the German Federal Office for Information Security (BSI) (see Fig. 4.2). The last certificate refers to the mySAP.com component of the R/3 system, Release 4.0b, which was assessed according to the following criteria:

- Information Technology Security Evaluation Criteria (ITSEC) V.2.1
- IT Security Evaluation Manual (ITSEM) V.1.0

For this certification, SAP transactions and RFC function groups (RFC = Remote Function Call) were assessed; assessment was according to evaluation level E2, and the certified minimum strength of the relevant security mechanisms is "medium." For details, see the certification report. This certificate is recognized in the following countries by comparable authorities: Germany, Finland, France, UK, Italy, The Netherlands, Norway, Portugal, Sweden, Switzerland, and Spain.

4.2 Compliance-Relevant Guides

Finding your way in the mass of official online sources of information about compliance in an SAP environment is not easy. In Sect. 4.2.1, "SAP Online Resources," we therefore look at the most important sources that refer to a number of documents.

SAP AG has, both independently and in its role as co-author in DSAG e.V. (German-speaking SAP user group), explained various compliance-relevant topics in publications. Three publications in particular are important from a practical perspective (see Sect. 4.2.3, "DSAG Guides: Audit Guides, Data Protection Guides").

It may be that you will have to adjust your expectations with regard to the content of compliance-related sources of information published on the SAP websites: they generally only address topics regarding IT general controls, such as security, access protection, and change management.

4.2.1 SAP Online Resources

The Internet contains sources of information and documents about the security of SAP systems. The generally accessible information is available on the official SAP Help Portal (http://help.sap.com/). As you can see in Figs. 4.3 and 4.4, there are separate security guides for the individual SAP products.

help.sap.com/

In SAP Service Marketplace, accessible for customers and partners, under service.sap.com/security, there are two particularly relevant sections in the SECURITY area:

SAP Service Marketplace

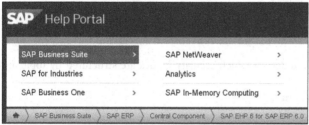

help.sap.com

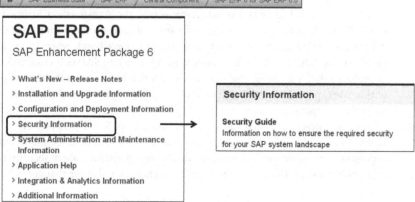

□ Figure 4.3 SAP Help Portal – Security Guides

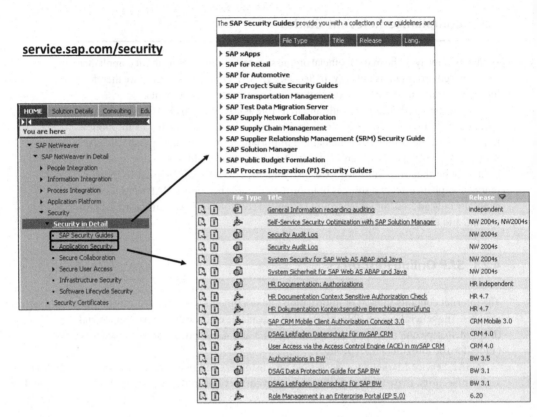

Figure 4.4   SAP Service Marketplace – "Security" area

- SAP Security Guides, in which security guides are structured by topic and SAP product
- Application Security

Under the link GENERAL INFORMATION within the APPLICATION SECURITY area, you will find links to the compliance-relevant tools and sources of information. The information about the tools in particular must be treated with reservation: it is not up-to-date or complete; Sect. 4.3, "Integrated Approach in SAP GRC 10.0 and Further Compliance-Relevant Solutions," also deals with this topic and, at the time of printing of this book, provides a valid overview of tools and applications that are relevant for audit and compliance.

SAP Security Notes   A further practice-related source of information are SAP Notes (see Fig. 4.5). Assigned to an SAP application component, these SAP Notes describe the treatment of certain security aspects in SAP products or contain information about security-relevant changes in these products as a result of release changes and other changes.

https://websmp109.sap-ag.de/securitynotes

Released SAP Security Notes list based on the date range selected			
59 SAP Security Note(s) found.			
Nu...	Application Area	Short text	Priority
751806	BC-TWB-TST-CAT	Missing confirmation prompt in CATT function modules	Correction with high priority
821875	BC-CST-MS	Security settings in the message server	Recommendations/additional info
830528	BC-MID-RFC	RFC logon: Security problems	Correction with high priority
888889	SV-SMG-SER	Automatic checks for security notes using RSECNOTE	Recommendations/additional info
1012066	BC-DWB-TOO-ABA	Security note: Authorization check when executing reports	Correction with high priority
1060643	BC-BSP	Security note: Hijacking/sys. login: New login after refresh	Correction with high priority
1133739	BC-SEC	Security note: Security gap in Data Browser (SE16)	HotNews
1168120	GRC-SAC-SCC	Risk Analysis and Remediation 5.3 Support Package (VIRCC)	Recommendations/additional info
1175239	BC-JAS-SEC	XSS attacks protection	Correction with high priority
1235367	SCM-APO-FCS-BF	Missing authority check in APO transaction.	Correction with low priority
1262016	SCM-APO-FCS-BF	Missing authority check in APO transaction.	Correction with low priority
1298433	BC-CST-GW	Security note: Bypassing security in reginfo & secinfo	Correction with medium priority
1324684	BC-DB-ORA-DBA	Creating encrypted RMAN backups using BR*Tools	Recommendations/additional info
1357370	BW-BEX-OT-DBIF	No authorization check for editor	Correction with high priority
1363371	FS-CD	FS-CD: Missing authorization checks SAPRGEN_CD	Correction with medium priority
1363788	EP-PIN-PB-PRT	Security Note: Vulnerable Page Builder	Correction with medium priority
1372831	BC-ESI-WS-JAV-CFG	WS Navigator help page can be misused for XSS	HotNews
1385621	BC-FES-ITS	Security: XSS vulnerability in ITS 6.20	Correction with medium priority

Figure 4.5 SAP Notes on security

Important Websites

For a summary of relevant SAP Notes, see https://websmp109.sap-ag.de/securitynotes and http://service.sap.com/securitynotes. You can also search for notes using keywords or uniquely assigned ID numbers.

http://www.sap.com/germany/about/company/revis/infomaterial/index.epx is another important link.

Here you will find information from the DSAG Audit/Risk Management working group, with various audit guides and guidelines.

4.2.2 Security Guides

The white paper "Secure Configuration of SAP NetWeaver Application Server ABAP" from SAP summarizes the most important security-relevant facts. The other, more detailed white paper, "SAP Standard for Security" (published initially in June 2009), offers a good, cross-solution overview of standard mechanisms, processes, and services that exist in the area of security in the SAP environment. As far as the content is concerned, the document covers more than security in the classic sense: from the perspective of an ICS concept, within the area IT GENERAL CONTROLS, this document covers sub-areas

ICS coverage

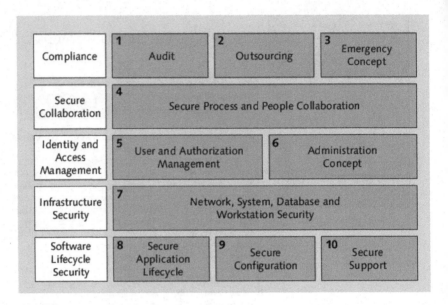

☐ **Figure 4.6** Secure Operations Map

such as access protection (at all relevant levels, such as application, databases, network, etc.) or change/incident management.

Focus   If you look at this document from the view of the life cycle of an application, it focuses in particular on the phase of live operation and on optimization; the design and implementation phases are only addressed marginally.

In the Security Guide, the activities and measures are grouped by topic (see Fig. 4.6). The relevant mechanisms and processes are grouped in five areas:

- Compliance
- Secure Collaboration
- Identity and Access Management
- Infrastructure Security
- Software Lifecycle Security

These areas contain ten sub-areas, the content of which is explained below:

Audit

Three groups of   This section describes general objectives of a security-related audit in the SAP environ-
audit activities   ment, and mentions three groups of audit activity:

- Initial analysis of the auditability of an SAP system. This is the evaluation of the central security-relevant system settings.
- Detailed audit of the security-relevant processes, operations, system settings, etc.
- Additional audit procedures, such as penetration tests, etc.

This section also contains a directory of SAP training courses related to compliance, as well as links to external sources of information, such as the publication on regular security audits for SAP systems from the BSI (see Sect. 4.2.3, "DSAG Guides: Audit Guides, Data Protection Guides").

Outsourcing

In addition to possible types of outsourcing and a list of typical security measures, this section describes mandatory components of Service Level Agreements. The link to further information resources contains SAP links to Application Management Services (AMS, SAP services) and to the description of the External Service Desk (functions within SAP Solution Manager).

SLA components, links to AMS and BSI

External links refer to both relevant BSI publications and to auditing standard 70 of the US professional association of auditors (the "SAS 70 Report" standard). This standard describes the treatment of control mechanisms in the event of outsourcing.

> **SAS 70 Is Being Superseded**   SAS 70 is being superseded internationally by the *International Standard on Assurance Engagements 3402* (ISAE), "Assurance Reports on Controls at Service Organizations"; on a national level, for example, in Germany, the topic is considered in IDW PS 951 (auditing the internal control system at service providers for functions outsourced to the service provider).

Emergency Concept

This section describes activities as part of an operative emergency concept that consists of two steps:

Emergency concept in two steps

1. Ongoing preparation and prevention
2. Notification functions and management of an emergency in accordance with the predefined measures plan

The section also describes points that must be noted as part of a documented emergency concept. The external links refer to relevant BSI publications.

Secure Process and People Collaboration

This section looks at communication both in the sense of distributed automated business processes (interfaces), and in the sense of exchange of information between participants in these processes (users) in the SAP environment. It describes the following parts in detail:

- Continuous maintenance and operation of a Public Key Infrastructure (PKI), user and authorization management, e-mail security, and anti-virus software
- Continuous monitoring of security settings
- Monitoring of compliance with directives and contract-specific agreements with employees, customers, and suppliers (for example, with regard to authentication, limitation of data storage, evaluation of activities, etc.)
- Monitoring and analysis of various activity logs

Numerous references to various SAP sources of information concern technical guidelines for the security of web services, collaboration with SAP NetWeaver and Process Integration, B2B security aspects, and much more.

User and Authorization Management

Six activity groups   This section describes the treatment of both internal and external SAP users. The standard processes and mechanisms that exist for this purpose in the SAP environment are divided into six activity groups and are described in the following structure:

- **Workflows**
  This part lists possible scenarios and requirements that affect user-related and authorization-related operations in SAP. They can be supported by workflows: one tool for this is SAP NetWeaver Identity Management (IdM).
- **Infrastructure maintenance**
  This section describes typical administration tasks undertaken as part of the maintenance of IdM, User Stores, and SSO mechanisms.
- **Administration authorizations**
  This part deals with the special treatment of administration authorizations.
- **Risk analysis**
  This aspect is particularly important from an ICS perspective. The document refers to SAP Access Control; for more information, see Sect. 4.3.1, "SAP Governance, Risk, and Compliance Suite 10.0."
- **Monitoring**
  This section describes monitoring activities within IdM and other access management solutions.
- **Maintenance of authorization roles**
  Here you can find information on the maintenance of roles in PFCG (Profile Generator).

The document also describes a possible structure and the content of an authorization concept in the SAP environment. It also contains a useful collection of sources of information on topics such as single sign-on and authentication, Identity Management, and relevant SAP standard training courses.

Administration Concept
(Authorization Concept for System Administration)

Administration   This section is dedicated to the treatment of authorizations for the various administra-
authorizations   tors in the SAP environment, who normally have extensive access rights. In addition to examples of critical activities in an SAP system, there are references to tools and mechanisms in the SAP environment that can minimize the risk associated with extensive authorizations, for example:

- Audit Information System
- SAP Access Control
- Special logging and review functions, etc.

In this book, we address these topics in Sect. 4.3, "Integrated Approach in SAP GRC 10.0 and Further Compliance-Relevant Solutions", and in Chap. 7, "General Application Controls in SAP ERP."

The section describes a special user administration and authorization concept for various administrator groups and for review processes, specifying it as a prerequisite for compliant treatment of administrator authorizations.

Network, System, Database, and Workstation Security

This section deals with the security of the infrastructure – that is, it looks at security aspects that, although SAP-relevant, are actually outside the SAP applications. The description of the security-relevant activities and the references to further information resources are divided up into the following areas:

— Operating system
— Database
— Network
— End-user workstations

Infrastructure security

Secure Application Lifecycle

This section describes standard mechanisms and activities that ensure compliant treatment of SAP software within an application lifecycle. It addresses not only security controls, but also change management. Three phases are considered differently between SAP standard software and customer SAP developments: design phase, implementation phase, and ongoing operation.

Change management aspects

Numerous SAP-internal and external links to information resources refer to developer guidelines (SAP Community Network, http://www.sdn.sap.com/irj/sdn/devguide, or help.sap.com, keyword SECURE PROGRAMMING) and to BSI publications etc. The section also mentions the following relevant tools:

— Transport Management System (TMS)
— Software Deployment Manager (SDM)
— SAP Solution Manager
— SAP NetWeaver Development Infrastructure (DI) for Java
— SAP Code Inspector

Secure Configuration

This section looks at the configuration not from a content perspective but from a process perspective: it refers to mechanisms that, on one hand, have to guarantee that the security-relevant configuration settings follow an established change management process, and on the other hand, are monitored with regard to changes.

Secure configuration as a process

With regard to monitoring the settings, the Security Guide refers to the Visual Administrator and the SAP NetWeaver Administrator within each individual application server (both the ABAP and the Java part of SAP NetWeaver are relevant), but also lists the following functions in SAP Solution Manager that enable monitoring in a distributed system landscape:

— Configuration validation functions
— Security Optimization Service (SOS)
— Integration of all customer-accessible EarlyWatch Alert services with SAP Solution Manager

The section also refers to the option of having additional monitoring activities performed by SAP employees via remote connections.

The monitoring of configuration settings is an important part of an ICS system and is covered in Chap. 16, "ICS Automation Using SAP Process Control."

Secure Support

Support   This section describes both general requirements of the internal organization at customers, as well as standard processes and mechanisms that SAP provides customers with to solve SAP product-related problems:

- Handling of OSS error messages
- Remote connections to the SAP customer systems

4.2.3 DSAG Guides: Audit Guides, Data Protection Guides

The publications of the German-speaking SAP user group (DSAG) that we will look at in this section have been created in collaboration with SAP AG and can be found both on the DSAG website and in SAP Service Marketplace (see Sect. 4.2.1, "SAP On-line Resources"). For the purposes of this book, the following guides are particularly relevant:

- SAP ERP 6.0 Audit Guide
- SAP ERP 6.0 Data Protection Guide

Both publications must be understood as recommendations that give interested parties points of reference. They are not binding directives or standards. In spite of this, note that the quality and competence of these publications is high, as confirmed by their high acceptance in practice (including by the Big Four auditing companies).

The SAP ERP 6.0 Audit Guide was created by the "Audit Roadmap" working group and consists of two parts:

- *Basic part*: explains IT general controls and cross-process application controls from an ICS perspective
- *Business part*: describes process-related or module-related application controls (and the procedure for auditing them) for FI, MM, CO, and SD

The SAP ERP 6.0 Data Protection Guide is based on the German Data Protection Act (BDSG), which regulates the treatment of personal data. The guide focuses on the SAP module Human Capital Management (HCM; previously Human Resources, HR); the control mechanisms it covers concern above all the security and the cross-process application controls that are also relevant in the compliance context of this book.

4.3   Integrated Approach in SAP GRC 10.0 and Further Compliance-Relevant Solutions

The three letters GRC (governance, risk, and compliance) have become firmly fixed in the vocabulary of top management levels and on the agenda of the CFO. However, whilst previously, compliance and the associated requirements of an internal control system (ICS), such as US SOX etc., have generally been considered in isolation, today we talk about an integrated GRC approach: this is evident both in the development of theoretical framework concepts and in the GRC software solutions.

But how can we achieve a good balance between theory and a software-supported implementation of this theory? What does SAP offer here? And what can we achieve

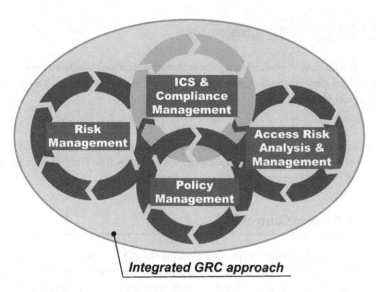

Integrated GRC approach

□ Figure 4.7 Integrated GRC approach with SAP GRC 10.0 (source: Chuprunov, CFO World)

with efficient automation of GRC processes based on the GRC solutions provided by SAP? In this section we address the most important points using a simple structure.

4.3.1 SAP Governance, Risk, and Compliance Suite 10.0

In July 2011, SAP launched its new product, SAP GRC 10.0, consisting of the main components Process Control (PC), Risk Management (RM), and Access Control (AC). For the first time, all existing GRC components have been integrated technically on one platform (SAP NetWeaver ABAP 7.02) and based on a common data model:

- SAP Process Control (previous version 3.0) – this product supports the ICS and Compliance Management process
- SAP Access Control (previous version 5.3) covers the Access Risk Analysis and Management topics. It has the following sub-components:
  - Access Risk Management (formerly RAR or Risk Analysis and Remediation)
  - User Access Management (formerly CUP or Compliant User Provisioning)
  - Business Role Governance (formerly known as ERM or Enterprise Role Management)
  - Centralized Emergency Access (formerly known as Superuser Privilege Management (SPM), for many customers also Firefighter)
- SAP Risk Management (previous version 3.0)

Figure 4.7 shows a simplified view of the integrated approach in SAP GRC 10.0. As you can see, the four elements are closely interlinked.

> **Note: Policy Management**
>
> From a process view, the Policy Management component can be considered separately as an independent component, even though from a licensing perspective, it is usually part of Process Control.

What does automating the GRC processes mean? Let us start with the ICS – that part of governance, risk, and compliance that most of you will be familiar with and that is supported by SAP Process Control.

4.3.2 SAP Process Control 10.0

The best way to explain the concept of automating the ICS is to abstract it to two views that are to be merged in a software-supported solution: the content view and the process view. For a detailed explanation of this concept, see Chap. 15, "ICS Automation: How to Set the COSO Cube in Motion."

Process Control contains all documentation elements of an ICS framework (processes, risks, controls, G/L accounts, etc.) that are often summarized in a risk and control matrix. For the implementation of Process Control, questions about the mass management of content are particularly relevant:

- For example, content can be uploaded: one way of doing this is using MDUG (Master Data Upload Generator, a function integrated in Process Control) or various consultancy solutions (for example, the tool provided by Riscomp GmbH).
- Another option for data uploads is the CLM (Content Lifecycle Management) component. It is delivered free with SAP GRC and enables primarily a transfer (for example, from one system to another) or a versioned backup of the GRC content.
- In daily operations, data maintenance is generally manual.

From a technical perspective, automation of content primarily means reducing the administrative effort required on the part of the ICS and any persons responsible for compliance. Higher efficiency is achieved thanks to a standardized structure and reusable elements, such as:

- Centralized documentation templates
- Parallel use of multiple ICS dimensions, e. g., for compliance and operational controls
- Mapping of shared services
- Referencing function

Automation also creates advantages for an authorization-controlled access to the individual elements, for logging changes to these elements, and for the use of the elements in reporting.

From the view of the processes, automation primarily relates to various activities that are applied to individual elements of an ICS framework (surveys, tests, evaluations, etc. – see Chap. 15). In summary, these activities can be represented as shown in Fig. 4.8.

The main activities are a number of recurring, manual ICS activities, such as confirmation of the execution of controls, design assessment, efficiency test, risk assessment,

Figure 4.8 Simplified presentation of the ICS management process in SAP Process Control (source: Chuprunov, CFO World)

etc. Above all, automation of the manual ICS activities means simple handling of these activities, predefined procedures, and automated notifications and reminders. Workflows in particular allow individual tasks to be processed intuitively. Thanks to workflows in Process Control, you can achieve the main objective of ICS and compliance management – structured and efficient procurement of information and close collaboration with specialist departments.

Efficient planning is the key factor of Process Control. In the Planner, you can trigger various workflow-supported operations en masse. There are two main points:

1. **Selection of organizational units**
   As required, you can select all or specific reporting units based on certain characteristics.
2. **Selection of processes, controls, or risks**
   Options that select objects according to specific characteristics, for example, risk level, control category, etc. are important.

A further advantage of process automation is the electronic storage of the results of activities. On one hand, this enables fast or real-time reporting of the compliance status. On the other hand, the use of attachments allows you to fulfill the principle of paperless compliance and supporting evidence.

However, one of the greatest additional benefits is achieved in the ICS process through the automated test and monitoring scenarios (also known as the Continuous Control Monitoring approach). Here, the SAP GRC system integrated with a business application automatically identifies deviations from the target status by evaluating master data, movement data, and control parameters, as well as update logs, according to specific rules.

▬ In scenarios that focus on compliance and fraud, GRC generally strengthens the ICS with higher accuracy and an almost unlimited capacity for evaluating large quantities of data.

Table 4.1 Automated ICS management using SAP Process Control: efficiency drivers

Content	Processes
Use of central reference catalogs and templates for individual elements of an ICS framework Multiple framework dimensions (for example, US SOX compliance, profitability, FDA compliance) Shared services concept	Simple and intuitive information procurement (for example, workflow-based) Continuous compliance monitoring (no manual evaluations required) Paperless compliance and supporting evidence Up-to-date reports at the push of a button (no consolidation work necessary)

- Where the focus is on efficiency, scenarios can strive for direct savings, for example, by detecting inefficiencies (e. g., operations that have been shipped but not billed) or by monitoring the quality of master data.

To summarize, the main characteristics of an automated ICS management can be represented as shown in Table 4.1.

Which modules can you use to develop an automated ICS process further in the direction of a comprehensive GRC approach? To answer this question, let us begin with authorization topics covered by the Access Control component.

4.3.3 SAP Access Control 10.0

Even though, from the ICS view, controls in business processes and access authorizations should form a consistent framework, in practice, these two areas often represent two independent silos. This is due above all to the organizational aspect:
- The access authorizations are usually managed in IT (security departments).
- Responsibility for the content of controls in business processes (even if these are completely IT-based) lies with the specialist departments.

In user and authorization management, GRC automation therefore consists primarily of designing the operative processes such that they conform to the ICS and supplementing them with additional ICS-relevant activities. These are, for example, the analysis of existing and the simulation of potential violations of segregation of duties; the module of Access Control described below is responsible for this.

Authorization Process for the Assignment of Authorizations – Access Risk Management (ARM)

Core of the Access Control suite

You may be familiar with the "old names" of this component: Risk Analysis and Remediation (RAR) and Compliance Calibrator. This function is the core of the Access Control suite.

It is impossible to detect authorization risks without using tools. The primary objective of the ARM component of Access Control is to detect critical authorizations or combinations of authorizations (segregation of duties). One example would be if the same person could execute program changes in a development environment and transfer them to the live environment. You can upload the content (segregation of duties, or SoD rules) or maintain it directly in the system. In the maintenance process, the trace-

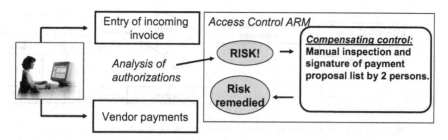

◻ Figure 4.9 Core functions of Access Risk Management

ability of changes and the principle of segregation of duties are guaranteed (for example, by means of notifications or release approval procedures for changes). The efficiency in the risk analysis results from the following points:

- **Fast processing of vast quantities of data**
  Broken down into authorization objects and values, millions of lines are analyzed.
- **Cross-system risk analysis**
  Authorizations are often distributed across several different systems. ARM allows you to harmonize different access logics and concepts at one central point.
- **Organizational rules**
  The organizational rules allow you to avoid false positives in situations where, in the case of violations of functional segregation of duties, organizational separation compensates. For example, the combination of authorizations for maintenance of vendor master data and invoicing may be critical, but the risk is modified if the two activities take place in different company codes.

Authorization risks are analyzed both in real-time and offline and the analysis can be performed across systems – that is, you can analyze the combination of critical authorizations within a risk in more than one system. For mitigation purposes, you can assign *compensating controls* to the risks identified (see Fig. 4.9). The documentation and management of these controls represents a further core function.

Analysis of authorization risks

As already stated, from the ICS perspective, authorization topics should form a standardized framework. Therefore, the existing *integration* of Access Control with Process Control is important:

- Risk analysis results from the ARM component can be passed on from Access Control to Process Control, meaning that from an ICS perspective, Process Control plays a central role.
- Controls that are assigned as mitigation in the risk analysis (i. e., violations of segregation of duties are considered as eliminated in the analysis result reports) can also be a component of the ICS framework in Process Control – that is, they can be integrated in the ICS management process as a whole.

From the process view, the benefit of the analysis of authorization risks and the mitigation of these risks are more visible in the interaction of ARM with other Access Control components when considered as part of the workflow.

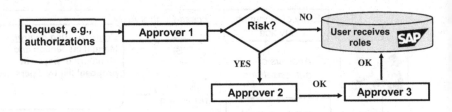

Figure 4.10 Provisioning workflows of User Access Management

User Access Management (UAM)

Centralized user administration

This component has also recently been renamed – you may still know it under the name Compliant User Provisioning (CUP) from Release 5.3. You can use UAM to achieve centralized user administration.

Project experience shows that the process of assigning access authorizations is faster and more reliable if it is supported by a workflow – the UAM (User Access Management) component is used for this purpose. The integration with Organizational Management (OM) from SAP ERP HCM and with identity management solutions (both from SAP and other providers) offers additional synergies if existing information about the organizational assignment of users can be reused.

You can design the workflows flexibly. As illustrated in Fig. 4.10 by means of a real project example, one way of designing the approval paths is dependent on authorization risks identified in the system (or based on various details in the request, on attributes or owners of selected authorization roles, etc.).

ARM-UAM integration: risks of a change request

The integration of UAM and BRG (Business Role Governance, see next section) with the risk analysis functions of the ARM component allows a preventive analysis of the risks in a change request before the rights are actually assigned. The simulations and the assignment or use of compensating controls are further properties that the integration enables.

From a compliance perspective, you can also use workflows to log and trace all approval steps.

The UAM component also offers workflows designed specifically for compliance purposes: the User Access Review Workflow and the Segregation of Duties (SoD) Review Workflow. You can use them to assign pure security and compliance tasks to the persons responsible and to monitor the processing of these tasks.

User Access Review

User Access Review (UAR) is not an independent Access Control component but a function or type of workflow within the UAM component. The aim of this function is to check that the assignment of authorizations is up-to-date at regular intervals and, where applicable, to reduce the authorization risks to a minimum.

In a workflow-based procedure, the person responsible receives information about the roles assigned to a user and the frequency of the use of these roles. The latter information is intended to make it easier to decide whether certain roles should be withdrawn and thus the associated risks can be minimized – the roles are withdrawn automatically once the review has been completed and the withdrawal of roles confirmed.

Review of authorization risks

The *Segregation of Duties Review* is also not an independent Access Control component but a function or type of workflow within UAR and is possible with the integration

◻ **Table 4.2** Comparison – ICS-relevant properties of selected workflows in User Access Management

Functions/types of workflow in UAM	I: Roles	I: Frequency of use	I: Risks	F: Risk mitigation	F: Role with-drawal
Classic user admin-istration	Yes	No	Yes	Yes	Yes
User Access Review	Yes	Yes	No	No	Yes
Segregation of Duties Review	No	Yes	Yes	Yes	No

I = Information about …
F = Functionality

of UAR with ARM. As part of this review function, authorization risks are analyzed at the level of individual users.

In addition to information about risks (segregation of duties conflicts or critical authorizations), the workflow provides you with details about the frequency of use of *functions* (groups of transactions that form the individual components of risk rules). The following options are available for handling risks:
- Assignment of a compensating control
- Proposal to clean up the corresponding segregation of duties violation (reduce the authorizations of a user by withdrawing roles or adjusting the content of roles)
- Acceptance of the risk

The segregation of duties violations are cleaned up manually or outside the Segregation of Duties Review Workflow.

Table 4.2 shows which ICS-relevant properties the three functions described in this section have within UAM.

ICS-relevant properties in UAM

For example, a processor of a UAR workflow can see which SAP roles a user has and how often the individual roles have been used within a specific time period (based on calls of the transactions in a role). He cannot see the authorization risks in UAR. The UAR function was designed to allow withdrawal of unused or infrequently used authorizations from a user where applicable.

Business Role Governance (BRG)

You may know this component under the old name of Enterprise Role Management (ERM) from Release 5.3.

The efficiency of workflow-supported management of roles in the BRG component is primarily achieved by the use of mapping rules in the specification of organization-specific authorization objects and by other features. However, the enrichment of authorization roles in BRG with additional attributes (functional area, process, subprocess, etc.) that enable you to search for and assign them later in UAM is part of this important efficiency driver.

Maintaining authorization roles based on a workflow

The integration of BRG with ARM has the advantage that you can define the roles free of segregation of duties conflicts. This represents a central prerequisite of ICS compliance in reporting, as critical authorizations can only be differentiated at user level

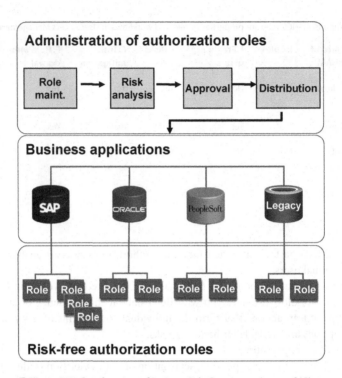

□ Figure 4.11   Core functions of Business Role Governance (source: SAP)

when the roles are "clean": you can only separate activities from one another if they are contained in different roles.

The core functions of the BRG component are illustrated in Fig. 4.11.

Centralized Emergency Access (CEA)

Emergency user concept using CEA

You will know this component under the name of Superuser Privilege Management (SPM) from the earlier Release 5.3, although you may also remember an even earlier name: Firefighter.

The CEA component of SAP Access Control helps you to establish an emergency user concept conform to an ICS.

If a user needs additional authorizations to execute certain critical activities, he can use an emergency user ID temporarily (provided the user has the authorization for such an emergency user ID) without having to log off or on to an SAP application again. The reason for requesting this emergency user ID is documented and the person responsible is informed via e-mail. All activities of the emergency user are logged.

Integration of CEA and UAM

The integration of CEA with the UAM component allows you to request and execute the assignment of authorizations for use of emergency user IDs as part of a workflow-based approval procedure.

To summarize, we can highlight the following important elements in the GRC integration of user and authorization management (Table. 4.3).

▣ Table 4.3 User and authorization management as part of GRC

Content	Process
Forwarding of risk analysis results from Access Control to Process Control Use of controls from Process Control for mitigation purposes in ARM Cross-system analysis rules Reuse of OM data	Integration of the ICS activities in operative processes (for example, application and approval processes, risk analyses, mitigation, audit trail, etc.) Intuitive analysis of the authorizations assigned (for example, using workflows) Automation of SoD and authorization review process Automation of the emergency user concept Traceability and auditability

▣ Table 4.4 Policies as part of GRC

Content	Process
Central repository for all policies, including version management etc. Integrated data model (linking individual policies with the ICS framework) Active use of policies in risk management (e. g., risk reduction) and in authorization management (mitigation of missing segregation of duties)	Workflow-supported life cycle (design, review, approval, publication, etc.) Distribution of policies to end users (including documentation of formal acknowledgment, confirmation of compliance, etc.)

4.3.4 Policy Management

Policy management is an independent process. Automating this process primarily means designing the entire life cycle of a policy efficiently. To enable you to do this, the Policy Management component is now available for the first time in the SAP GRC 10.0 solutions. The establishment of this component is an important milestone in the GRC suite and generally covers the letter "G" for Governance in the term "Governance, Risk, and Compliance."

In the Policy Management component, you can map the entire life cycle of a policy: documentation, agreement, release, and distribution to relevant employee groups who can confirm compliance with the respective policies formally. Using surveys, you can also ensure that employees have understood the contents of the policy.

From the ICS view, policies are also important control mechanisms. Therefore, integration with the ICS framework is necessary at this point. Integration options with Risk Management are also interesting if you consider further GRC modules. Thus, policies actively contribute to minimizing risks. Table 4.4 summarizes the most important efficiency drivers in the policy management process.

4.3.5 SAP Risk Management 10.0

We have already looked at the Process Control component in Sect. 4.3.2. Within the scope of compliance management, Process Control offers a risk-oriented approach through qualitative risk assessments or control risk assessments that are part of the

◻ **Table 4.5**   Risk Management: efficiency drivers

Content	Process
Integrated data model Reusable templates for risks, response etc. "Active" role of controls and policies in Risk Management (for example, use for the purposes of risk reduction)	Intuitive procurement of information about risks via workflows Reuse of the results from other components such as Access Control or Process Control KRI automation (manual as well as based on inte- gration with ERP and BW systems)

scoping process. If you want to take the risk analysis further (for example, quantitative risk analyses, simulations, collaborative risk assessments, bow-tie risk builders, risk heat maps, etc.), the Risk Management component offers automation of the risk management process as a whole.

In general terms, this component supports the risk management process through the sequence of the following steps:

1. Planning the risk environment
2. Identification of risks
3. Assessment and analysis of risks
4. Risk response
5. Monitoring of risks

Similarly to SAP Process Control, Risk Management offers integration with other applications. Whilst in Process Control the integration is with the Continuous Monitoring Framework (see Chap. 17), Risk Management offers automation of risk identification based on the *Key Risk Indicator* (KRI) function.

If we look at risk management in the context of integrated GRC processes, we can recognize further synergy effects: on one hand risks play an important part in the ICS, and on the other hand, depending on the level (strategic vs. operative), they are integrated directly in various processes as part of the risk management process.

Both applications – Process Control and Risk Management – are integrated with one another and have a common data basis, both with regard to the risks and with regard to common reporting. Figure 4.12 gives a high-level overview of the possible integration scenarios.

From the content and process views mentioned earlier, we can summarize the most important efficiency drivers as shown in Table 4.5.

Risk Management functions for the financial sector   With Release 10.0, the Risk Management component offers more extensive functions that support the Operational Risk Management (ORM) process that can be employed in the financial sector within the scope of requirements from Basel II and III and Solvency II (see Sect. 1.4, "ICS Requirements in the Financial Sector"). In particular, these are specific functions such as:

- Risk Control Self-Assessment
- Static Data Management
- Workflow-supported loss recording
- Loss Database

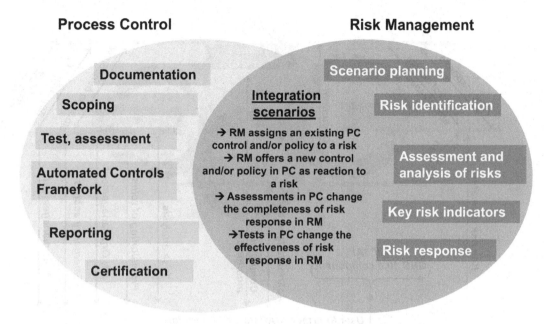

□ Figure 4.12   Core functions and integration scenarios – Risk Management and Process Control

4.3.6 Summary Overview of Integration Scenarios in SAP GRC 10.0

The integrated approach of GRC automation presented at the beginning of this chapter, in which four important elements represent individually self-contained processes but offer sufficient integration points, has become possible with SAP GRC 10.0 solutions. Now that you have gained an impression of the individual components of SAP GRC 10.0 and the individual integration scenarios, Fig. 4.13 summarizes them.

The integration scenarios behind the term *Continuous Monitoring* in this illustration are described in detail in Chap. 17, "Implementation of Automated Test and Monitoring Scenarios in the SAP ERP Environment."

4.3.7 SAP Audit Management

In addition to the SAP GRC 10.0 solutions that you have learned about already, there are other SAP applications that are relevant for an ICS.

SAP Audit Management (AM) supports the process of various audits. In practice, various areas of application, such as quality audits (for example, according to ISO standards), supplier audits, environmental protection audits, and security audits, have become established.

Process support for audits

This AM functionality supports the following audit phases:

1. Planning the audit
2. Executing the audit

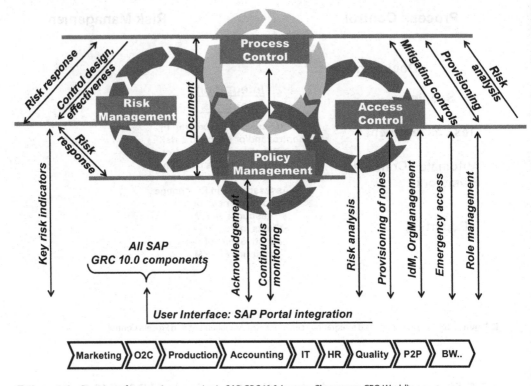

Figure 4.13 Overview of integration scenarios in SAP GRC 10.0 (source: Chuprunov, CFO World)

3. Follow-up and corrective measures
4. Reporting

Integration aspects   From a functional perspective, the integration with other SAP applications is restricted to the assignment of various objects outside Audit Management to the audit objects within Audit Management (for example, a supplier created in SAP ERP can be audited in Audit Management).

Service Pack 8 for the SAP GRC solutions is the first to offer integration with Audit Management. Figure 4.14 shows the existing integration options. These concentrate primarily on the link from GRC documentation objects (organizations, processes, risks, controls, etc.) with relevant documentation objects in Audit Management.

The graphical integration should also be mentioned here: regardless of whether the access takes place via SAP NetWeaver Portal or NWBC interface (NWBC = SAP NetWeaver Business Client), the user can see both applications: the SAP GRC solutions and Audit Management.

You have to enter the check operations in Audit Management itself manually; there is no comparable integration in the delivery scope as there is for the Continuous Monitoring Framework of Process Control (see Chap. 17, "Implementation of Automated Test and Monitoring Scenarios in the SAP ERP Environment"). Therefore, Audit Management can be considered a pure audit management tool. Its special feature is the option to define customer-specific audit reports.

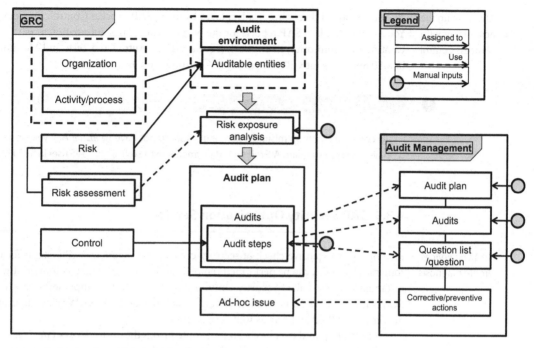

Figure 4.14 Integration of SAP GRC 10.0 and Audit Management

4.3.8 SAP Audit Information System

The official source of information for this tool is SAP Note 77503. As the name indicates, SAP Audit Information System (AIS) is an information tool. It is available in every SAP ERP system and offers options for executing report-based evaluation of various data for business audits, system audits, and tax audits.

SAP Note 77503

SAP Audit Information System provides a collection of standard reports (in total, over 600) grouped by the areas specified. These reports are also distributed across the standard menu tree of the SAP system. AIS offers added value through the presentation of audit-relevant analysis options based on financial statement items and processes. Furthermore, it offers variants to the SAP reports, with the variants providing points of reference for possible selection criteria. You can also use the variants directly.

Structured analysis options

AIS also offers preconfigured options for extracting audit-relevant data. You can then use this data for analysis purposes in various CAAT applications (CAAT = Computer-Assisted Auditing Techniques) such as IDEA, ACL, etc. (see Sect. 17.1.1, "Offline CAAT Tools").

Data extracts

AIS does not contain any additional information in connection with the analysis options offered – either with regard to interpretation of the analysis results or with regard to the control objectives or risks that would be relevant from an ICS perspective. A further disadvantage is that in AIS, you cannot reuse analysis results beyond the display of spool lists, for example, to log or document the results or to collect audit findings.

Overcoming the disadvantages with Process Control

You can avoid these two disadvantages by using SAP Process Control, for example. You use the standard SAP reports for the purposes of control automation as part of the Continuous Monitoring Framework (see Sect. 17.2, "Automated Tests and Monitoring in SAP Solutions for GRC Release 10.0 – Introduction").

Use of SAP Audit Information System

To correct a common misunderstanding – you do not have to *install* AIS; you simply have to assign standard AIS roles (or adjustments to the roles) to an AIS user in SAP ERP.

4.3.9 SAP Security Optimization Service

SOS services: remote diagnosis

SAP offers an extensive check of security-critical parameters in SAP systems for customers. This check can be performed remotely and to a large extent, automatically. It is a standard service called Security Optimization Service (SOS, http://service.sap.com/SOS). It comprises an evaluation of various settings on SAP NetWeaver Application Server (AS) ABAP and Java as well as in SAProuter.

Once the required data has been transmitted from the customer system via a secure remote connection and analyzed in SAP's own environment, the customer is provided with a result report and details of a contact partner in case there are any questions.

From a compliance perspective, the check of the settings in AS is highly relevant because the focus is on the SAP application logic. Issues such as the treatment of SAP standard users and their passwords, the analysis of profile parameters, certain critical authorizations, etc. are analyzed.

4.3.10 RSECNOTE Tool

SAP Note 888889

The RSECNOTE tool enables you to automatically check the implementation of security-relevant Notes in an SAP system. For a description of the installation and the use of the tool, see SAP Note 888889.

You can transfer the results of the analysis with the RSECNOTE tool to the Early-Watch Alert report (see SAP Note 863362).

4.4   Compliance-Relevant Content

Initial questions

The central questions when setting up and operating an ICS in an ERP environment are as follows:

- What do the business processes and value flows look like exactly?
- What risks are present in these processes, and what control measures can counteract these risks?

The definition and documentation of organization-specific processes, risks, controls, control objectives, etc. is a very time-consuming process. As SAP ERP is standard

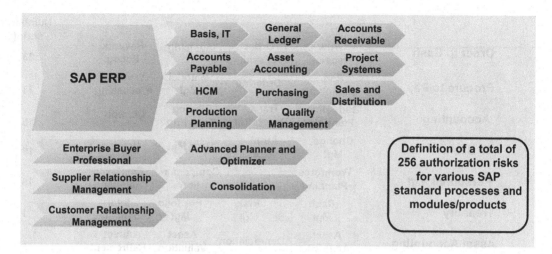

□ Figure 4.15 Scope of the predefined rules for identification of authorization risks in Access Control

software, you would expect ICS-relevant standard documentation that is useful in this process. Unfortunately, SAP has not yet been able to catalog the *application controls* (at least, not to the extent that would be interesting for many SAP customers), and the existing sources of information are somewhat lacking.

> **Orientation – Definition of Controls**   ❶
>
> Part II of this book, "From Concept to Content: Audit Guide for SAP ERP," is dedicated to the definition of controls in the SAP environment. There are also some sources of information available to both SAP customers and the public that we will address here. This information can be used both for the documentation of controls and, where applicable, in the technical definition of automated control tests.

4.4.1 Direct ICS Content: What Controls Are Available in SAP?

Direct ICS content is the description and, where applicable, the technical definition of control mechanisms that are relevant for the purposes of ICS compliance in an SAP ERP environment.

Risk Definitions in SAP Access Control

Within the framework of the out-of-the-box rule set, the Access Control component Access Risk Management (Release 10.0) contains approximately 260 risk definitions for SAP applications (there are also risk definitions for Oracle and PeopleSoft products).

Out-of-the-box rule set

These risk rules cover most processes within SAP applications that are relevant for compliance (see Fig. 4.15) and contain the following:

Contents of predefined check rules

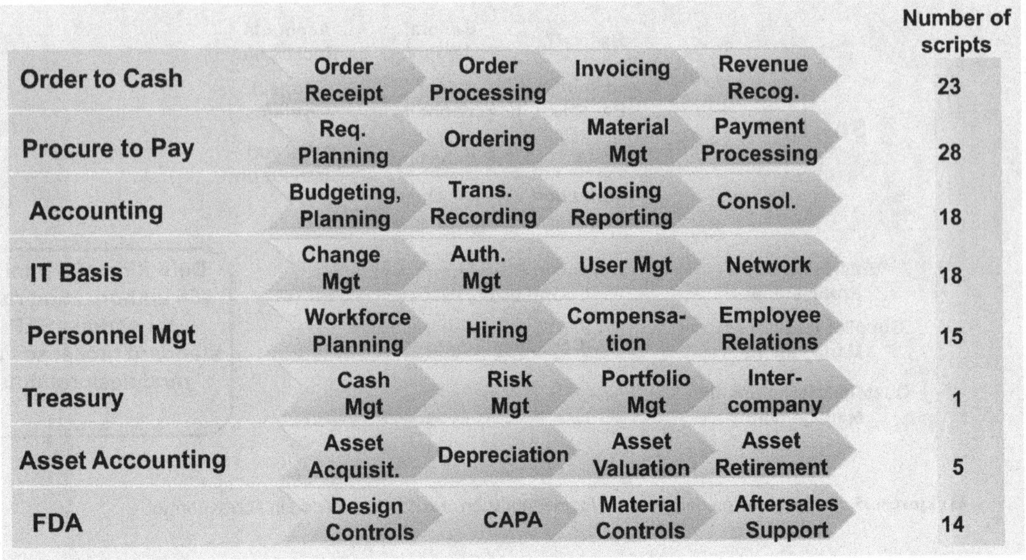

					Number of scripts
Order to Cash	Order Receipt	Order Processing	Invoicing	Revenue Recog.	23
Procure to Pay	Req. Planning	Ordering	Material Mgt	Payment Processing	28
Accounting	Budgeting, Planning	Trans. Recording	Closing Reporting	Consol.	18
IT Basis	Change Mgt	Auth. Mgt	User Mgt	Network	18
Personnel Mgt	Workforce Planning	Hiring	Compensation	Employee Relations	15
Treasury	Cash Mgt	Risk Mgt	Portfolio Mgt	Inter-company	1
Asset Accounting	Asset Acquisit.	Depreciation	Asset Valuation	Asset Retirement	5
FDA	Design Controls	CAPA	Material Controls	Aftersales Support	14

Figure 4.16 Predefined scripts in Process Control for automated control execution and tests in the SAP ERP environment

- Description of typical segregation of duties risks
- Qualitative assessment of risks as high, medium, or low
- Description of individual functions that create risks and the assignment of these functions to a specific process.
- Technical definition of check rules to the detailed level of authorization objects and the specification of the values of these rules

The predefined check rules for the identification of authorization risks are helpful for offering points of reference for the implementation of Access Control. In practice, you have to adjust risk definitions in order to take account of organization-specific processes. Furthermore, an SAP system often contains transactions developed independently by customers and you have to take these into account when specifying check rules (see Sect. 5.2.3, "Determining Authorization Objects").

Predefined Controls in SAP Process Control

Automated controls   The *Process Control* application provides two lots of content: on one hand, a predefined check rule for automated tests of application controls in SAP ERP (as part of the Automated Rules Framework, ARF). The more than 100 scripts delivered with Process Control 3.0 partly cover the "classic" SAP audit topics. However, Process Control can be integrated not only with SAP; scripts for Oracle and PeopleSoft are also delivered with the product.

As you can see in Fig. 4.16, the scripts cover SAP processes that are relevant for compliance as well as FDA-specific controls. For more information on automating controls using Process Control, see Chap. 16, "ICS Automation Using SAP Process Control."

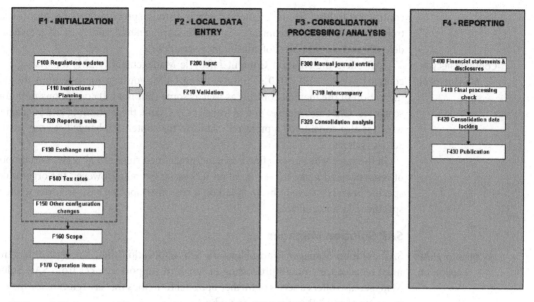

□ Figure 4.17 Structure of the Process Control Starter Kit with the control hierarchy for consolidation and financial reporting

The approach of SAP AG has changed to some extent with the GRC content for Release 10.0. All predefined rules in Process Control 10.0 come from Release 3.0 and remain in the old "Legacy Framework" within Process Control 10.0. The new Continuous Monitoring Framework in Process Control 10.0 does not contain any predefined scenarios.

Expertise required from the implementation partner

The reason for this is explained below. The information given is based on discussions with SAP Solution Management employees and on content from SAP presentations at events such as SAP Insider and SAP GRC Conference:

SAP wants to focus on its own core competence – in particular, on software and the greatest possible flexibility in the Continuous Monitoring Framework for the definition of various test and monitoring scenarios. In SAP ERP, application controls must be considered on a very customer-specific basis, as business processes at organizations are often as individual as human fingerprints – even if there are a certain amount of scenarios that are valid generally. Therefore, expertise at the implementation partners, who have their own content-relevant products that have matured in numerous projects (for example, RAMS – Riscomp Automated Monitoring Scenarios), is increasingly demanded. This means that the role of SAP will change towards offering a platform that enables various content providers to exchange content that partner companies are prepared to make available.

SAP is relying increasingly on partners even for "manual" content, that is, for the documentation of ICS frameworks.

One of the few examples for which SAP offers own content is from the Process Control area: the Starter Kit, with a hierarchy of controls that are usually relevant as part of an SAP-supported process of financial reporting (see Fig. 4.17).

With the exception of the Starter Kit, SAP partners that specialize in the GRC solutions from SAP often provide various best practice offers for predefined process and control hierarchies – from IT general controls, through process-related application controls, up to entity level controls. Such offers are generally not part of the standard delivery and are the object of consultancy services.

Content Lifecycle Management

SAP offers the solution Content Lifecycle Management (CLM) for managing the contents of SAP GRC 10.0 solutions: using CLM, you can manage both the documentation of the manual controls as well as some (but not all) continuous monitoring scenarios. CLM also enables you to transfer GRC data, the versioning and packaging of which is also considered a preferred platform for content exchange between partners, across systems.

In the same way as predefined content, predefined rules can also give certain points of reference and make the set up of an ICS easier overall. However, the organization-specific processes have to be analyzed on a customer-specific basis in order to identify specific risks and controls.

SAP Solution Manager

Obligatory SAP application

SAP Solution Manager is an obligatory SAP application that, amongst other things, must be used for smooth processing of standard support services from SAP. Solution Manager also offers a series of further optional functions that are relevant for the entire life cycle of an SAP application, including:

- Functions involved in the implementation of SAP solutions, such as test management, blueprinting, global rollouts, etc.
- Application monitoring, beginning with service level reporting up to monitoring of business processes
- Service desk
- Change request management and standard support services
- Upgrade management

Within the scope of application monitoring in particular, the Solution Manager functions can provide direct input with regard to control mechanisms relevant in the SAP environment. Experience indicates that this source of information is relatively unknown in compliance-oriented interest groups, possibly because many customers treat SAP Solution Manager rather contemptuously due to lack of know-how. The objective of most monitoring objects may well be efficiency in operational business processes, but many of these monitoring objects are also highly relevant for ICS compliance.

[e.g.]   Monitoring Objects in Solution Manager

The following objects can be monitored in SAP-supported sales processes:
- Monitoring of the number of open or blocked customer orders or overdue deliveries etc. focuses primarily on efficiency and profit.
- Monitoring of sales documents created in the SD module but not transferred to the FI module due to an interface error is directly relevant for compliance: the completeness of the sales figures posted in the general ledger is monitored. This completeness has a direct effect on the external financial reporting and the internal control of the organization.

The business process and monitoring catalog in SAP Solution Manager comprises numerous monitoring objects with alert or notification function:

- Cross-application interface monitoring (ALE/IDoc, qRFC, SAP Batch Input, Workflow Monitoring, XI/PI Monitoring, etc.)
- ERP Logistics Monitoring (evaluation of various critical constellations within sales documents and incoming invoices, monitoring of material movements and warehouse stock, purchase requisitions, purchase orders, errors in order feedback, etc.)
- Monitoring in ERP Financial Accounting (various open item monitoring, monitoring of payment runs and incompletely posted account statements, etc.)
- Various monitoring objects in SAP CRM, SAP APO, SAP Extended Warehouse Management
- Various monitoring objects for mass processing in the industry solutions SAP for Utilities, SAP for Banking, SAP for Insurance, SAP for Telecommunications
- Monitoring of SEM BCS (tasks and BI queries)

Monitoring functions

The *Data Consistency Cockpit* is a further relevant function area in SAP Solution Manager. The monitoring objects it contains cover, for example, the consistency of material stocks with regard to reconciliation of the general ledger and subledgers, and various consistency checks of FI/CO data, etc.

Data Consistency Cockpit

The monitoring functions of SAP Solution Manager are overall highly relevant for compliance; not only as a source of content for setting up an ICS, but also as a means for automating the ICS. For example, the monitoring objects in SAP Solution Manager can be replicated in SAP Process Control; however, there is as yet no direct integration between SAP Solution Manager and SAP Process Control.

ICS potential

SAP Training: GRC330 SAP Process Control

Here you can learn how to automate an ICS using SAP Process Control. This five-day training course covers both technical implementation details and ICS methodological topics.

SAP Training: GRC340 SAP Risk Management

Here you can learn how to automate a risk management process using SAP Risk Management. This three-day training course covers both technical implementation details and ICS methodological topics.

SAP Training: GRC030 and GRC300

These training courses deal with the implementation of SAP Access Control.

SAP Training: FIN900 Auditing with SAP ERP

The SAP training course "FIN900 Auditing with SAP ERP" provides audit-relevant SAP basic knowledge; in particular, it explains the selected control mechanisms and how they are audited based on processes. The course focuses on the following topics:

- SOX and further legal bases
- Basic principles of the SAP authorization concept
- Checking authorizations (segregation of duties)
- Organizational structures in SAP

Auditing with SAP ERP

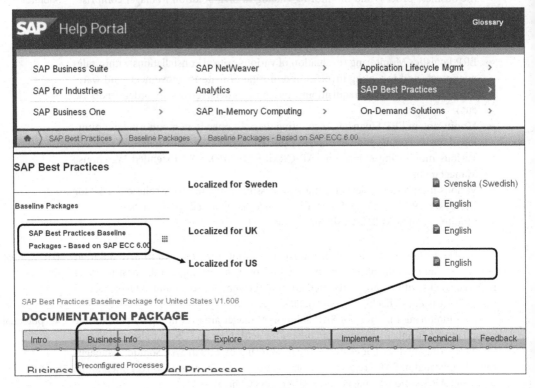

Figure 4.18   Process documentation for SAP Best Practice scenarios

- Selected controls and audit procedures in business processes (procurement, costing, sales and distribution)
- Selected audit topics within the scope of period-end closing (make-to-stock production, asset accounting, external accounting)
- Checking evaluations (warehouse stock, actual costing, transfer prices)
- SAP audit products and tools

Further Sources

AIS and SOS as ICS-related content sources

The Audit Information System explained in Sect. 4.3.8 can also provide input for the application controls in SAP: under certain circumstances, both the structure of the menu tree and its content – various reports – can be seen as control mechanisms.

For the security-related ICS content, see the Security Optimization Services described in Sect. 4.3.9. The individual points in the results report, in particular with regard to SAP NetWeaver AS ABAP, are "audit classics."

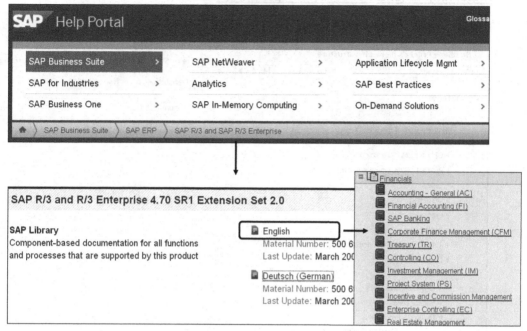

Figure 4.19 SAP Library – documentation on the functions of individual modules

4.4.2 Content with ICS Relevance: Standard Business Processes and Controls in SAP

The control mechanisms that compliance focuses on are components of different business processes. In order to identify the relevant risks and, where applicable, controls, you require knowledge of these processes. In an ideal case, corresponding process documentation produced during the SAP implementation is available in the organization (for example, compressed overviews in the form of flow charts, blueprints, etc.). However, this ideal case is rare. In practice, the documentation and control work is often reduced to a minimum, as the process and application owners frequently measure the necessity for documentation on how well they understand their plant themselves. In a situation in which organization-specific process descriptions are not available, the existing standard documentation of the standard processes in SAP can be the last resort.

Rather standard than nothing

In addition to standard training courses offered by SAP Education on the various SAP modules in processes, further sources of information are available.

SAP Best Practice Process Documentation

The official website help.sap.com provides two sources that can be helpful for understanding standard processes in SAP applications. One of these sources is the Best Practice process documentation: SAP offers country-specific and industry-specific preconfigured scenarios that make both the evaluation and implementation of possible scenarios easier.

Source of information for process flows

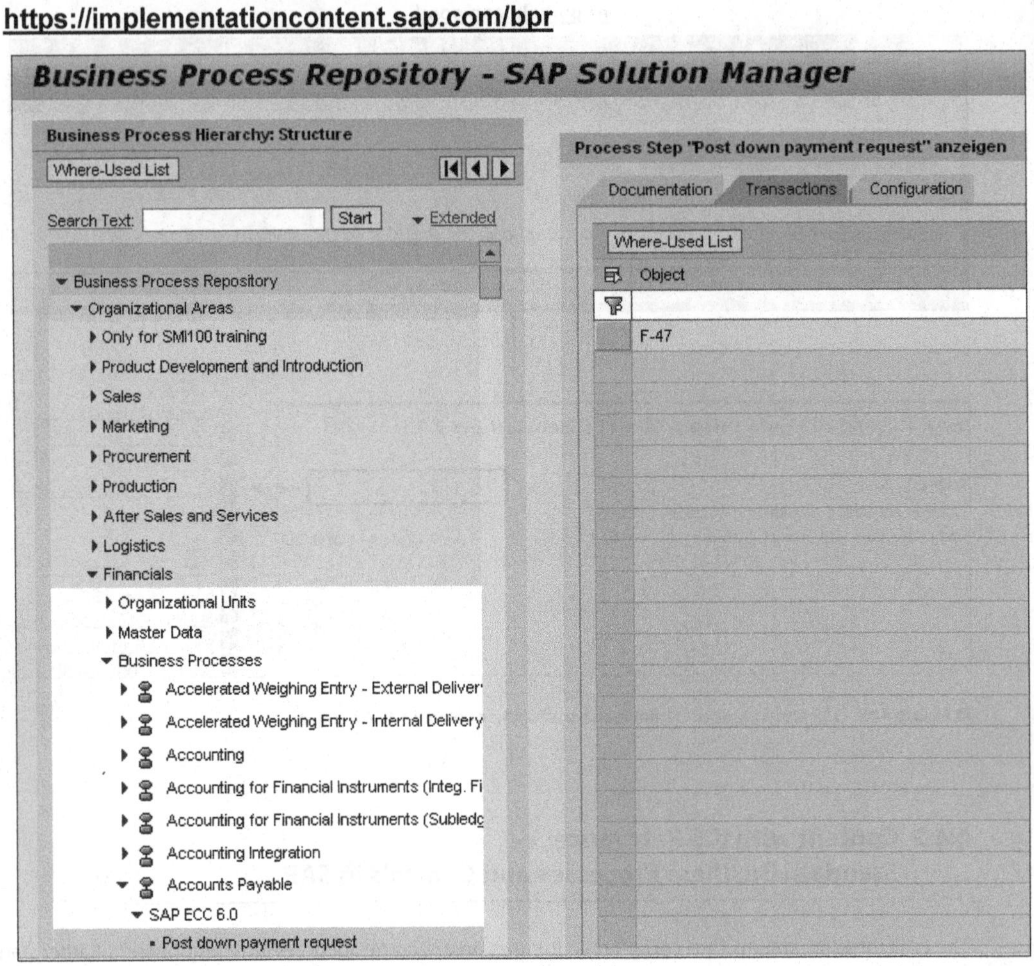

https://implementationcontent.sap.com/bpr

Figure 4.20   Business Process Repository in SAP Solution Manager

Process description for SAP Best Practice scenarios

The other source of information is the process descriptions for business processes. As shown in Fig. 4.18, these are available at help.sap.com under SAP Best Practices. For example, in the section Baseline Packages, you can select a country-specific localized package in the required language. The corresponding process documentation is located in the section Business Information under Preconfigured Processes • Full Scope.

SAP Library

In the SAP Library on the same website (help.sap.com), you can find the documentation for the functions of individual modules.

As you can see in Fig. 4.19, the SAP Library contains, for example, the description of standard functions in SAP-supported financial accounting.

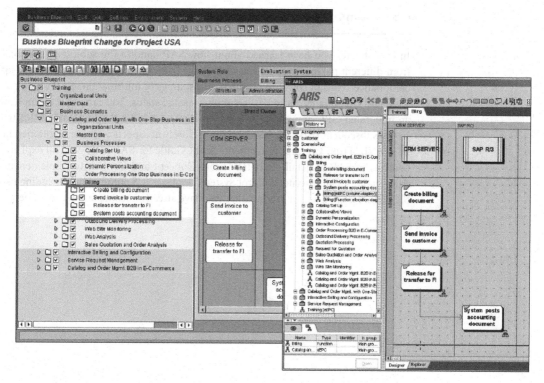

☐ **Figure 4.21** Graphical illustration of the process flows in SAP Solution Manager using the example of ARIS

SAP Solution Manager

We explained the monitoring functions of SAP Solution Manager in Sect. 4.4.1, "Direct ICS Content: What Controls Are Available in SAP?" A further area of Solution Manager, the implementation content, can provide useful information about the standard process and structure of SAP-supported business processes: to simplify the implementation of SAP products, Solution Manager contains product-specific and process-specific templates that you can use, for example, when creating business blueprints.

Blueprint templates as source

Figure 4.20 shows the Business Process Repository, which is freely accessible via the Web. In total, the predefined process descriptions contain up to four levels arranged hierarchically:

1. Business scenario level (for example, Requirements Planning)
2. Business process level (for example, Customer Order Processing as Part of Customer Order-Related Production)
3. Process step level (for example, Creating a Supplier Request)
4. SAP transaction level (VA11 – Create Inquiry, VA12 – Change Inquiry, VA13 – Display Inquiry, VA15 Inquiries List, V.03 – List of Incomplete Inquiries)

A graphical illustration of the process flows documented in Solution Manager is also helpful and can be achieved, for example, as shown in Fig. 4.21, through integration with ARIS.

4.5   Summary

In this chapter you have learned about how SAP handles the subject of compliance from different perspectives. The aspects range from the certification of software up to compliance-relevant software products and sources of information. SAP Governance, Risk, and Compliance Suite 10.0 assumes a special status. You can use it to implement an integrated GRC approach. This information concludes the first part of this book. In the subsequent parts, we will look more closely at aspects we have mentioned here: in Part II, "From Concept to Content: Audit Guide for SAP ERP," we will explain the controls in SAP in detail. Part III, "From Concept and Content to Implementation: Automation of an Internal Control System," looks at ICS automation, including use of SAP Process Control – a product that you have already become familiar with here.

Part II From Concept to Content: Audit Guide for SAP ERP

The first part of this book provided you with the theoretical information you need about ICS compliance in the SAP ERP environment.

Armed with this knowledge, you can now get to work! Your task is to design the content of your own ICS framework.

In this part of the book, we present the underlying compliance-relevant connections in the SAP system and explain how you can trace these connections independently and find the relevant control mechanisms in the SAP system. We then explain the most important control mechanisms in SAP ERP, according to the structure that you already know. Separate chapters are dedicated to the topics of fraud, FDA compliance, and data protection compliance. In particular, we consider the as yet unusual perspective that control mechanisms in the ERP environment can help you to detect inefficiencies in business processes: a detailed description, supported by examples, of how to automate such control scenarios independently awaits you.

Audit-Relevant SAP Basics

It is impossible to know everything. In a complex ERP system such as SAP ERP in particular, you have to know about the possible sources of information and be proficient in search techniques, provided you already understand the basic connections, of course.

Auditing an SAP system often requires "hacker"-like skills to be able to see behind the scenes of an application. To enable you to do this, the SAP system offers a wide range of search options and analysis tools. From a compliance perspective, two large areas in the SAP ERP environment are important (see Fig. 5.1):

- The *application logic* of SAP, consisting of the interaction of transactions, programs, and database tables
- Protection of the *access* to the application logic

Following the structure shown in Fig. 5.1, in this chapter you will learn:

- The advantages of table control in SAP
- The types of data and application checks that exist in SAP
- What the basic connections between transactions, ABAP programs, and tables in an SAP application look like
- How to trace these connections independently using various search tools and options and, where necessary, how to find relevant application checks
- How to test application controls in SAP
- How the authorization concept in SAP works
- How to find the audit-relevant authorization information independently
- How to test the user authorizations

This "find-it-yourself" approach will help you to better understand the information in the subsequent chapters of Part II of this book, as well as the approaches for automating the test and monitoring scenarios described in Part III.

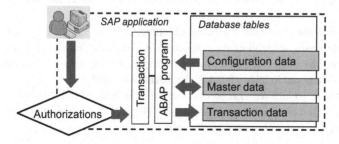

◻ **Figure 5.1** SAP in a nutshell

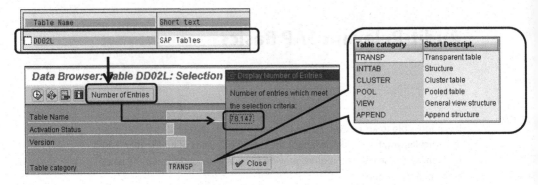

☐ **Figure 5.2**   Database table in an SAP system (ECC 6.0)

5.1   In the Beginning Was the Table: SAP as Table-Controlled Application

SAP has around
80,000 database
tables

The number of *database tables* in SAP ERP speaks for itself: there are around 80,000, depending on the modules in use – filled with master data, control data, and transaction data (see Fig. 5.2). To appreciate audit-relevant tasks in an SAP system means first of all understanding the logic of the application; and this logic occurs above all in the complex connections reflected in the structure and the connections between the individual tables.

SAP can therefore be called a table-controlled application.

> ❶   Table-Controlled Application
>
> *Table-controlled* means that the main parts of the program that determine the flow of data processing are partially outsourced as contents of database tables. This means that the ABAP code of the programs contains references to the contents of fields in database tables.

Tables control
programs

Controlling the program logic by means of the contents of tables enables you to adjust the processes mapped in SAP to the requirements of each individual customer. Many of the customizing options affect the compliance-relevant application controls directly:

- You can define the maximum permitted difference between the value for tax on sales and purchases (sometimes also referred to as VAT (value added tax)) entered manually and the value calculated by the system as a percentage rate. You define this tolerance amount in table T007A in the TOLERANCE field.
- If you want to introduce segregation of duties for maintaining vendor master data, you have to make corresponding entries in table T055F so that a second person has to approve a new vendor before it can be used.

These are just two examples of checks that are relevant for compliance. As you can imagine, the number of tables in SAP means that there can be further application controls. The dependency of the program logic on table content requires stronger controls over changes to that content (see Chap. 6), as well as a restriction of system access with change authorization.

From the *audit view*, the table control aspect of SAP provides the following advantages:

Table control – advantages from the ICS and audit view

- Transparency and traceability of application logic
- Possibilities for setting up application controls with no programming effort
- The basis for automating the evaluation of the design of application controls through the evaluation of table content
- Multiple replication of the same data at different levels of aggregation (e. g., customer line items, general ledger documents, general ledger account balances). This provides higher security against various manipulations: these would lead to a loss of consistency in the data, but consistency must be given across several tables.

Depending on the content, the SAP tables can be divided into master data tables, transaction data tables, and configuration data tables.

5.1.1 Data in an SAP System

When differentiating the data in an SAP system, if we look at criteria such as the volume of data and the contents or the processing, we generally differentiate between master data, control data, and transaction data.

Master Data

In an SAP system, master data is the basic data required to record the business transactions. From an audit perspective, the most important master data in SAP is in the general ledger and the subledgers:

Basic data for recording business transactions

- General ledger: general ledger accounts, cost centers, profit centers
- Subledgers: specific master data
  - Accounts receivable accounting: customer master data
  - Accounts payable accounting: vendor master data, payment terms
  - Asset accounting: asset master data
  - Materials management: material master data
  - Human resources: HR master data

As you can see in Fig. 5.3, master data in SAP is usually divided into two segments:

Segments in the master data

- **A segment**
  This segment contains that part of the data of a master data object that is not specific to an organizational unit (e. g., cross-company code data). The data is valid in all clients of an SAP system (e. g., table LFA1 with the vendor master data. Here, each vendor is included only once.)
- **B segment**
  This segment contains master data that is specific to an organizational unit (e. g., table LFB1 with the vendor master data. Here you can find additional data that can be maintained for a vendor in every organizational unit or in every company code.)

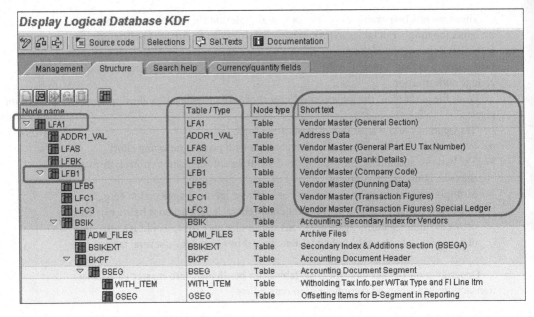

Figure 5.3 Example: Table structure of the vendor master data

Both segments are connected to one another (A:B = 1:n; LFA1 for a vendor: always only once (in one client); LFB1 for a vendor: in every organizational unit (e. g., company code) in which this vendor is created). When you create new master data, you have to create the central data (the A segment) first.

Transaction Data

Transaction data represents the result of the recording of business transactions and is referred to as "electronic documents." In SAP systems, the transaction data is broken down according to the structure of the business transactions. Some examples:

- **Financial Accounting**
  Postings in the general ledger and from the subledgers: accounts receivable and accounts payable postings, asset transactions and depreciation, etc.
- **Purchasing**
  Purchase requisitions, purchase orders, material movements, etc.
- **Sales and Distribution**
  Sales documents, distribution documents

Document header and document segment

The basic structure of the transaction data in an SAP system is similar across all modules and processes: in the SAP system, a document consists of a *document header* that is linked to one or more related *document segments*. In Fig. 5.4, you can see the structure of the transaction data in the general ledger, primarily tables BKPF (Document Header) and BSEG (Document Segment). There are standard rules for the general structure of transaction data in the SAP system; it consists of a document header and related segments or items (see Fig. 5.5).

Display Logical Database BRM

[🖉] [⟲] [⟳] | [🗐 Source code] [Selections] [🗫 Sel.Texts] [ℹ Documentation]

| Management | Structure | Search help | Currency/quantity fields |

[🗋][🗐][≫][🗐][🗑] [⊞]

Node name	Table / Type	Node type	Short text
▽ ⊞ BKPF	BKPF	Table	Accounting Document Header
⊞ BSET	BSET	Table	Tax Data Document Segment
▽ ⊞ BSEG	BSEG	Table	Accounting Document Segment
⊞ BSEC	BSEC	Table	One-Time Account Data Document Segment
▽ ⊞ EKKO	EKKO	Table	Purchasing Document Header
▽ ⊞ EKPO	EKPO	Table	Purchasing Document Item
⊞ EKBE	EKBE	Table	Purchasing Document History

◻ Figure 5.4 Table structure of the transaction data in Financial Accounting

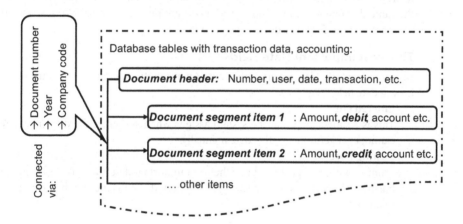

◻ Figure 5.5 Structure of an accounting document in the SAP system

- The *document header* contains general information about the business transaction. For example, the person who created the document, date, transaction (with which the business transaction was entered), document number, and organizational unit (depending on the process: company code, plant, sales organization, etc.).
- The *document segment* contains more detailed information about the business transaction: for example, amount, quantity (where applicable), debits/credits indicator, G/L account, etc. In the case of accounting documents, the system logic provides for at least two document segments per document, whereby the total of the debit amounts is always equal to the total of the credit amounts within one document. This safeguards the principle of double-entry accounting in the SAP system.

The document header and document segment are connected to one another by the document number, the fiscal year, and the ID of the relevant organizational unit. This is

Identifying a document uniquely

Technical field name

BUKRS	AUGDT	GJAHR	BELNR	BUDAT	BLDAT	CPUDT	ZFBDT

Field description

Company Code	Clearing	Fiscal Year	Document Number	Posting Date	Document Date	Entered on	Baseline Date
0100	15.12.2003	2003	0000150108	15.12.2003	15.12.2003	12.12.2003	15.12.2003
0100	20.01.2004	2003	0000191562	31.12.2003	12.12.2003	05.01.2004	12.12.2003
0100	20.01.2004	2004	0000150208	20.01.2004	20.01.2004	20.01.2004	20.01.2004
0100	17.08.2004	2004	0000192495	30.06.2004	24.06.2004	06.07.2004	24.06.2004
0100	17.08.2004	2004	0000192570	28.07.2004	22.07.2004	28.07.2004	22.07.2004
0100	17.08.2004	2004	0000150942	17.08.2004	17.08.2004	17.08.2004	17.08.2004
0100	30.08.2004	2004	0000192623	13.08.2004	29.07.2004	13.08.2004	29.07.2004
0100	30.08.2004	2004	0000192624	13.08.2004	06.08.2004	13.08.2004	06.08.2004
0100	08.11.2004	2004	0000151246	08.11.2004	08.11.2004	04.11.2004	08.11.2004
0100	22.11.2004	2004	0000193059	15.11.2004	24.10.2004	15.11.2004	24.10.2004

◘ Figure 5.6 Example of date fields in vendor documents

the result of the logic for assigning document numbers in the SAP system. In this logic, the same document number can be assigned multiple times in the SAP system – the same also applies for other document attributes.

The Most Important Date Fields

In a document, the date is very important. An accounting document contains the following date fields (Fig. 5.6):

— **Entered On**
    This is a time stamp that the system assigns when you enter the document. You cannot change/influence this date manually.

— **Posting Date**
    From an audit perspective, this is the most important date – it is used to assign the business transactions to a specific posting period. You can enter the posting date manually.

Further date fields   Depending on the process or subledger, further date fields can be relevant:

— **Document Date**
    This is a reference date that you can transfer manually from the underlying external document (e. g., incoming vendor invoice).

— **Clearing Date**
    For items managed according to the open item principle (e. g., invoices, incoming vendor invoices, goods receipts, payments, etc.), the system enters the date of clearing or manual or automatic assignment of the related items in this field.

— **Due Date**
    The due date, also called the *baseline date for payment*, determines when an open vendor or customer invoice is due. If cash discount percentage rates (and days) are not defined in the document, payment is due on the baseline date for payment. The evaluation (and where applicable, write-off) of open customer line items based on an aging structure is based on this date, for example.

These fields ensure that the basic requirements for a document, such as sequential numbering, unique assignment, and timeliness are met. For more information about

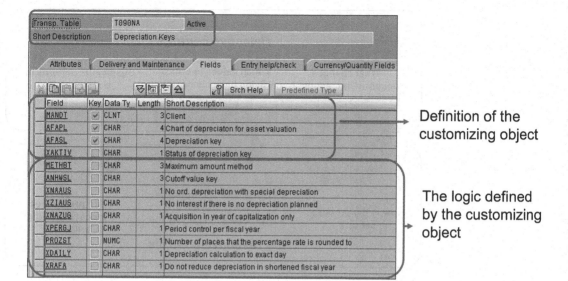

Figure 5.7 Configuration table for depreciation keys

compliance with the corresponding basic principles of an accounting-relevant document, see Chaps. 7 and 8.

Configuration Data

The majority of tables in the SAP system contain configuration data and determine the procedures and processes in the SAP application. They are known as the customizing tables. This ability to determine procedures and processes is possible because the logic of the ABAP programs contains references to the contents of corresponding customizing tables. In turn, this enables you to adjust the business processes mapped in the SAP system flexibly.

Customizing tables control processes in SAP

Depending on the process and module, the structure of the configuration tables can vary. However, the following general properties of a configuration table usually apply in the SAP system:

- A *configuration table* (e. g., table T090NA, Depreciation Keys, see Fig. 5.7) consists of:
  - Definition of a *main customizing object* (e. g., depreciation keys in Asset Accounting)
  - Where applicable, a link to other *related customizing objects* (e. g., chart of depreciation in Asset Accounting). Amongst other things, this link enables automatic determination of the main customizing object.
  - The *processing logic* assigned to the customizing object (e. g., daily calculation of the depreciation)
- A *further table*, with the name of the respective main customizing object (e. g., table T090NAT, Name of Depreciation Key), is assigned to a configuration table. All languages supported by SAP are taken into account.

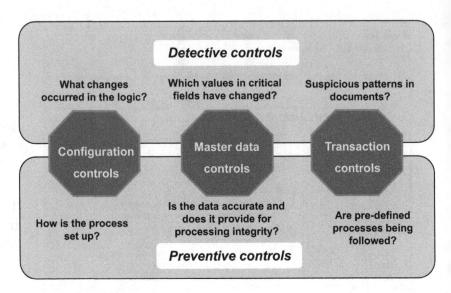

□ **Figure 5.8**   Types of control activities in the SAP environment

Changes to
configuration
tables

Changes to the contents of configuration tables *should* be subject to strict rules as part of Change Management (see Chap. 6). The contents must be protected against direct changes.

> **SAP Table Manual**
>
> You can use program RSSDOCTB (Table Manual) to view the documentation defined in SAP ERP for the individual tables.

5.1.2   Controls in the SAP System

Corresponding to the breakdown of the content of data in an SAP system into master data, transaction data, and configuration data, when you set up controls or check these controls in the SAP environment, the controls can be *configuration controls, master data controls, or transaction controls* (depending on the object of the control procedures) (see Fig. 5.8).

Questions in system
audits

The following are a few examples of typical questions that arise in connection with the system audit and the assessment of the ICS in the SAP environment:

━ **Questions about configuration controls**

Configuration controls control the data processing logic and therefore have a central ICS role in ERP-supported business processes:

━ Do the customizing settings correspond to the control objective in the business process?

Completeness: Is the ALE audit function used when transferring documents via an interface?

Evaluation: Are settings for the automated devaluation of material stock in accordance with the lowest value principle correct?

Reporting: Has the account determination for the automated splitting of the goods received/invoice received balance into "goods in transit" and "invoice in transit" been maintained correctly?

Correctness: Are the values for the calculation of the sales tax maintained in tax keys correct?

Segregation of duties principle: Has the review function for the creation of vendors been activated?

- Have the changes to the configuration data been executed in accordance with the defined change management process? Have they been approved/tested?

- **Questions about master data controls**

Some fields in the master data adopt a control function, influence the process of recording the business transactions, and are therefore relevant from an ICS view:

- Do the values contained in the master data support the control objective?

Evaluation: Have the credit limits been maintained completely, reducing the risk of depreciation of receivables as a result of their low intrinsic value?

Reporting: Have correct reconciliation accounts been assigned to the vendors in the master records?

Segregation of duties principle: Was the recording of the bank details approved in the same step as the invoice entry?

Have critical changes (bank details, reconciliation account, etc.) been checked and approved? Are there any signs of irregularities?

- **Questions about transaction controls**

The business transactions recorded can subsequently be assessed individually, e. g., to determine the effectiveness and correctness of the ICS:

- Have the authorization controls been implemented correctly? For example, have goods receipts and purchase orders for the same material been entered by the same person?

- Where business transactions have been entered manually, have guidelines been complied with (where there are no application controls or these are insufficient): are there instances of incorrect account assignment, exceeding the amount limit when entering one-time account invoices, etc.?

- Are there signs of possible irregularities with potential for fraud: postings at weekends, use of employees' own bank details when entering incoming one-time account invoices, splitting of purchase orders, etc.?

You can answer many of these questions using the search options in SAP. They can help you to understand basic connections in SAP. In the following sections you will learn about the most important search options.

5.1.3 Table-Specific Search

Suitable transactions or reports are not always available to provide you with the required information for audit-relevant questions. You will often have to obtain direct access to the contents of database tables to get the information. A few examples of such questions are:

Questions for the table-specific search

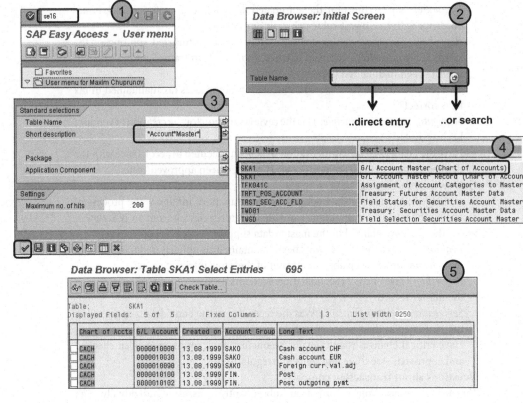

Figure 5.9 Table search using the Data Browser (transaction SE16)

- Which tables and fields contain the data you are looking for?
- How are the tables connected to one another? Which data/tables would also be important in connection with the information you are looking for?
- In which tables is configuration data managed?
- Where are the general attributes of the tables located?

These questions are also relevant for analyzing control mechanisms and can be answered by the table-specific or data-specific search.

Search using transaction SE16, Data Browser

The most common and frequently used search option is transaction SE16 (Data Browser). It enables you to search for table names as well as display the table contents (see Fig. 5.9); equipped with this basic tool you will get a long way: after calling up transaction SE16 (see ❶ in Fig. 5.9), you can either enter a technical table name directly or search using the short description of the table (❷ and ❸). If the search result is a list of tables ❹, you can double-click individual tables to display their contents ❺.

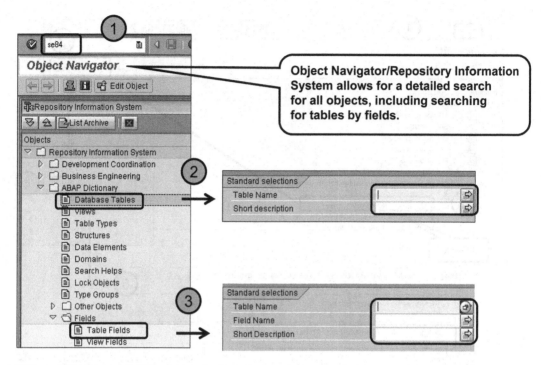

> Object Navigator/Repository Information System allows for a detailed search for all objects, including searching for tables by fields.

D Figure 5.10 Table search via data fields in the Object Navigator/Repository Information System (transaction SE84)

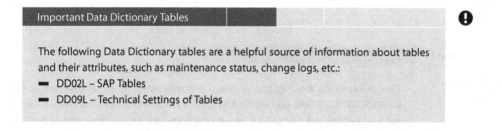

Important Data Dictionary Tables

The following Data Dictionary tables are a helpful source of information about tables and their attributes, such as maintenance status, change logs, etc.:

- DD02L – SAP Tables
- DD09L – Technical Settings of Tables

Deeper search and analysis options for tables are available in the Repository Information System (see Fig. 5.10). In addition to a direct table search and display, transaction SE84 (Repository Information System) allows you to search for tables using the data fields within the tables.

Search via data fields

When you call up this transaction (see ❶ in Fig. 5.10), two options are available:

- Option 1: via ABAP DICTIONARY • DATABASE TABLES, search for the technical table names or the table description (❷, similar to the previously mentioned transaction SE16)
- Option 2: via ABAP DICTIONARY • FIELDS • TABLE FIELDS ❸, search for tables based on the data fields (components of tables)

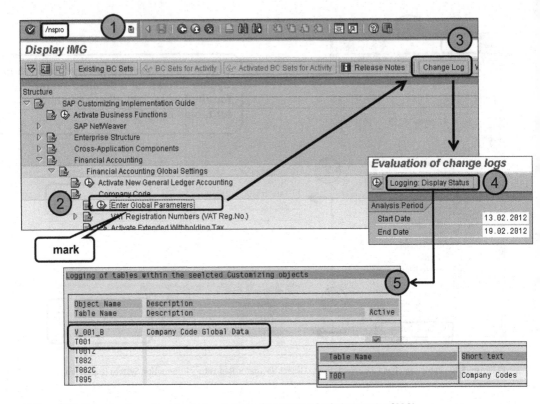

□ **Figure 5.11** Searching for customizing tables via the Implementation Guide (transaction SPRO)

[e.g.]

Table Search via Fields

If, as shown under ❸ in Fig. 5.10, you were to start a search for tables that contain the VENDOR NUMBER field, you would find tables LFA1 and LFB1 with the vendor master data; you would also find table BSIK with the open vendor line items, and table BSAK with the cleared vendor line items.

These are the most important tables that help you to understand the application logic in Accounts Payable Accounting.

Search for the configuration or control tables

A further important type of search that is useful, particularly for analyzing application controls, is the search for the control tables in the Implementation Guide. All customizing settings are summarized in these tables and are integrated in a menu tree according to processes and topics. As shown in Fig. 5.11, you would be able to determine, for example, that the company codes and their attributes are maintained in table T001. To do this, proceed as follows:

1. Call up transaction SPRO ❶ and click SAP Reference IMG.
2. Select a node in the configuration menu tree ❷.

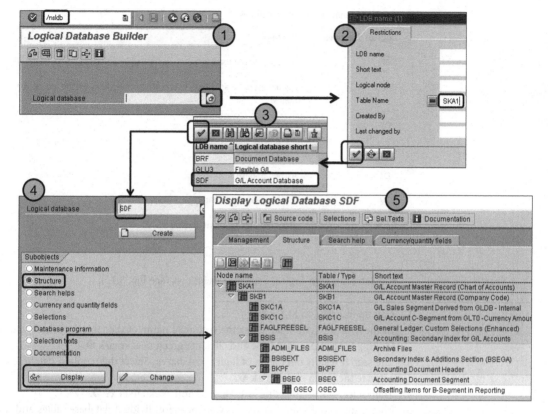

◘ **Figure 5.12** Searching for tables and understanding the data models using logical databases (transaction SLDB)

3. Click CHANGE LOG ❸.
4. In the dialog box that appears, click LOGGING: DISPLAY STATUS ❹.
5. The search result ❺ shows the name of the table you are looking for. You can use this table to save or maintain the corresponding configuration settings.

The information displayed when you click CHANGE LOG informs you about the status of the logging of the respective table.

Logical databases are a very useful source of information with regard to the basic connections between the tables and the data in SAP. Here, the connections are displayed graphically. On a process-specific basis, they explain the connections, primarily for the *master and transaction data*.

For example, if, via the keyword search (see Fig. 5.9), you have found out that the G/L accounts are located in table SKA1 (G/L Account Master Data, A Segment), you would be able to use the logical database SDF (G/L Account Database) to determine independently where the information about G/L accounts is used when you enter business transactions (table BSEG, Fig. 5.12). The logical databases provide valuable information in particular when you are developing the data analysis scenarios or automated control mechanisms that focus on *master data and transaction data*.

Logical databases

◘ **Table 5.1**   Examples of logical databases

Logical database	Content
SDF	G/L account database
BRF	Document database (in particular, the connection with the master data tables)
KDF	Vendor database
DDF	Customer database
ADA	Asset database
VRV	Invoice verification database: invoices
BMM	Materials management database

Search for logical databases

You can search for logical databases as follows (see Fig. 5.12):

1. Call up transaction SLDB ❶.
2. In the TABLE NAME field, enter the technical name of the table for which you are looking for a logical database and click the green checkmark ❷.
3. The search results offer a list of logical databases. Select the required database and activate the green checkmark ❸.
4. Then select the STRUCTURE radio button and click DISPLAY ❹.
5. The result of the search is an overview of the individual database tables and how they are connected to one another within the corresponding logical database ❺.

The most important logical databases are shown in Table 5.1.

Graphical overview of the table connections in the Repository Information System

Another useful source for the graphical representation of the connections between the database tables is the Repository Information System. In particular, it is the source for tracing the connections in the control data, but is also helpful with regard to master data. From the overview in Fig. 5.13, you can see that table SKA1 is connected to the following tables (amongst others):

— T004 – Directory of Charts of Accounts
— T077S – G/L Account Groups
— T880 – Global Company Data (for CONS Ledger)
— TFKB – Functional Areas

To display the graphical overview, proceed as shown in Fig. 5.13:

1. Call up transaction SE84 ❶.
2. Choose ABAP DICTIONARY • DATABASE TABLES and proceed to the required database table. Double-click to access the attributes of this table and click GRAPHIC ❷.
3. The result ❸ is the graphical display of the connections of the required table with other tables.

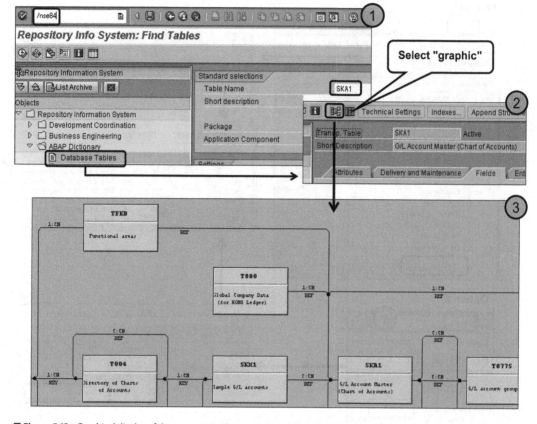

Figure 5.13 Graphical display of the connections between the tables in the Repository Information System

5.1.4 Transaction-Specific Search

In the SAP system, processes represent a chain of transactions that in turn represent a sequence of the individual steps in a business process.

Business process as a sequence of transactions

[e.g.]

The Purchasing Process as a Sequence of Transactions in SAP

In the SAP system, the purchasing process is mapped as follows (simplified illustration):
- Entry of a purchase requisition (transaction ME51)
- Release of a purchase requisition (transaction ME54)
- Entry of a purchase order (transaction ME21)
- Release of a purchase order (transaction ME28)
- Entry of a goods receipt (transaction MIGO)
- Invoice receipt and verification (transaction MIRO)
- Payment (transaction F110)

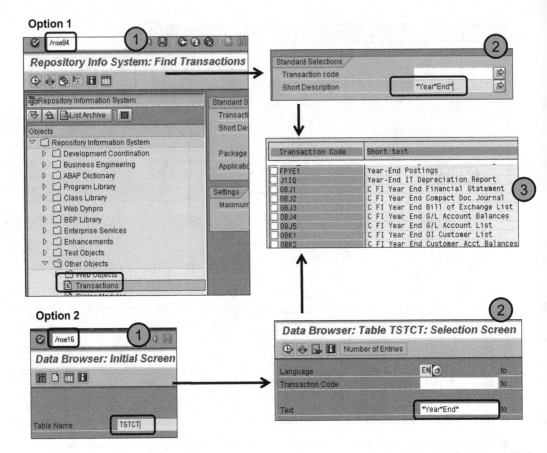

□ **Figure 5.14** Search for the names of the transaction in the Repository Information System (SE84) or the Data Browser (SE16)

Search for transactions

You can search for transactions using their short description or text in the Repository Information System (transaction SE84, see Fig. 5.14), for example. Table TSTCT contains information about the transaction names, which means that as an alternative, you can search for the transactions directly using this table (transaction SE16).

Perform the search as follows (see Fig. 5.14):

- With the first option, start transaction SE84; then, via the menu tree, call up OTHER OBJECTS • TRANSACTIONS ❶.
- With the second option, call up transaction SE16, enter "TSTCT" in the TABLE NAME field, and start the search ❶.
- In each subsequent step (❷ and ❷), you can enter the required keyword in the SHORT DESCRIPTION or TEXT search fields.
- The result ❸ is the list of transactions.

Transactions: search in the user menu

When you enter business transactions in the SAP system, you usually call up transactions via the SAP standard menu or the user menu. In the menu tree, transactions are structured according to their association to the individual modules or business processes. This enables an intuitive search.

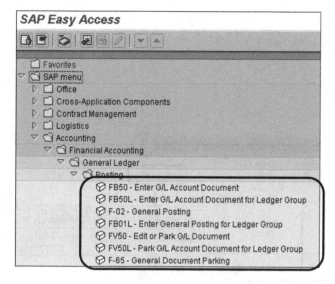

■ **Figure 5.15** Transactions in the menu tree

You can view the technical name of a transaction via the menu item EXTRAS • TECH-
NICAL DETAILED INFORMATION, or generally make the name visible for all transactions
via the setting EXTRAS • SETTINGS, checkbox DISPLAY TECHNICAL NAME. If you make
the technical transaction names visible, you can see the transaction codes in the menu
tree, as shown in Fig. 5.15.

As you can see, there are various transaction-specific search options in SAP. They
enable you to trace the flow of the business processes.

5.1.5 Program-Specific Search

In SAP, ABAP programs contain the processing logic. Transactions SE38 (ABAP Editor)
or SE84 (Repository Information System) enable you to search for programs using their
technical name or title (see Fig. 5.16).

Proceed as follows: Call up transaction SE84 and in the menu tree, choose PROGRAM
LIBRARY • PROGRAMS ❶. Another option would be to start transaction SE38 (or transaction SA38, ABAP: Program Execution, which can be used as an alternative), select
the search in the PROGRAM field, and then click INFORMATION SYSTEM ❶. Both options
enable you to then ❷ search either for the name of the program (PROGRAM NAME field)
or for a specific keyword in the SHORT DESCRIPTION field ❸.

Program search via
SE84 or SE38/SA38

5.1.6 The Relationship Between Programs and Transactions

You can find a link from the transaction to the related ABAP program when you execute
the transaction, for example.

Option 1

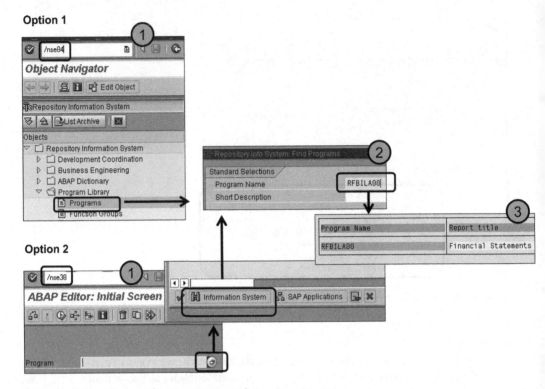

Option 2

☐ Figure 5.16 Program search for program names or designation

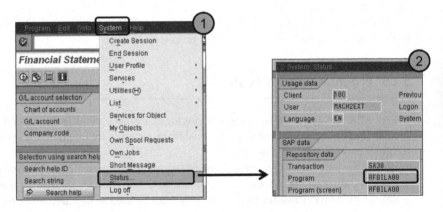

☐ Figure 5.17 Determining the transaction/program assignment from the transaction

If, for example, as shown in Fig. 5.17, you are on the screen with the selection criteria for displaying the financial statement values (i. e., in the previous step you called up the corresponding transaction or the program directly), via the menu path SYSTEM • STATUS, you can call up an additional window. In the REPOSITORY DATA section, you can see the names of both the transaction and the program.

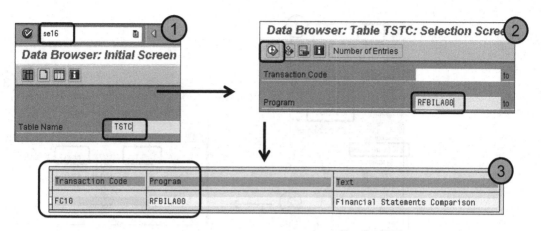

◘ Figure 5.18 Connection between transactions and programs via table TSTC

You can also trace the connection between transactions and programs via table   Table TSTC
TSTC. Using transaction SE16 (see ❶ in Fig. 5.18), call up table TSTC; in the PROGRAM
field, enter the name of the corresponding ABAP program ❷, then click EXECUTE to
get the result ❸.

In this way, you can find out that program RFBILA00 (Financial Statements) is
called up via transaction FC10. You can also perform the search, based on table TSTC,
in the opposite direction (from a transaction to a program).

5.1.7 The Relationship Between Programs and Tables

A central question in understanding the application logic in SAP is which data or con-   Link from programs
tent of which tables is used or changed when you execute a program.   to data

The simplest way to make the link from a program to the related tables visible is via
the ABAP source code (see Fig. 5.19).

Proceed as follows:

1. Call up transaction SE38 ❶.
2. On the entry screen, enter the program name in the PROGRAM field, activate the
   SOURCE CODE radio button, and then click DISPLAY ❷.
3. The result is the ABAP source code ❸. In the top section, directly after the general
   description of the program, the tables used are declared. Therefore, via the source
   code of program RFBILA00 (Financial Statements), for example, you would be
   able to determine that this program reads the information about G/L accounts from
   table SKA1.

This procedure can only give you a general view of the tables used, as the TABLES   Search for tables in
instruction that you see in Fig. 5.19 under ❸ is only one possible declaration type in   the ABAP source
ABAP. From an audit perspective, it may be necessary to search specifically for tables   code
whose contents are changed by a program. In some circumstances, this search can be at

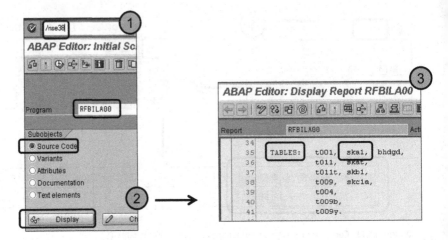

Figure 5.19 From program to table via the program source code

multiple levels if your objective is a complete analysis. This is described in the following note.

❗ Search Options for Tables in the ABAP Source Code

Common search options for tables in the ABAP source code are:
- In addition to being available in a TABLES instruction, the information about tables can also be taken from the TYPE referencing.
- In the object-oriented environment, tables can also be processed without an explicit declaration.
- A further option is the search for UPDATE, INSERT, or MODIFY commands in the program and the related includes (e. g., via the RS_ABAP_SOURCE_SCAN search program).
- Furthermore, in the ABAP code and the related includes, you must also search for the SUBMIT, CALL FUNCTION, or CALL TRANSACTION commands; in the includes/subroutines/etc. called up, you also search for the UPDATE, INSERT, or MODIFY commands.

Where-used list: from the table to the program   Another search often used in practice is the *where-used list*. This enables you to find programs and transactions that address data in specific tables. There is a differentiation between a reading and a changing use of data.

[e.g.]   Where-Used List Audit Treatment

During an SAP system audit, a program that was developed in-house was found – specifically, a program that can deactivate the logging of the table changes en masse (this is controlled by a field in table DD09 L).

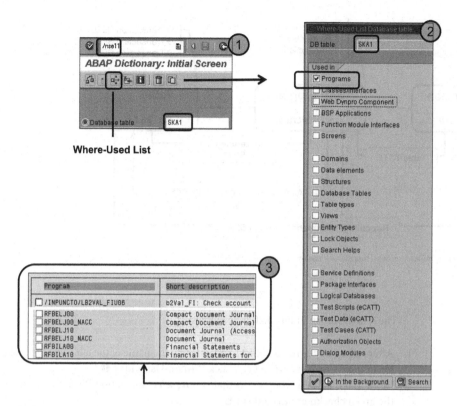

□ Figure 5.20 From the tables to the relevant programs via the where-used list

The authorizations for calling up the programs directly (transaction SA38) had been assigned very generously in the system being audited. In a strongly distributed system landscape, this represented a high risk: postings to the general ledger were made via several interfaces and the account assignment logic was controlled via maintainable conversion tables. It would not have been possible to trace changes to this logic if someone had changed the content of these maintainable tables via the direct table maintenance using transaction SM30.

In Fig. 5.20 you can see "regular reports" using the SKA1 table. These read-only reports are quite harmless but in some cases, auditors may find "update" or "delete" reports developed in-house that are sometimes used during implementation and transported by mistake into the live environment. From a compliance perspective, such programs should only be used with extreme caution, as the risk of error would have increased, for example, in manual posting transactions where the user relies on the names for the account search.

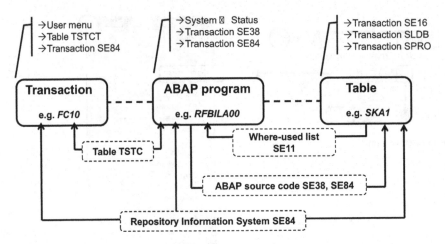

The search shown in Fig. 5.20 is as follows:

1. After calling up transaction SE11 and entering the name of the table you are looking for in the DATABASE TABLE field, click WHERE-USED LIST ❶.
2. In the USED IN field group in the dialog box, select the option PROGRAMS and click the green checkmark to confirm ❷.
3. The result ❸ is the list of programs that address the table in question.

> ❗ **Where-Used List for Tables**
>
> This procedure allows you only a general, and in some circumstances, incomplete view of the use of the tables in programs. Depending on the type of programming, the object list for the where-used list may be incomplete, particularly with regard to evaluations for SAP standard tables in SAP standard programs. You can only achieve a reliable statement with the where-used list for simple programs with low complexity.

5.1.8 Summary of the Search Options in SAP

Search options for tracing the connections in SAP

The options for tracing the connections in an SAP system described in the previous sections are summarized in Fig. 5.21.

The tools described should generally suffice to answer many of the questions about application controls in the SAP environment that arise during a system audit (see the other chapters in Part II of this book).

5.1.9 Organizational Structures in the SAP System

The structure of an organization is mapped in the SAP system using organizational structures. The individual components within the organizational structure are various organizational units that are linked with one another dependent on the process and SAP module. They form hierarchical structures.

The best way to obtain an overview of the organizational structures mapped in the SAP system is via the Implementation Guide (IMG). Choose transaction SPRO, click SAP Reference IMG and then follow the menu path ENTERPRISE STRUCTURE • ASSIGNMENT AND ENTERPRISE STRUCTURE • DEFINITION.

The organizational objects are as follows depending on the modules and processes:

- Client (higher-level organizational unit, technical view)
- Controlling area, operating concern, company code, business area (financial view)
- Plant, storage location, purchasing organization (Materials Management, Logistics)
- Sales area, sales organization, distribution channel, division, sales office, sales group (Sales and Distribution)
- Personnel area, employee group, employee subgroup (Personnel Management)

Organizational objects in the SAP system

When considering the financial reporting from a compliance perspective, as an independent accounting unit, the company code plays a central role.

The use of organizational units in SAP is very diverse. Figure 5.22 shows a simplified overview of the most important organizational units. The logistics structures (plants, purchasing organizations, etc.) can also be defined differently to the illustration, for example, more generally; the prerequisite for a cross-company code controlling area is that both company codes use the same chart of accounts.

You use the organizational units to assign the business transactions, whereby the related *master and control data* is often also defined specific to the organizational unit.

Organizational Structures in SAP Business Transactions   **[e.g.]**

An incoming invoice (transaction data: posting document) is entered in plant 2000, which is assigned to company code 1000 (organizational units: plant, company code).

When the invoice is entered, the first item of the account assignment is taken from the vendor master record (organization-specific master data: vendor) and the second is entered manually (organization-specific master data: G/L accounts).

In the background, the system checks whether the tolerance (organization-specific control data: tolerance limits for invoice verification) for the deviation of the invoiced amount from the amount in the corresponding purchase order has been exceeded.

Furthermore, when a business transaction is entered or a transaction is called up in the SAP system, an authorization check takes place to determine whether the user is permitted to execute this transaction. Here, organizational units play a further role: differentiation of the business transactions based on authorizations also considers the organizational structures.

Organizational structures in SAP authorizations

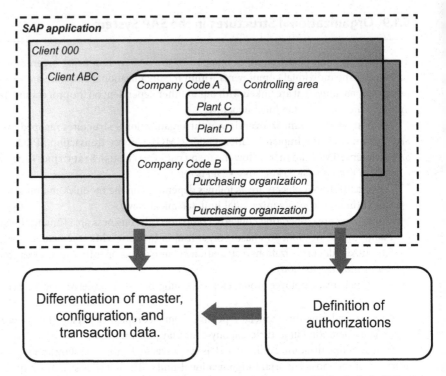

□ Figure 5.22 Simplified illustration of the organizational structures and their roles in the SAP system

Authorizations therefore represent a second important domain in addition to application controls. This second domain is the main focus of an internal control system, and we will look at this in the next chapter.

5.2   Authorizations

The controls described in Sect. 5.1 can only fulfill the compliance requirements if the access to these procedures is sufficiently protected. You will now learn about the basic principles of authorization protection in the SAP system. However, this book does not claim to provide answers to all questions on the topic of SAP authorizations. The compliance analysis focuses on only a few issues within the very complex application area around SAP authorizations. It is concerned primarily with correctness.

❶   Recommended Literature

For more in-depth questions, particularly regarding the design and efficient implementation of an authorization concept, see "Authorizations in SAP Software: Design and Configuration" by Volker Lehnert and Katharina Bonitz. It is published by SAP PRESS.

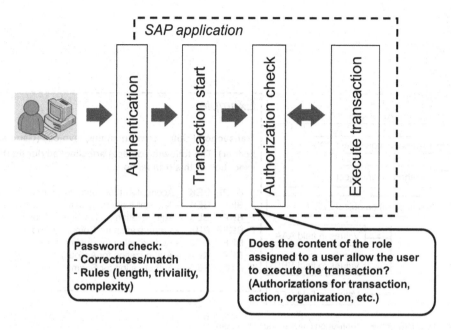

Figure 5.23 Simplified illustration of the authorization check in the SAP system

5.2.1 Flow and Hierarchy of Authorization Controls

For a user to successfully pass the security controls when logging on, he must have the authorization to execute a specific action in the SAP system. From an ICS perspective, the interaction of a user with an SAP system can be summarized as shown in Fig. 5.23. The authentication controls are explained in detail in Sect. 6.3. This illustration shows in simple terms which security checks take place in SAP – divided into authentication and subsequent authorization check.

When you call up a transaction, the individual components of the authorization check are as follows (simplified illustration):

Authorization check

1. Check transaction call
2. Check authorization object
3. Check role/profile
4. Check user

The following sections explain the individual parts of this sequence in more detail.

5.2.2 Authorization Objects

The authorization objects represent the lowest level within the architecture of the SAP authorization concept. Each authorization object is linked to specific data. Furthermore, access to this data is differentiated by the values in the (up to ten) value fields for

Role of the authorization objects

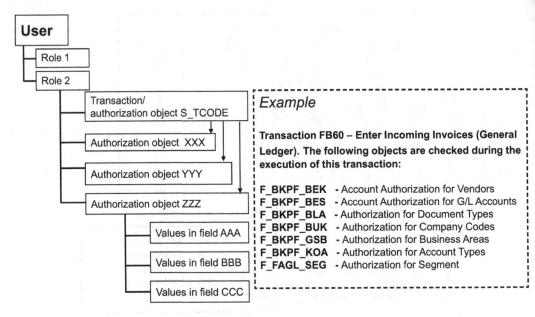

◘ **Figure 5.24**   Hierarchy of the authorization check in the SAP system

each authorization object. These value fields permit a specific type of access (e. g., read, write, etc.), activity, or organizational unit.

When a user processes a business transaction or calls up a transaction, the system first checks the authorization object S_TCODE as shown in Fig. 5.24. This object has only one field – for a transaction code. This means that the system first checks whether the user has a general authorization for calling up a specific transaction. After checking this higher level authorization object, the system checks further authorization objects determined by the transaction called up.

[e.g.]

Authorization Object F_BKPF_BUK

Authorization object F_BKPF_BUK (Accounting Document: Authorization for Company Codes) is checked when transaction FB60 is called up. It determines which activities with posting documents are allowed in which company code. The fields within this authorization object are ACTIVITY and COMPANY CODE.

Activities within an authorization object

The ACTIVITY field appears in most authorization objects and determines which activities are permitted with a specific data object, i. e., which actions are permitted within a specific business process. The most important activities in the SAP system are:

- 01 – Create (e. g., a document = post, create a master record)
- 02 – Change
- 03 – Display

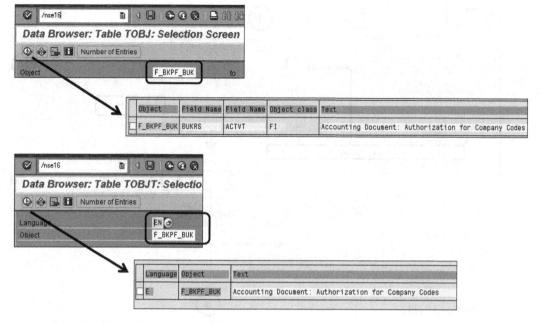

Figure 5.25 Tables TOBJ and TOBJT as source of information for authorization objects

- 05 – Lock/Unlock
- 06 – Delete[1]

From an audit perspective, the activities 01 and 02 are particularly important. For authorization purposes, other fields in the authorization objects separate the data to be processed using its attributes. For example, the accounting document has attributes such as the document type, G/L account, company code, business area, etc. The corresponding authorization objects are present for all attributes.

For a general overview of the authorization objects, in particular their names and fields, see tables TOBJ and TOBJT (see Fig. 5.25).

You can use transaction SE16 (Data Browser) to perform the following evaluation:

- Table TOBJ shows the existing fields for each authorization object (e. g., the COM-PANY CODE and ACTIVITY fields for object F_BKPF_BUK).
- Table TOBJT contains the description of the corresponding object.

Tables TOBJ and TOBJT

For detailed documentation on the individual authorization objects, see transaction SUIM (User Information System) as shown in Fig. 5.26.

Proceed as follows:

Documentation about authorization objects

1. First call up transaction SUIM and in the menu tree, choose AUTHORIZATION OB-JECTS • AUTHORIZATION OBJECTS BY COMPLEX SELECTION CRITERIA ❶.
2. Enter the name of an authorization object ❷. There is a technical limit in the system: you can query a maximum of three authorization objects simultaneously.

---

[1] Not the physical deletion of the data; that would be a very high risk from an audit view.

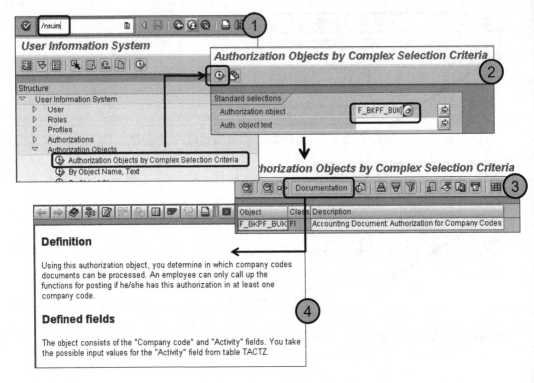

▣ Figure 5.26 Documentation for authorization objects

3. Then, from the search result ❸, click DOCUMENTATION to display the detailed documentation for the respective object ❹.

Naming conventions for authorization objects   The technical name of an authorization object can have a maximum of ten characters. The first character of the technical name generally represents the data protected by the object or operations for a specific area or module in the SAP system, for example:

- A – Asset Accounting
- S – Basis
- F – Financial Accounting
- K – Controlling
- L – Logistics
- M – Materials Management
- P – Personnel Management etc.

5.2.3 Determining Authorization Objects

From an audit perspective, you often have to know which authorization objects are checked when a transaction is called up. Only an analysis of the authorization check using tracing (transaction ST01) can provide a precise answer to this question, partic-

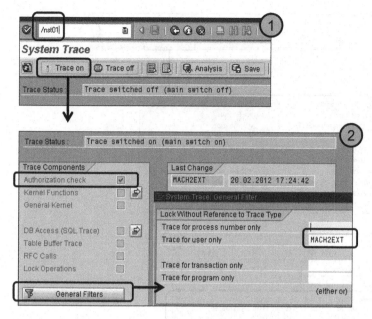

◘ Figure 5.27 Activation of the system trace

ularly in the case of transactions or programs developed in-house. This is because the check logic is defined in the source code of a program assigned to the transaction.

We will look at this option first and a further option later on.

System Trace

To use the system trace, you must first activate it (see Fig. 5.27). Proceed as follows:

Activating the system trace

1. Call up transaction ST01 and confirm TRACE ON ❶. The result is the message TRACE IS SWITCHED on in the TRACE STATUS field.
2. You must then define the system events to be analyzed ❷. The checkmark must be set for the AUTHORIZATION CHECK option. You can also use the GENERAL FILTERS button to refine the analysis criteria (e. g., restrict the analysis to a specific user).

Once you have activated the system trace, all activities that correspond to the selection criteria entered are recorded. Figure 5.27 therefore shows all authorization checks for user MACH2EXT right down to the level of the individual values of the authorization objects.

To analyze the system trace, proceed as follows (see Fig. 5.28):

Analyzing the system trace

1. Click ANALYSIS ❶.
2. Then define the analysis criteria for the system trace log ❷; here, the SAP system automatically adopts the selection criteria entered in the system trace filter as default values.
3. The result ❸ is a list of all authorization checks that took place in the system within the selection criteria. You can see, for example, that user MACH2EXT has called up

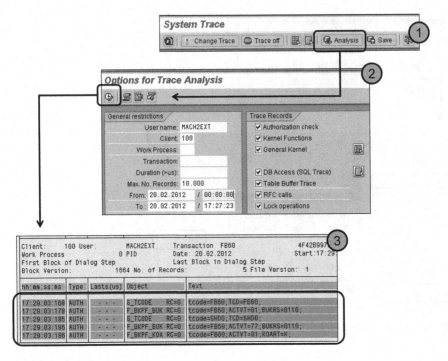

Figure 5.28 Analysis of the system trace

transaction FB60 (Enter Incoming Invoices) and that in executing this transaction, the SAP system has checked the following authorization objects: S_TCODE (transaction check), F_BKPF_BUK (company code check), and F_BKPF_KOA (account type check).

The system trace is not merely an important source of information for the authorization checks that take place in the SAP system; it is also an important audit event in itself.

[e.g.]   Checking a Control Using the System Trace

An organization uses many in-house and modified programs, including in the ordering process. Using the system trace analysis for transaction Z*, which was used to enter a purchase order, it has been possible to find out that it was not possible to restrict this transaction for organizational units by means of authorizations: there was no system check of authorization objects (e. g., authorization object M_BEST_WRK, Plant in Purchasing) that would have enabled such a restriction. The authorization control therefore had no effect.

For more information about "protecting in-house developments," see Sect. 6.4.1.

Data Browser: Table USOBT Select Entries   20

`&r` 🔍 🖨 🖩 📑 🗐 🔄 ℹ️   Check Table...

```
Table:          USOBT
Displayed Fields:   9 of   9      Fixed Columns:        | 5      List Width
```

Name	Test status type	Object	Field Name	Value
☐ FB60	TR	F_BKPF_BEK	ACTVT	01
☐ FB60	TR	F_BKPF_BEK	ACTVT	03
☐ FB60	TR	F_BKPF_BEK	BRGRU	
☐ FB60	TR	F_BKPF_BES	ACTVT	
☐ FB60	TR	F_BKPF_BES	BRGRU	
☐ FB60	TR	F_BKPF_BLA	ACTVT	01
☐ FB60	TR	F_BKPF_BLA	ACTVT	03
☐ FB60	TR	F_BKPF_BLA	BRGRU	
☐ FB60	TR	F_BKPF_BUK	ACTVT	01
☐ FB60	TR	F_BKPF_BUK	ACTVT	03
☐ FB60	TR	F_BKPF_BUK	BUKRS	$BUKRS
☐ FB60	TR	F_BKPF_GSB	ACTVT	01
☐ FB60	TR	F_BKPF_GSB	ACTVT	03
☐ FB60	TR	F_BKPF_GSB	GSBER	$GSBER
☐ FB60	TR	F_BKPF_KOA	ACTVT	01
☐ FB60	TR	F_BKPF_KOA	ACTVT	03
☐ FB60	TR	F_BKPF_KOA	KOART	$KOART
☐ FB60	TR	F_FAGL_SEG	ACTVT	
☐ FB60	TR	F_FAGL_SEG	GLRRCTY	
☐ FB60	TR	F_FAGL_SEG	SEGMENT	

□ Figure 5.29 Default values for authorization objects within a transaction

Default Values for the Profile Generator

For reasons of efficiency, in practice, table USOBT is generally used as a source of information instead of the system trace (see Fig. 5.29).

Table USOBT contains the list of authorization objects for each transaction that the SAP system uses in the maintenance of roles (see Sect. 5.2.4) via the Profile Generator (transaction PFCG): if a new transaction is added to a role, the related authorization objects are automatically transferred to table USOBT as well. This table contains only experience values that are delivered as a standard part of the SAP ERP software. The contents of an actual authorization check in SAP are determined not by this table but by the underlying ABAP programs for a transaction. Figure 5.29 shows, for example, authorization objects that are queried when transaction FB60 (Enter Incoming Invoices) is called up.

Default values for authorization objects – table USOBT

The default values delivered in the standard SAP system cover approx. 90 % of all cases and must be maintained, in particular to cover the role maintenance for transactions and programs developed in-house (logically, there can be no default values for these).

5.2.4 Roles in the SAP System

Roles can be described as a type of container that contains authorization objects as well as values for the fields of these objects. Since roles are the image of the operational and organizational structure within an organization, they are defined on an organization-specific basis. Another type of container is profiles. The SAP system generates these automatically from the roles and uses them to "pack" the authorization objects. In

Roles as a container for authorization objects

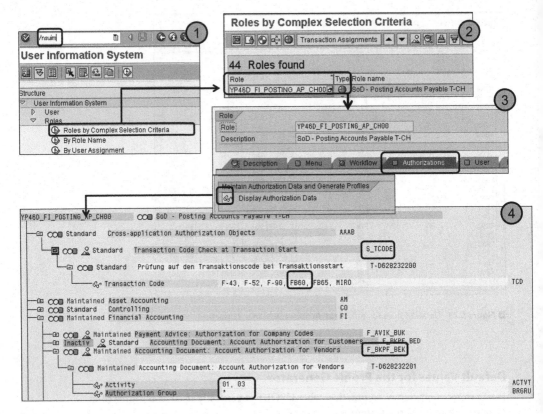

Figure 5.30 Example of a role and its contents

practice, however, authorization concepts based on roles predominate. Profile-based authorization concepts have now become obsolete.

When analyzing authorizations, you may want to know which roles contain authorizations for executing specific transactions. One of the most common analysis options for this would be transaction SUIM (User Information System); it is also recommended for many other authorization-relevant analyses. Perform the following steps (as shown in Fig. 5.30):

1. First call up transaction SUIM and choose ROLES • ROLES BY COMPLEX SELECTION CRITERIA ❶.
2. You can then search for roles using their technical names, their titles, the user assignment, or their content (down to the level of individual authorization objects). Double-click the role found ❷ to display it.
3. The role has various tab pages; for the analysis of the role content, the AUTHORIZATIONS tab is particularly relevant. Click DISPLAY AUTHORIZATION DATA ❸.
4. The result ❹ is a menu tree of authorization objects grouped by module. Their values are also part of the menu hierarchy.

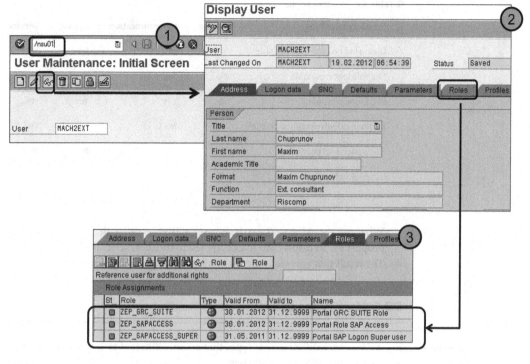

◘ Figure 5.31 User master record and the roles assigned to it

As you can see in Fig. 5.30, the role Accounts Payable Clerk contains a general authorization for calling up transaction FB60 (entering a vendor invoice in the general ledger) and the postings (*activity 01 Create/Post* in combination with *activity 03 Display*). The use of all vendor master records is also allowed under consideration of further restrictions in other authorization objects (the value in the AUTHORIZATION GROUP field has an asterisk, i. e., all possible values for this field are allowed).

Authorizations within a role

5.2.5 Users in the SAP System

From the view of the authorization check hierarchy shown in Sect. 5.2.1, a *user* would be the highest node. In an SAP system, users are managed as master records that have a series of attributes spread over various tab pages. Attributes are either used for information purposes (e. g., contact data) or they adopt a control function (e. g., user or license type). The most important control attributes of a user master record include the roles assigned to it (see Fig. 5.31).

You can analyze a user master record and the authorizations assigned to this user as follows:

Analyzing user master records

- Call up transaction SU01 and enter the user ID in the USER field. Then click DIS-PLAY **❶**.

◻ Table 5.2 Properties of user types

Property/user type	Dialog	Communication	System	Service
Dialog log on (SAP GUI) possible	Yes	No	No	Yes
Multiple logon possible	No	Yes	Yes	Yes
RFC logon possible	Yes	Yes	Yes	Yes
Background job execution possible	Yes	No	Yes	Yes
Force password change	Yes	Yes	No	No
Logon ticket can be created	Yes	Yes	No	No

What you see in the next step is the user master record with all related attributes and properties. To display the roles assigned to the user, select the ROLES tab page ❷.

— The result that you see is the list of all roles assigned to the user ❸.

5.2.6 User Types in SAP

User types   In SAP there are different user types that assume different task types. In detail, an SAP system has the following user types:

— A *dialog user* is used by exactly one person for all types of logon and is a primary focus from a compliance perspective. Persons involved in SAP-controlled business processes are dialog users in SAP.

— The *system* user type (a "technical" user) is used for system-internal (e. g., background processing, batch jobs, etc.) and system-defined (ALE, workflow, TMS, CUA) operations. This user cannot perform a dialog logon (using SAP GUI).

— The *communication* user type is used for non-dialog communication with the systems (e. g., for interfaces); a dialog logon (using SAP GUI) is not possible.

— A *service* user is a dialog user that is available to an anonymous, larger group of users. It is used, for example, for an ITS service or a public web service. After an individual authentication, an anonymous session started with a service user can be continued as a person-specific session with a dialog user.

— The *reference user* is, like the service user, a more general, non-person-specific user. It is not possible to log on with a reference user. The reference user is used only for additional assignment of authorizations.

Table 5.2 contains a summary of the properties of the individual user types.

Special users in SAP   When SAP systems are installed, the system automatically generates a series of special users that are equipped with several permissions: SAP*, DDIC, EARLYWATCH, SAPCPIC. The treatment of these permissions is important from a compliance view and is explained in Sect. 6.3.3.

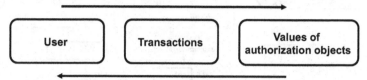

System checks: are the user's authorizations sufficient for XYZ?

| User | Transactions | Values of authorization objects |

Auditor checks: which users have authorizations for XYZ?

◻ **Figure 5.32** Authorization check

5.2.7 Example of an Authorization Analysis

Whilst an SAP system checks whether a user has the authorizations for specific activities, during an audit from a compliance perspective, this question is reversed: you want to find out which users are authorized for specific activities in the SAP system.

Analysis of authorizations

Therefore, you are dependent on search options that help to determine the users via authorization objects and field values. As Fig. 5.33 shows, one such option is transaction SUIM (User Information System). This tool is generally sufficient in the case of low analysis volumes and low analysis complexity. For analyses based on segregation of duties with multiple transactions however, you need additional tools such as SAP Access Control.

Tool for analyzing authorizations

The objective of the analysis described in Fig. 5.33 is to find out which users have authorization for entering incoming invoices via transaction FB60 in company code 1000.

1. Firstly, start transaction SUIM ❶ (User Information System). In this transaction, choose USER • USERS BY COMPLEX SELECTION CRITERIA.
2. Then maintain the selection criteria ❷; the following specifications were given in the example in Fig. 5.33:
   - For the authorization object S_TCODE, the value FB60 was entered. The system thus checks which users have a general authorization for transaction FB60.
   - Furthermore, for authorization object F_BKPF_BUK (Accounting Document: Authorization for Company Codes), company code 1000 and activity 01 (Create/Post) were entered.
   - Since an account assignment must be made when the incoming invoice is entered in the general ledger, the user must also have the authorization for account types K (vendors) and S (G/L accounts) and for activity 01 (Create/Post) in authorization object F_BKPF_KOA (Accounting Document: Authorization for Account Types).
   - Further authorization objects would be important (source: see Fig. 5.29) depending on whether these are further restricted as part of role maintenance or not.
3. The result ❸ is the list of all users who have the corresponding authorizations.

You now know how to perform one of the most important authorization analyses in SAP that is required as part of system audits. The tools available on the market (see, for

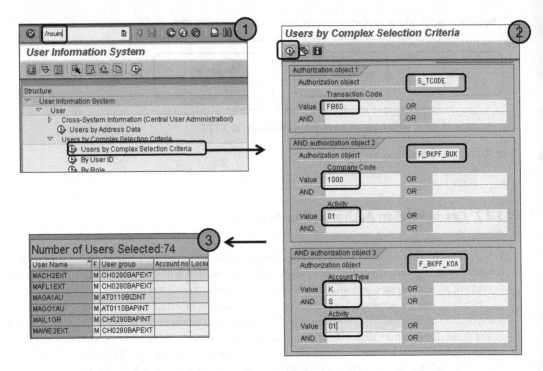

◻ Figure 5.33 Analysis of users based on authorization objects and their values

example, Sect. 4.3.3) use the same analysis principle with the (considerable) difference that in the authorization analysis, where applicable, an unlimited number of authorization objects can be used as analysis criteria.

5.3   Summary

In this chapter you have acquired a basic understanding of the data and types of controls in the SAP system. The breakdown into process or application controls and authorization controls reflects two large control areas. From an ICS and process view, these are closely connected; however, from a technical point of view, they are completely different.

Furthermore, you have learned about tools and search mechanisms in the SAP system that help you to trace the basic connections in SAP. These tools and search mechanisms can be just as useful in various audits in the SAP environment as in setting up efficient control mechanisms in SAP-supported processes.

IT General Controls in SAP ERP

IT general controls represent the very foundation of every ICS framework that covers ERP-supported business processes. In this chapter we will look at this foundation more closely.

In order to be able to rely on the processes in SAP ERP and to ensure the consistency of the data and the processing logic, a number of prerequisites that require efficient IT general controls (ITGC) must be fulfilled (see Sect. 3.1.4). Risks that IT general controls focus on are relevant in virtually all ICS compliance frameworks – regardless of whether the requirements relate to financial reporting or quality, for example. In this chapter, you will learn about the most important controls that form the ITGC part of an ICS framework in the SAP ERP environment and that IT auditors generally examine first. Remember that there are also reference models such as GAIT and CobiT (see Sect. 3.2.4 and 3.2.2) that you can use in practice as templates for executing checks.

6.1 Organizational Controls

The first thing to do is to get an overview of the IT organization and answer the general questions: Who does what? Are the organizational conditions sufficient to ensure operative, IT general controls? Are the existing guidelines and documentation appropriate? Do the guidelines consider the issues that are critical from an ICS perspective? In the following sections we will look at the most important IT general controls (with no claim of completeness).

6.1.1 IT Organization

In larger organizations, IT is often organized in *shared services* (service organizations) to guarantee the required infrastructure and operational support for business applications such as SAP ERP within an organization. As already mentioned in Sect. 4.2.2, the ICS view of the outsourcing of IT into service organizations is covered by auditing standards such as SAS 70, ISAE 3402, and IDW PS 951. In general terms, from a compliance perspective, the situation regarding control mechanisms in service organizations can be summarized as follows: the operational side of the processing of operative processes can be delegated to service organizations; however, the compliance-relevant questions with regard to control mechanisms in these processes remain the responsibility of the client.

Another important term is the *competence center*: this is a unit within an organization that supports business applications (usually according to a geographical principle); it does not cover the hardware aspect, as the *computer centers* look after this.

IT functions

If we look at the organization of IT in organizations as a whole, we see the following typical IT functions for supporting SAP-based business processes:

- Management and operation of the computer center. This center contains the servers and other components required for SAP applications, including physical controls (access security, fire protection, air-conditioning, etc.).
- Data backup, storage, and archiving
- Maintenance and administration of hardware, databases, and networks
- Maintenance of SAP software (importing Support Packages, upgrades, etc.)
- Monitoring and maintenance of the interfaces and connections between different systems
- Help desk functions for recording and processing SAP-related problems
- SAP application support is concerned with solving problems, implementing requirements, and processing projects that require changes to configuration or programming.
- Maintenance and administration of user access, such as network and application users, IDs, and passwords
- Strategic planning processes in IT in agreement with the business strategy, decisions with regard to the IT budget, the release strategy of the existing applications, where applicable the implementation of new, IT-supported processes

Foundation of
SAP-supported
processes

The functions mentioned are required as a whole for the SAP-supported processes to work reliably and without any problems. If, for example, the database management cannot ensure the consistency of the data, all other control mechanisms in the SAP application become irrelevant: for example, if the network and interface security is weak, in some circumstances the authorization and segregation of duties controls can be bypassed. If interface-based data processing is not complete, for example, data processing within an SAP application cannot be complete either. All of these elements are located in different IT functions within the IT organization. As you can see, the field of action for an IT auditor with regard to the IT organization is very broad, and it is important to get an overview of the organization at the beginning.

6.1.2 IT Outsourcing: Who Is Responsible for the Controls?

Responsibility in
the case of
outsourcing

When an organization outsources functions, it loses the immediate sovereignty over important control mechanisms. The question is, in an outsourcing scenario, who is responsible for the outsourced controls? The answer is extremely clear: the organization remains responsible. This is not only derived from numerous auditing standards – it is also immediately evident from the obligations of the business management. These cannot be transferred to third parties when processes are outsourced.

Unfortunately, when selecting an IT service provider, many organizations underestimate the importance of the compliance requirements and do not take the "hidden" costs of compliance into account in the price-performance ratio. There are certain control mechanisms that must be observed when selecting IT service providers.

Service Level Agreements (SLA)   ❗

An SLA is a standard contract for the recurring services of a service organization whose objective is to make the control options transparent for the client. SLAs contain precise descriptions of promised performance characteristics, such as scope of services, response time, and speed of processing. An important component here is the quality of service that the agreed service quality describes. In addition to the content of SLAs, auditors must also pay attention to regular reporting by a service provider (e. g., key figures, such as average actual availability, system performance, failure events, etc.).

Certification

Another means of control is very widespread, even if it does not guarantee complete coverage of the ICS topic: *certification*. Here there are ISO standards, for example, ISO 9000 ff., that are quality-oriented, or other standards that cover security (see Sect. 3.2.10). Today, certification is a common practice and a good marketing tool for many service providers.

An SLA standard contract or certifications typically do not address the relevant control mechanisms, or only address a few of them. Therefore, there are other tools that cover the ICS topic specifically for service providers. These tools are reports on ICS questions that auditors can create for service organizations.

SAS 70 Report   ❗

An SAS 70 report enables you to have the control mechanisms within a service organization certified by an independent auditor. In full, SAS 70 stands for "Statement on Auditing Standards No. 70: Service Organizations." This standard was issued by the *Auditing Standards Board* of the *American Institute of Certified Public Accountants* (AICPA) in the US and provides for two types of reports:

— **Type 1**
   As part of a type 1 report, the existence of an ICS at the IT service organization is confirmed.
— **Type 2**
   This type of report additionally contains the evaluation of the effectiveness of the controls.

Even though SAS 70 originates from the US, this type of report has also asserted itself in the non-US GAAP countries that do not have their own standards. From the view of an auditor, an SAS 70 type 2 report is the only option that allows you to rely on an internal control system at a service provider. In general, however, some separate audit procedures are still necessary even with a type 2 report.

> **Examples of International Standards**
>
> Further relevant international standards are:
> - Canada: Canadian Institute of Chartered Accountants (CICA) 5970
> - UK: Audit and Assurance Faculty Standard (AAF) 01/06
> - Australia: Guidance Statement (GS) 007
> - Hong Kong: HKSA Statements – Auditing Practice Note 860.2
> - Japan: Audit Standards Committee Report No. 18
> - Germany: Auditing Standard (PS) 951 from IDW

From SAS 70 to ISAE 3402

In order to standardize the wide range of country-specific standards, and to offer an alternative to the now rather old standard (SAS 70 was released in 1992), the *International Auditing and Assurance Standards Board* (IAASB) has introduced a new standard, the *International Standard on Assurance Engagements (ISAE) 3402*, Assurance Reports on Controls at a Service Organization. As part of the *International Framework for Assurance Engagements* from IAASB, this standard cannot replace the country-specific standards; instead, it represents a further alternative for service organizations to report on their own ICS. Nevertheless, *ISAE 3402* can be seen as a basis for future adjustments to the country-specific standards or as default standard for countries that do not have their own comparable standards.

> **Report According to ISAE 3402 vs. SAS 70**
>
> On one hand, ISAE 3402 introduces important new features; on the other hand, it has some similarities with SAS 70:
> - In comparison to an SAS 70 report, which refers only to the controls relevant to financial reporting, an ISAE 3402 report can extend to further compliance areas, for example, quality.
> - Another considerable difference to SAS 70 is that an ISAE 3402 report contains the formal confirmation of the responsibility for the ICS on the part of the management of a service organization.
> - Furthermore, an ISAE 3402 report should also contain the description of the audit procedures executed by the auditor, which is not the case in an SAS 70 report.
> - With an ISAE 3402 report, there is a differentiation between type A and type B. From a content perspective, these correspond to the SAS 70 type 1 and type 2 reports respectively.

The requirements for external reporting and auditing for US auditors of service organizations have also been adjusted based on *ISAE 3402: Statement on Standards for Attestation Engagements (SSAE) No. 16, Reporting on Controls at a Service Organization*. This standard replaces SAS 70.

The two new standards ISAE 3402 and SSAE 16 apply for reports on periods that end on or after June 15, 2011. Over time, ISAE will probably become the preferred standard for all non-US service organizations, whereas SSAE 16 will be the preferred option in the US. From a content perspective, there is little difference between the two standards.

6.1.3 Guidelines and Documentation

In Sect. 2.2.2, you have already seen that an auditor uses supporting documents to obtain an overview of the most important IT general controls. In particular, documentation is necessary for controls performed by an employee manually. Execution of the control should be documented so that, for example, an auditor can subsequently determine (using the documentation) that the control has actually been executed.

In practice therefore, the following types of documentation are typically required: *Types of documentation*

- **Documentation regarding physical safety, fire protection, and air-conditioning**
  This documentation should generally cover overview diagrams, current maintenance contracts, and maintenance logs.
- **Data backup and restart procedures**
  Here, documentation should show how the operations are logged and how long ago the last restart test based on backup copies took place.
- **Security guidelines**
  In the SAP environment, the issue of security is very complex. It extends far beyond the SAP application itself, and includes security of the database, network, and interfaces.
- **Authorization concept and user administration concept**
  Here, documentation should cover the definition and handling of critical authorizations, including the authorizations at operating system level. It should also cover the emergency user concept and the rules for segregation of duties (at role and user level). See also Sect. 6.4.1.
- **Change management guidelines**
  Issues such as system changes of any type are the typical focus of an audit (see Sect. 6.2). This is because events such as system changes can also affect the consistency of the processing logic and the data relevant for the ICS.
- **Developer guidelines**
  In an audit you concentrate on matters such as naming conventions, logging flags for tables developed in-house, consideration of the authorization checks in programs developed in-house, and assignment of programs to transactions.
- **Blueprints, tests, and acceptances**
  The documentation of implemented business processes, the acceptance logs (for example, functional tests, integration tests, user acceptance tests), and the documentation of tests that arise as part of the implementation projects conclude the list of documents generally required by the auditor.

You may think that the list of documents mentioned above is a matter of course. In practice, however, auditors do encounter some surprises.

In an audit, get an overview of the existing system and process documentation. In practice, the documents above are the minimum requirements, whereby the appropriateness of the content of the documentation is related to the complexity of the processes in IT and the ERP-supported business processes.   *Check: important process and system documentation*

6.2   Controls in the Area of Change Management and Development

Regardless of the legal compliance requirements – be they SOX or FDA etc. – the controls in the area of change management are always relevant. The same also applies for the type of audit or review performed: regardless of whether it is a GAPCAS check, a SOX audit, or a post-implementation review, you want to be convinced that the changes to configuration or the developments in an SAP system take place properly and thus represent a solid basis for the consistency of the data and the processing logic. In this section, you will learn about the most important change management controls that an auditor usually examines and that are a fixed component of every ICS framework.

6.2.1 SAP System Landscape

Making changes directly in a live SAP system in which various business processes are running is similar to performing surgery without an anesthetic. Naturally, there are exceptions: in practice, you change currency exchange rates, posting periods, or menu trees directly in the SAP system. For all other changes the following applies: in order to avoid endangering the life expectancy of a patient, or rather, an SAP system, you usually perform changes first in a *development system*, transport them to a *quality assurance system*, and then import them into the *live system* after successful tests. Transport paths can be as follows:

- From the quality assurance system to the live system
  (summarized: D → Q → L)
- From the development system to the live system
  (summarized: D → Q and D → L)

Three systems as standard   In the SAP ERP world, a system landscape with three systems is standard. For "smaller" implementations with a more manageable number of processes and no major developments or modifications of the SAP standard, you may find system landscapes with two systems in practice.

The easiest way to get a view of the SAP system landscape is using transaction STMS (Transport Management System, see Fig. 6.1).

Experience shows that in the system landscape area, there are very few issues, as here not only the requirements of auditors are affected but primarily an organization's very own interests.

Transport request as carrier of changes in SAP   In Fig. 6.1, you can see the individual systems and the connections between these systems. In SAP language, a connection is called a *transport route*. The transport routes transport *transport requests*. Individual configuration changes, program changes, and other changes in an SAP system are "packaged" in these transport requests. The procedures for handling transport requests are summarized under the term *Transport Management System* (TMS).

Check: SAP system landscape   Using the documentation and transaction STMS, get an overview of the appropriateness of the system landscape and transport paths that have been set up. Of particular interest are mechanisms that ensure that the quality system and live system have the same status with regard to configuration and development – with the exception of any

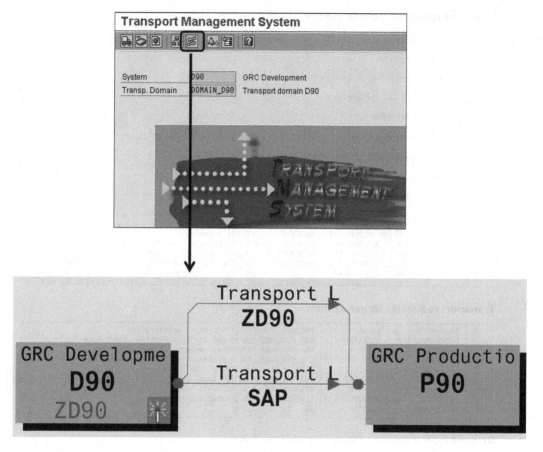

Figure 6.1 Overview of connections in the Transport Management System

functionality currently in the test phase. In technical jargon, the word *refresh* is often used: in a refresh operation, a system (live system) or a client is copied to the other system or client. Check how long ago the last refresh operation took place.

6.2.2 Change and Transport Management

You already know how a transport management system works in general terms. A *transport request* carries changes to various objects in an SAP system. The effective control mechanisms around these transport requests are essential to prevent risks to data and program consistency and system availability. To identify the relevant control mechanisms, let us go through the life cycle of a transport request together.

In an SAP system, you create a transport request and assign a short text to it. Use appropriate names for the transport request (for example, "Tax key adjustment") so that the name reflects the purpose of the change. This is important for assigning the transport request and making it easier to check the changes. It is also important, for

Control: naming transport requests

Transport requests: source system

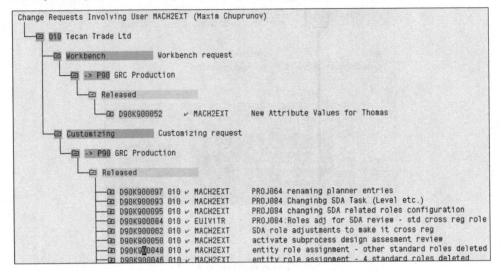

```
Change Requests Involving User MACH2EXT (Maxim Chuprunov)
   └─ 010 Tecan Trade Ltd
       └─ Workbench              Workbench request
           └─ -> P90 GRC Production
               └─ Released
                   └─ D90K900052    ✔ MACH2EXT    New Attribute Values for Thomas
       └─ Customizing            Customizing request
           └─ -> P90 GRC Production
               └─ Released
                   ├─ D90K900097 010 ✔ MACH2EXT    PROJ064 renaming planner entries
                   ├─ D90K900093 010 ✔ MACH2EXT    PROJ084 Changinbg SDA Task (Level etc.)
                   ├─ D90K900095 010 ✔ MACH2EXT    PROJ084 changing SDA related roles configuration
                   ├─ D90K900084 010 ✔ EUIV1TR     PROJ084:Roles adj for SDA review - std cross reg role
                   ├─ D90K900062 010 ✔ MACH2EXT    SDA role adjustments to make it cross reg
                   ├─ D90K900050 010 ✔ MACH2EXT    activate subprocess design assesment review
                   ├─ D90K900048 010 ✔ MACH2EXT    entity role assignment - other standard roles deleted
                   └─ D90K900046 010 ✔ MACH2EXT    entity role assignment - 4 standard roles deleted
```

Transport requests: target system

25	D90K900078	☐	EUIV1TR	PROJ084: GRC PC Configuration Notification	△
26	D90K900080	☐	EUIV1TR	Note:1588820 Shared Service Organization is not Shown Correc	△
27	D90K900082	☐	EUIV1TR	PROJ084:Note:1590029 Assessment: no header informa.	△
28	D90K900084	☐	EUIV1TR	PROJ084:Roles adj for SDA review - std cross reg role del	△
29	D90K900095	☐	MACH2EXT	PROJ084 changing SDA related roles configuration	△
30	D90K900093	☐	MACH2EXT	PROJ084 Changinbg SDA Task (Level etc.)	△
31	D90K900089	☐	EUIV1TR	PROJ084:SEC:Roles	✔
32	D90K900097	☐	MACH2EXT	PROJ064 renaming planner entries	✔
33	D90K900106	☐	EUIV1TR	SEC: table logging	△

◘ Figure 6.2   SAP transport requests in a source and target system

example, to use referencing if possible (e. g., the number of an SAP Note that has been implemented).

The top part of Fig. 6.2 shows individual transport requests and some examples of naming. You can call up this list with transaction SE01 (Transport Organizer).

Control: packaging transport requests

Since you can package multiple changes in one transport request, it makes sense to keep these separate. This results in a further control. The contents of a transport request must belong to related functions that can be tested individually. For example, you would summarize the activation of BC Sets as part of the implementation of SAP GRC Suite within one transport request (see Chap. 16, "ICS Automation Using SAP Process Control").

The information in the name of a transport request is in no way sufficient to justify its origin and right to exist and to document the test results and formal releases.

Control: standard forms and test documentation

Furthermore, from an ICS perspective, you must test every change in the system for its effects on security, the effectiveness of existing controls, or the necessity for new controls. In practice therefore, standard forms or tools have been established to take over this documentation function. You can also create the documentation using SAP Solution Manager.

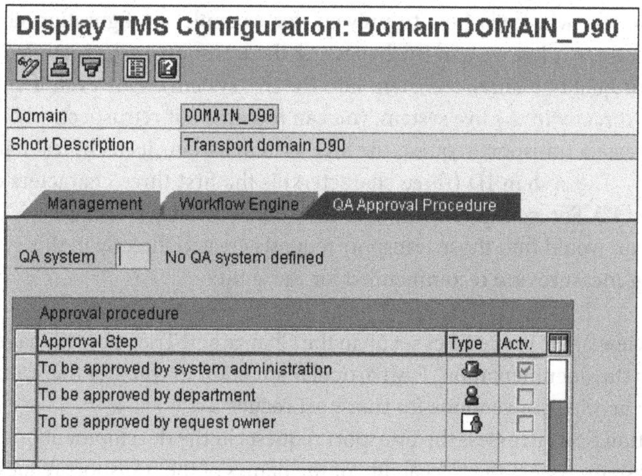

□ Figure 6.3 Configuration of the approval procedure for transport requests

The transport requests generated are released in the SAP source system and automatically distributed to the intended target systems via transport paths. In an SAP target system, these transport requests are available for an import transaction. The bottom part of Fig. 6.2 shows an example of an import queue.

In addition to the release and import transactions, you can establish an *approval procedure for transport requests*. Figure 6.3 shows an example of where you can make the corresponding settings in SAP.

To see this overview in SAP, call up transaction STMS and then navigate to the corresponding settings via System OVERVIEW • GOTO • TRANSPORT DOMAINS.

A correct organizational and technical procedure must be defined (above all the documentation and notification of superiors) for cases where a change has to be executed urgently (for example, to correct an error). From a technical perspective, you use the *preliminary import* function in such cases. This imports a transport request but simultaneously leaves it in the import queue so that you can import it at a later point in time in correct order with any other related transports.

Control: emergency production changes

The execution of two operations – release and import of transport requests – by the same person can lead to a conflict of interests. Therefore, these two operations must be kept separate using authorizations.

Control: segregation of duties

The authorization object S_TRANSPRT is responsible for the import and export operations in change and transport management. The following values are relevant:
- Activity 43: Release (in source system, transaction SE01)
- Activity 60: Import (in target system, transaction STMS)

To import transport requests, you also need authorization object S_CTS_ADMI, with the values IMPA and IMPS for the field CTS_ADMFCT.

To guarantee segregation of duties between the import and release operations, a user must not have authorization for release and import simultaneously.

Controls: transport
requests created in
the live system

In Sect. 6.2.3, you will learn how to prevent, for example, configuration changes being made directly in a live system (by bypassing the transport paths intended from a development or quality assurance system into the live system). However, if changes have been made directly in the live system, you can find this out retrospectively.

When you create a transport request, the SAP system assigns its technical name or ID automatically. The system ID (three characters) is the first three characters of the transport request ID. For example, if you were to search for transport requests XYZ* in a system XYZ, you would find those transport requests created directly in this system.

Check: Change and
Transport Manage-
ment System

The following measures are recommended for the audit:

1. Get an overview of the procedures set up in the Change and Transport Management System from the documentation. Pay particular attention to whether there are clear rules for the naming conventions for transport requests.
2. Use transaction SE01 to assess the transport requests in the development or quality assurance system. Assess the traceability of the names of the transport requests.
3. Check whether the release and import authorizations for transport requests are used in compliance with the principle of segregation of duties.
4. Check whether an approval procedure has been set up for transport requests.
5. In the live system, use transaction SE01 to check, using the naming conventions for the transport requests in this system, whether any transport requests have been created directly in this system.

6.2.3 Client Control

Clients in the
SAP system

A client is an SAP-specific "technical" organizational unit. It allows you to separate master data, transaction data, and configuration data, as well as authorizations, globally within an SAP system. A client has an important control function. It determines whether and how changes can be made in an SAP system. You use transaction SCC4 (Client Administration) to make the relevant settings. The parameters shown in Fig. 6.4 are determined for each client.

The following settings are required from an audit view:

■ In the area CHANGES AND TRANSPORTS FOR CLIENT-SPECIFIC OBJECTS, the option AUTOMATIC RECORDING OF CHANGES is set ❶ because the system is a development system. In a live system, this parameter should be set to No CHANGES ALLOWED.
■ The area Cross-Client Object Changes is set to Changes to Repository and Cross-Client Customizing Allowed ❷. In a live system, the option No Changes to Repository and Cross-Client Customizing Objects should be set.
■ In a live system, the area PROTECTION: CLIENT COPIER AND COMPARISON TOOL should be set to No OVERWRITING; settings that you see under ❸ in the example would be more probable in a development system.
■ The area CATT AND eCATT RESTRICTIONS should be set to eCATT AND CATT NOT ALLOWED (CATT = Computer Aided Test Tool, eCATT = Extended CATT). If you find the settings under ❹ in a live system, question this critically.

> ❯ **CATT** In addition to their actual purpose of testing scenarios that have been set up, in SAP, CATT functions are also often used for data transfer. Since, under some circumstances, changes can thus be made at database level, the use of these functions in a live system represents a risk.

Display View "Clients": Details

Client	010 Riscomp GmbH	
City	Rothenthurm	Last Changed By: MUPI1EXT
Logical system	D90CLNT010	Date: 08.02.2011
Std currency	CHF	
Client role	Test	

Changes and Transports for Client-Specific Objects
- ○ Changes without automatic recording
- ⦿ Automatic recording of changes
- ○ No changes allowed
- ○ Changes w/o automatic recording, no transports allowed

Cross-Client Object Changes
Changes to Repository and cross-client Customizing allowed

Protection: Client Copier and Comparison Tool
Protection level 0: No restriction

CATT and eCATT Restrictions
eCATT and CATT Not Allowed

Restrictions
- ☐ Locked due to client copy
- ☐ Protection against SAP upgrade

⬛ **Figure 6.4** Client settings

You can use transaction SCC4 to check the client settings or you can check them directly in database table T000 (transaction SE16 (Data Browser)).

Check: client settings

The (temporary) changes to the client settings are permitted; however, they should be documented and justified with reasons that can be traced. Checking a change that has taken place against its documented justification represents a "classic" audit procedure.

You can use program RSTBHIST to evaluate changes to the client settings in table T000. For individual changes, depending on the content (for example, opening a live client for direct changes), you would expect documented reasons.

Check: changing client settings

The following steps are recommended for the audit:

Check: client settings

1. Check the client settings, especially in the live SAP system, using transaction SCC1 or directly in table T000.
2. Evaluate any "openings" of the live system that have taken place in the past as described above. The prerequisites for evaluating table T000 are described in Sect. 7.2.2.

6.2.4 Maintenance and Updates

The software is "alive"

SAP AG maintains and develops the SAP software further by providing new software releases, Support Packages, and Enhancement Packages (EhPs). Furthermore, remote or service connections are set up for the purposes of monitoring and problem resolution. SAP employees can use these connections to access SAP systems at the customer's location and SAP can also offer automated remote services (such as EarlyWatch Alert). SAP Notes for resolving specific known problems are also published.

Getting an overview of the organization and the status of the SAP ERP software is one of the regular audit procedures in an SAP audit.

Actuality of SAP ERP

As an auditor, for the purposes of ensuring (even) higher security and consistency of the data and program logic, you would expect and recommend an up-to-date level of *Support Package* – there is often a direct connection between the software release and compliance with legal requirements. In the module Human Capital Management (HCM) in particular, where legal requirements with regard to taxation of income etc. frequently lead to special Support Packages, up-to-date software is very important from an ICS view.

Check the software is up-to-date

You can check the release level of the individual components ❶ and the level of Support Packages ❷ in an SAP ERP system, as shown in Fig. 6.5, via the menu item System: Status. Alternatively, you can use transaction SPAM (Support Package Manager).

Control: actuality of SPs

You can compare the current level of an SAP ERP system with the information about Service Packs available that is published online or on SAP Service Marketplace (https://sapneth2.wdf.sap.corp/ocs-schedules).

When you are assessing whether the SPs are up-to-date, remember that due to organizational restrictions, many organizations only have one time frame each year in which they can perform SAP maintenance tasks, such as importing SPs etc.

Control: release and SP levels in the SAP landscape

The SAP standard system landscape with three systems gives rise to a further control that you must check: a general principle to be observed would be that all systems in the SAP landscape have the same release and Support Package level.

Control: access data in the secure area

An audit can produce many questions about the maintenance of SAP systems. Interviews with SAP Basis specialists would be recommended to clarify, for example, how, by whom, and how often SAP Notes are monitored and whether these are distributed consistently to all systems. One of the more critical points thereby is the maintenance of access data for SAP ERP systems for the purpose of access via remote support connections used by SAP employees. The standard procedure would be to publish the user name and password in the *secure area* that is only accessible for the person processing the corresponding error message. In interviews, you can clarify how access data is communicated to SAP for the purpose of remote access. Communication via e-mail or telephone would not be ideal, but really critical is access data published in the text of an error message itself and thus visible to a wide audience. Therefore, you can also perform random tests to check texts in OSS error messages. You should also check whether and how tests are performed for system updates.

Check: maintenance and updates

In addition, the following procedures are recommended for the audit:

1. Get an overview of the procedure that has been set up for updating SAP software.
2. Use transaction SPAM to check the SP level of the SAP system. In doing so, consider the SPs available officially and, where applicable, the underlying legal regulations.

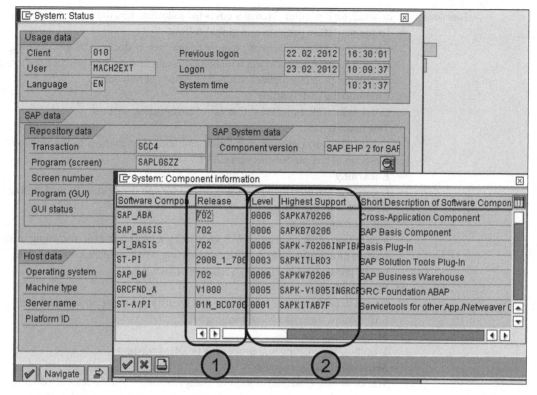

Figure 6.5 Release and Support Package information in SAP ERP

3. Check that remote access to the SAP systems is being handled properly.
4. Use transaction SPAU (Display Modified Objects) to get an overview of the modifications that have been performed in SAP and whether they have been performed properly.
5. Also check deviations to SAP standard objects that arise following repairs. You can do this using transaction SE03 (Transport Organizer Tools) and the DISPLAY REPAIRED OBJECTS button. When doing so, remember that objects with a repair indicator cannot be overwritten, and this would happen when a new Support Package is imported. Where applicable, use the documentation to check the reasons for the repairs.

6.2.5 SAP Solution Manager

SAP Solution Manager is a central system for managing and documenting a complex and distributed solution landscape. It supports the complete life cycle of a software solution, from the business blueprint, through the implementation projects, right up to live operation. SAP Solution Manager offers access to tools, methods, and pre-configured content. Use of SAP Solution Manager is included in the maintenance charge and the software is provided free of charge to all SAP customers.

Functions

In detail, SAP Solution Manager offers the following functions:

- **Implementation projects and global rollout**
  Creation of a blueprint; management of the project documentation, training material; test cases; access to implementation roadmaps and best practice documents; creation of project templates that can be reused in rollouts
- **Customizing distribution**
  Cross-system alignment and transfer of customizing settings
- **Test management**
  Organization and execution of functional tests after changes to the software; automation of test procedures via eCATT
- **E-learning**
  Creation of learning materials using SAP Tutor and distribution of the learning materials in learning maps
- **Solution monitoring**
  Monitoring of all connected SAP systems by a central system, including business process monitoring and service level reporting. We have already looked at the content of pre-defined monitoring scenarios in Sect. 4.4.2.
- **Service delivery**
  Access to performance, availability, and security optimization-oriented services of SAP to minimize risks when running SAP
- **Service desk**
  Workflow for creating and processing problem messages
- **Managing change requests**
  Workflow-based administration of change requests. All changes are documented such that they can be traced; correction and transport procedure functions are called up in the background.

Solution Manager as obligation

The importance of SAP Solution Manager as central node for the administration of a complex system landscape has grown continuously. Even though just a few years ago, opinion was divided as to whether SAP Solution Manager should be seen as an obligation, the position has now become clear: from audit and compliance perspectives, the absence of SAP Solution Manager results in a negative finding. This is because the elementary maintenance of an SAP system – downloading support backups, defining access data in the secure area, etc. – requires the use of SAP Solution Manager. Organizations that do not use it often have to use "creative" (and thus error-prone) workarounds (for example, manual download of support backups from SAP Service Marketplace etc.).

  Clarification Is Necessary

Many SAP customers do not use SAP Solution Manager beyond the minimum required. This is generally due to a lack of know-how. SAP is doing a lot to counteract this deficiency. Documentation is available free of charge on the Internet: http://www.sap.com/platform/netweaver/components/solutionmanager/index.epx.

In addition, SAP training and certification courses for SAP Solution Manager are recommended.

6.3 Security Controls for Access to the SAP System and for Authentication

Access protection is one of the foundations of IT general controls. Ensuring that business transactions and other events in an SAP ERP system can be uniquely assigned to an authorized person requires logical access controls. Here we must differentiate between access *to the system* and *within the system*. In this section, you will learn which control mechanisms exist for access to SAP ERP, whereas Sect. 6.4 will show how access authorizations are restricted within SAP ERP.

6.3.1 Identity and Life Cycle of the User

From an ICS perspective, users who can access SAP ERP in a "normal" dialog mode are particularly interesting, above all dialog users.

Access is either via entry of the user ID and password or automatically by means of the single sign-on procedure (SSO). Although the principle of a unique cross-system identity of a user is not necessary from a technical perspective for the first option, it is a requirement for SSO. In an SAP audit, you must make sure that from a compliance perspective, the principle of identity is fulfilled across all systems: this is the only way to enable, for example, an automated cross-system analysis of impermissible authorization combinations.

Principle of identity

The realization of the identity principle in user administration is the prerequisite for fulfilling the requirements for traceability and accountability in an ICS. Therefore, you should use, for example, interviews, walkthroughs, and, where applicable, system evaluations to clarify whether and how it is assured that across all systems and networks, one person has the same technical user identification number or the same user name.

Controls: cross-system user identity

SAP NetWeaver Identity Management is one of the software solutions available on the market that can guarantee consistent compliance with the identity principle through centralized user administration. Further relevant SAP products are Central User Administration (CUA) and SAP Access Control. Organizational Management (OM) in SAP is addressed in Chap. 11, "Data Protection Compliance in SAP ERP Human Capital Management." Organizational management is the management of information about a person, their contractual status, and tasks. This function is present in three SAP applications: SAP ERP HCM, SAP SRM, and SAP CRM.

SAP IdM and OM

As part of the identity principle, a user account must be traceably assigned to one person. Occasionally, anonymous or collective user IDs may be used in an SAP ERP system (e. g., for student employees). This is something that is unacceptable in a live environment, as, for example, it can violate a license agreement with SAP and it may be the case that postings in SAP cannot be uniquely assigned to a user.

Control: anonymous user accounts

In table USR03 (Address Names of Users), you can check the plausibility of the names of the users and determine how far they can be assigned to one person uniquely.

Furthermore, an organization should establish a process that efficiently replicates organizational changes connected to an employee (recruitment, transfer, or resignation) in IT applications. From an audit perspective, the transfer and resignation events are particularly relevant.

Controls: user changes

Check: identity and life cycle of the user

Check compliance with the identity principle in the organization and in particular, in SAP systems: Are there any anonymous user accounts? Are user IDs standardized in all systems?

Perform the following audit procedures with regard to the user life cycle:

1. Record the process. How does the organization handle organizational changes? Which tools are used to process these changes?
2. Ask the personnel department of the organization being audited for a list of all employees who have left the organization and who had an SAP ERP account. Then check this list against tables USR03 and USR02 (Login Data) in the system. This enables you to determine whether changes are considered on a timely basis and completely.
3. In the case of a change (e. g., change of department), you can trace the changes in the authorization assignments using transaction SUIM (User Information System) under the CHANGE DOCUMENTS menu item.
4. You can validate the usual procedure in the user life cycle of locking users that have been inactive for a longer period in table USR02 (analyze the LAST LOGIN ON and USER LOCK STATUS fields).

6.3.2 Password Protection

A password is the key to an SAP ERP system and must be protected. As an auditor, you would expect security guidelines that cover the relevant facts.

Control: security guideline

Security guidelines should document requirements for password protection. In general, the requirements issued by the Big Four as part of IT audits correlate to the recommendations communicated by the German Federal Office for Information Security (BSI) (www.bsi.de), including with regard to the password length of eight characters. These recommendations are not legal specifications; in case of doubt, the recommendation of an independent IT auditor would be decisive.

   Security Standards

Traditionally, standards for secure IT systems have been developed by national standardization agencies, such as DIN (Deutsche Industrienormen) in Germany, and federal IT agencies, such as the BSI in Germany or NIST (National Institute of Standards and technology) in the US (the NIST recommendations and guidelines first applied to government IT and their scope was then extended to commercial installations). With the harmonization of standardization efforts, national standards then became European Norms (EN) or international standards (of the ISO). In some cases, technical specifications became codified law.

You define the security level for password protection using SAP profile parameters. The profile parameter settings apply across the system in SAP ERP, and thus for all clients and all users of an SAP instance.

> ## Password Protection-Relevant Profile Parameters
>
> ❗
>
> The most important profile parameters are listed below:
> - `Login/min_password_lng`
>   This parameter determines the minimum length of the logon password. This can be up to 40 characters, whereby the recommendation is a minimum of eight characters.
> - `Login/password_expiration_time`
>   Period of validity for the passwords in days
> - `Login/fails_to_session_end`
>   The number of incorrect logons by the user before the logon procedure is terminated or the logon window is closed
> - `Login/fails_to_user_lock`
>   If the number of incorrect logon attempts exceeds the value defined in this parameter, the user account is locked.
> - `Login/min_password_digits`
>   This parameter controls the minimum quantity of numbers (0 to 9) a password must contain.
> - `Login/min_password_letters`
>   This parameter determines the minimum quantity of letters in a password.
> - `Login/min_password_lowercase`
>   This parameter determines the minimum number of lower case letters in a password. (It has no effect if another profile parameter, `Login/password_downwards_compatibility`, is set to the value 5.)
> - `Login/min_password_uppercase`
>   The minimum number of upper case letters is set in this parameter. (It has no effect if another profile parameter, `Login/password_downwards_compatibility`, is set to the value 5.)
> - `Login/min_password_specials`
>   This parameter determines the minimum quantity of special characters in a password.
> - `Login/min_password_diff`
>   This parameter can be used to define the minimum number of different characters a new password must contain compared to the old password when the user changes his password.
> - `Login/password_change_waittime`
>   This parameter can be used to define the number of days after which a user can change his password again. Changes to the password by another user (e. g., when a password is reset) are not taken into account.
> - `Login/password_history_size`
>   This parameter defines the size of the password history, the purpose of which is to prevent passwords being reused.

You check the settings in the profile parameters using program RSPARAM. Alternatively, you can list security-relevant profile parameters using program RSUSR003 and selecting the DISPLAY PROFILE PARAMETERS option.

Control: check with program RSPARAM

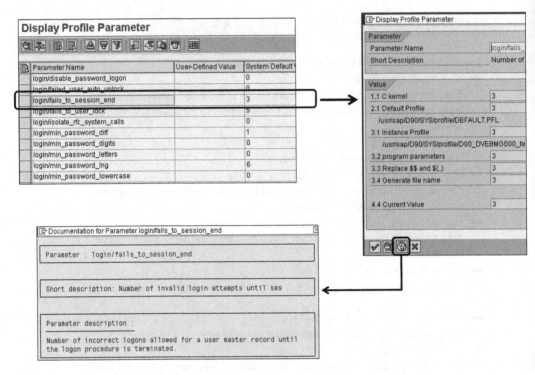

Figure 6.6 Profile parameters and their description in SAP ERP

Find descriptions
for profile
parameters

As shown in Fig. 6.6, you can use program RSPARAM (e. g., call up via transaction SA38, ABAP Reporting) to view the documentation for each profile parameter. The list generated contains further profile parameters relevant for security using login*.

Control: impermis-
sible passwords

A risk that cannot be covered by the profile parameters is the use of trivial passwords. You maintain the list of prohibited passwords in table USR40 in SAP. The table should also contain trivial passwords, such as the name of the organization and days of the week/month.

With profile parameters that ensure a highly complex password and high level of security overall, you reduce the risk of trivial passwords.

6.3.3 Handling Standard Users

The SAP ERP software is delivered with standard users. These are created automatically when the system is installed. The standard users are:
- SAP*
- EARLYWATCH
- DDIC
- Other users, such as SAPCPIC, WF_BATCH, or TMSADM

Check the Passwords of Standard Users in All Clients

Client	User	Lock	Password Status	Lock	Inc.Logons	Valid from	Valid to
000	DDIC	🔓	Exists; Password not trivial.				
	SAP*	🔓	Exists; Password not trivial.				
	SAPCPIC	🔓	Password ADMIN well known. See SAP Note 29276				
001	DDIC	🔓	Exists; Password not trivial.				
	SAP*	🔓	Exists; Password not trivial.				
	SAPCPIC	🔓	Password ADMIN well known. See SAP Note 29276				
010	DDIC	🔓	Exists; Password not trivial.				
	SAP*	🔓	Exists; Password not trivial.				
	SAPCPIC	🔓	Password ADMIN well known. See SAP Note 29276				
066	DDIC		Does not exist.				
	EARLYWATCH	🔓	Password SUPPORT well known.				
	SAP*	🔓	Password 06071992 well known.				
	SAPCPIC		Does not exist.				

Figure 6.7 Checking the standard users with program RSUSR003

These standard users represent a risk: firstly, they are anonymous and thus violate the identity principle; secondly, they are equipped with wide-ranging authorizations (in some cases, even unlimited).

The SAP* user is intended for the installation phase and is available as standard in clients 000, 001, and in every new client created. In older SAP releases, the SAP* user had the widely known password 06071992, and with effect from ERP 6.0 with ECC 6.0, the initial password is "pass." The situation is similar for the SAPCPIC user, which is delivered with the standard password "admin."

Standard passwords

You can check the standard passwords for the standard users with program RSUSR003 (see Fig. 6.7). Table USR02 also provides audit-relevant information (Status of User Lock and Number of Incorrect Logons fields).

Control: changing the standard password for standard users

The program runs the analysis for all clients; this is absolutely essential from an audit perspective: with the far-reaching authorizations of, for example, SAP*, it is possible to make system changes that take effect for all clients.

You can use the profile parameter Login/no_automatic_user_sapstar to make the standard user SAP* "less powerful." The SAP* user is firmly anchored in the ABAP source code of an SAP system. Deleting this user (for example, with transaction SU01, User Maintenance) means that you can use it to log on with the initial password PASS. SAP* then has the following properties:

Control: profile parameters for handling SAP*

- The user has all authorizations as no authorization checks are performed.
- The standard password PASS cannot be changed.

From an audit perspective, the target value of the profile parameter mentioned is "1" (automatic user SAP* is deactivated) – meaning that deleting the SAP* user presents no risks.

6.3.4 Emergency User Concept

Emergency users and risks

In principle, authorizations in business applications should be created according to the principle of least privilege. However, there may be emergencies that require fast access to an SAP ERP system and thus a user account with far-reaching permissions. In such cases, which are outside the usual system operation, emergency users are used. Since, by definition, these user accounts are not assigned to one person and their permissions are not assigned according to the principle of least privilege, the far-reaching risks connected to the emergency user are obvious. However, these compliance-related risks are also accompanied by high operative risks: due to the (potentially high) requirements for system availability, an emergency user may have to be available at very short notice for urgent troubleshooting and correction measures.

Emergency user process

Therefore, organizations must establish a process that ensures that, in the case of fast access to emergency user IDs, sufficient controls are in place to ensure that these users are used compliant with the ICS:

- A documented emergency user concept
- Where possible, restriction of the authorizations of emergency users (for example, separate users for IT and for business processes)
- Restriction of access to the login data (password) for the emergency user
- Clearly defined prerequisites for use of an emergency user
- Complete logging of the actions of the emergency user
- Approval or notification process for use of the emergency user ID
- Regular analysis of the logged activities of the emergency user

SAP customers are rather unenthusiastic about the procedure often recommended by auditors in the past of keeping the password for an emergency user in a sealed envelope in a safe. SAP now offers not only tools for covering individual requirements (for example, logging when a Security Audit Log is used, see Sect. 7.3.2), but also a product that supports the emergency user process as a whole: the product is SAP Superuser Privilege Management (see Sect. 4.3).

Check: use of the emergency user

In addition to reviewing the content of a documented emergency user concept, an auditor must convince himself that this concept actually works. To do this he can use program RSUSR100 (in the menu tree of transaction SUIM) to find evidence of the use of the emergency user and then verify the individual uses (cause, notification, etc.) by means of the documentation.

6.4   Security and Authorization Controls within SAP ERP

In Sect. 6.3 we explained the most important risks, controls, and audit procedures with regard to logical access to the SAP system. Now we will show you what is important with regard to authorizations within SAP ERP from an ICS and audit perspective. Knowledge of the basic features of the authorization concept in SAP ERP (see Sect. 5.2) will be useful. At this point we will focus on the most important compliance-relevant issues.

6.4.1 Protecting Programs and Transactions – Basic Level

Authorization checks in SAP ERP must work so that when users are assigned, authorizations can be restricted in accordance with the principle of least privilege and the principle of segregation of duties. You already know that authorization objects, authorization roles, and users are the most important elements within the authorization concept. The check for authorization objects and field values is included in the ABAP source code (AUTHORITY - CHECK command) of every transaction. The authorization check always takes place for SAP standard programs and transactions. However, care must be taken when using standard transactions in the source code of in-house developments: if the CALL TRANSACTION command is used, unfortunately you cannot assume that a correct authorization check takes place in the background when the user calls up a transaction developed in-house.

Authority check command

▶ **Command "Call Transaction"** If a transaction is called up in the ABAP source code of a program indirectly, i. e., by another transaction, it may be the case that no authorization check takes place. For example, authorizations are not checked when a transaction calls up another transaction with the instruction CALL TRANSACTION (**SAP Note 358122**).

For programs and transactions developed completely in-house (they begin with Z*, Y*, or/*), authorization protection must be incorporated using the AUTHORITY - CHECK command.

The following procedures are recommended for the audit:

Check: authorization protection for programs developed in-house

1. Look at the documented developer guidelines and determine whether and how security-relevant topics are considered when programs are developed, in particular, whether mandatory tests for correct authorization check are planned.
2. As shown in Fig. 6.8, use program RSABAPSC to check whether a program developed by a customer contains the language command AUTHORITY - CHECK and whether the relevant authorization objects are considered appropriately.
3. Where the CALL TRANSACTION command is used, check whether the relevant issues detailed in SAP Note 358122 have been implemented.

```
Statistical program analysis to find ABAP lang. commands

⊕ 🗐

○ Report                    [                              ]
○ Function module          [                              ]
⦿ Transaction code          MK02|              🔄
○ Dialog module            [                              ]

ABAP language commands      AUTHORITY-CHECK    to  [              ] ➡
```

```
Statist. program analysis
TRANSACTION MK02 Change vendor (Purchasing)

MODULE TRANSAKTIONS_INIT OUTPUT
  PERFORM BERECHTIGUNG_PBO
    AUTHORITY-CHECK OBJECT 'F_LFA1_APP' ID 'ACTVT' FIELD B_ACTVT ID 'APPKZ' FIELD CHAR1
    PERFORM AUTHORIZATION_GENERAL_DATA
      AUTHORITY-CHECK OBJECT 'F_LFA1_GEN' ID 'ACTVT' FIELD P_ACTVT
MODULE KONTO_LESEN
  PERFORM KREDITORENSTAMM_LESEN
    PERFORM BERECHTIGUNGS_PRUEFUNGEN
      AUTHORITY-CHECK OBJECT 'F_LFA1_BEK' ID 'BRGRU' FIELD LFA1-BEGRU ID 'ACTVT' FIELD '02'
      AUTHORITY-CHECK OBJECT 'F_LFA1_BEK' ID 'BRGRU' FIELD LFA1-BEGRU ID 'ACTVT' FIELD B_ACTVT
      AUTHORITY-CHECK OBJECT 'F_LFA1_GEN' ID 'ACTVT' FIELD B_ACTVT
      AUTHORITY-CHECK OBJECT 'F_LFA1_GRP' ID 'KTOKK' FIELD HLP_KTOKK ID 'ACTVT' FIELD B_ACTVT
      AUTHORITY-CHECK OBJECT 'F_LFA1_BUK' ID 'BUKRS' FIELD LFB1-BUKRS ID 'ACTVT' FIELD B_ACTVT
      AUTHORITY-CHECK OBJECT 'F_LFA1_BEK' ID 'BRGRU' FIELD LFB1-BEGRU ID 'ACTVT' FIELD B_ACTVT
      AUTHORITY-CHECK OBJECT 'M_LFM1_EKO' ID 'EKORG' FIELD LFM1-EKORG ID 'ACTVT' FIELD B_ACTVT
MODULE KONTOGRUPPE
  PERFORM KONTOGRUPPE_BEARBEITEN
    AUTHORITY-CHECK OBJECT 'F_LFA1_GRP' ID 'KTOKK' FIELD RF02K-KTOKK ID 'ACTVT' FIELD '01'
MODULE DYNTAB_AUFBAUEN
  PERFORM X055_AUFBAUEN
    AUTHORITY-CHECK OBJECT 'F_LFA1_AEN' ID 'VGRUP' FIELD WA_T055G-GRUPP
```

◻ Figure 6.8 Checking the language command "Authority Check" in transactions

If the analysis of the ABAP source code can provide theoretical information about whether a system authorization check takes place, check the actual execution of the check using the system trace.

Check: system trace for transactions developed in-house You can generate the main unit of the transactions developed in-house for the check detailed below by evaluating the contents of table TSTCT for Y*, Z*, or/*.

In parallel to executing a relevant transaction, you can switch on the system trace to trace the authorization check that has actually taken place at object level and assess whether this is appropriate, complete, and correct. For details, see Sect. 5.2.3.

No direct program access for business users A transaction is not the only way of calling up processing logic in SAP ERP; you can also call it up by starting a program directly (for example, via transaction SA38). There is a high risk involved in doing this because in practice, user access to programs is usually only restricted at transaction level, meaning that users who have a general authorization for transaction SA38, for example, could also start programs not intended for them – including critical service programs that execute mass changes or even deletion of certain data. Checking the restriction of direct access to programs is therefore an important audit procedure.

Check: authorizations for calling up programs directly Check (see Sect. 5.2.7) whether business users have direct access to programs (for example, transactions TSA38, SE18). The relevant authorization object is S_PROGRAM. If business users do have these authorizations, check to what extent access to programs is limited:

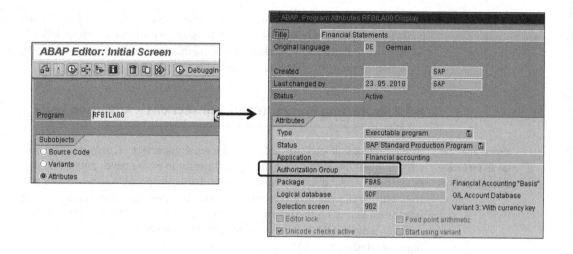

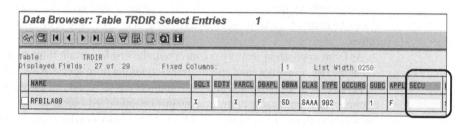

Figure 6.9 Assignment of authorization groups to programs in SAP

1. Check the content of the authorization roles and determine the extent to which the field P_GROUP for the object S_PROGRAM contains useful values and not "*" (this value would allow all possible values).
2. Also check whether authorization groups are assigned to the individual programs. The relevant tables are TPGP (Overview of Existing Authorization Groups) and TRDIR (Programs and Authorization Groups). Program-specific authorization groups allow you to assign authorizations for program execution in more detail.

Figure 6.9 shows how authorization groups are assigned to the programs (transaction SE38); you can also see here that in the standard, no authorization group is assigned to program RFBILA00. Alternatively, you could trace the same results via table TRDIR: field SECU contains no entry for program RFBILA00.

As a general rule, business users should only receive access to the program logic via dedicated transactions, and not via programs.

You can trace the assignment of transaction codes to the programs as follows:

1. As described in Sect. 5.1.5, generate the list of programs developed in-house using transactions SE84 (Repository Information System) or SE38 (ABAP Editor) by selecting "Z*" or "Y*" in the PROGRAM NAME field.

Check: assignment of transaction code to programs

2. You assign transactions to programs in table TSTC. Table TSTCT would also be helpful; it provides information about the name of the individual transactions.
3. You can find programs developed in-house that have not been assigned to a transaction by comparing the lists specified above.

6.4.2 Protecting Programs and Transactions – Advanced Level

Comprehensive analysis for extensive developments

In the previous chapter, we addressed the most important security and compliance-relevant questions within SAP, including those for in-house developments. In the case of extensive ABAP developments, and considering the possible access to SAP systems from outside (for example, "technical" access via remote function call destinations or intentional access via the Internet, for example, as part of SAP Supplier Self-Service, etc.), the topic of *ABAP code security* is worthy of more detailed examination due to the high complexity of the SAP world.

In all common programming languages, faults during development may lead to immense security vulnerabilities in the live application. ABAP is no exception. The sharp rise in the number of SAP Security Notes in the past few years shows the need for further action.

As far as application security is concerned, the first important thing to understand is that the risk comes not from specific transactions but from special ABAP commands.

Let us look at the creation and the execution of ABAP reports on a live system as an example. Conventionally, protection against unauthorized execution means restricting access to transactions SE38 and SE80, not giving any developer authorizations for S_DEVELOP, and configuring the SAP server as a live system. Indeed, all of these measures are necessary in order to stop the creation and the execution of ABAP reports through transactions SE38 and SE80. However, these measures are not sufficient alone. From a technical perspective, ABAP code is not created through transactions SE38 und SE80 but by the command `INSERT REPORT`. However, this command neither performs an authorization check nor checks whether it is run on a live system. These checks do take place explicitly in the source code of the transactions SE38 and SE80. However, any program developed in-house may use the command `INSERT REPORT` to write further ABAP programs without performing any authorization check. Figure 6.10 shows this clearly.

The explicit authorization model that SAP designed for ABAP gives rise to the general problem that authorization checks during runtime can only be executed if the authorization objects are indeed explicitly checked in the ABAP programs. If, as in this example, the check is missing in the ABAP code, even critical commands and actions are executed without the user being authorized to do so. Thus, any potentially dangerous actions and commands in the ABAP code must be examined as a matter of course.

A False Sense of Security

More and more organizations are introducing modern GRC software (governance, risk, compliance). An added value here is the automation of the ICS processes as well as the possibility to hardwire them with relevant procedures in risk management, user and authorization management, policy management, etc. The integration of GRC applications with ERP systems is very promising: master data, transaction data and control data in

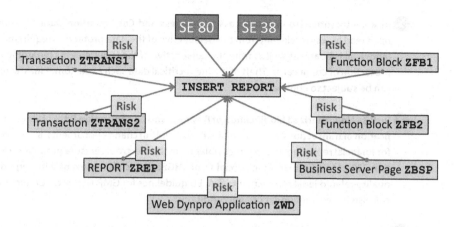

☐ **Figure 6.10** Application security risk – it is not the transactions that are dangerous but the ABAP commands

ERP systems are efficiently monitored, the risks and vulnerabilities are thereby recognized with the click of a button, and measures for correction are initiated automatically (see Chap. 17). This approach, called Continuous Control Monitoring (CCM), reaches technical limits with classical GRC software when it comes to checking ABAP code.

With manually driven ICS processes, the situation is very similar: on one hand, manual checking involves a lot of effort – even if only spot checks are performed; on the other hand, auditors usually do not have any tools available for full testing. Furthermore, such audits require specific expertise.

Regardless of whether ICS processes run on an Excel basis or whether they are supported by GRC software, the live ABAP code is still a black box. As a result, many organizations have insufficient security measures in the area of ABAP development.

Security Flaws in ABAP

Which dangers arise from security flaws in the ABAP code? The risks due to insecure programming can be classified into six areas: they describe the respective impact of security defects on compliance and the *legal* rights that are violated if insecure code finds its way into a live system.

> **Risk 1 – Unauthorized Execution of Business Logic** Most compliance requirements referring directly or indirectly to data and processing logic in IT systems include questions regarding access privileges:
>
> Accuracy and reliability of financial reporting (SOX, GAPCAS, etc.)
> - Quality (FDA)
> - Data protection/data privacy
> - Tax law
>
> Adherence to the principles of least privilege and segregation of duties can be affected in these domains.
> Under such circumstances, criminal law could also be relevant.

❯ **Risk 2 – Unauthorized Read Access to Business and Configuration Data** Unauthorized read access is relevant from the perspective of the data protection requirements (above all HR data) as well as from the perspective of the requirements regarding the protection of credit cards. Theft of business-critical data such as customer master data can be subject to criminal law.

❯ **Risk 3 – Unauthorized Modification of Business and Configuration Data** Direct modification of transaction data can violate the principle of change documents, in particular for financial reporting. It is in direct violation of the electronic erasure prohibition Section 239 of the German Commercial Code (HGB) and is also relevant with regard to quality-related legal requirements (DA, EU guidelines for GMP, GLP, etc.). Criminal law can also be relevant under certain conditions.

❯ **Risk 4 – Denial of Service** For critical systems, the compliance requirements in the area of financial reporting are relevant because when he sees a threat to the continued existence of the company, an auditor – to protect the investors – must communicate the findings in question. Where violation is intentional, criminal law can take effect.

❯ **Risk 5 – Repudiation of Business Processes** Legal requirements such as Section 239 of the German Commercial Code (HGB) and other provisions require non-repudiation regarding the creation of and change to the business transactions recorded (document principle) as well as master and control data.

❯ **Risk 6 – Identity Theft** The principle of accountability and non-repudiation can be affected (financial reporting, quality, data protection). Identity theft, aiming at acquiring additional authorizations, is moving in the same direction regarding compliance relevance as described in **Risk 1**.

The abuse of most of the (security) flaws implies bad faith, criminal energy, and often also internal offenders (see Chap. 12). This does reduce the likeliness of an occurrence, but looking at the high damage potential, the corresponding risks should be taken seriously.

These risks can increase if development is outsourced to consulting organizations. In this case, the developers' know-how, as well as their loyalty to the customer, is no longer present. Company acquisitions raise the risk too, since huge quantities of ABAP code are added to the company. Developers in subsidiaries should not be allowed to have access to data of the parent company via back doors.

Examples of security defects

There are many different types of vulnerabilities that could arise from ABAP code. To show the technical risks, let us use the example of the BIZEC APP/11 list (The Business Security Initiative, http://bizec.org) as a basis (Tab. 6.1).

The most obvious security problem in ABAP code is presented by missing or technically faulty authorization checks (APP-03). Since ABAP has an explicit authorization concept, any program executing authorization-relevant actions must also explicitly check the appropriate authorization objects itself. If this check in the ABAP code is missing or faulty, the program will execute the action even though the user does not have the required authorization.

Another fundamental but less obvious problem is the *injection* vulnerabilities. Through them, malicious users can manipulate certain (dynamic) ABAP commands

◻ Table 6.1 BIZEC APP/11 – the current most dangerous/most common security issues in ABAP code and their corresponding risks

ID	Vulnerability	Description	Risks
APP-01	ABAP Command Injection	Execution of arbitrary ABAP code	1–6
APP-02	OS Command Injection	Execution of arbitrary operating system commands	1, 4
APP-03	Improper Authorization (Missing, Broken, Proprietary, Generic)	Missing or flawed authority checks	1
APP-04	Generic Module Execution	Unauthorized execution of modules	1
APP-05	Cross-Client Database Access	Access to business data on a different SAP client	2, 3
APP-06	SQL Injection	Malicious manipulation of SQL commands	2, 3, 4, 5
APP-07	Unmanaged SQL	Usage of native SQL commands	4, 5
APP-08	Cross-Site Scripting	Manipulation of the browser UI, Identity theft	6
APP-09	Cross-Site Request Forgery	Execution of business logic in the name of another user	6
APP-10	File Upload (Malware)	Storage of malicious data on an SAP Server	1, 4
APP-11	Directory Traversal	Unauthorized write/read access to files on the SAP server	2, 3, 4

to make them behave in unexpected ways. This manipulation of dynamic ABAP commands works even if correct authorization checks are performed. Very often, ABAP developers do not know which risks occur with the use of dynamic programming techniques and unintentionally open the door to hackers. The following figure shows what a command injection (a special type of injection vulnerability) looks like in ABAP.

The code example (Fig. 6.1) shows how user input (lv_name) is processed at runtime in order to create and subsequently execute a new report. An attacker can manipulate the program through this command injection vulnerability and execute arbitrary ABAP code. In this case, this even works on a live system and without any developer authorization (S_DEVELOP) because the ABAP command that actually creates the program (INSERT REPORT) neither performs an authorization check nor checks whether it is a live system.

From an ICS or compliance view, the best control mechanisms are preventive in nature. For general IT controls (ITGC) in the area of change management with custom developments, the following mechanisms are recommended:

Preventive measures

- Proper developer guidelines and standards
- Use of static code analysis tools (quality assurance)

```
REPORT Z_RISIKO.
DATA lt_prog(72) OCCURS 0 WITH HEADER LINE.
PARAMETERS lv_name  TYPE string.
lt_prog = 'REPORT ZFT.'.
APPEND lt_prog.
CONCATENATE
  `DATA lv_tmp(80) TYPE c VALUE '`
  lv_name
  `'.`
  INTO lt_prog  .
APPEND lt_prog  .
lt_prog = 'WRITE / lv_tmp.'.
APPEND lt_prog.
INSERT REPORT 'ZFT' FROM lt_prog  .
SUBMIT ('ZFT').
```

◘ **Figure 6.11** Example of an ABAP Command Injection (APP-01) vulnerability

Standards Without development standards, security-oriented programming is not possible. All developers and third party providers must adhere to these development standards. Important: fixing security bugs can be much more complex (and costly) than modifications to configuration or user roles, for example. The more custom code a company has written, the greater the potential risk. Development standards regarding security must be designed properly at an early stage in order to avoid the list of problems increasing continuously through new code.

Quality Assurance Tools Adequate quality assurance processes are a must. In order to detect inconsistencies and differences to the target state in advance, tools for static code analysis, such as Virtual Forge CodeProfiler, can be integrated into the SAP Transport Management System (TMS) of SAP. This is a central measure to prevent insecure code from entering a live system. This tool can also scan all ABAP code in the live system for a large variety of security and compliance violations – and thus mitigate the immense compliance risk that originates from custom ABAP code.

For more information on the topic of ABAP security, see the book Secure ABAP-Programming, published in 2009, available from SAP Press.

6.4.3 Protecting Tables

In SAP, you can maintain table content that controls the data processing logic directly, in particular, configuration tables. This maintenance is one of the critical, risky operations in an SAP system and, if controls are ineffective, can have serious consequences for the consistency of the processing logic and the data. Therefore, the assignment of corresponding authorizations must be handled particularly strictly.

Check: authorizations for table maintenance

Business users must not have any authorization for general table maintenance, for example, using transactions SE11 (ABAP Dictionary Maintenance) or SM30 (Table Maintenance). Investigate the following:

1. Check the authorization assignment for table maintenance for transactions SE11, SM30, and SM31, as explained in Sect. 5.2.7 (in connection with the authorization object S_TABU_DIS). Values in the ACTIVITY field are restricted to 01 or 02.
2. However, if you want the general maintenance transactions to be present in the business user role, you must ensure that there is an effective authorization restriction one level lower – with authorization object S_TABU_DIS in the field DICBERCLS (Authorization Group).
3. Check that authorization groups are continuously assigned to the maintainable tables with the ICS-critical content. Use tables TDDAT (Assignment Table-Authorization Group) and TBRG (Authorization Groups) as the source of information for this check.
4. If authorization controls for table maintenance are not effective, additional authorization controls must be set up.

Protecting tables by means of authorization groups requires a lot of effort when assigning authorizations for transactions for general table maintenance (SM30 etc.). In practice, the following procedure has become established:

Alternative procedure for table protection

1. General standard transactions such as SM30 are not made available to business users; instead, the users receive dedicated table-specific maintenance transactions developed in-house.
2. For maintenance purposes, maintenance views are created for tables and these prevent direct maintenance of the tables technically.

6.4.4 Controlling Authorization Checks

The central prerequisite for a functioning authorization concept is that the system performs checks at authorization object level. SAP ERP has functions that enable you to switch off the check of authorization objects (for example, using transaction SU24, Authorization Object Check under Transactions). The risk from an ICS perspective is obvious: the specific switching off of the check of individual objects can make the entire authorization concept in an SAP system ineffective.

From the example in Fig. 6.12, you can see that for transaction FB60 (Enter Incoming Invoices), the SAP system can check all relevant objects (if this is provided for in the ABAP source code). However, these checks could be specifically prevented in SAP; the relevant information for each authorization object is in the CHECKIND (check indicator) column.

Check the underlying settings in SAP that control the scope of authorization checks:

Check: profile parameters

1. Use program RSPARAM to check the setting for the profile parameter Auth/no_check_in_some_cases. If the value is Y, it is theoretically possible to switch off the authorization check for individual objects (except for objects belonging to Basis or SAP ERP HCM).
2. If it should be possible to switch off the check on a transaction-specific basis, check whether this has actually taken place. To do this, evaluate tables USOBX_C (settings undertaken by SAP customers) and USOBX (SAP standard settings).

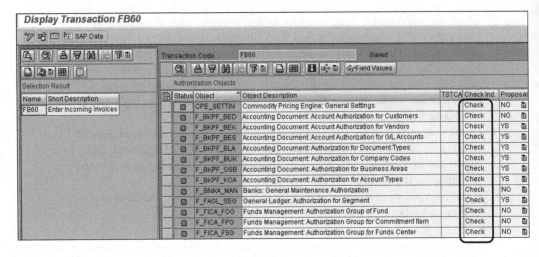

■ **Figure 6.12** Switching off the authorization check at object level with transaction SU24

Authorization objects can be switched off on a transaction-specific basis and also centrally, i. e., for all transactions. Therefore, investigate the following:

- Check the value of the `Auth/object_disabling_active` profile parameter. If the value is Y, not maintained, or empty, individual authorization objects can be switched off globally, i. e., for all transactions.
- If it should be possible to switch off the check centrally, check whether this has actually taken place. Use transaction AUTH_SWITCH_OBJECTS to get the overview required.

Further profile parameters for controlling authorization checks

In SAP, there are further profile parameters that control the degree of effectiveness of controls for access security and password protection. The most important ones are summarized below:

- **Auth/new_buffering**
  For details of the possible values of this parameter, see program `RSPARAM`. A value lower than "4" bears the risk that in some circumstances, inconsistencies can arise between maintained authorization values and the actual access permissions of the user.
- **Auth/rfc_authority_check**
  This parameter determines whether there is an authorization check for the authorization object S_RFC for RFC actions.
- **Auth/system_access_check_off**
  You use this parameter for fine control of the authorization checks for ABAP language elements. If the value is "0" all authorization checks are switched on.
- **Auth/tcodes_not_checked**
  The authorization object S_TCODE is checked whenever a transaction is called up. This parameter can be used to enter transactions excluded from the check. In practice, transaction SU53 (Evaluate Authorization Check) is often defined here; otherwise, S_TCODE should apply for all transactions for security reasons.

- **Bdc/bdel_auth_check**
  This object refers explicitly to the deletion of batch input sessions, in particular, the extent to which the object S_BCD_MONI is considered in this activity: if the value is "true" this authorization object is active, for example, for the use of transaction SM35 (Batch Input Monitoring).
- **Rspro/auth/pagelimit**
  In an environmentally conscious organization, this parameter should definitely be used: it controls whether it is possible to restrict the number of pages in a print request based on authorizations. If the value is "1" authorization object S_PRO_PAGE is considered.

6.4.5 Critical Administration Transactions

You have already learned about some critical authorization combinations in the area of IT general controls. These are access permissions that, in practice, are summarized under the collective term *Basis authorizations*. However, it is not only the assignment of Basis authorizations in critical combinations that is alarming from ICS compliance and risk perspectives; the abuse of the principle of least privilege for the individual Basis authorizations can also represent a high risk for the availability of SAP systems and for the integrity and consistency of the data and the processing logic.

Principle of least privilege

Table 6.2 shows some examples of critical transactions.

In practice, there are various strategies for handling the principle of least privilege in the Basis area. Depending on the organization, some of the critical Basis authorizations can be outsourced to the role of an emergency user so that no employee has permanent use of these authorizations, thus enabling increased logging mechanisms to take effect (see Sect. 6.3.4).

6.4.6 Consideration of the Principle of Segregation of Duties

We have already used the key term segregation of duties several times in this book; critical authorization combinations also exist in IT general controls (or in Basis).

The following authorization combinations must be seen as critical because where such a combination exists, there is a risk of unauthorized changes:

Check: segregation of duties, development and authorizations

- Development (e. g., transaction SE38) and other program changes (e. g., Customizing)
- Release and import of transport requests

Furthermore, due to an increased risk of errors (but also because of possible fraud), in practice, the combination of the following two authorizations is questionable:

- User maintenance (including assignment of authorization roles), for example, transaction SU01 (User Maintenance) or SU10 (User Mass Maintenance)
- Authorizations for the maintenance of role content via PFCG (Profile Generator)

Table 6.2 Overview of the critical Basis authorizations in SAP

Transactions	Description of Critical Activities	Authorization Objects
SCC4, SE06	Maintenance of client modifiability	S_ADMI_FCD
SE38, SA38	Modification and development of programs (developer key necessary); web dynpro development must be considered.	S_DEVELOP SP_PROGRAM
SM30, SM31, SE16, SE16N	Table maintenance	S_TABU_DIS S_TABU_CLI
SCC6, SE01, SE06, STMS	Administration of the Transport Management System	S_CTS_ADMI
RZ04	Administration of SAP instances (CCMS – Computer Center Management System)	S_RLZ_ADM
RZ10, RZ11	Administration of profile parameters	S_RLZ_ADM
Programs RSCDOK99 and RSCDOK*	Deletion of change documents	S_SCDO
SM59	Administration of RFC connections	S_ADMI_FCD
SM49	Immediate execution of the operating system command	S_LOG_COM
SM13	Update administration	S_ADMI_FCD
SM35	Administration of BI folders	S_BDC_MONI
SNRO	Administration of number range intervals and levels	S_NUMBER

❶ Compensating Controls

Some possible compensating controls must be mentioned here:
- At authorization object level, it is usual to restrict the maintenance of own authorizations (or those of an IT department) by an administrator through the restriction of values for the User Group field in the object S_USER_GRP based on technical authorizations.
- Direct assignment of the roles using transaction SU01 (User Maintenance) is no longer a best practice scenario: organizations are increasingly using *provisioning tools* where the assignment of authorization roles to the users is subject to an automated approval procedure, and in addition, a *risk analysis* can take place (see Sect. 4.3.3 and 4.3.4).

Thus far, we have looked at the topic of segregation of duties from a *content* perspective, i. e., which actions should be kept separate (at role and user level) in SAP ERP from a risk perspective. This view continues in Chap. 8 through 11, where you will learn about process-specific application controls. However, what do you have to do to ensure general compliance with the principle of segregation of duties from a *process perspective*?

The main points are summarized below:

Processes to guarantee segregation of duties

— **Documentation**

Organizations should analyze their own SAP-supported processes and documented risks – especially with regard to critical authorization combinations.

Check: segregation of duties, users and authorizations

The core of such documentation is the *segregation of duties matrix*. This is a two-dimensional representation of all authorizations subject to risk and is created based on the processes of the organization. The following are decisive in the definition of the segregation of duties requirements: organization size, process risk potential, size of the department in which the respective process step is located, etc.

If segregation of duties cannot be achieved, for example, for organizational reasons, alternative controls must be implemented and documented.

— **Role management process**

The basic prerequisite for the assignment of authorizations in SAP compliant with the principle of segregation of duties is conflict-free authorization roles. Segregation of duties can only be achieved at user level if the maintenance of critical authorizations is kept separate at role level (for example, via transaction PFCG, Profile Generator). The correspondingly documented procedure is a mandatory component of an authorization concept.

— **Authorization assignment process**

Once the SAP authorization roles are "clean," (no segregation of duties conflicts), the subsequent assignment of roles to the users must consider the segregation of duties risks.

6.5 Summary

You now know what the greatest risks and most important relevant control mechanisms in the area of IT general controls in the SAP environment are and how to check them: you have learned valuable information about the possible organizational controls and measures in the ERP environment as well as the requirements of change management processes and the security of user access to an SAP system. You have also learned about the most important compliance requirements and how to fulfill these in the area of user and authorization management. Furthermore, you now know about the most dangerous "back doors" in the ABAP code and about the ways to deal with those potential threats.

This knowledge should help you to build up a reliable "foundation" for your ICS. Looking at the individual life phases of an SAP application, you can apply this knowledge above all in the initial implementation of an SAP system, but also for the changes that take place continuously. It is also indispensable when executing system audits of all types in the SAP environment.

General Application Controls in SAP ERP

Traceability, unalterability, and completeness – the task is to ensure that these comprehensive compliance principles are fulfilled in SAP. This chapter is dedicated to this task.

In Sect. 3.1.4, you learned that general application controls (IT general controls) have an important function in IT systems, primarily in fulfilling the requirements for ensuring *traceability, unalterability*, and *completeness*. These requirements are not only the result of the application of common sense to generally applicable and internationally standardized GAAP (Generally Accepted Accounting Principles) or their translation into the language of IT; they exist legally in every country in one form or another (see Chap. 1). The most explicit mention of these requirements in the IT environment in official law is to be found in Germany, where the following are particularly relevant:

- *Section 239 Para. 3 German Commercial Code*, according to which, entries or recordings may only be changed such that their original content can still be determined.
- *Section 257 German Commercial Code:* From this part of the legislation, we can derive that all document information recorded in tables, all data and programs connected to this information that control or describe the invoice collection procedure, and all changes to this data and these programs must be documented as part of the procedure documentation and stored for a period of at least ten years.

From an ICS view, ignoring the risks in SAP ERP that endanger compliance with the above-mentioned basic principles can place doubt on the reliability of the external financial reporting. In this chapter, you will learn about the cross-module and cross-process risks that are present in every SAP ERP system and about effective control mechanisms to counteract these risks.

The topics in this chapter are differentiated from the topics in Chap. 6, "IT General Controls in SAP ERP," that refer to the same objects, for example, tables, according to the following principle: IT general controls (Chap. 6) are relevant for tables for authorizations; with general application controls (Chap. 7), the focus is on traceability of the data changes in tables.

Differentiation between ITGC and general application controls

7.1 The Principle of Unalterability

The principle of *unalterability* requires little comment: as you learned in Sect. 3.1.1, this principle represents one of the prerequisites for a proper *document function* because only an electronic document that cannot be changed can be seen as a document. In the following sections, we will show some of the risks that can endanger fulfillment of the document function in SAP ERP, as well as the related control mechanisms.

7.1.1 Protecting Data in Tables

Risks, SE16N
and SAP_EDIT

In Sect. 6.4.3, you learned how to protect SAP tables in daily system operation. However, these control mechanisms are not sufficient for all options for maintaining table contents. Transaction SE16N (General Table Display) offers a "hidden" option. If, after calling up an SAP table with transaction SE16N, you also call up the function &SAP_EDIT (requires far-reaching SAP authorizations), you can change the contents of this table. This means that you can also maintain important document tables directly (that is, without creating a change document), which violates the document principle.

For the following tables, where changes can be made via transaction SE16N and the function &SAP_EDIT, you can verify these changes:

- SE16N_CD_KEY – Table Display of Change Documents: Header
- SE16N_CD_DATA – Table Display of Change Documents: Data

The solution in SAP
Note 1420281

You can see the individual change documents in these tables – however, you can also delete the change documents with transaction SE14 (Utilities for Dictionary Tables). Thus, transaction SE16N in combination with the &SAP_EDIT function represents a serious risk. To close this loophole, SAP has published Note 1420281. You can use it to control the risk described. When you implement this SAP Note, the &SAP_EDIT function is deactivated (the implementation of the source code adjustments contained in SAP Notes and the manual steps is a standard process in SAP).

From SAP ERP version ECC 6.0 (ECC stands for ERP Central Component) and Support Packages 17 and 18, the corresponding correction is "installed" as standard.

Check:
maintenance

To assess the appropriateness of the treatment of the risks specified, perform the following steps:

1. Via SYSTEM • STATUS, check the release and the SP level of the SAP system in question. Does this indicate that the above-mentioned function &SAP_EDIT is deactivated?
2. If necessary, check whether the correction contained in SAP Note 1420281 has been implemented.

7.1.2 Debugging

Direct violation

Debugging activities in a live SAP ERP system represent the most serious violation of the requirements for unalterability of accounting documents and of compliance with the principle of traceability (in Germany, Section 239 Para. 3 of the German Commercial Code on "prohibition of electronic erasure" would be relevant). The activities may indeed sometimes be required for fast problem solution, but in particular, the option of changing the field content of all tables (including tables with accounting documents) as part of debugging or even deleting complete data records represents a high risk. One of the reasons for this is that the corresponding activities are generally not logged (exception: system log, see Sect. 7.3.1).

Changing/deleting
table contents

Figure 7.1 shows an example of how to activate debugging mode ❶:

1. After calling up table GRFNTASKPLAN with transaction SE16 (Data Browser), enter "/h" in the transaction row and then confirm twice with the ENTER key.

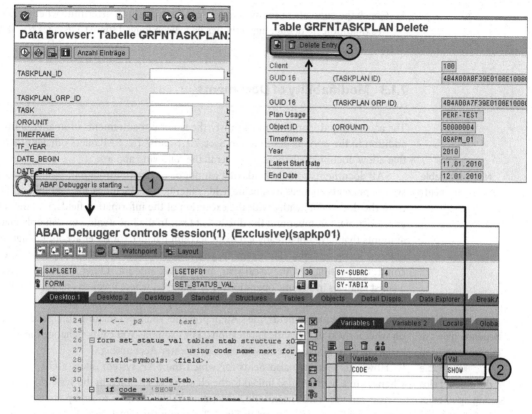

Figure 7.1 Deletion of table entries using the debugging function

2. In the variant, `code show` ❷ is replaced by `delete`, which makes the deletion ❸ of a corresponding data record in table GRFNTASKPLAN possible.

This risk requires effective *controls* that focus on three important areas:
— Restriction of the debugging authorizations
— Emergency user concept
— Configuration and evaluation of the system log

The handling of debugging authorizations is one of the mandatory audit procedures in an SAP audit and you must take it into account when setting up an ICS.

Check: debugging authorizations

1. Check whether authorizations for debugging activities are handled restrictively. In your evaluations, consider in particular authorization object S_DEVELOP, object type DEBUG, and activities 02 (change) and 06 (delete).
2. Check whether debugging activities are provided for in the emergency user concept (see Sect. 6.3.4). In an ideal case, only the emergency user may have debugging authorization in a live SAP ERP system.

3. Check the contents of the system log (see Sect. 7.3.1) to determine whether activities that indicate debugging activities have been logged there (messages A1 4 and A1 9).

7.1.3 Modifiability of Documents

The accounting documents must satisfy the general requirements of unalterability. In addition to the options described in Sect. 7.1.1 and 7.1.2, SAP offers official functions that allow document changes. In general, the following applies:

Non-modifiable
fields

SAP documents contain fields that cannot be changed: through in-built checks, the system prevents changes to specific field contents. This includes, for example, all fields from the document header with the exception of the information fields, i. e., the reference document number and the document text. In the line items, you can only change amounts that have not already led to an account balance (or other account assignment objects) being updated. For example, you cannot change the amount posted, the account, the posting key, the fiscal year, and the tax amount. Other fields are protected against changes in specific operations. For example, where invoices are posted net, you cannot change the cash discount amount when posting the payment.

Modifiable
depending on the
components used

In some document fields, the system prevents you from making changes depending on whether you use specific applications. For example, you cannot change the account assignment to a cost center if you use Cost Center Accounting.

Modifiable
document fields

However, there are also fields for which the SAP system offers a change option. Changes to a field are also linked to the change rules defined in the system.

Setting up rules for
field changes

You can use transaction OB32 (Maintain Table TBAER) to set up change rules for specific fields. As you can see in Fig. 7.2, for one-time customer documents, you can change the bank account retrospectively (for example, if a credit memo has been paid for a one-time customer). You can also consider prerequisites, for example, the possibilities for making a change exclusively for line items that have not been cleared or posting periods that are open.

Check: document
change rules

It is advisable to adopt the standard change rules included in the delivery scope. You can check the rules that have been set up as follows.

1. Use transaction OB32 to check the fields in documents for which changes are permitted (as an alternative, you can also do this directly via table TBAER); consider the existing general modifiability rules. Extensive modifiability options require explanation.
2. Use transaction FB04 (Document Changes) or program RFBABL00 to evaluate the document changes that have been made.

 Exception

There is an exception to the rules described above: for sample and recurring entry documents (see Sect. 8.3.2), you can change all additional account assignments.

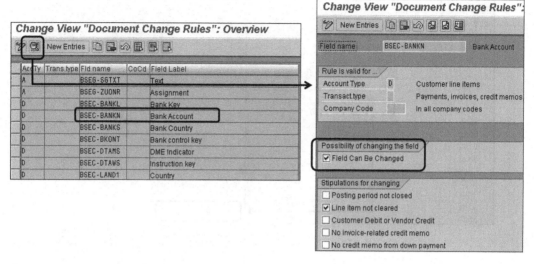

Change View "Document Change Rules":
New Entries
Field name   BSEC-BANKN   Bank Account
Rule is valid for ...
Account Type   D   Customer line items
Transact.type   Payments, invoices, credit memos
Company Code   In all company codes
Possibility of changing the field
☑ Field Can Be Changed
Stipulations for changing
☐ Posting period not closed
☑ Line item not cleared
☐ Customer Debit or Vendor Credit
☐ No invoice-related credit memo
☐ No credit memo from down payment

◘ Figure 7.2 Change rules for SAP documents

7.2 Controls for Data-Related Traceability

SAP ERP offers mechanisms for recording and evaluating changes that have taken place in the system. They represent a technical basis for fulfilling the principle of traceability. The mechanisms enable controls that can assess and minimize some risks (*detective controls*). In particular, these are the risks that result from missing segregation of duties, errors in master data maintenance, etc. The controls include reports in Financial Accounting that show changes to G/L accounts, vendors, and customers, etc. as part of closing activities (see Sect. 8.1.4).

Technical basis for traceability

7.2.1 Change Documents in SAP

The recording of change documents is already "installed" as standard for the most important master data and must be considered in in-house developments in SAP ERP. For example, if you change the bank details for a vendor, G/L account, or a material master, *change documents* are stored in SAP for these changes. You can evaluate them using various programs, for example, program RFKABL00 for changes to vendor master data, program RFSABL00 for changes to G/L account master data, the CHANGE DOCUMENTS section in the menu tree for transaction SUIM (User Information System), to name just a few options.

Document for a change = change document

These change documents are located in the following SAP tables:

SAP tables

— CDHDR – Change Document Header
— CDPOS – Change Document Items

What are the prerequisites for recording change documents? You must first create a change document object using transaction SCDO (Display Change Document

Setting up change documents

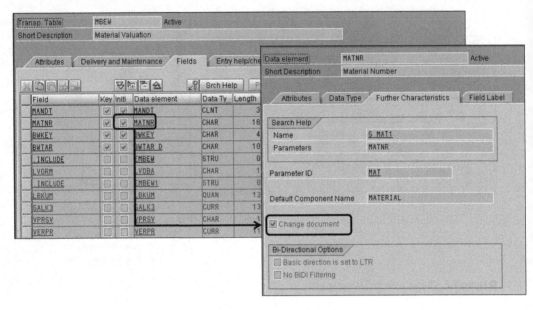

□ Figure 7.3   Properties of data elements as a prerequisite for recording change documents

Objects). Then, as you can see in Fig. 7.3 from the example with table MBEW, you must activate the CHANGE DOCUMENT option in the technical properties of every relevant data element (e. g., Material Number). In our example, this allows you to log valuation-relevant changes in the material master. The last technical steps for activating the recording of change documents would be the generation of updates for relevant objects in transaction SCDO and the addition of the corresponding function calls in the relevant update programs.

Check: change documents   To check the change documents, proceed as follows:

1. Get an overview of the main developments in the SAP system, for example, for maintaining own master data, and check the corresponding tables, as shown in Fig. 7.3, to determine whether the recording of change documents is activated.
2. Use transaction SCDO and the analysis of the source code of the relevant update programs to analyze the accuracy of the treatment of change document objects.
3. Check the contents of the developer guidelines to determine the extent to which the use of change document functions for the purpose of fulfilling traceability requirements is prescribed.
4. Check whether critical authorizations for deleting change documents (for example, using programs RSCDOK91, RSCDOK95, RSCDOK99) are assigned restrictively. One of the most important authorization objects for this is S_SCDO.

7.2.2 Table Logging

A further technical option in SAP is recording changes in database tables – *table logging*. The aim of this logging is to implement the traceability principle in the SAP system, similarly to the change document function that you already know. From a technical perspective, it is easier to activate the table logging than the logging using change documents. For accounting-relevant tables developed in-house in particular, table logging is the usual method in practice.

What should be logged? Compliance vs. performance

During audits, however, auditors often find that tables developed in-house are not logged; as a counter-argument, organizations often state that including lots of tables in logging is not feasible for performance reasons.

Experience has shown that the following is recommended for the *scope of logging*: what must be logged are changes in maintainable tables with master data and control data that have a content reference to one of the following compliance requirements:

Recommended scope of logging

- **External financial reporting**
  The criterion for selecting the relevant data is that it is directly involved in processes that lead to changes to the G/L account balances or to details relevant to the notes for the financial statements.
- **Processes with potential for fraud**
  Processes connected to the handling of asset values (payment transactions, materials management, fixed assets, etc.) or to the granting of advantages to business partners (credit memos, contracts, payment terms, etc.) have a risk of fraud.
- **Other compliance relevance**
  Data with *other* compliance relevance at discretion or in the industry-specific environment of an organization (e. g., FDA requirements etc.)

As you can see, tables with transaction data are not mentioned. The reasons are as follows:

Tables with transaction data

- By definition, it should not be possible to maintain tables with transaction data (registered business transactions, logs, or processing logs).
- If there are legitimate reasons that should make it possible to maintain tables with transaction data, this could cause system performance problems or an increased amount of work required due to a usually high transaction volume.

How do you implement table logging from a technical perspective? Two SAP Notes are recommended here: SAP Note 1916 refers to the older releases of SAP and is generally somewhat out of date; SAP Note 112388 gives a more detailed and up-to-date description of the relevant issues (https://service.sap.com/sap/support/notes/112388).

SAP Notes for table logging

The SAP system must fulfill two prerequisites for *table logging*:

Prerequisites for table logging

- The profile parameter `rec/client` should allow logging in the relevant client (you can maintain this parameter via transaction RZ10, Maintain Profile Parameters).
- Logging must be activated for each table individually with transaction SE13 (Maintain Technical Settings (Tables)). In many SAP standard tables this logging flag is already set. However, in some circumstances it may be necessary to include further standard tables in the logging.

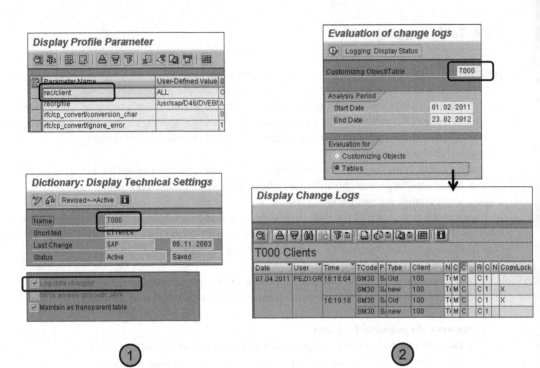

Figure 7.4   Technical prerequisites and evaluation results for table logging

If these prerequisites are fulfilled, use program RSTBHIST or RSVTPROT to evaluate the changes made in the tables (alternatively, use transaction SCU3).

Figure 7.4 shows the summary of the technical prerequisites ❶ for table logging using the example of table T000, as well as the evaluation of the changes in this table ❷.

Check: table logging

Perform the following steps to check table logging:

1. Use program RSPARAM to check whether the profile parameter rec/client is set for the productive client.
2. Determine the tables developed in-house (Z* or Y*) and assess their accounting relevance via interviews etc. Use program RDDPRCHK to check that the logging settings are correct. Alternatively, you can use SAP table DD09 L.

❶   **Logging in SAP Process Control**

With SAP Process Control, you can use a snapshot function to monitor changes to the contents of a specific database. The advantage of a Process Control-based logging is that you can involve changes to important objects in the ICS process immediately. For example, if a control field in table T001 (Company Codes) is changed, in Process Control, a notification and a workflow for problem resolution can be generated and forwarded to the person responsible automatically. However, from a technical perspective, options described in Sect. 7.2.1 and 7.2.2 are preferred due to the requirements for completeness from logging. The Process Control logging options would be a useful supplement.

In Sect. 17.2.1 you will learn about another logging option for recording and evaluating data changes with SAP Process Control.

7.2.3 Document Number Assignment

In an SAP system, the individual business transactions are recorded as documents (*transaction data*, see Sect. 5.1.1). Technically, there are generally two options for numbering documents:

— **External document number assignment**
   The document numbers are assigned "externally," i. e., by other SAP modules or from other systems via interfaces.
— **Internal document number assignment**
   With this option, the SAP system assigns a document number itself.

Both options have something in common: the SAP system checks whether the document numbers lie within a specific interval assigned. However, the system only ensures that the numbering is *sequential* when document numbers are assigned internally. Unfortunately, even sequential document numbering can have *gaps* in SAP for various reasons, and this could adversely affect the fulfillment of the principle of traceability.

Therefore, in SAP ERP, controls that prevent gaps in the document numbering or at least justify gaps are essential. The usual causes for gaps in document numbering are summarized below.

— **Document archiving**
   If a number range interval to be checked contains numbers for documents that have been reorganized (or archived), these numbers are reported as a document gap. Therefore, document archiving must be documented such that document numbers can be traced.
— **Document number buffering**
   For performance and other reasons, a shared memory on the application server contains a technical option for "bundling" document numbers in the update process. When you start an SAP instance, several document numbers are loaded to the main storage simultaneously, creating a *buffer*. If the SAP system is shut down at a time when not all document numbers from the buffer have been used, gaps arise. Therefore, buffering must not be activated for critical number range objects such as RF_BELEG (Number Ranges for Accounting Documents).
— **Document parking**
   In SAP, a parked document receives a number from the "real" *number range interval*. However, as long as the parked document has not been posted, there is a gap. This gap cannot be corrected even when a parked document is deleted (see also Sect. 8.3.1).

Traceability of transaction data through numbering

Gaps in document numbering

- **Fraudulent actions**
  Gaps can also arise from intentional deletion of entries in document tables (at database level or via debugging, see Sect. 7.1.2). In certain circumstances such deletion would be classified as a criminal act.
- **Manual maintenance of number ranges**
  Improper manual maintenance of document number range intervals can lead to gaps (e. g., if the current number of the last document saved is increased by one or more).
- **Update terminations**
  Update terminations also lead to gaps in the document number assignment if the update is not restarted in good time and the corresponding operation has been entered again (see Sect. 7.4.1, "Monitoring Update Terminations").

Check: no gaps in document number assignment

Perform the following audit procedures for document number assignment:

1. Get an overview of the document number ranges that have been set up (table NRIV).
2. Use program RFBNUM00 to evaluate the document numbers for gaps. Request supporting documents for any gaps you discover (e. g., for document archiving, deletion of parked documents, or update terminations).
3. In table TNRO, check whether buffering of the document numbers is activated for the relevant document number range objects (RF_BELEG, RV_BELEG, MATBELEG, etc.).
4. Check whether authorizations for maintaining the number ranges with transaction FBN1 (Accounting Document Number Ranges) or for direct maintenance of table NRIV are assigned restrictively.

7.3   Traceability of User Activities in SAP

The activities that take place in an ERP system must also satisfy the principle of traceability – regardless of whether these are transaction calls, user activities, critical system events, or configuration changes. SAP offers some control mechanisms that help you to monitor and, where necessary, document ICS-critical activities. We will look at the most important of these controls in this section.

7.3.1   System Log

What does the system log do?

The system log is the most important log in an SAP system and is the starting point for problem analysis. In the system log, messages, warnings, and errors are documented with different colors. From the numerous system events documented in the system log, there are some that are important from an ICS view because, for example, the following is documented there:

- Debugging activities (message A1 9) that led to table content being changed (see Sect. 7.1.2)
- Update terminations (message R6 5)

```
08:29:27 DIA  000 010 STPE16R                        ⊘  D0 1 Transaction Canceled 00 671 ( SAPSQL_ARRAY_INSERT_DUPREC 2012022
08:29:28 DIA  000 010 STPE16R                        ⊘  R6 5 Update terminated
08:29:28 DIA  000 010 STPE16R                        ⊖  R6 6 > Update key: 4F42766F0DRC2F3RE10000000A0R020C
08:29:28 DIA  000 010 STPE16R                        ○  R6 7 > Update module: CO_RU_VB_CONFIRMATION_POST
08:29:28 DP                                          ⊘  Q0 J work process type required for request handling is not available
08:29:28 DP                                          ⊘  Q0 G Request (type UPD) cannot be processed
08:51:00 DIA  004 010 DIKL1AU                        ⊘  AB 0 Run-time error "MESSAGE_TYPE_X" occurred
08:51:00 DIA  004 010 DIKL1AU                        ○  AB 1 > Short dump "120221 085100 tecan001_P46_00 DIKL1AU " created
09:01:38 S-A       000 p46adm                        ⊘  E0 7 Error 000104 : Connection reset by peer in Module rslgsend(027)

10:29:23 DIA  002 010 MAFL1EXT      SE38              ⊘  A1 9 Field contents changed: LS_WERKSDISPO-WERKS -> 2850
10:29:23 DIA  002 010 MAFL1EXT      SE38              ○  A1 4 > in program ZZ_UNCONF_PO_FORMS   line 0304  event SEND_UNCONF
10:29:23 DIA  002 010 MAFL1EXT      SE38              ⊘  A1 9 Field contents changed: LS_WERKSDISPO-WERKS -> 2850
10:29:23 DIA  002 010 MAFL1EXT      SE38              ○  A1 4 > in program ZZ_UNCONF_PO_FORMS , line 0304, event SEND_UNCONF
10:38:05 DIA  000 010 INKA16R       SU01              ⊘  R0 P Entries in the number range buffer were deleted (count: 1 )
```

◻ Figure 7.5 Messages in the system log: update termination and change to table content in debugging mode

━ Immediate and unrestricted transmission of operating system commands from the SAP user interface via program RSBDCOS0 (message LC 0)

You can see examples of these and other messages in Fig. 7.5.

You can call up the system log with transaction SM21 (Online System Log Analysis). By selecting EDIT • EXPERT MODE in the menu bar, you can expand the selection criteria available. After the optional restriction to periods, users, transaction code, process start, problem class, etc. and reading of the system log, the results are presented in list form.

Using the system log

Correct configuration of the system log is very important. The system log is written locally for every application server. Unless defined otherwise explicitly in a system parameter, it is written to the *SLOG<instance number>.log* file. Each log entry has 192 bytes, which means that the standard size of 500 Kbytes corresponds to 2,065 entries. In a larger SAP system, this limit would be exhausted after less than one day. When the defined limit is reached, every new entry displaces the oldest entry in the log file. To ensure that system events can still be traced, you also define a backup file in the system log. When the maximum size is reached, the content of the actual log file is shifted to this backup file. The log file is then written again beginning with an empty file. This can all be controlled using settings for the profile parameters. For the most important settings, see Table 7.1.

How do you configure the system log?

In UNIX systems, a *global system log* is also available. The entries of all local system logs of the configured instances can be merged in this log.

Unix: global system log

The most common audit procedures in connection with the treatment of the system log are summarized below:

Check: SAP system log

1. Check whether the procedure for evaluating the system log is documented: Frequency? What is checked? How are critical messages further processed? In addition, check whether the documented procedure is also adhered to in practice.
2. Check the settings for the profile parameters (see Table 7.1) and whether they are maintained appropriately; consider the size of the system (number of users, transaction volume, etc.). You can evaluate the profile parameters with program RSPARAM.
3. In the context of other audit procedures (monitoring the update terminations or detecting debugging activities), use transaction SM21 to analyze the contents of the system log.

◘ Table 7.1 Relevant profile parameters for the system log

Profile parameter	Meaning
`rslg/max_diskspace_local`	Determines the maximum size of the local log file
`rslg/local/file`	Determines the location of the local log file on the application server
`rslg/local/old_file`	Determines the location of the backup file for the local log file on the application server
`rslg/max_diskspace_central`	Determines the maximum size of the central log file
`rslg/central/file`	Determines the location of the central log file on the application server
`rslg/central/old_file`	Determines the location of the backup file for the central log file on the application server

7.3.2 Security Audit Log

Logging security-relevant activities

The Security Audit Log (SAL) enables you to log security-relevant activities by users in the SAP system. It is neither technically possible nor useful, nor permitted for reasons of data protection, to log all actions of all users in this way. With regard to the audit, emergency, support, and other privileged users (e. g., SAP standard users) should be logged in the Security Audit Log. The following information can be documented in the Security Audit Log, for example:

- Successful and failed dialog logon attempts
- Successful and failed RFC logon attempts
- RFC calls
- Changes to user master data
- Successful and failed transaction starts

Setting up SAL

Once you have activated the Security Audit Log via corresponding profile parameters (see Table 7.2), you have to create an *audit profile* (transaction SM19). In this profile, you have to define one or more *SAL filters*. These filters determine which audit classes are logged for which users in which clients. You have to select each filter explicitly using the FILTER ACTIVE checkbox.

Check: Security Audit Log

Perform the following evaluations to check the Security Audit Log:

1. Using profile parameter `rsau/enable`, evaluate whether SAL is activated and whether the other profile parameters (see Table 7.1) are set appropriately. You can evaluate the profile parameters with program `RSPARAM`.
2. Use transaction SM19 to check the contents of the filter settings in SAL and the extent to which emergency users, support users, and standard users are included in logging. Where applicable, check the requirements of the data protection regulations.
3. You can analyze the log contents of SAL with transaction SM20 (Analysis of Security Audit Log).

◘ **Table 7.2** Security Audit Log – relevant profile parameters

Profile Parameter	Definition
rsau/enable	Activation of the Security Audit Log on the application server
rsau/local/file	Determination of the location of the Security Audit Log on the application server
rsau/max_diskspace_local	Maximum space that may be assigned to audit files
rsau/selection_slots	Number of filters permitted for the Security Audit Log

4. Check whether authorization for the above-mentioned transactions, including SM18 (Reorganize Security Audit Log) is assigned restrictively.

7.3.3 History of Transaction Calls

Information about transaction calls (statistical records or statistics file) that are part of the Computer Center Management System (CCMS) of SAP represents a valuable source for various evaluations – for example, it can be used for RBE tools (Reversed Business Engineering), in various checks, determinations, and performance analyses as well as many other options. Since this data is person-specific data, the information must be handled in accordance with the *data protection regulations*.

Who did what and when?

You can evaluate the contents of the statistics file (file name *stat.DAT*) with transaction STAD or program RSSTAT26. Examples of general information in the statistics file are:

Statistics file

- Date, transaction start, transaction end, transaction code, program, screen
- Database statistics: Inserts, Updates, Selects, Fetches, Deletes
- Table-specific statistics etc.

Each time you change screen, a statistics record is written to a file specified by the profile parameter stat/file. The *SAP work processes* first create local buffers for the data. When these buffers are full, the content is emptied to the statistics file.

You can check the treatment of the history of transaction calls as follows in SAP:

Check: statistics file

1. Check the specification of the statistics file-relevant profile parameters, including stat/file. You can evaluate the profile parameters with program RSPARAM.
2. Consider the relevant data protection requirements and check whether access to the statistics file is sufficiently restricted (transactions STAD, ST03, etc.). Access to global statistical entries is based on authorization object S_TOOLS_EX. Without this authorization, users can only access their own statistical entries recorded. The object contains a field for the authorization name. If you enter the value "S_TOOLS_EX_A" you can display other statistical entries.

☐ Table 7.3   CTS-relevant transports and directories

Log (Directories or Tables)	Description
`<transport_directory>/bin`	Configuration file of the transport program `tp`
`<transport_directory>/data`	Data files for the transport requests
`<transport_directory>/sapnames`	One log file for each CTS user. It documents the transport activities for this user's transport requests.
`<transport_directory>/buffer`	One import buffer per system. The buffer lists the requests pending import for this system, including all work steps required for the import.
`<transport_directory>/cofiles`	Control files for the transport requests. The object classes, import steps required, and return values are noted here.
`<transport_directory>/log`	General and request-specific log files
Table E070	Request/task headers
Tables E071 and E071K	Object entries and key entries of requests/tasks

7.3.4 Traceability of System Changes in the Change and Transport Management System (CTS)

Change and Transport Management System

In addition to the technical options already explained for documenting changes in the system, the *Change and Transport Management System* (CTS) offers some mechanisms for logging changes to the program logic and other system changes. You have already learned about the basics of CTS in Sect. 6.2.2. The most important elements are:

- CTS directories with corresponding information about the individual transport requests
- SAP database tables with transport-relevant content
- CTS parameters that determine the entire CTS process, including the contents of the above-mentioned CTS directories

Table 7.3 summarizes the most important CTS directories and SAP database tables. CTS directories represent central storage of the most important information about CTS-controlled system changes. You should archive the contents of the directories on a regular basis.

Parameters in transport control program tp

Program `tp` performs the actual control and execution of transports between SAP systems at operating system level. This program triggers both the export of data from one SAP system and the import into other systems. The logic is determined by, for example, parameters that you can find in CTS as follows: Transaction STMS • Overview • Systems • SAP System • Change • Transport Tool. (These are *not*, therefore, parameters that you can maintain with transaction RZ11 and evaluate using program RSPARAM.)

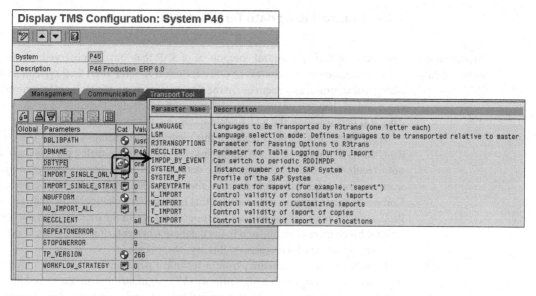

Figure 7.6 Evaluation of the transport parameters

Figure 7.6 shows an example of the list of relevant CTS control parameters, including:

— RECCLIENT: Recording of the changes to the contents of Customizing tables in table logs (as described in Sect. 7.2.2)
— *IMPORT: Control of the validity of imports of different types of change requests

In addition to the organizational controls in CTS described in Sect. 6.2.2, there are further important application controls:

Check: traceability in CTS

1. In collaboration with the person responsible for Basis, assess the procedure for archiving the contents of the CTS directories and the appropriateness of the authorization-based restriction of access to these directories and the relevant database tables.
2. Check the transport parameters as shown in Fig. 7.6.

7.4 Cross-Process Processing Controls

Compliance with the principles of completeness, accuracy, and traceability of data processing can be impaired in an SAP system where there are update terminations and errors in interface processing. Below you will learn which controls you can set up and test for update processes in SAP. You will also learn what is important for monitoring cross-system processes that have been realized using common SAP interface technologies.

7.4.1 Monitoring Update Terminations

Asynchronous writing of data

The update system is a central component of SAP that must be observed, not in isolation, but always in the context of other technical *services* of an SAP system, such as dialog, background, and enqueue. In the SAP environment, the term *update* means the execution of changes at database level that is performed after the entry of or changes to data. It is performed by the SAP update system for the most part *asynchronously*.

What does asynchronous mean in this context? For example, when a user enters data, this is first received by the *dialog process*. However, the dialog process itself does not execute the required changes to the database. Instead, specially designed *update work processes* execute the changes; thus, the changes are implemented asynchronously. Compared to *synchronous data changes*, that is, immediate change by the dialog process itself, asynchronous writing means higher performance for the user: he does not have to wait for his changes to be updated in the database when entering, changing, or deleting data. The update work processes do this asynchronously.

V1 and V2 operations

In asynchronous processing, from a technical perspective, there is a differentiation between postings with a high priority (*V1 operations*) that are processed first (for example, operations entered in the general ledger), and postings with lower priority (*V2 operations*) that are used for statistical purposes, for example. V2 updates can only be executed after V1 updates.

Risks during the update

Errors can occur during the execution of updates. On one hand, in some circumstances, business transactions can only be entered incompletely in SAP; on the other hand, bigger problems can also occur: in some circumstances, failure of the updates can mean a shutdown of the entire system, even after a short time – the objects to be changed in the update remain blocked and the *update tables* continue to grow (VBHDR: update headers, VBMOD: update modules, VBDATA: data transferred to the modules, VBERROR: error information in the case of an update termination).

Which control mechanisms does SAP offer to minimize errors in update processes? Firstly, there are in-built controls that you can set up using profile parameters. The most important of these parameters are summarized in Table 7.4.

You can find further relevant profile parameters using program RSPARAM. In the list of all parameters that this program creates, search for Rdisp/vb*. All parameters that start with Rdisp/vb* relate to update processes in the SAP system.

In addition to ICS-conform configuration settings, regular monitoring of the update terminations should be a fixed part of the administration of any SAP system. Figure 7.7 shows how you can perform this monitoring with transaction SM13 (Administrate Update Records) ❶ or transaction SM14 (Update Program Administration) ❷.

Monitoring update terminations

In addition to transaction SM13, which basically returns the contents of table VBLOG, you can use program RFVBER00 (FI Document: List of Update Terminations). It also lists a history of incorrect updates (including updates that have already been deleted). The following update records can appear with the respective status in the list of results:

- INIT – the record is waiting for the update
- AUTO – if the update is active again after the update server has stopped, the record is updated automatically
- RUN – the record is currently being processed
- ERR – an error occurred and led to the termination

◻ Table 7.4 Overview of the important profile parameters in update administration

Profile Name	Meaning
rdisp/vbmail	Specifies whether a message is sent to a user automatically if there is an error in their update request
rdisp/vb_mail_user_list	Here you can also enter persons responsible for the update administration who are always informed in the case of an update error.
rdisp/vbdelete	Number of days after the expiry of which the unfinished update requests are deleted when the SAP system or instance is restarted (table VBLOG). The default is 50. Recommendation: > 365 days.
rdisp/vbreorg	This controls whether incomplete update requests are deleted when the SAP system or instance is restarted. There are alternatives for deleting incomplete update requests, see Fig. 7.7.
rdisp/vb_stop_active	This parameter defines whether the update can be deactivated manually or, in the case of a serious database problem, automatically.

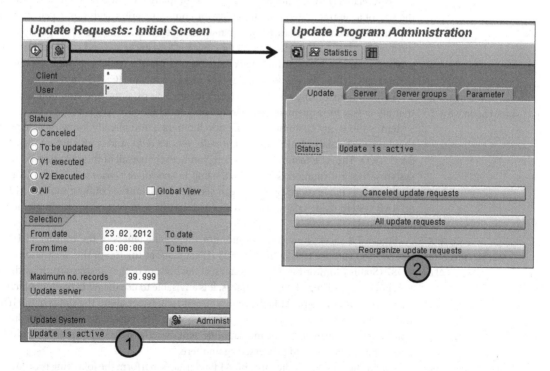

◻ Figure 7.7 Overview: access to the analysis of update terminations and to update administration

Status "Err"   In particular, you must analyze the entries with status Err. The posting processing must be repeated and the treatment of errors documented such that it can be traced.

Check: update   Checking the treatment of update terminations in SAP ERP is essential. In this context, perform the following procedures:

1. Get an overview of the procedures and control mechanisms established in the organization for minimizing risks with regard to updates: profile parameter settings, system log evaluations (messages R0 R, R0 S, R0 U, R0 X, etc.), monitoring of update terminations with transaction SM13, and program RFVBER00.
2. Check the treatment of update terminations – are they processed on a timely basis? Is there clear definition of who has to restart the update (IT or accounting department employee)?
3. Check whether authorizations for update administration are assigned restrictively (in particular for transactions SM13 and SM14, administration of the update process, as well as authorization object S_ADMI_FCD).

7.4.2 Completeness of the ALE Interface Processing

Cross-system communication   It is rare for all business processes to be mapped in one single central system. For various reasons, constant data comparison and exchange can be necessary: information flows between relatively independent branches of a company, technical bottlenecks caused by the size of a central system, the necessity for communication with other, generally independent systems (e. g., warehouse management system etc.). One of the possible and most widespread technical solutions for constant data exchange and comparison in the SAP environment is *Application Link Enabling* (ALE). Due to the very high complexity of this topic, below we will look at only the most important ICS-relevant issues.

ICS-relevant information via ALE   ALE contains business scenarios (e. g., for invoice receipts) and function modules that allow you to implement the transfer and comparison of data from or to an SAP system without any customer-specific developments. You already know that there are three types of data in SAP: *transaction data, master data,* and *configuration data* (see Sect. 5.1.1). The ALE technology can help you to exchange all of this data between SAP systems. The information is exchanged using *Intermediate Documents* (IDoc) that belong to a specific *message type*. You can see the details of the configuration of ALE in an SAP system using transaction SALE (ALE has its own section in the Implementation Guide).

Control mechanisms with ALE   Figure 7.8 shows how you can monitor the completeness of the transfer of IDocs in SAP. You can use transactions WE05 (IDoc Lists; at the top of the illustration) and BD87 (Status Monitor for ALE Messages; at the bottom of the illustration). In addition to regular monitoring of ALE interfaces, it is advisable to use the *ALE auditing function*: using ALE message type ALEAUD, you can send a message about the status of the IDoc transfer from a receiver system to the sender system. The advantage of this procedure is that in the case of an error, the messages are sent directly to the department responsible and can be corrected and processed again there.

Check: Application Link Enabling   When checking the topics around ALE interfaces, perform the following procedures:

1. In an interview, find out whether ALE functions are used. Where applicable, use transaction SALE to get an overview of the configuration of ALE functions (in

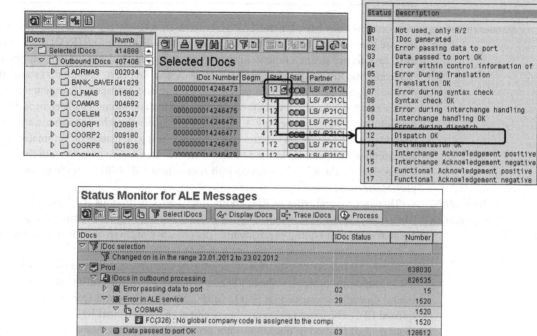

Figure 7.8 Monitoring of IDocs in ALE functions

particular, with regard to the message types used). Check whether message type ALEAUD is used.

2. Check the consistency of the configuration of ALE using transaction IDOC (IDoc: Repair and Check Programs).

3. Check whether the monitoring of a complete and error-free transfer of IDocs is organized appropriately and takes place regularly. As shown in Fig. 7.8, use transactions BD87 (Status Monitor for ALE Messages), WE05 (IDoc Lists), and BDM2 (Monitoring: IDocs in Receiving System) to get an independent overview of the status of the transfer of IDocs.

4. Check whether authorizations for ALE administration are assigned restrictively (in addition to the transactions stated, authorization object S_IDOCMONI is also relevant here).

7.4.3 Remote Function Call Connections

Standard interface log

Many connections between two SAP systems or an SAP system and an external system are based on the SAP interface log of the *Remote Function Call* (RFC). As part of RFC, specific pre-defined function modules are called up that support different interface concepts. RFC is therefore the basis for ALE and BAPIs; RFC is used as standard for exchanging object contents as part of the Change and Transport Management System (see Sect. 6.2.2 and 7.3.4). In the automation of test and monitoring scenarios using the Automated Rules Framework, RFC is used to transfer the selection criteria and test results back to SAP Process Control (see Chap. 17, "Implementation of Automated Test and Monitoring Scenarios in the SAP ERP Environment"). You can maintain the RFC connections or the *RFC destinations* with transaction SM59 (RFC Destinations (Display/Maintain)).

Types of RFC communication

There are several types of RFC communication: synchronous RFC, asynchronous RFC, transactional RFC, queued RFC. The use of different types of communication necessitates different control mechanisms. The objective of these control mechanisms is above all the completeness of the data transfer via RFC interfaces.

Figure 7.9 shows two examples of monitoring transactions: you can use transaction SM58 to monitor the transactional RFCs, and transaction SMQ1 (qRFC Monitor (Outbound Queue)) or transaction SMQ2 (qRFC Monitor (Inbound Queue)) to monitor queued RFC. The latter type is an enhancement of transactional RFC. In this variant, requests are collected in queues and not processed by a transactional RFC until there is certainty that all predecessors have been handled correctly. On one hand, this procedure guarantees the processing of requests in the order of their receipt; on the other hand, it requires monitoring of the individual requests in the queue to ensure the completeness of the transfer.

RFC and security

Security questions are also relevant in connection with RFC: on one hand, RFC communication must be sufficiently protected (e. g., use of the *trusted system* option in the individual RFC destinations, which does not require identification data between connected systems); on the other hand, the maintenance of RFC destinations themselves must also be sufficiently protected. Attention must also be paid to the use of *RFC users*: dialog users must be avoided; instead, separate user types specifically for this purpose should be used, for example, communication users (see Sect. 5.2.6).

RFC inventory advisable

Experience shows that organizations use many RFC destinations, including those about whose purpose no information can be provided. Since RFC represents a type of open door into an SAP system, proper documentation of the individual RFC destinations is essential and is a further important prerequisite for proper actions in the RFC area.

Check: Remote Function Call

Perform the following audit procedures in connection with RFC interfaces:

1. Get an overview of the RFC destinations that have been set up; use transaction SM59 or table RFCDES. Check whether the purpose of individual destinations is traceably documented and whether the live system contains only destinations actually used.
2. Check whether the monitoring of the completeness of the RFC data transfer is organized appropriately.
3. Check whether security questions in the RFC area are considered sufficiently. In authorization analyses with regard to the maintenance of RFC destinations, con-

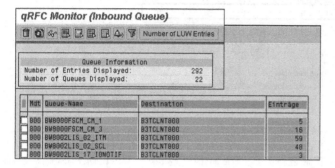

Figure 7.9 RFC – monitoring transactions

sider the object S_ADM_FCD. The following values in the SYSTEM ADMINISTRATION FUNCTIONS field are relevant:

- NADM (network administration) including transaction SM59
- RFCA (RFC administration)
- QDEL (execution of program RSTRFCQDS)
- RSTRFCIDS for deleting a queue in SMQ1 or SMQ2

7.4.4 Completeness of Batch Input Processing

The *batch input procedure* is a further standard technology that has been used for a long time and is very widespread in the SAP environment. Via simulation of a user dialog, it transfers data to the SAP system or executes mass updates. The data transfer takes place in two steps:

Batch processing made by SAP

1. Creation of a batch input session that contains all relevant data (transactions, screens, fields, field values).
2. Processing of this session in the system. The *processing* of the batch input session imports the data into the SAP system.

The creation of a batch input session is either triggered externally (e. g., via standard interfaces for account statements or interfaces developed in-house) or as part of SAP-internal operations that use the same technology, for example, splitting the balance of

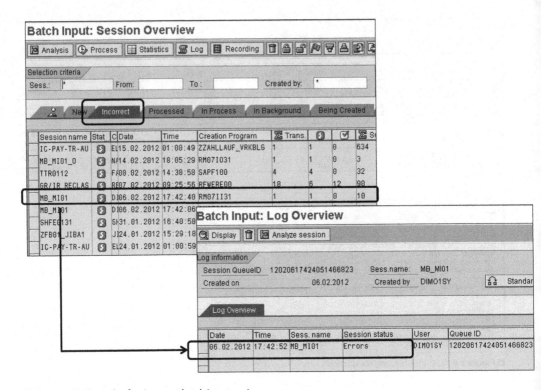

□ **Figure 7.10**   Example of an incorrect batch input session

a GR/IR account etc. When a batch input session is processed (either in *dialog mode* or in the *background*), all consistency checks take place that also take place for normal transaction calls. However, since, in some circumstances, sufficient consistency, accuracy, and completeness of the data that comes from external sources cannot be given for all transactions within a session for a posting, the transactions are terminated.

In this case, the batch input session is reported as PROCESSED WITH ERRORS. The individual transactions (a batch input session can contain many transaction lines) that could not be processed are visible in the log (all other data records have been posted). The incorrect batch input sessions must therefore be reprocessed on a timely basis to ensure the *completeness* of the recording of the business transactions.

As an example, Fig. 7.10 shows batch input session MB_MI01. The transaction, MI01 (Create Physical Inventory Document) ran with errors.

Check: batch input processing

To check the handling of batch input operations in SAP, perform the following audit procedures:

1. Get an overview of the operations that take place in the SAP system in question based on the batch input technology. In particular, *naming conventions* of the batch input sessions are important (programs that create the batch input sessions assign the names automatically).

2. Check the organization of the batch input processing: Are the different batch input operations assigned to specialist contact persons? Are redundant, incorrect etc. sessions monitored on a timely basis and, where applicable, deleted?
3. Check whether authorizations are assigned based on the principle of least privilege (transaction SM35, authorization object S_BDC_MONI with field values: DELE – Delete; IMPO – Import; AONL – Process sessions in dialog mode; ABTC – Pass on sessions to background processing; etc.). Check whether authorizations are restricted according to the naming conventions of batch input sessions.
4. Use transaction SM35 to evaluate incorrect batch input sessions (in particular, those that are relevant for accounting purposes – you can assess this from the transactions listed in the log). Check whether they are reprocessed on a timely basis and whether incorrect sessions that are no longer relevant are flagged for deletion in good time.

7.5 Summary

In this chapter, you have learned about the general application controls in SAP. The main difference between these controls and the IT general controls is that general application controls are primarily geared towards compliance with the basic principles (completeness, traceability, unalterability) of the processing of data when recording business transactions and therefore have a direct reference to business processes. In this area, a specific risk can often be assigned to an *assertion*: for example, incomplete transfer of incoming invoices from an external system to SAP via an interface can influence the completeness of the payables in external financial reporting.

In contrast, IT general controls play a supporting role and can rarely be assigned to an assertion. An approval procedure for transport requests would apply across all objects for all system changes. The differentiation in the example above for the interface for incoming invoices would not be possible.

Controls in Financial Accounting

We primarily associate ICS and auditing with financial reporting. Therefore, we will begin the diverse topic of SAP process controls in this book with financial accounting.

One of the main causes and triggers for ICS compliance requirements is the external financial reporting that certain target groups outside an organization rely on. Some elements of this financial reporting, for example, the financial statements, are created almost "at the touch of a button." Here, primarily the following FI components of SAP ERP are relevant:

- General Ledger Accounting (FI-GL and, where applicable, New General Ledger)
- Accounts Payable Accounting (FI-AP)
- Accounts Receivable Accounting (FI-AR)
- Bank Accounting (FI-BL)
- Asset Accounting (FI-AA)

In order for this reporting to be reliable, and for an SAP system to comply with the principles described in Sect. 3.1.1, any risks that exist must be recognized and addressed with effective controls. Without claiming to provide a complete list of all relevant issues, in this chapter we will address the most important risks and control mechanisms. We will also describe audit procedures that are an "absolute necessity" in every SAP system in practice.

In describing the audit procedures, we will look closely at relevant data models (i. e., database tables). This information will help you in the third part of the book to establish a connection to possible automated test and monitoring scenarios in SAP. For this type of scenario, data must be read directly from database tables and thus understanding the underlying data models is very important.

8.1 Underlying Control Mechanisms in General Ledger Accounting (FI-GL)

From an ICS perspective, General Ledger Accounting (FI-GL) is the "heart" of the SAP ERP application. All information relevant for financial reporting comes together here. This section should provide you with a basic understanding of the transactions in FI-GL and will address selected control areas.

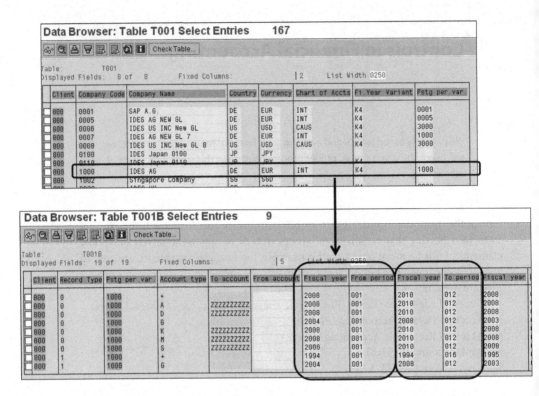

□ Figure 8.1   Evaluation of the open posting periods

8.1.1   Principle: Real-Time Postings

Period-specific
posting

In SAP ERP, the principle of real-time display of business transactions in reporting is realized by the fact that the fiscal year is divided into posting periods. The fiscal year can correspond to a calendar year or be mapped as a shortened fiscal year or fiscal year alternative to the calendar year. On the system side, you have to configure the *fiscal year variant* and *variant for posting periods* and assign them to a company code – an independent accounting unit in SAP. In general, the individual posting periods correspond to a calendar month and usually, at any one time, only one posting period may be open (or a maximum of two, as, for example, postings relating to the previous month can still be made at the beginning of a month).

Special periods

Special periods are an exception: you usually set up further auxiliary periods in addition to the "normal" posting periods (generally twelve) – up to four additional periods. These additional posting periods are intended for corrections and manual postings at the end of the year during year-end closing. Posting period 12 is closed when the special periods are open for posting.

Figure 8.1 shows that posting period variant 1000 is assigned to company code 1000. The entries evaluated for this variant in table T001B show that for most account groups, all main posting periods are open. The negative example in Fig. 8.2 comes from a development system; in a live SAP system it would lead to a major query.

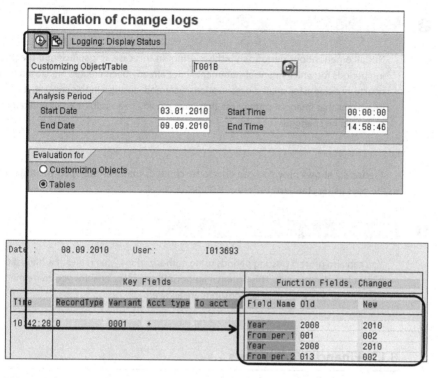

□ Figure 8.2 Checking the change of posting periods in the past – negative example

The individual G/L accounts are differentiated using the following account groups:
- A – Assets
- D – Customers
- G – Special ledger
- K – Vendors
- M – Material
- S – G/L accounts

Check compliance with the principle of real-time recording of business transactions as follows:

Check: principle of real-time postings

1. Get an overview of the fiscal year variants that have been set up (transaction OB29, Fiscal Year Variants, or table T009) as well as their assignment to the relevant company codes (table T001).
2. Check whether more than one posting period is open at the same time (table T001B) and whether the one month rule (or maximum two) has been complied with in the past (evaluate changes in table T001B with program RSTBHIST).

No Monthly Closing

Not all organizations perform monthly closing. In this case, it is sufficient if the posting periods for which financial statements have already been created are closed (e. g., quarterly closing; for smaller organizations, year-end closing). In this context, it is also important that financial statements that have already been published or audited can no longer be changed.

Figure 8.2 shows how you can check the changes made to the open posting periods in the past using standard program RSTBHIST.

 Authorization Object F_BKPF_BUP

You can also protect posting periods using authorizations – the relevant authorization object is F_BKPF_BUP. This optional authorization object enables you to define the open posting periods in which postings are allowed.

8.1.2 Financial Statements

Creating the financial statements
How do you create financial statements? When you enter a manual posting, you have to assign the individual items in a document to G/L accounts. *G/L accounts* are main account assignment characteristics in an SAP ERP system: when you enter a posting, it must contain at least two items, with one debit and one credit amount respectively. These amounts must balance to zero for each document (this "zero control" is built into the system, i. e., coded in the program logic, and cannot be changed without great effort).

Total of all accounting-relevant transactions
The total of all accounting-relevant transactions that make up the transaction data (see Sect. 5.1.1) in an SAP system must be presented at the end of the year, structured according to G/L accounts, as financial statements. The correct and complete assignment of the individual G/L accounts to the structure of these reports is an important prerequisite for the accuracy of the external financial reporting.

Figure 8.3 shows the example of a financial statement hierarchy maintained with transaction OB58 (Maintain Table T011/T011 T).

Check: financial statement version
You must check that the financial statements have the correct structure and that the accounts are assigned completely. Call up the financial statement version using transaction OB58 or in the IMG (transaction SPRO) via FINANCIAL ACCOUNTING • GENERAL LEDGER ACCOUNTING • BUSINESS TRANSACTIONS • CLOSING • DOCUMENT • DEFINE FINANCIAL STATEMENT VERSIONS.

- Expand the hierarchy within the relevant node. It is the duty of the auditor to assess the *accuracy of the assignment of the G/L accounts*.
- The unassigned G/L accounts are listed as such outside the financial statement hierarchy. They can indicate an incomplete financial statement version.

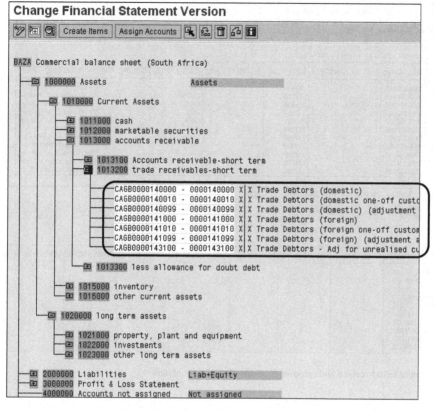

Figure 8.3 Financial statement version

There can be exceptions to the assignment of G/L accounts to the financial statement hierarchy: when mapping parallel accounting, for example, to implement country-specific (e. g., German GAAP) and internationally recognized (e. g., US GAAP or IFRS) accounting guidelines simultaneously based on the G/L account solution, it is usual to have "dummy" auxiliary accounts that are not required in the financial statements. However, such G/L account solutions have become superfluous with the advent of New General Ledger.

Parallel accounting

8.1.3 G/L Account Master Data

Where do you find G/L accounts? In SAP ERP, at database level they are in tables SKA1 (central G/L account data) and SKB1 (company code-specific data, see Sect. 5.1).

The individual fields in the G/L account master – Fig. 8.4 shows some examples – each have an important control function. Some of these functions have associated risks and must therefore be checked from an ICS perspective.

Checking the plausibility and accuracy of the G/L account master data is very important in a system audit.

Check: fields in G/L account master

Data Browser: Table SKA1 Select Entries   454

Check Table...

Table: SKA1
Displayed Fields: 8 of 8   Fixed Columns: 3   List Width 0250

Chart of Accts	G/L Account	Balance sheet acct	G/L account	P&L state. acct	Account Group	Deletion flag	Short Text
IKR	0000300000	X	300000		SAKO		Ordinary share capit
IKR	0000310000	X	310000		SAKO		Share premium accoun
IKR	0000321000	X	321000		SAKO		Capital redemption r
IKR	0000322000	X	322000		SAKO		Provisions for own s
IKR	0000323000	X	323000		SAKO		Reserves required by
IKR	0000324000	X	324000		SAKO		Other reserves
IKR	0000332000	X	332000		SAKO		Retained Earnings
IKR	0000333000		333000	X	SAKO		Withdrawal from capi
IKR	0000334000		334000	X	SAKO		Activated carried fo
IKR	0000334100		334100	X	SAKO		Deferred carried for
IKR	0000337000		337000	X	SAKO		Transfer of profits

Data Browser: Table SKB1 Select Entries   200

Check Table...

Table: SKB1
Displayed Fields: 11 of 11   Fixed Columns: 3   List Width 0250

Company Code	G/L Account	Authorization	E/R diff. key	Tax category	Interest indic.	Rel. cash flow	Auto. posting	Line items	OI manageme
1000	0000100128					X	X	X	
1000	0000100129					X	X	X	
1000	0000100130					X	X	X	
1000	0000100131					X	X	X	
1000	0000101000					X		X	
1000	0000102000					X		X	
1000	0000102009					X		X	X
1000	0000110000					X		X	
1000	0000110002					X		X	X
1000	0000110005					X		X	X

Figure 8.4   Control fields in central and company code-specific G/L account data

1. Use table T001 to find the relevant chart of accounts assigned to the organization or company code being audited. Table SKA1 contains important control information for each G/L account.
2. One of the control fields is the AUTOMATED POSTINGS ONLY field. If manual postings are not permitted to an account, this field must contain the value "X" in that account (for example, some accounts in Materials Management or sales accounts that may only be posted to in an invoicing run).
3. The assignment of correct field status groups is also important (see Sect. 8.2.2). Compare the assigned field status groups with the settings defined in the blueprint and check individual field status groups in samples.

Security tip: protecting G/L accounts

SAP enables you to protect important master data objects individually. Table SKB1 (G/L Account Master Record (Company Code)) contains the AUTHORIZATION GROUP field. In this field you can assign authorization groups to the individual accounts. These authorization groups can be used to restrict access in user roles to specific accounts.

8.1.4 Checking that Transaction Figures Are Consistent with the Accounting Reconciliation

During month-end closing, important activities from an ICS perspective are executed periodically in SAP-supported accounting. These are activities that check the consistency of the accounting-relevant transaction data.

Consistency check: two options

You can check consistency with the accounting reconciliation. There are two options:

- If you use New GL, you can use program TFC_COMPARE_VZ; it executes the evaluation for each *ledger* set up.
- If you do not use New GL, use program SAPF190 (Financial Accounting Comparative Analysis) for the reconciliation.

> **Activating New General Ledger**
>
> Use table FAGL_ACTIVEC to check whether New GL is activated. If it is, the value in the ACTIVE field should be "X."

The programs mentioned execute an enhanced reconciliation in Financial Accounting. They perform the following consistency checks:

Consistency checks

- Debit and credit transaction figures of the customer accounts, vendor accounts, and G/L accounts are consistent with the debit and credit totals of the documents posted.
- Debit and credit transaction figures of the customer accounts, vendor accounts, and G/L accounts are consistent with the debit and credit totals of the application indexes (the application indexes are used within the system for accounts with open item management or line item display).

The results of the reconciliation are stored, meaning that you can trace previous runs of these programs in the system.

In some circumstances, executing the reconciliation analysis can take several hours. Therefore, you should execute the data selection in the background (as a batch job). Differences in the application indexes are often caused by changes to the LINE ITEM DISPLAY setting of the G/L account. For more information, see SAP Note 31875.

SAP Note 31875

In practice, there is a common misconception that the accounting reconciliation checks whether the general ledger and subledger agree. This is not the case. To check this, you should perform additional (manual) checks as part of the ICS. For further information, see Sect. 8.1.6.

8.1.5 Selected Controls for Closing Operations

In addition to executing the accounting reconciliation, as part of closing operations, it is highly advisable to execute a series of programs that list changes to important master data in FI-GL. Table 8.1 shows the most important programs.

Programs with changes

◘ **Table 8.1** Overview of the control programs to be executed in General Ledger Accounting in closing operations

Description	Program	Comment
Accounting reconciliation/comparison of documents/transaction figures	SAPF190 TFC_COMPARE_VZ	Discuss error messages with Basis
Changes to G/L account master data	RFSABL00	Also check "templates" for other accounts
Changes to accounting documents	RFBABL00	Particular caution with recurring entries
Evaluation of canceled posting records	RFVBER00	Store documents
Evaluation of parked documents	RFPUEB00	Post or reverse
Evaluation of held documents	RFTMPBEL	Post or reverse
Control for recurring entry original documents	RFDAUB00	Beginning, end, and plausibility
Control for changes to vendor master data	RFKABL00	Check the plausibility of the changes and the person entering them
Control for changes to customer master data	RFDABL00	Check the plausibility of the changes and the person entering them
Control for changes to bank master data	RFBKABL0	Check the plausibility of the changes and the person entering them
Control for changes to accounting documents	RFBABL00	Check the plausibility of the changes and the person entering them
Evaluation of FI postings	RFBELJ00	Check the plausibility of the person entering the postings
Credit management change display	RFDKLIAB	Check changes to the limits and blocks

Depending on the compliance environment, it may be necessary to store or archive (e. g., in the form of spool lists) the results of the programs in Table 8.1 as evidence of the control procedures executed.

8.1.6 Reconciliation Work in FI-GL

As part of month-end and year-end closing, you perform other reconciliation work with the main objective of checking that the financial statement items are accurate.

Balance Confirmations

This important audit procedure is performed both by organizations (where applicable, in coordination with auditors) or under the supervision of auditors. Its primary aim is to address the risks of the overvaluation of receivables and sales revenue as well as the undervaluation of payables.

> **Collaboration Between Organizations and Auditors**   **[e.g.]**
>
> For example, the organization prints and sends balance confirmation letters to vendors and customers, who then send their answers to the auditing company.

You can generate confirmation letters with SAP transactions F.17 (for customers) and F.18 (for vendors).

Comparing FI-GL and Subledgers

Further control procedures relate to the reconciliation of figures, for example, from Asset Accounting, Accounts Payable Accounting, and Accounts Receivable Accounting with General Ledger Accounting. In our opinion, here there are few if any risks on the system side in SAP ERP 6.0: the degree of integration of the individual FI components ensures the uniformity of the posting data. For example, in Asset Accounting, the depreciation results are no longer passed on using the batch input method; they are posted to FI-GL directly. Furthermore, you can only enter customer and vendor operations in SAP if you have defined reconciliation accounts in customer and vendor master data – meaning that postings are made to FI-GL automatically.

Low risk – but still useful

Nevertheless, the following reconciliation work can be helpful:

Helpful reconciliation work

- Reconciliation of the total of the documents with account balances: comparison of the results of program RFSSLD00 (G/L Account Balances) with the results of program RFHABU00 (General Ledger from the Document File).
- Reconciliation of the results of program RFKKBU00 (Open Item Account Balance Audit Trail from Document File) with program RFKSLD00 (Vendor Balances in Local Currency) and RFDSLD00 (Customer Balances in Local Currency).

The reconciliation of FI-GL or the entry of figures that arise outside the FI component is more complicated: for example, figures from the material valuation in MM or the WIP calculation (WIP = work in progress) in product cost accounting or in order accounting in PS. We will address further reconciliation work with figures from outside FI in Chaps. 9 and 10.

8.2   Controls over the Accuracy and Quality of Data in General Ledger Accounting

Posting transactions in the SAP system

In Sect. 5.2, you learned basic information about posting documents and transaction data in an SAP system. This will help you to understand the information in the following section. To generalize, we can assign posting transactions in an SAP system to one of two groups:

▬ *Non-routine transactions*
   In SAP, an accountant generally enters these based on his own judgment or expert opinion (for example, financial statement items for provisions)
▬ *Routine transactions*
   These are generated en masse in the SAP system, to a large extent automatically.

Both groups contain risks that endanger the accuracy and completeness of posting data in SAP. In auditing, risks of non-routine transactions are addressed by substantive audit procedures (i. e., individual check of transactions). With the second group – routine transactions – the focus is on application controls (these are primarily evaluated as part of a system audit). These application controls can prevent inaccuracies accumulating, for example, due to poor data quality as a result of mass data processing. You can counteract these risks with controls that we will look at below (see Sects. 8.2.2 and 8.2.4).

8.2.1 Accurate Account Determination

Automatic assignment of G/L accounts

Manual document entry, in which the accountant assigns *all* G/L accounts based on his own judgment, represents only a fraction of the transaction data in an SAP ERP system. Most instances that belong, from an accounting view, to the subledgers, are posted to pre-defined accounts automatically in SAP ERP. From an ICS perspective, you have to check the completeness and accuracy of the maintenance of the *account determination* for relevant transactions. In coordination with contact persons, you can select relevant operations subject to risk and check them. Checking the accuracy of the account determination requires a good basic understanding of accounting and knowledge of the relevant chart of accounts.

Transaction FBKP (Maintain Accounting Configuration) offers a good option for checking the account determination (see Fig. 8.5).

In this example, you can see where the automatic postings section in transaction FBKP is located (click AUTOMATIC POSTINGS ❶) and how to get an overview of the individual account determination groups. Double-click one of the GROUPS ❷ to see the individual transactions within this group. Double-click a TRANSACTION ❸ to navigate to the overview of the accounts defined.

Check: posting logic and account determination

For selected transactions in the automatic account determination, use transaction FBKP to check the accuracy and completeness of the G/L accounts defined.

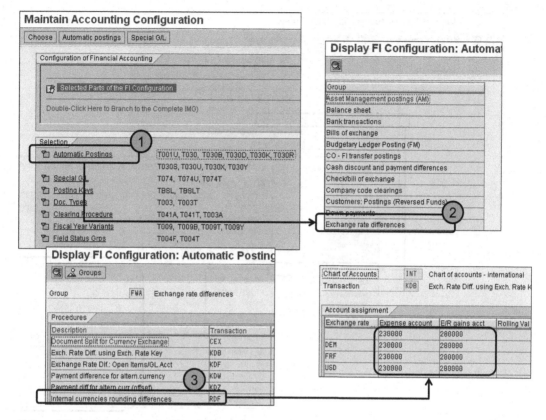

Figure 8.5   Checking the account determination with transaction FBKP

8.2.2 Field Status Groups

In SAP, to maintain master data or enter postings, you have to enter certain information. With default configuration settings, the scope of information required is not always sufficient to guarantee complete and/or correct processing, particularly if considerable changes have been made to standard processes as part of the SAP implementation. To guarantee the required quality and completeness of the data, SAP enables you to set up transaction-specific and data-specific *field status groups*.

In Fig. 8.6, you can see, for example, that a separate field status group G004 has been set up to record postings in which expense accounts (cost accounts) are used. This field status group ensures that when a posting is entered, the cost center must also be entered as additional account assignment (required entry). This is essential for the transaction to also be taken into account in Controlling or Management Accounting (for example, in cost center accounting). Field status groups that you see in Fig. 8.6 are assigned to the G/L accounts in the master data of these accounts. The system uses them if a corresponding G/L account is selected during document entry.

As part of an SAP system audit, you should analyze and check the definition of field status groups.

Force required entry on the system side

Check: field status groups

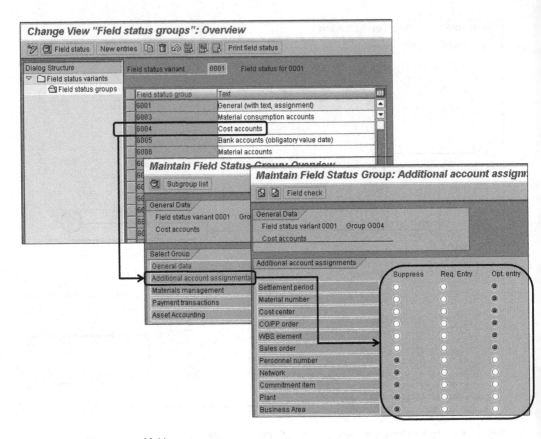

◻ Figure 8.6   Maintenance of field status groups

1. Using transaction OBC4 (Maintain Table T004 V), check whether, for the field status groups set up for the relevant transactions, data is defined as required entry
   fields.
2. Furthermore, SAP offers consistency check programs that can check the quality of
   the data controlled by field status groups in cross-module transactions. For example,
   you can use program RM07CUFA (Field Selection Comparison: Movement Type –
   G/L Account) to check the consistency of the field status groups for accounts from
   MM and FI views.

8.2.3   Calculating Taxes for Manual Postings

Programs   From an ICS perspective, the correct valuation and reporting of tax liabilities due to the
state or tax authorities is very important. In SAP ERP, you can rely on the accuracy of the
ADVANCE RETURN FOR TAX ON SALES/PURCHASES program (RFUMSV00). It presents
the cumulative tax amounts at the end of a period.

These cumulative amounts comprise individual documents that are created when
you enter various transactions. The most important transactions are:

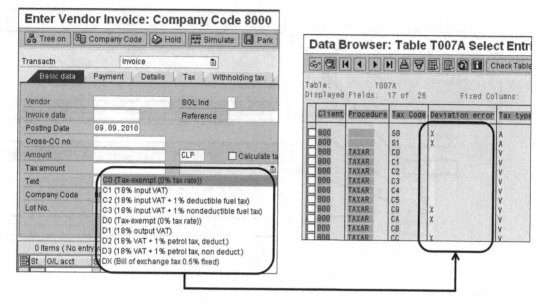

□ Figure 8.7   Controlling the error message for an alternative tax amount

— *Invoice Receipt*
  Here, the tax is generally determined by the manual entry of the input tax code.
— *Invoicing*
  The sales tax determination is defined separately in connection with invoicing. It defines which tax rate is applied for the output tax.

Program RFUMSV00 takes data about the individual transactions from table BSET (Tax Data Document Segment). Program RFUMSV10 (Additional List for Advance Return for Tax on Sales/Purchases) also takes data that is updated by individual postings from the SAP tables with G/L account line items.

In SAP ERP, for transactions relevant for tax (output tax and sales tax), the system calculates the tax amount automatically when you enter individual postings manually (i. e., the invoicing transaction is not relevant here). However, in some circumstances you can change it manually: the decisive factor is how the tax code selected is configured.

As you can see in Fig. 8.7, for each tax code, you decide whether the system should issue an error message if the tax amount is not correct. The system performs the check as follows:
SAP check for the accuracy of the tax amount

For each tax code, the system calculates the correct tax using the base amount and the percentage rate. If there is a deviation of more than one currency unit (for example, cent), the system issues an error message for each relevant line item. If, in the tax code, there is no entry in the DEVIATION ERROR field, a warning message appears instead of the error message and you can continue entering the posting.

Using table T007 A or transaction FTXP (Maintain Tax Code), you can evaluate tax codes to determine whether settings in the DEVIATION ERROR field are appropriate:
Check: settings for tax calculation

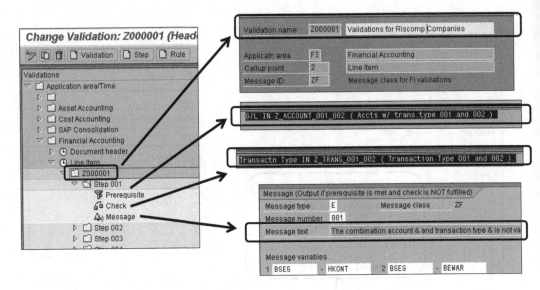

Figure 8.8 Example for setting up a validation

"empty" entries mean that you are allowed to manually enter an amount different to the amount calculated by the system.

8.2.4 Validations in SAP

Customer-specific logical rules

For various transactions, with SAP, in addition to the existing standard consistency checks, you can set up customer-specific logical rules that check the accuracy, for example, of data entered manually. This option is called *validation*, and the corresponding functions allow you to set up validation and substitution rules that can strengthen the controls in financial accounting.

In practice, you set up rules as follows, for example:

- To exclude an invalid combination of G/L accounts
- To prevent the use of invalid business areas
- To favor useful entries in comment fields (e. g., through minimum length)
- To correct automatic entries for specific information (substitution)
- To restrict the maximum amount for a posting (alternatively, you can set up tolerance groups, see Sect. 8.4.2)

Validations

You can also use validations as an alternative to the SAP authorization roles to restrict the access to certain transactions on a user-specific basis. Figure 8.8 shows an example of a validation.

The validation in Fig. 8.8 is intended to ensure that certain G/L accounts are not permitted by the system when a posting is entered for transaction types 001 and 002. If the user tried to enter these G/L accounts, the system would issue an error message.

Check: validations and substitutions

When you set up validations, there are three possible levels for checking the rules: on entry of data in the document header, in line items, or when the document is saved.

There are two options for the output of a check: a warning message or an error message. A warning message is informative in nature and from an ICS view, does not represent an effective control.

1. Validations and substitutions are important from an ICS view. Get an overview of the purpose and content of the validation rules set up in an interview and through transaction GGB0 (Validation Maintenance).
2. With regard to substitutions, note that even "well intentioned" rules have associated risks: if no messages are set up, the user may not realize that the system automatically changes or replaces data he has entered.

8.2.5 Foreign Currencies

In SAP, you can enter business transactions in foreign currencies based on the exchange rates defined in the system. The system translates the amount into the local currency assigned to a company code. You can imagine the dramatic effects incorrectly maintained exchange rates can have: for example, if the decimal point is in the wrong place in the exchange rate, the amount in local currency would be ten times higher or lower and this error would multiply across several transactions. From an audit perspective, there are two important aspects with regard to foreign currencies: on one hand, maintenance of the currencies; on the other hand, the foreign currency differences.

High risk with incorrect translation

Maintaining Currencies

In SAP, you can maintain exchange rates manually in table TCURR, for example, as shown in Fig. 8.9, using transaction SM30 (Call View Maintenance) and using the maintenance view V_TCURR.

There are two principle exchange rates depending on which exchange rate entry is maintained for each currency pair selected (e. g., GBP/USD).

— *Direct quotation*
  The price in the "to" currency to be paid for one (ten, hundred, …) unit(s) of the "from" currency.
— *Indirect quotation*
  The quantity in the "from" currency that you receive for one (ten, hundred, …) unit(s) of the "to" currency.

Manual maintenance should be an exception: organizations usually import exchange rates on a daily basis as provided by, for example, the central banks of the respective country.

From an ICS view, the maintenance of exchange rates is associated with high risks and therefore deserves special attention.

Perform the following procedures:

Check: maintenance of exchange rates

1. Conduct interviews to establish the procedure for maintaining exchange rates. Check whether the import of the file with the currency exchange rates is sufficiently protected (for example, access to the directory where the file is stored).

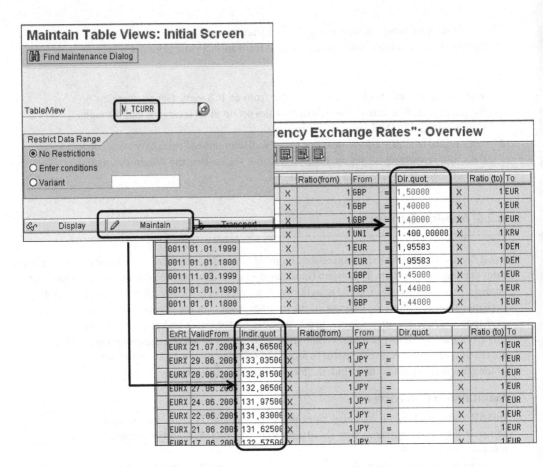

□ **Figure 8.9**   Direct maintenance of currency exchange rates

2. Check the scope of the assignment of authorizations for direct maintenance of the exchange rates (transaction SM30, maintenance dialog V_TCURR). This should be handled very strictly.

Date field: weak encryption   SAP has installed a built-in control in the logic for table TCURR: the date field has been encrypted to make direct table maintenance (e. g., in maintenance dialog or at database level) difficult. However, the control is weak: with targeted manipulation, you can easily get around the generally known encryption logic. If, for example, the date field contains the value 80009688, subtract 99999999 from this; the result will be the required date (80009688 – 99999999 = 19990311 = 1999.03.11).

Maximum Foreign Currency Differences

In addition to the maintenance of exchange rates, a further control is very important: in SAP, when you enter a document, you can correct the exchange rate manually. To restrict the scope of such corrections, SAP offers tolerances for foreign currency differences. There are two options:

- Tolerance limit per company code
- Tolerance limit per currency pair

If the deviation exceeds a defined tolerance limit (in percent), the system generates an error message.

To check that foreign currency differences are treated correctly, perform the following steps:

Check: tolerance limits

1. Use table T001 to check whether the maximum tolerance limit is set up for relevant company codes (cross-currency) and whether the amount is appropriate.
2. Use table TCURD to check whether maximum exchange rate deviations are defined for currency pairs (cross-company code or for all clients).

8.3 Completeness of Processing in General Ledger Accounting

In Chap. 7, you learned about risks that can compromise the principle of completeness across topics, thus also in financial accounting. In this section, we will look at specific risks that can endanger the completeness of processing in the FI module and controls that counteract these risks.

8.3.1 Document Parking

From an ICS perspective, document parking is a double-edged sword. On one hand, this function offers additional useful control mechanisms; on the other hand, it requires further control procedures for it to be used properly and with no risks.

Document parking: double-edged sword

It can be helpful to implement a principle of segregation of duties technically for document entry, specifically in the following case:
- The first person can enter documents but not post them, only "park" them.
- A second person checks that the parked documents are correct (amount, account assignment, additional information, etc.) and posts them where applicable.

You can control document parking technically by means of the amount. This means that, depending on the amount, for example, in local currency, the SAP system would start a workflow-based procedure to post a document. You have to configure this procedure in the Implementation Guide.

In SAP, you can set up a general, amount-based restriction of postings at user level – as an alternative to the segregation of duties principle described above – using tolerance groups (see Sect. 8.4.2).

The following audit procedures are recommended:

Check: use of document parking

1. In interviews, find out whether the organization uses document parking to implement the principle of segregation of duties in accounting.
2. If applicable, check the Implementation Guide under FINANCIAL ACCOUNTING • FINANCIAL ACCOUNTING GLOBAL SETTINGS • DOCUMENT • DOCUMENT PARKING to establish whether the desired control strategy has been implemented correctly.

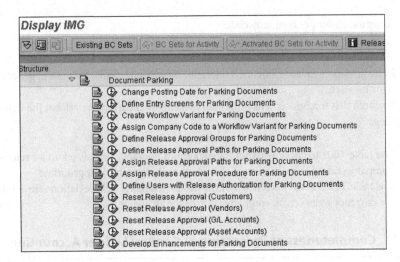

□ **Figure 8.10**   Configuration of workflow-based document parking

Note that where this procedure is used, release groups must be assigned in customer and vendor master data, for example.

Risk: "forgotten" postings

However, document parking can not only strengthen the control system but is also associated with risks. In practice, document parking is often used to enter documents for which you still require information (for example, the correct account for the expense posting).

A parked document is not a posted document. That is, the G/L account balances have not been updated and the corresponding business transaction has not been entered for accounting purposes. Therefore, where document parking is used, controls are necessary to ensure that at the end of the month, no parked documents are "forgotten."

You can use the tables listed in Table 8.2 to check for the presence of parked documents in SAP.

Check: presence of parked documents

To check the completeness of processing for parked documents, perform the following audit procedures:

1. In interviews, clarify whether control mechanisms that ensure complete consideration of parked documents in closing operations (e. g., month-end closing) are set up.
2. Use program RFPUEB00 (List of Parked Documents), RFTMPBEL (List of Documents Entered Which Are Incomplete), or the tables listed in Table 8.2 to check for the presence of parked documents.

A further traceability risk in connection with parked documents results from the fact that deleted parked documents leave gaps in the document number assignment (see Sect. 7.2.3). Therefore, the use of parked documents results in additional documentation requirements.

☐ Table 8.2 SAP tables with parked documents

Table	Documents
VBKPF	Document header for document parking
VBSEC	Document segment for one-time account data for document parking
VBSEGA	Document segment for document parking – database for assets
VBSEGD	Document segment for document parking, customers
VBSEGK	Document segment for document parking, vendors
VBSEGS	Document segment for document parking – database for G/L accounts
VBSET	Document segment for document parking, taxes

8.3.2 Recurring Entries

To enable you to map regularly recurring business transactions such as rent payments efficiently, SAP offers the *recurring entry* function. This works as follows: program SAPF120 (transaction F.14) calls up the recurring entry documents set up (these are not real documents but merely templates) at regular intervals (for example, by scheduling a job) to create "real" posting documents. This does not take place immediately but via generation of a batch input session. Documents are not posted in SAP until this session has been run. You can use recurring entry documents both periodically and according to a pre-defined plan.

Templates for regular postings

With the latter option, you have to configure the *run schedules* and define the *execution dates* behind each plan. You do this in the Implementation Guide under Financial Accounting • Financial Accounting Global Settings • Document • Recurring Entries.

You can get an overview of the recurring entry documents set up using program RFDAUB00 (transaction F.15, List Recurring Entries) (see Fig. 8.11).

The risks associated with the use of recurring entry documents are obvious: when postings are generated, the processor is generally excluded, which makes controlling the accuracy of postings more difficult. Therefore, control mechanisms should be set up, including a periodic review to ensure that recurring entries are up-to-date and to check the execution dates set up.

To get an overview of the control mechanisms for recurring entry documents, check the following:

Check: treatment of recurring entries

1. In interviews, find out whether recurring entry documents are used and whether there are regular evaluations to check that they and the execution dates are up-to-date (in the IMG: Financial Accounting • Financial Accounting Global Settings • Document • Recurring Entries).
2. Use program RFDAUB00 to check whether there are any recurring entry documents in the system.

```
┌──────────────────────────────────────────────────────────────────────────────────────────────────┐
│ Recurring Entry Documents                                                                          │
├──────────────────────────────────────────────────────────────────────────────────────────────────┤
│ [icons]                                                                                            │
│                                                                                                    │
│ Riscomp  Ltd.                              Recurring Entry Documents                        Time   │
│ Jännedorf                                                                                   RFDA   │
│                                                                                                    │
│ CoCd DocumentNo Type Pstng Date First run  Next run   Last run   Inter Dte Run  Number DID ATx Reference    Document Header Text │
│ Itm PK SG SI AccTy Account     Tx    LC Tax Amount      Amount in LC LCurr      Amount in FC Crcy  │
│                                                                                                    │
│ 0100 990000     SA  13.02.2003 31.01.2003 31.01.2003 30.11.2003    1   31        0  X  X  KER BUCHUNGEN │
│ 001 40      S      780100    V0                        6.666,67 CHF            6.666,67 CHF         │
│ 002 40      S      750000    V0                        5.000,00 CHF            5.000,00 CHF         │
│ 003 40      S      780000    V0                       41.666,67 CHF           41.666,67 CHF         │
│ 004 40      S      620500    V0                       17.916,67 CHF           17.916,67 CHF         │
│ 005 40      S      770500    V0                       12.500,00 CHF           12.500,00 CHF         │
│ 006 40      S      600040    V0                       33.166,67 CHF           33.166,67 CHF         │
│ 007 40      S      600040    V0                       10.750,00 CHF           10.750,00 CHF         │
│ 008 40      S      600040    V0                        6.083,33 CHF            6.083,33 CHF         │
│ 009 40      S      600040    V0                          708,33 CHF              708,33 CHF         │
│ 010 40      S      600040    V0                        8.583,33 CHF            8.583,33 CHF         │
│ 011 40      S      600040    V0                        7.500,00 CHF            7.500,00 CHF         │
│ 012 40      S      600040    V0                        3.833,33 CHF            3.833,33 CHF         │
│ 013 50      S      220800                            154.375,00- CHF          154.375,00- CHF      │
│                                                                                                    │
│ 0100 990001     SA  13.02.2003 31.01.2003 30.04.2003 30.11.2003    1   31        3  X     KER BUCHUNGEN │
│ 001 40      S      780100    V0                        6.666,67 CHF            6.666,67 CHF         │
│ 002 40      S      750000    V0                        5.000,00 CHF            5.000,00 CHF         │
│ 003 40      S      780000    V0                       41.666,67 CHF           41.666,67 CHF         │
│ 004 40      S      620500    V0                       17.916,67 CHF           17.916,67 CHF         │
│ 005 40      S      770500    V0                       12.500,00 CHF           12.500,00 CHF         │
│ 006 40      S      600041    V0                       33.166,67 CHF           33.166,67 CHF         │
│ 007 40      S      600041    V0                       10.750,00 CHF           10.750,00 CHF         │
└──────────────────────────────────────────────────────────────────────────────────────────────────┘
```

□ Figure 8.11 Evaluation of recurring entry documents with RFDAUB00

3. Check the treatment of batch input sessions generated when recurring entries are created (see Sect. 7.4.4).
4. Check whether authorizations for changing recurring entry documents are assigned appropriately.

8.3.3 Reconciliation Ledger

FI and CO – financial and management accounting

The SAP CO module (Controlling) maps value flows primarily required for internal purposes, namely as part of management accounting. The CO postings are either created at the same time as the FI postings (for example, for expense-relevant transactions there is usually an account assignment to one or more CO objects – cost center, order, etc.) or in internal CO transactions. The latter can also trigger postings in FI in some circumstances.

[e.g.]

CO-Internal Transactions Trigger Postings in FI

The costs of a centrally managed fleet of vehicles are distributed to the individual companies at the end of a period within the module CO-OM (Overhead Management). Since different companies can be assigned to different company codes in some circumstances, an additional (transfer) posting would be necessary in the FI module. Depending on whether or not New GL is used in the company concerned, two scenarios would be possible:

> ▬ **Additional steps without New GL**
> If New GL is not active, additional activities are required to reflect the CO transactions in the FI module. This is done using the reconciliation ledger. At the end of the month, all FI-relevant values collected in the reconciliation ledger are transferred to FI-GL using transaction KALC (Cost Flow Message).
> ▬ **With New GL**
> If New GL is used, reconciliation work is no longer necessary: provided the settings are correct, there is real-time integration between FI and CO and the transactions in CO do not have to be replicated in FI.

Let us stay with the first option and assume that New GL is not available. You can check the settings in the SAP Implementation Guide under FINANCIAL ACCOUNTING (NEW) • FINANCIAL ACCOUNTING GLOBAL SETTINGS • LEDGERS • REAL-TIME INTEGRATION OF CONTROLLING WITH FINANCIAL ACCOUNTING.

Check: configuration in the reconciliation ledger

Amongst other things, here you can check whether all relevant transactions for the automatic generation of FI postings are selected, whether the integration is activated, and whether the correct accounts are defined in the account determination, etc. You can also use the program that can check the completeness of the document transfer (TRANSFER CO DOCUMENTS INTO EXTERNAL ACCOUNTING). Alternatively, you can call up program FAGL_COFI_TRANSFER_CODOCS.

With regard to the transfer of values from CO to FI, the focus is on completeness.

Check: transfer values from CO to FI

1. Log review: In transaction KALC, you can use the menu path EXTRAS • LOG to display the processing results from the past. For the date fields, note that the relevant date relates to the period of the transfer of the CO values to FI (the reconciliation ledger run) and not the posting date of the FI documents.
2. Use transaction KALC or the option in the Implementation Guide, TRANSFER CO DOCUMENTS INTO EXTERNAL ACCOUNTING, to check that the values are transferred completely to FI. Do not forget to select the TEST RUN option.

8.4 Data Security and Protection in General Ledger Accounting

To protect financial data against undesired changes, user authorizations must be handled in accordance with the principle of least privilege. In addition to authorizations, further control mechanisms are available in the Implementation Guide: application controls (see Sect. 5.1.2). We will look at some of the important controls for protecting the data in Financial Accounting below.

8.4.1 Protecting Company Codes

As an independent accounting unit, the company code is one of the most important elements of the SAP organizational structures. Some important settings for financial accounting are made at company code level, for example, the assignment of the chart of accounts, the fiscal year variant, and the maximum exchange rate deviation (foreign

Company code: important element

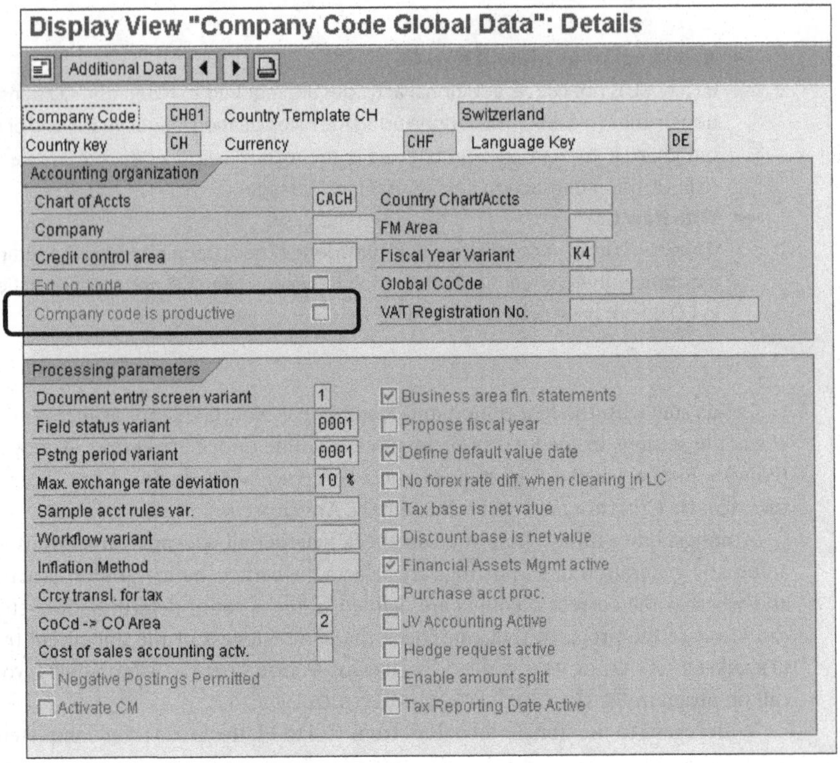

Figure 8.12   Global settings in the company code

currency rates, see Sect. 8.2.5). For an overview of the most important settings, see Fig. 8.12.

Productive indicator in the company code

You make these settings in the Implementation Guide under FINANCIAL ACCOUNT-ING • FINANCIAL ACCOUNTING GLOBAL SETTINGS • COMPANY CODES • GLOBAL PA-RAMETERS (alternatively via transaction SM30 and the maintenance dialog V_001_B). It is obvious that access to these functions – as well as generally to the configuration and direct table maintenance – must be handled restrictively. Note also one setting in particular in the company code: the *productive indicator* (see Fig. 8.12). This indicator is required above all to protect data relevant for accounting.

Productive indicator not set

During the SAP ERP implementation – for example, in the test phase – it may be necessary to delete data (master and transaction data) in Asset Accounting in a company code. You can use transaction OABL (Reset Company Code) to do this. It causes the following:

- All asset master records are deleted
- All asset transactions are deleted

To avoid such a surprise – in live operation particularly unpleasant – (sudden disappearance of data in Asset Accounting), the above-mentioned productive indicator must be set in the company code. Special attention must also be paid to the assignment

◻ Figure 8.13 Message when a company code is reset and for the check regarding whether the productive indicator has been set

of authorization object A_ADMI_ALL, which is checked when transaction OABL is called up.

Figure 8.13 shows the message that appears when you try to reset a company code. It also shows the PRODUCTIVE field, which controls whether such a reset is possible. You can trace the values of this field in the table directly. If the field has the value "X" for a company code, the company code is protected against deletion programs.

Perform the following steps to check the company code protection:

Check: company code protection

1. In table T001, check whether the productive indicator is set for the company codes used in live operation.
2. Check whether the assignment of authorizations for transaction OABL and authorization object A_ADMI_ALL is handled restrictively.

8.4.2 Tolerance Groups

User-specific tolerance groups
In Sect. 8.2.4, you learned how to set up complex rules that help you to establish additional controls for entering accounting documents. SAP also offers an easier option for setting up user-specific maximum amounts allowed: assigning *tolerance groups* to the individual users. These groups restrict the maximum amount in a document. For example, if a user with a tolerance group set to USD 10,000 tries to enter a credit amount of USD 10,001 in the "Marketing Costs" account, the system issues an error message. There are other limits that you can set. You can determine the following in the Implementation Guide (FINANCIAL ACCOUNTING (NEW) • FINANCIAL ACCOUNTING GLOBAL SETTINGS • DOCUMENT • TOLERANCE GROUPS • DEFINE TOLERANCE GROUPS FOR EMPLOYEES):

- The maximum amount for which an employee may post a document
- The maximum amount for which an employee may enter a line item in a customer or vendor account
- The amount of cash discount (in percent) an employee may grant in a line item
- The maximum amount for which payment differences may be accepted

Maximum amounts for payment differences are also defined in these tolerance groups.

Business partner-specific tolerances
In addition to user-specific tolerance groups, there are also tolerance groups for business partners, customers, and vendors. You define these in the Implementation Guide under ACCOUNTS RECEIVABLE AND ACCOUNTS PAYABLE • BUSINESS TRANSACTIONS • INCOMING PAYMENTS • MANUAL INCOMING PAYMENTS • CLEARING DIFFERENCES • DEFINE TOLERANCES FOR CUSTOMERS/VENDORS. The purpose of these tolerances is primarily to restrict the "leeway" in dealing with payment differences and residual items that can arise in payment clearing.

Figure 8.14 shows an example of how to define and assign ❶ a tolerance group for users. Under ❷, you can also see the contents of a business partner-specific tolerance group.

Check: user and business partner tolerance groups
Perform the following steps to get an overview of the treatment of tolerance groups:

1. In the Implementation Guide (as described above) or in table T043T, check whether tolerance groups are defined appropriately (the AMOUNT PER DOCUMENT limit ❶ in the example in Fig. 8.14 should raise some questions). Then check whether these groups are used – use table T043, where tolerance groups are assigned to individual users.

2. In the Implementation Guide or in table T043GT, check whether the tolerance limits for business partners are appropriate. In tables LFB1 (for vendors) and KNB1 (for customers), check whether and for which business partners these tolerances are used.

8.4.3 Protecting Master Data

The master data in Financial Accounting covers objects such as G/L accounts, assets, banks, vendors, and customers. The meaning of the master data was explained generally

Display View "FI Tolerance Groups For Users"

Group	0001
Company code	0001	SAP A.G.		Walldorf
Currency	EUR

Upper limits for posting procedures

Amount per document	1.000.000.000.000,00
Amount per open item account item	1.000.000.000,00
Cash discount per line item	5,000 %

Permitted payment differences

	Amount	Percent	Cash discnt adj.to
Revenue	100,00	10,0 %	10,00
Expense	100,00	10,0 %	10,00

Change View "Customer/Vendor Tolerances": Details

New Entries

Company Code	0001	SAP A.G.	Walldorf
Currency	EUR
Tolerance group	DEB3	Example

Specifications for Clearing Transactions

| Grace days due date | 3 | Cash Discount Terms Displayed |
| Arrears Base Date | |

Permitted Payment Differences

	Amount	Percent	Adjust Discount By
Gain	200,00	5,0 %	3,00
Loss	100,00	1,0 %	3,00

Permitted Payment Differences for Automatic Write-Off (Function Code AD)

	Amount	Percent
Rev.		%
Expense		%

Specifications for Posting Residual Items from Payment Differences

☐ Payment Term from Invoice Fixed payment term
☐ Only grant partial cash disc
Dunning key

Tolerances for Payment Advices

	Amount	Percent
Outst.receiv.from		%
Outst.payable from		%

Change View "Assign Users-->Tolerance Groups

New Entries

User name	Tolerance group	
SMITH	0001	

① ②

☐ **Figure 8.14** Examples for tolerance groups for users and business partners

in Sect. 5.1.1; the special feature of the master data in FI is its direct involvement in postings that make up the entirety of external financial reporting.

| Master Data for a Posting | | **[e.g.]** |

For manual invoice entry with transaction FB60 (Enter Incoming Invoices), the following master data is required: a *vendor* and an *expense account* (whereby for a vendor, a further G/L account – the *reconciliation account* – is defined).

Figure 8.15 shows the most important FI master data tables in SAP and how they are connected.

You generally establish controls over the quality of the master data on the system side by setting up field status groups (see Sect. 8.2.2). However, the actions of setting up and changing this data must be sufficiently protected by authorizations.

Permissions for executing master data maintenance transactions must, from an *organizational perspective*, only be assigned to qualified persons from specialist areas in accordance with the principle of least privilege. From a *technical* perspective, roles must

Master data maintenance transactions

Table Name	Short text
ANLA	Asset Master Record Segment
ANLB	Depreciation terms

| SKA1 | Table | G/L Account Master Record (Chart of Accounts) |
| ▽ SKB1 | Table | G/L Account Master Record (Company Code) |

LFA1	Table	Vendor Master (General Section)
LFBK	Table	Vendor Master (Bank Details)
▽ LFB1	Table	Vendor Master (Company Code)
LFB5	Table	Vendor Master (Dunning Data)
LFC1	Table	Vendor Master (Transaction Figures)
LFC3	Table	Vendor Master (Transaction Figures) Special Ledger

KNA1	Table	General Data in Customer Master
KNBK	Table	Customer Master (Bank Details)
▽ KNB1	Table	Customer Master (Company Code)
KNB4	Table	Customer Payment History
KNB5	Table	Customer Master (Dunning Data)
KNKK	Table	Credit Management Cust. Mstr. Control Area Data
KNC1	Table	Customer Master (Transaction Figures)
KNC3	Table	Customer Master (Special G/L Transaction Figures)

| BNKA | Table | Bank Master Record |

◻ Figure 8.15 Overview of the most important data tables in Financial Accounting

be set up. Using authorization objects and their values (see Sect. 5.2.2), these roles provide sufficient protection for the access to master data.

Table 8.3 summarizes the most important master data-related authorization objects.

In Table 8.3, the special feature of customer and vendor master data is clear: it has both an *FI view* and *Sales and Distribution-relevant* or *Purchasing-relevant* view.

Authorization groups

Beyond the values that are built in as standard in the SAP logic for the authorization check for objects that are always present (e. g., organizational units), you can summarize master data in specific groups that can be protected individually. To achieve this additional flexibility in the design of the authorizations, you set up *authorization groups* of master data.

No authorization groups for master data are included in the scope of the SAP delivery. It is generally up to the SAP customers to use them. In Fig. 8.16 you can see, for example, that there is an additional AUTHORIZATION column in the master data of G/L accounts and customers: here ❶ you can assign new groups as required and use them in the maintenance of the authorization role authorization objects ❷.

❗   Check: Master Data Protection in FI

For the transactions and authorization objects shown in Fig. 8.16, use an evaluation (e. g., in program RSUSR002 – see Sect. 5.2.7) to get an overview of the extent to which authorizations are handled according to the principle of least privilege.

■ **Table 8.3** Overview of authorization objects for protecting FI master data

Transactions	Object	Aim of Authorization Object
FI01, FI02, FI06 Create and maintain bank master data	F_BNKA_BUK	Restriction for house banks and bank accounts – company code level
	F_BNKA_MAN	General maintenance authorization for bank master data
FD01, FD02, FD06 – Accounting VD01, VD02, VD06 – Sales and Distribution Create and maintain customers	F_KNA1_APP	Restriction to Financial Accounting or Sales and Distribution
	F_KNA1_BED	Restriction to individual customers via specific groups
	F_KNA1_BUK	Restriction to company code level
	F_KNA1_GRP	Restriction to customer account groups
	F_KNA1_KGD	Restriction of general modifiability for account groups
FD32, F.34 Maintain customer credit limit	F_KNKA_KKB	Restriction for control area-related data
	F_KNKK_BED	Restriction to customer account numbers
FK01, FK02, FK06 – Accounting MK01, MK02, MK06 – Purchasing, create and maintain vendors	F_LFA1_APP	Restriction to Financial Accounting or Purchasing
	F_LFA1_BEK	Restriction of vendors via authorization groups
	F_LFA1_BUK	Restriction to company code level
	F_LFA1_GRP	Restriction to account groups
FS00, FSP0, FSS0, Create and maintain G/L account groups	F_SKA1_AEN	Restriction to specific fields
	F_SKA1_BES	Restriction to individual accounts via authorization groups
	F_SKA1_BUK	Restriction to company code level
	F_SKA1_KTP	Restriction for charts of accounts
AS01, AS02, AS06, AS21, AS22, AS26 Create and maintain assets	A_S_ANLGR	Restriction to company code level
	A_S_ANLKL	Restriction to level of asset classes and company codes
	A_S_KOSTL	Restriction to level of cost centers and company codes
	A_S_WERK	Restriction to level of plants and company codes

8.4.4 Critical Transactions

In SAP-supported financial accounting, there are transactions that require special protection due to the associated high risks. In particular, this affects transactions that change, delete, or reverse important data in FI en masse – but also the transactions you know for changing posting periods or resetting company codes.

Mass maintenance and deletion actions

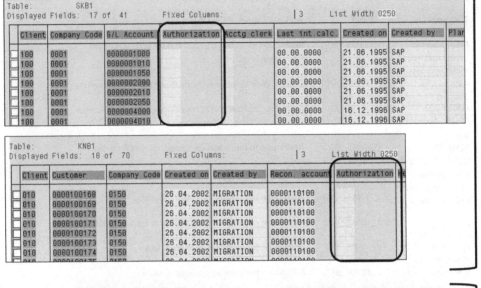

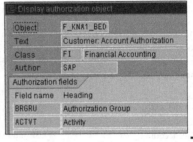

☐ **Figure 8.16**   Use of authorization groups for individual protection of master data

Check: critical   Check whether the transactions from the list below are handled appropriately,
authorizations in FI whether they are sorted into roles that are handled restrictively, and whether these
roles are assigned to a restricted person subgroup.

- Transactions F.80, FP22 – mass reversal of documents
- Transactions XK99, XD99 – mass maintenance of customers and vendors
- Transaction FPVC – mass reversal of dunning notices
- Transaction F.34 – mass maintenance of credit limit data
- Transactions OB_GLACC11, OB_GLACC12, and OB_GLACC13 – mass mainte-
  nance of G/L accounts
- Transaction MASS – central transaction for numerous mass changes. This transac-
  tion must be specially protected with the object B_MASSMAIN.
- Transaction OABL – reset company code
- Transaction S_ALR_87003642 – maintenance of posting periods

▢ Table 8.4 Segregation of duties requirements in financial accounting

Authorizations for the following activities ...	... should not be combined with authorizations for the following activities:
Maintenance of posting periods	All postings that lead to the G/L accounts being updated
Maintenance of substitution and validation rules	
Maintenance of exchange rates for foreign currencies	
Bank or cash reconciliation	
Maintenance of all FI master data	
Entering incoming invoices in the general ledger (e. g., via FB60)	Maintenance of the FI view of vendor master data
Entering invoices or credit memos in the general ledger	Maintenance of the FI view of customer master data
Maintenance of depreciation areas	Postings in asset accounting
Maintenance of asset master data and capitalization	

8.4.5 Segregation of Duties in General Ledger Accounting

The principle of segregation of duties must always be observed when the activities combined in one person would bear the risk of fraudulent activities or show an increased potential for error. Where possible, these activities should not be executed by the same person. However, experience shows that it is very difficult to implement segregation of duties requirements in financial accounting by means of authorizations – usually due to the organizational circumstances: the efficient ERP-supported processes often do not allow additional persons to be employed simply for propriety. Nevertheless, you should avoid a combination of the authorizations in Table 8.4 in one person.

Risk of fraudulent activities

How do you handle these requirements? Due to the organizational conditions already mentioned, in audit practice, the focus often shifts from compliance with the requirements for segregation of duties to checking that the *compensating controls* work properly. In Sect. 8.1.5, we saw some examples of controls that regularly check the legitimacy of master data changes.

Compensating controls

Check whether the SAP roles have been defined in compliance with the segregation of duties requirements listed in Table 8.4.

Check: segregation of duties in FI-GL

If the technical prerequisites for segregation of duties at role level are given, check whether this is also the case for the users and whether the authorization combinations subject to risk have been assigned to users.

If the segregation of duties requirements cannot be implemented organizationally, check whether there are documented compensating controls and whether these are executed.

> **Orientation**
>
> The topic "segregation of duties for payment transactions" belongs in this section from a content perspective, but due to its special features will be handled separately in Sect. 8.6.2.

8.5 Controls in Asset Accounting (FI-AA)

Asset accounting is that part of financial accounting where you enter and manage long-lasting assets in the fixed assets of an organization. The task of asset accounting is to evaluate and post acquisitions and disposals of assets and determine and post the depreciation values. In SAP, asset accounting is usually referred to as FI-AA.

Sections 8.1.1, 8.1.6, 8.2.2, and 8.4.3 have already mentioned control mechanisms that are also relevant in asset accounting. Below we will describe some selected FI-AA-specific control mechanisms and how to check them.

8.5.1 Basics of Asset Accounting in SAP

Creation of an asset
The capitalization of tangible fixed assets and the determination of depreciation for these assets are the core functions in FI-AA. An asset can arise in various ways:

- Purchase of an asset: this involves an external supplier (purchase).
- Own manufacture of an asset: the values for assets produced in-house can come from materials management, production, or plant maintenance if other SAP modules are used (production, capital investment measure).

The wear on tangible (fixed) assets (table ANLP) is taken into account in regular (usually monthly) depreciation on a value basis.

Main elements of depreciation
The main elements in SAP-supported asset accounting are master data (assets) and various basic data from the configuration.

- **Asset**
  The individual fixed assets are the central master data in FI-AA. You can use program RAAEND01 (Changes to Asset Master Records) to analyze changes to this master data; to analyze values in the fixed assets, you can use transaction AW01N (Asset Explorer) or the asset history sheet program RAGITT01.
- **Asset class (table ANKA)**
  The individual assets are structured by groups that, on one hand, contain separate rules for depreciation, account determination, etc., and on the other hand, are used for reporting.
- **Depreciation area (table T093)**
  The fixed assets can be evaluated on a value basis according to different principles. These principles generally reflect country-specific (valuation and financial

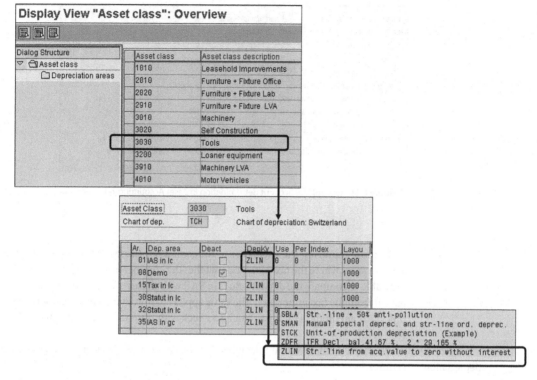

◻ Figure 8.17   Overview of default values for asset classes

statement rules), tax, and other (arithmetical) special features. In FI-GL (and therefore in the financial statements), the values of only one depreciation area can be forwarded immediately or online. The values for the other depreciation areas are forwarded to FI-GL via batch input during the monthly posting of the values.
- **Chart of depreciation (tables T096, T093C)**
The chart of depreciation is a superior FI-AA element that summarizes country-specific depreciation areas. A chart of depreciation must be assigned to a company code during configuration.

8.5.2 Default Values for Asset Classes

You control the asset-relevant flows in Financial Accounting using asset classes. Here you define important parameters, particularly those that control the depreciation logic. You can determine many of the parameters manually when you create a new asset, but you often adopt *default values* defined in asset classes. Therefore, it is important to check that these default values are correct – particularly for the *depreciation key* and useful life.

Figure 8.17 shows how you can use transaction OAYZ (Asset Class: Depreciation Areas) to check the default values defined. By double-clicking one of the asset classes you can display the default values.

Controlling value flows for depreciation in FI-AA

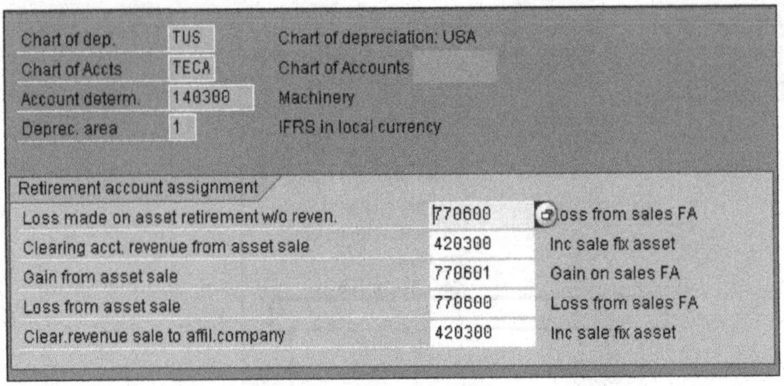

□ **Figure 8.18** Example for account determination in Asset Accounting-retirement

In most countries, the useful life of different asset classes is pre-defined from a tax view. In cases where the tax valuation matches the commercial valuation, it makes sense to be able to compare the default values in SAP with these regulations (e. g., depreciation tables) from the tax authorities. The same applies to the default values for permitted depreciation methods, which you can also check with transaction OAYZ (DEPRECIATION KEY field).

Check: depreciation-relevant parameters in asset classes

To check the ICS-relevant default values of asset classes, perform the following procedures:

1. Use transaction OAYZ to check the default values for the useful life and the depreciation key for relevant asset classes.
2. Check whether the actual values maintained in the USEFUL LIFE field deviate from the legally prescribed values in individual asset classes. To do this use tables ANLA (information about assets and asset classes) and ANLB (information about assets and their useful lives).

8.5.3 Account Determination in Asset Accounting

Reflection of values from AA

In SAP General Ledger Accounting, the values from Asset Accounting are generally reflected automatically by means of account determination. Whether the FI-AA transactions are displayed correctly in FI-GL depends on the correct assignment of the G/L accounts and the consistency of the field values in these G/L accounts. Table 8.5 shows the list of transactions that you can use to check that the G/L accounts defined in the account determination are correct.

You can also find these transactions in the menu tree of the Implementation Guide. Figure 8.18 shows an example of how to define G/L accounts as part of a sample chart of accounts for USA in the depreciation area IFRS for various retirement transactions.

Check: account determination in FI-AA

To check the account determination in FI-AA, perform the following steps:

1. Use the transactions listed in Table 8.5 to check that the account determination for the relevant transactions in FI-AA is correct and complete.

2. In addition to checking that the account determination is correct manually, you can execute an automated consistency check of the settings relevant for account determination and the field values in the G/L account master (see Sect. 8.5.4).

8.5.4 Consistency Check for Account Determination and Configuration

The SAP Implementation Guide (transaction SPRO) offers a function for FI-AA that, in addition to providing a general overview of the relevant settings, determines inconsistencies automatically. The consistency check function is available under FINANCIAL ACCOUNTING (NEW) • ASSET ACCOUNTING • PRODUCTION PREPARATION • CHECK CONSISTENCY.

Consistency check for the configuration

As you can see in Fig. 8.19, in addition to checking the FI-AA-relevant fields in the G/L account master, here you can also check the consistency of other configuration settings in FI-AA. When you call up the options highlighted, the system executes programs RACKONT1 (FI-AA: Customizing Consistency Check for G/L Accounts) and RACHECK0 (Consistency Check Report FI-AA Customizing). The following consistency check transactions are available:

- OAK1 – Consistency: Chart of Depreciation
- OAK2 – Consistency: Company Code
- OAK3 – Consistency: Depreciation Area
- OAK4 – Consistency: G/L Accounts
- OAK5 – Customizing Reconciliation Account Control
- OAK6 – Consistency: G/L Accounts

In addition to this automatic evaluation that relates to the configuration and the G/L account master, use program RAABST01 to detect reconciliation problems between the value update in FI-AA and the account update in FI-GL (related to a specific account). In particular, this program is helpful when differences arise between the balance list in FI-GL and the values reported in the asset history sheet.

Reconciliation of the values with FI-GL

The following audit procedures are recommended:

Check: consistency check in FI-AA

1. Execute transactions OAK1 to OAK6 to check the consistency of the configuration and the field values in the G/L account master for FI-AA.
2. Use program RAABST01 to check whether there are any differences between FI-GL and FI-AA.

8.5.5 Depreciation

To map special features of local financial statement requirements, SAP offers some country-specific pre-configured scenarios, including some for asset accounting. However, these *localized* SAP scenarios are not always available at the same time as a new release and do not always cover all countries.

Country-specific scenarios

Table 8.5   Overview of the account determination transactions for Asset Accounting

Transaction	Short Description
AO86	Account Assignment Retirements
AO87	Account Assignment Revaluation on APC
AO88	Account Assignment for Investment Support
AO89	Account Assignment Not to Current Account Assignment Share
AO90	Account Assignment Acquisitions
AO93	Ordinary Depreciation Account Assignment
AO94	Special Depreciation Account Assignment
AO95	Account Assignment Unplanned Depreciation
AO96	Account Assignment Transfer of Reserves
AO97	Account Assignment Revaluation of Depreciation
AO98	Account Assignment Interest
AO99	Account Assignment Derived Depreciation Areas

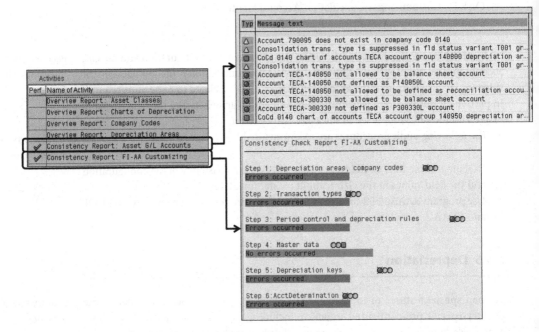

Figure 8.19   Consistency checks for configuration and the account determination-relevant G/L account master in Asset Accounting

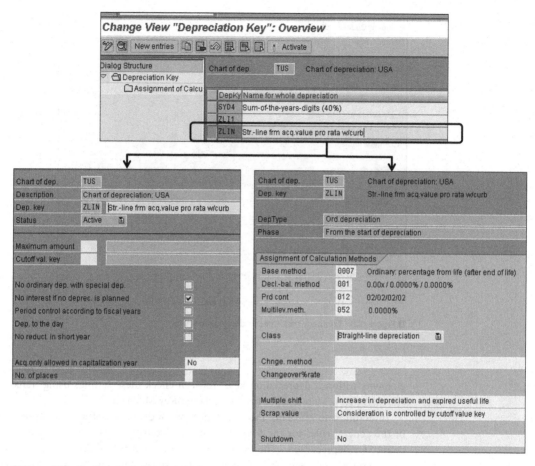

■ **Figure 8.20** Configuration of depreciation keys

In 2007, the author of this book was faced with the challenge of implementing the valid legal requirements in Latvia in Asset Accounting (FI-AA) for an organization. The rules to be observed were heavily based on local tax law and required, for example, that the foundation of a building be depreciated differently to the roof of the same building. Furthermore, the residual value had to be taken into account across all valuation areas in the calculation of the depreciation amounts.

In other words: the basic elements of FI-AA (see Sect. 8.5.1) had to be set up again completely from scratch, including the depreciation keys.

To understand the calculation logic of custom-defined depreciation keys, an auditor must put his love of details and his affinity with mathematics to the test again. Figure 8.20 shows an example of how to define individual calculation methods in the   Depreciation keys are not easy

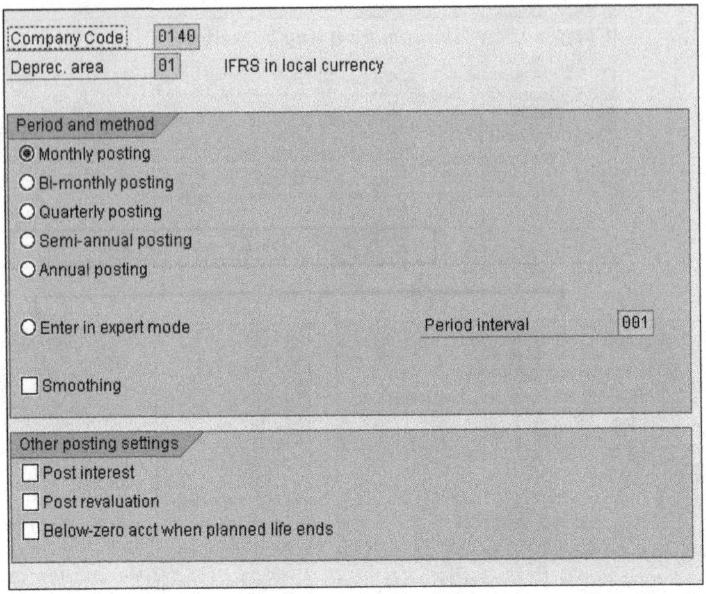

□ **Figure 8.21** Company code-specific depreciation rules

elements within a depreciation key. You can check these settings using transaction AFAMA (View Maintenance for Depreciation Key Method).

In addition to checking the calculation methods, it is useful to get an overview of the general rules for the frequency of the automatic entries to reconciliation accounts for depreciation. The frequency of the forwarding of depreciation values to FI-GL and other settings are defined for each company code and depreciation area (see Fig. 8.21).

You can generate this overview with transaction OAYR (Posting Rules for Depreciation).

Check: depreciation rules
For depreciation, perform the following selected audit procedures:

1. Check that the calculation rules in the depreciation keys are correct – in particular the custom-defined depreciation keys, which begin with Z or Y. Use transaction AFAMA to do this. Alternatively, you can use the following tables:
   - T090NA (Depreciation Keys)
   - T090NAT (Names of Depreciation Keys)
   - T090NAZ (Depreciation Keys – Method Assignment)

2. Use transaction OAYR to check the general company code-specific rules for transferring the depreciation values to FI-GL. The critical rules would include, for example, the non-admissibility of posting below zero depreciation; this is not allowed according to the German Commercial Code and IFRS or in most countries according to tax law.

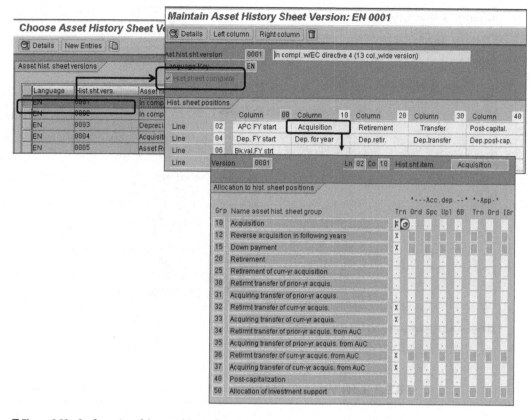

■ Figure 8.22 Configuration of the asset history sheet

8.5.6 Asset History Sheet

One of the most important sources of information in SAP-supported asset accounting is the *asset history sheet*. In SAP, this is defined in the form of standard report RAGITT01 and offers a compressed overview of all accounting-relevant asset-related value flows in SAP. You must check the completeness and accuracy of the values considered in this report critically, particularly if adjustments have been made to the standard system during the SAP ERP implementation. You maintain the structure and composition of the asset history sheet with transaction OA79 (Maintain Asset History Sheet Definition).

Figure 8.22 shows how the individual transactions (e. g., acquisitions) are assigned to the items in the asset history sheet. The HISTORY SHEET COMPLETE indicator is important; it must appear as "selected" in the relevant history sheet version.

The following actions are relevant when checking the asset history sheet:

Check: completeness of the asset history sheet

1. Check whether the individual transactions in the asset history sheet have been considered completely, and check in particular the completeness indicator in the relevant history sheet version (transaction OA79).
2. Alternatively, use table TABWP to check the completeness indicator.

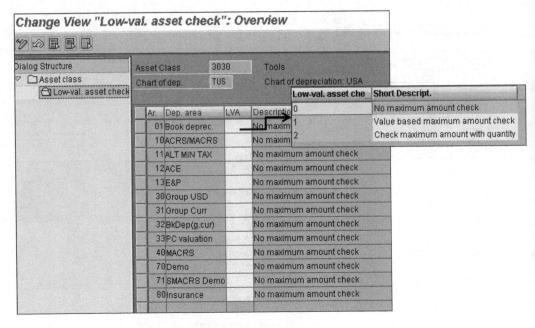

□ Figure 8.23   Asset class – control of the low value asset value check

8.5.7 Low Value Assets

Error reduction
through configu-
ration control

Low value assets do not have to be capitalized; instead, they can be entered as operating expenses in the year they are acquired. Technically, this requirement is implemented in SAP using the special depreciation key LVA (low value assets) and the useful life (1 month). Correct accounting treatment of low value assets can also be strengthened by a configuration control: this is a maximum amount check that rejects an acquisition posting in FI-AA if the amount is below a specific level.

Options for the
value check

Figure 8.23 shows how you can set up such a check in SAP for each asset class and each depreciation area using transaction OAY2 (Asset Class: Low Value Asset Check). You have three options:

- *No entry:* The maximum amount check is inactive.
- *1:* The system checks the entire acquisition and purchase costs (APC) of the asset against the LVA maximum amount defined.
- *2:* The system checks the average APC of the assets in a collective posting against the LVA maximum amount defined.

In your evaluation, do not forget that only one depreciation area in the overview of all depreciation areas listed can transfer values to FI-GL online (a *real depreciation area*).

You maintain the LVA maximum amounts with transaction OAYK (Low Value Assets). As you can see in Fig. 8.24, they can also be defined on a company code-specific basis for each depreciation area.

Check: LVA configu-
ration control

Find out whether the LVA issue is relevant for the organization you are auditing and, if applicable, how these assets are to be treated according to accounting guidelines.

Change View "Amount for low-value assets": Overview

Dialog Structure
▽ ☐ Company code selection
    🗁 Amount for low-value

Company Code   0360   China

Ar.	Name of depreciation area	LVA amount	MaxLVA pur	Crcy
01	Book depreciation --> IFRS in Tecan	2.000,00	2.200,00	CNY
20	Cost-accounting depreciation	2.000,00	2.200,00	CNY
30	Consolidated balance sheet in local cu	2.000,00	2.200,00	CNY
31	Consolidated balance sheet in group c	2.000,00	2.200,00	CHF
32	Book depreciation in group currency	2.000,00	2.200,00	CNY

◨ Figure 8.24   Low value asset maximum amounts per company code

8.5.8 Authorization Control in Asset Accounting

You already know from Sect. 5.2 how authorization controls work in SAP. In order to set up the assignment of authorizations in FI-AA according to the principles of segregation of duties and least privilege, it may be necessary to differentiate at the level of individual values in authorization objects. One of the special features of SAP-supported accounting transactions in FI-AA is that there are corresponding *movement types*. You can see the individual transaction types in tables TABW (Movement Types) and TABWT (Names of Movement Types). Movement types have three characters and for simplification, can be summarized in four main categories:

   Movement types

- 1* – Acquisition
- 2* – Retirement
- 3* – Transfer/reposting
- 4* – Post-capitalization

    With regard to movement types, two authorization objects interact in FI-AA:

   Authorization objects

- A_B_ANLKL
  This authorization object is the first part of the MOVEMENTS IN AN ASSET MASTER RECORD object. At this level, you define whether a user may post movements to an asset master record of an asset class in a specific company code. The following fields are assigned to the authorization object: ASSET CLASS, COMPANY CODE, and ACTIVITY CATEGORY.
- A_B_BWART
  This authorization object is the second part of the MOVEMENTS IN AN ASSET MASTER RECORD object. At this level, you define whether a user may post movements to an asset master record with a specific movement type within an asset class. Defined fields here are ASSET CLASS and MOVEMENT TYPE.

    In addition to distinguishing between movement types, FI-AA also distinguishes between different activities as part of the closing activities. Authorization object

   Activities

`A_PERI_BUK` defines whether the respective system user may perform the following periodic tasks in FI-AA:
- Post depreciation (ACTVT 30)
- Recalculate depreciation (ACTVT 31)
- Post asset values (ACTVT 32)
- Post planned depreciation to cost accounting (ACTVT 33)
- Create new depreciation area (ACTVT 34)
- Fiscal year change (ACTVT 35)
- Year-end closing (ACTVT 36)
- Archiving (ACTVT 37)
- Reload archive (ACTVT 38)

Check: authorizations in FI-AA

Check the following main points in connection with authorizations in FI-AA:

1. Check the extent to which the principle of segregation of duties has been considered in the assignment of authorizations in FI-AA (see Sect. 8.4.5).
2. Check whether the authorizations described in this chapter are assigned in accordance with the principle of least privilege.
3. Get an overview of the movement types used (e. g., via tables TABW and TABWT) and check whether critical movement types, for example, retirement due to scrapping, are specially protected.

8.5.9 Critical Authorizations in Asset Accounting

Auxiliary transactions – only for implementation

SAP-supported asset accounting contains some service transactions that may be used exclusively during implementation – not in live operation. If these transactions are not locked in the system being audited, the assignment of authorizations must be handled very strictly. The transactions are:

- **OABL – Reset Company Code**
  Executing this transaction deletes all asset master records and movements. This could be helpful for testing the data transfer, but would have disastrous consequences in live operation (see also Sect. 8.4.1).

- **OAGL – Reset Posted Depreciation**
  This transaction resets posted depreciation in the asset subledger. The system deletes the corresponding values of all assets of a company code. The depreciation is not reset in the accounting sense: no documents or posting sessions are created that reverse depreciation postings that have already been entered in Financial Accounting. Therefore, the reset in FI-AA causes differences between the accumulated depreciation of the asset in the subledger and the related accounts in Financial Accounting.

- **OAAR and OAAQ – Take Back Year-End Closing Activities**
  To take back year-end closing activities that have already taken place in FI-AA, there are two transactions: OAAR (Year-End Closing by Area) and OAAQ (Take Back FI-AA Year-End Closing (per company code)).

- **OABK – Delete Asset Class**
  This transaction is only necessary in the implementation phase if asset classes created are no longer required.

- **OAMK – Change Reconciliation Accounts**
  This transaction is useful because it lists all FI-AA reconciliation accounts. However, this transaction contains the critical option DELETE RECONCILIATION INDICATOR FOR ALL ACCOUNTS.

Check whether the authorizations for the service transactions listed above are assigned according to the principle of least privilege.

Check: critical authorizations

8.6 Controls in Accounts Payable (FI-AP) and Accounts Receivable (FI-AR)

The Accounts Receivable and Accounts Payable components in FI represent, on the processing side, the subledger part of receivables/sales revenues and payables/expenses in the year-end closing. Where further ERP components are used, further processes come into play; in this book, these will be dealt with as part of the Procure to Pay process (Chap. 9) and the Order to Cash process (Chap. 10).

Some of the topics relevant to FI-AP and FI-AR have already been dealt with in the previous sections as part of the overall FI-GL controls. The following section looks at control mechanisms specifically for FI-AP and FI-AR.

8.6.1 Accuracy of the Reconciliation Accounts

How does the SAP system "know" which G/L account in FI-GL is automatically posted to in the background in a business transaction involving a customer or vendor? The answer is: through the *reconciliation account*. This is defined in the master record of a customer or vendor and used for a posting.

Figure 8.25 shows the following example: Account 210000 (AP Trade, 3rd) is assigned to vendor 15670 (COLLECTOR OF REVENUE SAINT LOUIS). The assignment of a reconciliation account in the FI view of the business partner master data is mandatory (required entry field); in practice, the risks result from an incorrect assignment. In the financial statements, the receivables and payables are usually summarized in groups, for example, domestic/foreign receivables/payables. If, for example, a foreign payables account is assigned to a domestic vendor, this will appear under an incorrect item in the year-end closing. In the subsequent devaluation of receivables items according to country-specific risks (country-specific del credere), this can lead to the devaluation being calculated incorrectly. Overall, the risk is of incorrect display of payables and receivables.

Incorrect display in the financial statements

In special G/L transactions, it is not the reconciliation accounts directly assigned that are used; in special postings (e. g., down payment, bill of exchange), the reconciliation account defined in the master record of a business partner is replaced by another account (e. g., DOWN PAYMENTS RECEIVED instead of RECEIVABLES). This replacement is based on the special G/L indicator that must be specified for such postings.

Special G/L transactions

The rules for deriving the special G/L accounts are defined in the Implementation Guide under FINANCIAL ACCOUNTING (NEW) • FINANCIAL ACCOUNTING GLOBAL SETTINGS • ACCOUNTS RECEIVABLE AND ACCOUNTS PAYABLE • BUSINESS TRANSACTIONS • POSTINGS WITH ALTERNATIVE RECONCILIATION ACCOUNT • DEFINE ALTERNATIVE RECONCILIATION ACCOUNTS AND OTHER SPECIAL G/L TRANSACTIONS.

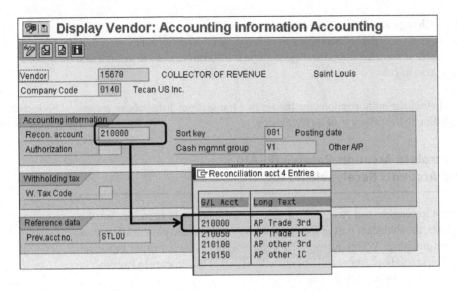

■ **Figure 8.25**   Example for the reconciliation account of a vendor

Check: reconcilia-
tion accounts in
business partner
master data

With regard to the assignment of reconciliation accounts, perform the following audit procedures:

1. Execute plausibility checks to determine the accuracy of the reconciliation accounts: you can take the country indicators of the business partners from tables LFA1 and KNA1, and the G/L accounts assigned are in tables LFB1 and KNB1.
2. Check that alternative reconciliation accounts for special G/L transactions are assigned correctly (see the path in the Implementation Guide above).

8.6.2 Payment Functions

Before we look at control mechanisms as part of the SAP standard payment run function, here are a few tips about how to address payments generally in SAP from an ICS and audit perspective.

Payment options

In practice, auditors often overlook the fact that transaction F110 (Parameters for Automatic Payment) is not the only step in the sequence of actions for payment processing and not the only payment option.

—   The results of a payment run in SAP are often forwarded to another application (including non-SAP software) designed for payment transactions where the payments are processed further. In these applications, individual payments can generally also be entered manually. The applications also often have separate release and approval procedures (additional control mechanisms) – this must all be taken into account in the audit.

—   The payment transactions require interaction with banks: for example, the banks collect files with payment instructions via the network/FTP, which means that control mechanisms for payment files require special consideration.

- In SAP, payment by check or payment instructions (transaction FIBLAPOP) is also possible; and do not forget the possibility of online transfers.
- In larger organizations, it is generally difficult to set up efficient controls for payment runs: daily checks of hundreds, even thousands of transactions in payment proposal lists are virtually impossible. The recommended setting, seen from an auditor's view, would therefore be as follows: once the invoice has been entered, it is paid. The audit focus shifts to the previous step, invoice verification.
- It is easy to forget that payments in SAP sometimes go to customers (credit memo) and not just to vendors.

Using the due date, the SAP payment program (transactions F110 and F111) determines the vendor and customer items to be paid. From the specification of the date for the next payment run, SAP "knows" whether an item is to be included in the current or the next payment run. Processing generally takes place in two steps:

(margin note) SAP payment program

1. **Preparation of a payment proposal list**
   You can determine manually which proposed items are paid.
2. **Execution of the payment run**
   The results are created as print lists, forms (e. g., checks), data media, etc.

From a risk perspective, it is usual to separate these two steps with authorizations: one person would be responsible for the proposal list and another for the execution of the payment run. From an authorization perspective, you can use objects F_REGU_BUK (restriction at company code level) and F_REGU_KOA (restriction at account type level: D – customers, K – vendors, S – G/L accounts) to do this. The values for the actions regarding these two objects are identical, as you can see in Table 8.6.

(margin note) Authorizations in the payment run

The assessment of the control mechanisms for the payment run is essential. The most important audit steps in this context are listed below:

(margin note) Check: controls for the SAP payment run

1. Check whether the assignment of authorizations for the payment program and for entering and releasing invoices is separate (segregation of duties).
2. Check whether the same persons have authorization for preparing payment proposal lists and for executing the payment run (segregation of duties).
3. The REGU* tables can help you to execute various evaluations regarding payment functions (e. g., table REGUA, Changes to Payment Proposals: User and Time).
4. Check whether, in the case of missing segregation of duties, there are sufficient compensating controls. For example, the payment proposal lists can be printed out and checked and signed by two persons (segregation of duties).

With regard to operative controls for the payment program, there are some options for benefiting from the configuration of periods for payments:

(margin note) Optimizing payments

- On a company code-specific basis, *tolerance days* can be defined for payables and added to the payment periods determined, thus enabling payments to be delayed.
- A *minimum cash discount percentage rate* can also be defined. If this is not reached, payment is not made until the due date for net payment (the date on which the open item is to be paid without cash discount deduction).

Table 8.6 Actions for the payment run in SAP

	Action Code	Description
Prepare payment proposal list	02	Edit parameters
	03	Display parameters
	11	Execute proposal
	12	Edit proposal
	13	Display proposal
	14	Delete proposal
	15	Create proposal payment medium
Execute payment	21	Execute payment run
	23	Display payment run
	24	Delete payment run payment data
	25	Create payment run payment medium
	26	Delete payment run payment orders
	31	Print payment medium manually

8.6.3 One-Time Customers and Vendors – Caution!

Risks of one-time account business partners

If you think that, as soon as the requirements for segregation of duties between the maintenance of business partner master data and entering invoices and credit memos is implemented by means of authorizations, the segregation of duties risk is dealt with, you will be disappointed. Unfortunately (from an ICS perspective, or fortunately, with regard to the flexibility in operative business), with SAP, you can enter an incoming invoice for a one-time vendor, enter the required bank details at the same time, and thus bypass the authorization controls (and thus, also segregation of duties). This one-time account function is also available for customers; the use of alternative payment recipients or payers in a document also offers a similar function. What risks does this create?

- **Generally: traceability**
  Since an "anonymous" business partner master record is used instead of a regular one, more work is involved in assigning the one-time account transaction to a specific vendor or customer.

- **One-time customers**
  An anonymous customer has no specific credit limit. There is a risk of fraudulent actions with payment transactions to one-time customers.

- **One-time vendors**
  Here the risk is primarily one of fraud. Transactions connected to cash outflow are generally subject to risk – in particular, those that take place with disregard for the requirements for segregation of duties.

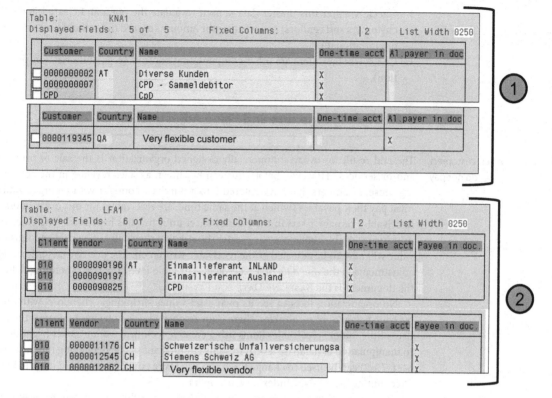

Figure 8.26 Fields relevant for segregation of duties in the business partner master record

You define a business partner as a one-time business partner when you create it (master data maintenance). Since one-time account functions can have wide-reaching consequences from an ICS perspective, corresponding controls must be executed during master data maintenance (regulated one-time accounts) or during invoice and credit memo entry. In practice, the latter are often handled organizationally (rules regarding the maximum amount limit for one-time account partners) or, with somewhat more effort, using authorizations (see Sect. 8.4.3).

Compensating controls

In Fig. 8.26 you can see how to evaluate business partner master data for one-time vendors and for alternative payment recipients and payers: table KNA1 ❶ contains the required information for customers, and table LFA1 ❷ the required information for vendors.

The most important audit steps with regard to one-time business partners are summarized below:

1. Evaluate tables KNA1 and LFA1 to check whether one-time business partner master records exist. Do the same for master records that permit the use of alternative payment recipients or payers.

Check: one-time account functions and alternative bank data in a document

2. Check whether this master data is used (evaluate the open and cleared items for customers and vendors) and whether the amounts exceed the amount limits defined organizationally.
3. Check whether there are other compensating controls (e. g., authorization protection).

8.6.4 Ageing Structure and Value Adjustments

When customers do not pay

The end result for every commercially designed organization is the sale of products and/or services. However, before this can be shown as sales revenue in the accounting sense, customers that have entered into a purchase contract with an organization must pay their payables (which at the same time, are receivables for this organization). Receivables remain assets in the balance sheet until this has happened. The older the overdue receivables balances, the greater the risk that they will not be paid and thus the value will have to be adjusted or the receivable written off. The decisive factor for value adjustments is the *due date* of a receivable. (At table level, the corresponding field in the document is the BASELINE DATE FOR PAYMENT.)

No organization likes to see its own asset values shrinking. Therefore, with large overdue balances of receivables, there is an associated risk of trying to change the due date of the "older" receivables items using creative technical workarounds (right down to manipulation at database level). In some circumstances, the debugging function (see Sect. 7.1.2) can be used to change the BASELINE DATE FOR PAYMENT field in table BSID (Accounting: Secondary Index for Customers).

Check: detecting fraud from the due date

Perform the following analysis steps to identify possible manipulations of the due date:

1. Find out the extent to which considerable overdue balances of receivables were observed in the past and whether they were devalued. Use SAP programs (RF-DOPR00, RFDOPR10, RFDOFW00) to get an overview of the ageing structure of receivables.
2. Evaluate the system log to establish whether debugging activities have taken place in the past (see Sect. 7.3.1).
3. Execute plausibility checks using CAAT tools – even if the situation in the organization you are auditing indicates low risk of fraud: evaluate the contents of table BSID. Larger time differences within individual documents between the *baseline date for payment* and, for example, the *entry date* can indicate irregularities.

8.6.5 Segregation of Duties for Master Data Maintenance

Sensitive fieldds

The maintenance of business partner master data, in particular for vendors, can be seen as a critical activity in itself. You should especially protect critical fields in vendor master data, including those you have learned about in Sect. 8.6.3, as well as, for example, the bank details. SAP enables you to do this using *sensitive fields*. If you define a field in the customer or vendor master record as sensitive, any changes to the field entry blocks the account of the respective customer or vendor. To remove the block, a second authorized person must check the change and confirm or reject it.

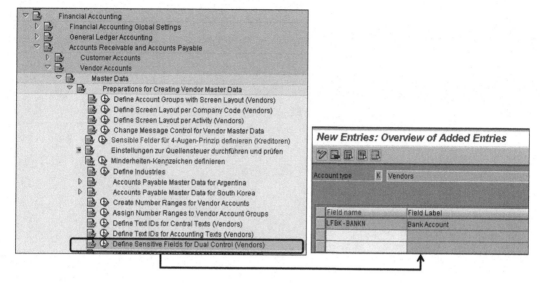

◻ Figure 8.27 Configuration of sensitive fields

Figure 8.27 shows the path in the Implementation Guide for setting up the principle of segregation of duties for vendor master data (alternatively, you can perform evaluations directly in table T055 F). In the example, the BANK ACCOUNT field in the Customizing table has been defined as sensitive. If the accounting clerk responsible changes the entry in this field in the customer or vendor master record, the account is blocked for the payment run until a second authorized person confirms the master data change.

Check: definition of sensitive fields in master data maintenance

The protection of sensitive business partner fields is one of the important control mechanisms in SAP ERP and must be analyzed in every system audit.

8.7 Summary

In this chapter, you have learned about a number of important control mechanisms in SAP-supported financial accounting. They represent the "core" of every ICS framework whose purpose is to ensure the reliability of external financial reporting. In addition to general ledger topics, the areas asset accounting, accounts payable accounting, and accounts receivable accounting have been dealt with here.

The processes in accounts payable accounting are closely linked with the Procure to Pay process, which we will explain in the next chapter.

Control Mechanisms in the SAP ERP-Supported Procure to Pay Process

For organizations that make products, purchasing and materials management are vital parts of the value-added chain: the organizations cannot produce anything without the basic materials. In this chapter, we will look at the procure to pay process from an audit perspective.

The SAP-supported purchasing process, referred to as "procure to pay process" (P2P process) below, includes the following subprocesses:

- Identification of procurement sources and management of these sources (procurement) with reference to the subprocesses of vendor and material master data maintenance
- All internal processes for preparing the purchase order at the vendor, for example, releasing purchase requests; creation, shipping, and administration of purchase orders; outline agreements and other common types of agreement in the purchasing process
- Administration of other data relevant for the purchasing process (e. g., vendor rating, maintenance of purchasing info records, quota arrangements, or simple information regarding material planning)
- Order-related goods receipts and the accounting valuation of these receipts
- Invoice receipts and outgoing payments with reference to purchase orders

Figure 9.1 shows a simplified overview of the SAP-supported purchasing process.

As, on one hand, the P2P process is connected to the procurement of goods or services, and on the other hand leads to payments, under some circumstances, the risks involved can be associated with fraudulent activities. In addition to these risks of fraud, the P2P process bears further risks in connection with financial reporting. Therefore, organizations depend on controls to ensure the correctness, completeness, or valuation of balances, payables, or provisions for outstanding invoices.

In this chapter, you will learn about some selected control mechanisms and audit procedures for detecting ICS weaknesses in the SAP-supported P2P process. Remember that the risk situation must always be adapted to the organization-specific environment. Experience shows that control mechanisms different to those described in this chapter can be in place if procurement processes take place between two organizations *within a corporate group* or if *down payment requests* are used to a large extent.

SAP-supported purchasing process

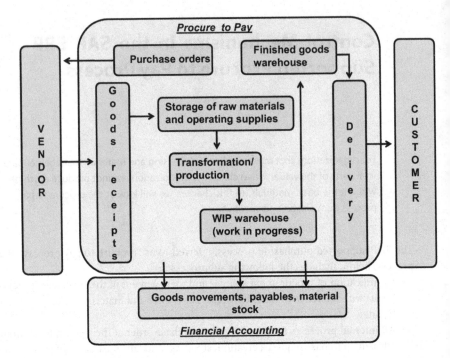

☐ **Figure 9.1** Simplified illustration of the SAP-supported purchasing processes

9.1   Ordering

Here we will address the common controls in the SAP-supported ordering process.

9.1.1 Maintenance of the Organizational Structures Consistent with Authorizations

Risk: organizational structure vs. authorizations

In larger SAP systems in particular, in which numerous company codes are run live, appropriate segregation of duties is important. However, this segregation of duties can only be implemented in the authorization administration if the current organizational structure of the operative units is maintained in the SAP system. If this is not the case, for example, if the organizational structure changes, authorizations assigned would not match the planned areas of responsibility, meaning that a proper, authorization-based segregation of duties in purchasing would not be effective.

[e.g.]   Local and Central Purchasing Processes

The purchasing process can be set up *locally* (i.e., one purchasing organization and the related purchasing groups serve one plant) or *centrally*. The central purchasing process (one purchasing organization serves several plants) is typical, for example, of the purchasing strategy for raw materials; with this procedure, organizations can often achieve better purchasing conditions.

You maintain the organizational structure in purchasing in the Implementation Guide. In particular, the assignment of the plants to the purchasing organizations should correspond to the authorizations assigned, i. e., role content. The corresponding settings in Customizing are located as follows: ENTERPRISE STRUCTURE • DEFINITION • LOGISTICS, GENERAL and MATERIALS MANAGEMENT. You can analyze the roles defined with transaction SUIM (User Information System) or directly with transaction PFCG (Profile Generator) (see Sect. 5.2.5, "Users in the SAP System").

Perform the following audit procedures to assess the effectiveness of the authorization controls in purchasing:

Check: organizational structures in purchasing

1. In the Implementation Guide, check the settings for the organizational units in Logistics. Alternatively, you can do this using tables T001W (Plants), T024E (Purchasing Organization), T024 W (Permitted Purchasing Organizations), and T001 K (Valuation Areas).
2. Get an overview of the authorization concept, in particular of the authorization roles used and the extent to which the segregation of roles corresponds to the organizational structure in SAP. The roles that contain the following authorization objects are particularly relevant: M_BAN_* (Purchase Requisitions) or M_BES_* (Purchase Orders) with the suffix *WRK for plant, *EKO for purchasing organization, and *EKG for purchasing group.

9.1.2 Segregation of Duties in Ordering

The main risk in the ordering process is from unauthorized purchase orders and the associated outflow of funds. To counteract this risk, many organizations have developed procedure instructions or guidelines that limit purchasing capabilities. SAP enables you to map such controls at the point in the system where a purchase order is to be released by different persons on a graded scale in accordance with specific value limits.

Risks in the ordering process

SAP Release Strategy

The release strategy contains the approval procedure for purchase requisitions. The strategy specifies the release codes that have to be used to approve a total purchase requisition or a purchase requisition item. It also specifies the sequence in which the approvals have to take place. A maximum of eight release codes may be defined.

The release strategy can be configured as an option in the ordering process.

The release strategy allows you to set up segregation of duties control mechanisms for complete purchase orders, contracts, scheduling agreements, requests for quotations, or sheets for recording services (these forms are all types of purchasing documents in

Release strategy: with and without classification

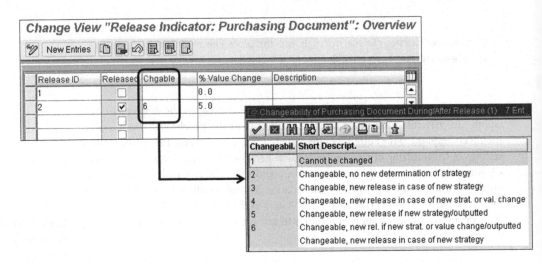

□ **Figure 9.2** Maintenance of release indicators for purchasing documents

SAP, i. e., possibilities for generating a purchase order). This procedure is called *release strategy with classification*.

Alternatively, the release strategy can take place at item level (i. e., for each item within a purchase order), that is, *without classification*. From a risk perspective, with regard to the release strategy, note that a purchase requisition or purchase order is deemed released as standard even if the conditions for a release strategy, i. e., the conditions for the release, are not fulfilled.

The *release with classification* (i. e., per purchase order/for all items within a purchase order) offers considerably greater flexibility than the release strategy without classification. However, the release conditions, for example, value, material group, account assignment, and plant must also be maintained. You maintain the release strategy in the Implementation Guide by setting the purchasing document types for the release strategy and setting the release criteria (MATERIALS MANAGEMENT • PURCHASING • PURCHASE REQUISITION/PURCHASE ORDER • RELEASE PROCEDURE (FOR PURCHASE ORDERS) • DEFINE RELEASE PROCEDURE FOR PURCHASE ORDERS/PURCHASE REQUISITIONS).

Release indicator   As part of the release strategy, you can also assign values for *release indicators*, i. e., maximum deviations after release (see Fig. 9.2). You can also define that a purchase requisition or purchase order has to be re-released if specific upper limits defined during configuration are exceeded.

SAP Business   In addition to the release strategies, you can also use *SAP Business Workflow*. In the
Workflow   system illustrated in Fig. 9.2, the roles (release levels) have been adapted to customer-specific requirements. The person performing the release is determined in a user exit by means of a separately maintained cost center and release hierarchy.

▶ **Common Mistakes in Connection with Workflows** In practice, reference is often made to the SAP Business Workflow function in connection with SAP application controls. On its own, this function does not represent an independent control: it is merely an aid so that the person performing the release does not have to enter the purchase

☐ **Figure 9.3** Field control for purchase requisitions and purchase orders

☐ **Figure 9.3** Field control for purchase requisitions and purchase orders

requisition number or purchase order number manually. The data is still processed with regular SAP transactions. This means that the assignment of authorizations for corresponding transactions continues to be a decisive factor from an ICS view even when SAP workflows are used. Therefore, effective controls can only be achieved via the interaction of system settings (Customizing) and authorizations.

Value entries are important where the release strategy is used. As you can see in Fig. 9.3, you can define the entry control via the setting in Customizing: MATERIALS MANAGEMENT • PURCHASING • PURCHASE REQUISITION/PURCHASE ORDER • DEFINE SCREEN LAYOUT AND DOCUMENT LEVEL • FIELD SELECTION KEY (e. g., NBB for purchase requisitions/NBF for purchase orders) • SELECTION GROUP *Quantity and Price*.

Value entries

The following audit procedures are recommended in connection with release strategies in an SAP system:

Check: release strategies in the ordering process

1. Clarify whether release strategies are used in the ordering process. If applicable, use the Implementation Guide to get an overview of the release strategies. You can also view the settings for the release strategies in table T16FS.
2. Check the screen control settings for values for each item in the field selection groups PURCHASE ORDERS and PURCHASE REQUISITIONS; you can use table T162 (field group MATERIAL PRICES) to do this.

9.2   Goods Receipts and Invoice Verification

The recording of goods receipts and incoming invoices leads to liabilities (payables) for an organization and thus is vitally important in the P2P process. Below we will address selected risks and control mechanisms in this area.

9.2.1 Goods Receipts: Critical Movement Types

Risks of movement types 561 and 501   In SAP, material movements, including goods receipts, are controlled by means of movement types. These have an important control function and ensure, for example, that when a goods receipt is recorded, the relationship to a prior purchase order is established. Therefore, movement types 561 (Data Transfer) and 501 (Goods Receipt without Purchase Order) should be handled restrictively.

- **Movement type 561**
  The initial transfer of material stocks is used in the SAP standard system, for example, to transfer materials from a legacy system to the SAP stocks. If this movement type is not used correctly, there is a risk, for example, that stock values in MM do not agree with the values in the general ledger. This movement type is not required in a live system.

- **Movement type 501**
  This movement type posts the balances to the material subledger but thereby disables some preliminary business process controls. Furthermore, transactions cannot be recorded correctly in the GR/IR account and valuation prices for materials (in the case of moving average price) may be determined incorrectly in some circumstances.

As movement type 561 is not required in everyday business processes, it should be blocked. The authorization for posting goods movements with movement type 501 should be assigned restrictively. Alternatively, you can implement a downstream business process control. For each plant, the movements with movement type 501 are analyzed and compared with the organizational specifications. In SAP, you use transaction MB51 (Material Document List) to analyze movements for each movement type.

Check: critical movement types   To check the effectiveness of the application controls in connection with the material movement types, perform the following procedures:

1. Using table T156, get an overview of the SAP system information about movement types.
2. Authorization object M_MSEG_BWA is used to restrict movement types on the basis of authorizations. Check whether the relevant values are defined in the role definitions.
3. In SAP, movement types can be blocked in two ways: using transaction OMJJ (Customizing: New Movement Types): there, the permitted transactions must be removed from movement type 561; alternatively, in the account determination – this can remain unmaintained for critical movement types (blank fields for G/L accounts).
4. Use transaction MB51 to evaluate material movements with critical status.

9.2.2 3-Way Match and Payment Blocks in Logistics Invoice Verification

The recording of incoming invoices is one of the closing steps in the P2P process. Payment and clearing of open items follow this step – see Sect. 8.6.5 "Segregation of Duties for Master Data Maintenance." In addition to the operative risks of entry errors or fraudulent actions, in this area there are risks for year-end closing with regard to the accuracy, completeness, and reporting of payables for goods and services.

In most cases, the *Logistics invoice verification* (transaction MIRO) is used in SAP; it is part of SAP Materials Management. Here, you can enter incoming invoices before or after goods receipt. To control variances effectively (e. g., if the invoice contains a higher amount or lower quantity than the purchase order), it is important that the incoming invoice has a reference to the purchase order or a purchase order item, but also to the goods receipt. This link has become an established term in the ICS lexicon: *3-way match*.

However, SAP also offers configuration controls for incoming invoices with no purchase order reference. These controls can reduce the risks associated with invoice entry. The following configuration controls are relevant:

- Invoice blocks due to a variance of the invoice item (quantity/price/purchase order price quantity variances, etc.) from the purchase order
- Invoice blocks due to the absolute amount of an invoice item with or without purchase order reference
- Stochastic (randomly determined) invoice blocks with and without purchase order reference

In addition to automated controls, you also have the option of a manual invoice block.

In the Logistics incoming invoice verification, the related items from the purchase order, goods receipt, and incoming invoice operations are compared with one another. If the tolerances set are exceeded, the entire incoming invoice is posted, but the *payment block* "R" (invoice verification) is set in the vendor item of the accounting document.

Blocked incoming invoices must be released with transaction MRBR (Release Blocked Invoices). You configure the Logistics incoming invoice verification in Customizing by maintaining the tolerance limits per company code (see Fig. 9.4, Materials Management • Logistics Invoice Verification • Invoice Block • Set Tolerance Limits).

The system differentiates between the blocking reasons and handles them accordingly. Some blocking reasons can be deleted; others remain in place. The blocking reasons can also be differentiated in the authorization concept (e. g., in the case of *quality-related blocking reasons* vs. *variances from estimated price*).

Margin notes:
Checking/blocking variances

Tolerance limits in invoice verification

Handling blocking reasons

> **Switching off "Bypasses"** The function for posting incoming invoices to G/L or material accounts should be deactivated for the Logistics invoice verification to prevent the controls mentioned above from being bypassed (MATERIALS MANAGEMENT • LOGISTICS INVOICE VERIFICATION • INCOMING INVOICE • ACTIVATE DIRECT POSTING TO G/L AND MATERIAL ACCOUNTS). Of course, incoming invoices can also be entered manually outside of the Logistics invoice verification (see Sect. 9.5, "Corporate Governance").

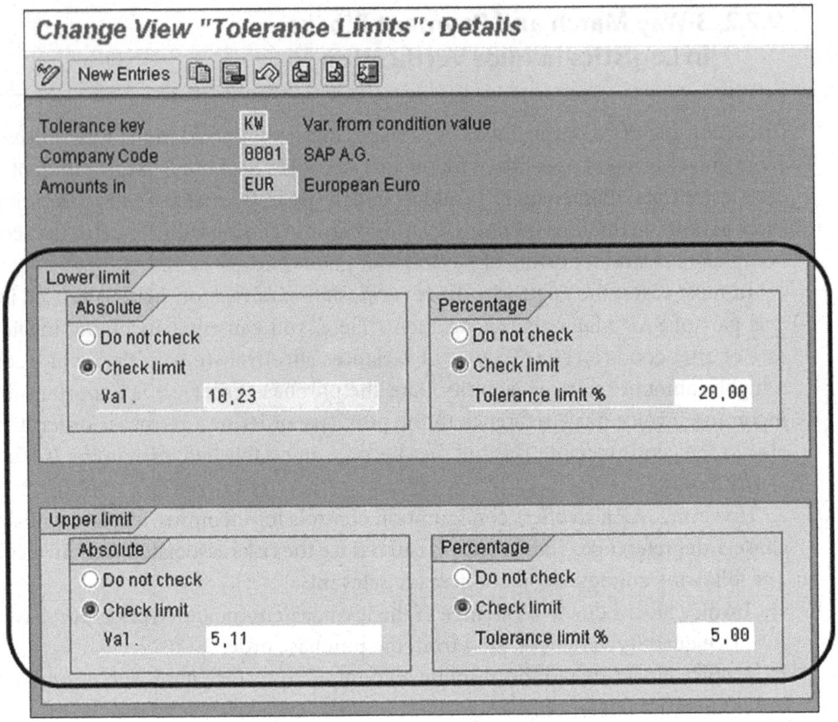

Figure 9.4 Tolerance limits for invoice verification

Stochastic or amount-based blocks

The system uses *stochastic blocks* for incoming invoices even though there are no variances between the purchase order, goods receipt, and invoice receipt. As a result, the incoming invoice also has to be released for payment. This control is based on a psychological effect that deters fraudulent activities. You activate stochastic blocks per company code in the Implementation Guide: MATERIALS MANAGEMENT • LOGISTICS INVOICE VERIFICATION • INCOMING INVOICE • INVOICE BLOCK • STOCHASTIC BLOCKS.

Absolute item amounts can also lead to a block if an absolute amount is exceeded. You can also configure this function in the Implementation Guide under Materials MANAGEMENT • LOGISTICS INVOICE VERIFICATION • INCOMING INVOICE • INVOICE BLOCK • ITEM AMOUNT CHECK.

Check: controls for invoice verification

Perform the following steps to assess the controls in invoice verification:

1. In the Implementation Guide or in table T169G, check the tolerance limits considered automatically in the Logistics invoice verification in SAP.
2. In the Implementation Guide or in table T169P, get an overview of the stochastic or amount-based blocks set up.
3. Appropriate segregation of duties must be ensured between the individual actions in the assignment of authorizations for entering purchase orders, goods receipts, and incoming invoices and for blocking invoices. Check whether this is guaranteed organizationally based on authorizations and whether, if there is no segregation of duties, appropriate compensating controls are in place.

9.2.3 Check for Duplicate Invoice Entry

A check for duplicate invoice entry can prevent accidental duplicate entry of incoming invoices. The system compares the reference number, invoice data, and amount and issues a warning message if applicable.

Accidental duplicate entry

The prerequisites for checking duplicate invoice entry are as follows:

- In the vendor master record, the indicator must be set in the CHECK DUPL. INV. (check for duplicate invoice entry) field.
- The check for duplicate invoices must also be set in Customizing.

For each company code, you can define whether the system should search for duplicate invoices in the respective company code only, or in all company codes. You configure this in the Implementation Guide under MATERIALS MANAGEMENT • LOGISTICS INVOICE VERIFICATION • INCOMING INVOICE • SET CHECK FOR DUPLICATE INVOICES.

The following evaluations are useful in connection with the risks associated with duplicate invoice entry:

Check: duplicate invoice entry

1. Check whether the system prerequisites for the automatic warning in the case of a duplicate invoice entry are fulfilled (vendor master record and configuration settings).
2. You can use CAAT evaluations (see Sect. 17.1.1 "Offline CAAT Tools") to check posted invoices for duplicate entries.

9.3 GR/IR Account

Proper handling of mass routine transactions can be a real challenge for many organizations in practice. A common situation is that at the end of the month, the GR/IR clearing account has a balance far from zero and thousands of uncleared items.

As an interim account between the balance sheet account and the vendor account, a *GR/IR clearing account* fulfills an important control and assignment function. In a GR/IR account, goods receipts (GR) and invoice receipts (IR) are entered for a purchase order. In the first case (GR), the GR/IR account is cleared by the posting of the invoice, and in the second case (IR), by the posting of the goods receipt.

Goods receipt/ invoice receipt

Improper treatment of the GR/IR account can affect the reporting and valuation of the receivables and payables items as well as the price difference accounts.

9.3.1 Clearing the GR/IR Account

The first challenge for many organizations is a complete and correct assignment of related open GR and IR items in the GR/IR account. With a high volume of transactions, the standard transaction intended for this purpose, MR11 (GR/IR Account Maintenance) may be insufficient. You can use SAPF124 to clear GR/IR items automatically. The program assigns relevant items using the rules maintained in table TF123 (Additional Rules for Running Program SAPF124 (Clearing)).

Complete and correct assignment

Data Browser: Table TF123 Select Entries   19

[Check Table...]

```
Table:              TF123
Displayed Fields:  10 of  10      Fixed Columns:              | 4    List Width 0250
```

Client	Chart of accts	Account Type	From acct	To account	Criterion 1	Criterion 2	Criterion 3
100		D	0000000001	9999999999	ZUONR	GSBER	VBUND
100		D	A	Z	ZUONR	GSBER	VBUND
100		K	A	Z	ZUONR	GSBER	VBUND
100		S	0000000000	9999999999	ZUONR	GSBER	VBUND
100	TECA	D	0000000001	0000106046	ZUONR	VBUND	
100	TECA	K	0000000001	0000010300	ZUONR		
100	TECA	K	0000010301	0000010301	XBLNR		
100	TECA	K	0000010302	9999999999	ZUONR		
100	TECA	K	10301AT	10301AT	XBLNR		
100	TECA	K	10301DE	10301DE	XBLNR		
100	TECA	K	10301NL	10301NL	XBLNR		
100	TECA	K	10301US	10301US	XBLNR		
100	TECA	S	0000000000	0001130399	ZUONR		
100	TECA	S	0001130400	0001130400	XREF3		
100	TECA	S	0001130401	0000220449	ZUONR		
100	TECA	S	0000220450	0000220450	XREF3		
100	TECA	S	0000220451	0000220499	ZUONR		
100	TECA	S	0000220500	0000220520	ZUONR		
100	TECA	S	0000220521	0000999999	ZUONR		

◻ Figure 9.5   Assignment criteria for automatic clearing with program SAPF124

Automatic clearing   As shown in Fig. 9.5, you can define assignment criteria (maximum of five) for individual G/L accounts or for a G/L account number interval. The ZUONR (assignment number) criterion is decisive for the GR/IR account: this field is made up of a purchase order number and purchase order item and enables the assignment of the goods receipts and invoice receipts. Program SAPF124 clears the related items if there are no value-based variances between the goods receipts and the invoice receipts. This creates *clearing documents*.

Tolerance limits for clearing   Furthermore, program SAPF124 also enables you to clear GR and IR if there are price variances within defined threshold values and to enter the differences in a price difference account. The prerequisites are:

- A *tolerance group* is maintained with permitted values for absolute and/or percentage rate price variants.
- A tolerance group is assigned to the GR/IR account.
- The account determination is maintained for the *price difference account*.

Maintenance and assignment of tolerance groups   Figure 9.6 shows where you can configure tolerance groups in the Implementation Guide, which absolute and percentage tolerance values you define, and where you can assign the relevant tolerance group (unique within a company code) to the master data of a GR/IR account.

Check: GR/IR account clearing   Perform the following audit procedures in association with GR/IR account clearing:

1. Look at the account determination (transaction FBKP, Maintain Accounting Configuration, operation WRX) to determine which G/L account is defined as GR/IR account.
2. Use transaction FS00 (assignment to a tolerance group, manual vs. automatic maintenance of the GR/IR account etc.) to get an overview of the settings in the master data of the GR/IR account. The details of the contents of the tolerance groups are

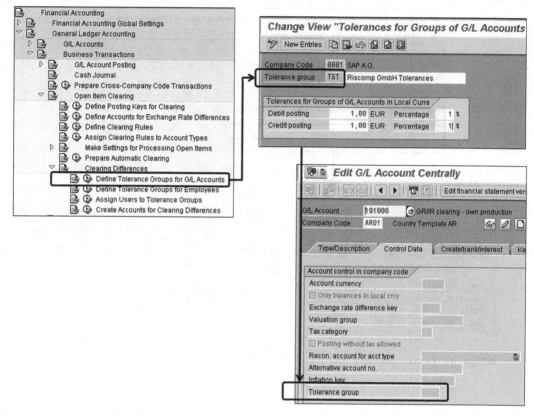

◘ Figure 9.6 Definition and use of tolerance groups

available in tables T043S and T043ST. Transaction OMR3 (MM-IV Default Account Maintenance) or table T169 K contain further settings relevant for the maintenance of the GR/IR account.

3. Use transaction FBL3 N (G/L Account Line Items) to evaluate the status of the maintenance of the GR/IR account.

4. Get an overview of the assignment criteria set up in table TF123 for automatic clearing.

9.3.2 Closing Operations and Reporting of the GR/IR Account in the Balance Sheet

Provided the GR/IR account has been maintained correctly and completely, and assuming that no goods receipt-based invoice verification is used, during closing operations (monthly), the balance of the GR/IR account must be split into two open items to ensure correct accounting treatment (reporting and valuation). These two components correspond to two transactions in the account determination:

- BNG (invoiced but not yet delivered): outstanding deliveries
- GNB (delivered but not yet invoiced): outstanding invoices

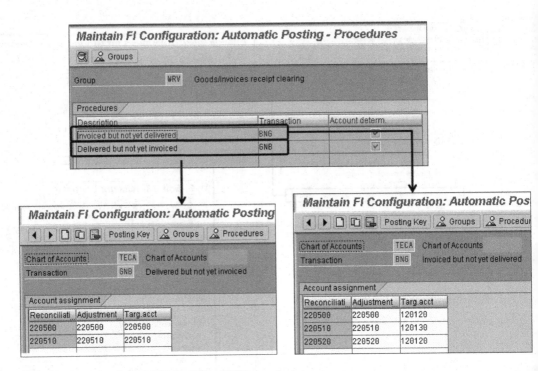

□ Figure 9.7   Account determination for GNB and BNG transactions

Splitting the GR/IR balance

Figure 9.7 shows how you can maintain and check the account determination for these transactions (via transaction FBKP, Maintain Accounting Configuration). You use program RFWERE00 to split the GR/IR balance. At the end of the month, it generates a posting that brings the balance on the GR/IR account to zero and posts to two further accounts (BNG and GNB). At the same time, it generates a further posting that reverses this first posting on the first day of the following month. You can use program RFWERE00 for the accounting split and to analyze the GR/IR account (without posting).

Program RM07MSAL

In practice, a further program, RM07MSAL (List of GR/IR Balances) is often used. This program compares the goods receipt quantities and values of a purchase order with the invoice receipt quantities and values of this purchase order if the balance is not zero, enabling you to trace variances. If there are variances, you can also see which purchase orders are affected.

Check: reporting the GR/IR account at the end of the month

To check the correct accounting treatment of the GR/IR account balance, perform the following evaluations:

1. Evaluate the balance of the GR/IR account at the end of a month. If this is not zero, clarify whether the invoice verification is on a goods receipt basis. If not, clarify how the balance of the GR/IR account is treated in closing operations.
2. Use transaction FBKP to check whether the correct G/L accounts are assigned in the account determination for the BNG and GNB transactions.

9.4 Controls for Stocks

From master data maintenance to the valuation – as current assets on the asset side of the balance sheet, stocks are the core of the ICS-relevant topics in the P2P process.

9.4.1 Maintenance of Material Master Data

We have already explained some important P2P-relevant controls in the master data area in Sect. 8.6.1, "Accuracy of the Reconciliation Accounts." The final topic is the material master: maintenance of this object influences many important processes in the organization. In addition to the P2P process, the *sales process* (order to cash, O2 C) is also affected. From the view of the internal control system, the valuation of current assets and the calculation and reporting of input tax are also relevant. Therefore, the maintenance of material master data should be integrated in an ICS-conform change process.

Important role of material master data

In some organizations, a combination of authorizations is used in connection with the SAP Business Workflow function. The restriction of authorizations for company codes, plants, material master views, and maintenance status ensures that only authorized users can maintain materials. The workflow functionality informs the authorized users which material masters are ready for maintenance.

Controls for the material master

The workflow is initiated by *events*. In this case the event is the creation of a new material master record, i. e., the maintenance of basic data. As a result, a change order is created – Fig. 9.8 shows an example.

SAP Business Workflow

This change order is sent to a local material master administrator. After release, the order is forwarded to all local organizational units for maintenance of the relevant material master views (see ❶ in Fig. 9.9).

The material master administrator can trace the progress of the material master maintenance at any time. For each view in the material master, there is a subsequent release to ensure appropriate segregation of duties. You can display the material mas-

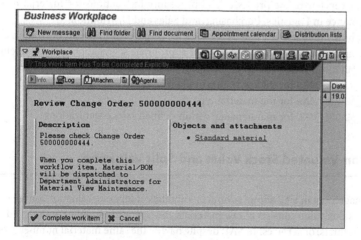

◻ Figure 9.8 Change order for the material master

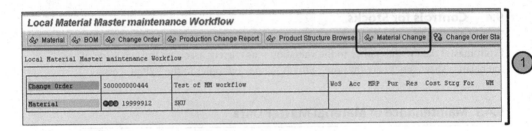

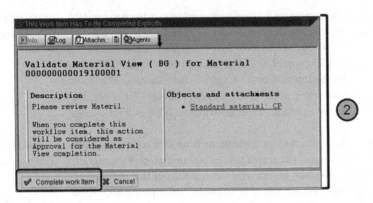

□ Figure 9.9 Workflow-based processing of material master data

ter via the MATERIAL CHANGE button. The material master change is completed with confirmation of the workflow task COMPLETE WORK ITEM ❷.

You can configure standard SAP workflows via SAP MENU • TOOLS • BUSINESS WORKFLOW • ADMINISTRATION.

Check: maintenance of material master data

Perform the following evaluations in connection with the treatment of the material master data:

1. Get an overview of the processes and procedure instructions for material master maintenance in Logistics, Purchasing, and Sales and Distribution.
2. Check how the material master maintenance is reflected in the authorization concept. Important authorization objects for appropriate segregation of duties include:
   - M_MATE_STA for changing the maintenance status
   - M_MATE_WRK for the restriction at plant level
   - M_MATE_MAR for the material type
   - M_MATE_VKO for maintenance within defined sales organizations

9.4.2 Non-Valuated Stock Value and Split Valuation

Valuated vs. non-valuated stock

Stock management in SAP allows several possibilities of separate valuation for the stock value. The stock value consists of raw materials and operating supplies, unfinished and finished products, or services. In SAP, despite having the same material number, stocks can have a different accounting value. For example, a material with an expiration date that has passed is managed mostly as *non-valuated*. Material is reclassified between valuated and non-valuated stock in the following cases:

- Goods are first received in quality assurance and only released to the unrestricted warehouse stock after quality assurance release.
- (Un)finished products exceed their shelf life or materials are managed as non-valuated project stock.
- Materials are shifted between valuated and non-valuated stock due to stock transfer or reposting.

The classification of the stock value bears the risk of incorrect reporting, i. e., over-valuation or undervaluation in the financial statements.

If the expiration date check is activated, the SAP *batch management* function can automatically change the status of the stock from Free to Not Free, including the creation of a material document. Using the account determination, you can configure the relevant movement type such that the entire book value of the batch is posted as an expense. You activate the expiration date check with transaction OMJE (table T159 L as well as per movement type in table T156). You must also maintain movement type 341 (unfinished activities, free to not free in the account determination, table T156 ff.). *Configuration for reclassification of stock*

In addition to batch management, materials can also be valuated differently in manual material movements. This is relevant for organizations that purchase (externally) as well as produce and store raw materials, unfinished products, and finished products. As the acquisition and production costs of the materials are different in this case, the stocks must be *valuated separately*. *Treatment of the split valuation*

The risk involved in split valuation is comparable with the valuation risk for non-valuated stock.

You configure the split valuation in Customizing under Materials Management • Evaluation and Account Assignment • Split Valuation • Activate/Configure Split Valuation or using transaction OMW0/OMWC. You use these configuration settings to configure, amongst other things, valuation categories (for example, whether the material is produced in-house or purchased externally). *Configuration of the split valuation*

Perform the following audit procedures in connection with material valuation: *Check: valuation of the stock value*

1. Get an overview of whether split valuation and batch management are used.
2. You can check the activation for the expiration date in batch management in tables T159 L and T156.
3. Check the settings for split valuation of stock values in Customizing with transactions OMW0 (MM-IV Control Valuation) and OMWC (MM-IV Split Material Valuation).

9.4.3 Account Determination for Material Movements

The logistical processes in warehouse management are assigned to the main processes purchasing, production, and sales. The necessary material movements must update on one hand the quantities in the storage locations, and on the other hand the corresponding values in accounting. In an SAP system, this is achieved by means of *movement types*. Each material movement has a movement type in the material document. *Material movements in SAP*

Movement types and account determination

Amongst other things, a movement type controls whether only quantities, only values, or both are updated in the system. For example, for a goods receipt for a purchase order, the material stocks in the storage locations must be increased and the stock value adjusted. In contrast, a *transfer* within a plant or a valuation area requires only the update of the quantities, but not the book values. It is essential that the account determination is accurate: if the settings are incorrect, this can have a negative impact on the accuracy of the stock values in the financial statements.

Configuration of the account determination

From an ICS perspective, the accuracy of the account determination and the system restriction that G/L accounts cannot be selected manually for material movements are very important. In SAP Materials Management, the account determination consists of the following elements:

- Valuation control
- Valuation area
- Valuation class
- Account modification

In the valuation control and valuation area, you define which plants are created with or without adjustment of the account assignment (account modification); in the valuation class, you define which account is finally posted to. You can use the *valuation class* to set up material-specific automatic account determination. For example, the inflows for raw materials can be posted to different stock accounts to the inflows for semi-finished products, even though in both cases the same transaction is entered. The *account category reference* links valuation classes with material types, thus defining which valuation classes are permitted for a material that is itself always assigned to a specific material type.

To prevent errors in the recording of material movements, the check indicator in the account modification (table: T156X to XPKON) should *not* be set. This setting also prevents G/L accounts entered on the entry screen from being used for the accounting document.

Check: account determination for material movements

Perform the following procedures in connection with the account determination for material movements and to reconcile the general ledger with the values in MM:

1. Get an overview of the system settings for account determination, in particular the account modification for movement types. Also get an overview of the connection of the charts of accounts (transaction OMWD or using the fixed account table T030).
2. In samples, check the account assignment of the movement types for important material types. To do so, use transaction OMWB (MM-IV Automatic Account Assignment (Simulation)) and then choose the Simulation or G/L Accounts button.
3. Note: program RM07MMFI executes a balance comparison between SAP Materials Management and SAP Financial Accounting. Program RM07MBST also compares the totals of the warehouse stock with the stock account in Financial Accounting. You should check the consistency of the stocks regularly with program RM07KO01.

9.4.4 Correction of Stock Values: Inventory and Material Devaluations

As part of monthly, quarterly, or year-end closing activities, stock must often be valued in accordance with country-specific requirements. In the USA, the lower of cost or market value principle applies. To comply with German Commercial Code, stock must be checked for any devaluation requirement. Other accounting regulations, for example, IAS 2, require a valuation at lower, historical costs or at net sales value (at net sales price, net distribution costs, etc.). Variances in quantities as a result of the inventory count results or the necessity of a value adjustment (entry of additional acquisition and production costs) represent further possible causes of value adjustments.

Adjusting values – when and why?

SAP supports different inventory procedures. For example, *permanent, key date-related, or annual inventory count*. However, the objective of all procedures is to find differences between the quantities in the SAP system and the actual quantities in the warehouse. These inventory differences are entered in the system (*count confirmation*) and then written off.

Inventory

To prevent a variance as a result of material movements during the inventory count, the stocks should be frozen by means of a block on the storage locations. You can activate this block in Customizing (MATERIALS MANAGEMENT • INVENTORY MANAGEMENT AND INVENTORY • PHYSICAL INVENTORY • ALLOW FREEZING OF BOOK INVENTORY BALANCE IN STORAGE LOCATION).

Inventory control: blocking storage locations

Another important inventory control is the segregation of duties between the count and recording of the counted results on the one hand, and the authorization for writing off the inventory differences on the other. Authorization object M_ISEG_WDB in activity 01 is required for recording the count. Authorization for writing off inventory differences is given by authorization object M_ISEG_WDB. You can also define upper limits for the maintenance of inventory differences in system customizing.

Inventory control: segregation of duties

To ensure the completeness of the inventory, the inventories created should also be closed after closing.

Adjustments to the book value can occur on an ongoing basis if, for example, transport invoices are recorded as additional acquisition and production costs. In the case of materials manufactured in-house for assets under construction, the costs are recorded indirectly at the end of the month. Corresponding controls of the materials that are valuated with the *standard price* and the assessment of manufacturing costs are explained in Sect. 9.4.6, "Product Cost Accounting."

Value adjustment based on acquisition and production costs

For trading goods or externally procured materials (valuated mostly with the *moving average price*), you must determine whether there is any need to devalue the stock value. For this purpose, SAP offers several procedures that have to be configured in the system. In addition to the price control (standard price (S)/moving average price (V)), you can also perform a lowest value test on the basis of the periodic moving average price, the average inward movement price, through determination of the lowest market prices, of consumption monitoring procedures (LIFO/FIFO), the range of coverage, or the warehouse range of coverage.

Devaluation of the stock value

The valuation of the stock value allows significant leeway in the reporting of the values in the financial statements. Therefore, the following controls are recommended:

- **Controls for devaluation**

  Important parameters for calculating the determination of lowest value must be set correctly in Customizing at program start:

- Range of coverage reductions in the determination of lowest value in Customizing (transactions OMW5 and OMW5 W)
- Selection of the document types and movement types considered in determining lowest values using market prices for the calculation of the inward movement prices (transaction OMWI for movement types/transaction OMWJ for document types)
- Reduction values for the determination of lowest value according to movement rate (transactions OMW5 and OMW5 W)
- Valuation level for LIFO/FIFO (transaction OMWL) as well as the definition of LIFO/FIFO-relevant movement types

▬ **Controls for segregation of duties**

Appropriate segregation of duties should also be ensured. SAP enables you to create a batch input session as well as directly update of the valuation prices in the material master. Appropriate segregation of duties can be achieved in two different ways.

- *Preventive control*

  The value adjustment is performed exclusively with a batch input session. The user who prepares and executes the valuation must not be authorized to update the material master. Furthermore, the user should not be authorized to process the batch input sessions.

- *Detective control*

  The changes to prices in the material master are evaluated after the update using transactions MRN9 (Balance Sheet Values by Account) and CKMPCD (Display Price Change Documents).

> **Important for Transaction CKMPCD** Choose the LINE ITEMS PER MATERIAL option, otherwise the value changes are not output.

Finally, the definition of the steps for the determination of lowest value is important. However, these must be defined organizationally before you can start transactions MRN0 (market prices), MRN1 (range of coverage), MRN2 (movement rate), and MRN3 (loss-free valuation), etc. for determination of lowest value.

Check: value adjustment of the stock value

You must check the following in connection with value adjustments in materials management:

1. Get an overview of the inventory procedures used and clarify whether storage locations are blocked during the inventory. Evaluate relevant change documents. Check whether segregation of duties requirements are implemented via authorizations.
2. Considering the relevant accounting regulations, check the procedure for devaluations and, where applicable, analyze the relevant configuration settings. Check whether segregation of duties requirements are considered.

9.4.5 Release of Scrapping

Writing off stocks conform to the ICS

Most organizations regularly check their warehouse stock. Stocks that are no longer required or can no longer be sold are written off in "scrapping actions" as a goods issue from stock to expenses in the profit and loss statement. In the SAP standard, the movement types 551, 553, and 555 are defined for this purpose. If the scrapping actions are not performed, in most cases the quantity in the stock value has to be corrected.

With regard to the use of critical movement types, the control should take place in two parts:

1. The preliminary control consists of the restrictive assignment of authorizations.
2. As the SAP standard system unfortunately does not support a more effective control at process level (preliminary release of scrapping), you can subsequently check manually whether the critical movement types have been used on an authorized basis.

With regard to the treatment of scrapping, check the following:

Check: release of scrapping

1. The movement types are restricted with authorization objects M_MSEG_BWA, M_MSEG_BMB, M_MSEG_BWE, M_MSEG_BMF, and M_MSEG_LGO. Check whether movement types 551, 553, and 555 are handled restrictively.
2. You can use transaction MB51 (Material Document List) to analyze material movements with specific movement types. Evaluate the material documents with scrapping movement types 551, 553, and 555 and compare the result with the released scrapping actions.

9.4.6 Product Cost Accounting

In many cases, the valuation of the stock value within the value-added chain of organizations is performed with the SAP module Controlling (CO) and its components Product Cost Controlling (CO-PC) and Profitability Analysis (CO-PA). Various types of orders, for example, internal orders or production orders, act as cost objects or cost collectors. These cost collectors are debited by the individual transactions in the business process, for example, by the raw material withdrawal. At the end of the production process, these cost collectors are then credited by the (production) confirmation of the material and, for example, the stock is debited on make-to-stock production or customer order.

Value flow for goods from in-house production in SAP

The semi-finished products or finished products are mostly confirmed at standard price. In this case, at the end of the period, the variances between standard price (from the planned costs) and the actual costs arising must be compared. Any variances must be analyzed and the standard price must be adjusted. The main risk for the inventory valuation is that Controlling as internal accounting cannot be reconciled with external accounting. Errors in Controlling would then be inherited into the stock value through revaluation of the stock or the work in process.

In principle, the CO module must be integrated in two directions. The FI module must be integrated in Controlling so that all relevant business transactions are replicated in the correct reconciliation accounts (Fig. 9.10). In Customizing for the CO module, you must also check which cost collectors the organization uses. This determines whether all important business transactions recorded in FI have been transferred to the CO module. Generally, for a goods removal (picking) for a production order, "Production expense to raw materials" is posted in FI. Account assignment also takes place to the corresponding cost collector, for example, the production order.

Integration of FI in CO

Display View "Posting Rules in WIP Calculation and Results Analysis":

CO Area	Comp	RA Ver	RA category	Bal./Cre	Cost Elem	Record	P&L Acct	BalSheetAcct	Accounting P
0001	0001	0	WIPR			0	891000	791000	
1000	0105	0	WIPR			0	500300	120180	
1000	0105	0	WIPO			0	500300	120180	
1000	0105	0	RUCR			0	500300	120180	
1000	0105	0	RUCP			0	500300	120180	
1000	0105	TP1	WIPR			0	500300	120180	
1000	0105	TP1	WIPO			0	500300	120180	
1000	0105	TP1	RUCR			0	500300	120180	
1000	0105	TP1	RUCP			0	500300	120180	
1000	0105	TP2	WIPR			0	500300	120180	
1000	0105	TP2	WIPO			0	500300	120180	
1000	0105	TP2	RUCR			0	500300	120180	
1000	0105	TP2	RUCP			0	500300	120180	
1000	0110	0	WIPR			0	500300	120180	
1000	0110	0	WIPO			0	500300	120180	
1000	0110	0	RUCR			0	500300	120180	
1000	0110	0	RUCP			0	500300	120180	
1000	0110	TP1	WIPR			0	500300	120180	
1000	0110	TP1	RUCR			0	500300	120180	

☐ **Figure 9.10** Account determination for CO-FI integration

Integration of CO in FI   In the opposite direction, the CO module can transfer the costs to FI real-time or using a reconciliation ledger. This applies for primary and secondary cost types. The ICS-relevant questions in this regard have already been explained in Sect. 8.3.3, "Reconciliation Ledger." If New GL is active, you should also check the Customizing settings for the posting of the Financial Accounting documents and align the settings with the organization of the valuation areas. Thus the stocks, costs, and company codes to which the Controlling module posts should be aligned (transaction CKM9). You should also use samples to check the accuracy of the account determination (transaction OKGB or table V_KKAB).

Segregation of duties   Appropriate segregation of duties should also be implemented within the Controlling module. Therefore, the creation of cost collector, internal orders, and production orders must be separate. You must also ensure that the different cost objects are closed again on a timely basis to ensure that all costs are allocated to the stocks in the correct period.

Check: P2P product cost accounting   In connection with product cost accounting, perform the following audit procedures:

1. Check the cost objects used and check which primary cost elements are posted to them. Assess the risk situation of the organization and whether the valuation of stocks for balance sheet purposes is based on figures from Controlling.

This is the case, for example, when the organization valuates its finished products with planned prices and at period end, compares the actual costs arising in Controlling with the planned costs. If the stock values are then adjusted based on the figures from Controlling, cost recording and allocation should be complete and accurate.

2. If New GL is not active (see also Sect. 8.3.3, "Reconciliation Ledger"), use transaction KALC to evaluate the posting documents. Using samples, check whether the costs have been transferred completely. Make sure that you start the transaction in test mode. If documents are missing in the evaluation, this must be analyzed.

3. Check whether segregation of duties requirements are considered sufficiently in the authorization concept.

9.4.7 Goods Issues from Non-Valuated Stock

Many organizations use *non-valuated material* to manage quantities or to procure materials and services. For example, advertising materials or test products can be managed in the system on a quantity basis, but the acquisition and production costs for these stocks are posted from the warehouse to expenses directly on goods receipt for the purchase order or on the withdrawal of the raw and auxiliary materials. To prevent an unauthorized goods issue, the goods issues should be subject to an operative control. The risk of an unauthorized goods issue is relevant if the non-valuated materials have a free market value if the goods are, for example, test products subject to duty on tobacco or spirits.

Within the procurement process, it is important that return deliveries for non-valuated materials can only be performed with reference to purchase orders. This is particularly important as the expense is reversed. Note that free of charge deliveries in the sales process represent a similar risk, but other automated controls are used. *Returns items* are processed by setting a checkmark (RETPO field for returns item) in the purchase order item. As soon as you post the goods issue for this "returns order" using transaction MIGO (Goods Movement), the system determines the required movement type (161 in the standard system). You perform the relevant settings in the Implementation Guide: MATERIALS MANAGEMENT • PURCHASING • PURCHASE ORDER • RETURNS ORDER • RETURNS TO VENDOR.

Having non-valuated goods issues under control

9.5   Corporate Governance

In Sect. 8.6.5, "Segregation of Duties for Master Data Maintenance," we looked at the ICS-relevant questions regarding payment transactions. Here we will address the importance of these transactions from the view of external requirements. In the international environment, the requirements with regard to transparency and control of payments are increasing. Reasons for this can be negotiated agreements (tobacco industry in Europe), legislative requirements (as in the Foreign Corrupt Practices Act in the USA), or legislation for preventing money laundering or tax evasion. Organizations should implement appropriate effective controls over outgoing payments and payment recipients to satisfy these external requirements.

External requirements of payment transactions

Most legal actions against organizations that have violated any of the above requirements are often settled out of court in practice. However, in addition to the financial loss, the damage to the reputation of an organization can be serious.

High risk

In addition to the controls regarding one-time vendors and critical fields in the vendor master as already covered, the corporate governance controls should include special measures with regard to the direct recording of vendor payments and customer credits.

Automatic control   In addition to a restrictive assignment of authorizations for recording general vendor invoices using transactions FB60 (Enter Incoming Invoices) or F-43 (Enter Vendor Invoice), the following measures or system settings should be performed to enable an automated control:

- Maintenance of a payment block for FI vendors and FI customers in the master record
- Definition of a sales document type for customer credit memos, which automatically creates and blocks a credit memo. This automated control is explained in detail in the order to cash (O2C) sales process, see Chap. 10.

9.6 Summary

This chapter has provided an overview of ICS-relevant topics in the procure to pay process. From an ICS perspective, the main risks, for which appropriate control mechanisms have been explained, are in the subprocesses ordering, invoice verification, treatment of the GR/IR account, and in the area of inventory valuation.

Control Mechanisms in the SAP ERP-Supported Order to Cash Process

The objectives of every economically functioning organization are sales and profit. Sales and distribution is very important here. Let us consider the risks and controls in the process chain from the purchase order to payment of the invoice.

The sales and distribution process, "order to cash" (O2C), has a central role in market-oriented organizations. All inquiries and orders come together in the sales and distribution process and this process provides the customer with the relevant goods and services. In most organizations, the sales and distribution process is comprised of the following parts:

1. Quotation/order entry
2. Provision of goods or services
3. Billing (invoicing)
4. Incoming payment

Figure 10.1 illustrates the SAP-supported sales and distribution process.

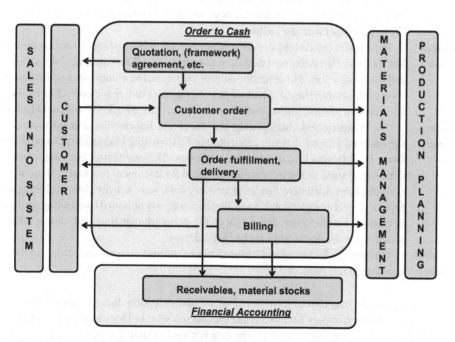

◻ Figure 10.1 Simplified illustration of the SAP-supported order to cash process

Sales & Distribution
(SD)

The Sales & Distribution (SD) module in a standard SAP ERP system supports a number of different variants of the business process: for example, for the sale of services (service master record), for handling down payment requests in plant engineering and construction (special G/L transactions), or for partial and collective payments.

In the following we will illustrate common control mechanisms that, viewed simply, can be summarized in two groups:
- Controls in the preparatory sales and distribution phase
- Controls in order fulfillment and revenue recognition

10.1 Controls in the Preparatory Sales and Distribution Phase

There are various prerequisites for sending an invoice to the customer: there must be an order, the customer must have been created, and the customer's creditworthiness must have been evaluated. In this chapter, you will learn about the risks and control mechanisms in the preparatory sales and distribution phase.

10.1.1 Controls during Order Entry

Sales order as basis

In most cases, the initial order receipt is the starting point for subsequent sales revenues and incoming payments. When an order is received, the customer master and the materials or services are summarized in a *sales document/sales order* and processed in the O2 C process. All further process steps in the delivery of goods and in billing are based on the sales order. The sales order is generally the system representation of a legally binding contract with the customer.

Risks during order entry

In SAP, you can create sales documents directly or by copying an existing quotation. The transfer of the document data from the quotation reduces the probability of an error and the input effort. However, for control purposes, the *automatic completeness check* is very important. The main risk when entering sales orders is incorrect or incomplete sales documents that, under some circumstances, can lead to lower sales or to bad debts.

Controls during order entry

The completeness check checks the document information entered according to a predefined scheme that you can define in Customizing (SALES AND DISTRIBUTION • BASIC FUNCTIONS • LOG OF INCOMPLETE ITEMS • DEFINE/ASSIGN INCOMPLETION PROCEDURE). If some of the information required for document processing is missing (for example, sales document header or delivery data, sales activity data, business partner data, or delivery header data), a warning message may be issued (depending on the configuration). Furthermore, depending on the status group maintained, certain follow-up activities for the document may be blocked.

Check: sales documents

Perform the following audit procedures in connection with sales orders in the SAP-supported O2C process:

1. Get an overview of the types of sales and distribution documents used (SALES AND DISTRIBUTION • SALES • SALES DOCUMENTS • SALES DOCUMENT HEADER • DEFINE SALES DOCUMENT TYPES). The data is stored in table TVAK.

2. Check whether the completeness procedure is configured (see the IMG path above) and whether documents are regularly checked for incompleteness (transaction V.02, List of Incomplete Sales Orders) and reworked where necessary.
3. The following evaluations can also be helpful to get an overview of the existing sales documents:
   - Evaluation of duplicate orders (transaction SDD1, Duplicate Sales Documents in Period)
   - Analysis of orders with a delivery date a long time in the past (transaction V.15, Display Backorders)
   - Evaluation of pickings for sales orders without goods issue (VL06O, Outbound Delivery Monitor)

   If you find orders with an unclear status, clarify the order status with the specialist department. Sales orders should be entered and processed real-time.
4. Transactions VKM1 (for displaying blocked sales documents) and VKM2 (for displaying released sales documents) can also provide a useful overview.

10.1.2 Quality of Customer Master Data

In the sales and distribution process, customer master data is the basis for regular business relationships. For every sales order, SAP requires a minimum level of customer master data. However, to ensure that business operation is regulated, an organization-specific process for customer master data maintenance should be defined.

Process for customer master data maintenance

This process begins with checking whether a master record already exists for the customer. Where applicable, sales and distribution supplements existing customer master records or creates new customer data. Good quality, complete customer data is very important. For example, if the credit limit maintenance is overlooked (see Sect. 10.1.4), there is a risk of payment defaults; partner roles that are not maintained lead to unclear information and sales figures. If the organization is subject to additional requirements, for example, the Prevention of Money Laundering Act, good quality customer master data can only be ensured with a controlled customer master data management.

Controls for customer master data

You can perform a more extensive, qualitative analysis of the customer master data using SAP Query Painter or other CAAT options (see Sect. 17.1.1). Figure 10.2 shows the data model for this type of evaluation.

[e.g.]

Analysis with SAP Query Painter

In a practical example, this analysis for a tobacco products manufacturer revealed that, despite strict money laundering constraints, valid bank details were only maintained for 8 % of all customers.

You can identify duplicate customer masters using transaction S_ALR_87012180 (List of Customer Addresses).

Further operative controls in customer master data maintenance can be the release or even just the monthly check of the change log for critical fields in the customer master record (see Sect. 8.1.5). SAP supports the segregation of duties in the maintenance of

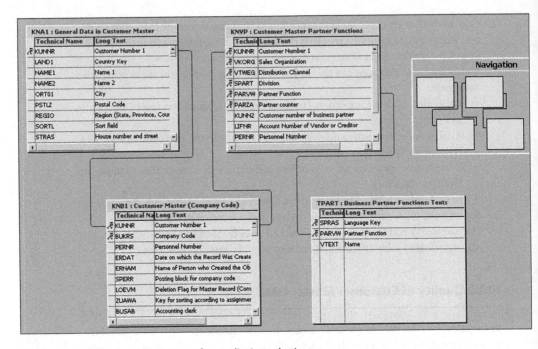

■ **Figure 10.2**   Customer master data query for a qualitative evaluation

customer master data by allowing you to define critical fields in the customer master record. If one of these fields is changed, there is an immediate block. Any change to the master record must be released by a second person.

Customizing   You can set the sensitive fields in Customizing under FINANCIAL ACCOUNTING • AC-COUNTS RECEIVABLE AND ACCOUNTS PAYABLE ACCOUNTING • CUSTOMER ACCOUNTS • MASTER DATA • PREPARATIONS FOR CREATING CUSTOMER MASTER DATA • DEFINE SENSITIVE FIELDS FOR DUAL CONTROL, see Sect. 8.6.5.

Check: mainte-   When checking customer master data, get an overview of the process for main-
nance of customer   taining this data. Pay particular attention to whether the controls for ensuring the
master data   completeness and accuracy of the relevant data are appropriate.

10.1.3 Segregation of Duties for Master Data Maintenance

The basis for ICS-conform master data management is appropriate segregation of du-ties. In the sales and distribution process, the following requirements should be met:

— **Segregation: maintenance of customer master data from the entry of sales orders and from credit limit maintenance**

The maintenance of customer master data must be segregated from the entry of sales orders and from credit limit maintenance. The following authorization objects provide authorizations for maintaining customer master data:

  — V_KNA1_BRG for customer authorization groups

  — V_KNA1_VKO for authorization for sales organizations

- V_KNKK_FRE for processing and release of blocked vendor documents
- The authorizations for maintaining dunning data in the customer master record are restricted by the authorization objects F_KNA1_BUK (Company Code) and F_KNA1_APP (Activities for Customer Master Records).
- **Segregation: authorization for credit limit maintenance from the posting authorizations in financial accounting**
  For appropriate segregation of duties, authorizations for credit limit maintenance should not be combined with posting authorizations in financial accounting (also: billing and credit memo entry). Authorization objects V_KNKK_FRE and V_VBUK_FRE control the authorizations for releasing sales orders.

As is always the case where segregation of duties is concerned, where this is not in place (and is difficult to implement in practice), the ICS focus must be on compensating controls.

10.1.4 Credit Limit Assignment and Control

In the sales process, there are various options for clearing receivables from goods and services. The option with the lowest risk is the exchange of goods and money (cash sale); other variants are prepayment or electronic bank collection. In plant engineering and construction, in most cases a bank guarantee is used to safeguard receivables. Here, the bank guarantees the outstanding receivables should the customer become insolvent.

When customers do not pay

If the customer is granted a credit period, the organization should limit and actively manage the risk of a bad debt by implementing a credit control.

The maintenance of customer master data also covers the entry, evaluation, and management of the credit default risk. In the standard system, SAP supports risk minimization in this area by providing different credit limit controls. SAP differentiates between *static* and *dynamic* credit limit control to deal with the default risk.

Credit default risk

The credit limit control is based on two pillars:
- Maintenance of the credit limit and the risk category in the customer master record
- Activation of the credit limit assignment in sales document types

You maintain the credit limit in the customer master record within the respective *credit control area*. You can display the relevant data using transaction FD32 (Change Customer Credit Management).

Credit Control Area ❶

In SAP, credit control areas are an organizational criterion for managing credit limits. You assign credit control areas to the company codes in Customizing.

Figure 10.3 shows credit limit data for a customer in SAP. The credit limit data is stored in SAP table KNKK. You can make a statement about the quality of the credit control data by evaluating this table.

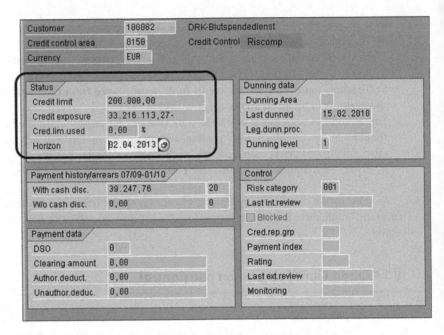

Customer	100002	DRK-Blutspendedienst
Credit control area	0150	Credit Control Riscomp
Currency	EUR	

Status		Dunning data	
Credit limit	200.000,00	Dunning Area	
Credit exposure	33.216.113,27-	Last dunned	15.02.2010
Cred.lim.used	0,00 %	Leg.dunn.proc.	
Horizon	02.04.2013	Dunning level	1

Payment history/arrears 07/09-01/10			Control	
With cash disc.	39.247,76	20	Risk category	001
W/o cash disc.	0,00	0	Last int.review	
			☐ Blocked	

Payment data		Cred.rep.grp	
DSO	0	Payment index	
Clearing amount	0,00	Rating	
Author.deduct.	0,00	Last ext.review	
Unauthor.deduc.	0,00	Monitoring	

◻ Figure 10.3   Credit limit data in the customer master record

Maintenance of the customer master data and credit limit controls

From the view of credit limit controls, customer master data maintenance, as already mentioned in Sect. 10.1.2, is vitally important. On one hand, credit limits must be completely maintained; on the other hand, there must be no customer "duplicates" if possible: multiple master records for one customer can lead to the risk of the overall organization credit limit increasing above an acceptable level due to the accumulation of several credit limits.

Check: credit limits in sales and distribution

Check the following in connection with credit limit maintenance:

1. Get an overview of the use of credit control functions in the SAP-supported sales and distribution process: maintenance of the credit limits, procedure for credit limit check (for example, the use of the credit vector function that allows a credit limit check on order entry).
2. Evaluate the completeness of the maintenance of credit limit data in table KNKK. Consider the plausibility of the assigned limit. Entries such as USD 999,999,999 for the credit limit do not represent an effective control.
3. You can display and evaluate changes to the credit limit using transaction FD24 (Credit Limit Changes). Evaluate the changes for plausibility.

10.2   Controls in Order Fulfillment and Revenue Recognition

The whole range of risk types is represented in the process of revenue recognition: from operational risks, through financial reporting risks, right up to fraud risks.

10.2.1 Controls for Delivery of Goods

Most organizations deliver their goods to logistics partners of the customer or to the customer directly by creating a *delivery*. If the delivery is put together within the organization (picking), picking documents are generally created as well. Depending on the goods delivered, a number of organizations also offer free of charge deliveries or replacement deliveries. Free of charge deliveries bear a considerable risk of uncontrolled or unauthorized goods issues (potential for fraud). Further ways of delivering goods supported by SAP are also interesting from an ICS view: the option in SAP of triggering *goods issues without reference to sales documents*, which can be used to process return deliveries, normal deliveries, or cancellations, must be seen as critical.

Risk areas

| Sales Document Type | DS | Scheduling Agreement | Sales document block | A |

Field	Value		Field	Value
Sales Document Type	DS	Scheduling Agreement		
SD document categ.	E		Sales document block	A
Indicator				

Number systems

Field	Value		Field	Value
No.range int.assgt.	07		Item no.increment	10
No. range ext. assg.	08		Sub-item increment	10

General control

Reference mandatory			Material entry type	
Check division			☐ Item division	
Probability	100		☑ Read info record	
Check credit limit	A		Check purch.order no	
Credit group			☐ Enter PO number	
Output application	V1		Commitment date	

Shipping

Delivery type	LF	Outbound delivery	Immediate delivery	
Delivery block				
Shipping conditions				
ShipCostInfoProfile				

Billing

Dlv-rel.billing type	F2	Invoice	CndType line items	
Order-rel.bill.type			Billing plan type	
Intercomp.bill.type			Paymt guarant. proc.	
Billing block			Paymt card plan type	

◻ **Figure 10.4** Sales document type with automatic delivery block

System controls   You have already learned about movement types in connection with the P2P process (see Sect. 9.2.1, "Goods Receipts: Critical Movement Types"). However, movement
types are also relevant in connection with the O2C process. You define the movement
types in table T156; using authorization object M_MSEG_BWA allows you to restrict the
movement types using authorizations. You can access the Customizing for movement
types with transaction OMJJ (Customizing: New Movement Types). We would recommend removing transactions from movement type 561 (goods issue, initial entry of
stock balances (into SAP System)).

If deliveries are not based on sales documents, the sales document type used must
automatically trigger a block of the sales order (see Fig. 10.4). You define the sales document types in table TVAK. The block can be by means of a user exit or by setting block
types in Customizing (transaction VOV8, Document Type Maintenance).

Check: delivery of   Check the following in connection with goods movements:
goods

1. Get an overview of the treatment of free of charge deliveries. Check the settings for
    the corresponding movement types.
2. Check whether deliveries with specially configured sales document types, for ex-
    ample, free of charge deliveries, have an automatic delivery block. This ensures that
    free of charge deliveries require a separate release.
3. Use transaction VL14L to evaluate sales orders blocked for delivery. Make sure that
    the block status has been updated beforehand. To do this, the specialist department
    should execute program SDSPESTA to ensure that the block information is up-to-
    date.

10.2.2 Pricing and Determination of Sales Tax

Order-related and   As already mentioned, the operative sales process also contains the billing (invoicing)
delivery-related   step. Here, SAP differentiates between *order-related and delivery-related* billing. Whilst
billing   delivery-related billing is based on a specific delivery item, order-related billing references an order item, meaning that a delivery, including the transfer of risks, does not
necessarily have to have taken place. Partial and collective billing documents are possible for both types of billing.

Incorrect billing   During billing the price is determined. The condition technology in SAP uses *con-
documents   dition types* to define surcharges and discounts based on the gross price. *Surcharges and
discounts* are necessary, for example, to consider a flat rate discount in defined sales
channels, such as the Internet, or for major customers. Further common criteria for
material price determination are materials or customers (Fig. 10.5).

In addition to the sales price, during billing the sales tax is also determined. Another
frequent problem here is that chain transactions and triangular deals are not reflected
correctly. Incorrect determination of the sales tax has a negative impact on the accuracy
and completeness of the sales tax liabilities. The organization is also liable for the sales
tax not calculated.

A further operative risk is the incorrect determination of net prices, which can lead
to the loss of sales and profit.

Risk of   In addition to unintentional errors, there is also a risk of fraudulent actions: if it is
manipulation   possible to enter individual items in the access sequence manually, for example, a percentage discount, the sales price can be influenced in favor of the customer; if an or-

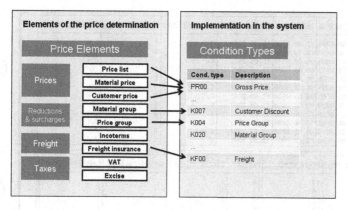

■ **Figure 10.5** Components of pricing as represented in the SAP system

ganization's products are subject to consumption tax, the tobacco tax, spirit tax, or petroleum tax can also be determined during billing.

Compare the processes and controls in the area of sales prices and materials with the Customizing settings in the system and then check Customizing for the pricing procedure (transaction: VCHECKT683, Customizing Check Pricing Procedure).

Use samples to check the automatic determination of sales prices (see Fig. 10.6). To do so, proceed as follows:

Samples for automatic sales price determination

1. For one of the sales document types used (field AUART), use transaction SE16 in table VBAK (restrict field VBTYP to C, Order) to search for entries for a specific period ❶.
2. Determine the pricing procedure used for the customers concerned (table KNVV, field KALKS) ❷.
3. From the sales document types used, determine the corresponding pricing procedure (table T683 V) ❸.

Note that condition types and access sequences are mostly identical.

To find out which access sequences are assigned to a costing type, evaluate table T682I (see Fig. 10.7). Even in table T682, only the data records with *application indicator* V may be considered. Alternatively, you can view the setting for the access sequences in Customizing (SALES AND DISTRIBUTION • BASIC FUNCTIONS • PRICING • PRICING CONTROL • DEFINE ACCESS SEQUENCES).

Determining the access sequence assigned to the costing type

For each individual step in the access sequence, the "Table" column contains a reference to the table that contains the condition records. In the SAP condition technology, this is an *access*. To find the relevant table in the ABAP Dictionary, insert "A" in front of the number. For example, 617 becomes table name A617.

In summary, the relevant audit procedures for pricing and sales tax determination consist mainly of getting an overview of the billing types used and the system for price determination. In some circumstances, a sample check also enables you to identify incorrect condition types and implausible entries in condition tables.

Check: price determination during billing

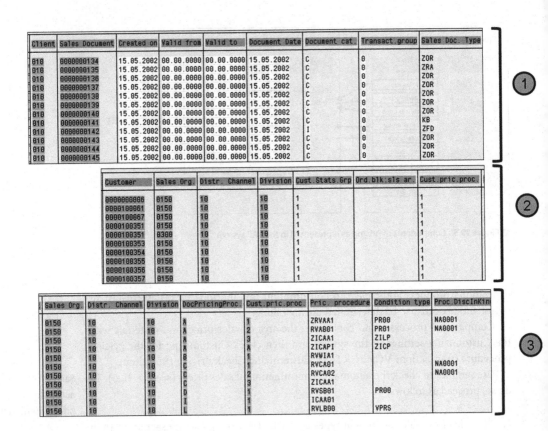

Client	Sales Document	Created on	Valid from	Valid to	Document Date	Document cat.	Transact.group	Sales Doc. Type
018	0000000134	15.05.2002	00.00.0000	00.00.0000	15.05.2002	C	0	ZOR
018	0000000135	15.05.2002	00.00.0000	00.00.0000	15.05.2002	C	0	ZRA
018	0000000136	15.05.2002	00.00.0000	00.00.0000	15.05.2002	C	0	ZOR
018	0000000137	15.05.2002	00.00.0000	00.00.0000	15.05.2002	C	0	ZOR
018	0000000138	15.05.2002	00.00.0000	00.00.0000	15.05.2002	C	0	ZOR
018	0000000139	15.05.2002	00.00.0000	00.00.0000	15.05.2002	C	0	ZOR
018	0000000140	15.05.2002	00.00.0000	00.00.0000	15.05.2002	C	0	ZOR
018	0000000141	15.05.2002	00.00.0000	00.00.0000	15.05.2002	C	0	KB
018	0000000142	15.05.2002	00.00.0000	00.00.0000	15.05.2002	I	0	ZFD
018	0000000143	15.05.2002	00.00.0000	00.00.0000	15.05.2002	C	0	ZOR
018	0000000144	15.05.2002	00.00.0000	00.00.0000	15.05.2002	C	0	ZOR
018	0000000145	15.05.2002	00.00.0000	00.00.0000	15.05.2002	C	0	ZOR

①

Customer	Sales Org.	Distr. Channel	Division	Cust.Stats.Grp	Ord.blk:sls ar.	Cust.pric.proc.
0000000006	0150	10	10	1		1
0000100061	0150	10	10	1		1
0000100067	0150	10	10	1		1
0000100351	0150	10	10	1		1
0000100351	0300	10	10	1		1
0000100353	0150	10	10	1		1
0000100354	0150	10	10	1		1
0000100355	0150	10	10	1		1
0000100356	0150	10	10	1		1
0000100357	0150	10	10	1		1

②

Sales Org.	Distr. Channel	Division	DocPricingProc.	Cust.pric.proc.	Pric. procedure	Condition type	Proc.DiscInKin
0150	10	10	A	1	ZRVAA1	PR00	NA0001
0150	10	10	A	2	RVAB01	PR01	NA0001
0150	10	10	A	3	ZICAA1	ZILP	
0150	10	10	A	A	ZICAPI	ZICP	
0150	10	10	B	1	RVWIA1		
0150	10	10	C	1	RVCA01		NA0001
0150	10	10	C	2	RVCA02		NA0001
0150	10	10	C	3	ZICAA1		
0150	10	10	D	1	RVSB01	PR00	
0150	10	10	I	1	ICAA01		
0150	10	10	L	1	RVLB00	VPRS	

③

◘ Figure 10.6 Evaluations in the area of sales price determination

Usage	Application	Access sequence	Access	Table	IndexNumber key	Exclusive	Cond.module p1	Requirement	Header condit.	Access category
A	RV	VST	20	011	0			000		
A	RV	WT01	05	090	0			000		
A	RV	WT01	10	384	0	X		000		
A	RV	WT01	20	004	0			000		
A	RV	WT03	10	383	0			000		
A	RV	WT04	10	004	0			000		
A	TP	TP00	10	141	0	X		000		
A	TP	TP00	20	142	0	X		000		
A	TP	TP00	30	143	0	X		000		
A	TP	TP00	51	501	0	X		000		B
A	TX	BRB1	10	392	0	X		000	X	
A	TX	BRCI	10	349	0	X		000		
A	TX	BRCI	20	392	0	X		000	X	
A	TX	BRCO	05	346	0	X		000		
A	TX	BRIB	01	344	0	X		000	X	
A	TX	BRIB	05	382	0	X		000		
A	TX	BRIB	98	382	0	X		000		
A	TX	BRIB	99	392	0	X		000	X	
A	TX	BRIC	05	382	0	X		000		
A	TX	BRIC	98	382	0	X		000		
A	TX	BRIC	99	392	0	X		000	X	
A	TX	BRID	05	382	0	X		000		
A	TX	BRID	98	382	0	X		000		

◘ Figure 10.7 Determining access sequences

10.2.3 Return Deliveries and Credit Memos

An established aspect of retail trading, as well as the asset and consumer goods industry, is the treatment of goods returned by customers. This process ensures that goods that are returned by customers are accepted properly. It mostly includes checking whether the goods can be resold or must be disposed of. If the goods are taken back into the warehouse stock, they must be posted as an inward goods movement. In addition, a credit memo must be issued to the customer or new goods delivered.

Risk factor: credit memos

The entry of *customer credit memos* can represent a direct cash outflow if they are paid out to the customer. If the credit memos are offset against outstanding receivables, this represents an indirect outflow of funds. In both cases there is a risk of fraudulent activities. There is a further risk with regard to the accuracy of the receivables.

Valuated goods movements should be used to record goods receipts. Whilst this does lead to an increase in current assets, a scrapping movement type can adjust the stock again and is therefore subject to appropriate SAP controls. The SAP system offers the option of recording return deliveries of goods using return delivery orders. From a technical perspective, these are a type of sales order. Instead of a billing document, the system creates a credit memo at the time of goods receipt. In Customizing, you should define that these credit memos are blocked automatically (similar to a billing block) and require a separate release. For the configuration of material movement types, see Sect. 9.2.1 regarding controls in the purchasing process.

System controls for return deliveries

You configure the returns documents and the automatic creation of credit memos in Customizing using transaction VOV8 (Document Type Maintenance). Figure 10.8 shows an example of how sales document type RE is configured for returns processing. The billing-related settings are particularly important from an ICS perspective.

10.2.4 Billing Due List

The creation of billing documents is an important step in the sales and distribution process. The billing document triggers the posting of the sales (sales revenue) and receivables (open items in the customer account). The differentiation between delivery-related and order-related billing, as explained in Sect. 10.2.2, can also be relevant for service order items or maintenance contracts.

When invoices are not issued at the correct time

The *billing due list* represents a risk with regard to the completeness of sales. It includes all delivery-related or order-related billing documents that can be billed but are not. However, the sales costs are due to the full extent.

Billing due list

The billing due list can be released for billing manually or automatically. However, if there are errors or a posting block has been set for the customer, unbilled sales document items can arise.

The following audit procedures are recommended in connection with the billing due list:

Check: billing due list

1. Check the billing due list (transaction VF04) with regard to timeliness and compliance of the billing items with the internal procedure guidelines.
2. Check whether appropriate segregation of duties is implemented between billing, customer master data maintenance, credit management, and order entry. For

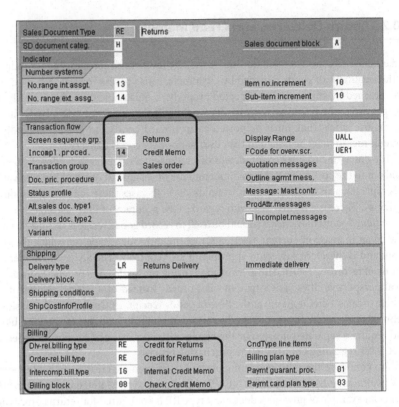

□ Figure 10.8 Customizing for a returns document type with credit memo proposal and automatic block

billing, authorization objects V_VBRK_FKA, V_VBRK_VKO, and transaction codes VF01, VF02, VF04, or VF11 are relevant.

10.2.5 Completeness of Accounting Entry of Billing Documents

Errors in the transfer to General Ledger Accounting

Once the billing documents have been created in SAP, the billing items are transferred to SAP Financial Accounting and posted to the corresponding accounts, for example, sales revenue. If the billed items are not transferred to General Ledger Accounting, or are transferred incompletely, these sales revenues are missing from the profit and loss statement at the end of the period. In addition to the actual billing document line items, credit memos can also remain unprocessed on the interface.

To check the completeness of the transfer of billing documents, use transaction VF03 (Display Billing Document) (see Fig. 10.9). Using the value search help, you can determine the billing documents that have not yet been transferred to accounting.

Check the sales documents determined and the reasons why they have not been transferred. Alternatively, you can use transaction SE16 to evaluate table VBRK. The field POSTING STATUS contains the status of the billing document and the error reason (see Fig. 10.10).

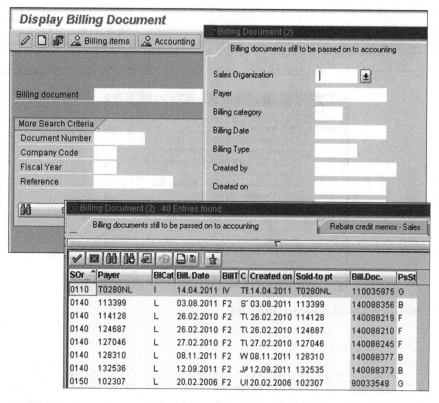

◻ Figure 10.9 Determination of billing documents that have not yet been transferred to General Ledger Accounting

The posting statuses 0, A, B, F, G, I, and K are relevant. Organizations should use appropriate procedures to detect billing items with these statuses in good time.

Perform the following audit procedures in connection with the completeness of the billing document transfer to Financial Accounting:

1. Find out whether appropriate controls are established to regularly check the complete transfer of billing documents to accounting.
2. Evaluate table VBRK for the relevant posting status.

Check: incorrect billing documents

10.2.6 Dunning

After the delivery or performance of services and billing, the receivables remain open until payment is received. They are therefore called "open items." In most cases, the receivables are cleared by bank payment, bank collection, cash payment, or transfer. However, in some cases, the customer does not pay his liabilities on time. For the organization, on the one hand it is important that any default risk is recognized in good

Dunning process

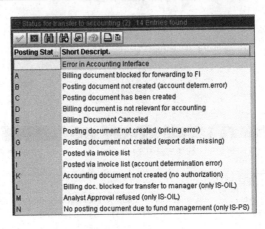

le: VBRK								
played Fields: 17 of 85		Fixed Columns:			2	List Width 0250		
Billing Doc	Billing Type	Document cat.	Distr. Channel	Pric. procedure	Shipping Cond.	Customer group	Incoterms	Posting Status
0140045631	F2	M	10	ZRVAUS	99	03	EXW	C

Status for transfer to accounting (2) 14 Entries found

Posting Stat.	Short Descript.
	Error in Accounting Interface
A	Billing document blocked for forwarding to FI
B	Posting document not created (account determ.error)
C	Posting document has been created
D	Billing document is not relevant for accounting
E	Billing Document Canceled
F	Posting document not created (pricing error)
G	Posting document not created (export data missing)
H	Posted via invoice list
I	Posted via invoice list (account determination error)
K	Accounting document not created (no authorization)
L	Billing doc. blocked for transfer to manager (only IS-OIL)
M	Analyst Approval refused (only IS-OIL)
N	No posting document due to fund management (only IS-PS)

☐ **Figure 10.10**   Status list for billing documents not transferred

time and further purchase orders or deliveries stopped. On the other hand, these open items must also be actively requested. In SAP, this task is performed in dunning.

The programs in SAP Dunning select the overdue items that result in a debit balance. In addition, they select the customers and vendors whose master record permit a dunning notice. The programs then determine the reminder or dunning level and print the dunning letter.

The sending of the dunning notice and the active management of the customer relationship by the sales and distribution department should lead to fast receipt of payment without having a negative effect on the customer relationship.

Risks   In addition to the risk of loss of receivables already mentioned, the intrinsic value of the receivables in the financial statements must be ensured. To take account of loss of receivables, either a flat rate provision is posted or the individual open items are analyzed with regard to age and whether they can be collected and then individual provisions are posted.

At this point we will look only at the controls in dunning. The dunning settings are defined in Customizing and in the vendor and customer master records.

Controls   Check whether the organization uses the SAP dunning functions and if so, whether the dunning procedure configured covers all relevant risk areas in receivables management.

Basic settings in dunning   Check whether the parameters configured conform to the relevant organizational guidelines. You can also get an overview of the settings for the dunning procedure by calling up transaction OBL6. The settings for the dunning procedure are located in SAP Customizing (transaction: SPRO • FINANCIAL ACCOUNTING • ACCOUNTS RECEIVABLE AND ACCOUNTS PAYABLE ACCOUNTING • BUSINESS TRANSACTIONS • DUNNING • BASIC SETTINGS FOR DUNNING/DUNNING PROCEDURES). Here you can find, for example, as

Change View "Dunning Areas": Overview

New Entries

Co	Area	Text
0001		Default dunning area
S001		Riscomp dunning area for domestic customers

Change View "Dunning Block Reasons": Overview

New Entries

Lock	Text
	Freed for dunning
*	Dunning interface
A	Open customer reclamation
B	3rd Dunning notice issued
C	Customer at collection agency
D	Intercompany customers
E	AAA customer
H	Block reason H
L	Block L/C
R	Blocked by invoice verification

Change View "Dunning Keys": Overview

New Entries

Dunn.key	Max.level	Print sep	Text
1	1	☑	Triggers maximum dunning level 1-Mittlerer Mahnweg
2	2	☑	Triggers maximum dunning level 2 - Kurzer Mahnweg
2		☑	Payment has been made, separate item display

◻ Figure 10.11 Basic settings in dunning

shown in Fig. 10.11, the settings for the dunning areas, dunning keys, and the dunning block reasons.

You can also define the entire dunning procedure, and in particular the parameterization, in SAP Customizing (transaction: SPRO • FINANCIAL ACCOUNTING • ACCOUNTS RECEIVABLE AND ACCOUNTS PAYABLE ACCOUNTING • BUSINESS TRANSACTIONS • DUNNING • DUNNING PROCEDURE • DEFINE DUNNING PROCEDURE) or directly via transaction FBMP. An example for a dunning procedure in which a payment reminder is sent after 14 days is shown in Fig. 10.12.

In connection with the master data and open items, perform the following audit procedures in the dunning process:

Check: dunning process

- Evaluate the vendor and customer master data to determine the extent to which non-associated third party organizations and business partners are blocked for dunning and which dunning levels individual customers and vendors have. Use transaction SE16 to evaluate tables LFB5 and KNB5 (the DUNNING BLOCK field is relevant). The automatic dunning run does not capture vendors or customers for which a block indicator is set. Note, however, that the evaluation can also contain blocked customers and associated organizations. Use table KNB5 to evaluate the customers.
- Then check the list of receivables and, if applicable, down payments made, using transactions FBL3N (vendors) and FBL5N (customers). In the layout, select the ARREARS BY NET DUE DATE field.
- Compare the overdue open items with the settings for the dunning run to determine whether the receivables are dunned at the correct time and in accordance with the organization guidelines.

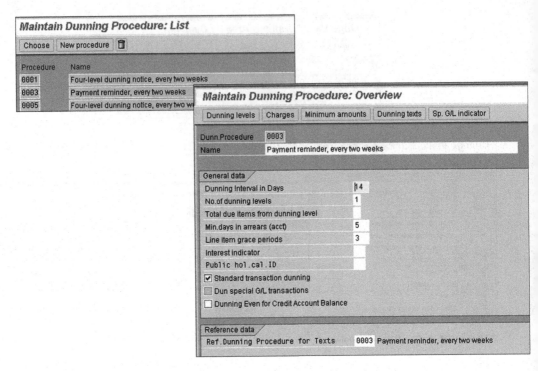

Figure 10.12 Definition of the dunning procedure in Customizing

> ❗ **Configuration of the Dunning Procedure**
>
> You can get a good overview of the settings for the automatic dunning procedure in Customizing with transaction OBL6 (Consistency Check: Dunning Program Configuration). The block indicators are saved in tables KNB5 for the customer master record and LFB5 for the vendor master record. You can evaluate the open items with transactions FBL3N (vendors) and FBL5N (customers).

10.3 Summary

From the view of external financial reporting, the risks and control mechanisms in the order to cash process, which you have learned about in this section, are very clear. Divided into the preparatory phase and the phases for order fulfillment and revenue recognition, the compliance view of the O2C process focuses heavily on the operative organization objectives. This is because sales and profit are the prime interests of organizations. The risks of fraud in the O2C process must not be overlooked: for more information, see Sect. 12.4.

Data Protection Compliance in SAP ERP Human Capital Management

Personal data must be treated with special care: explained here under the generic term "data protection," this issue is important not only for compliance experts but also for most people reading this book.

The risks and relevant control mechanisms in the SAP-supported processes of personnel management and payroll – the module Human Capital Management, SAP ERP HCM – are very clear from the perspective of external financial reporting: in general, the issue is the correct and complete transfer of the results of a payroll run for wages and salaries and provisions for outstanding salaries (for example, 13th monthly salary) to the general ledger. As a result, the personnel costs are posted right up to the level of the individual cost centers. Further relevant issues could arise where time data entry is used and where travel expense management is integrated.

Data protection as a further compliance view

In this chapter, we will move away from the financial reporting-driven aspect of compliance – with the exception of the ever-present topic of security and authorizations – to look at the compliance of HCM processes from the data protection perspective.

The requirement and the wish to protect employee data within the scope of the legal *data protection regulations* is a defining feature of the SAP ERP HCM-supported processes: the focus is on personal data and this requires special treatment. In this chapter, we will present the most important legal data protection aspects with regard to SAP ERP HCM.

> **Recommended Literature**
>
> For more detailed information on this topic, see the book "Authorizations in SAP Software: Design and Configuration" by Volker Lehnert and Katharina Bonitz. It is published by SAP PRESS.

11.1 Legal Data Protection Requirements

When describing the legal data protection requirements in this chapter, we will refer above all to the EU data protection directive but also to US-specific regulations, as these have an undeniable, immediate influence on most internationally active companies.

The EU directive requires that member states of the EU implement certain requirements in national law. For the purpose of legibility, we will not refer each time to the fact that the directive must be implemented in national law; we will only mention a few country-specific laws as examples.

11.1.1 Data Protection

Data protection legislation is modern legislation. Therefore, in comparison to other sources of law, it is fortunately very specific. Furthermore, data protection is not predominantly the subject of national regulations; it is always connected to proposals or even binding directives from international organizations.

Data protection directive of the Council of Europe
In Europe, the directive from the Council of Europe is the first item to mention (COE, 1981). It has the potential of achieving worldwide importance: the Council of Europe has requested that all states sign up to the directive, and this is also being discussed seriously in, for example, Australia and Mexico. For many EU countries, the directive became valid law to be implemented in national law as a result of the ratification by the respective national parliaments.

EU data protection directive
The "EU Data Protection Directive" (EU, 1995) is actually effective worldwide, although indirectly. It requires that an appropriate level of protection must be demonstrated for exchanging data with third countries (that is, states that are not member states of the European Union). According to Article 25 (6) of the directive, the EU Commission may find that a third country ensures an appropriate level of protection. To achieve this, the USA, for example, has concluded an agreement with the EU: US companies can demonstrate an appropriate level of protection if they "voluntarily" sign up to the Safe Harbor Principles (see Gola, Klug, Körffer, 2010, Section 4 b RN 15).

To execute the data protection directive, national legislative bases have been created that demonstrate systematic similarities. In addition to general data protection legislation, there are often specific regulations or regulations for individual sectors. In this case, the more specific (i. e., more detailed) regulation applies.

Supplements for Germany
Let us look at Germany as an example: here, in addition to the German Data Protection Act (BDSG), the German Penal Code (StGB), the German Social Welfare Code (SGB), German labor law, and in particular the Works Council Constitution Act (BetrVG) all contain regulations on data protection.

Figure 11.1 illustrates how German legislation is embedded in the international legislative pyramid. For companies that process personal data originating in electronic form from parts of companies within the EU in any automated procedure, regulations apply that in general must comply with at least the EU directive.

A company that has its registered office in the EU is subject to national legislation that is also based on the EU directive. There may also be standards for individual sectors regulating individual facts more specifically, as is the case, for example, in the Austrian and German data protection regulations.

National Legislation in Germany

A company that has its registered office in Germany is subject to the regulations of the German Data Protection Act (BDSG). For employee data, regulations from the German Social Welfare Code (SGB), labor law, etc. also apply. In many areas, the processing of personal (employee) data is subject to co-determination of the works council in accordance with the Works Council Constitution Act (BetrVG). Within the scope of social insurance and tax law, personal data that the employer has to make accessible to the authorities in electronic form is mentioned explicitly.

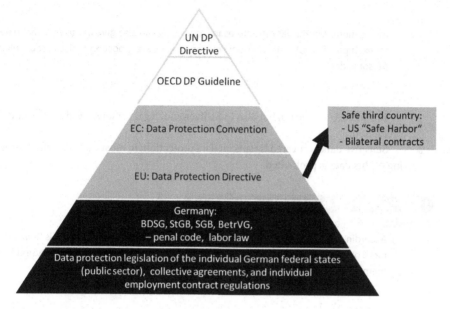

Figure 11.1 Data protection pyramid

11.1.2 Basic Principles: European Union Directive

In the following we refer to the EU directive. It obliges the member states of the EU to implement certain requirements in national legislation.

Implementation of the EU Directive in Valid National Legislation ❶

For the purposes of legibility, we will not specify each time that EU decisions must be implemented in national legislation and thus represent an immediate legal effect that is otherwise not given naturally.

The details in this section refer to the EU directive from 1995: "Directive 95/46/EC of the European Parliament and of the Council of 24 October 1995 on the protection of individuals with regard to the processing of personal data and on the free movement of such data, Official Journal L 281, 11/23/1995 P. 0031–0050."

Personal Data

Article 2 a) of the EU directive refers the data protection to natural persons.

Definition: Personal Data ❶

Personal data is on one hand every individual detail about a person (e.g., residence) or on the other hand, details that can be assigned to a person (e.g., the ordering of medication). Master data structures in a company can also give rise to personal data: for example, if a cost center has only one employee, every posting to this cost center is personal data.

In some EU countries, but also in Switzerland, legal persons are also subject to data protection.

Sensitive data   Sensitive data is covered by special data protection; in most cases therefore, processing of this data is prohibited.

Definition: Sensitive Data

According to Article 8 (1) of the EU directive, sensitive data refers to details "revealing racial or ethnic origin, political opinions, religious or philosophical beliefs, trade-union membership, and [...] of data concerning health or sex life."

However, there are exceptional cases in which processing of this data is also permitted. These exceptions are regulated on a case-by-case basis.

Definitions and Explanations of Data Processing

The processing of personal data covers the saving, changing, transmitting, blocking, and deletion of this data. These terms are defined as follows (see Article 2):

- **What is meant by "processing"?**
  The processing of data covers the collection, recording, storage, adaptation or alteration, retrieval, disclosure by transmission, alignment or combination, or deletion of personal data. Note that the processing, and above all the combination or alignment of personal data, may create new personal data. When you analyze the ordering behavior of a customer (natural person), for example, a new personal data record is created.

- **What is a file with personal data?**
  A file with personal data is any structured set of personal data that can be evaluated according to specific criteria. It is sufficient for one single criterion to be capable of evaluation for this definition to apply. The file does not necessarily have to be available in electronic form.

- **Who is responsible for processing and in what form?**
  The *controller* (person responsible for processing) is the natural or legal person who determines the purposes and means of the processing of personal data.
  The *processor* is the natural or legal person who processes personal data on behalf of the controller. The processor can be another legal person from the same company.
  The *recipient* is the natural or legal person who receives the data. An exception applies for individual examination orders from authorities.

- **When is processing permitted?**
  According to the directive, any freely given specific and informed indication of his wishes by which the data subject signifies his agreement to personal data relating to him being processed is sufficient consent. Even if the EU directive does not require

written consent in principle, it is strongly advised; written consent is required in some national legislation and/or with reference to specific data. You must be able to demonstrate the circumstances under which and for which data consent has been given – written consent is advisable, where applicable electronically.

More Precise Definition of "Person Responsible" in a Group Structure

In practice, in complex group structures questions often arise about responsibilities. The person responsible is the independent legal person who has, has had, or is initiating a work contract with the subject concerned.

Before a legally independent subsidiary makes data available to other legally independent subsidiaries or the head office (recipient), clarification of whether the registered office of the recipient is in the EU is required.

Within or outside the EU

- If the registered office of the recipient is in the EU, then the data processing can be deemed *commissioned data processing*. In this case, the person responsible does not change. However, commissioned data processing requires that the recipient is completely bound by instructions with regard to the data processing and that this can also be proven.
- If the registered office of the recipient is not in the EU, the data processing cannot be commissioned data processing. In this case, *data transfer to third parties* must be assumed (see Gola, Klug, Körffer, 2010 Section 2 RN 21).[1]

Commissioned Data Processing

[e.g.]

Imagine a corporate group in which a legally independent shared service center manages employee data within the EU. In this case, the data processing is commissioned data processing. If the shared service center is not in the EU, it must be in a safe third country. Accordingly, the responsibility in the sense of any protective measures to be set up or instructed lies with the person responsible, that is, the actual employer.

Rights of the Subject/Limitations on Use

Only permissible (Article 6 (1)) personal data may be stored. This means that there must be a legal or contractual basis for storing the data. A contractual basis does not negate the protection of sensitive data. It also means that the data may only be collected with reference to the previously defined purpose and within the required scope. Only factually correct data may be stored. This includes the right of the subject to have the data cleaned up.

Permissibility

The organization is observing correct procedure if it can prove that there is a legal basis and/or consent from the subject. It is in the organization's own interests to obtain written or electronic consent. This consent should also document how the subject has been informed of the purpose of the data processing. It must also be possible to prove that the consent was given voluntarily.

Legislation, consent, information

In some cases, in particular with regard to employees, there are clear legislative bases for data processing: an employee does not have to declare consent if the employer for-

---

[1] Check whether it is a case of commissioned data processing or transfer of functions (see Gola, Klug, Körffer, Section 11 RN 9).

wards personal data to social insurance or tax authorities. However, this does not mean that the data collected for this purpose can be provided for any other purposes.

Where data is processed without consent, for example, to fulfill legal requirements, the subject must be informed of the data processing.

Check: processing of personal data

The following basic questions must be answered during the audit with regard to the *processing of personal data*:

1. Is the processing of the data determined by law?
2. If this is not the case: has the subject given a written declaration of consent?
3. Was this consent given voluntarily and in full knowledge of the purpose of the data processing?

Purpose with regard to content and time

With regard to the processing of personal data, in every case, the data may only be processed for one or more specific purposes. Any other use without a renewed written declaration of consent from the subject is not permitted. The purpose also determines how long data may be stored for or how long it must be stored for: data that is no longer required for the specified purpose must be deleted provided it is not required to document, for example, data changes (postings, releases).

Check: purpose

To check compliance with the principle of purpose, the following questions must be answered:

1. Is there a clear purpose for each procedure?
2. Does the purpose define which data is to be stored and for what period?
3. Is exclusively data required for the purpose processed?
4. Can it be demonstrated that data no longer required is archived (if necessary) or deleted (if possible)?

Right to information

In general, the subject must be informed of the storage and the planned data usage (Article 10). This point is particularly interesting if the data may be processed within the scope of other legal conditions without the consent of the subject or if the data is to be provided for a purpose other than that originally declared.

Right of access

In principle, the subject has the right to view any data collected about him and to be informed about the type of data processing (Article 12). One example of a facility for this purpose is the register of processing operations that details the IT systems used, the data qualities, and the security measures.

Factual accuracy and inspection

Only factually correct personal data may be processed. Where applicable, the subject has the right to request a correction.

Check: factual accuracy

To check compliance with the principle of factual accuracy, the following questions must be answered:

1. How is the factual accuracy of the personal data guaranteed?
2. Is there an automatic procedure for requesting that subjects evaluate their data and correct it where necessary?
3. How can subjects have data corrected?
4. Can subjects see their data on request?

Further Principles of Processing

Article 16 of the EU directive regulates the confidentiality of processing: this is generally only permitted on instruction by the person responsible. Therefore, it must be possible to prove that instructions were given beforehand for every type of access to personal data.

Article 17 provides that "appropriate technical and organizational measures" must be taken to guarantee the protection of data against destruction, loss, unauthorized alteration, unauthorized forwarding, and unauthorized access. These measures must be appropriate with regard to the risks, latest technology, and costs.

Before personal data may be processed in one or more automated procedures, a "designated supervisory authority must be notified" (Article 18 (1)). Different processing purposes are possible.

Article 18 (2) provides for a simplification of the obligation to provide notification provided there is an operational data protection officer who maintains a register of processing operations.

Data transfer to third countries (i. e., non-EU countries) is regulated in Article 25. Transfer is only permitted if the third country has an appropriate level of protection in place. This is demonstrated, for example, through agreements of the EU Commission with the country in question. For data transfer to the United States, the US Safe Harbor Principles represent the basis for permitting personal data to be transferred to the USA from companies with registered office in the EU.

As soon as a "person responsible" (i. e., a natural or legal person) collects data in the EU, an appropriate level of protection must be given for data transfer to a third country. In this context, in addition to payroll accounting, Gola, Klug, and Körffer refer explicitly to communication directories and skills databases (see Gola, Klug, Körffer, 2010, Section 4 b RN 13).

Confidentiality of processing

Protective measures

Obligation to provide notification

NotificationData protection officer

Data transfer to third countries

From What Point Must an Appropriate Level of Protection be Given?	[e.g.]

The requirement for an appropriate level of protection in connection with a third country means that even a standard communication data directory or a standard database for user information in a corporate group can be deemed data transfer to a third country. This makes the EU directive the most legally binding worldwide source of law for data protection.

The Safe Harbor Principles (US Department of Commerce, 2000) represent a compromise between the EU and the United States of America. In accordance with these principles, US states that process personal data from European states can "voluntarily" commit to meeting the seven Safe Harbor Principles:

Safe Harbor Principles

- **Notice**
  The organization must notify the subject about the processing of his data, the purposes of the processing, and the specific data, as well as inform the subject of the options for viewing the data and options for objections.
- **Choice**
  The organization must grant the subject the opportunity to prohibit a use beyond that of the original purpose or transfer to third parties.

- **Transfer to third parties**
  A transfer to third parties is only permitted provided the principles of notice and choice have been complied with. The third party must also have subscribed to the Safe Harbor Principles or be able to prove in some other way that they comply with these principles (this applies to every country that has subscribed to the directive of the European Council or is a member state of the EU).

- **Access**
  Subjects must be able to receive access to their data in order to request, where applicable, corrections, supplements, or deletions.

- **Security (protective measures)**
  The organization must commit to take reasonable precautions to protect personal data against loss, misuse, unauthorized access, disclosure, alteration, and destruction.

- **Data integrity**
  The organization must commit to ensuring that only correct and relevant data is processed for the defined purpose.

- **Enforcement**
  By means of appropriate controls and sanctions, the organization ensures that the afore-mentioned principles are observed. Failure to comply with the principles means that the organization no longer falls within the EU regulations for safe third countries

Consequences of protective measures

The protective measures demanded in Article 17 of the EU directive are set out differently in the national legislation of different countries. In German data protection law, for example, they are regulated in detail in an annex to Section 9 of the German Data Protection Act (BDSG). The important terms of the German legislation are listed below; they are valid in the same sense in Austria and almost word-for-word in Switzerland.[2]

- **(Physical) Access control**
  Unauthorized persons must be prevented from gaining (physical) access to the data processing systems.

- **Logical access control**
  General access to the systems used must be restricted to authorized persons only.

- **Least privilege control**
  Access must be restricted to persons formally (from an organizational view) entitled to have access. Furthermore, these persons must have access only to the minimum amount of data they need in order to complete their tasks.

- **Disclosure control**
  It must not be possible for data transfers (technical interfaces, transmissions) to be accessed by unauthorized persons. It must be possible to prove this at all times.

- **Input control**
  It must be possible after the fact to check and ascertain whether personal data has been entered into, altered, or removed from data processing systems and if so, by whom.

---

[2] In Austria they are regulated in detail in Section 14 (2) of the Austrian Data Protection Act. In Switzerland (non-EU), they are regulated in detail in the implementing regulation of the Swiss Data Protection Act Article 9 (1) and refer to the control objectives detailed in the text above.

■ **Job control**
Where commissioned data processing takes place, the person responsible must guarantee that the processor complies with the instructions.
■ **Availability control**
Personal data must be protected against accidental destruction or loss.
■ **"Combination not permitted"**
There must be a guarantee that data collected for different purposes can be processed separately. (The term "combination not permitted" is used here but does not originate from the EU directive.)

11.1.3 Co-Determination and Employee Data Protection

In both Germany and Austria, for example, there are laws that grant works councils and employee committees a right of participation and co-determination with regard to the processing of employee data.

Co-determination

> **Co-Determination of Works Councils and Employee Committees** ❶
>
> In Germany, the relevant law is the Works Council Constitution Act (BetrVG); see Däubler, Klebe, Wedde, Weichert (2010) and Gola, Klug, Körffer (2010) for further information.
>
> The employee committee is the employee representation in the public sector in Germany. Its tasks are regulated not in the BetrVG, but in the Federal Employee Representation law (BPersVG) and the employee representation laws of the individual German states.

> **Works Council Agreement Required** ❶
>
> In some areas, agreement by the works council is required before a respective IT-supported procedure can be introduced or changed. This is the case in Germany. Without exception, it must be assumed that the introduction and use of an SAP ERP HCM system in an organization in Germany is subject to co-determination by the works council.

The limitations on use detailed above do not explicitly define the period after which data must be deleted. This question is very important, including with regard to job application procedures, skills databases, and appraisal procedures.

Storage of data

With regard to an employee, in principle, personal data may be recorded and stored; the EU data protection directive does not contain any detailed instructions regarding employees. However, depending on the respective national labor legislation, we can assume that there are either legal or contractual regulations or case law that further

Employee

regulate employee data protection.[3] The German Data Protection Act (BDSG), for example, contains explicit rules on employee data protection in Section 32.

In principle, therefore, the following applies: personal data may be collected and processed within the scope of an employment relationship. Without exception, the principle of purpose and the principle of a legal basis or the explicit consent of the subject apply.

Job application
procedure

Data relating to job applications must be destroyed after completion of the procedure. As far as in-house applicant databases are concerned, this means that a clear declaration of consent must be obtained from the subject. This consent should be renewed on a regular basis. Transfer of data to third parties (even within the same corporate group) is not legally permitted without explicit permission from the subject. For Germany, it must be assumed that the data is collected directly from the subject, meaning that a link from data collected directly from the subject to publicly accessible details, such as Xing or Facebook, is not legal (see Däubler, Klebe, Wedde, Weichert, 2010, Section 32 RB 56).

❗ Direct Collection

Even though direct collection is not mandatory in all EU countries, with regard to employees, it is the most sensible method as it is the most suitable way of ensuring that the employee is informed of the data collection and of ensuring the data quality. Accordingly, in the case of direct collection, a declaration of consent can be obtained or, where necessary, right of objection granted.

Collecting sensitive
data

Within the scope of a work relationship, it may be necessary to collect sensitive data, for example, for health protection (across Europe or specifically for Germany) due to legislation regarding protection against unlawful dismissal.

In Germany, since 2009, as an exception, personal data of an employee may be collected to detect criminal activities if there are actual indicators for suspicion that can be documented. This was a reaction of the German legislature to a scandal at a large German transport company.

Once the prerequisites no longer apply (purpose, legal basis, consent), all data collected must be deleted. This does not include data that must be stored based on other legal, bye-law, or contractual requirements.

[e.g.] Storage

For example, the German Radiation Protection Ordinance dictates that the data regarding an employee's exposure to radiation must be stored until the end of the employee's 75th year, and for at least 30 years. Data must be deleted at the latest 95 years after birth.

---

[3] See Oberhofer (2009) for the legal situation in Austria. For the legal situation in Switzerland (the EU data protection directive does not apply here), see Maurer-Lambrou, Vogt (2006) Art. 328b/362 OR.

With regard to skills databases and appraisal procedures, we can assume that this data is relevant for the entire term of the work relationship and is therefore only deleted once the work relationship has terminated, as it is only then that the purpose no longer applies.

Skills databases and appraisal procedures

Treatment of Skills Databases

The treatment of skills databases is bound to the information under "More precise definition of 'person responsible' in a group structure" in Sect. 11.1.2, "Basic Principles: European Union Directive" of this book.

The following questions are relevant in connection with employee data protection:

Check: employee data protection

1. Is there a legal basis for every item of data collected and/or a declaration of consent from the subject?
2. Has the retention period been clarified for every item of data collected?
3. Are declarations of consent available for transfer of the data to third parties?
4. Are there special protective measures for sensitive data?
5. Can it be demonstrated that data no longer required is archived (if necessary) or deleted (if possible)?
6. Is there a guarantee that the data is used exclusively within the scope defined for the purpose?
7. With regard to the purpose in particular, is there a guarantee that only queries defined in advance in systems defined in advance are possible?

11.1.4 Excursion: Protection of Patient Data

Patient data enjoys special protection worldwide. The legislation of most countries contains relevant regulations. This data protection focus, alongside the corresponding SAP software products used in hospitals and clinics, is a side issue that will not be explicitly addressed in this book. However, a general insight into the pertinent regulations in the USA is relevant:

- The Health Insurance Portability and Accountability Act of 1996 (HIPAA) Privacy and Security Rules
- The Patient Safety and Quality Improvement Act of 2005 (PSQIA) Patient Safety Rule

The *Standards for Privacy of Individually Identifiable Health Information* ("Privacy Rule") establishes a set of US-national standards for the protection of certain health information. The U.S. Department of Health and Human Services ("HHS") issued the Privacy Rule to implement the requirement of the Health Insurance Portability and Accountability Act of 1996 ("HIPAA"). The Privacy Rule standards address the use and disclosure of individuals' health information – called "protected health information" – by organizations subject to the Privacy Rule – called "covered entities" – as well as standards for individuals' privacy rights to understand and control how their health information is used. Within HHS, the Office for Civil Rights ("OCR") has responsibility for implementing and enforcing the Privacy Rule with respect to voluntary compliance activities and civil money penalties.

A major goal of the Privacy Rule is to assure that individuals' health information is properly protected while allowing the flow of health information needed to provide and promote high quality health care and to protect the public's health and well being. The Rule strikes a balance that permits important uses of information, while protecting the privacy of people who seek care and healing. Given that the health care marketplace is diverse, the Rule is designed to be flexible and comprehensive to cover the variety of uses and disclosures that need to be addressed.

The regulation implementing the Patient Safety and Quality Improvement Act of 2005 (PSQIA) was published on November 21, 2008, and became effective on January 19, 2009. See the Patient Safety Rule (42 C.F.R. Part 3). PSQIA establishes a voluntary reporting system to enhance the data available to assess and resolve patient safety and health care quality issues. To encourage the reporting and analysis of medical errors, PSQIA provides Federal privilege and confidentiality protections for patient safety information called *patient safety work product*. Patient safety work product includes information collected and created during the reporting and analysis of patient safety events.

For more detailed information, see the official website of the U.S. Department of Health & Human Services (http://www.hhs.gov/ocr/privacy/).

11.2   General Data Protection-Relevant Control Mechanisms in SAP

Principle of traceability

From the view of data protection requirements, the fulfillment of the principle of traceability in SAP must be considered from two aspects:

- **Logging required**
  On one hand, the option of performing relevant evaluations immediately for support purposes is provided. Data protection law itself, or rather, the annex to Section 9 (1) of the German Data Protection Act (BDSG) defines this uniquely: it states that measures must be taken "to ensure that it is possible after the fact to check and ascertain whether personal data have been entered into, altered or removed from data processing systems and if so, by whom." Such requirements affect primarily data in SAP ERP HCM.

- **Logging is not always a conscious decision**
  On the other hand, thanks to the logging mechanisms that you already know (for example, the recording of all transaction calls by users in SAP ERP – see, for example, Sects. 7.3.2 and 7.3.3), personal data that is relevant for data protection purposes arises outside SAP ERP HCM and in further SAP-supported business processes. This fact is heavily neglected in practice.

We will address both aspects of the traceability issues below.

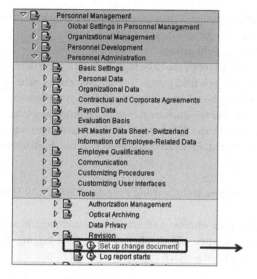

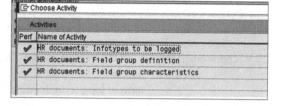

▣ Figure 11.2   Settings for logging infotypes

11.2.1 Tracing Changes to Personal Data

We will look at the concept of infotypes in more detail in Sect. 11.4.2, "Personnel Events." At this point, it is sufficient to state that all personal master data in SAP ERP HCM is contained in tables called *infotypes*. Tracing changes to personal data in SAP would therefore require logging these infotypes. You can achieve this using *HCM-specific change documents* (not to be confused with the change documents from Sect. 7.2.1, which are relevant to other SAP-supported processes).

HCM-specific change documents

You set up these change documents in the SAP Implementation Guide under PERSONNEL MANAGEMENT • PERSONNEL ADMINISTRATION • TOOLS • REVISION/AUDIT • SET UP CHANGE DOCUMENTS.

> **❯ Caution – No Default Values!**   The standard SAP system does not contain any infotype log, which means that the control tables required are delivered empty.

As you can see in Fig. 11.2, three steps are necessary to set up HCM change documents:

Setting up change documents

1. **Define infotypes to be logged**
   A change to an infotype defined as *to be logged* triggers the creation of an infotype log. Therefore, infotypes that are not defined as to be logged are not logged. Transaction class A applies for the creation of an infotype log for HR master data management; transaction class B applies for the creation of an infotype log for Applicant Data Administration.
2. **Define field groups** ·
   Within an infotype, all fields to be logged must be specified. Via the FIELD LIST, you can display and select all fields of an infotype. Furthermore, within an infotype, you

can group fields in differentfield groups. When the infotype log is created, all fields in a field group are treated as one unit and logged together.

3. **Define the characteristics of the field groups**

In this step you define which field groups are to be logged. You can also define SUP-PLEMENTARY FIELD GROUPS for each field group. The supplementary field groups are always logged if a field within the relevant "triggering" field group has changed. Here you must also define whether the document is to be recorded as a long-term document (L) or short-term document (S). Long-term documents are retained in SAP until they are explicitly deleted. From an ICS perspective, the short-term documents are sufficient.

You can display changes to infotype records using program RPUAUD00 (Logged Changes in Infotype Data).

Check: logging of infotypes   In the Implementation Guide, check whether, as described above, change documents have been set up for all relevant infotypes. Check whether the type of logging (short-term or long-term documents) has been selected appropriately.

11.2.2 Logging Report Calls in SAP ERP HCM

In SAP ERP HCM, you can log calls of reports that use personal data in SAP. You make the corresponding settings in the Implementation Guide under PERSONNEL MAN-AGEMENT • PERSONNEL ADMINISTRATION • TOOLS • REVISION/AUDIT • LOG REPORT STARTS (the prerequisite is that reports to be logged use logical database PNP). For each report, you can define whether it is logged when started online, in the background, or for both variants. The following data is included in the log: report, report title, user, start date, start time, report parameters, and selection options.

You can view the results of the logging using program RPUPROTD.

Check: logging of report calls   The following audit procedures are useful in connection with logging report calls:

1. In the settings in the Implementation Guide, check whether report calls are logged.
2. If report calls are logged, check whether access to program RPUPROTU is handled restrictively.

11.2.3 Deleting Data and Making it Unrecognizable

Anonymizing data   In Sect. 6.2.1, you learned about the usual structure of the SAP landscape. In practice, a live SAP system is often used as a copy template, for example, for a quality assurance system or a training systemIn a copy operation (depending on the system copy profile), in some circumstances all data can be transferred, even data from SAP ERP HCM. As authorizations are assigned less strictly in a quality or sandbox environment, here there is a risk that personal data (as well as customer and vendor data) can fall into the wrong hands. Therefore, in these systems, data (contents of infotypes) is made anonymous using various programs.

Check: making data anonymous   It is useful to get an overview of the system landscape in the SAP ERP HCM en-vironment. Check whether, when the live system is copied, personal data is made anonymous.

In addition to the question regarding the system copy, deletion of data in a live HCM system is also relevant: the Recruitment module thus contains corresponding programs that, for example, delete data of applicants and other persons who enter their own data in the HCM system via the Internet. Check the use of such programs (for example, scheduling in the Job Scheduler, contents of program variants used, etc.). Program RCF_DELETE_EXT_CAND is used for external candidates to be deleted in E-Recruiting.

Applicant data

As far as employee data is concerned, at the time of printing of this book, in the standard SAP system, the HCM module does not contain any functions that would allow the deletion of employee data en masse. Neither is it always possible to delete individual employees: as soon as SAP ERP HCM contains payroll results for an employee, the employee can no longer be deleted.

Employee data

11.2.4 Personal Data Outside SAP ERP HCM

Due to the further requirements for traceability, personal data can arise outside SAP ERP HCM – many companies are often not aware of this. From a data protection view, many of the logging actions in SAP are less critical: for example, the user ID is logged in all documents entered in SAP. A flexible mass analysis of documents would be possible, for example, through the further evaluation of information that is stored as a file and that can be generated by a direct table access or starting a program. Since local storage of SAP data can be restricted by means of authorizations, this option should be used.

However, from a data protection view, some logging methods are associated with a higher risk:

Higher risk logging methods

- **Security Audit Log**
  Here, for example, you can set up filters that log all of a user's actions. For data protection reasons, logging activities of other users beyond a recommended scope of anonymous emergency users, standard users, support users, etc. is questionable (and in Germany, for example, must be agreed with the works council) (see Sect. 7.3.2, "Security Audit Log").
- **History of transaction calls**
  The data stored in the statistics file about all transaction calls within a specific period is relevant with regard to data protection. Therefore, access to this file must be handled strictly (see Sect. 7.3.3, "History of Transaction Calls").
- **SQL trace**
  As long as this trace is activated, all database activities of a user or a user group are logged. Access to the SQL trace functions and the log file in particular should therefore be handled restrictively.

With regard to the handling of data protection-relevant information, check the following:

Check: handling of data protection-relevant data in SAP ERP

1. Clarify whether any data arising outside SAP ERP HCM is classified from a data protection view.
2. Check whether the authorizations for saving data locally are assigned restrictively.

3. Check whether activities of business users are logged in the Security Audit Log and whether the access to the statistics file is sufficiently restricted. Also check the handling of the SQL trace functions.

11.3 Special Requirements of SAP ERP HCM

The special requirements that SAP ERP HCM has to satisfy are due to the handling of employee data. Personal data contains general data about a person, but also sensitive data in the sense of the EU directive (see Sect. 11.1.2, "Basic Principles: European Union Directive").

Protection standards
The special protection of all personal data is a legal requirement; it must be protected against any undesired access. This protection must be specific; intentional access to several tens of thousands of employees does not meet this requirement. It must be possible to demonstrate who has been able to view or change personal data, at what time, and for what reason.

Other reporting obligations
In addition to the restriction of access for users, the HR area is also subject to legal requirements that specific personal data must be reported to social insurance authorities, tax authorities, or supervisory authorities. This is regulated in a number of legal sources that can differ strongly from country to country and depending on the industry (for example, reporting obligations in the food industry or the energy industry).

Self-maintenance
The next special feature is that data that is processed can, in principle, be the user's own data. The employee in payroll accounting also receives his salary via SAP ERP HCM, and is therefore also an employee in the system. Here, measures must be taken to ensure that nobody can maintain their own income or similar critical data.

Abuse of information
Finally, there is another special feature that sometimes leads to employee data and payments being managed by third party providers: improper use of employee data can disrupt peaceful operation.

Technical special features
Figure 11.3 shows a summarized illustration of various requirements for protecting employee data as well as a simplified structure of this data. The different requirements have led to some special technical features:

- Individual exclusion option (instead of the usual positive authorization) with regard to a user's own personnel number
- Structural authorizations
- Context-sensitive authorizations

These issues are presented in the following section.

11.4 Authorizations and Roles in SAP ERP HCM

Authorizations are particularly important in SAP ERP HCM. They are used to set up a considerable proportion of the required protective measures, the access controls:

> [M]easures … shall be taken to prevent data processing systems from being used without authorization [and] to ensure that persons authorized to use a data processing system have access only to those data they are authorized to access (source: German Data Protection Act (BDSG)).

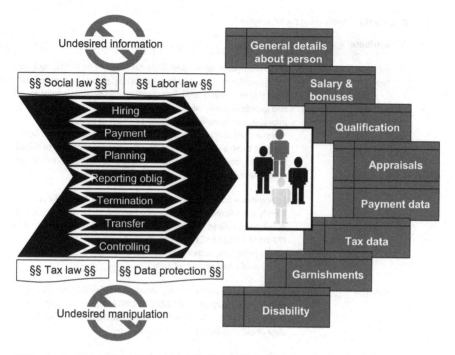

□ **Figure 11.3** Standards, processes, and data in SAP ERP HCM

A principle of least privilege without exception is necessary from both a functional and an organizational perspective. Only data required as a result of formal responsibility may be accessed.

Recommended Reading		❗

For more in-depth questions regarding the design of an authorization concept in SAP ERP HCM, see the book "Authorizations in SAP Software: Design and Configuration" by Volker Lehnert and Katharina Bonitz. It is published by SAP PRESS.

11.4.1 Differentiating Attributes in SAP ERP HCM

In the HCM system, data is defined in infotypes and frequently given attributes. Table 11.1 shows some of the required attributes.

The information defined in the infotypes can be evaluated in the infotype tables, including the following tables:

- PA0000 (IT0000) to PA0998 (IT0998)
- HRP1000 (IT1000) to HRP1990 (IT1990)
- PA2001 (IT2001) to PA3893 (IT3893)
- HRP5003 (IT5003) to HRP6200 (IT6200)

SAP ERP HCM attributes

Infotype tables

◻ Table 11.1 Attributes in the HCM system

Attribute	Description
Infotype (information type)	Personal, organizational, and other data in SAP ERP HCM is defined in infotypes: the primary data for a person is defined in infotype 0002, the basic pay in infotype 0008, family and related persons in infotype 0021, and qualifications in infotype 0024. Infotypes can be defined for specific periods of time. The standard SAP system contains several hundred infotypes, and many of them are country-specific. From the point of view of the authorization concept, a restriction of each infotype based on a sensitivity assessment is required.
Subtype	Subtypes are further subclassifications of the infotype. Infotype 0021 (family and related persons) specified above can be differentiated in detail using various subtypes, for example, SPOUSE, DIVORCED SPOUSE, PARTNER, CHILD, EMERGENCY CONTACT. Where necessary, authorizations must be assigned using a precise combination of infotype and subtype.
Subtype	For example, for an emergency situation, it is feasible that the information under subtype EMERGENCY CONTACT is provided to security personnel, but that security personnel have no reason to see further data about children, divorced spouses, etc.
Object type	Each element of an organization can be portrayed as an independent object. Important object types are, for example, organizational unit (O), position (S), and person (P). There are further object types for the indirect function assignment: role (AG), user (AG). You maintain objects in infotype 1000.
Plan variant	Since planning is very important in SAP ERP HCM, it is usual to define various plan variants that can be protected accordingly. Future-based planning with reference to personnel is definitely sensitive; however, it is rare.
Planning status	In connection with planning, it may also be necessary to differentiate between the different possible statuses (active, planned, requested, approved, rejected) that an object can have by means of authorizations. In the industry solution SAP for Defense & Security, the planning status is very important.
Personnel area	The personnel area is an organizational characteristic for grouping the employees of an organization according to administrative criteria and for allowing restriction of authorizations to specific areas.
Employee group	The employee group is a further grouping characteristic independent of the personnel area. Usually there is a differentiation between at least active employees, pensioners, external employees, and early retirees.
Employee subgroup	Employee subgroups are differentiated within the employee group. This means that active employees can be classified into hourly paid employees, salaried employees, and non-pay-scale employees.
Organizational key	The organizational key is a further characteristic for differentiating the personnel and company structure. You can define default values for the organizational key.

◻ **Table 11.2** Authorization objects

Object	Description	Field	Description
PLOG	Personnel planning	INFOTYP	Infotype
		ISTAT	Planning status
		OTYPE	Object type
		PLVAR	Plan variant
		PPFCODE	Function code
		SUBTYP	Subtype
P_ORGIN	Master data	AUTHC	Authorization level
		INFTY	Infotype
		PERSA	Personnel area
		PERSK	Employee subgroup
		SUBTY	Subtype
		VDSK1	Organizational key
P_PCLX	HR: clusters	AUTHC	Authorization level
		RELID	Area ID for clusters in tables PCLx
P_PERNR	Master data – personnel number check	AUTHC	Authorization level
		INFTY	Infotype
		PSIGN	Interpretation of an assigned personnel number
		SUBTY	Subtype

Inspection of these structures can be used in individual cases to control which data the structures contain in the sense of checking sensitivity. You can evaluate the infotypes used with program RPDINF01.

Check: contents of the infotypes

11.4.2 Personnel Events

In SAP ERP HCM, the term *personnel event* is a collective term for various events that can be recorded in personnel administration (employment, change, termination, etc.). For example, in personnel administration, the employee data can be processed using transaction MAINTAIN HR MASTER DATA (PA30). Alternatively, you can use transaction PERSONNEL ACTIONS (PA40). The authorization objects shown in Table 11.2 are associated with this transaction.

Infotypes for
transaction PA30

To define the authorizations for a personnel event, for example, hiring, you need information about which infotypes are to be maintained. These settings depend on the configuration of the process flows in SAP ERP HCM. With regard to transaction PA30 (Maintain HR Master Data), at least the following infotypes are required:

- IT0000 – Events
- IT0001 – Organizational Assignment
- IT0002 – Personal Data

The following infotypes are also frequently maintained:

- IT0003 – Payroll Status
- IT0007 – Planned Working Time
- IT0008 – Basic Pay
- IT0009 – Bank Details
- IT0012 – Fiscal Data – Germany
- IT0013 – Social Insurance – Germany
- IT0016 – Contract Components
- IT0021 – Family
- IT0105 – Communication

Subtypes in
authorizations

Further infotypes may be necessary depending on the configuration.

If you maintain infotype IT0105 (Communication), you must also maintain the type of communication via the subtype. To determine the subtype for an infotype, in the Subtype Characteristics table (T591A), you can use the infotype to determine the subtypes assigned (see Fig. 11.4).

For the personnel event, you also need the details of the personnel area (field PERSA), the employee group (field PERSG), the employee subgroup (field PERSK), and the organizational key (field VDSK1). This would provide you with all details for the authorization object HR: Master Data (P_ORGIN). (You have to activate the check, see Sect. 11.4.4, "Authorization Main Switches.")

Restriction to
personnel numbers

To control the authorizations for the personnel event further, depending on further settings, you can define a specification with regard to the authorization object HR: Master Data • Personnel Number Check (P_PERNR). There, using the Interpretation of Assignment – User/Personnel Number field (PSIGN), you can define whether an employee is permitted to access the data for his own personnel number; to be more precise: here you define whether the user assigned to a personnel number via infotype 0105, subtype 0001 may access this personnel number. The field PSIGN can take the following forms:

- I – additional authorizations for the user's own personnel number
- E – excluded authorizations for the user's own personnel number

E overrides I. The form * is not supported. The Authorization Level field (AUTHC) controls the type of access (read, write, write locked record).

❗ Special Feature: Authorization Object P_PERNR

The authorization check against object P_PERNR represents a real exception. In all program flow checks, it checks whether a specific authorization is present: the principle

```
Table:              T591A
Displayed Fields:    6 of   6        Fixed Columns:              | 3      Li
```

MANDT	INFTY	SUBTY	ZEITB	OBJRQ	STEXT
010	0006	1	2		Permanent residence
010	0006	4	2		Emergency address
010	0006	FPCB	2		Addresse pendant le congé bonifié
010	0006	FRRT	2		Residence Address for Ticket Restaurant
010	0006	HKTX	2		HK:Tax Consultant Address
010	0006	R1	2		Accomodation provided by employer
010	0006	R2	2		Hotel accomodation provided by employer
010	0008	0	1		Basic contract
010	0008	1	2		Increase basic contract
010	0008	2	2		Comparable domestic pay
010	0008	3	2		Refund of costs in foreign currency
010	0008	4	3		Local weighting allowance
010	0008	BR01	3		Increase Basic Contract - Brasil
010	0008	DEBV	2		Assessment Basis Prohibited Activities
010	0008	DUBE	2		Incapacity to Work Civil Servant
010	0008	ERA	2		Germany Only
010	0008	FA	2		Previous Superior Employer
010	0008	FBNL	2		Flexible Benefits (NL)
010	0008	FI01	3		
010	0008	FS	2		Secondary assignment
010	0008	HG	2		Up. Limit Income from Wages/Pension Imp.
010	0008	HG54	2		Upper Limit Additional Pension Payment

Figure 11.4 Subtype characteristics

is that the access is positively authorized. Using authorization object P_PERNR, the authorization for access to data with reference to a user's own personnel number can be granted for specific infotypes or activities (positive authorization) but can also be prohibited (negative authorization).

To enable the check of the user's own personnel number, an authorization main switch must be set (see Sect. 11.4.4).

Personnel events make up a large part of personnel administration. Provided logging is defined for the relevant infotypes, you can check changes in the infotype data using transaction S_AHR_61016380 (Logged Changes in Infotype Data). From a data protection perspective, even just displaying the data requires protection. From an accounting perspective, personnel events must be correct as they can also be associated with changes in pay. This is particularly critical with regard to possibilities for self-maintenance.

Check: personnel event

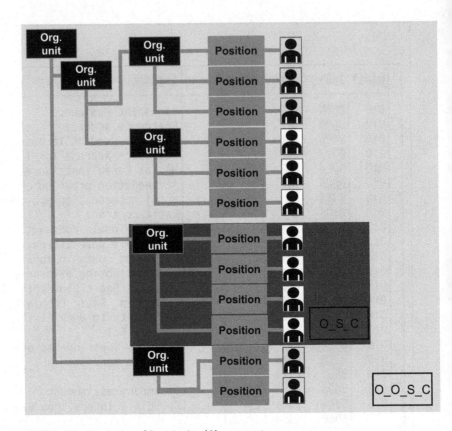

□ **Figure 11.5** Simple view of Organizational Management

11.4.3 Structural Authorizations

Structural
authorizations

Structural authorizations are a special feature of SAP ERP HCM authorizations; however, this feature is now also accessed in other solutions. The special feature is that a structural profile is assigned to a separate table via a separate transaction – thus, independently of transactions SU01 (User Maintenance) and PFCG (Profile Generator).

The structural authorizations are based on Organizational Management within SAP ERP HCM and allow restriction of organizational access to a specific part of the organization. This restriction is ICS-relevant as on the one hand, it restricts organizational access of authorizations, thus following the principle of least privilege for the purposes of data protection. On the other hand, it is also required for accounting in order to comply with the principle of least privilege and, where applicable, segregation of duties here. To make this clear, Fig. 11.5 shows a simplified view of Organizational Management.

Evaluation paths

You can see that an organizational structure can consist of any number of hierarchically structured organizational units. Positions are assigned to the organizational units, and in turn, a person is assigned to the position. The gray areas represent the result quantity for an evaluation path. In our context, these would be the areas of an organization for which an access is explicitly granted.

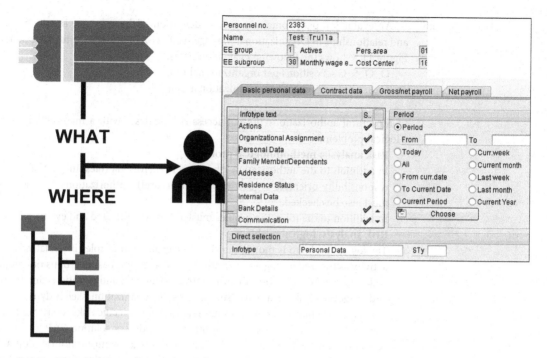

□ Figure 11.6 Structural authorizations and roles

Evaluation paths can evaluate this information "along" the structure. The evaluation paths illustrated would represent the information for all displayed organizational units, a position, the (further) objects, and the person with reference to the user.

Structural authorizations enable you to differentiate between organizational accesses in accordance with data protection requirements. This principle is made clear in Fig. 11.6. In this type of approach, the role contains two views:

- The process organizational view that provides answers to the question "What?" (actions and measures)
- The responsibility-oriented organizational view that, with the help of structural authorizations (shown as a reporting structure), answers the question "Where?"

Structural authorizations – responsibility-oriented organization

This shows that structural authorizations must be assigned in addition to roles.

A *structural profile* combines one or more evaluation paths with the designated start object, the evaluation depths, and the period restrictions within one or more plan variants: this means that you can define precisely to which part of the organization access is granted for actual and plan information and for which periods. The responsibility-oriented organizational access thus defined is made more specific at runtime (depending on further settings); this means that at runtime, the system determines which jobs, positions, persons, etc. the user has access to.

Structural authorization profile

You use transaction OOSP (Authorization Profiles) to maintain a structural authorization profile. You assign structural profiles to users using transaction OOSB (USER (STRUCTURAL AUTHORIZATION); the relevant table is T77UA, USER AUTHORIZATIONS.

Maintenance and assignment of the structural authorization profile

Evaluation path   An evaluation path contains a precise definition of the sequence in which objects and relationships in Organizational Management in SAP ERP HCM must be evaluated. Figure 11.5 shows the following evaluation paths:
- O_O_S_C – Positions per organizational unit
- O_S_C – Positions of one organizational unit

Structural authorizations present access risk analyses with a methodological and a logical problem.

- **Risk analysis: methodological problem**
  In addition to the authorizations that a user receives via roles, in SAP ERP HCM, responsibility-oriented organizational (structural) authorizations for each user must also be checked.
  In addition to the roles, the profiles must also be investigated and evaluated.

- **Risk analysis: logical problem**
  The logical problem is more extensive. The evaluation of roles is a relatively static activity as the underlying authorizations are static: purchasing groups or company codes do not change at runtime. In contrast, structural authorizations are dynamic and are generally determined at runtime. As the organization itself is dynamic, part of the organization that demonstrates relatively few specific risks today can be critical tomorrow. A good example of this is the industry solution SAP for Defense & Security for organizations for domestic and foreign security: information about units sent on a tour is naturally more sensitive than information about units at home and this can change on a daily basis.

SAP Access Control   SAP Access Control offers the technical option of including structural profiles in the risk analysis. The use of Access Control therefore leaves "only" the logical problem of useful definition of risks resulting from structural profiles.

Check: structural authorizations   Using transaction OOAC (HR: Authorization Main Switch), you can evaluate which objects a structural profile contains at runtime. This evaluation enables you to estimate the parts of an organization that an owner of this profile may access.

This can only ever be a sample. You should define critical parts of an organization separately and then use these samples such that the actual content is checked for the "critical" parts of the organization (context solution in HCM authorizations).

Basic concept of the context solution   In simple terms, the *context solution* is the combination of the role-based concept with the structural profiles. Structural profiles are entered in specific authorization objects.

Figure 11.7 shows this principle. The structural profile is included in the role. The user who receives the role (directly or indirectly) has, via the role, process organizational and responsibility-oriented organizational authorizations.

Authorization objects of the context solution   Table 11.3 shows an authorization object for the context solution. In comparison to the corresponding authorization object without context solution, this authorization object contains an additional field: the Authorization Profile field (PROFL), in which the structural profile is entered.

Check: structural authorizations – context solution   Firstly, check which authorization concepts are used in SAP ERP HCM. Based on this, check whether the settings have been configured accordingly. Finally, use samples to check the extent to which SAP ERP HCM authorizations provide sufficient organizational restriction, i. e., usually excluding access to the entire HR data of an organization.

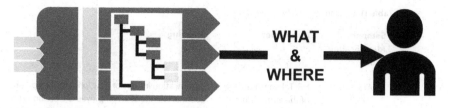

◻ Figure 11.7   Context solution

◻ Table 11.3   Authorization objects of the context solution

Object	Description	Field	Description
P_ORGXXCON	HR: Master data – enhanced check with context	SUBTY	Subtype
		SBMOD	Administrator group
		SACHZ	Administrator for time recording
		SACHP	Administrator for HR master data
		SACHA	Administrator for payroll
		PROFL	Structural profile
		INFTY	Infotype
		AUTHC	Authorization level

11.4.4 Authorization Main Switches

In SAP ERP HCM, authorizations are controlled to a considerable extent via *authorization main switches*. We have already mentioned this in reference to the objects P_ORGIN and P_PERNR.

Authorization main switches mainly control the following procedures:

- Use of a master data check on the infotype (see Sect. 11.4.2, authorization object P_ORGIN)
- Use of the enhanced master data check on the infotype
- Use of the check for the user's own personnel number (see Sect. 11.4.2, authorization object P_PERNR).
- Use of structural authorizations (Sect. 11.4.3)
- Tolerance period after transfer
- Test procedure
- Combination of various checks

Control function of the main switches

You configure the authorization main switches using transaction OOAC (HR: Authorization Main Switch). These are illustrated in Table 11.4.

Because of their importance for an authorization concept, the authorization main switches must be included in a check of the authorization concept: these switches are

◻ Table 11.4　Main switch check relevance

Semantic identification code	Description	Meaning
ADAYS	HR: Tolerance time of the authorization check	Specification in days of how long after an organizational change of an employee the previous user responsible still has access to this employee's data.
APPRO	HR: Test procedure	You use this switch to activate the check of IT0130 (employee data check). The test procedure must be defined in Customizing for personnel administration.
DFCON	HR: Default position (context)	Within the context solution: definition of the handling of personnel numbers that are not linked to Organizational Management in SAP ERP HCM, i. e., personnel numbers that are not assigned to a position or are only assigned to a default position.
INCON	HR: Master data (context)	Within the context solution: activation of the use of authorization object P_ORGINCON.
NNCON	HR: Customer-specific authorization check (context)	Within the context solution: activation of the use of customer-specific authorization objects.
NNNNN	HR: Customer-specific authorization check	Activation of the use of customer-specific authorization objects.
ORGIN	HR: Master data	Activation of the standard check on infotypes, authorization object P_ORGIN
ORGPD	HR: Structural authorization check	Activation of the structural authorization check
ORGXX	HR: Master data – enhanced check	Activation of enhanced check on infotypes with authorization object P_ORGXX.
PERNR	HR: Master data – personnel number check	Activation of the check for the user's own personnel number.
XXCON	HR: Master data – enhanced check (context)	Within the context solution: activation of the enhanced check on infotypes.

directly associated with both data protection risks and commercial risks. For example, if the check against the user's own personnel number is suppressed in these switches, relevant role settings are bypassed and the administrator can adjust his own pay.

Check: authorization main switches

The comparison of the conceptually defined values with the actual settings is particularly important. If a company has defined the check for the user's own personnel number in certain areas to avoid self-maintenance (part of the personnel event), you must regularly check whether this setting is also active. In the same sense, but more extensively, this also applies for the context solution and the structural authorizations (see Sect. 11.4.3, "Structural Authorizations"): the protection is only effective when the switches are set. Therefore, get a regular overview of the settings with transaction OOAC (HR: Authorization Main Switch).

11.5 Summary

In this chapter, you have learned how personal data in SAP ERP, particularly in the Human Capital Management module, can be protected, and the legal regulations that are the basis for this protection. You protect the data using authorization controls in HCM – these are very different to the "usual" ERP authorizations as described in Sect. 5.2, "Authorizations." The high complexity of the topic is a result, amongst other things, of the fact that in practice, the area of HCM authorizations contains extensive customer-specific technical adjustment options via BAdIs.

We have not looked at the financial reporting-relevant processes in HCM, but the authorization and traceability controls that you have learned about are relevant from the view of external financial reporting as well as in respect of data protection regulations.

Fraud in an SAP System

A powerful ERP system such as SAP ERP offers many options for safe handling of data and information. However, these options can also be used to hide criminal activities.

Fraud is a risk that is difficult to avoid for an organization of any size: despite well-known penal consequences, in practice, there is plenty of criminal energy for such activities. A modern ERP system such as SAP can represent a risk, but at the same time it offers solutions for fraud prevention and detection. We have already mentioned fraud topics frequently in the second part of this book – in this chapter we will look at the topic as a whole and for specific processes.

12.1 Introduction to "Fraud"

In the fourth "Global Economic Crime Survey," a study run every two years globally by PricewaterhouseCoopers (source: www.pwc.com), more than 43 % of organizations surveyed stated that they had been affected by fraud. Amongst other things, fraud can have a negative impact on an organization's economic position (affecting the balance sheet and profit and loss statement), the organization's culture, and the reputation of an organization. Organizations generally find it difficult to quantify the risk because many scenarios are also based on speculation that questions the integrity of the employees. A climate of mutual mistrust is not a good environment for cooperation in an organization.

Increasing risk

Fraud can take place at various levels and have various objectives. In recent history, cases of fraud in financial reporting have provided headlines worldwide. Some cases have been so extreme that large organizations collapsed or disappeared (see Sect. 2.2.2, "Selected Auditing Principles").

12.1.1 Types of Fraud

Let us first explain the term *fraud* in more detail and look at the individual types of fraud.

Fraudulent financial reporting can be defined as follows: intentional incorrect reporting of the financial position of an organization – through a deliberate false statement or incorrect presentation of the financial, asset, or revenue position. The objective of this incorrect presentation is to deceive the addressees of the information.

Fraudulent financial reporting

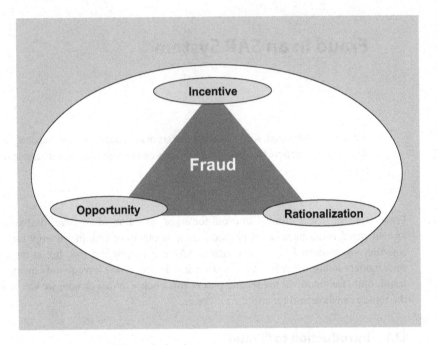

◻ Figure 12.1   Favorable factors for fraud

The purpose of such a fraud can be, for example, to improve the organization's results (e. g., sales) so that the organization can negotiate better refinancing conditions. This type of fraud can occur in various places in the financial reporting, for example:

- Assets, sales revenue, or profit could be reported too high.
- Amounts due, expenses, or losses could be reported too low.

Fraudulent financial reporting is rarely done for the direct enrichment of the criminal, in contrast to embezzlement.

Asset embezzlement

Asset embezzlement means that an individual or a group of individuals misappropriates the assets of an organization illegally for their own purposes.

This type of embezzlement is done to achieve a direct financial benefit. It is often done by means of theft (e. g., from the warehouse) or by means of impermissible use of funds (e. g., through the transfer of liquid funds of the organization to a private bank account).

Three factors that favor fraud

The fraud theory defines three prerequisites for criminal acts (see Fig. 12.1):
- The opportunity to commit fraud
- The incentive to commit fraud
- The ability to rationalize your own actions

An organization must restrict all three factors in order to proactively minimize the potential for fraud.

Information technology (and special networked, integrated, and powerful ERP systems such as SAP) offers opportunities for exercising certain types of fraud and concealing these illegal activities. At the same time, information technology also offers

◪ **Table 12.1** Types of automated anti-fraud controls

Type of control	Property	Examples of controls that can prevent/detect fraud
Access controls	Preventive	Can restrict access to critical tasks or information (e. g., maintenance of transfer prices) Can force the separation of incompatible activities (e. g., between master data maintenance of vendors and the execution of payments)
Application and configuration controls (see Sects. 3.1.4 and 5.1.2)	Preventive	Can contribute to the systematic suppression of certain behavior patterns or acts (e. g., goods issue can only be posted if there is a customer order)
Semi-automated controls with a manual aspect, automated monitoring (see Sect. 3.1.4 with regard to the structure of controls in the ERP environment)	Detective	Used to identify exceptions within specific transaction types (e. g., inspection of manual journal entries) Allow transactions to be checked using data analysis (e. g., analysis of direct manual postings in the general ledger)

considerable control and monitoring mechanisms that reduce the risk of fraud efficiently and effectively.

However, two of the three factors are not associated with technological components. Fraud at a higher management level is often caused by the desire to achieve the highest targets and the associated bonus payments. Therefore, in addition to realistic objectives, organizations should also define acceptable or unacceptable (e. g., dishonest) behavior in their guidelines. They should also specify the consequences of actually committing fraud. Efficient communication of such regulations reduces the possibility of justifying fraud.

12.1.2 Fraud and the SAP System

On one hand, the SAP system can be used to execute and conceal fraudulent activities. With the introduction of ERP systems, activities that were previously performed by numerous employees can now be concentrated on a few or even individual persons. Integrated and networked ERP systems whose existence is justified by the aim of achieving increased efficiency in processes often present organizations with the challenge of finding a balance between an efficient and a secure organization when assigning authorizations in practice. In many cases, security means segregation of duties (which generally has a negative effect on efficiency). *SAP system can create opportunities for fraud*

On the other hand, with the right application, the SAP system can be used for early detection or even prevention of fraud. To do this, the SAP system offers numerous types of (semi-)automated controls (see Table 12.1). *An SAP system can prevent fraud*

The control types specified are present in the different SAP modules and can be applied in combination to minimize the risks of fraud in an SAP system environment proactively. In principle, preventive, automated controls are preferred over detective *Preventive controls are preferred* controls, as it is difficult to bypass preventive IT controls, making them more effective. Furthermore, automated controls only cause an initial, one-time effort (setting the system parameters) and use up only low or even no personnel resources in executing the control activity. Remember that there are also non-automated preventive controls (e. g., organizational controls).

The following sections describe fraud risks using different business processes as examples.

Note on the Following Examples		

For each fraud scenario, we present a selection of combinations of preventive and detective control activities that can prevent or reduce fraud. We do not guarantee to illustrate the complete range of control activities as for every risk of fraud, the SAP configuration and the ICS environment of a business process must be analyzed individually and extensively.

12.2   Fraud Scenarios in SAP Basis

The SAP Basis component, SAP NetWeaver Application Server ABAP, is the basis for most SAP products. Fraud in the environment of the SAP Basis component is mostly due to users having too many rights and to the abuse of support and administration functions in SAP that enable automated application controls to be bypassed. The fraud does not take place in the SAP Basis component itself, but the extensive access to the support functions can allow access to the various business processes.

Frequently misused functions

In this area, fraud can take place due to misuse of the following functions:
- "Write-debugging" authorizations
- Processing a batch input session under a different user ID

We will now look at these functions in more detail and show how fraud can be detected and prevented in an SAP system.

Orientation	

Here, familiarity with the contents of Chap. 6, "IT General Controls in SAP ERP," and Chap. 7, "General Application Controls in SAP ERP," can be very helpful. These chapters describe Basis-relevant controls in more detail (with some direct references to fraud).

12.2.1 "Write-Debugging" Authorizations

Types of debugging

You already know the dangers of debugging from Sect. 7.1.2; here we will address the corresponding risks again because of their importance. *Debugging* is a function that allows experienced users to solve a problem in a program or with reference to data step-by-step. In the SAP system there are two types of debugging:

- *Read-debugging* enables you to correct program errors and shows the content of program variables during runtime.
- *Write-debugging* also enables you to correct program errors, shows the content of program variables during runtime, and allows additional changes.

As far as fraud is concerned, there are two important points to note regarding write-debugging:

Write-debugging and fraud

- Anyone who can correct program errors has a deep knowledge of the SAP system and can bypass all authorization queries. The debugger has free access to the SAP system.
- During the correction of a program error, user fields that the SAP system needs for logging can be changed to make it look as if another person executed the transaction. This function can be used to conceal fraud.

12.2.2 Processing a Batch Input Session under a Different User ID

In the batch input procedure (see Sect. 7.4.4), one or more transaction calls can be merged with associated data. This function can be used for various transactions, for example, creating vendor master data, recording manual journal entries, or creating user master data.

To run a batch input session, the user requires the necessary authorizations. However, the SAP system can be configured such that the batch input session can be run using a background job *under a different ID*. With regard to fraud, there are two important aspects to be considered in this case:

Opportunities for fraud

- If a user has authorization to run batch input sessions as a background job, he can select any other user and add that user's authorizations to his own.
- All batch input business transactions that have been created under a different user ID as part of a background job are also logged under this ID.

In an SAP system, you can control the processing of background jobs under another user ID using authorizations. The most important authorization object is S_BTCH_NAM. This authorization object contains only one authorization field. This field defines the authorized user ID that is permitted to enter such background jobs. Without this authorization, users may only enter background jobs under their own ID. This authorization should be assigned very restrictively, if at all.

Preventive control: restrictive assignment of authorizations

The SAP system records all background jobs executed (including batch input sessions run) in a log. This log contains all of the information about a background job. To identify who has triggered a background job under another ID, you can analyze SAP table TBTCP (Background Job Overview) (see Fig. 12.2).

Detective control: batch job log files

In all background jobs where the field name SDLUNAME (Job Scheduler) is different to the field name AUTHCKNAM (Background User ID), this is an indicator that the job was run by a different person. Note, however, that this job log only lists the program or report executed; it does not provide any information about the business content of the business transactions executed. Therefore, you must find out which processes within an organization are processed via the corresponding BI operation.

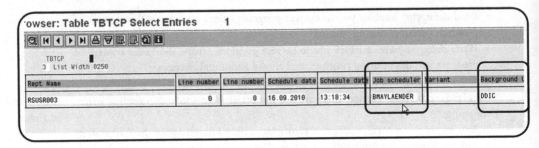

Figure 12.2 Background job log

12.3   Fraud Scenarios in the General Ledger

Most fraud scenarios in SAP-supported financial accounting relate to falsified, manually executed document postings and changes. This type of fraudulent journal entry is often executed during period closing.

Balance sheet fraud/falsification

This type of fraud is known as *balance sheet fraud/falsification*, and the following actions are particularly prevalent in financial reporting:

- Posting of fictitious sales and receivables
- Incorrect presentation of fixed assets
- Incorrect presentation of payables and expenses

12.3.1 Fraudulent Manual Document Postings in the General Ledger

The SAP system has various control mechanisms that can contribute to preventing unauthorized manual journal entries in the general ledger.

Blocking manual postings

For example, some general ledger accounts can be configured such that only automatic entries are permitted and the SAP system rejects manual postings (for example, sales revenues posted from SD via billing transactions). In practice, where necessary, it is useful to establish an account that you can post to manually and monitor specifically.

You can see accounts with the setting AUTOMATED POSTINGS ONLY (table field INTB) in table SKB1. Check closely whether all relevant accounts are blocked for manual posting. In practice, however, you often need to be able to post to accounts manually, meaning that only a detective analysis of the accounts can identify any unauthorized postings.

Restricting manual postings

A further measure in the SAP system is the restrictive assignment of authorization for manual entry of documents in the general ledger. Transactions that allow manual entry of documents in the general ledger include:

- FB01 – Post Document
- FB50 – G/L Account Posting
- FB50L – Enter G/L Account Document for Ledger Group
- FB01L – General Posting for Ledger Group

Since even transactions developed in-house could be used, all transactions developed in-house that are used to enter documents manually must be subject to appropriate controls.

12.3.2 Identification and Analysis of Manual Journal Entries

It is not the primary aim of external or internal auditors to detect fraudulent actions, but in the course of their work they must address the risks of fraud, for example, by analyzing journal entries. Whilst a number of audit standards (e. g., SAS99, ISA240) define the requirements that external auditors have to meet with regard to the risks of fraud when auditing financial statements, internal requirements have to be considered on a case by case basis.

Although auditors are not primarily concerned with detecting fraud, forensic investigators focus on cases of fraud.

Definition of "Forensic Science" ❶

The term *forensic science* is the application of a broad spectrum of sciences to answer questions of interest to a legal system (source: http://en.wikipedia.org/wiki/Forensic_science).

The greatest challenge in analyzing journal entries in the general ledger is in differentiating between manual entries and automatic entries. SAP treats all transactions as journal entries; manual entries are not identified separately. In practice therefore, CAAT-based data analysis scenarios are often used (see Sect. 17.1.1, "Offline CAAT Tools"). These scenarios are based on extracts from the document tables (BKPF and BSEG, see Sect. 5.1.1, "Data in an SAP System"). *[Analysis at table level]*

The elements listed below can be helpful in identifying manual journal entries. However, to interpret the results, you need specific ERP process knowledge and accounting and auditing expertise.

- Transaction: Code, table BKPF, field TCODE
- Document type: Table BKPF, field BLART
- Business transaction: Table BKPF, field GLVOR
- User ID: Table BKPF, field USNAM
- General ledger: Table BSEG, field HKONT

Depending on the audit objective, the focus is on different fields. However, as a minimum requirement, consider the fields from Table 12.2 when analyzing the SAP accounting documents.

Common CAAT-supported queries can include the following scenarios: *[CAAT-supported queries]*

- List of users who have made journal entries
- List of journal entries above a specific amount
- List of journal entries made after the closing date
- List of backdated documents
- List of entries made at unusual times
- List of entries made during vacation absences

◻ Table 12.2 Useful fields for analyzing document data in the general ledger

Table	Field	Description
BKPF	MANDT	Client
BKPF	BUKRS	Company Code
BKPF	BELNR	Document Number
BKPF	GJAHR	Fiscal Year
BKPF	BLART	Document Type
BKPF	BLDAT	Document Date
BKPF	BUDAT	Posting Date
BKPF	MONAT	Period
BKPF	CPUDT	Entered On
BKPF	CPUTM	Entered At
BKPF	USNAM	User ID
BKPF	TCODE	Transaction Code
BKPF	BSTAT	Document Status
BKPF	GLVOR	Business Transaction
BKPF	PPNAM	Parked By
BSEG	MANDT	Client
BSEG	BUKRS	Company Code
BSEG	BELNR	Document Number
BSEG	GJAHR	Fiscal Year
BSEG	BUZEI	Item
BSEG	KOART	Account Type
BSEG	SHKZG	Debit/Credit
BSEG	DMBTR	Amount in Local Currency
BSEG	WRBTR	Amount
BSEG	PSWBT	General Ledger Amount
BSEG	HKONT	General Ledger Account

12.4   Fraud Scenarios in the Sales Area

In the sales area, fraudulent activities are mostly caused by incentives for achieving a sales target (for example, in the case of a high variable and sales-dependent salary component). To achieve their inflated sales targets, employees commit fraud in the SAP system by, for example, executing the following actions:

- Issuing fictitious invoices to fictitious customers
- Granting unapproved credit memos/discounts or reporting discount agreements incorrectly at the end of the fiscal year
- Giving away free goods without permission
- Reporting a receivable as paid even though it has not been paid or not been paid in full

Incentives to commit fraud

We will now look at these cases of fraud in more detail. We will show how they can be detected and prevented in an SAP system.

12.4.1 Issuing Fictitious Invoices to Fictitious Customers

As sales are often decisive for paying sales personnel, this can be an incentive for committing fraud by issuing fictitious invoices to a non-existent customer to achieve the sales target. Monitoring the *due date breakdown* of unpaid invoices has proven to be a good method for detecting fictitious invoices (see also a further risk of fraud in Sect. 8.6.4, "Ageing Structure and Value Adjustments").

Analyzing due dates

SAP offers various standard reports for executing such monitoring. A report commonly used in practice is the Due Date Analysis for Open Items (transaction S_ALR_87012168); other useful reports are:

- S_ALR_87012175 – Open Items: Customer Due Date Forecast
- S_ALR_87012178 – Customer Open Item Analysis (Overdue)

Overdue and unpaid invoices should be analyzed regularly by a third person who is not involved in either the invoice or payment process.

To reduce the risk of fraud addressed in this chapter, you should assign the relevant SAP authorizations separately and not in combination to one person:

Segregation of duties

- Maintenance of customer master data (all views), and
- Creation/posting of outgoing invoices (FI and SD modules)

Furthermore, select the system settings such that an invoice can only be created in connection with an existing customer purchase order or based on a delivery note, and such that the invoice data (quantity of goods, invoice price, etc.) cannot be overwritten manually. One SAP function that controls the document flow for this data is *copying control* (IMG path: Sales and Distribution • Billing • Billing Documents • Maintain Copying Control for Billing Documents). Under the menu item Maintain Copying Control for Billing Documents, for each type of invoice you can specify which data is to be copied from the reference documents into the billing document.

Copying control and manual processing

To ensure that the copied data cannot be overwritten manually, for the condition types you must set the condition Not possible to process manually (IMG path

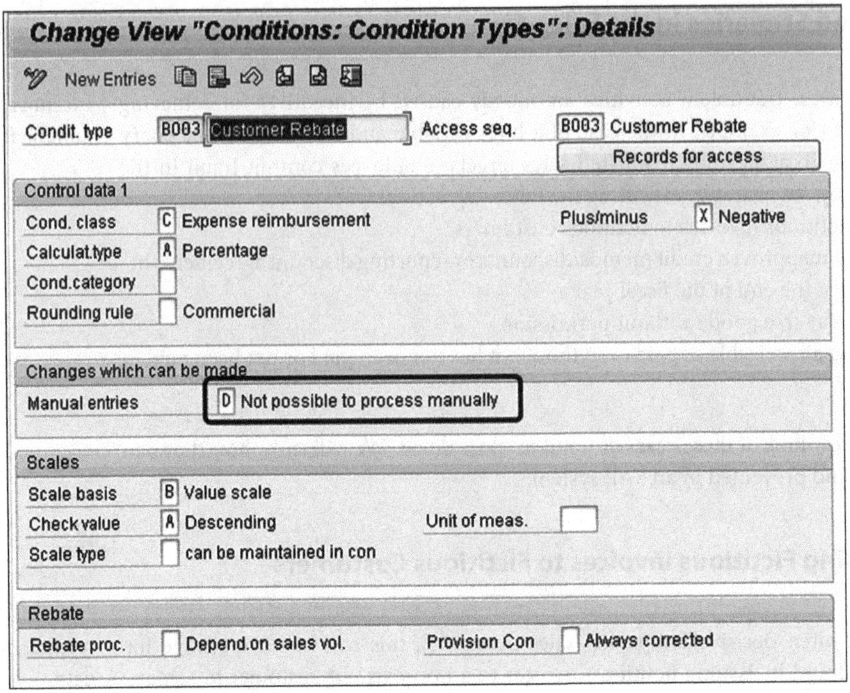

Figure 12.3 Configuring condition types

SALES AND DISTRIBUTION • BASIC FUNCTIONS • PRICING • PRICING CONTROL • DE-FINE CONDITION TYPES) (Fig. 12.3).

12.4.2 Granting Improper Credit Memos or Discounts

Formalizing the treatment of credit memos and discounts

Both credit memos and discounts have a direct influence on the profit margin. Therefore, the granting of credit memos and discounts should be documented in detail in a guideline and observance of the guidelines monitored.

Credit Memos and Discounts

Normally, a *credit memo* should be paid out to a customer based on an existing invoice, triggered by a damage report or similar.

Discounts are marketing instruments for improving customer satisfaction, sales, etc. They can be granted on goods or payments.

The following fraud scenario occurs frequently in practice: together with the customer, the sales employee arranges a discount or credit memo that does not meet the official guidelines in order to enrich both customer and employee (the discount/credit memo is shared between all parties involved).

It is also imaginable that sales personnel agree to discounts demanded by the customer in order not to endanger the conclusion of a contract, even though the discount would violate internal regulations.

Therefore, in the authorization concept, for example, you should assign the following SAP functions as restrictively and separately as possible:

- Issuing/changing credit memos
- Releasing credit memos for posting and thus payment
- Possibility of entering manual discounts

Segregation of duties

Analyze table VBRK, for example, with regard to the following fields, to check credit memos created manually:

- **Field FKART (Billing Document Type)**
  Select the billing document type
- **Field ERNAM (Created By)**
  Only a defined person subgroup should have created credit memos.
- **Field FKDAT (Billing Document Date)**
  This field shows the period in which the credit memos were posted. For example, an unusually high number of credit memos after year-end closing/change of fiscal year is suspicious.

Check: table VBRK

Using system settings, you can also define that credit memos have to be released under observance of segregation of duties before a posting and thus payment may occur.

You can also configure the SAP system such that rebate settlements can only be activated up to a pre-defined amount (IMG path; SALES AND DISTRIBUTION • BILLING • REBATE PROCESSING • REBATE AGREEMENTS • DEFINE ARRANGEMENT TYPES). Payment mode C (no restriction for manual payments) should not appear in any arrangement type.

Arrangement types

12.4.3 Excessive Use of Free Goods

To strengthen the customer relationship, sales personnel often offer free goods (see Sect. 10.2.1, "Controls for Delivery of Goods"). If the use of free goods is not monitored, this good marketing instrument can be abused:

- The goods are taken for private consumption and may even be sold on
- The giving of free goods may not be proportionate to the customer margin
- Customers are provided with unofficial free goods instead of a discount

"Free of charge" is dangerous

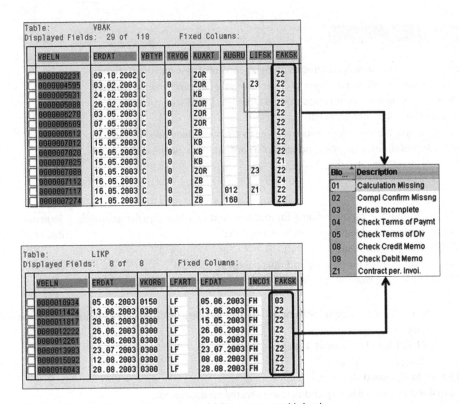

◻ Figure 12.4   Checking sales documents and delivery notes at table level

Controlling free
goods

You can control the handing over of free goods by checking goods delivered but not invoiced. To do this, check field FAKSK (Block) in table VBAK (Sales Documents) and table LIKP (Delivery Notes) (see Fig. 12.4).

If there is no entry in the field FAKSK (Block), the delivery note can be used to issue an invoice. If there is an entry, the issue of an invoice is blocked. These cases should be analyzed regularly by a third person.

Furthermore, you should monitor the goods not invoiced regularly using the MAINTAIN BILLING DUE LIST function (transaction VF04).

Get an overview of the following settings that control the treatment of free goods:

- SALES AND DISTRIBUTION • SALES • SALES DOCUMENTS • SALES DOCUMENT ITEM • DEFINE ITEM CATEGORIES
- SALES AND DISTRIBUTION • BASIC FUNCTIONS • PRICING • PRICING CONTROL • DEFINE AND ASSIGN PRICING PROCEDURE

12.4.4 Improper Write-Off of Open Customer Receivables

Segregation of
duties

To prevent improper write-off (i. e., the customer payment is lower than the customer receivable and the difference amount is written off without further measures in violation of the organization's guideline), the authorizations for the incoming payment process and the CREATE/CHANGE INVOICE process should not be assigned to one person.

If incoming payments are processed automatically, you should check those payments that cannot be cleared automatically, and, if necessary, clarify them in good time.

You should also configure the tolerance value of the system for automatic/manual write-offs (the difference between the outstanding amount and the incoming payment) appropriately.

12.5 Fraud Scenarios in Personnel Accounting

Personnel accounting, in particular payroll and expenses accounting, appears to be a predestined environment for fraudulent activities. If fraudulent actions in personnel accounting are successful over a longer period, considerable damage can be caused. The following scenarios explain a selection of SAP ERP HCM settings that can restrict fraudulent activities in payroll accounting.

12.5.1 Fictitious Employees

Fictitious employees represent a considerable risk that a non-existent person or a non-existent salary claim could be entered in the SAP ERP HCM system and, depending on how the internal control system (ICS) is set up, not recognized as fictitious. Changes in the employee relationship, for example, a termination or hiring of new personnel can favor this type of fraudulent activities.

Ending/changing a work relationship

Fraud by Means of a Fictitious Employee	[e.g.]

If, for example, an employee leaves or is sacked, but the data record remains active in the system and the bank details are changed, the current payments can be transferred to this incorrect account.

In addition to this example, there are further opportunities for executing fraudulent activities using a fictitious employee, for example:

Further opportunities

- Fictitious employee – the person does not exist
- Temporary employees who are often not subject to the normal internal controls as these are designed for permanent employees

To reduce the danger of fictitious employees, an appropriate control environment is required – both within and outside the SAP system. This should consist of an appropriate documentation of all relevant employee information, including proof and documents for all information in the system. In practice, spontaneous checks of employee data have proven to be a useful instrument in strengthening the control environment.

Documentation of employee information

Possible controls within the SAP ERP HCM system are, for example:

Controls

- Inspection of changes to employee data records and information types (see Sect. 11.1.2, "Basic Principles: European Union Directive")

- Separation between access to the master data of the employees and the transaction data, for example, time recording
- Comparison of wage and salary statements with those of previous periods (is the data displayed appropriate in comparison to previous periods?)

12.5.2 Limited Access to Own HR Data

In addition to separating tasks for the employee subgroup to be processed, you should restrict access to users' own HR data so that employees cannot edit their own data records. In this case, prevention is more effective than a detective control.

Preventive control   Access to own data records would mean that employees could manipulate payments and deductions, which could lead to a direct financial impact for the organization.

Control steps   You should therefore block users' own HR data by means of the following three SAP settings:

1. **Check configuration**
    You can check the personnel number with the following setting: PERSONNEL MANAGEMENT • PERSONNEL ADMINISTRATION • TOOLS • AUTHORIZATION MANAGEMENT • MAINTAIN AUTHORIZATION MAIN SWITCHES. Within this Customizing function you should activate the PERNR setting (HR: Master Data – Personnel Number Check) by setting the value to 1.

2. **Infotype linking**
    Once you have activated the check of the personnel numbers, you must link it with the respective SAP user account so that the SAP system "knows" which personnel number belongs to which account and blocks it accordingly. To configure this, enter the SAP user account for each item of HR data in the infotype (0105) and subtype 0001 (System User ID). The subtype links the SAP user account with the respective HR data, thus blocking it.

3. **Authorization restriction**
    To define the user access (in this case, access to the user's own data), you have to maintain authorization object P_PERNR for each SAP account. In particular, set the object field PSIGN (interpretation of the respective personnel number) to E (exclude).
    This type of restriction always requires a second person to make changes in a user's own HR data.

12.5.3 Segregation of Duties for Confidential Data

Fraud in respect of extra hours, vacation credit, etc.   In the personnel area, fraud is not necessarily restricted to the manipulation of direct wage data. Although it is less common in practice, extra hours, vacation credit, work scheduling, and approved absences are also manipulated. Therefore, access to such sensitive and confidential data should be very limited, in particular with regard to the fact that many countries have very strict data protection legislation (see Chap. 11, "Data Protection Compliance in SAP ERP Human Capital Management") and this requires that data in IT systems is sufficiently protected.

From a technical perspective, the configuration of correct segregation of duties in SAP ERP HCM is realized differently to that in other SAP modules. The concept of the authorization object does exist, but as the master data is designed differently, the configuration is also different. The following options explain how segregation of duties (for maintaining the infotypes that refer to the master data) can be realized in SAP ERP HCM.

Segregation of duties

Changes to the infotypes in an SAP ERP HCM system require the approval of a second person. You can configure this in the approval settings of the SAP ERP HCM system (authorization objects P_ORGIN or P_ORGXX). There are two variants for this setting:

- **Asymmetric setting**
  One user group processes the data (maintenance) and a separate group has to approve these changes (approval). The group of "approvers" can only approve existing entries and has no access to the system to enter changes.
  - For the asymmetric setting, the "maintenance" group needs the combined approvals E (enqueue) and R (read), but not W (write).
  - The "approval" group needs the combined approvals D (dequeue) and R (read), but not W (write).
- **Symmetric setting**
  Two separate users are also required in this setting, but both have the same roles. Both have restricted write authorizations, whereby the user who processes an infotype first blocks it. Only the second user can remove this block. For the symmetric setting, both groups (maintenance and approval) need the combined approvals S (symmetric) and R (read), but not W (write).

12.6   Summary

In this chapter you have learned about selected fraud scenarios in SAP ERP and the relevant control mechanisms. The topic of fraud is very diverse – as is the criminal energy behind it. Not all deliberate irregularities take place in the SAP system, even when processes are SAP-supported. Therefore, this chapter has only covered a few issues.

Based on the principles conveyed in this chapter, where necessary, you should be able to address the risks of fraud in your organization or at your customer independently.

Excursion: FDA Compliance and Controls in SAP

Risks that can be present in the IT-supported manufacturing process for food and medicinal products affect all readers: either directly as consumers or, where applicable, also in a professional capacity.

So far, in Part II of this book, you have learned about the implementation of cross-industry requirements – generally within the scope of external financial reporting and for the protection of personal data in the SAP ERP environment. In this chapter, we will show you the legal regulations that the activities of manufacturers of food and medicinal products have to comply with. Furthermore, we will provide an overview of what these requirements mean in practice for IT-supported processes, in particular in the SAP environment.

13.1 Legal Requirements in the Manufacture of Food and Medicinal Products

You will almost certainly have heard of the US government agency the *Food and Drug Administration* (FDA). You will now learn details about regulations issued by this agency and how they are connected to similar regulations in other countries. We will also show you which respective FDA-relevant *principles* have become established in practice, and which three phases in the life cycle of an IT application are relevant from the perspective of the corresponding requirements.

Origin and Objective of FDA Regulations

The Food and Drug Administration (FDA) is the authority for food inspection and the medicinal product approval authority of the United States that is subordinate to the Department of Health and Human Services.

It was founded in 1927 with registered office in Rockville (Maryland, USA) and given the task of protecting public health in the USA. The FDA checks the quality, safety, and effectiveness of human and veterinary medicinal products, biological products, medicine products, food, and devices that emit radiation. It does so for devices manufactured in the USA and for imported products.

Another task of the FDA is improving public health. It does this by helping to accelerate innovations intended to make food and medicinal products more effective, safe, and affordable. The FDA also publishes precise, scientific information on the use of food and medicinal products to improve health. All medication approved in the USA must be produced by pharmaceutical manufacturers who have been inspected by the FDA and whose manufacturing systems meet the corresponding regulations. The same applies to manufacturers of medicinal products.

13.1.1 FDA-Relevant Legal Requirements in an International Comparison

CFR – Code of Federal Regulations in the USA

The Code of Federal Regulations (CFR) is the summary of the administrative laws of the United States of America. It is published in the Federal Register by the departments and agencies of the Federal Government and consists of 50 titles. In this chapter we will focus on the regulations contained in Title 21, "Food and Drugs (administered by the US Food and Drug Administration and the US Drug Enforcement Administration)."

"FDA compliance" as common term

However, a restriction to the requirements of the Code of Federal Regulations 21 of the USA would be an incorrect approach to take, as the approval and control authorities of almost all countries have introduced corresponding regulations for the food, pharmaceuticals, biotechnology, and medical device industries. However, many of these countries follow the example of the FDA, although with a time delay, and therefore it is common in the industry to use the term *FDA compliance*, even if products of non-US organizations are not intended for the North American market. The following are examples of authorities with tasks similar to those of the FDA:

- ICH – *International Conference on Harmonization of Technical Requirements for Registration of Pharmaceuticals for Human Use*
- EMA – *European Medicines Agency* (formerly EMEA)
- HPFB – *Health Products and Food Branch* (Canada)
- BMGS – *Federal Ministry for Health and Social Affairs* (Germany)
- NPCB – *National Pharmaceutical Control Bureau* (Malaysia)
- TGA – *Therapeutic Goods Administration* (Australia)
- MDEC – *Medical Device Evaluation Committee* (Australia)
- FOPH – *Federal Office of Public Health* (Switzerland)
- SHI – *Swiss Agency for Therapeutic Products*
- MHLW – *Ministry for Health, Labour and Welfare* (Japan)
- PMSB – *Pharmaceutical and Medical Safety Bureau* (Japan)

Harmonization of FDA compliance

These are just a few examples of authorities similar to the FDA. It is only logical that as part of cross-border trade in the products concerned, a harmonization of the legislation became necessary. Therefore, in November 1995, the *Pharmaceutical Inspection Cooperation Scheme* (PIC/S) was founded – an international program for cooperation in the field of pharmaceutical inspection. It focuses on the development of standards, cooperation with the specialist body at EU level, and exchange of experiences. For the member states of the EU, the EMA (the European Medicines Agency) has taken over the lead role – although worldwide there are 37 member authorities in PIC/S.

13.1.2 GxP – The FDA Basic Principles

In Sect. 3.1.1, "ICS Basic Principles in the ERP Environment: From GAAP to GAP-CAS," you learned about the generally accepted accounting principles that are applied worldwide due to their universal nature. The FDA field also has basic principles that are recognized internationally.

In 1980, the *International Society for Pharmaceutical Engineering* (ISPE) was founded – a professional organization for employees active in the pharmaceutical industry. As an industry initiative, in 1994, ISPE published "Good Automated Manufacturing Practice" (GAMP), a guide to validating automated systems in pharmaceutical production. The basic principles of "Good Manufacturing Practice" (GMP), also issued by the ISPE, have since been extended by "Good Laboratory Practice," "Good Clinical Practice," and further guidelines; the abbreviation *GxP* is now used, whereby "x" represents the various fields concerned. These principles are the basis for validation.

Origin of good manufacturing practice

In 1991, the European Commission issued two directives that specified the principles and guidelines of good manufacturing practice for medicinal products for human use (91/356/EEC) and for veterinary medicinal products (91/412/EEC). The guideline for good manufacturing practice (GMP) contains detailed guidelines that correspond to these basic principles. These guidelines are intended to make the evaluation of applications for a manufacturing permit easier, and form the basis for inspections at medicinal product manufacturers. The basic principles of good manufacturing practice and the detailed guidelines apply for all activities for which a permit is required in accordance with Article 16 of Directive 75/319/EEC and Article 24 of Directive 81/851/EEC in the respective amended version. They also apply for all other procedures for large-scale medicinal product manufacture, for example, in hospitals, and for the manufacture of products for clinical trials (for example: The Rules Governing Medicinal Products in the European Union. Volume 4. Guidelines to Good Manufacturing Practice. Medicinal Products for Human and Veterinary Use. 1999 Edition, available at http://ec.europa.eu/health/documents/eudralex/vol-4/index_en.htm).

Good manufacturing practice in the EU

One example for cross-border cooperation between authorities observing identical basic principles is the collaboration between the German Federal Office of Public Health (BAG), the Federal Office for the Environment (FOEN), and the Swiss Agency for Therapeutic Products (swissmedic): these authorities work according to a common GLP (good laboratory practice) program. The *good laboratory practice* (GLP) is a quality assurance system concerned with the organizational process and conditions under which non-clinical health and environmental safety studies are planned, performed, monitored, recorded, archived, and reported. The basic principles of GLP were developed by a GLP panel of experts founded in 1978. Their work was based on the GLP regulations for non-clinical trials, which were published by the US FDA in 1976. In 1997, the GLP guidelines were updated to reflect the latest technology.

Good laboratory practice

The term *good clinical practice* (GCP) designates internationally recognized rules for the performance of clinical studies issued according to ethical and scientific viewpoints. The focus is on the protection of the participants in the trial and their informed consent, as well as the quality of the results of the study. GCP is part of the above-mentioned guidelines for "good working practice" in the development and manufacture of medicinal products (see, for example: http://en.wikipedia.org/wiki/Good_Clinical_Practice). In the European Union, the first GCP rules were published in 1989 (for exam-

Good clinical practice

ple, *EU-GCP Note for Guidance*). Through harmonization between the USA, Europe, and Japan as part of the ICH, in 1996 the detailed ICH GCP Guideline E6 was produced and approved by the Committee for Medicinal Products for Human Use (CHMP) of the European Medicines Agency (EMA) as a European guideline. In some aspects, the requirements of the European GCP guidelines go beyond ICH GCP: for example, the requirement that all test apparatus must be manufactured according to GMP see, for example: http://de.wikipedia.org/wiki/Good_Clinical_Practice).

13.1.3 IT from the View of FDA Compliance

FDA vs. IT   All basic principles mentioned in Sect. 13.1.2, "GxP – The FDA Basic Principles," must be fulfilled in an environment that today is dominated by IT-supported processes. What does that mean for IT systems that control FDA-relevant procedures? In practice, we can project the FDA compliance requirements onto IT systems and differentiate between three phases:

1. Implementation: FDA-conform validation of a system
2. Operation of an IT system: FDA-relevant application controls
3. System maintenance: updating the validation

In all three phases, there is a risk that the system will not achieve or will lose the stated objectives of patient or consumer safety, product quality, and data integrity.

Validation of an IT system   If business processes at organizations subject to FDA regulations are supported in part or in whole by computer systems, these systems must be "validated" during implementation. During operation they must also meet specified conditions defined by law and monitored by regulatory bodies.

Operation of an IT system   Validation of a system as part of the implementation is without doubt the most important phase. However, operation of the system also bears the risk that, for example, changes to certain master data or configuration settings can cause a risk to patient safety. Examples are the extension of the cleaning intervals for production systems or the extension of the shelf life of a medicinal product. Therefore, efficient control mechanisms for relevant master data, control data, and transaction data of an IT system are essential.

Maintenance of an IT system   Chapter 5.8 of the introduction to Part 11 of CFR Title 21 represents a special challenge to the operators of validated systems: it states explicitly that changes due to "software upgrades," "fixes," or "service packs" require a revalidation of the system by means of regression test. Therefore, from an FDA compliance perspective, the running maintenance of an IT system must be separated as an independent phase (or as a separate control area).

13.2   Validation of IT Systems

Validation is relevant for all life phases of an IT application, but the validation effort is highest during the initial introduction. Therefore, the following section describes the content and meaning of the FDA-specific validation of an IT system primarily for the implementation phases.

13.2.1 Validation Procedure

What does validation mean in the context of FDA compliance requirements?

> **Definition of Validation** ❗
>
> Documented evidence in agreement with the basic principles of good manufacturing practice that procedures, processes, equipment, materials, working operations, or systems actually produce the expected results.

First of all, this definition implies a documentation of "the expected results" against which the computer system (or other equipment, materials, working operations, etc.) must be tested. Specifications are derived from this description, and these specifications are the template for configuring or programming the computer system. Program modules are tested against these specifications and *integration tests* are performed to validate the entire system. The tests, together with the user requirements, must be carefully documented so that changes to the documents can be demonstrated and traced. If an electronic *document management system* is used to manage the documents, this must also be validated.

Focus on documentation

In practice, the procedure for the validation is often illustrated graphically in the form of a "V" model, as shown in Fig. 13.1.

In principle, the framework of the V model for the implementation of an FDA-relevant system corresponds to the well-known ASAP implementation approach of SAP. However, the procedure in the V model is much more formal, in particular with regard to the documentation of the different project phases. The illustration also shows that there is a strong formal connection between tests and the underlying documents.

Risk-based approach

In August 2003, the FDA changed the rules for validation by introducing *risk-based validation*. This change allows the industry to restrict (based on a well-documented risk analysis) the business processes to be validated in such a way that the validation is possible with an effort appropriate to the industry. This approach has parallels to the similar risk-based approaches mentioned in Part I of the book in connection with the ICS approaches from the view of external financial reporting.

It is important to understand that all current FDA requirements refer to the documentation, and not only for the installation of a computer system, but also in the operation of such a system, whereby, for example, changes to master data could have consequences for patient safety, product quality, or data integrity (see Sect. 13.3 "FDA Compliance in IT-Supported Business Processes"). The tools delivered with the standard SAP system allow organizations to meet these documentation requirements: for example, the Documentation Management System (DMS) that is part of SAP Solution Manager (see Sect. 6.2.5, "SAP Solution Manager"). This has been confirmed in practice by numerous vendor audits by customers from the life sciences industry or their agents.

As well as being required to document the user requirements, technical specifications, programming, configuration, and corresponding tests, organizations must also connect these documents to one another. This means that for a configuration setting – for example, an entry in a table – an auditor must be able to look for and find the relevant technical specification that was the basis for this entry being made, as well as the related user requirement.

From a setting to the documentation

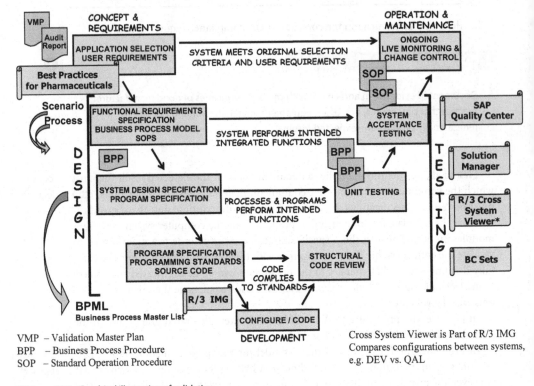

Figure 13.1   Graphical illustration of validation

13.2.2 Controls in Implementation Processes

ICS-relevant control mechanisms

The previous section explained the extensive documentation requirements during the implementation of an FDA-relevant IT system. The design of an implementation process in itself – including change and test management, consideration of safety questions, and fulfillment of cross-system requirements for traceability, completeness of processing, etc. – should generally correspond to the requirements that you have already learned about for the "usual" ICS criteria using the example of SAP ERP (see Chap. 6, "IT General Controls in SAP ERP," and Chap. 7, "General Application Controls in SAP ERP"). The usual SAP-specific tools and mechanisms that should be used are also relevant in the FDA environment (system landscape with three systems, change and transport management, etc.).

"Bundling" of configuration settings in BC Sets

A considerable difference to the usual practice is that in the GxP-relevant environment, there is a strong recommendation to group configuration settings in BC Sets that can be linked traceably to the specifications described. For example, the naming of the BC Sets could make it much easier for an auditor to trace documents.

Continuous monitoring of settings

Continuous monitoring of the (properly documented and tested) settings (see Fig. 13.1) concludes the process of introducing an FDA-relevant application and thus represents a smooth transition to the next phase that we will address in Sect. 13.3: operation and compliance in IT-supported business processes. With the introduction of SAP's GRC products onto the market, in particular *Process Control*, proactive controls for configuring systems that have to comply with the regulations of the FDA or similar authorities are now available for the first time. This is considerable progress compared to pure documentation. These controls prevent errors being made during configuration whereas previously, it was only possible to document who had made what errors and when. For details on this topic, see Chap. 17, "Implementation of Automated Test and Monitoring Scenarios in the SAP ERP Environment."

13.3 FDA Compliance in IT-Supported Business Processes

In this section, we will use examples to show which control mechanisms you can establish when operating an SAP application. The examples given are based partly on preconfigured test and monitoring scenarios of SAP Process Control (see Sect. 4.3.2 and Chap. 17).

13.3.1 Examples: Controls in Procurement

With regard to the manufacture of medicines and medicinal devices, the rules for good manufacturing practice require the use of qualified materials and suppliers, that is, materials and suppliers that meet the predefined quality requirements. In particular, customers in the life sciences and food industries must purchase materials only from qualified suppliers. The quality metrics in the configuration of SAP Quality Management can be set up such that materials can only be procured from suppliers who have been qualified and accepted through an audit. This type of application control can ensure that, in the case of materials that are used directly in production and labeling and packaging materials, only qualified and accepted suppliers are used.
Purchasing from "good" suppliers

Materials that are procured from non-qualified or non-approved suppliers bear the risk that specifications for the end product are not met. Contamination can also have a direct effect on patient and consumer health. The relevant control objectives are set down in law:
Risks and control objectives

- 21 CFR Parts 210 and 211 for the pharmaceuticals industry, 211.22 Responsibilities of the quality control unit
- 21 CFR Part 820 for medical devices, 820.50 Purchasing controls

In an SAP system, you can set up monitoring scenarios that ensure that only qualified suppliers can be selected when you order raw materials (components, labels, and packaging materials). This type of control mechanism would enable you to prevent the immediate risk as well as the corresponding negative consequences for the reputation of the organization.

13.3.2 Examples: Controls in Production Management

No further comment is required regarding the FDA-relevance of IT-supported processes that control the production of food and medicinal products and medical devices.
Proving required knowledge

In the product creation phase, several control mechanisms are used: one example is monitoring the level of knowledge of the production personnel. In the life sciences industry, all production processes are described by instructions called *Standard Operation Procedures* (SOP). These instructions are continuously updated, and management is responsible for ensuring that personnel that operate the systems always have the most up-to-date knowledge of the instructions. Management must also ensure that personnel attend the planned training measures.

Risks and control objectives

If employees in the manufacture of chemical components, pharmaceutical production, or packaging of medication do not regularly attend required training measures with regard to good manufacturing practice, there would be a risk that the FDA-relevant products would be manufactured by unqualified personnel, not be compliant with FDA, and these products could endanger the health of the consumer. SAP ERP Human Capital Management (HCM) is configured such that employee training can be planned; completion of training courses is registered in SAP. The fulfillment of corresponding control objectives directly addresses the following legal requirements: 21 CFR Parts 210 and 211 for the pharmaceuticals industry, 211.25 paragraphs a) and b) organization and personnel.

The person responsible for production can use evaluations of relevant data in SAP ERP HCM to monitor participation of personnel in predefined training courses to fulfill this control objective. These controls enable you to take measures at an early stage if employees have not attended the training courses.

13.3.3 Examples: Controls in Quality Management

Check quality regularly

Quality management is one of the most important functions for ensuring patient safety per se. One example of a possible control is the *inspection interval*: in SAP, raw materials and products are managed as material master records. In SAP Quality Management, *regular quality inspections* of materials can be triggered based on the *inspection interval* (the time between two recurring quality controls in days) in the material master record.

Risks and control objectives

If components with an overdue quality control are used for production of medicinal products, resulting products can pose a health risk. The FDA requirements and rules require the execution of an appropriate quality inspection at regular intervals to ensure consistent quality. To avoid the use of outdated or contaminated materials, and to satisfy the legal requirements (21 CFR Parts 210 and 211 for the pharmaceuticals industry, 211.87 Retesting of approved components; 21 CFR Part 820 for medical devices, 820.72 Inspection, part a)), control mechanisms are required in SAP to check the presence of the required information about the inspection interval in the material master record (days in the period until the next quality inspection of the material).

13.3.4 Examples: Controls in Asset Maintenance

Maintaining assets

Using the SAP module Enterprise Asset Management, (EAM, formerly Plant Maintenance, PM), you can control measures in the form of, for example, cleaning or other maintenance tasks that maintain the manufacturing assets and machines in an FDA-conform state. Such operations are not only planned in SAP; their actual execution is also registered in Enterprise Asset Management.

Extending the period between two planned cleaning operations or other maintenance tasks (for example, to save costs) can influence the quality of medicinal or food
products manufactured with these plants. Therefore, it is important to monitor changes
to such data. Proper execution of cleaning and maintenance tasks is prescribed by law
in 21 CFR Parts 210 and 211 for the pharmaceuticals industry, 211.67 a) and b2) Equipment cleaning and maintenance. One of the possible control scenarios in SAP would be
to monitor the execution of planned tasks on time. The reconciliation of the cleaning
and maintenance cycles with the maintenance calendar can be automated using corresponding configuration data. *Risks and control objectives*

13.3.5 Examples: Controls for Batch Traceability

In the event of product complaints, and for questions with regard to product safety etc.,
it is important to document the composition of semi-finished products and finished
products across all production levels in order to be able to provide evidence where necessary. In SAP, manufactured products are grouped in *batches* and the history of a batch
is documented in the *batch where-used* list. This list traces how a batch is created and
processed over the different production levels. The "batch where-used" list is required
to determine the batch production in which another batch is used or from which other
batches a batch is produced. *Guaranteeing product history*

If the batch where-used list is changed frequently, it is difficult to trace the movement
of goods, which results in inconsistent goods movement data records. To ensure batch
traceability, control mechanisms are required for which the legal requirements in 21
CFR Parts 210 and 211 for the pharmaceuticals industry, 211.188 Batch production
and control records, and 211.192 Production record review are relevant. *Risks and control objectives*

One possible control mechanism would be to monitor changes to the batch where-
used list. Remember the functions described in Sect. 7.2, "Controls for Data-Related
Traceability," which ensure the traceability of changes in SAP: for example, you could
monitor a change to the batch where-used list or the frequency of changes.

Another possible control would be checking a general setting in SAP: the batch
where-used list function itself must first be activated in the SAP configuration and any
changes to the corresponding settings can be evaluated regularly.

13.3.6 Examples: Controls in Warehouse Management Processes

SAP-supported warehouse management processes are FDA-relevant as the configuration of the permitted *stock withdrawal strategies* has a direct influence on the age of the
products delivered – medicines are generally subject to an aging process that influences
their effect on the patient. Furthermore, in many businesses in the pharmaceuticals and
medical devices industry, products are sterilized in the warehouse immediately before
delivery and the sterilization thus becomes part of the warehouse management process – although it is actually a production step. Which stock withdrawal strategies does
the SAP component Warehouse Management support? The flow of goods can be organized in accordance with the following standard strategies: *Stock withdrawal strategies*

- First in, first out (FIFO)
- Last in, first out (LIFO)
- First expired, first out (FEFO)
- Partial quantities first

From an FDA compliance perspective, the first strategy in the list is preferred.

Risks and control objectives   The expiry of a use-by date is a serious problem in the life sciences industry, as the potency of the active components reduces with age and there is potential for harmful decomposition products to arise. There is a risk not only for patient safety but also for the brand image and for the image of the entire manufacturing company. The use of the FIFO withdrawal strategy means that the oldest materials in the warehouse are withdrawn first, which in turn ensures that older material is not left on the shelf and the use-by date exceeded. The relevant legal regulations are:

- 21 CFR Parts 210 and 211 for the pharmaceuticals industry, 211.150 Distribution procedures
- 21 CFR Part 820 for medical devices, 820.150 Storage, 820.160 Distribution

Monitoring the configuration settings that regulate the use of the FIFO withdrawal strategy can counteract the above-mentioned risks.

FEFO   As an alternative to FIFO, the withdrawal strategy according to remaining life – *first expired, first out* – can be used in SAP. It is based on the shortest remaining life (field SLED, Shelf Life Expiration Date, is the decisive factor). This strategy would be even safer than FIFO, as when a material is returned, the date of goods receipt (decisive for FIFO) could be overwritten, but the use-by date not changed.

13.4 Observing FDA Compliance for System Maintenance, System Updates, and System Changes

As already explained in Sect. 13.2.2, "Controls in Implementation Processes," any change to a validated system represents a challenge to the persons responsible; the FDA regulations stipulate that proof is required that the system still delivers the expected results despite the change. In Chapter 5.8 of its "Guidance for Industry" to part 11 of 21 CFR *Change Control (Configuration Management)*, the FDA writes:

- Systems should be in place to control changes and evaluate the extent of revalidation that the changes would necessitate. The extent of revalidation will depend upon the change's nature, scope, and potential impact on a validated system and established operating conditions. Changes that cause the system to operate outside of previously validated operating limits would be particularly significant.
- Contractor or vendor upgrades or maintenance activities, especially when performed remotely (i. e., over a network), should be carefully monitored because they can introduce changes that might otherwise go unnoticed and have an adverse effect on a validated system. Examples of such activities include installation of circuit boards that might hold new versions of "firmware" software, addition of new network elements, and software "upgrades," "fixes," or "service packs." It is important that system users be aware of such changes to their system.
- You should arrange for service providers to advise you regarding the nature of such revisions so you can assess the changes and perform appropriate revalidation.

- We consider regression analysis to be an extremely important tool that should be used to assess portions of a system that were themselves unchanged but are nonetheless vulnerable to performance/reliability losses that the changes can cause. For instance, new software might alter performance of other software on a system (e. g., by putting into place new device drivers or other code that programs share).

These statements clearly show that the SAP-specific control mechanisms described in Chap. 6, "IT General Controls in SAP ERP," and Chap. 7, "General Application Controls in SAP ERP," as part of change management, general traceability of system changes, and security are also important with regard to the FDA. These control mechanisms would be a good example of how, in the event of *multi-domain requirements* of an ICS (see Sect. 15.2.3, "Controls"), ICS automation can achieve synergies for areas that are relevant for cross-domain or cross-compliance purposes (see Sect. 16.3.8, "Multiple Compliance Framework Concept"). | Cross-compliance requirements

In order to cover additional FDA-specific requirements, SAP has developed a tool that allows operators to break down business processes configured on a system into a "technical bill of material." If he does the same with the new software to be installed, by comparing the two technical bills of material, the operator can identify business processes affected by the new software. If processes considered GxP-relevant are affected, they must be subjected to a regression test. This tool is the *Business Process Change Analyzer*, which is part of SAP Solution Manager (from SAP Solution Manager 7.0 EhP1). This solution can reduce the revalidation effort considerably. | Business Process Impact Analyzer

13.5 Summary

This chapter has provided a brief overview of the specific legal requirements for manufacturers of medicinal and food products. It has also shown how these regulations are implemented in the ERP environment. The requirements focus on protecting the consumer, who is dependent on the high quality of the products.

The example of the FDA clearly shows that ERP systems are subject to requirements that are valid from many compliance aspects: these are the general IT controls and the general application controls that form the foundation of any ICS framework. However, within this foundation, the FDA compliance has particularly high standards that are expressed in the form of validation requirements.

Examples of Efficiency-Oriented and Profitability-Oriented Analysis Scenarios in SAP ERP

Saving money and optimizing processes are objectives in the ICS process: we will explain this as yet partially unusual perspective using relevant scenarios in SAP ERP.

As already described in Sect. 3.1.5, "Structure of the Efficiency-Oriented and Profitability-Oriented Controls in the ERP Environment," efficiency-oriented and profitability-oriented control mechanisms as applied to SAP ERP can be divided into four layers:

- Process controls
- Master data quality controls
- User input controls
- Reporting controls

The information presented in this chapter is based on this structure. We will give examples of efficiency-oriented and profitability-oriented controls that refer to these four layers.

In the context of this chapter, controls primarily mean scenarios for data analyses: the areas of application for such analyses stretch from internal audit, through process optimization, up to data governance. In this chapter, we will use examples to show how you can increase efficiency and profitability in SAP ERP-supported business processes. *Focus on data analyses*

From a content perspective, this chapter – more than all other chapters in the third part of the book – deals in particular with technical implementation options, that is, the implementation of corresponding analysis scenarios. The objective is to provide you with tools for implementing these scenarios based on the Continuous Monitoring Framework of the SAP GRC 10.0 solutions (see Chap. 17).

14.1 Process-Related Data Analyses

The principle of process-related data analyses is only marginally different from case to case.

In the first step of these analyses, you connect the SAP transaction data tables and master data tables with one another. You do this either directly in the SAP system using queries, or download the tables manually from the SAP system and then link them using one of the widespread table processing tools (Excel, Access, ACL, etc.). *Step 1*

In a second step, you then use the same tools to check the data for anomalies. In order to be able to check business processes and master data for efficiency, consistency, and correctness, the following basic prerequisites must be met: *Step 2*

— **Understanding of the process**
Understanding of your own business processes as well as SAP Best Practice processes.

— **SAP data structures**
Understanding of the SAP data processing logic and about how this data must be linked for analysis purposes.

— **Analysis capability**
Extensive knowledge of and competence in use of the respective analysis tool (Excel, Access, ACL, etc.).

Optimizing the analysis   Even if your organization has one or more employees with these capabilities, it is still important to verify the results of such analyses in detail with the business areas affected – at least the first time they are run. The consequence of this check is that you usually have to adjust the analyses because you need to refine the selection criteria to eliminate false positives. At the end, you should have an analysis that delivers reliable results and that you can repeat as often as required in the future. Depending on the effort required for the analysis, the question is then to what extent full or at least partial automation of such analyses is useful (see Chap. 17).

The aim of the following examples is to explain the principle of the control. Above all, it is important to understand the data structures of the business processes. Whether you use an SAP query, manual download, Excel, or ACL to implement analysis scenarios is secondary; the principle is the same for all of these methods.

Recognizing trends and main features   In principle, the purpose of such analyses is generally not to determine the precise number of exceptions, but to check whether the business processes allow certain conditions or whether certain trends or inconsistencies are recognizable. As the analyses enable you to identify the symptoms (inefficiencies in the process, deviations from planned or expected targets, etc.), these tests often lead to interesting discussions or even to further analyses that can identify the cause.

In the following pages, we will discuss some examples of efficiency-oriented and profitability-oriented process controls.

14.1.1 Comparison of the Purchase Order Date with the Goods Receipt Date

In this analysis, the aim is to identify purchase order items created just before the goods receipt. As far as the purchase order items identified are concerned, the suspicion is that the purchase orders were triggered without entry of a corresponding purchase order in the SAP system, and the purchase order was only entered in the SAP system when the subsequent goods receipt could not be executed due to the missing purchase order.

If purchase orders have been approved outside the SAP system, then in the purchase order operations identified, it is highly probable that the approval process has been bypassed.

Creating an SAP query   Due to the complexity and number of tables involved in this analysis, it makes sense to create an SAP query (SAP transaction SQVI or SQ01).

With an SAP query, you can connect SAP tables without having any ABAP knowledge. Thanks to a largely graphically-supported user interface, data is merged directly in the SAP system and can then be analyzed further in Excel, Access, ACL, etc. (At

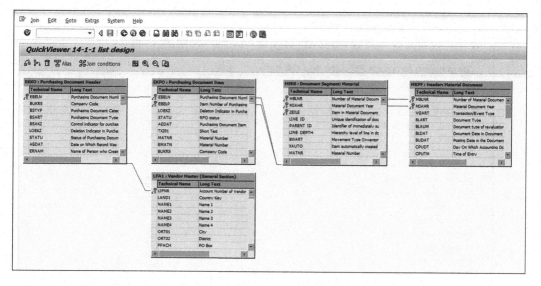

◘ Figure 14.1 SAP query

◘ Table 14.1 Links between table EKPO and other relevant tables

Connected data	Table/field	Table/field	Join
PURCHASING DOCUMENT HEADER · PURCHASING DOCUMENT ITEM	EKKO-EBELN	EKPO-EBELN	Inner
PURCHASING DOCUMENT HEADER · VENDOR MASTER (GENERAL SECTION)	EKKO-LIFNR	EKKO-LIFNR	Inner
PURCHASING DOCUMENT ITEM · DOCUMENT SEGMENT: MATERIAL	EKPO-EBELN	MSEG-EBELN	Inner
	EKPO-BBELP	MSEG-EBELP	Inner
DOCUMENT SEGMENT: MATERIAL · HEADER: MATERIAL DOCUMENT	MSEG-MBLNR	MKPF-MBLNR	Inner
	MSEG-MJAHR	MKPF-MJAHR	Inner

the end of this section we will also describe how to perform this analysis without a query.)

Figure 14.1 shows a graphical illustration of the query with the required SAP tables and their structure.

As the connections between the respective tables in Fig. 14.1 are only visible to a limited extent (i. e., without their properties), Table 14.1 shows how these tables have to be merged.

Merging tables

◻ Figure 14.2   SAP query – purchase order date vs. goods receipt date

You can usually link tables with one another using fields. Table 14.1 contains a list of the fields that you should use to connect the tables. With each connection, you must also define whether the connection is an "outer join" or "inner join."

[e.g.]   Example: Outer Join or Inner Join

If, for example, you are checking whether goods receipts have been entered on the same day that the corresponding purchase order was created, the *inner join* has the effect that purchase orders with no goods receipt are not listed in the analysis. In contrast, an *outer join* would have the effect that all purchase orders are listed, including those for which no goods receipts have been registered.

Selecting list and selection fields   In the SAP query, for the tables selected you have to define which fields are list fields (fields portrayed in the SAP query as column heading and the contents of which are listed as a result) and which are selection fields (fields that should be available on the selection screen before the execution of the respective query). You can make this decision on an individual basis, and you can define a field as both a list field and a selection field. For example, the "Plant" field can be relevant both for the selection and as a list field for analysis results.

The following database tables are relevant for comparing the purchase order date and goods receipt date:

◻ **Table 14.2** Recommended selection criteria

Table/field	Description	Recommended selection
EKKO-EBELN	Purchasing Document Number	No selection
EKKO-BUKRS	Company Code	The company codes relevant for the analysis
EKKO-BSTYP	Purchasing Document Category	Enter "F" to restrict the analysis to purchase orders.
EKKO-BSART	Purchasing Document Type	Purchasing document types relevant for the analysis
EKKO-LOEKZ	Deletion Indicator in Purchasing Document (Header)	Press F2 to call up the selection options and then choose ▰. This ensures that only purchase orders that have not been deleted are selected.
EKKO-AEDAT	Date on which Record Was Created	No selection
EKKO-LIFNR	Vendor Account Number	No selection
EKKO-EKORG	Purchasing Organization	Purchasing organizations relevant for the analysis
EKPO-LOEKZ	Deletion Indicator in Purchasing Document (Item)	Press F2 to call up the selection options and then choose ▰. This ensures that only purchase orders that have not been deleted are selected.
EKPO-MATNR	Material Number	No selection
EKPO-WERKS	Plant	Plants relevant for the analysis
MSEG-BWART	Movement Type	Enter "101" to restrict the analysis to goods receipts.
LFA1-KTOKK	Vendor Account Group	Vendor account groups relevant for the analysis

- Table EKKO – Purchasing Document Header
- Table EKPO – Purchasing Document Item
- Table LFA1 – Vendor Master (General Section)
- Table MSEG – Document Segment: Material
- Table MKPF – Header: Material Document

Once you have created the query, defined the relevant fields, and then execute the query, the selection screen shown in Fig. 14.2 appears.

Which selection criteria should you enter now? Experience indicates that, in addition to restrictions at organizational level, you should make the further selections shown in Table 14.2.

Recommended selection criteria

Once you have run this query, you can save the results list in a local file and then compare, in Excel, Access, or ACL, when the purchase order was created (field EKKO-AEDAT, DATE ON WHICH RECORD WAS CREATED) and when the corresponding goods receipts were posted (field MKPF-BUDAT, POSTING DATE).

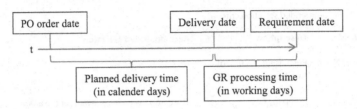

□ Figure 14.3 Purchase orders vs. purchase requisitions over time

Alternatives for technical implementation   If you do not have the option of creating this analysis as an SAP query, you can save the tables listed above (table connection/structure) in local files manually using SAP transactions SE16 or SE16N, and then connect and analyze the individual tables in Excel, Access, or ACL accordingly. What is important is that you download the contents of the relevant fields of the tables specified completely.

If you need to use the analysis described regularly, and your organization uses the SAP GRC suite, you can automate the scenario using the Continuous Monitoring Framework.

14.1.2 Timely Release or Creation of Purchase Requisitions and Purchase Orders

Comparison of transaction data and master data   The aim of this analysis is to check whether purchase requisitions are released promptly. Therefore, you compare transaction data (purchase requisitions, releases) with master data (planning parameters). This enables you to check how efficiently and effectively the procurement process harmonizes with the master data created. However, remember that all analyses in which you compare transaction data with master data can be adversely affected by the fact that you compare master data at the time of the analysis with transaction data from the past. Thus, if master data (in this case planning parameters: planned delivery time, goods receipt processing time) has been adjusted after purchase requisitions and purchase orders have been created, the analysis is not useful.

However, experience shows that this happens in only a few cases. Furthermore, as explained in the previous example, the aim is not to determine the precise number of such cases, but generally to get an impression of how efficient and effective the procurement process is. In spite of this, for this type of analysis, it is always important to verify the results with specialists from the respective operative business areas.

Backward scheduling   This analysis is based on the backward scheduling function provided by SAP. Viewed simply, it works as shown in Fig. 14.3.

Starting with the requirement date, the SAP system uses the goods receipt processing time to determine the delivery date for the goods ordered. Based on the delivery date, the SAP system then uses the planned delivery time to calculate the latest date by which the purchase order must be placed for the goods to be available for the date requested.

Timely release and creation   The aim of the first part of this analysis is to test whether the purchase requisition was released on time. It is only relevant if purchase requisitions are subject to a release strategy in your organization. In the second part of the analysis, the aim is to check whether the purchase order was created on time.

Timely Release of the Purchase Requisition

This analysis uses cluster tables. As you cannot use these in queries, you have to download the tables from SAP manually first. In a second step, you can then merge and analyze them using Excel, Access, or ACL.

When selecting tables manually, save the respective selections as variants so that if you want to run the analysis again, you do not have to enter all of the selection values again.

Table EBAN (Purchase Requisitions) contains all of the information in a purchase requisition. Using the selection in Table 14.3, you can therefore select all purchase requisitions that have been successfully released.

Recommended selection criteria for table EBAN

Once you have run the transaction, you can download the results to a local file (spreadsheet).

In order to determine when a purchase requisition was released, you have to analyze the corresponding change documents. Almost every creation, change, or deletion of data in SAP, whether it be master data or transaction data, is registered in change documents and saved in tables CDHDR (Change Document Header) and CDPOS (Change Document Items). As these tables are used for all changes, the volume of data they contain is correspondingly high.

There are two options for selecting change documents. They are described in detail below.

Selection of change documents – two options

Variant A

Variant A uses a standard SAP program in which tables CDHDR (Change Document Header) and CDPOS (Change Document Items) are linked. The disadvantage of this method is that you receive all changes for the selected change object in the selected period. You can select by type of change in a second step, as described below. To do this, call transaction SE38 and enter program name RSSCD100 (Display Change Documents).

In addition to the object class and the table name, on the selection screen shown in Fig. 14.4, the date fields (From/To) should also be used for selection.

Once you have run the program, use the filter function (▼) on the FIELD column to restrict the list to all entries with the value FRGZU. This selection restricts the list to all changes in which the release status was changed. Then download the results to a local file (spreadsheet).

Variant B

With this method, you download tables CDHDR (Change Document Header) and CDPOS (Change Document Items) manually. You therefore also have to connect the tables with one another manually. With this method, you can only select those changes from table CDPOS that influence the release status.

As almost all data changes (master data and transaction data) are recorded in tables CDHDR and CDPOS, the tables are correspondingly large.

Recommended selection criteria

A meaningful selection is therefore even more important. The selection in Table 14.4 restricts the selection to all change documents that have changed the release status.

Once you have run the transaction, you can download the results to a local file (spreadsheet).

◘ Table 14.3 Recommended selection criteria for table EBAN

Field	Description	Recommended selection
BANFN	Purchase Requisition	No selection
BNFPO	Purchase Requisition Item	No selection
BSART	Purchasing Document Type	Document types relevant for the analysis
BSTYP	Purchasing Document Category	Enter "B" to restrict the analysis to purchase requisitions.
LOEKZ	Deletion Indicator in Purchasing Document	Press F2 to call up the selection options and then choose ▤. This ensures that only purchase requisitions that have not been deleted are selected.
STATU	Status of Purchasing Document	No selection
FRGKZ	Release Indicator	Enter "2" to restrict the analysis to finally released purchase requisitions.
FRGZU	Release Status	No selection
FRGST	Release Strategy	No selection
EKGRP	Purchasing Group	No selection
ERNAM	Name of Person who Created Purchasing Document	No selection
TXZ01	Short Text	No selection
MATNR	Material	Press F2 to call up the selection options and then choose ▤. This ensures that only purchase requisitions with a material number are selected. It indirectly excludes materials for which this analysis is less meaningful.
WERKS	Plant	Plants relevant for the analysis
MENGE	Scheduled Quantity	No selection
MEINS	Unit of Quantity	No selection
BADAT	Requisition Date	No selection
FRGDT	Release Date	No selection

With table CDPOS (Change Document Items), you can select all changes that have changed the release status, but to analyze whether the release was on time, you also need the information about when the release took place. This information is available in table CDHDR (Change Document Header).

Recommended selection criteria   The selection from Table 14.5 therefore selects all CDHDR table entries for which a CDPOS table entry has been identified.

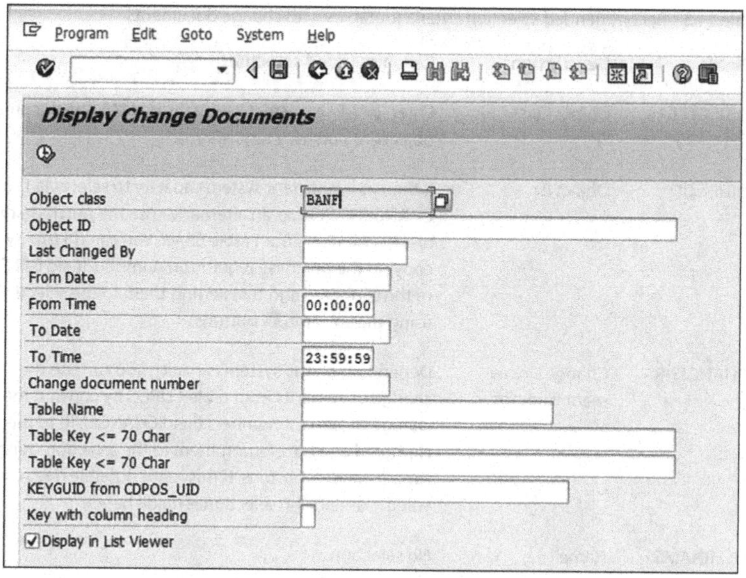

◻ Figure 14.4 Analysis of change documents

◻ Table 14.4 Recommended selection criteria for the tables with change documents

Field	Description	Recommended selection
OBJECTCLAS	Object Class	Enter "BANF" to restrict the analysis of change document objects to purchase requisitions.
OBJECTID	Object ID	Depending on the system capacity, you can use the purchase requisitions from table EBAN by copying the purchase requisition numbers (field BANFN) to the clipboard and transferring them to the selection using the ⬛ and 🖩 (Insert) icons. If this is not possible due to the volume of data, you should at least restrict the number range of the purchase requisitions using the From/To function.
CHANGENR	Change Document Number	No selection
TABNAME	Table Name	Enter "EBAN" to restrict the analysis to the correct table.
TABKEY	Table Key	No selection
FNAME	Field Name	Enter "FRGZU" to restrict the analysis to release indicators.
CHNGIND	Change Indicator	No selection
VALUE_NEW	New Value	No selection
VALUE_OLD	Old Value	No selection

▢ Table 14.5 Recommended selection criteria for tables with change documents

Field	Description	Recommended selection
OBJECTCLAS	Object Class	Enter "BANF" to restrict the analysis of change document objects to purchase requisitions.
OBJECTID	Object ID	If there is insufficient system capacity to select via the CHANGENR field, as an alternative use the purchase requisition numbers from table EBAN. You can do this by copying the purchase requisition numbers (field BANFN) to the clipboard and transferring them to the selection using the ⬚ and 🖼 buttons.
CHANGENR	Change Document Number	Depending on the system capacity, you can use the change documents from table CDPOS by copying the change document numbers (field CHANGENR) to the clipboard and transferring them to the selection using the ⬚ and 🖼 buttons. If this is not possible due to the volume of data, no selection is made here.
USERNAME	Name	No selection
UDATE	Date	No selection
UTIME	Time	No selection
TCODE	Transaction	No selection

Tables CDHDR and CDPOS

You can link tables CDHDR and CDPOS to one another uniquely using the change document number (field CHANGENR). You should also link the field UDATE (Date) from table CDHDR with table CDPOS. It can also be useful to make the field USERNAME (Name) available in table CDPOS.

Regardless of whether you have downloaded the change documents with variant A or B, you must now perform the following steps:

1. In the New Values (VALUE_NEW) column, delete all blank spaces. To do this, use the Replace All function (key combination Ctrl + H)
2. Sort the New Values (VALUE_NEW) column in descending order.
3. Sort the Date (UDATE) column in descending order.

These steps ensure that the last release that took place is selected.

Comparison

To now compare the effective release of the purchase requisitions (field UDATE) with the latest date on which the purchase requisition should have been released, compare the field UDATE (change date) from the change table (table CDPOS or CDHDR) with the field FRGDT (release date) from the purchase requisition table (table EBAN).

Timely Creation of the Purchase Order

Creating an SAP query

In this analysis, create a query (transaction SQ01 or SQVI) to connect tables EKKO, EKPO, EKET, and MARC with one another (see Fig. 14.5).

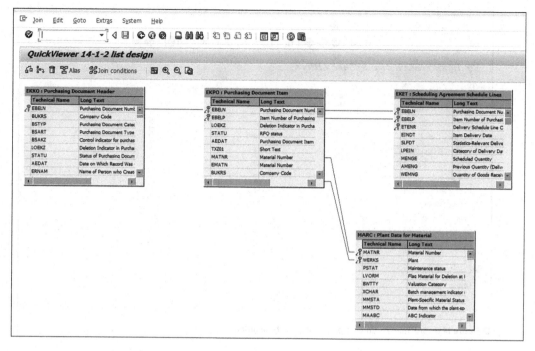

Figure 14.5 SAP query – timely creation of a purchase order

Table 14.6 Linking of the tables for the analysis of purchase orders

Table/field	Table/field	Join
PURCHASING DOCUMENT HEADER · PURCHASING DOCUMENT ITEM		
EKKO-EBELN	EKPO-EBELN	Inner
PURCHASING DOCUMENT ITEM · PLANT DATA FOR MATERIAL		
EKPO-MATNR	MARC-MATNR	Inner
EKPO-WERKS	MARC-WERKS	Inner
PURCHASING DOCUMENT ITEM · SCHEDULING AGREEMENT SCHEDULE LINES		
EKPO-EBELN	EKET-EBELN	Inner
EKPO-EBELP	EKET-EBELP	Inner

As the connections between the respective tables are only visible to a limited extent in Fig. 14.5, Table 14.6 contains a list of the fields that you can use to link these tables with one another. For each connection, you must also define whether it is an "outer join" or "inner join."

You can take the individual fields to be included in the query from the following tables according to your individual requirements:

Relevant tables

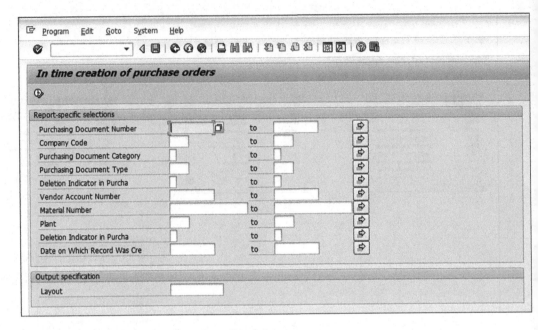

◘ Figure 14.6   SAP query – timely creation of a purchase order

◘ Table 14.7   Recommended selection criteria for the analysis of purchase orders, Table EKKO

Table/field	Description	Recommended selection
EKKO-EBELN	Purchasing Document Number	No selection
EKKO-BUKRS	Company Code	Company codes relevant for the analysis
EKKO-BSTYP	Purchasing Document Category	Enter "F" to restrict the analysis to purchase orders.
EKKO-BSART	Purchasing Document Type	Purchasing document types relevant for the analysis
EKKO-LOEKZ	Deletion Indicator in Purchasing Document (Header)	Press F2 to call up the selection options and then choose ▤. This ensures that only purchase orders that have not been deleted are selected.

- Table EKKO – Purchasing Document Header
- Table EKPO – Purchasing Document Item
- Table MARC – Plant Data for Material
- Table EKET – Scheduling Agreement Schedule Lines

Selection
Recommended
selection criteria

Once you have created and run the query, the selection screen appears (see Fig. 14.6). The following selection criteria are recommended (see Table 14.7).

■ **Table 14.8** Recommended selection in table VBAK (Sales Document: Header Data)

Field	Description	Recommended selection
VBELN	Sales Document	No selection
ERDAT	Creation Date	Here you can define the time period for the sales documents to be analyzed (for example, a year or a quarter).
ERNAM	Creator	No selection
VBTYP	Sales Document Category	Enter "C" to restrict the analysis to sales orders.
AUART	Sales Document Type	Sales document types relevant for the analysis
NETWR	Net Value of Sales Order in Document Currency	No selection
WAERK	Document Currency	No selection
VKORG	Sales Organization	Sales organizations relevant for the analysis
VTWEG	Distribution Channel	Distribution channels relevant for the analysis
SPART	Division	Divisions relevant for the analysis
VKGRP	Sales Group	Sales groups relevant for the analysis
VKBUR	Sales Office	Sales offices relevant for the analysis
GSBER	Business Area	Business areas relevant for the analysis
BSTNK	Customer Purchase Order Number	No selection
BSARK	Customer Order Type	No selection
BSTDK	Customer Purchase Order Date	No selection
KUNNR	Customer Number	No selection

14.1.3 Time between Incoming Purchase Order and Confirmation of the Customer Order

When you enter a sales order in the SAP system, you generally enter the purchase order number and purchase order date of the customer in the header data of the sales document. This allows to you analyze how long it takes for a customer order to be confirmed in the SAP system. The entry of the customer order triggers the clarification of the availability of the customer requirements in the system and the corresponding confirmation. Therefore, it is important for both the customer and for internal requirements planning that customer orders are processed as efficiently as possible.

For this analysis you only need one table – VBAK. Table 14.8 shows a useful selection of fields.

Recommended selection criteria for table VBAK

To now analyze the time from the customer purchase order date to the recording of the sales order, you have to compare fields BSTDK (Customer Purchase Order Date) and ERDAT (Creation Date). You can refine the time calculated with the above-mentioned field selection even further by comparing, for example, whether there are major differences depending on the customer order type or the sales organization.

In comparison to the previous example, this rather simple analysis illustrates particularly clearly how effectively and efficiently you can test processes.

14.1.4 Ten Further Examples of Possible Data-Based Process Analyses

Understanding of the processes and data models

In this section, you have seen some examples of how you can assess selected efficiency-relevant issues in business processes by analyzing data in SAP ERP. The number of business processes is almost infinite. In order to be able to assess the business processes critically, you need both process expertise and a deep understanding of the data models.

The list below shows further examples of data-based process analyses:

- Time between invoice receipt and invoice entry
- Planned goods receipt processing time in comparison to the actual goods receipt processing time
- Analysis of on-time delivery performance and quantity reliability of supplier deliveries
- Analysis of order reasons in customer credit notes: pattern for
  - Users
  - Date of entry (for example, at the beginning or end of a reporting period) etc.
- Material standing times (for materials managed in batches)
- Bypassing of the release strategy
- Predictable deviations between the purchase order price and material standard price (purchase order price deviation)
- Transfer price validation
- Missing scans of invoices
- Development of purchase order price and delivery time

14.2 Analysis of Master Data Quality

Poor master data quality as a source of errors

Missing, incorrect, or inconsistent master data leads to processes with errors and standard analyses containing unreliable information. Therefore, the quality of the master data is very important. In the following examples, the aim is to show how you can use simple methods to assess the quality of the master data.

As already stated in Sect. 8.2.2, "Field Status Groups," the configuration of the field status groups can have an important influence on the quality of the master data as a preventive control.

14.2.1 Quality of Customer Master Data

There are many factors that have a direct influence on business success, such as quality of the products, production capacity, the strength of sales, etc. However, there are also factors that you can check critically using data analyses. Thus, the quality of the customer master data has an immediate influence on sales-relevant operations of an organization and can influence the business success directly.

The most important tables for the analysis of customer master data are listed below. You can select different fields for the analysis depending on whether or how you use the processes/fields in the analysis.

- Table KNA1 – Customer Master (General Section)
- Table KNB1 – Customer Master (Company Code)
- Table KNVV – Customer Master Sales Data

Relevant tables

In practice, there are some typical analysis scenarios that you can use, for example, to identify duplicated customer master data or to assess the completeness of the maintenance of address data (city, postal code, etc.). The most important of these analyses are listed below.

Important analyses

- **Duplicated customer master data**

  The aim of this analysis is to check whether customers have been duplicated within an account group (KTOKD). To perform this analysis, you have to link the following fields:

  - KTOKD (Account Group)
  - NAME1 (Address Line 1: Name 1)
  - NAME2 (Address Line 2: Name 2)
  - STRAS (Street)
  - PSTLZ (Postal Code)
  - ORT01 (City)

  To make sure that similar names and streets are also recognized as duplicates, you should only use the first five to eight characters of the fields NAME1 (Address Line 1: Name 1), NAME2 (Address Line 2: name 2), and STRAS (Street). If you do not do so, minimal differences such as Street/St. or Ltd/Ltd. are interpreted as different values.

- **Standardized maintenance of customer address data**

  Here you can check, for example, whether there are customers where the following fields are not maintained or are not maintained in a standardized way: ORT01 (City), PSTLZ (Postal Code), TELF1 (Telephone), SORTL (Sort Field), or STCD1 (Tax Number 1).

  For the following fields you can check, for example, whether the format (length etc.) of the entries within the respective country is standardized: PSTLZ (Postal Code), TELF1 (Telephone Number 1), or STCD1 (Tax Number 1).

  In some countries, there are different telephone number or postal code formats within the country and therefore you cannot use these analyses here. However, you should be able to perform the analysis for most countries.

- **Accuracy of the reconciliation account**

  Here you can check whether the reconciliation account within an account group is maintained consistently. The field ACCOUNT GROUP comes from table KNA1 and must be connected to table KNB1 via the field KUNNR (Customer Number). In practice, the same reconciliation account is often used within an account group, otherwise the sales are not posted correctly.

A reconciliation account is usually always maintained – the corresponding field is defined as a required field in the configuration of the field status variants in the SAP standard ERP system. You can also make the accuracy of a reconciliation account plausible by, for example, making the reconciliation account plausible in connection with the country of the customer. For example, for an organization in the USA, a customer from Germany with the reconciliation account "Domestic Receivables" would be an incorrect constellation that would have to be corrected.

- **Missing or incorrect Incoterms**
  Here you can check whether the Incoterms within the relevant account group are maintained correctly. The field ACCOUNT GROUP comes from table KNA1 and must be connected to table KNVV via the field KUNNR.

- **Reconciliation of the payment terms between the company code and sales organization**
  For this analysis you compare the payment terms (field: ZTERM) from table KNB1 with table KNVV. Here it is important to understand how the company code is assigned to a sales organization. You can check this assignment with transaction OVX3.
  The master data can also provide for payment terms not having to be agreed between the company code and sales organization, but this is rare.

14.2.2 Produced Materials with No Bill of Materials

The aim of this analysis is to identify materials that, according to the procurement indicator in the material master (E = in-house production), are produced in the plant but no bill of materials has been defined for these materials. In SAP ERP, you can also cost manufactured parts without a bill of materials – you can identify these cases from the special procurement indicator in the costing view. However, a bill of materials is generally used to cost a manufactured material.

Missing bill of materials
If a bill of materials is missing, the system issues error messages in costing. These materials have either not been completely created yet, or are about to be set to inactive. However, both situations should be reflected in the plant-specific material status in order to avoid errors in costing.

You need the following tables for this analysis:
- Table MARC – Plant Data for Material
- Table MAST – Connection of Material to Bill of Materials

Recommended selection criteria for table MARC
For this analysis you must select at least the fields shown in Table 14.9 from table MARC (Plant Data for Material).

To make troubleshooting easier, you could add further organizational fields, such as the MRP Controller (field DISPO) to the selection.

Recommended selection criteria for table MAST
Table MAST (Connection of Material to Bill of Material) is very simple as far as the number of columns is concerned. Therefore, you generally do not need to restrict the selection here. However, if you do want to do so, select the fields shown in Table 14.10.

◻ Table 14.9 Selection from table MARC (Plant Data for Material)

Field	Description	Recommended selection
MATNR	Material	No selection
WERKS	Plant	Plants relevant for the analysis
LVORM	Flag Material for Deletion	Press F2 to call up the selection options and then choose ▥. This ensures that only customers that have no deletion flag are selected.
MMSTA	Plant-Specific Material Status	Select material statuses for which the material must be completely maintained.
BESKZ	Procurement Indicator	Enter "E" to restrict the analysis to produced materials.
SOBSL	Special Procurement Type	No selection

◻ Table 14.10 Selection from table MAST (Connection of Material to Bill of Materials)

Field	Description	Recommended selection
MATNR	Material	No selection
WERKS	Plant	Plants relevant for the analysis
STLAN	Bill of Materials Usage	No selection

To now determine whether there are materials that are produced in a plant according to the procurement indicator, you have to check that all materials with procurement indicator "E" also have a corresponding entry in table MAST.

These materials have either been created in the respective plant accidentally, or the bill of materials is actually missing for these materials. If the bill of materials is missing, this should be reflected accordingly in the plant-specific material status, otherwise errors would occur for these materials in the next valuation run.

14.2.3 Reconciliation of Material Costs within a Company Code

Materials that are transferred from one plant to another within the same company code (stock transfer) must have the same value in both plants. Table 14.11 shows a simple example of how these materials have to be set up in the respective plants in order to support correct material valuation. You can see the differences in the settings in the material master.

Different valuations indicate that the material is not set up correctly – probably in the receiving plant – or at least was not set up correctly at the time of costing. It could also be the case that the price units have not been aligned between the manufacturing plant and receiving plant (see Table 14.12: here there is a resulting difference of USD 0.11 per unit).

◻ **Table 14.11**   Values in the material master for stock transfers

Field in material master	Values in manufacturing plant Plant: xx01	Values in receiving plant Plant: xx02
Procurement Indicator	"E" In-house production	"F" External procurement
Special Procurement Type	"50" Standard production	"A1" Stock transfer from plant xx01
Special Procurement Type for Costing	"Blank"	"A1" Stock transfer from plant xx01

◻ **Table 14.12**   Example – valuation differences due to unreconciled price units

Material valuation manufacturing plant	Material valuation receiving plant
USD 110.11 × 1 unit	USD 1.10 × 100 units
Difference: USD 0.11/1 unit	

◻ **Table 14.13**   Selection for table MBEW (Material Valuation)

Field	Description	Recommended selection
MATNR	Material	No selection
BWKEY	Valuation Area	Valuation areas relevant for the analysis; generally there is a 1:1 relationship between the valuation area and the plant.
LVORM	Flag Material for Deletion	Press F2 to call up the selection options and then choose ▤. This ensures that only customers that have no deletion flag are selected.
LBKUM	Total Valuated Stock	No selection
SALK3	Value of Total Valuated Stock	No selection
VPRSV	Price Control Indicator	Enter "S".
STPRS	Standard Price	No selection
PEINH	Price Unit	No selection

Recommended selection criteria for table MBEW

For this analysis – the reconciliation of material costs within a company code – you need table MBEW (Material Valuation) (see Table 14.13).

If you find valuation differences in this table, you can investigate these differences further either with SAP standard transaction MB51 or with table MSEG (Document Segment: Material).

Recommended selection criteria for table MSEG

Table 14.14 shows the most important selection criteria in table MSEG (Document Segment: Material).

These stock transfer movements simultaneously create an incoming posting in the receiving plant. The values of these two postings are derived from the standard price

◘ Table 14.14 Selection for table MSEG (Document Segment: Material)

Field	Description	Recommended selection
MBLNR	Material Document Number	No selection
MJAHR	Material Document Year	No selection
ZEILE	Material Document Item	No selection
BWART	Movement Type	Enter "641" (stock transfer to stock in transit).
MATNR	Material Number	No selection
WERKS	Plant	Plants relevant for the analysis
DMBTR	Amount in Local Currency	No selection

of the respective plant. Therefore, if the standard prices have been aligned between the plants, the values in the sending and receiving plants are the same.

14.2.4 Ten Further Examples of Possible Master Data Analyses

In this section, you have seen some examples of how you can discover statuses that can have a negative effect on business processes by analyzing master data in SAP ERP. The list below contains further examples:

- Cross-plant reconciliation of planning parameters
- Analysis of master data duplicates (materials, customers, suppliers, etc.)
- Reconciliation of payment terms defined in master data of suppliers who are also customers
- Analysis of the correlation between the credit limit and credit risk (for example, a high credit limit with a low risk is correct; a high credit limit with a high credit risk is not correct)
- Identification of missing master data views (materials, customers, suppliers, etc.)
- Search for missing purchasing info records for purchased materials
- Analysis of the material special procurement keys that indicate plants in which the material has not been created or has not been created completely
- Reconciliation between planning group and supplier type (internal/external) in the purchasing info record
- Missing sales and transfer prices for materials sold externally and internally

14.3 Manual Data Changes

These analyses should help you find out whether and how frequently users change data in SAP. On one hand, the aim is of course to check whether the corresponding users are authorized to make these changes. On the other hand, the aim is above all to check how frequently such manual changes are required.

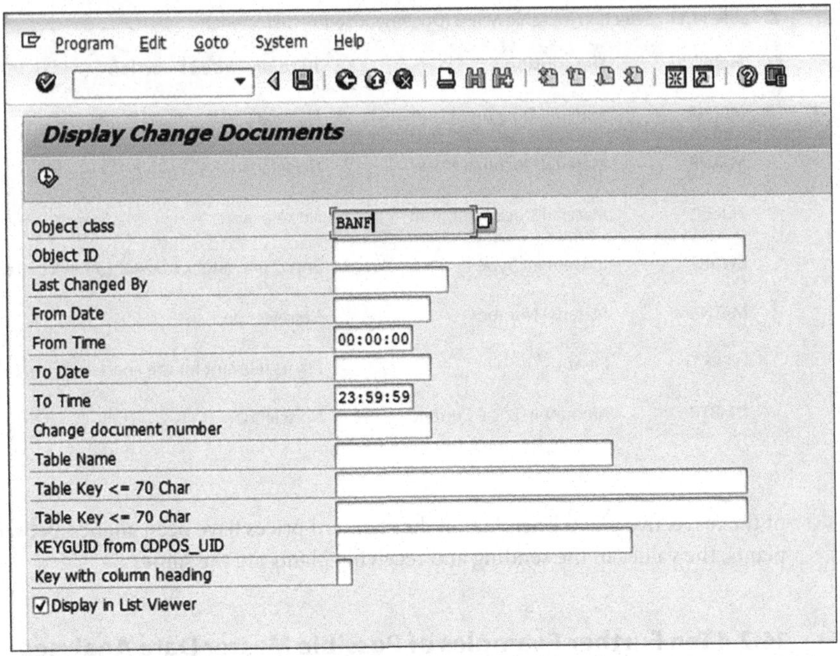

□ **Figure 14.7**   Analysis of change documents for purchase requisitions

Are the users authorized to make changes?
The user profile determines whether a user is technically authorized to change data in the system. However, when you check the user profiles for possible conflicts, this is always just a snapshot of the authorizations assigned to the user at the time of the analysis. The aim of the analyses presented here is to check which data has been changed in a period.

Time of changes
It may be that a user is authorized to make changes, but that these changes take place at the wrong time. For example, if a user changes purchase order texts after the purchase requisition has already been released, this is at least questionable – even though, based on the user profile, the user is authorized to make such changes.

Change tables
In all of these tests you work with change tables. All data changes are registered in these change tables, and the tables are therefore very large. There are generally two options for investigating these change tables (see variants A and B in Sect. 14.1.2, "Timely Release or Creation of Purchase Requisitions and Purchase Orders"). The following examples each describe the method with the SAP standard report (variant A).

14.3.1 Changes to Purchase Requisitions

Manual adjustment of planning parameters
The aim of this analysis is to determine to what extent and how frequently purchase requisitions have to be adjusted manually. As purchase requisitions are based on the planned requirements and the system usually generates the underlying planning parameters automatically, you can use this analysis to check how well these planning parameters have been set up. Ideally, the manual interventions are restricted to a min-

Table 14.15 Recommended selection criteria for program RSSCD100 – analysis of purchase requisitions

Field	Description	Recommended selection
Object Class	SAP data object	Enter "BANF" to restrict the analysis to purchase requisitions.
Last Changed By	User ID of the person who made the change	No selection
From Date	The date from which changes are to be considered	Due to the size of the table, it is important to restrict the period for the analysis meaningfully.
From Time	The time from which changes are to be considered	Specify 00:00:00 to ensure that all changes within the selected period are considered.
To Date	The date to which all changes are to be considered.	Due to the size of the table, it is important to restrict the period for the analysis meaningfully.
To Time	The time to which all changes are to be considered.	Specify 23:59:59 to ensure that all changes within the selected period are considered.
Table Name	Table to be analyzed within the SAP data object.	EBAN (Purchase Requisitions)

imum. However, if you discover that, in particular, quantity and date fields often have to be adjusted manually, this can be an indicator that the planning parameters do not support the planning process ideally and that there is potential to increase efficiency.

To track changes, call up SAP transaction SE38 and enter program name RSSCD100 (Display Change Documents) (see Fig. 14.7).

Table 14.15 shows some recommendations for the choice of selection criteria for the analysis of changes using program RSSCD100.

Recommended selection criteria

Once you have executed report RSSCD100, if necessary you can save the results in a local document and then, for example, analyze them further in Excel. You can take information about the type of change from the output list based on the FIELD.

Table 14.16 shows a selection of the most important fields within table EBAN (Purchase Requisitions).

Fields: purchase requisitions

You can see the complete list of fields in table EBAN in transaction SE11 (ABAP Dictionary: Initial Screen).

Depending on the volume of the changes, manual changes to the contents in the fields listed above indicate how efficiently the processes are set up/run; or, however, to what extent the master data, in this case the planning parameters, correspond with reality.

14.3.2 Changes to Purchasing Documents

The aim of this analysis is to identify manual changes to purchasing documents. As the reasons and the risk of such adjustments can be very different, Table 14.17 shows a selection of possible changes and the risks they bear.

◘ **Table 14.16**   Important fields in table EBAN (Purchase Requisitions)

Field	Changes
LOEKZ	Deletion indicator
FRGZU	Release status
EKGRP	Purchasing group
TXZ01	Short text
LGORT	Storage location
MENGE	Purchase requisition quantity
LFDAT	Item delivery date
LIFNR	Preferred supplier
KONNR	Number of higher level contract
DISPO	MRP controller

◘ **Table 14.17**   Overview of risks involved with changes to purchasing documents

Change to	Risk	Cause
Purchase order quantity	Process inefficiency Adverse effect on correctness	Incorrect planning parameters in the material master Bypassing the release (depending on the system configuration, no further release is required if the purchase order quantity is increased)
Purchase order price	Process inefficiency Adverse effect on correctness	Prices in the info record or purchase order contracts are not up-to-date Bypassing the release (depending on the system configuration, no further release is required if the purchase order price is increased)
Over-delivery tolerance or indicator for unlimited over-delivery	Adverse effect on correctness	Bypassing the release (no further purchase order release is required if the tolerance is adjusted or the indicator for unlimited over-delivery is set)
Delivery address	Adverse effect on correctness	Fraud
Purchase order text	Adverse effect on correctness	Fraud Bypassing the release (adjustment of the purchase order text does not require further purchase order release)
Release	Adverse effect on correctness	Release of the purchase order by the same person who created the purchase order.

◻ **Table 14.18** Recommended selection criteria for the analysis of changes to purchasing documents with program RSSCD100

Field Name	Description	Recommended selection
Object Class	SAP data object	Select the entry EINKBELEG to restrict the analysis to purchasing documents.
Last Changed By	User ID of the person who made the change	No selection
From Date	The date from which changes are to be considered	Due to the size of the table, it is important to restrict the period for the analysis meaningfully.
From Time	The time from which changes are to be considered	Specify 00:00:00 to ensure that all changes within the selected period are considered.
To Date	The date to which all changes are to be considered.	Due to the size of the table, it is important to restrict the period for the analysis meaningfully.
To Time	The time to which all changes are to be considered.	Specify 23:59:59 to ensure that all changes within the selected period are considered.
Table Name	Table to be analyzed within the SAP data object.	The most common tables here are: EKKO (Purchasing Document Header) EKPO (Purchasing Document Item) EKET (Scheduling Agreement Schedule Lines) EKES (Purchase Order Confirmations) EKKN (Account Assignment in Purchasing Document)

To analyze changes to purchasing documents, proceed as follows: call up transaction SE38 and enter program name RSSCD100 (Display Change Documents).

Make the following selections as shown in Table 14.18.

The purchasing document header (table EKKO) generally contains information that is valid for every item. The purchase order currency, supplier, or release status of the purchase order are classic examples of fields that appear in the purchasing document header. Table 14.19 shows the most important fields and what they mean.

The purchasing document item (table EKPO) contains details about what was ordered, in what quantity, and under what conditions. Table 14.20 shows the most important fields

As a purchasing document item can have several different delivery dates, the schedule line (scheduling agreement) table (EKET) contains information about the delivery date with the expected delivery quantity. Table 14.21 lists the most important fields in table EKET.

Table EKES (Purchase Order Confirmations) contains details for the purchase order confirmation. Table 14.22 shows the most important fields in table EKES.

Recommended selection criteria

Fields: purchasing document header

Fields: purchasing document item

Fields: schedule line (scheduling agreement) table

Fields: purchase order confirmations

◘ **Table 14.19** Important fields in table EKKO (Purchasing Document Header)

Field	Changes
ZTERM	Terms of payment key
EKGRP	Purchasing group
WAERS	Currency key
WKURS	Exchange rate
INCO1	Incoterms part 1
INCO2	Incoterms part 2
KTWRT	Cumulative planned value
FRGZU	Release status

◘ **Table 14.20** Important fields in table EKPO (Purchasing Document Item)

Field	Changes
LOEKZ	Deletion indicator in purchasing document
TXZ01	Short text
LGORT	Storage location
KTMNG	Target quantity
MENGE	Purchase order quantity
NETPR	Net price in purchasing document in document currency
UEBTO	Tolerance limit for over delivery
UEBTK	Indicator: unlimited over delivery permitted

◘ **Table 14.21** Important fields in table EKET (Scheduling Agreement Schedule Lines)

Field	Changes
EINDT	Item delivery date
SLFDT	Delivery date relevant for statistics
MENGE	Scheduled quantity

Fields: account assignment in purchasing document

For standard, direct purchasing purchase orders, you determine the account assignment via the account determination of the material ordered in the corresponding organization. For indirect purchase orders, or purchase orders entered via assets, projects, or orders, table EKKN (Account Assignment in Purchasing Document) contains the relevant details. Table 14.23 shows the most important fields in table EKKN.

◘ **Table 14.22** Important fields in table EKES (Purchase Order Confirmations)

Field	Changes
ETENS	Sequential number of purchase order confirmation
EINDT	Purchase order confirmation delivery date
MENGE	Purchase order confirmation quantity
LOEKZ	Purchase order deletion indicator

◘ **Table 14.23** Important fields in table EKKN (Account Assignment in Purchasing Document)

Field	Changes
ZEKKN	Sequential number of the account assignment
LOEKZ	Deletion indicator for purchasing document account assignment
MENGE	Quantity
KOSTL	Cost center
ANLN1	Asset main number
ANLN2	Asset sub-number
XBAUF	Post to order
XBPRO	Post to project
KSTRG	Cost object

You can display all fields in tables EKKO, EKPO, EKET, EKES, and EKKN with transaction SE11.

Due to the various usage options of the purchasing processes and the complexity of these data elements, the first time you run this analysis you should analyze all change documents over a shorter period for a data object to then identify the relevant fields based on the results.

14.3.3 Changes to Sales Documents

The aim of this analysis is to identify manual changes to sales documents. As the reasons and the risk of such adjustments can be very different, Table 14.24 shows a selection of possible changes and the risks they bear.

◘ **Table 14.24** Overview of the risks of changes to sales documents

Change to	Risk	Cause
Sales price	Process inefficiency, correctness/control	Sales price conditions are not updated Bypassing of the sales price release
Terms of payment	Correctness/control	Bypassing of the agreed standard conditions
Deletion flag	Correctness/control	Fictitious sales orders inflate the expected sales

◘ **Table 14.25** Recommended selection criteria for the analysis of changes to sales documents with program RSSCD100

Field	Description	Recommended selection
Object Class	SAP data object	Select the entry VERKKBELEG to restrict the analysis to sales documents.
Last Changed By	User ID of the person who made the change	No selection
From Date	The date from which changes are to be considered	Due to the size of the table, it is important to restrict the period for the analysis meaningfully.
From Time	The time from which changes are to be considered	Specify 00:00:00 to ensure that all changes within the selected period are considered.
To Date	The date to which all changes are to be considered.	Due to the size of the table, it is important to restrict the period for the analysis meaningfully.
To Time	The time to which all changes are to be considered.	Specify 23:59:59 to ensure that all changes within the selected period are considered.
Table Name	Table to be analyzed within the SAP data object.	The most common tables here are: VBAK (Customer Order Header Data) VBAP (Customer Order Items Data) VBEP (Customer Order Delivery Data) VBKD (Customer Order Commercial Data)

Recommended selection criteria   To restrict program RSSCD100 (Display Change Documents, can be called up, e. g., via transaction SA38) to sales documents, make the selections as shown in Table 14.25.

Fields: customer order header data   The header data of the customer order table (table VBAK) contains information that is valid for every sales document item. Table 14.26 shows the most important fields in the customer order header data.

Fields: customer order item data   The customer order item data (table VBAP) contains information on the article(s) sold, as well as the quantity and net price. Table 14.27 lists the most important fields.

Table 14.26 Important fields in table VBAK (Customer Order Header Data)

Field	Changes
NETWR	Net value
WAERK	Sales document currency
KALSM	Sales and distribution: pricing procedure
VSBED	Shipping condition

Table 14.27 Important fields in table VBAP (Customer Order Items Data)

Field	Changes
MATNR	Material number
PSTYV	Sales document item type
NETWR	Net value of order item in document currency
KWMENG	Cumulative order quantity in sales units

Table 14.28 Important fields in table VBKD (Purchase Order Confirmations)

Field	Changes
INCO1	Incoterms part 1
INCO2	Incoterms part 2
ZTERM	Terms of payment key
KURSK	Exchange rate for pricing

As a customer order item can be distributed across various delivery dates, table VBEP (Customer Order Delivery Data) contains the corresponding details – field EDATU (Delivery Date) is particularly relevant.

Purchase order confirmations are documented in table VBKD (Purchase Order Confirmations). Table 14.28 shows the most important fields in this table.

Fields: purchase order confirmations

You can display all of the fields in the tables using transaction SE11.

Due to the various usage options of the sales processes and the complexity of these data elements, here too, the first time you run this analysis you should analyze all change documents over a shorter period for a data object to then identify the relevant fields based on the results.

14.3.4 Manual Data Changes – Ten Further Examples

SAP ERP has a vast amount of master data and transaction data that you can change manually. In addition to the examples described above, the following scenarios are possible:

- Analysis of conspicuously large changes to material standard prices
- Analysis of changes to prices and terms of payment in the customer invoice
- Analysis of changes to terms of payment in supplier invoice recording
- Check of changes to delivery addresses in purchase orders
- Analysis of changes to over-delivery tolerances in purchase orders
- Analysis of activities of emergency users (or "Firefighters," see Sect. 4.3.3)
- Check of correctness when opening and closing posting periods
- Analysis of changes to user access rights
- Analysis of changes to credit limit data and risk data in the customer master
- Analysis of manual release of payments

14.4 Supplementing SAP ERP Standard Reports

Adding data to standard analyses

The aim of these analyses is to add data from other reports, master data, or transaction data to SAP standard analyses. This supports the validity of these reports and the root cause analysis. The requirements of such reports are generally very individual, in the same way that the local processes and organizations are set up individually in the system.

14.4.1 Planning Parameters Added to Stock Analyses

Standard analyses

SAP provides a number of useful standard analyses for analyzing the warehouse stocks. The following are examples of corresponding SAP transactions:

- Transaction MC46 – Analysis of Slow-Moving Items
- Transaction MC42 – Range of Coverage by Usage Value
- Transaction MC43 – Range of Coverage by Requirements
- Transaction MC44 – Analysis of Inventory Turnover

Supplementing standard analyses

These reports do identify materials that are managed inefficiently; however, they only analyze the symptoms and not the cause of the problem. You can make these reports much more meaningful by adding planning parameters relevant for you. In most cases, the planning parameters are the cause of the inefficient management of materials. To analyze the cause of the problem as well as the symptoms, proceed as follows:

1. First run the required SAP standard report and save the results lists in a local file. To do this, choose the path SYSTEM • LIST • SAVE • LOCAL FILE.
2. In a second step, save the planning parameters relevant for you in a local file as well. The following is a list of the most common planning parameters in table MARC (Plant Data for Material):
   - Field EKGRP – Purchasing Group
   - Field DISPR – Material: MRP Profile
   - Field DISMM – MRP Type
   - Field DISPO – MRP Controller
   - Field PLIFZ – Planned Delivery Time in Days
   - Field DZEIT – In-House Production Time

- Field WEBAZ – Goods Receipt Processing Time in Days
- Field DISLS – MRP Lot Size
- Field MINBE – Reorder Point
- Field EISBE – Safety Stock
- Field BSTMI – Minimum Lot Size
- Field BSTMA – Maximum Lot Size
- Field BSTFE – Fixed Lot Size
- Field FEVOR – Production Scheduler
- Field UEETO – Tolerance Limit for Over-delivery

As table MARC refers to plant level, you can easily connect it using the above-mentioned transactions MC42, MC43, MC44, and MC46. This enables you to see not only how well the materials are managed, but also the corresponding planning parameters that strongly influence the administration of the materials.

14.4.2 Customer Master Data Added to Credit Management Analysis

The aim of this analysis is to add customer master data to a credit management analysis. This enables you to compare customer master data such as terms of payment and Incoterms with the credit limit and credit risk. There is usually a certain correlation between this data; under certain circumstances it is even prescribed in guidelines. You can therefore use this analysis to check whether the prescribed guidelines are being adhered to.

You execute the analysis with transaction F.31 (Credit Management – Overview). This report shows customers with their risk class, credit limit, and utilization of this credit limit. You can use the CUSTOMER button (shift key + F5) to call up the individual customer details. However, you cannot display this customer data in a table in the report. To display the data in this way, you first have to save the report in a local file. You can do this via the path SYSTEM • LIST • SAVE • LOCAL FILE. | Step 1

In a second step, you have to save the customer and credit data in a local file. The following is a selection of possible tables: | Step 2

- The *terms of payment in the customer master* are defined at both sales organization level (table KNVV) and in table KNB1. Generally, these terms of payment keys should be reconciled with one another.
- The *terms of payment at company code level* are located in table KNB1 (Customer Master (Company Code)), in the field ZTERM (Terms of Payment Key).
- The *terms of payment and delivery at sales organization level* are located in table KNVV (Customer Master Sales Data). Table 14.29 shows the corresponding fields.
- Details of the *customer master from the credit management view* are located in table KNKK (Customer Master Credit Management: Control Area Data). Table 14.30 lists the most important fields.

As tables KNB1 and KNVV are at company code level and sales organization level, before you link the tables with the report, you must check how the individual organizational units are connected to one another. | Tables KNB1 and KNVV

This enables you to analyze whether the credit limit corresponds to the risk category or payment and delivery conditions, as well as the last time the credit limit was checked

◻ **Table 14.29**   Important fields in table KNVV (Customer Master Sales Data)

Field	Description
INCO1	Incoterms part 1
INCO2	Incoterms part 2
ZTERM	Terms of payment key

◻ **Table 14.30**   Important fields in table KNKK (Customer Master Credit Management: Control Area Data)

Field	Description
AEDAT	Date of last change
UEDAT	Date on which the credit limit was exceeded
DTREV	Last check (internal)
REVDB	Last check (external)
NXTRV	Next check

and the last time changes were made to the credit master. This information is only available in the SAP standard report indirectly and is therefore difficult to analyze.

14.5 Summary

In this section you have learned that in the SAP ERP system, you can use data analyses to check the flow of the business processes for efficiency, anomalies, and inconsistencies. In numerous examples you have seen that you can analyze master data and transaction data almost manually or using tools such as SAP Query (also MS Access or Excel) if you work with the individual SAP database tables. This work requires a good understanding of the data model in SAP ERP.

The analyses described are quite time-consuming when you first set them up, but on the other hand they are very efficient and effective for detecting improvement potential that can have a measurable effect for the success of an organization. You can also automate the analyses described by, for example, starting them directly in SAP queries, programming reports, or setting up corresponding scenarios in Process Control as part of the Continuous Monitoring Framework (see Chap. 17).

Part III   From Concept and Content to Implementation: Automation of an Internal Control System

Imagine that, as a consultant, you are supporting a crude oil company in an Arabian desert state in the automation of an internal control system. Your previous research has shown that this company belongs to the king of this state, does not actually have to fulfill any legal ICS regulations, and the financial reporting of this company is not accessible to the public.

You set off for this project, leave the airplane in the Arabian desert, and learn the following: the risks and controls, to date documented on paper, refer primarily to the processes relevant for financial reporting; from this, you conclude that there is a balance sheet and profit and loss statement for this company, even if they are only intended for a select group of people. You learn that there is an internal audit team, and are referred to the COSO cube, with the expectation that this "thing" is "active" and can be used at the push of a button. How do you handle this situation?

As adventurous as this scenario may sound, I found myself in this situation somewhere in the desert and would like to share with you how I overcame these challenges.

In the last part of the book, I explain the theoretical concept of ICS automation and show how you can implement this concept with the help of an SAP product. Particularly interesting is the procedure for the "real" automation, when business processes are monitored to a large extent with no human participation. This is the continuous monitoring approach that is based on the integration of GRC software with ERP systems. A chapter with examples from practice will then show how organizations of different size have efficiently implemented the topics of ICS and compliance management.

ICS Automation: How to Set the COSO Cube in Motion

The concept of an internal control system that works at the push of a button is very simple but at the same time very abstract: reason enough to dedicate a separate chapter to it.

Concepts for implementing the internal control system (ICS) are heavily influenced by the COSO study, the internationally recognized standard in the ICS field. Many ICS implementation concepts are based on the theoretical construct of the COSO cube, with its 26 basic principles, five core components, and three dimensions. Concepts that, in practice, are offered by various consultancy firms or are designed in-house, frequently represent a high-quality framework from a content and design perspective – however, the framework is unfortunately usually based on Microsoft Excel and SAP users have to transfer it to the SAP platform. It is clear that such an approach does not offer any visions for automation.

What does automating an ICS mean, and how can you close gaps between concepts and efficient implementation of these concepts? In searching for core competences in the area of process automation you would look at software manufacturers, and SAP also provides suitable solutions. Before we look at these solutions in Chap. 16, "ICS Automation Using SAP Process Control," and Chap. 17 "Implementation of Automated Test and Monitoring Scenarios in the SAP ERP Environment," this chapter will provide you with an initial basic understanding of the concept of ICS automation.

15.1 Basic Concept of ICS Automation

As is usual for basic concepts and as the term already indicates, the basic concept of ICS automation is simple and understandable for most people.

Note for the Following Explanation ❶

Some readers who have experience with compliance could see the following explanations as too simple and general. We cannot completely deny this. Note therefore that in the following explanations, the complex topics have intentionally been broken down and made simple. They serve merely to make the meaning of ICS automation more specific and to answer the basic question of how to set the COSO cube in motion.

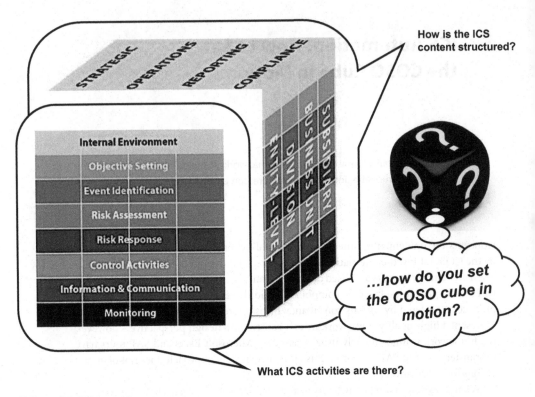

Figure 15.1   ICS automation

15.1.1 COSO Cube in Action

Execute activities as simply as possible

As you can see in Fig. 15.1, the COSO model has content and activities. *Automation* would mean that the persons involved would execute the activities as simply as possible, for example, by making entries in certain fields in a template or by analyzing data received in the form of an e-mail message or task that can be closed and sent back with a simple click. Thus, with reference to ICS, "automated" cannot be understood as "person-independent."

Content = object

ICS activities process *ICS content* and therefore, here we introduce a new term: the *object*. In a software solution, an object corresponds to an item of master data (see Sect. 5.1.1, "Data in an SAP System") and is involved in various activities and transactions (Fig. 15.2). Together, ICS objects and ICS activities create ICS results.

---

❶   Parallels Between SAP and ICS Software

If we were to project data in SAP ERP onto data in an ICS application, this would look as follows:
- SAP ERP: master data + transactions = transaction data
- ICS application: ICS objects + ICS activities = ICS results

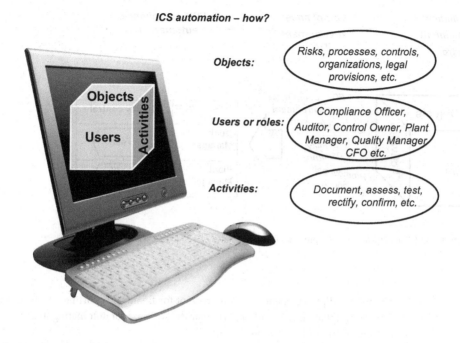

■ **Figure 15.2**   Approach to ICS automation

To describe the meaning of *ICS results* more precisely, we can look at an individual   ICS results
ICS result, for example, a log entry in the system that contains the following information:

- Object: Control "Expiry date on the milk carton is OK"
- Test date: 07:30, 12/01/2010
- COSO domain: Operations
- COSO component: Control activities
- Activity: Control execution
- Activity result: Negative

15.1.2 Concept of ICS Automation

Automation of an ICS generally involves an application that maps ICS-specific *objects*   Three dimensions
and enables a series of ICS-relevant *activities* with reference to these objects. This takes   of ICS automation
place from the perspective of the *persons* involved in the ICS process (see Sect. 15.2,
"ICS-relevant objects and documentation").

Thus, there are three important dimensions to ICS automation: objects, users, and
activities. They form the basic framework of an ICS application and you can use them
to model the compliance process.

The ICS is seen as a means for ensuring compliance (see Sect. 15.1.1, "COSO Cube   ICS automation =
in Action"). Therefore, with regard to ICS automation, we generally refer to *compliance*   compliance
automation. This is relevant as many readers primarily associate ICS with legal require-   automation

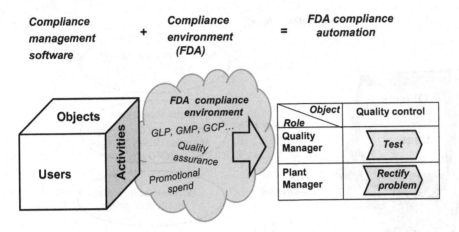

Compliance management software + **Compliance environment (FDA)** = **FDA compliance automation**

☐ **Figure 15.3**   Modeling of the compliance process – FDA compliance

ments for handling risks and controls relevant for financial reporting. It is important to understand that an ICS, and in particular the software for automating it, can handle various legal and in-house requirements.

Automating FDA compliance

As shown in Fig. 15.3, process steps such as tests of quality controls by the Quality Manager and the rectification of problems discovered during control activities by the Plant Manager are an extract from the quality management process that has to be established within the framework of implementing FDA compliance requirements. This example shows how you can merge the individual building blocks for FDA-specific compliance automation.

Automating SOX compliance

However, you could also use the individual ICS building blocks to implement an ICS process intended to guarantee compliance with the legal requirements for reliability of external financial reporting.

SOX compliance process

As illustrated in Fig. 15.4 (this example is simplified and in no way complete), by means of individual ICS modules, the SOX compliance process can contain the following subprocesses:

- The control owner executes the control steps in the business process and confirms this.
- The auditor checks the effectiveness of the controls. This means that he checks whether the control mechanisms achieve the control objectives and whether the controls are actually performed. The process owner ensures that the weaknesses detected by the auditor are rectified and assesses whether the design of established control mechanisms is up-to-date.

Depending on the legal, organizational, and industry-specific environment, the scenarios for ICS automation can be different; the basic contexts in the construct that enables ICS automation can therefore be considered generally valid.

However, this book concentrates primarily on the ICS model based on the requirements relevant for financial reporting, and therefore does not claim to be complete. In the next section, you will learn about the basic properties of individual building blocks that you can use to model an automated ICS process.

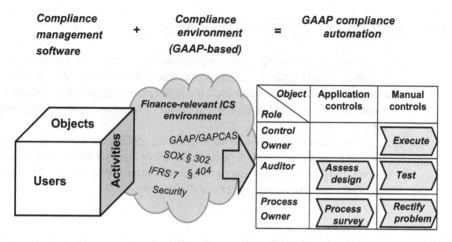

Figure 15.4 Modeling of the compliance process – SOX compliance

15.2 ICS-Relevant Objects and Documentation

Objects are the central building blocks of an ICS. On one hand, they have a static *documentation function* (for example, a control, consisting of its descriptions, various attributes, etc.) and thus fulfill the requirements for the existence of an ICS. On the other hand, these objects are the subject of various assessments (for example, assessment of the suitability of the design of a control for achieving the control objective). One of the purposes of this *dynamic function* of ICS objects is to provide a period-based statement about the *effectiveness* of the control that is documented as an object.

The design of the ICS data model, at the center of which are various objects, is of central importance in the ICS automation. In the description of the ICS objects that follows, their business importance is reduced to a minimum; instead, we focus on their functional properties that have a practical importance for the ICS implementation.

15.2.1 Organizational Units

The purpose of organizational units is to map the structure of an organization. This generally takes the form of a *hierarchy*. The level of detail of the individual hierarchy levels is aligned primarily with reporting requirements: in a group that is active internationally, this generally corresponds to a division along business lines within a country. Depending on the specific details, the organizational structure in an ICS can also be aligned according to further requirements, for example, sign-off responsibilities (see Sect. 15.3.9, "Sign-Off"), according to independent accounting entities, or according to the mapping of shared service organizations, etc.

Organizational hierarchy – properties

[e.g.] | Shared Services Organizations

A control may be relevant for multiple organizational units. A typical case is the general IT controls: if the IT application used by "organization A" and "organization B" is managed by a central IT service organization, from a compliance perspective, organizations A and B are reliant on the effectiveness of change management controls with regard to this IT application.

Organizations A and B have no influence on the controls, but must show them in their own ICS reporting and are de facto responsible for them (see Sect. 6.1.1, "IT Organization"). If an IT service organization in an organization does not act as an independent unit, it will have to be reported "fictitiously" as if it were.

HCM
Organizational
Management vs.
ICS structure

The example of the shared services organizations clearly shows that the compliance-relevant organizational structures often have little to do with the operative structure of an organization – seen through the eyes of the auditor, the world sometimes looks rather different. Furthermore, if we consider the fact that even the division of ICS responsibilities does not necessarily match the personnel assignment of employees, the importance of the integration of an ICS application with SAP's *Organizational Management* decreases (see Sect. 11.4.3, "Structural Authorizations"). The demand for the integration with Organizational Management is frequently raised during the implementation of SAP Process Control because organizations often want to reuse the existing organizational structures from other SAP applications.

[e.g.] | ICS Responsibility Does Not Correspond to HR Assignment

An internal auditor employed at corporate level in Germany could also cover the entire EMEA region in his operative responsibility.

Multidimensionality
of the
organizational
structure

In practice, it is sometimes necessary to arrange the same organizational units in different hierarchies, grouped by geographical regions, by business fields, etc. Therefore, one of the main properties of the organizational hierarchy in ICS automation is the multidimensionality. This principle is partly achieved in SAP Process Control 10.0.

15.2.2 Processes

Business processes
as ICS objects

From an ICS perspective, business processes are a container with a control function for the process steps they contain. The primary aim of the processes is to ensure the integration of controls in the business processes. Similarly to organizational units, for reporting reasons, you can display processes in a hierarchy (for example, in the "process → subprocess → process step chain"); you may also have to map the process steps as objects in a flow chart diagram in order to illustrate all of the dependencies between the individual process steps. Processes in the data model of an ICS application can also be a medium for connecting organizational units with controls.

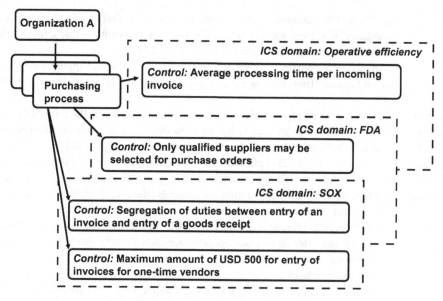

□ Figure 15.5 Multiple domain principle in an ICS application

15.2.3 Controls

Incorporated in the process hierarchy, controls are objects that can be seen as process steps with a control function. As central objects in an ICS application, controls have a series of properties and attributes that have both an informative and controlling function. These attributes are often specific to an organization; in practice, the following attributes have become established:

— *Control frequency*
That is, the frequency of the control procedures (several times per day/continuously, daily, weekly, etc.).
— *Trigger*
Is the control event-based or time-based?
— *Control purpose*
Are the controls preventive or detective controls?

Control attributes

We also differentiate between manual, semi-automated, and automated controls. As mentioned in Sect. 5.1.2, "Controls in the SAP System," automated controls can be divided into configuration controls, master data controls, and transaction controls.

Corresponding to the division of the COSO cube, there are controls that cover the strategic, operational, and reporting and compliance areas. In practice, there is often the requirement to consider the areas specified, also called domains, from a higher level perspective: in a similar way to the *multiple hierarchy principle* of the organizational units as mentioned in Sect. 15.2.1, "Organizational Units," at the highest hierarchy level in an ICS, control activities – with all other related objects, including organizational units – are divided into domains. Thus we can refer to a *multiple domain principle* (see

Multiple domain principle in the ICS

Fig. 15.5). For example, a control system can contain domains that cover not only compliance objectives, such as SOX, FDA, etc., but also controls that target efficiency in business processes or take place at the strategic level.

The multiple domain principle is supported in the respective applications – in SAP Process Control (from Release 3.0), for example, by the Multiple Compliance Framework.

Reusability of controls

Another major property of the multiple domain principle is the reusability of controls. This means that you can assign the same objects to the same or different organizational units, both within one domain and across multiple domains.

Integrative role: controls in the GRC concept

As an object in an ICS application, the control has an important integrative function when we consider the ICS as part of GRC in an organization from a concept perspective. As objects within a GRC application, the controls take over the following function:

- **Corporate Governance**
  Here, controls take on a similar role to that in the ICS. We differentiate between internal and external corporate governance controls (http://en.wikipedia.org/wiki/Corporate_governance).
- **Risk Management**
  Here, controls primarily take on a compensating role. They are intended to counteract (reduce) the probability of occurrence of a risk and/or its effects.

15.2.4 Control Objectives

Optional object

The term *control objective* is self-explanatory; the purpose of the control objective as an optional object in an ICS application is to make the ICS documentation more detailed. The necessity of the objects in an ICS application can be derived from the necessity of initiating activities on these objects (see Sect. 15.3, "Basic Scenarios of ICS Activities"). The ICS process generally requires targeted activities with regard to the control objective.

In practice, the necessity for this object is generally caused by a control objective being achieved by multiple control steps (1:n relationship).

[e.g.]   One Control Objective – Multiple Controls

The control objective is the traceability of changes to critical data, for example, in an in-house developed table in an SAP system. This objective can only be guaranteed by two effective application controls that work in parallel (see Sect. 7.2.2, "Table Logging"):
- The general handling of logging in a client by setting the profile parameter `rec/client`
- The consideration of the logging requirements in the change management process (the log flag for individual tables)

However, there can be other constellations, for example, if a control is used for multiple control objectives (n:1 relationship).

In practice, use of a specific ICS data model can necessitate documenting the control objective as an independent object: for example, an ICS data model in which risks and account groups are not assigned to a control directly but through use of a control objective. Alternatively, if we look at the control objective outside the ICS (as part of a GRC model), it can be understood as an object that is directly associated with the strategy of an organization.

Integrative role: control objectives in the GRC concept

15.2.5 Risks

From the view of an ICS application, a risk is at least as important as a control and is directly connected to the control. This means that in the data model of an ICS application, risks are connected with controls either directly or indirectly (using other objects). As in the case of control objectives, it must be possible to establish a 1:n relationship as well as an n:1 relationship.

One Risk – Multiple Controls

[e.g.]

The risk of fraudulent activities, caused in the purchasing process by missing or inefficient segregation of duties, can occur if one (or both) of the following controls is/are ineffective (or the risk cannot be minimized to the required extent):
- Deficient segregation of duties in the area of authorizations (such as the occurrence of transactions FK02 (Change Vendor Accounting) and MIRO (Logistics Invoice Verification) within the same role or same user master record)
- Inefficient controls in the area of one-time vendors, where it is possible to maintain the bank details directly when entering an incoming invoice

As an object a risk is interesting not only for ICS purposes; here it is generally only subject to qualitative assessments. In risk management, a risk can be included in both qualitative and quantitative assessments. There are also risk-specific activities.

Integrative role: risk object

15.2.6 Account Groups

Account groups are optional objects in an ICS application. Their existence is due to the fact that the most widespread compliance requirements demand efficient controls in external financial reporting. An account group incorporates one or more G/L accounts. The aim of the account groups is to connect this financial reporting in the business processes and beyond with the control steps in these processes (see Fig. 15.6).

Connection between reporting and processes

Financial Statement Structure

❶

Note that, within the IAS framework or, for example, in accordance with Section 266 of the German Commercial Code (HGB), the classification of liabilities into domestic and foreign is not mandatory; however, this classification is often undertaken in practice.

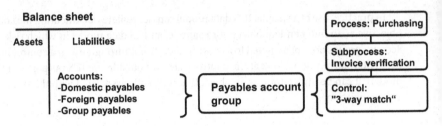

◘ Figure 15.6   Connection between the financial statements and a control

A control can also be connected to multiple account groups.

[e.g.]   One Control – Several Account Groups

A deficient automatic clearing of a GR/IR account can lead to an incorrect display of the figures in multiple accounts simultaneously:
- GR/IR account balance
- Goods in transit
- Outstanding invoices
- Price differences

Account groups as means of prioritization

You can also use the account groups in an ICS application to restrict the number of controls (or at a higher level, organizational units) to be tested depending on their relevance, whereby this relevance can be based, for example, on the value of certain financial statement items. If the value of a specific account group that is usually assigned to an organizational unit by means of other objects such as process, subprocess, or control exceeds a specific amount, these objects are preselected for a specific activity (usually a design or effectiveness test, see Sects. 15.3.4 and 15.3.5). Note that scoping based on materiality alone is usually not sufficient (see further scoping options in Sect. 15.3.2, "Selection and Prioritization of Control Activities").

15.2.7 Example of an ICS Data Model

The building blocks described form the basic framework of an ICS application. The interaction in the form of links between these modules makes up the data model or the ICS data scenario in an ICS application.

In practice, the ICS data models can vary; the diversity of the possible combinations of ICS objects is created above all by the numerous options for linking the risks, processes, and controls with one another. Figure 15.7 shows an example scenario in which the risks are assigned to the control both directly (risk 2) and indirectly (via control objective, risk 3). A scenario in which control objectives are assigned to controls via account groups is also possible. In practice, risks are assigned directly in two respects. In an ICS application, this is important from an informative aspect (in Sect. 16.3.2, "ICS Data Model in Process Control," you will find more details based on the example of SAP Process Control).

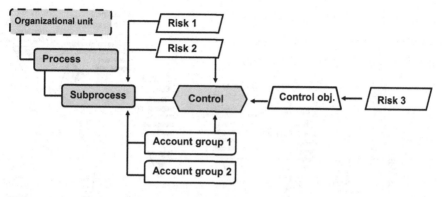

Figure 15.7 Schematic example of an ICS data model

ICS Data Model   **[e.g.]**

Let us stay with Fig. 15.7. You can see that one process step, in this case a subprocess, contains multiple risks (risk 1 and risk 2).

- The only control within this subprocess refers to only one of the two risks; this means that this risk – risk 2 – is neutralized or covered by the control (provided the control has been designed correctly and is effective).
- The other risk – risk 1 – is not covered by a control. In an ICS application, this would require action.

15.3 Basic Scenarios of ICS Activities

In this section we describe basic activities that make up the core functionality of a virtual ICS application; the focus is also on financial reporting compliance.

If the sequence of activities in business processes is clear – for example, from determination of requirements, through purchase order, goods receipt, and invoice verification up to payment in the P2P process – the ICS activities initially appear quite abstract and not integrated in the immediate value-added chain. Figure 15.8 shows typical activities as part of the definition of a SOX compliance process.

Recommended Literature   ❶

We recommend that you read the document "IT Control Objectives for Sarbanes-Oxley" published by the IT Governance Institute. It is available free of charge via the Internet (www.isaca.org) and contains illustrative explanations on the topic of ICS in the IT environment.

We will address the most important activities from Fig. 15.8 below.

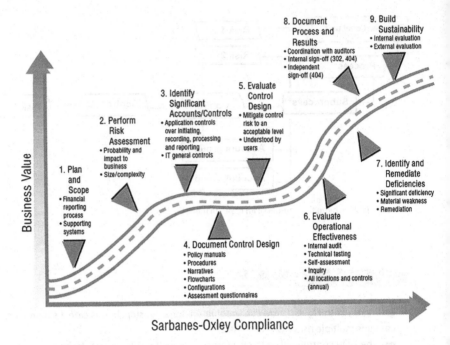

Figure 15.8 Compliance roadmap (source: IT Control Objectives for Sarbanes-Oxley, IT Governance Inst

15.3.1 Documentation

Documentation in an ICS application
In an ICS application, the documentation comprises the contents of the individual objects, as described in Sect. 15.2, "ICS-Relevant Objects and Documentation," and their connections. One of the widespread forms of ICS documentation is a risk and control matrix. In detail, the following activities can be part of the documentation function:
- Change to the object contents (for example, the description of a control or its specific attributes)
- Creation of a new object (for example, occurrence of a new risk due to a process change)
- Change in the assignment of objects (for example, introduction of a control within a process)

15.3.2 Selection and Prioritization of Control Activities

Scoping: prioritization of ICS activities
With regard to the designations for the selection and prioritization of audit procedures as one of the types of ICS activities, the term *scoping* has become established The aim of scoping is to plan the scope of audit procedures (primarily design and effectiveness tests) and to concentrate these activities on areas that require increased attention. Higher priority is required for the selection of controls that can most probably lead to a control objective not being achieved. In an ICS application, scoping is performed by determining certain object characteristics or values that are subsequently decisive in

the selection of ICS objects. In practice, characteristics such as the level of risk or the value of financial statement items and the materiality are used. Account groups are of central importance for the latter characteristic.

Scoping Scenarios

[e.g.]

The following are examples of scoping scenarios:
- To test the effectiveness of the controls, you generally only select organizational units where the balance sheet total exceeds a certain value limit.
- For the design test, you only select controls that were last performed more than two years ago.
- All controls associated with risks with status HIGH are subject to the effectiveness and design test.
- Controls for which performance has been positively confirmed, and that are associated with risks with status LOW, are excluded from the effectiveness tests.

15.3.3 Control Execution

By definition, the control execution concerns the control object and can be understood in one of the following ways:
- **Confirmation of control execution**
  This is the confirmation by a control owner that certain process steps have been executed, in accordance with the description in the text field of a control. This relates primarily to the manual control steps or control steps with a high manual aspect.
- **Automated control execution: monitoring**
  This refers to the triggering of a control execution in the ICS application itself. It involves the automation of the control execution in which the ICS application is used as a control medium (the ICS system provides the data to be analyzed automatically, or undertakes the analysis itself). It is achieved through integration of the ICS application with the respective ERP system. A widespread designation for automated control execution in practice is monitoring.

Monitoring

[e.g.]

An example of automated control execution in an ICS application is the daily inspection of manual postings above a specific value limit in the general ledger using the document journal (program RFBELJ00).

The list of documents from the SAP system selected by the respective program is forwarded to the ICS application and made accessible to a person responsible for inspection.

One of the objectives of results recording during control execution in an ICS application is that an independent compliance officer can use the corresponding information to assess the functional capability of controls. This person relies in part on statements

Reuse of confirmed control execution

by control owners as well as on any supporting documents provided and, in certain circumstances, can reduce the scope of their own work at their own professional discretion.

15.3.4 Design Test

Design test: assessment of state

The design test usually refers to the assessment of the state or the assessment of the change in state of a certain ICS object within a specific period. It primarily concerns the assessment of the design of controls. The aim is to determine whether the state (or the design) of the corresponding control is suitable for achieving the control objective.

[e.g.]

> **Design Test**
>
> Let us assume that a control is concerned with segregating activities between the recording of purchase orders (transaction ME21) and the recording of goods receipts (transaction MIGO). From an authorization perspective, this objective can be achieved by not having these transactions within one and the same role; that is, there must be separate roles that enable the assignment of the respective authorizations to different users. In this case, as part of the design test, you would analyze the roles to determine the extent to which their contents meet the requirements specified.

15.3.5 Effectiveness Test

Is the control objective achieved?

The result of an effectiveness test is a positive or negative statement about the achievement of the control objective. There is a differentiation between a manual and an automated effectiveness test.

- In *manual effectiveness tests*, business transactions are checked for compliance with defined control rules. Where applicable, the business transactions are tested in samples whose scope depends on the frequency of the controls. There are various methods for the examination, such as inspection, interview, observation, external confirmation, etc.
- In an *automated effectiveness test*, the question of whether the control objective was achieved is answered in an ICS application. The actual status in the ERP system is compared with predefined criteria for the target status.

Segregation of duties in the ICS application

Due to the principle of segregation of duties, the confirmation of the control execution and the execution of the effectiveness tests are formally separated.

- The *control execution* is confirmed by a person who has operative process and control responsibility.
- The control owner must not make any compliance-relevant statements: this means that only a person independent of the control execution may perform the *effectiveness test*.

Control Execution and Automated Effectiveness Tests

[e.g.]

Let us assume that the use of one-time vendors is permitted organizationally for recording incoming invoices to a maximum of USD 500.

- The corresponding *control execution* is manual: the control owner must observe the amount limit; if an invoice exceeds USD 500 and the vendor does not exist, he must ensure that a new vendor master record is created and then use this to record the business transaction.
- In an *automated effectiveness test*, an ICS application would read the documents with an invoice amount of more than USD 500 posted to one-time vendors from the SAP system and display them, or make them available for the auditor, as a negative deviation from the control objective.

15.3.6 Survey

Surveys are used in an ICS application to procure information that ICS owners later use to assess compliance.

Information procurement

Surveys

[e.g.]

The following are examples of types of surveys (or: *assessments, evaluations*).

- Entity level controls: The assessment of the effectiveness of this special area often requires interviews that can be logged in an ICS application.
- Results of surveys about changes in processes or in the design of controls are often used by ICS owners in the documentation or the design test.
- To identify new risks not yet recorded by an ICS application, surveys can be sent to the process or control owners or to management.

As in the case for confirmation of control execution and the effectiveness test, segregation of duties is used in a design test and a survey about the change to the design of a specific control. The two activities must not be performed by the same person.

Segregation of duties: design test vs. survey about design change

15.3.7 Risk Assessment

The risk assessment can be a qualitative and quantitative assessment of risks:

- The *qualitative risk assessment* comprises the assessment of the probability of occurrence and the effect of a risk. The end result is usually the classification of a risk as high, medium, or low.
- The *quantitative risk assessment* is usually a monetary assessment of the risk.

The functionality of an ICS application often contains only a qualitative assessment of risks that is usually used for planning purposes. If we look at the functionality of an ICS application as part of a GRC solution, the advantages of an integrated solution are

Integrative aspects of the risk assessment

visible: the results of the risk assessment as part of a risk management application can be reused in an ICS application.

Risk classification of ICS objects

In addition to the assessment of risks, risk categories are often assigned to the other ICS objects (for example, the organizational units or account groups). In an ICS application this can take place manually or can be calculated, for example, based on certain statistics or attributes of the objects. The role of the risk categories is to prioritize and they belong more to the area of scoping than to risk assessment.

[e.g.]

Risk Categories

The assignment of risk categories to the organizational units can be based on the following criteria, for example:
- Number of negative test results (design or effectiveness tests) in a specific period
- Balance sheet total
- Date of the last design and effectiveness test
- Percentage share of manual controls

15.3.8 Remediation

Content

Negative results of assessments and tests as part of ICS activities can be the following, for example:
- Discovery of unsatisfactory design or the ineffectiveness of a control
- Risk not covered by a control
- A control not performed consistently

These negative results must be logged. Follow-up activities are necessary for remediation.

15.3.9 Sign-Off

It may be necessary for management or the process owner to formally confirm activities executed. This confirmation refers to a specific group of ICS objects, the results of various activities, and in particular, to the weaknesses identified.

Meaning

In practice, this confirmation can have the following meaning from a content perspective:
- Confirmation of the effectiveness of controls
- Confirmation of the acknowledgment of existing problem cases (for example, ineffective controls) and steps introduced for rectification
- Confirmation that the process and control steps recorded are up-to-date and confirmation of the risks

In an ICS compliance environment shaped by SOX, this confirmation is mandatory and has become established under the name *sign-off*.

◻ Table 15.1 Simplified overview of ICS roles and connection to objects and activities

Roles	Objects	Activities
ICS owner	All	Documentation, scoping, effectiveness test, design test
Management	Own organizations, processes, and controls	Reporting, sign-off
Process owner	Processes, controls	Survey, rectification
Control owner	Controls	Control execution

15.3.10 Report Evaluation

In an ICS application, the aim of reporting is to get an overview of the ICS objects (organizational and process structures, risk and control matrixes, etc.) and the results of activities (primarily results of effectiveness and design tests).

The reporting function represents the essence of the automation of an ICS in which the status of compliance can be evaluated "real-time."

15.3.11 Persons as Links Between ICS Objects and Activities

All ICS activities mentioned are performed by different persons who thus connect the activities with objects. Which groups of persons (that is, which *roles*) are there in an ICS scenario? Table 15.1 contains some examples of typical roles in an ICS process.

> **Chief Compliance Officer – Not a New Profession**   ❶
>
> Frederick William I, King of Prussia and Margrave of Brandenburg, archgentleman and Elector of the Holy Roman Empire (1688–1740), was very aware of the need for controls when he appointed von Creutz as Controller General of all finances: he decreed that should the Controller General note any confusion or inaccuracy in the administration of the finances, or sense that those appointed were not fulfilling their duties with the utmost loyalty, diligence, and accuracy, then he must consult with their superiors without delay to remedy the situation, or to Frederick William himself.

Depending on the size of an organization and how it is organized internally, there can be a differentiation between the tasks of global and local ICS owners.

In the context of efficiency and profitability, (see Sect. 3.1.5, "Structure of Efficiency-Oriented and Profitability-Oriented Controls in the ERP Environment," and Chap. 14 "Examples of Efficiency-Oriented and Profitability-Oriented Analysis Scenarios in SAP ERP"), the usual limits applicable exclusively to compliance apply to the ICS role definition: the stakeholders participating in the ICS process can be given roles such as Process Owner, Data Governance Specialist, Controller, etc.

To conclude, we draw your attention to two typical misunderstandings with regard to ICS role definition that arise in practice:

- The role of *Controller* in a compliance-oriented ICS context in a compliance-oriented ICS context is often confused with the role of an ICS owner: this is because, in addition to their primary tasks (for example, in the area of management reporting or in efficiency-oriented and profitability-oriented ICS management processes), controllers sometimes also take on the role of ICS owner.
- Sometimes, *internal audit* and *ICS responsibility* are considered as two names for one function: note however, that internal audit can be involved in certain ICS activities, but is usually not involved in the design of the contents and process of the ICS.

15.4 Summary

With the theory of ICS automation, you are now best equipped for finding out how to proceed with ICS automation in practice. In this chapter, it was important to demonstrate that ICS automation means the merging of the ICS content, activities, and roles to form an ICS process.

ICS Automation Using SAP Process Control

From ICS automation theory to practice: now it's time to implement the theoretical basis using SAP Process Control.

In Chap. 15, "ICS Automation: How to Set the COSO Cube in Motion," we explained how to launch the COSO cube and how to automate an ICS process. You learned how to achieve this objective in theory by combining individual ICS-specific building blocks – objects, activities, and roles. Now that we have described the central properties of the ICS building blocks mentioned, it is time to put the individual pieces of the puzzle together and to show how you can model and technically implement an automated ICS process in practice using software.

In this chapter you will learn how to automate an internal control system (ICS) using SAP Process Control, and in particular, what the technical architecture of the solution looks like, how to get the basic functions of the application up and running, and how to implement ICS processes and models in SAP Process Control.

The functionality and technical details refer to SAP Process Control Release 10.0. In Sect. 4.3, "Integrated Approach in SAP GRC 10.0 and Further Compliance-Relevant Solutions," we described how SAP Process Control is embedded in the SAP solutions for Governance, Risk, and Compliance 10.0. We also described the most important functions of SAP Process Control. We will now present these functions in detail.

16.1　Introduction: ICS Implementation with SAP Process Control

Before you can implement an ICS process, you have to design it. As in every implementation project, the blueprint phase is vitally important. In this section, you will learn how to model the ICS process in the form of a matrix in practice when implementing SAP Process Control in order to create a basis for a subsequent technical implementation.

Describing ICS processes in the form of flow charts is a common practice. The process shown in Fig. 16.1 illustrates the confirmation of control execution by a control owner as part of a self-assessment.

Chapter 15, "ICS Automation: How to Set the COSO Cube in Motion," described the properties of the most important ICS objects and ICS activities. The other building block for the ICS implementation is the people, or rather, the roles: as a final link, they bring a third dimension to an ICS application and link ICS objects and activities to form an ICS matrix (see Fig. 16.2).

As you can see in Fig. 16.2, the process involves one object: the control. Activities that relate to the control are grouped by role:

From flow charts to the implementation matrix

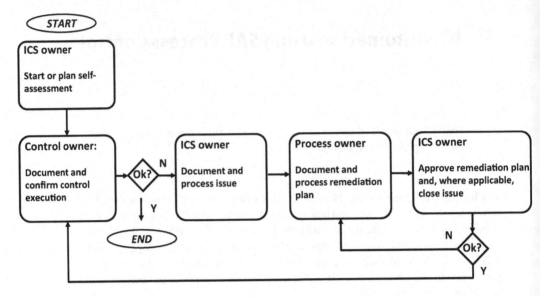

☐ **Figure 16.1** Confirmation of control execution in the ICS process

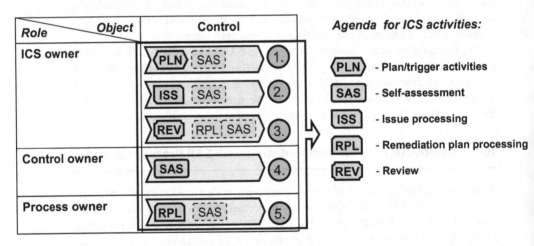

☐ **Figure 16.2** Implementation matrix for the ICS subprocess "Confirmation of control execution"

1. An ICS owner plans and triggers the control confirmation (SAS = self-assessment) ❶, processes an issue (ISS = issue) that relates to a self-assessment ❷, and approves or rejects a remediation plan (RPL = remediation plan) ❸ for rectifying this issue related to the self-assessment.

2. A control owner documents the execution of the control as part of the self-assessment (SAS) ❹ and, where applicable, reports an issue.

3. A process owner is responsible for processing the remediation plan ❺ created as part of the self-assessment as a result of the issue.

The design of the SAP Process Control functionality in the form of a matrix at the level of individual roles is very important. This importance can be traced back to the *object-related security concept* (see Sect. 16.5.2, "Object-Related Security in Action").

ICS implementation matrix

Although the objects and activities are relatively fixed, you can design the ICS process tailored to your organization by designing roles flexibly. From the matrix, we can derive two types of information that are required for the design of the *roles* as part of the object-related security concept:

- The activities determine the *content* of a role (answer to the question: what is the user allowed to do?).
- The objects determine the *level* of the assignment of the role to the users (answer to the question: where, or for which roles is the user allowed to execute the activities?).

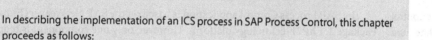

Structure of the Description of ICS Implementation in This Chapter

In describing the implementation of an ICS process in SAP Process Control, this chapter proceeds as follows:

- The technical part describes which components from the technical landscape are required and how you can launch the minimum standard functions of SAP Process Control (see Sect. 16.2, "Technical Implementation").
- When describing the implementation of an ICS approach, we also follow the approach outlined in Chap. 15, "ICS Automation: How to Set the COSO Cube in Motion," in which the ICS can be designed in the form of a matrix ("3D approach"): firstly, we address the properties of the *objects* – the master data and the possible models for the master data in SAP Process Control (see Sect. 16.2).
- The description of the implementation of the possible *activities* or scenarios (see Sect. 16.4, "Implementation of the ICS Process") forms the core of this chapter.
- The design of the *roles* introduces the final dimension into the ICS matrix and (logically) completes the description of the matrix by linking roles with activities and objects (see Sect. 16.5, "ICS and Compliance Implementation: Roles").
- In Sect. 16.6, "SAP Process Control as GRC Component – New Features and Developments," we describe, from the process view, the possible scenarios for integrating SAP Process Control with other components such as SAP Risk Management, SAP Access Control, etc.

16.2 Technical Implementation

In this section, you will learn which technical components are required to implement SAP process Control and which configuration steps you have to perform after completing the technical installation in order to launch the standard functions of SAP Process Control. We will then present sources of information about SAP Process Control.

16.2.1 Technical Architecture and Installation

From a *technical* perspective, SAP Process Control is a complex application (in contrast to the *functional* perspective, which, for example, is much simpler compared to SAP

ERP). Depending on the required scope of functions, it can contain multiple software components. We can differentiate between the mandatory software components that form the core of the application, and the optional components.

Mandatory Components of the Technical Architecture

Frontend client architecture

As far as the mandatory SAP Process Control components are concerned, we differentiate between components that enable interaction with the application (frontend client) and the application itself. Two frontend clients are required:

- Users access the application via a *web browser* (for example, Internet Explorer from Version 7 upward). Technically, SAP NetWeaver Portal or SAP NetWeaver Business Client can be used in the background.
- You configure and administer the application via the Implementation Guide, which you call up via the *SAP GUI*.

Process Control architecture

The SAP Process Control application is based on the SAP NetWeaver (Enhancement Package 2, EhP2) technology platform. However, only one component is required (the second component listed below is optional):

- *SAP NetWeaver Application Server ABAP (AS ABAP) 7.02*, including the required auxiliary applications
- *SAP NetWeaver Portal 7.01*, which runs on SAP NetWeaver Application Server Java, is optional in Release 10.0 (in contrast to Release 3.0): the web interface can also be called up with SAP NetWeaver Business Client as an alternative. This second option does not require any additional installation and is contained in AS ABAP.

To ensure smooth operation of SAP Process Control, you also need *SAP Solution Manager* (primarily so that you can download the SAP Process Control software) and the Support Package Manager (to download Support Packages).

Optional Components of the Technical Architecture

Depending on the functional scope required, further software components may be necessary:

- **Use Crystal Reports**
  From Release 3.0 of SAP Process Control, SAP offers the Crystal Reports technology in reporting. This technology enables you to present information visually in high-quality and with pixel accuracy. To use this technology, in Release 3.0, the components SAP BusinessObjects Enterprise XI 3.1 (now called SAP BusinessObjects BI Platform) and the Integration Kit for SAP XI 3.1 were required. In Release 10.0, these components are no longer necessary. Crystal Reports Adapters (CRA) enable the use of SAP Crystal Reports.
- **Find and version attachments**
  SAP Process Control enables you to upload various files as attachments, both for individual objects (see Sect. 16.3.2, "ICS Data Model in SAP Process Control") and when processing workflow-based tasks (see Sect. 16.4, "Implementation of the ICS Process"). For a more extensive search and versioning for these documents, you need SAP NetWeaver 7.02 Search and Classification (TREX).
- **Access tests and assessments in offline mode**
  In order to enter tests and assessments in offline mode, in Release 3.0, Adobe LiveCycle Designer 7.1 was required (no longer required in Release 10.0). This compo-

nent enabled you to document test and assessment steps in a PDF file. When you imported this PDF file into the application, the test results were transferred. Adobe Document Services was required in Release 3.0 to enable reports to be exported as PDF, and is required in Release 10.0 in order to use the offline functions specified.

— **Control automation**
In connection with the integration of the SAP solutions for GRC with further ERP systems, in Release 10.0, changes have been made compared to previous releases of the individual GRC components: previously, GRC component-specific Real Time Agents (RTA) had to be installed in target systems, but Release 10.0 refers to plug-ins that are also no longer GRC component-specific. Thus, in Release 10.0, the same plug-ins cover the integration requirements of SAP Process Control, SAP Risk Management, and SAP Access Control.

16.2.2 Initial Configuration of the Standard Functions

Once you have completed the installation and post-installation activities, the next task is to configure the application. Practice shows that there are configuration steps that you always have to perform at the beginning of the execution phase in the project. The configuration steps are listed in a proven order below. These steps are necessary to launch the core functionality present in the standard scope, to perform the first function test, and, where applicable, to experience the first success in the project.

Objective

> **Orientation**
>
> In the presentation below, the respective components are added in parentheses in order to differentiate between the configuration in *SAP NetWeaver Portal* and in *SAP GUI* via the Implementation Guide (transaction SPRO).

1. **Activate the application (SAP GUI)**
   The first step is to check, and where applicable, execute the activation of the relevant applications.
2. **Activate BC Sets (SAP GUI)**
   To speed up the implementation process, SAP has preconfigured some settings based on best practice experience. These settings are grouped in Business Configuration (BC) Sets.
3. **Create test users and assign roles (SAP GUI)**
   Secion. 16.5, "ICS and Compliance Implementation: Roles," explains the basic principles of users and roles in the SAP system.
4. **Check access to the application (SAP NetWeaver Portal)**
   You have to check that you can generally call up SAP Process Control in SAP NetWeaver Portal (provided this is used) or using SAP NetWeaver Business Client.
5. **Check Case Management configuration (cases) (SAP GUI)**
   In the next step, you have to check the consistency of the configuration in Case Management.

6. **Execute automated workflow customizing (SAP GUI)**
   All you have to do is activate the preconfigured workflows.
7. **Set the properties of the tasks to "general" (SAP GUI)**
   In this technical step, you configure tasks that are relevant for workflows in SAP Process Control.
8. **Activate event linkage (SAP GUI)**
   This step is also relevant in connection with workflows.
9. **Test workflows (SAP GUI)**
   Once you have completed all the necessary configuration steps related to workflows, you can perform the first workflow test.
10. **Delete incorrect entries and restructure the directory (SAP GUI)**
    SAP has left a series of entries in some master data tables in the standard delivery of SAP Process Control and established a configuration option for removing these superfluous entries.
11. **Schedule jobs (SAP GUI)**
    In the Implementation Guide, you have to schedule application jobs at various points (for example, sending e-mails, user replacements, etc.).
12. **Create root organization hierarchy (SAP GUI)**
    Using transaction GRFN_STR_CREATE (Administration SAP Process Control), you have to create the highest level node within the organization hierarchy.
13. **Create regulation/policy and assign organizational unit (SAP NetWeaver Portal)**
    Once you have performed the most important configuration steps via SAP GUI or in the Implementation Guide, you have to perform the preparatory work in SAP Process Control via SAP NetWeaver Portal.

Practical use of interim results

After completing the initial configuration, in practice you have the following options:

- Training and workshops on the standard functionality of SAP Process Control
- Fit/gap analysis (analysis of the requirements vs. standard functions) and blueprint
- Adjustment of the standard functions and implementation of the customer-specific scenario with the aim of performing a proof of concept, building a prototype, and preparing a live start

16.2.3 Information Sources on Implementing, Operating, and Upgrading SAP Process Control

In order to support customers in the various life phases of SAP software, SAP provides various sources of information (see Fig. 16.3).

Guides for SAP Process Control

The following documents are available online in SAP Service Marketplace for SAP customers:

- **SAP Process Control Sizing Guide**
  This document helps you to plan and select the size and performance of hardware on which the Process Control application is to be installed.

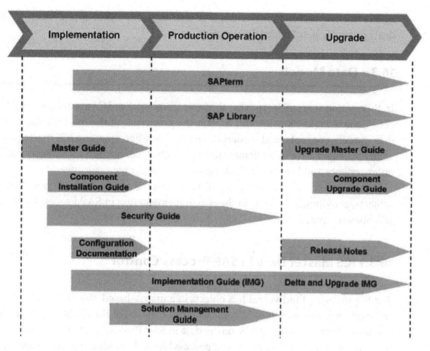

Figure 16.3 Information sources (source: SAP documentation, Master Guide for SAP Process Control)

- **SAP Process Control Master Guide**
  This document provides a rough functional overview of SAP Process Control, describes various relevant sources of information, such as further guides and SAP Notes, and also gives an overview of the individual software components and the technical architecture of the solution.
- **SAP Process Control Installation Guide**
  This document describes, in detail, the steps necessary as part of the preparation and execution of the technical installation and for the post-installation activities.
- **SAP Process Control Operations Guide**
  This document describes the typical activities involved in the administration and ongoing support of the Process Control application.
- **SAP Process Control Security Guide**
  This document gives a detailed view of the topics around the security and the authorization concept of SAP Process Control.
- **SAP Process Control Upgrade Guide**
  This document describes the procedure for technically upgrading the earlier releases of SAP Process Control to the latest release version (for example, from 3.0 to 10.0).
- **SAP Process Control Migration Guide**
  If an upgrade from an older release to the latest version is not possible for technical reasons, a migration is performed. This document describes the procedure for the migration to the current release version of SAP Process Control (for example, from MIC 2.0 to SAP Process Control 10.0).

We also recommend the five-day SAP training GRC 330 on SAP Process Control. It deals primarily with the implementation.

16.3   Data Model

In this section you will learn what the basic framework of ICS master data in SAP Process Control looks like. We will explain the properties of the master data, which ICS data models, concepts, and scenarios are possible when mapping ICS master data, and what challenges arise in implementation projects in connection with master data based on experience and how these challenges can be overcome.

At the end of this section, you will know how to use the first of three dimensions (objects, activities, and roles) in the ICS implementation in SAP Process Control – the ICS objects – practically.

16.3.1 ICS Master Data in SAP Process Control

Business view   The importance of individual ICS objects in a matrix-based model for ICS automation was explained in Chap. 15, "ICS Automation: How to Set the COSO Cube in Motion." The basic framework of the ICS master data in SAP Process Control has a similar structure: the organization hierarchy and process hierarchy (including the controls), which are connected to one another, form the core of the application.

Figure 16.4 shows these two main hierarchies; they are located in SAP Process Control in the navigation menu under MASTER DATA ❶ • work area ORGANIZATIONS ❷ and under BUSINESS PROCESSES ❸.

Organization and process hierarchies   The organization hierarchy can have any number of levels. The process hierarchy consists of processes that can also have an unlimited number of levels (even though in practice, it is rare to use more than two levels). The last link in the hierarchy chain is subprocesses and controls: the connection of one or more controls to a subprocess completes every hierarchy.

Properties of the objects   When we look at the individual objects – for example, organizations and controls (see Fig. 16.5) – we can quickly recognize their main properties:

- The objects contain documentation fields, for example, NAME (up to 40 characters) and DESCRIPTION (unlimited) ❶.
- You can add attachments or links to the individual objects (ATTACHMENTS AND LINKS tab) ❷.
- Organizations and controls have attributes ❸ that either have a pure documentation and reporting function (for example, control attribute CONTROL SIGNIFICANCE or NATURE) or control the logic of the application (for example, control attribute CONTROL AUTOMATION: AUTOMATED/MANUAL/SEMI-AUTOMATED).

These properties apply for all objects in SAP Process Control. Most objects are also time-dependent (see Sect. 16.3.4, "Time Dependency of ICS Master Data").

Main objects   From a functional perspective, the main objects in SAP Process Control – the organization and process hierarchies – play the following roles:

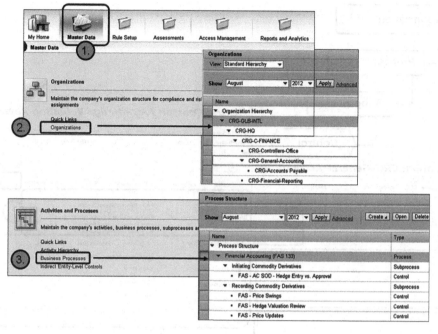

Figure 16.4 Organization and process hierarchies

- For *all objects* within the organization and process hierarchies, the following applies: based on authorizations, these objects allow access to ICS master data, reporting, and to ICS activities (see Sect. 16.3.6, "Concept of Object-Related Security").
- *Organizations* primarily map reporting and responsibility requirements in SAP Process Control. As part of the Continuous Monitoring Framework, organizations can determine the default selection criteria for organizational units in an SAP ERP system.
- *Processes*, *subprocesses*, and *controls* reflect reporting and responsibility requirements, as well as the structure of the ICS-relevant business processes.
  - *Subprocesses* can also be involved in surveys.
  - *Controls* are the focus of the ICS process and are involved in various assessments and tests, both manual and automated.

Orientation   ❶

Further SAP Process Control objects, such as risks, control objectives, account groups, test plans, surveys, etc. were dealt with in Chap. 15, "ICS Automation: How to Set the COSO Cube in Motion."

In the ICS process, you maintain the master data in the application, as shown in Fig. 16.4. For various administrative tasks, there are transactions such as GRFN_STR_DISPLAY (Display Process Control) or GRFN_STR_CHANGE (Change Process Con-

Technical details and administration

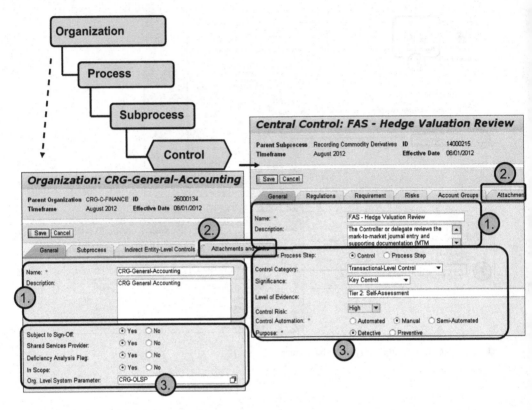

◘ Figure 16.5 Organizational units and controls

trol). You can use these transactions to maintain the master data directly in the backend (access to the master data is via SAP GUI).

As you can see in Fig. 16.6, the administration transaction contains three application areas:

- The left-hand side ❶ contains the search options for all objects.
- At the top right ❷, you can maintain the general properties of the objects (for example, assignments, definition of the validity period, etc.).
- At the bottom right ❸, the maintenance options for the contents of the individual objects are available.

> **User Restriction** Note that the administration functions mentioned must be restricted to a very small group of users as here, extensive changes can be made and the system generally provides no or only a few consistency checks in the backend (for example, objects for which there are tasks or user assignments can be deleted here without question).

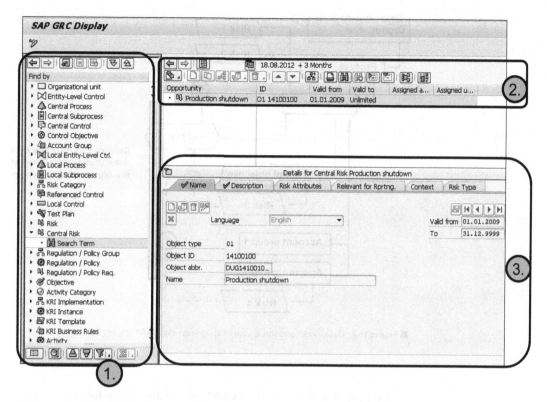

Figure 16.6 Administration transaction for SAP Process Control and SAP Risk Management

16.3.2 ICS Data Model in SAP Process Control

The central task of ICS master data in SAP Process Control is to map the ICS framework (in practice, the term risk and control matrix is often used). This framework is primarily to be understood as a composition of processes, controls, risks, control objectives, etc.

Figure 16.7 shows a rough approximation of the ICS data model. You can see that the account group and control objective objects can also be assigned to the subprocesses. The *risk* as an object has a special importance, and it can be mapped in the ICS data model in three different ways.

Business view

Use of risks in the ICS data model

- **Direct assignment**

  Risks can be assigned to the subprocesses and controls directly ❶. However, at the level of a control, only risks that have already been assigned to a subprocess one level higher can be assigned.

- **Indirect assignment**

  If a control objective or an account group has been assigned to a subprocess, and the account group in turn is associated with risks, the risks appear in the lower level control as assigned via control objective ❷ or account group ❸.

In summary, we can say that a control can only "see" and "recognize" risks that are assigned at the subprocess level.

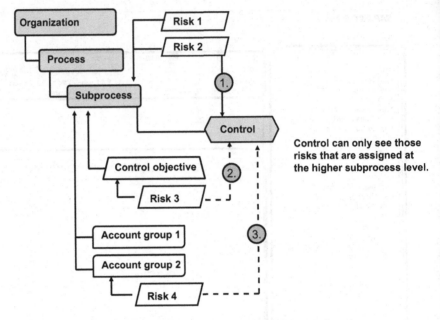

□ **Figure 16.7** Data model and three ways of assigning risks in SAP Process Control

The business importance of the direct risk assignment is as follows:

- The assignment of risks at the subprocess level answers the following question: What risks does the process bear or which risks are relevant?
- The assignment of risks at a deeper control level answers the following question: Which of the relevant risks are covered by control mechanisms?

Technical details and configuration   Experience has shown that the following technical background information is helpful in implementation projects: HR structures have been used in the technical software execution of the master data in SAP Process Control. All objects are contained in *infotype* 1000 (table HRP1000). The link to the long text fields (for example, the fields under DESCRIPTION) is located in infotype 1002 (table HRP1002, field TABNR), and the texts themselves in table HRT1002.

Configuration of the number ranges   You can configure the number ranges via SAP GUI in the Implementation Guide under GRC • GENERAL SETTINGS • DEFINE NUMBER RANGES. This step is optional, as you can use the existing default configuration of the number ranges.

16.3.3 Central vs. Local ICS Master Data

Business view   In the ICS master data concept, it is important to differentiate between *central* and *local* master data in SAP Process Control. From an ICS perspective, this differentiation between the centralized and decentralized approach affects the ICS documentation process (see Sect. 16.4.1, "ICS Documentation Process").

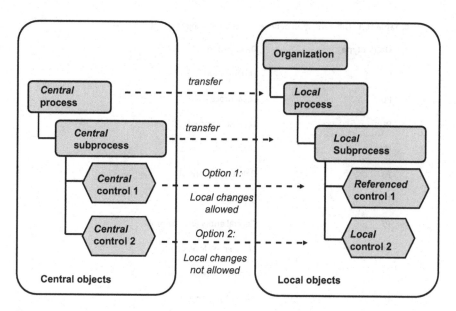

□ **Figure 16.8** Local vs. central ICS objects

- **Global ICS objects**
  Global ICS objects can generally be considered as the content of a central ICS catalog. They have a passive function, and are a type of master data template that is indirectly involved in the ICS process.
- **Local ICS objects**
  The local ICS objects are active master data that is directly involved in the ICS process. The local ICS objects arise when you link the individual hierarchies of global objects.

As you can see in Fig. 16.8, the distinguishing factor of the central master data is that it is not linked to an organization: when the process and control hierarchies are transferred from the catalog with central master data into an organization, the property of the central master data objects changes and they become local objects.

If the property of the ICS master data changes from central to local, from a system perspective, this means that new *objects* are created. If, when a central subprocess is assigned to an organization it is copied, a local subprocess is created, for example.

In Sect. 16.3.2, "ICS Data Model in SAP Process Control," we described how master data objects are contained in *HR infotypes*. Within these infotypes, the ICS master data is differentiated by object type, some of which are illustrated in Table 16.1.

Origin of local objects

Technical tips

16.3.4 Time Dependency of ICS Master Data

An ICS is not static: the organizational structures, business processes, responsibilities, and control mechanisms, etc. are constantly changing. In order to fulfill the important requirement of being able to reflect not only an image of the ICS at a specific key date

ICS status at any time

□ Table 16.1 Differentiation between master data objects by object type

Object type	Description
O	Organization
P0	Local process
P1	Local subprocess
P2	Local control
P3	Referenced control
P5	Central control
P7	Central entity level control
P9	Local entity level control
PK	Central process
PL	Central subprocess

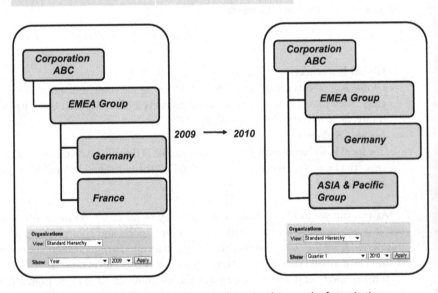

□ Figure 16.9 Time dependency of the ICS master data using the example of organizations

in SAP Process Control, but also the status of the ICS at any time in the past (or the planned status in the future), the concept of time dependency was developed: every object has a time-based validity that is documented in the VALID FROM and VALID TO fields.

Change to the organizational structure   For example, if the organizational structure changes, as shown in the example in Fig. 16.9, this can be portrayed using the time-based validity:

- For the organization FRANCE, the content of the field VALID To was changed from UNLIMITED to 12/31/2009.

■ Furthermore, a new organization Asia & Pacific Group was created with the value 01/01/2010 in the Valid From field.

This avoids, for example, ICS objects being deleted. It also ensures compliance with the principle of traceability. When you choose the required period in the overview of the organization hierarchy, the organizational structure valid for this period is displayed.

Once you have created the organization hierarchy, in the frontend (via SAP Net-Weaver Portal), the value in the Valid From field can no longer be changed. You can bypass this restriction using the administration transaction GRFN_STR_CHANGE (Change SAP Process Control). To ensure traceability, the corresponding authorizations must be assigned very restrictively.

16.3.5 Traceability of Changes

In a compliance management application such as SAP Process Control, the principle of traceability is very important. In SAP Process Control, you can use reports to evaluate the creation of new risks (as well as new processes, controls, etc.), changes in the organizational structures or the description of controls, and much more.

As you can see in Fig. 16.10, the standard reports in SAP Process Control enable various evaluations, for example, the comparison of ICS master data between two periods ❶ or the evaluation of all changes within a period ❷.

The master data changes can be evaluated in SAP Process Control because they are logged: for every change, a *change document* is stored in the SAP system. SAP Process Control is based on the platform SAP NetWeaver – just like SAP ERP. To enable the logging from a technical perspective, the same technical prerequisites as described in Sect. 7.2.2, "Table Logging," have to be fulfilled. In detail, this concerns the settings for relevant profile parameters and logging indicators that you have to set for the tables mentioned in Sect. 16.3.2, "ICS Data Model in SAP Process Control."

Change documents

16.3.6 Concept of Object-Related Security

The organizations and business processes mapped hierarchically in SAP Process Control cover the entire ICS-relevant structure of a company. In a large, internationally active organization with complex structures, the responsibilities within the scope of the ICS processes have to be delineated not only functionally (what/which actions a user may execute), but also on an object-related basis (where/in which organization and process hierarchies may the user execute actions). A further important concept implemented in SAP Process Control is therefore the concept of object-related security.

User/object assignment

Let us assume you want to separate responsibilities between two organization hierarchies and between two processes. As you can see in Fig. 16.11, the ICS owner in organization A is not authorized to access organization B (for example, to perform various evaluations in reporting or to perform a sign-off, see Sect. 16.4, "Implementation of the ICS Process"). Within organization A, process owner Y may only access the processes and controls that belong to the asset accounting area. She has no access to the accounts payable accounting area that is in the area of responsibility of process owner X.

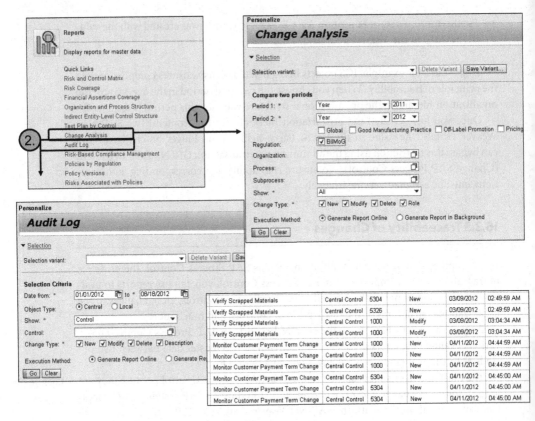

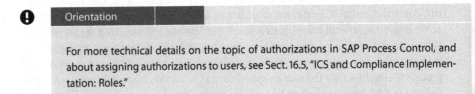

⬛ **Figure 16.10**   Reports for analyzing master data changes

You can ensure this separation by assigning the persons to objects within an ICS hierarchy directly. This enables certain actions to be executed along the hierarchy according to the *top-down principle* – the user receives authorizations of the lower hierarchy levels (provided the assignment is in place).

❗ | Orientation

For more technical details on the topic of authorizations in SAP Process Control, and about assigning authorizations to users, see Sect. 16.5, "ICS and Compliance Implementation: Roles."

16.3.7 Customer-Specific Fields

Documentation in objects and activities

An ICS has to be documented on one hand in the text fields of ICS objects (controls, risks, etc.), and on the other hand by the selection of predefined values in various *attributes*. The documented ICS framework represents the entirety of such information

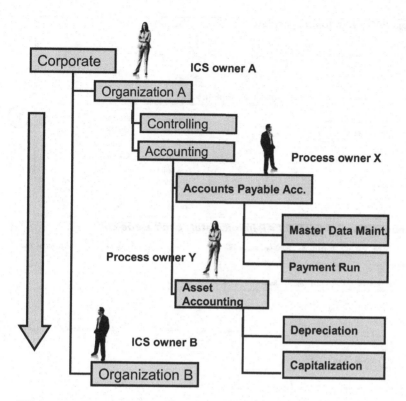

Figure 16.11 Principle of object-related security in SAP Process Control

across all objects. In addition to the documentation of the ICS, the execution of various surveys, assessments, and tests must also be documented.

In general, in SAP Process Control, we can differentiate between master data-related and activity-related documentation.

Figure 16.12 shows master data-related documentation ❶ (fields within a control) and activity-related documentation ❷ (fields within the task CONTROL EFFECTIVENESS MANUAL TEST). If you require further fields beyond the standard for master data-related or activity-related documentation, you can create customer-specific fields (custom fields).

The division of the documentation options into master data-related and activity-related documentation corresponds to the division of the options for their technical implementation. Here we refer to HR and non-HR fields:

Customer-specific fields in SAP Process Control

- Master data-related fields: HR fields
- Activity-related fields: non-HR fields

Background to the Differentiation

This differentiation in the technical execution options can be traced back to the underlying data model:

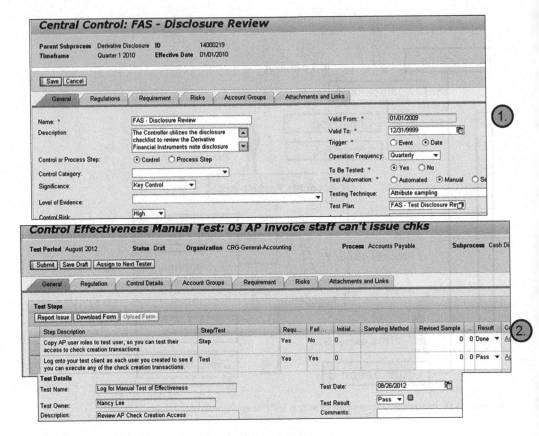

Figure 16.12 Master data-related and activity-related documentation

- As master data is contained in *HR infotypes*, (see Sect. 16.3.2, "ICS Data Model in SAP Process Control"), we refer to HR fields.
- For the technical software execution of assessment, test, and other workflows, the Case Management functionality is used (this is used, for example, in CRM), which means that the documentation fields are located in *cases* and not in the HR infotypes.

Procedure for HR fields

As the ABAP Dictionary is affected when you create new HR fields, you need a developer key for this activity. The steps you have to perform when creating HR fields are as follows:

1. Create the new data elements in the ABAP Dictionary
2. Create infotypes
3. Add fields in the SAP GUI administration transaction (optional)
4. Add fields in Web Dynpro ABAP and Java
5. Add fields in the reports (optional)

When you create non-HR fields, you have to perform the following steps:

1. Create the new data elements in the ABAP Dictionary
2. Create new fields
3. Add fields in Web Dynpro ABAP and Java
4. Add fields in the reports (optional)

Procedure for non-HR fields

16.3.8 Multiple Compliance Framework Concept

Section 15.2.3, "Controls," addressed the *multiple domain principle*. This important property of an ICS, derived from the COSO model, is used to cover multiple global ICS objectives (for example, compliance with certain legal requirements, such as SOX, BilMoG, or FDA, monitoring of operative effectiveness of the processes, or observing internal policies, etc.). In parallel, the content that addresses the ICS objectives globally, that is, across domains, should be reused as efficiently as possible. In SAP Process Control, the principle of multiple dimensions is implemented by the Multiple Compliance Framework concept.

Business view

Figure 16.13 shows this concept using the example of a control that is relevant for two compliance views simultaneously. The main idea behind this concept is achieving greater efficiency in the ICS process. This is to be achieved in two ways:

- By the reuse of the same controls in different *regulations*, such as SOX ❶ or BilMoG ❷ (in SAP Process Control, one domain corresponds to one compliance initiative)
- By the reuse of the test, survey, and assessment results for processes and controls that are relevant across multiple domains (for example, test results for IT general controls as part of SOX ❶ and BilMoG ❷)

The individual *regulations* can use the same master data (objects) but have different functions (for example, the "FDA" regulation contains a specific process for handling problems in which the CAPA functionality (CAPA = Corrective And Preventive Actions) and the e-signature are used, see Sect. 16.4.4, "Problem-Solving Process").

Properties of regulations

The Terms "Regulation" and "Compliance Initiative"   ❶

The terms *regulation* and *compliance initiative* are synonyms. The term "compliance initiative" is usually used in connection with the older GRC Release 3.0, and "regulation" mainly with reference to GRC Release 10.0.

You can implement the functional differences and the process differences by designing specific *activities* and *roles*. Two regulations are preconfigured in the standard delivery of SAP Process Control: SOX and FDA.

Technical details and configuration

To create a new regulation, perform the following steps:

Creating new regulations

1. SAP GUI: Create new regulation-specific roles (via PFCG)
2. SAP GUI: Create and configure new regulation (in IMG)
3. SAP GUI: Assign new roles to the new regulation (in IMG)
4. Frontend: Create new regulation within an existing or a new regulation group

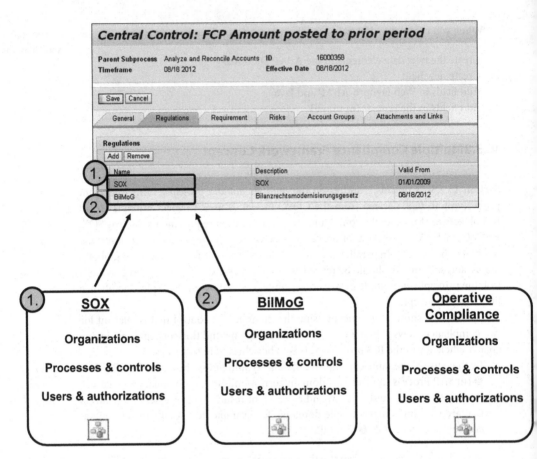

Figure 16.13 Multiple Compliance Framework concept in SAP Process Control

16.4   Implementation of the ICS Process

As you already know from Sect. 4.3.2 and 16.4, an ICS process can be represented simply as a sequence of ICS activities. Figure 16.14 shows an example of such a sequence.

Now that you have learned about the basic scenarios of the ICS activities in Sect. 15.3, in this section you will learn what the ICS standard scenario in SAP Process Control looks like, about the content of individual process steps, and how you can implement this content, and where applicable, adjust it, technically. However, we will restrict the explanations to the main questions that, based on experience, arise during the implementation of SAP Process Control.

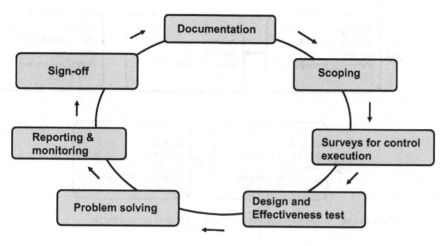

❏ **Figure 16.14**   ICS cycle – simplified presentation

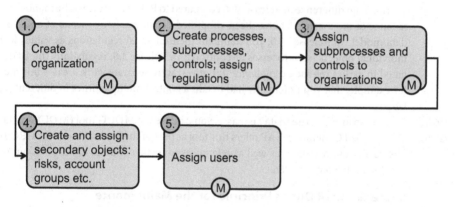

❏ **Figure 16.15**   Sequence for ICS master data maintenance

16.4.1 ICS Documentation Process

How do you implement the ICS framework in the system? This question is relevant not only during the implementation phase, during which you have to upload the ICS master data into SAP Process Control, but also during the operation of SAP Process Control. Business view

The organizational structures, business processes, control mechanisms, and responsibilities are constantly changing, and you have to update the ICS master data at regular intervals. The maintenance in SAP Process Control is intuitive, thanks to the web interface. An important prerequisite for the maintenance is knowledge of the data model (see Sect. 16.3.2, "ICS Data Model in SAP Process Control").

Figure 16.15 shows the sequence for maintaining the ICS master data in the central catalog (steps ❶ to ❺, work area MASTER DATA). Maintenance in the central catalog

Step ❹ is optional and depends on the ICS documentation requirements in the organization; the other maintenance steps are mandatory (see Fig. 16.15).

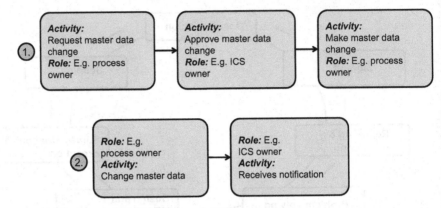

☐ **Figure 16.16**   Two options for reflecting the segregation of duties principle

The main difference in Release 10.0 compared to Release 3.0 is that the manual main-tenance of the master data has been simplified considerably by means of an adjusted data model. In Release 10.0, you maintain the individual regulations as values within individual objects (subprocesses or controls); in Release 3.0, regulations (or, as desig-nated in earlier releases, *compliance initiatives*) were separate work areas – this meant, for example, that you potentially had to edit a control multiple times in different regu-lations.

Technical details and configuration

To upload the master data en masse, you can use the MDUG tool (MDUG = Master Data Upload Generator). SAP offers this tool as part of the SAP solutions for GRC 10.0. The user documentation, as well as references to further sources of information, is lo-cated in SAP Note 1563286.

Segregation of Duties Principle for the Maintenance of the ICS Framework

Business view

When you are maintaining the ICS master data, you will often have to involve a second person in the changes, for example, from a quality or responsibility perspective (such as when creating a new control, assigning a risk, changing the process description, etc.).

[e.g.]

Segregation of Duties Principle for Control Documentation

In everyday ICS tasks, it is feasible to imagine a scenario in which a process owner wants to change the description of the design of a control. An ICS owner has to approve this change, and should at least be informed about it.

Both options are possible in SAP Process Control, as shown in Fig. 16.16.

In the first scenario ❶, an approval process is triggered before the objects can be changed. However, the second option ❷ can also be used; here, a notification is sent to the person responsible when the objects are changed.

To enable the options described, you have to activate workflows for master data changes. You do this in the Implementation Guide under GRC • Shared Master Data Settings • Activate Workflow for Master Data Changes.

Technical details and configuration

Centralized vs. Decentralized Documentation of the ICS

In practice, we differentiate between a decentralized and a centralized approach for the ICS documentation. This refers not only to the process itself – in the ICS process, some of the ICS activities, such as scoping, planning, independent effectiveness tests, etc. can be executed centrally (at corporate level) or decentrally (in the individual units). Furthermore, the management of ICS master data is also relevant, as is the mandatory use of a predefined minimum scope of centrally documented controls.

Business view

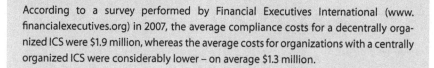

FEI Survey Results

According to a survey performed by Financial Executives International (www. financialexecutives.org) in 2007, the average compliance costs for a decentrally organized ICS were $1.9 million, whereas the average costs for organizations with a centrally organized ICS were considerably lower – on average $1.3 million.

Whilst you can use roles to ensure that activities in SAP Process Control are centralized, on the master data side, you have the option of assigning subprocesses to the organizational units either as a reference or a copy, as shown in Fig. 16.17. You make the assignment within an organization. To do this, in the Subprocess area, click Assign Subprocess ❶ and then select the required subprocess from the central catalog ❷. The selection of the assignment method is a separate step ❸.

Options for assigning subprocesses

Figure 16.18 describes the options available in SAP Process Control for maintaining the control:

- If a subprocess from the central catalog has been assigned as a reference ❶, you can no longer change the related controls.
- However, if a subprocess has been assigned as a copy ❷, you can change the existing controls ❸ or create new ones ❹.

A new functionality in Release 10.0 called "Field-Based Configuration" also allows you to set individual fields within a control to "Local changes are not allowed" when you are using the "Local changes allowed" assignment method – thus enabling a "semi-centralized" scenario.

Section 16.3.3, "Central vs. Local ICS Master Data," described the concept of local vs. global master data. The local master data arises after the subprocess has been assigned.

Technical details and configuration

Shared Services Concept in the ICS

The essence of the shared services concept mapped in SAP Process Control is the multiple reuse of the same process and control hierarchy, and in particular, the multiple reuse of the test and assessment results within a regulation.

Business view

From a business view, the reuse of process and control hierarchies, as well as test and assessment results, can be necessary in the two ICS scenarios outsourcing and IT general controls.

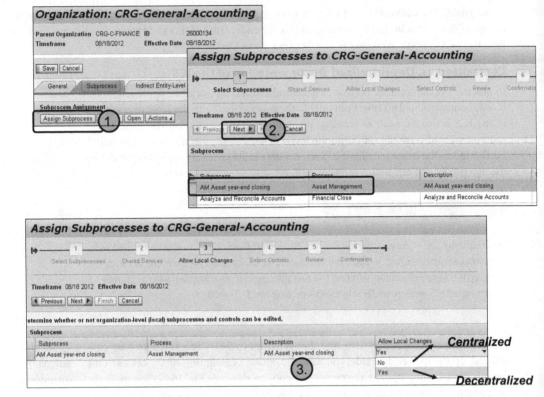

⬛ Figure 16.17   Prerequisites for implementing a centralized vs. a decentralized approach in master data management

[e.g.]   Outsourcing or Centralized Services

If certain services in an organization have been outsourced or centralized in-house within shared services facilities, this creates a challenge for the ICS process: as far as the centralized processes are concerned, the controls are processed in one location but remain (formally) the responsibility of all units that operate the corresponding processing (see Sect. 6.1.2, "IT Outsourcing: Who Is Responsible for the Controls?").

In an environment in which business processes are supported by IT, not only organizational but also ICS-specific challenges lead to a similar situation.

[e.g.]   IT General Controls Scenario

Let us assume the same IT application is used by several units within an organization. Every unit can be individually responsible for different business process-specific control mechanisms. The IT general controls, usually the responsibility of an IT department, are

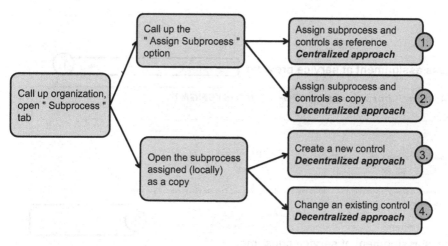

■ **Figure 16.18** Centralized vs. decentralized documentation approach in action

> centralized. These IT general controls are valid for the entire application, and therefore also for all units that use this application.

In both cases described, the results of the tests and assessments have to be made available for the same controls for multiple organizations. In SAP Process Control, the challenge of implementing this approach technically is solved via the shared services function.

As you can see in Fig. 16.19, the following prerequisites must be ensured to enable the use of the shared services functionality: **Prerequisites**

- The corresponding option must have been selected in a service provider organization ❶.
- Furthermore, the subprocesses used in the service provider organization must be released for reuse by the service consumer organizations ❷.
- When subprocesses are assigned to a service consumer organization, the released subprocesses are indicated accordingly ❸.
- In a further step ❹, the service provider organization has to be selected in a drop-down list.

You have now seen how to map the documentation of an ICS framework in SAP Process Control.

16.4.2 Scoping Process

In Sect. 1.2.1, "SOX in the USA," we mentioned the control selection process (top-down risk-based scoping). The aim of this process is to prioritize control areas. As legislation does not prescribe this process as mandatory and there are only general instructions, in

Subprocess assignment at service provider

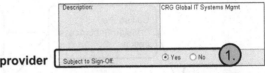

Assign Subprocesses to CRG-C-INFO-SYSMGMT

|◆———— 1 ————— 2 ————— 3 ———— 4 ———— 5 ———— 6 ———◀|

Select Subprocesses   Shared Services   Allow Local Changes   Select Controls   Review   Confirmation

Timeframe 08/18 2012 **Effective Date** 08/18/2012

[◀ Previous] [Next ▶] [Finish] [Cancel]

The orgunit is a Shared Services Provider, so it can share its Subprocesses and Controls. Please select if you would like to share the Subprocesses.

Subprocesses to offer as Shared Services

Subprocess	Description	Share
IT Change Management	IT Change Management Manage Transport Group	☑

Subprocess assignment at service consumer

Assign Subprocesses to CRG-General-Accounting

|◆———— 1 ————— 2 ————— 3 ———— 4 ———— 5 ———— 6 ———◀|

Select Subprocesses   Shared Services   Allow Local Changes   Select Controls   Review   Confirmation

Timeframe 08/18 2012 **Effective Date** 08/18/2012

[◀ Previous] [Next ▶] [Finish] [Cancel]

Shared-Services-Provider
CRG-C-INFO-SYSMGMT ▼
Shared Service nicht verw.
CRG-C-INFO-SYSMGMT

Subprocess

Subprocess	Process	Description	Shared Service
IT CHANGE*			
IT Change Management	IT General Controls	IT Change Management Manage Transp...	

Figure 16.19 Illustration of the shared services scenario

practice, various scenarios have become established. Some of these scenarios are offered in SAP Process Control.

Materiality-Based Scoping Process

Business view

Section 15.3.2, "Selection and Prioritization of Control Activities," explained scoping as one of the basic scenarios of the ICS activities. A materiality-based assessment that is based on the amount of the balances of individual accounts or their account groups is used – sometimes initially when a control framework is set up, but in some organizations this process also takes place regularly, for example, annually.

Account groups in SAP Process Control

The materiality-based selection process is supported in SAP Process Control (where the materiality is referred to as "significance"). As a connection between financial reporting and the processes, *account groups* play a central role here (see also Sect. 15.2.6). You create the hierarchy of the account groups in the work area MASTER DATA in the ACCOUNTS menu group. Section 16.4.1, "ICS Documentation Process," describes the role of the account groups in the data model of SAP Process Control.

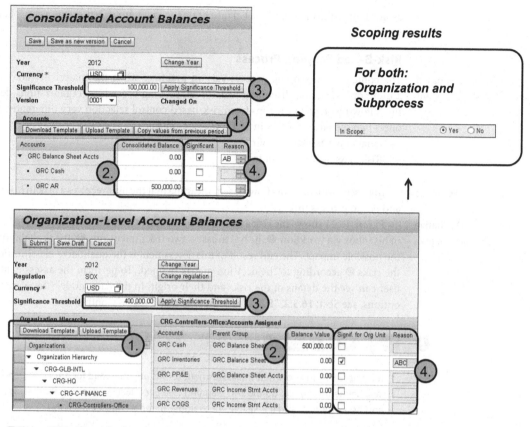

Figure 16.20 Materiality-based scoping process

Figure 16.20 shows how the materiality-based scoping process is implemented in SAP Process Control. Via MASTER DATA • ACCOUNTS you have access to two options:

Two options

- CONSOLIDATED ACCOUNT BALANCES (consolidated balances and significance)
- ORGANIZATION-LEVEL ACCOUNT BALANCES (organization-level balances and significance)

With both scoping options you have to perform the following steps:

Execution

1. Maintain the balances of the individual account groups manually either in Microsoft Excel form ❶ (can be downloaded and uploaded), or directly in the application ❷.
2. Then define and apply a threshold value for the materiality ❸.
3. The result is that both the relevant account balances ❹ and organizations and subprocesses are selected automatically (but you can also select them manually).
4. Per default, the scoping results are stored for each year, but you can configure this flexibly.

The difference between the two approaches described is that in the second option, you maintain the account balances for each organization. In the first option, you use

Difference between the options

an account group once, and the balance of this account group represents a consolidated value.

Risk-Based Scoping Process

Workflow-based risk assessment

The contents of a scoping process vary in practice: while the materiality analysis is a more or less standardized and widespread scoping procedure, organizations design the follow-on steps in the top-down risk-based control selection very differently. SAP offers two scenarios for this in SAP Process Control:

- Qualitative assessment of risks
- Risk classification of controls

Scenarios

Both scenarios are workflow-based, meaning that the user receives a task in his inbox and has to process this task.

Qualitative assessment of risks

Figure 16.21 shows the risk assessment procedure. Once the user has received a task in his inbox via workflow ❶, he has to assess two risk dimensions ❷: the probability and the possible impact. The end result of this assessment is the qualitative classification of the risks ❸ according to the decision matrix defined. To perform the assessment, the user can see the details of the risks and their origin in the data model (there are three options, see Sect. 16.3.2, "ICS Data Model in SAP Process Control").

> ❗ **Validity of the Assessment Results**
>
> It is important to know that the assessment results are only valid for a specific period. You define this period during the planning (see Sect. 16.4.3, "Planning Process, Tests, and Assessments") and it is visible, for example, in reporting (see Sect. 16.4.5).

Risk classification of controls

The Fig. 16.21 shows the procedure of the second scoping scenario, in which the controls are subjected to a risk classification. When processing a task (they are generated for each subprocess), you can see the details of the controls as well as the existing issues ❶. You can configure the criteria to be assessed flexibly, and can select the values via the drop-down list ❷. The end result is the risk classification of the controls ❸ in accordance with the decision matrix defined. The risk classification is transferred to the master data of the respective controls ❹. The results of the risk classification are transferred to the control attribute CONTROL RISK; if necessary, you can also maintain this attribute manually (if the configuration permits this).

Comparison

Two criteria – probability and impact – are prescribed for the risk assessment and you can only adjust the possible values. In contrast, for the risk classification of controls, you can define any number of assessment criteria. In both cases, you can define the derivation logic in a matrix. The respective settings are in the Implementation Guide under GRC • PROCESS CONTROL • SCOPING.

Derivation of combined risk assessment results

The field LEVEL OF EVIDENCE represents a further option for setting up a risk-based approach in the ICS. You can enter values in this field manually, or they can be determined automatically (as a combination of the values for control risk level and risk level). You maintain the derivation rules – *Control risk level + risk level = level of evidence* – in the IMG: GRC • PROCESS CONTROL • SCOPING • SET LEVEL OF EVIDENCE.

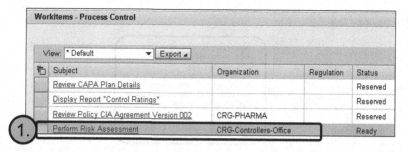

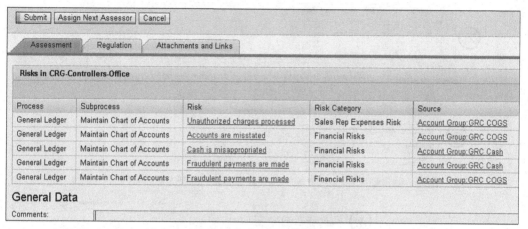

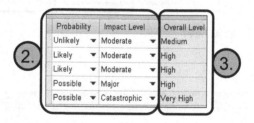

■ **Figure 16.21** Risk assessment as part of the scoping process

16.4.3 Planning Process, Tests, and Assessments

In SAP Process Control, workflow-based ICS activities are triggered using the planning function. This function is located in the work area ASSESSMENTS in the ASSESSMENT PLANNING menu group under PLANNER.

As a result of the harmonization of functions of individual components in GRC Release 10.0, the planning function now contains the activities of all GRC components for the first time, and not just activities for SAP Process Control.

As you can see in Fig. 16.22, planning begins with the selection of the activity to be executed, the period, the start date, and a due date (deadline) ❶.

Harmonized
Planner in
Release 10.0

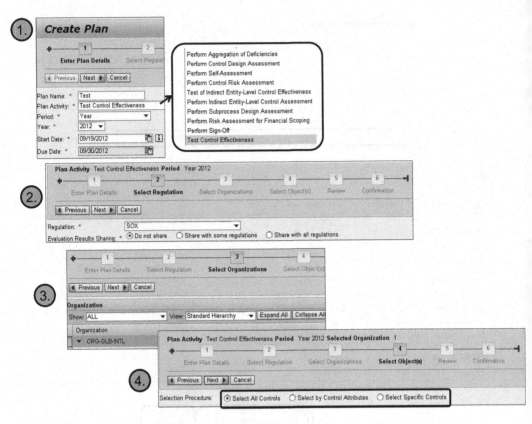

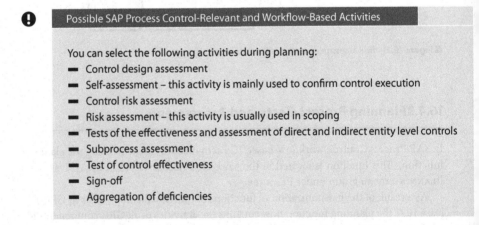

◻ Figure 16.22   Planning ICS Activities

> ❶   **Possible SAP Process Control-Relevant and Workflow-Based Activities**
>
> You can select the following activities during planning:
> - Control design assessment
> - Self-assessment – this activity is mainly used to confirm control execution
> - Control risk assessment
> - Risk assessment – this activity is usually used in scoping
> - Tests of the effectiveness and assessment of direct and indirect entity level controls
> - Subprocess assessment
> - Test of control effectiveness
> - Sign-off
> - Aggregation of deficiencies

Time dependency of ICS Activities   The selection of a test or assessment period is very important, as it is not only the objects that are time-based in SAP Process Control, but also the test and assessment results. These are stored in a *test log* that, analog to an ERP system, has the role of transaction data or individual documents.

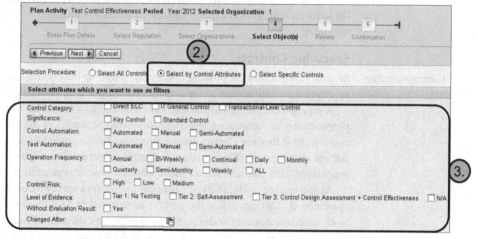

◘ Figure 16.23 Use of scoping results in planning

In the next step ❷, you have to define whether the test or assessment results are only used with one regulation or are shared with other regulations (where applicable).

You can also select one or more organizational units (see ❸ in Fig. 16.22) and then the objects to be assessed or tested (subprocesses or controls). There are three options:

- Select all controls within an organization
- Select controls using their attributes
- Select controls individually (see ❹ in Fig. 16.22)

The scoping process described in Sect. 16.4.2 continues logically in planning: as you can see in Fig. 16.23, when selecting organizational units ❶, you can restrict the selection to ORGANIZATIONS IN SCOPE. In addition, select the option SELECT BY CONTROL ATTRIBUTES ❷. You can then restrict the control risk or level of evidence ❸ that was determined in the control risk assessment.

Scoping results in planning

In practice, you often have to delete the entries in the planning function during the implementation or test phase. These are located in database table GRFNTASKPLAN.

Notifications

Not all persons involved in the ICS process use a compliance management application. Therefore, a notification function is essential. In SAP Process Control, e-mail notifica-

E-mail notifications

tions can be sent automatically (also applies for Lotus Notes). The trigger is a new task in the inbox defined for the planning function. A new task is generated once the *start date* of the activity is reached.

Reminder and escalation function

A further-reaching and separately configurable option is the sending of a reminder when the due date for a task is exceeded. You can also establish an escalation function that involves additional persons to the task owner.

You set up the e-mail notification function in the IMG under GRC • GENERAL SETTINGS • WORKFLOW • WORKFLOW E-MAIL NOTIFICATIONS. To do this you have to perform the SAPconnect configuration (standard transaction SCOT).

In practice, you often have to adjust the text that the user receives. You can do this in the IMG via GRC • GENERAL SETTINGS • WORKFLOW • WORKFLOW TASK NAMES when necessary.

Executing Controls

Control execution

Section 15.3.3 shows the possible options for mapping the control execution in an ICS application – confirmation of the control execution and automated control execution.

A separate chapter is dedicated to automated control execution (see Chap. 17, "Implementation of Automated Test and Monitoring Scenarios in the SAP ERP Environment"). SAP Process Control uses a workflow-based procedure for confirmation of control execution. In this procedure, a control owner receives a *self-assessment task* for processing. This task refers to a control within a specific organizational unit.

As you can see in Fig. 16.24, the user has to process a survey by answering individual questions ❶. You can define the surveys as required in SAP Process Control – in the work area ASSESSMENTS under SURVEYS. If necessary, the control owner can look at the control details ❷. An important function in SAP Process Control is the possibility to add attachments and links ❸. These are used as *supporting evidence* in the confirmation of the control execution.

Configuration

Just like all other workflows in SAP Process Control, the self-assessment workflow does not require any further configuration. The workflows are preconfigured and all you have to do is activate them (see Sect. 16.2.2, "Initial Configuration of the Standard Functions"). In practice, however, you can, for example, adjust the names of the individual assessment levels of self-assessments: you do this in the Implementation Guide via GRC • PROCESS CONTROL • ASSESSMENT CONFIGURATION • SPECIFY NAMES FOR RATINGS ❹.

Testing Controls

We described the importance of effectiveness tests in an ICS application in Sect. 15.3.5: the objective of an effectiveness test is to be able to make a statement regarding the achievement of the control objective. There is a differentiation between a manual and an automated effectiveness test.

Manual effectiveness tests

Automated tests are explained in Chap. 17, "Implementation of Automated Test and Monitoring Scenarios in the SAP ERP Environment." In SAP Process Control, manual effectiveness tests are implemented using a corresponding workflow.

As you can see in Fig. 16.25, the tester has a test plan to process ❶. This test plan was sent to him via workflow. You maintain test plans in the work area MASTER DATA under MANUAL TEST PLANS. You can define the logic of the test procedure in the individual test steps within a test plan.

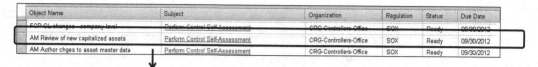

Object Name	Subject	Organization	Regulation	Status	Due Date
~~FSD GL changes - company level~~	~~Perform Control Self-Assessment~~	~~CRG-Controllers-Office~~	~~SOX~~	~~Ready~~	~~09/30/2012~~
AM Review of new capitalized assets	Perform Control Self-Assessment	CRG-Controllers-Office	SOX	Ready	09/30/2012
AM Author chges to asset master data	Perform Control Self-Assessment	CRG-Controllers-Office	SOX	Ready	09/30/2012

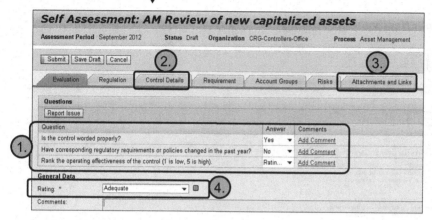

◻ Figure 16.24 Assessment of control execution (self-assessment)

Logic in Manual Test Plans		**[e.g.]**

The logic within a test plan defines, for example, whether a negative result of a test step leads to a negative overall result, which sample size is prescribed, which method is used for sample selection, etc.

You have to enter the test date, test result, and other comments in the general area of the test documentation ❷. If the effectiveness test is positive, you complete it by clicking Submit ❸. If the effectiveness test is negative, the system forces the creation of a problem case (button Report Issue ❹). The subsequent steps are described in Sect. 16.4.4, "Problem-Solving Process."

Offline Test

Effectiveness tests cannot always take place when the user's computer is connected to the network. Offline documentation of the test results is possible in SAP Process Control using SAP Interactive Forms by Adobe.   Business view

As you can see in Fig. 16.26, you can download the offline form within a task to be processed. You can then, for example, save the form locally and fill it out in offline mode. However, this option is less practical as once you have filled out the form, you have to access the workflow task in the inbox again.   Uploading results

To get around this limitation, you can send offline forms automatically via e-mail. Once the form has been completed, the user can simply send it back. For many users, this means that they do not have to log on to SAP Process Control. The system reads   Sending results via e-mail

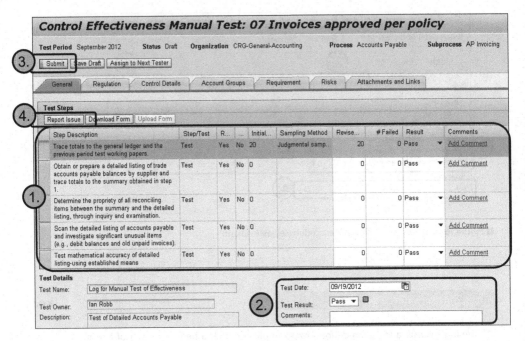

test and assessment results from the form automatically. However, this option requires additional configuration in the IMG.

Further Surveys and Assessments

Up to this point, you have learned about the ICS activities as part of scoping, control execution, and effectiveness tests. We have explained all main activities that are available with the planning function. There is a further planning function in the CERTIFICATION work center. In this function, you plan the sign-off and aggregation of issues. You will now learn more about selected main activities.

Control Design Assessment

Assessing the characteristic of the controls

In the control design assessment, you analyze the characteristic of a control as to how suitable it is for achieving the control objective (see Sect. 15.3.6, "Survey"). In SAP Process Control, just like the self-assessment, this activity is workflow-based, refers to the control as an object, and also uses a survey that you can maintain as a separate object.

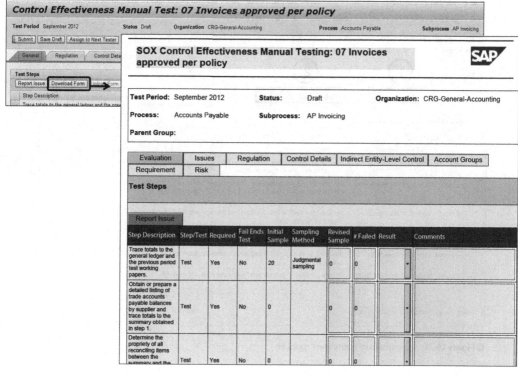

● **Figure 16.26** Offline assessment form

Activities with Regard to Entity Level Controls

The following two ICS activities refer to entity level controls (see Sect. 3.1.4, "Structure of a Classic ICS Framework in the ERP Environment") that form an independent hierarchy in SAP Process Control.

— Test of indirect entity level control effectiveness
— Indirect entity level control assessment

The necessity for entity level controls within an ICS framework results from the COSO study. From a business perspective, it is justified by the fact that there are control mechanisms that have a major influence on the control environment but are not a direct part of the business processes.

As you can see in Fig. 16.27, the entity level controls are not part of the "usual" process and control hierarchy ❶, but are assigned separately within organizational units on the INDIRECT ENTITY LEVEL CONTROLS tab ❷.

You maintain the entity level controls in the work area MASTER DATA under ACTIVITIES AND PROCESSES. The procedure for workflow-based tests and assessments of these ICS objects is identical to that for "normal" controls.

Assessing "high-level" controls

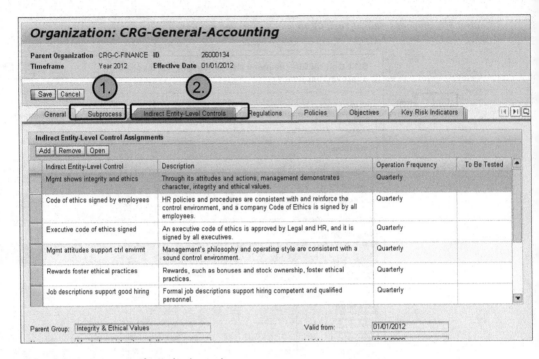

Figure 16.27 Assignment of entity level controls

Subprocess Design Assessment

Assessing subprocesses or groups of controls
Within a process control hierarchy, this action refers to the subprocess (the hierarchy node above the controls), displays usual assessment properties, and has the objective of considering control groups on a cumulative basis. In practice, you use this option, for example, to find out about the adjustment requirement or how up-to-date the ICS documentation is.

16.4.4 Issue Remediation Process

Business view
An ICS must be effective, and the core tasks of a compliance management process include efficiently rectifying issues identified. *Issues*, which in practice, depending on the area, are called *findings* or *problem cases*, can be caused as follows, for example:

- There are no or insufficient controls in a process, meaning that risks in a process are not covered.
- A control is inefficient or has been designed incorrectly, meaning that the control objective cannot be achieved.
- A control is not executed in the scheduled frequency, etc.

In SAP Process Control, processing issues is the functional core of the application. As you can see in Fig. 16.28, the issues arise in SAP Process Control if the result of a manual test, an assessment, or an automated control is negative. You then have

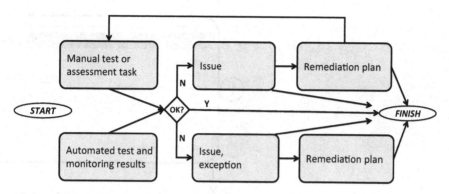

◻ **Figure 16.28** Procedure for issue rectification

to process the remediation plan to rectify the issues. Once you have completed this processing, the system can trigger a new assessment or test automatically (optional).

In practice, a reassessment is generally triggered automatically with a delay: this is useful particularly for an effectiveness test, because the effect of the control cannot be reassessed immediately after the issues have been processed and new samples have to be taken.

Automated reassessment

We can summarize the most important steps in the process of reporting and processing issues (see Fig. 16.30) as follows:

Process steps

1. The creation of an issue is mandatory and is forced by the system if the result of a test or an assessment is rated as negative.
2. You can report more than one issue in a test or assessment (see Fig. 16.29).
3. When you report an issue, you have to define its priority and the person responsible ❶. The system proposes a user for processing the issue. If necessary, however, you can overwrite this system proposal.
4. The issue reported is sent to the inbox of the user responsible via workflow ❷. There are three options for processing an issue ❸:
   - Create a plan for rectifying the issue
   - Cancel the issue (a reason has to be documented)
   - Forward the issue to another user
5. The plan for rectifying the issue is then processed. This plan is called a *remediation plan*.

The most important points in rectifying the issue can be summarized as follows:
- The remediation plan has a due date and a processor who, similarly to the reporting of an issue, is proposed by the system or defined manually (see ❶ in Fig. 16.29).
- The remediation plan is placed in the user's inbox ❷.
- The processing of the remediation plan is documented ❸.

Remediation plan

To make the process of issue rectification more flexible, the Implementation Guide offers a few options. As already stated, an automated triggering of a repeat assessment or a test is optional. You can configure this via GRC • PROCESS CONTROL • ASSESSMENT

Technical details and configuration

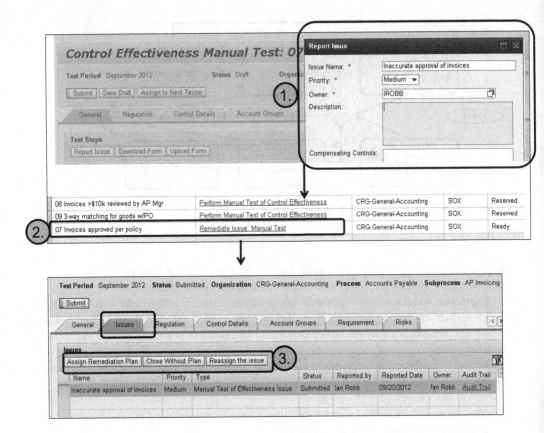

SETUP • SPECIFY REEVALUATION NECESSITY AND TIME LAG. You can also define the required time delay for a reevaluation/reassessment.

Configuring logic for the due date   In this setting, you can define how the due date is determined for a new assessment. Proceed as follows:

1. Select a certain number of days for the new assessment and the retest.
2. The due date for the new assessment (for example, a new effectiveness test or a new control design assessment) is calculated as follows:
    It is the last date of the following: original due date, the date trigger for the new assessment or the new test (taking account of any possible time lag), and the due date of error rectification plus the number of days that you specify when configuring the column DUE DATE SHIFT.

Necessity of issues for entity level controls   For assessments of entity level controls, SAP Process Control offers the option of making the reporting of an issue necessary only from a specific rating. You configure this option in the Implementation Guide as follows: GRC • PROCESS CONTROL • ASSESSMENT SETUP • DETERMINE ENTITY LEVEL CONTROLS: NECESSITY OF ISSUE REPORTING.

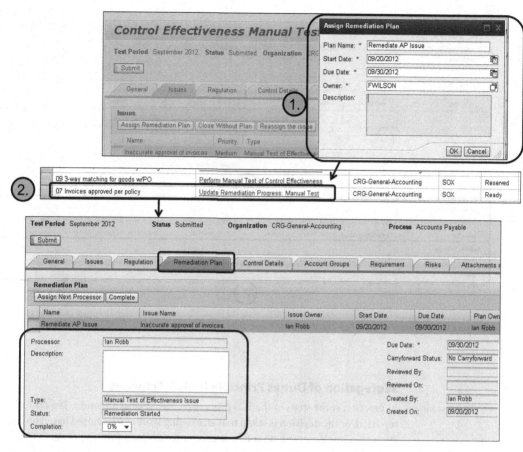

▣ Figure 16.30 Processing of a plan for issue rectification

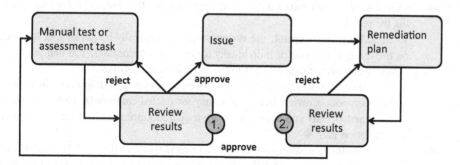

▣ Figure 16.31 Review steps in the test and assessment process

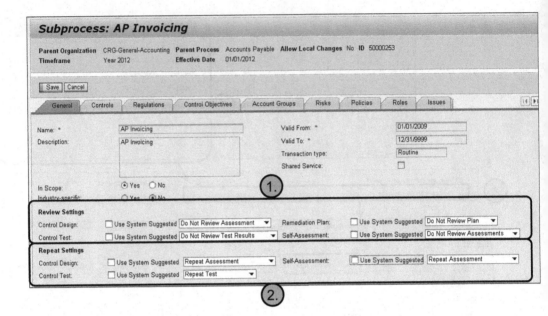

□ **Figure 16.32**   Control of the review and the test and assessment repetition

Segregation of Duties Principle for ICS Activities

Business view   In practice, some steps in the ICS process require special attention. If a critical issue is reported, or the decision is taken that an existing issue can be closed based on a remediation plan implemented, it is often necessary to involve a further person in the decision process (see Fig. 16.31).

Validation in the ICS process   In SAP Process Control, this segregation of duties principle is implemented in the form of review tasks that can be switched between the individual test and assessment steps. Via workflow, a reviewer receives the task of checking the test or assessment results (or *validating* them) ❶, or, for a completed remediation plan ❷, the task of deciding whether this plan was implemented and the issue can be closed, for example.

Reviewer   The reviewer can enter his own comments, and has the choice of accepting or rejecting the result.

In SAP Process Control, the review steps can generally be performed depending on the rating of an issue or individually for certain subprocesses. You define the latter option in the master data and not in the Implementation Guide.

As you can see in Fig. 16.32, at subprocess level, you can define whether, for tests and assessments, a review step is necessary for related controls ❶. Here you can also define whether tests and assessments are triggered automatically after completion of a remediation plan ❷.

Technical details and configuration   In the Implementation Guide, you can define whether the validation is necessary for specific ICS activities: GRC • PROCESS CONTROL • ASSESSMENT SETUP • SPECIFY WHETHER REVIEW IS NECESSARY.

Furthermore, SAP Process Control offers the option of forcing validation steps dependent on the rating of issues. To do this, in the IMG, choose GRC • PROCESS CONTROL • ASSESSMENT SETUP • SKIP REVIEW DEPENDING ON RATING.

Test Automation and Monitoring Through Integration

"Push the button and get results": the great vision of ICS automation has come true with the help of compliance management software – including SAP Process Control – based on the *Continuous Monitoring Framework*. A separate chapter is dedicated to this topic (see Chap. 17, "Implementation of Automated Test and Monitoring Scenarios in the SAP ERP Environment"). Here we will merely summarize the most important aspects and give answers to the most frequent questions.

For a business user whose task is to execute ICS activities rather than to set up the system, whether the controls in SAP Process Control are automated or manual is usually irrelevant:

- Automated controls are just as much part of the process and control hierarchy as manual controls.
- The test and assessment tasks, as well as the test results, are sent to users in the form of workflows for both manual and automated controls.

The situation is different for the *configuration* of the controls, which is not visible for a "normal" business user.

User view

Automated Controls

Automated controls are controls that can be executed without the involvement of a human being. For example, if a live client is opened for direct changes in an SAP ERP system, this means that an important preventive control has become ineffective – even if compensating controls are possible. SAP Process Control can detect this status, report it as an issue, and send it to the person responsible for processing.

[e.g.]

In this example, the effort that would be necessary to check all clients used in all SAP ERP systems in an organization would take up time and resources. In contrast, an automated test takes seconds and requires the attention of the person responsible only if an issue is detected.

Greater efficiency

In addition to this type of ideal scenario, in which the system "knows," based on predefined check rules, that there is an issue, less clear scenarios are also feasible in SAP Process Control. In these scenarios, the evaluation results must first be analyzed by a person responsible before an issue is created and processed (such as the manual posting to an account that permits only automatic postings).

Requirements in organizations

In practice, the testing of controls – such as *checking* their design or effectiveness – is often confused with the *execution* of these controls. The functionality available in SAP Process Control is suitable not only for testing the controls (and thus using this application not only for covering compliance requirements), but also, through the use of various monitoring scenarios, as a fixed part of the existing business processes. Compared to other monitoring tools and options (for example, the evaluation of ABAP reports or services or monitoring functions in SAP Solution Manager), the approach

Typical mistake

of monitoring control mechanisms in a centralized ICS management system has clear advantages: a formalized and workflow-based process for processing issues can ensure that problems identified are rectified more efficiently, and the "ICS overall view" allows a complete statement about the status of compliance (almost real-time).

Where do the users see the results of the test and monitoring transactions in SAP Process Control, and which measures are possible, where applicable, for rectifying inconsistencies identified?

Figure 16.33 shows that there are at least three access points for checking the results of automated test and monitoring scenarios:

- Regardless of whether controls were assessed manually or automatically, all results are stored in the controls themselves ❶. This means that when you open a local control, on the Assessment tab, you will find both the results of design surveys etc. and the results of automated tests (provided the control is defined and configured as automated or fully automated).
- The list of all active control monitoring scenarios and their results are located in the Job Scheduler ❷.
- Of course, you can also find the results in reports ❸.
- The results are issued via workflow. The basic concept that no issue is lost in the ICS and must be thoroughly documented and processed also applies to automated controls. For monitoring scenarios, exceptions are issued to the user responsible via workflow, and for test scenarios, issues ❹. The subsequent processing of the issues follows the standard process in SAP Process Control.

Technical details and configuration

For the technical details regarding the setting up of automated test and monitoring scenarios, see Chap. 17. Only the most important points are listed here:

- SAP Process Control can connect to SAP ERP, PeopleSoft, Oracle, and other business applications and can analyze master data, control data, and transaction data in these applications.
- The most important elements in the Continuous Monitoring Framework within SAP Process Control are scripts and rules that are assigned to the controls.
  - *Data sources* define which data is read from which system.
  - *Rules* define the selection values and contain, to some extent, analysis criteria and analysis logic.
- In the Continuous Monitoring Framework, you can use scripts and rules from SAP Process Control, as well as standard programs and queries in SAP ERP.

Aggregation of Deficiencies

Business view

In an ICS application, it can be necessary to consolidate multiple issues and deficiencies found. There can be many reasons for this:

- In the tests and assessments of controls within different processes, issues reported can relate to the same content.
- The same control can be tested in SAP Process Control in different periods and report the same issue in every period; multiple issues can even be reported for one test or assessment.
- Within the framework of legal regulations, such as US SOX, it can be necessary to consider the issues identified on a summarized basis and rate them formally as significant deficiency or even material weakness, where applicable. The criteria for

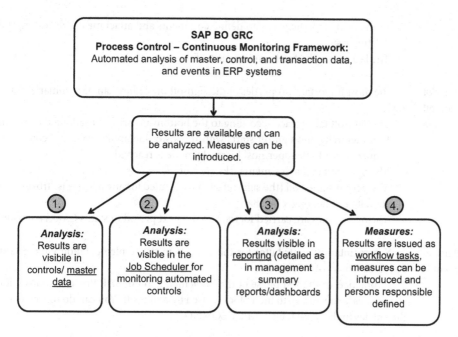

Figure 16.33 Automated control results in SAP PC

the grouping come from the external financial reporting: different issues can affect the same items in the financial statements and, viewed in total, cause a higher risk than when considered individually.

In SAP Process Control, this need is covered by aggregation of deficiencies. Just like most ICS activities, the aggregation of deficiencies runs on a workflow basis: the person responsible receives a task that contains an overview of the issues present. The individual issues have to be summarized in groups.

Sign-Off Process

The *sign-off* is the last step in the ICS cycle supported by SAP Process Control. This optional ICS activity can be traced back to formal legal requirements (such as in US SOX), according to which the management of an organization has to confirm that an ICS has been set up, along with measures for ensuring its effectiveness.

Necessity of sign-off

The sign-off procedure established in SAP Process Control is workflow-based and is usually scheduled simultaneously for all organizations within a corporate hierarchy. The person responsible has to process a sign-off task in several steps, guided by the system (buttons Continue and OK):

Process steps

1. The user has an overview of the organizational units involved in the sign-off, as well as of all open and closed issues reported during the assessment and testing of controls.
2. The user then processes the survey – you can define the individual questions as required.

3. In the next step, the user can define comments and attachments (for example, for existing issues).
4. The last step is the final confirmation of the sign-off.

Special features of the sign-off procedure

The most important properties of the sign-off procedure can be summarized as follows:

- The sign-off takes place according to the bottom-up principle. Along the organization hierarchy, the sign-off starts with the lower hierarchy levels and continues in sequence until the uppermost hierarchy node is reached.
- The open test and assessment tasks are closed.
- The period signed off (the sign-off can be executed for any period) is "frozen"; master data can no longer be changed.
- The open issues are carried forward to the next period in status CARRYFORWARD.

Technical details and configuration

You maintain the attributes for the sign-off in the Implementation Guide: GRC • PROCESS CONTROL • SIGN-OFF.

In practice, in the test phase of the implementation of SAP Process Control, it can sometimes be necessary to lift a block caused by a sign-off. You can do this by deleting the entries in database table GRPCCLOSING.

16.4.5 Reporting

Business view

The primary objective of reporting in SAP Process Control is to provide real-time information about the effectiveness of an ICS: about deficiencies detected, the status of processing, etc. Many user groups' use of SAP Process Control, such as top management or external auditors etc., can be restricted to reporting; for other user groups, the reporting and the execution of tests and assessments, or the processing of issues, etc., can also be very important. Therefore, the importance of reporting during an implementation project is very high. The reports in SAP Process Control are *theoretically* ready to use, but in real-world projects, configuration and adjustment work is always necessary: for example, the addition of new fields to a report, the creation of user-specific report variants, performance-optimizing configuration settings.

Main reports

In total, SAP Process Control offers around 40 standard reports that cover the following main areas, as shown in Fig. 16.34:

- **Master data**
  Master data-related and documentation-related reports, primarily aimed at the ICS framework established in SAP Process Control (risk and control matrix etc.)
- **Evaluation of test and assessment results**
  Results for checking the planned test and assessment scope, analyzing the test and assessment results, and tracing open issues as well as measures for rectifying them
- **Automatic monitoring**
  Reports designed especially for the topic of continuous monitoring
- **Management dashboards**
  Various summary presentations of test and assessment results (heatmaps, dashboards, etc.) with aggregation options

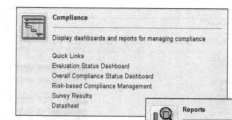

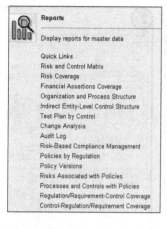

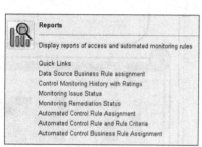

Figure 16.34 Standard reports in SAP Process Control

— **Roles and authorizations**

   User-related and authorization-related reports allow an evaluation of the responsibilities and user assignments in the ICS framework

Figure 16.35 shows some examples of reports that are available in SAP Process Control:

— Detailed presentation of master data hierarchies and test and assessment results, with statistical summaries, in the form of pie charts ❶, some reports with drilldown functions ❷

— Various dashboards with drilldown function ❷

— Documentation-oriented reports, for example, with control and risk descriptions ❸

— Heatmaps ❹ that establish a link to SAP Risk Management

In principle, there are two options for calling up a report in SAP Process Control:

— Generate the report online

— Generate the report in the background and have the system send the generated result to your own inbox as an attachment

Calling up reports

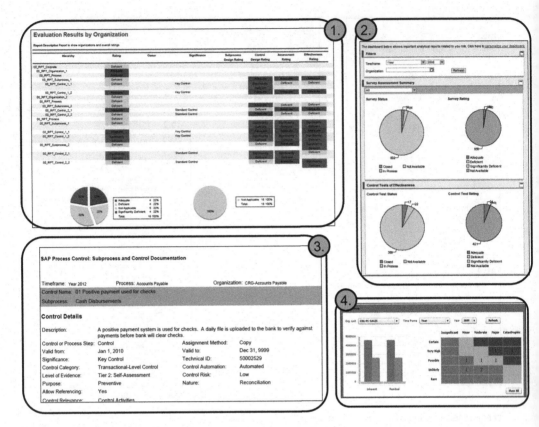

◻ Figure 16.35   Report types in SAP Process Control

Technical details
and configuration

In principle, two technologies for reports can be used in SAP Process Control:

- **SAP Crystal Reports**
  You can use this graphical, high-quality reporting technology (as described in Sect. 16.2.1, "Technical Architecture and Installation") in SAP Process Control via Crystal Report Adapters (CRA). An additional configuration of the application is necessary.

- **Web Dynpro**
  Calling up reports using Web Dynpro is available as standard in SAP Process Control and does not require any further components. When using this interface technology, users have access to the *Analysis Dashboard Report*, which SAP BusinessObjects Dashboards (formerly Xcelsius) uses.

Integration options of the reporting engine of SAP Process Control with Business Intelligence allow you to cover in particular the additional need for statistical summaries or trend analyses (presentation of test and assessment results on a time axis). The new BI reports can be integrated directly in the corresponding work center of SAP Process Control.

16.5 ICS and Compliance Implementation: Roles

You generally model a workflow-based ICS process by designing authorization roles. They bring a third dimension into the ICS model by linking ICS objects and activities and assigning them to a user.

Modeling the ICS process

From the following pages you will learn what the authorization model in SAP Process Control looks like, which predefined best practice authorization roles SAP Process Control offers, and how to assign the users to the authorization roles within the framework of object-based security. We will also show how you can adjust the roles or redefine them.

> **Source of Information**
>
> The *Security Guide* for SAP Process Control, which is available to SAP customers on SAP Service Marketplace, provides a detailed description of the authorization concept.

16.5.1 Authorization Model in SAP Process Control

Figure 16.36 shows the structure of the authorization concept in SAP Process Control:

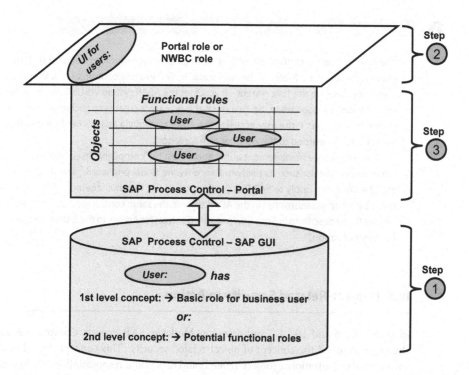

◻ **Figure 16.36** Overview of the role concept of SAP Process Control

- As part of level ❶, a user has to be created via SAP GUI and have a basic set of roles (the role SAP_GRC_FN_BUSINESS_USER, which is assigned to every user). This basic set can also contain functional roles necessary as part of the second level authorization concept.
- The second authorization level ❷ concerns either portal roles or SAP NetWeaver Business Client roles. These enable a user to see different areas and functions within SAP Process Control. Steps 1 and 2 are more part of the technical maintenance of the user that is usually performed by the security team – in contrast to step 3.
- The third level ❸ contains, on the Web interface of SAP Process Control (frontend), the assignment of a user within a matrix to ICS objects (such as organizations, processes, subprocesses, and controls) and simultaneously to the functional roles. At this level, the *concept of object-related security*, which primarily controls the ICS process, is implemented in SAP Process Control.

Process view of the authorization assignment
These levels are implemented in the live operation of SAP Process Control as follows: user and authorization administration is responsible for assigning the required authorization and portal roles to each user (via transaction SU01, User Maintenance, in the Implementation Guide (SAP GUI), and via the User Management Engine in SAP NetWeaver Portal).

The last maintenance step is part of the ICS process in SAP Process Control and in this application, is executed, depending on the scenario, by organization-specific ICS owners, for example.

 User Authentication and Security in SAP Process Control

The ABAP system is configured as User Store (user source of information) of the User Management Engine (UME) of the Java stack. In SAP Process control, user authentication takes place via the Java system – it accesses the ABAP system via UME to verify the user. If a user is logged on to the Java stack, the Java stack creates an SSO ticket (session cookie) for the user. If the user accesses the ABAP system via an Internet browser, this SSO ticket is forwarded to the ABAP system for logon.

The compliance management application must be "compliant" itself: the usual security requirements, such as password security, no trivial passwords, standard users, etc. therefore also apply to SAP Process Control. As the user management and the authentication mechanisms run in the ABAP system, the same control mechanisms apply here as those described in Sect. 6.3, "Security Controls for Access to the SAP System and for Authentication."

16.5.2 Object-Related Security in Action

In Sects. 16.3.6 and 16.5.1, "Authorization Model in SAP Process Control," we have already mentioned the concept of object-related security. This concept is used to determine the organizational (object-related) and functional responsibilities. As you can see in the example in Fig. 16.37, the user PAT SZAFRON has been assigned the order

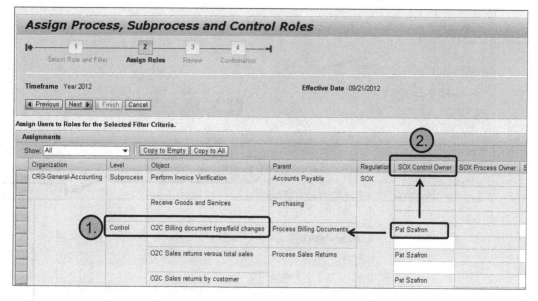

Figure 16.37 Assignment of the user to the objects and roles

to cash-related detective and configurative control BILLING DOCUMENT TYPE FIELD CHANGES ❶. This user also receives the functional role SOX CONTROL OWNER ❷.

What effect does the user assignment described have? In this example, SAP Process Control "knows" from the assignment that the task for self-assessment – an ICS activity contained in the SOX Control Owner role – for the assigned control has to be sent to Pat Szafron, for example. The role can also be configured such that the user only has access to his or her "own" hierarchy in reporting.

In SAP Process Control, you assign the user to the objects in two areas:

- For the central organization hierarchies, you perform the maintenance via ACCESS MANAGEMENT • GRC ROLE ASSIGNMENTS • ORGANIZATIONS.
- For the organization, process, and control hierarchies, you perform the maintenance via ACCESS MANAGEMENT • GRC ROLE ASSIGNMENTS • BUSINESS PROCESSES.

16.5.3 First Level vs. Second Level Authorizations

From a content perspective, you can assign the user to the objects and roles in two ways depending on which of the two possible authorization levels you selected in the Implementation Guide via GRC • GENERAL SETTINGS • MAINTAIN AUTHORIZATION CUSTOMIZING during the implementation. Here there are two options: *First Level* and *Second Level*.

If the setting for second level authorizations is active, the user selection for role assignments at entity level is restricted to users who have been assigned the corresponding authorization role in their user profile.

Second level authorizations

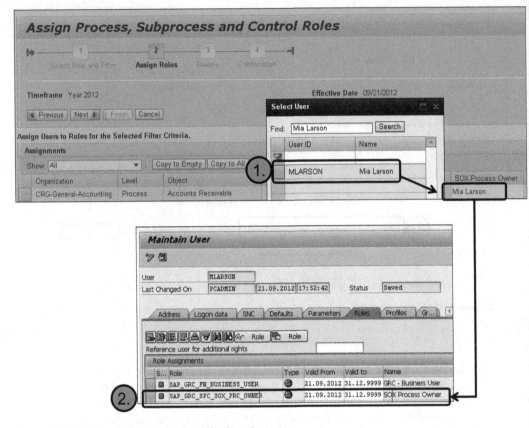

◻ Figure 16.38 Difference between level 1 and level 2 authorizations

Figure 16.38 shows the user assignment for this option. The user MIA LARSON receives the role SOX PROCESS TESTER and at the same time, the assignment to a process. In this option, Mia Larson is only available as one of the possible users ❶ because the role SOX PROCESS TESTER is also in her ABAP master record ❷. This means that the assignment of an ABAP role in ABAP ❷ "allows" the assignment of this role in SAP NetWeaver Portal ❶.

First level authorizations   In contrast, if you use the first level option, in SAP NetWeaver Portal, you can select any user in SAP Process Control for the assignment (the user must have the role SAP_GRC_FN_BUSINESS_USER in their ABAP master record).

Advantages and disadvantages   In practice, the second level authorization option offers on one hand greater precision and a lower error ratio during role assignment in SAP Process Control than the first level authorization option. For example, a control owner cannot be entered as an external auditor by mistake.

On the other hand, the effort required for the initial creation of a user in ABAP via SAP GUI (transaction SU01) increases with the second level option because this user must receive not only a generic role but also a function-specific role. This means that the user and authorization administrator must first receive additional input (where

Role	Type	Role name
SAP_GRC_SPC_GLOBAL_AUT_ADMIN	⊕	Global Automated Rules Customizing Admin
SAP_GRC_SPC_GLOBAL_CEO_CFO	⊕	Global CEO/CFO
SAP_GRC_SPC_GLOBAL_INT_AUD	⊕	Global Internal Auditor
SAP_GRC_SPC_GLOBAL_ORG_ADMIN	⊕	Global Organization Administrator
SAP_GRC_SPC_GLOBAL_ORG_OWNER	⊕	Global Organization Owner
SAP_GRC_SPC_GLOBAL_PRC_ADMIN	⊕	Global Process Admin
SAP_GRC_SPC_GLOBAL_REG_ADMIN	⊕	Global Regulation Admin
SAP_GRC_SPC_GLOBAL_SRV_ADMIN	⊕	Global Survey Admin
SAP_GRC_SPC_GLOBAL_TPL_ADMIN	⊕	Global Testplan Admin

SAP_GRC_SPC_SOX_AUT_SPECIALIST	⊕	SOX Automated Rules Specialist
SAP_GRC_SPC_SOX_CTL_OWNER	⊕	SOX Control Owner
SAP_GRC_SPC_SOX_ICMAN	⊕	SOX Internal Control Manager
SAP_GRC_SPC_SOX_ORG_TESTER	⊕	SOX Organization Tester
SAP_GRC_SPC_SOX_PRC_OWNER	⊕	SOX Process Owner
SAP_GRC_SPC_SOX_PRC_TESTER	⊕	SOX Process Tester
SAP_GRC_SPC_SOX_SIG_ADMIN	⊕	SOX Signoff Admin
SAP_GRC_SPC_SOX_SPR_OWNER	⊕	SOX Subprocess Owner

◘ Figure 16.39 Example standard roles in SAP Process Control

applicable in a request for user change) from the specialist department or team about the ICS-specific tasks of a user.

16.5.4 Predefined Best Practice Role Concept in SAP

SAP Process Control contains best practice experiences as BC Sets. This also applies to the authorization roles: activation of a corresponding BC Set makes predefined standard roles available (the ABAP authorization roles as part of the first and second authorization level, see Sect. 16.5.1, "Authorization Model in SAP Process Control"). | BC Sets

Figure 16.39 shows examples of standard roles in SAP Process Control. | Standard roles
- The upper section lists roles that apply for objects across all regulations.
- The lower section contains roles from the preconfigured regulation SOX.
- There are also roles that contain administration and configuration authorizations for SAP Process Control, as well as roles for an FDA, as further preconfigured regulation.

The practical benefit of predefined roles is obvious: a complete redesign of roles is time-consuming and expensive. In the design phase of an implementation project, you use standard roles as a comparison and subsequent adjustment basis.

16.5.5 Adjusting the Roles

The property of authorization roles of controlling workflow-based ICS activities (see Sect. 16.5.2, "Object-Related Security in Action") is the focus as far as changing existing | Assigning business events

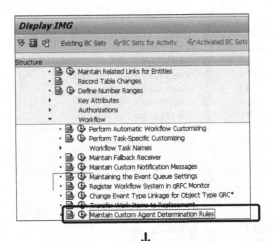

◻ Figure 16.40 Example for the role adjustment – assignment of workflow-based ICS activities

or designing new roles is concerned. You adjust this property in the Implementation Guide by assigning business events (see Fig. 16.40).

Figure 16.40 contains two examples for a role adjustment:

— Through the assignment of the business event GRC_PERF_SIGNOFF, the authorization role GLOBAL CEO/CFO ❶ receives the property of sending a user the workflow-based sign-off task.

— The authorization role SOX PROCESS TESTER ❷ is, analog to the described example of the business event GRC_PERF_TESTING, responsible for having the system send a scheduled effectiveness test to a user (see Sect. 16.4.3, "Planning Process, Tests, and Assessments").

Further example for role adjustments   A further property of the roles, which, based on project experience, is the focus of the adjustments, is the change of object or entity level during the assignment of users (see Sect. 16.5.2, "Object-Related Security in Action").

[e.g.]   Change of Object or Entity Level During Assignment

This type of adjustment is necessary, for example, if a user is to be assigned for processing the effectiveness test at subprocess level (that is, for all controls at a lower level in the hierarchy) and not one level higher at process level (this is the case for the standard role SOX PROCESS TESTER).

16.6 SAP Process Control as GRC Component – New Features and Developments

In Sect. 4.3 you learned about the structure of the SAP solutions for GRC in Release 10.0 and gained an impression of an integrated GRC approach. In this section we will address selected new features and integration scenarios of SAP Process Control in connection with other GRC components.

16.6.1 Policy Management and Other New Features in Release 10.0

One aspect of operative corporate governance is an efficient process for managing policies. From Release 10.0, SAP Process Control supports the complete life cycle of a policy (Policy Management) with workflow-supported procedures (see Fig. 16.41).

Process for managing policies

SAP Process Control offers a role-based scenario in which a policy undergoes the following levels:

— When *a policy is established*, it is reviewed after the initial documentation. Feedback can be collected from multiple persons responsible via workflow. After the feedback has been incorporated, the policy is sent for final *approval*, whereby multiple iteration loops are possible before a policy is released. The approver has three options: reject the policy, send it back for reworking, or publish it.

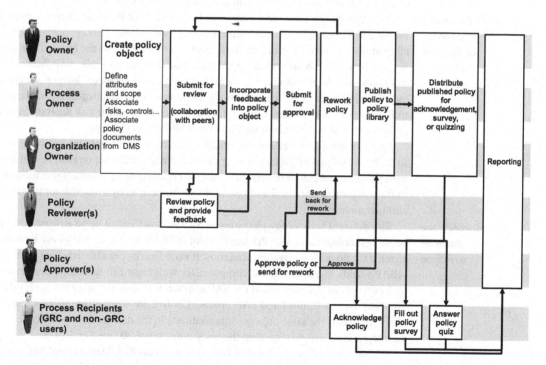

☐ **Figure 16.41** Policy Management functionality in SAP Process Control

▬ The *implementation of a policy* begins when it is officially published. A policy can then be sent to a relevant group of people (selection can be via roles, user groups, or on an individual basis) for formal acknowledgment or, where applicable, for acceptance. A further option is to use a survey or tests to check whether the contents of the policy have been understood. The degree of acceptance and other key figures with regard to the policy can be traced in reporting. Policy Management is one of the most important new features of SAP Process Control 10.0.

16.6.2 Integration with SAP Access Control

You can implement control automation in SAP Process Control using the Continuous Monitoring Framework. This enables an integration of SAP Process Control with other applications, whereby you can analyze master data, transaction data, and control data from other ERP applications.

In Sect. 5.2, "Authorizations," you learned that authorization controls is a special topic in SAP ERP. The special technical features of this area was one of the reasons why SAP Access Control (see Sect. 4.3.3, "SAP Access Control 10.0") was originally a separate product and was only gradually integrated with the remaining GRC components, in particular SAP Process Control. However, you also know that authorization controls are an essential part of an ICS framework. To look at this as a whole, we therefore have to bring two large areas together – application controls as part of business processes and authorization controls. For two corresponding software solutions, SAP Process Control and SAP Access Control, this would make integration necessary.

Central source of
information for
compliance
As you already know, and as shown in Fig. 16.42, SAP Process Control is responsible for the ICS compliance management process as a whole. This application contains all compliance-relevant information, in particular controls and the results of tests and assessments for both authorization controls and all other controls. SAP Access Control takes the role of a supplier. If we look at the existing technical integration options individually, we discover that previously, there was only one integration scenario (up to Release 3.0): SAP Access Control forwards the results of the risk analysis from the component *Risk Analysis & Remediation* to SAP Process Control.

From a content perspective, this situation can, corresponding to the two types of risk in SAP Access Control (segregation of duties risk and critical action risk) be concerned with the risks that can be traced back either to critical authorization combinations ❶ or to the assignment of critical authorizations ❷. You can analyze the risk for users or for authorization roles.

Java vs. ABAP – the
challenge
overcome
The different technology platforms of SAP Access Control up to Release 5.3 (Java-based technology) and SAP Process Control (SAP NetWeaver/ABAP) have heavily restricted the possible integration scenarios. It would not be possible to bring the Java and ABAP worlds together without compromises with regard to flexibility, performance, and expense. In Release 10.0 of the SAP solution for GRC, the situation is very different: SAP Access Control and SAP Process Control are harmonized to a large extent, share (partially) the same objects (organizations) in the data model, and offer above all an integration scenario regarding the *mitigating controls* ❸ (see Fig. 16.42).

Within the SAP Access Control component Access Risk Management, the mitigating controls are used to minimize the authorization risks from their assignment. From

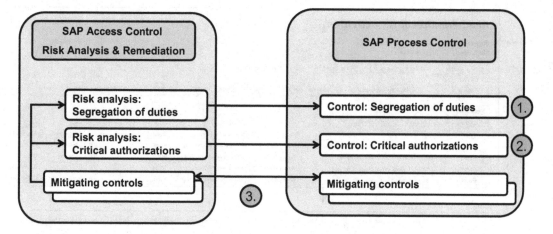

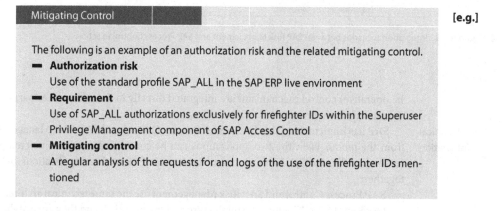

Figure 16.42   Existing integration scenarios between SAP Access Control and SAP Process Control

a content perspective, the mitigating controls are manual, semi-automated, or automated application controls within business processes.

Mitigating Control			**[e.g.]**

The following is an example of an authorization risk and the related mitigating control.
- **Authorization risk**
  Use of the standard profile SAP_ALL in the SAP ERP live environment
- **Requirement**
  Use of SAP_ALL authorizations exclusively for firefighter IDs within the Superuser Privilege Management component of SAP Access Control
- **Mitigating control**
  A regular analysis of the requests for and logs of the use of the firefighter IDs mentioned

It goes without saying that the need for ICS activities that are involved in the mitigating controls in SAP Access Control and SAP Process Control should be identical to ensure the unity of an ICS framework. From Release 10.0 this unity is ensured, and mitigating controls can be included in effectiveness tests or other assessments for SAP Process Control and can also be automated.

Identical controls

16.6.3 Integration with SAP Risk Management

The processes in risk and compliance management go hand in hand, as you have already learned from Sect. 4.3.5, "SAP Risk Management 10.0." On one hand, risks play an important part in the ICS, and on the other hand, depending on the risk level (strategic

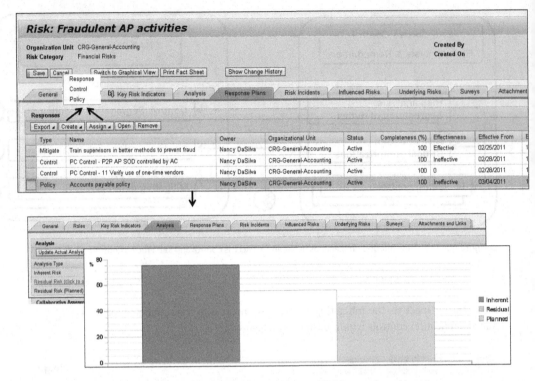

□ **Figure 16.43**   Integration scenarios between SAP Risk Management and SAP Process Control in action

vs. operative) control mechanisms are integrated directly in the processes as part of the risk management process.

Technical integration
SAP has implemented this fact in SAP Process Control and SAP Risk Management: from the *process view*, the two applications can be considered as two connected processes (see Fig. 16.43). However, from the technical view, these applications belong together:

- SAP Process Control and SAP Risk Management use the same technical architecture (see Sect. 16.2.1, "Technical Architecture and Installation") and they are installed at the same time.
- Both applications do have separate hierarchies in the Implementation Guide, but some of the configurations still apply for both SAP Risk Management and SAP Process Control.
- Both applications have the same authorization concept: a user can be a user of SAP Risk Management and SAP Process Control simultaneously.
- Both applications can use the same objects: organizational units, processes, risks, controls, policies. For the summary regarding the integration of SAP Process Control and SAP Risk Management at process level, see Sect. 4.3.5. You already know that the most important integration points enable you to minimize the risk in SAP Risk Management via integration of SAP Process Control.

As you can see in Fig. 16.43, there are two important integration scenarios:

- When processing remediation plans (risk response), you can use an existing control or policy as a risk-minimizing measure.
- If there is no suitable control or policy available for minimizing the risk, in SAP Risk Management you can generate a workflow-based request to assign a new control or policy in SAP Process Control.
- As well as the existence of a policy or control, you also need information, for example, about the effectiveness of the policy or control in order to come to a conclusion about the potential of a risk minimization. The information about the result of the effectiveness test from SAP Process Control and about the assessment of the design is forwarded to SAP Risk Management and displayed in the fields COMPLETENESS and EFFECTIVENESS.

The measurable effect of the risk minimization can be traced in the work area ANALYSIS (and in reporting): the net risk reflects the risk level after measures, and you can configure the degree of the effect in the IMG (example: by what percentage does the gross risk reduce if a control has been assigned and if, according to SAP Process Control test results, this control has been rated as effective?).

16.6.4 Merging GRC, Strategy, and Performance Topics

As well as GRC, *strategy and performance management* also belong on the agenda of C-level management, and the central questions cover the following areas:

- **Risks and opportunities**
  Which risks influence my organization and to what extent are these risks relevant for my performance objectives? How can we assess risks and opportunities? How do we have to consider risks when defining strategies and policies?
- **Internal control environment**
  Are the correct compliance, performance, and other controls established? Are they efficient? Can established controls minimize risks? How can we ensure that deviations from strategic objects are detected early?
- **Strategy**
  How can the strategy be translated into policies and performance plans? Which objectives are useful taking the given risk tolerance into account?
- **Performance**
  To what extent is my performance at risk? Are internal and external opportunities used optimally? Do the business activities correspond to the parameters planned in the strategy and business plan?

When faced with the challenge of finding a proper balance between risk orientation, fulfilling compliance requirements, and a performance that can be planned, whilst simultaneously maintaining sight of strategic objectives, software support can be very helpful.

If you consider the existing landscape of SAP applications, you will see that the business performance optimization products include applications that cover BPM and GRC objectives. Thus it is obvious that the two large areas BPM and GRC belong together. However, to what extent is this common theme supported by integration scenarios?

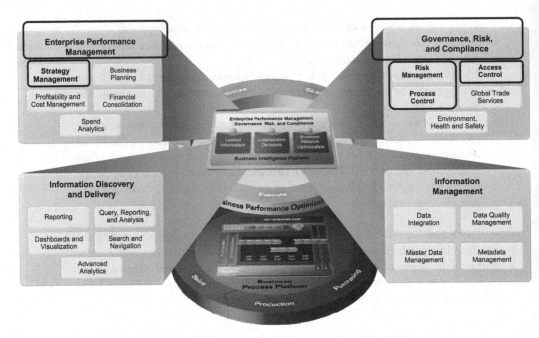

◘ Figure 16.44   SAP software products relevant for business performance optimization (source: SAP)

Figure 16.44 summarizes the products relevant for business performance. Whilst the individual GRC applications are integrated, connecting solutions for *Enterprise Performance Management* and *Governance, Risk, and Compliance* is still a challenge. Even in Release 10.0, the integration between SAP Process Control and Strategy Management is only possible to a limited extent.

[e.g.]   Integration Scenario

To enable the forwarding of aggregated risk exposure values (summarized values for all or selected risks within a risk category), you can implement the integration between SAP Strategy Management and SAP Risk Management by setting up and configuring web services. The result is visible as one of the key performance indicators (KPI) within a corresponding strategic objective in SAP Strategy Management.

The key figure "Total Risk Exposure" is used in SAP Strategy Management, in addition to other KPIs, to calculate an objective performance index. This integration scenario thus enables a two-dimensional view of strategic objectives:

Historical operational KPIs together with the risk exposure values that have a clear future reference allow a more comprehensive assessment of the goal achievement.

The scenario presented comprises only a very basic exchange of data between applications that, from the process perspective, largely represent isolated silos.

The great potential that would be opened up by bringing four categories together–*controls, risks, strategy, and performance* (already visible at the level of recognized refer-

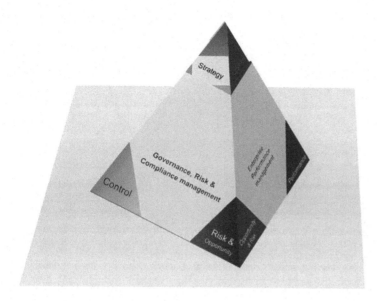

❏ Figure 16.45 High-level vision of an integrated BPM process

ence models, see Sect. 3.2.12, "Summary View of Reference Models") – for an integrated and interdisciplinary BPM process (BPM = Business Performance Management) revives a great vision (see Fig. 16.45).

16.7 Summary

In this chapter, you have learned how to automate an ICS process using SAP Process Control 10.0. This involves bringing two views of the ICS together based on the roles of the individual actors:

- Content view: in summary, this is called ICS documentation
- Process view: this refers to various workflow-controlled ICS activities

In Chap. 17, "Implementation of Automated Test and Monitoring Scenarios in the SAP ERP Environment," you will see a deeper presentation of one of the most important ICS automation scenarios: the integration of the ICS processes with the ERP systems in which compliance-relevant business processes take place.

16.2 Summary

Implementation of Automated Test and Monitoring Scenarios in the SAP ERP Environment

All preparatory work is complete: the legal compliance requirements, the controls in SAP ERP, and the ICS process view come together in automated test and monitoring scenarios.

In Chap. 16, "ICS Automation Using SAP Process Control," you learned how to automate an ICS process using SAP Process Control. The highest degree of automation in an internal control system (ICS) is creating test and monitoring results for IT-supported business processes "at the touch of a button." This great vision has now become reality in the SAP environment. In this chapter, you will learn about the options that are available for automating test and monitoring scenarios in the SAP environment. You will also learn how to implement one of these options, the integration of compliance management software with ERP systems, in Release 10.0 using the example of SAP Process Control (component of the SAP solutions for GRC).

In the second part of this book, you have become familiar with control and monitoring scenarios in the SAP ERP environment. The level of detail of the descriptions was high enough – combined with the knowledge that you will acquire in this chapter – to allow you to set up individual automated solutions based on SAP solutions for GRC independently (the descriptions were broken down to the level of the database tables and fields).

17.1 Automated Test and Monitoring Scenarios in the SAP Environment

Both external and internal audit have to react to the increased automation of ERP-supported business processes appropriately. Thus, in the last few decades, not only has a new audit approach become established (the transaction audit, see Sect. 2.1.2 "Transaction Audit as Audit Approach in the IT Environment"), but new tools and other integration options have also arisen.

Chapter 14, "Examples of Efficiency-Oriented and Profitability-Oriented Analysis Scenarios in SAP ERP," explained how not only legal compliance but also profitability and efficiency in business processes can be a reason for monitoring scenarios. This chapter gave you an impression of what expertise you need in the area of SAP ERP processes and controls to enable you to implement corresponding controls.

In the pages that follow, you will learn about three types of compliance-related automated test and monitoring options in the SAP environment. Each option is valid in its own right depending on the organizational and system framework conditions. In this section, you will learn about the properties, areas of use, and the advantages and disadvantages of the individual options.

17.1.1 Offline CAAT Tools

The first option is CAAT tools (CAAT = *Computer Assisted Auditing Techniques*), in particular, offline data analyses using CAAT tools. This type of data analysis is one of the options for automating test and monitoring operations.

Main characteristics of offline data analysis

What distinguishes this type of offline analysis?

— The auditor works with data extracts. These are imported into an analysis tool in **.txt* or **.csv format* and subjected to various analysis logic. Either the auditor extracts the data from the customer's system himself, or on request, and with a description of the required field structure, the organization provides the data.

— The analysis logic mentioned is either already available as predefined scripts or the auditor defines or adjusts it himself. Adjusting the analysis logic (queries) requires a certain level of technical knowledge about the analysis tool, but overall, the complexity of the query administration is relatively low and can be mastered by someone who is not a computer programmer.

— The object of the evaluations is primarily transaction data (electronic documents from the various business events: purchase orders, invoice receipts and goods receipts, asset and material movements, manual postings, etc.).

— The analysis and the interpretation of the results that cannot be automated are a main part of the work with CAAT. The analysis is generally independent and manual. The auditor completes his work "behind closed doors"; the results are generally only communicated to the customer as part of the communication of the audit findings.

Know-how requirements

In addition to the technical know-how for dealing with the corresponding tools (data import, implementation of the analysis scenarios and use of statistical functions, saving the analysis results, etc.), knowledge of the processes from which the data to be analyzed arose is primarily required.

[e.g.]

Required Knowledge in the SAP-Supported Order to Cash Process

Let us look at two examples that illustrate the knowledge that the auditor must have:

■ To evaluate open customer items, you have to know that the customer master data is located in tables KNA1 and KNB1, that the open items are in table BSID, and that the cleared items move from table BSID to table BSAD. Knowledge of the individual transactions that make up the process (invoicing, manual invoices, clearing transactions, etc.) is essential.

■ To perform plausibility checks in dunning, you have to know how dunning runs are executed and by which program, and which dunning levels are set up, etc. At data model level, you need an overview of the relevant tables, the master data, and the documents (for example, you have to know that table KNB5 contains relevant dunning data).

The auditor can acquire the corresponding process, data model, and control know-how in the SAP environment using the methods described in Chap. 5, "Audit-Relevant SAP Basics."

Why do we use offline data analyses? Above all, we use offline data analyses because the respective tools offer evaluation functions that are difficult to recreate with other means. For example, using the *Benford Law-based* analysis, you can detect conspicuous patterns in the distribution of figures (if the maximum tolerance limits for purchase orders have been deliberately bypassed by splitting the orders). Other various defined, statistical functions allow you to identify transactions entered at weekends, or to apply various sampling methods.

Advantages of offline data analyses

There are other notable advantages:

- The auditor often has to deal with several million transactions. The approach of taking samples is not appropriate for all audit procedures, and CAAT tools offer a great deal of assistance here.
- In offline mode, the auditor is generally independent, both with regard to the availability of contact persons and the system and with regard to system performance.
- The same scenarios can be used for data that comes from different systems. With flexible importing of data from different sources, the only remaining task is to ensure that the mapping is performed correctly.
- The specialized data analysis tools can process large quantities of data in fractions of a second. Compared with online evaluations, which can bring some systems to their knees, this is one of the greatest advantages.

Products from two leading manufacturers have established themselves on the market: ACL and IDEA. For simpler analyses, in practice, Microsoft Access or Excel is also used.

In practice, in addition to the necessity for data and process know-how, there are two great challenges: extracting the required data from the system, and converting this data into the format that can be used by the data analysis tools.

Challenges of working with data analysis tools

There are some technical means for *extracting* the data in the SAP environment:

Data extraction in the SAP environment

- The Data Browser (transaction SE16) is often used. You can use it to call up the contents of database tables individually. However, for performance reasons, this option is often not sufficient.
- The Audit Information System (AIS, see Sect. 4.3.8, "SAP Audit Information System") offers some common predefined scenarios for data extraction (for example, for accounting documents, from tables BKPF and BSEG).
- You can also use the DART tool (DART = Data Retention Tool) to extract further data. In practice, the functionality of this tool is used to provide data to tax authorities. However, this tool is rather inflexible, particularly with regard to changing the preconfigured data structures.
- In practice, ABAP programs are often written for complex data extracts involving multiple tables. Due to the simple logic, the programming effort is low and the programs can be reused.

With regard to the *format* of the data, note that you can generally reuse the extraction results with no further effort. However, if only spool lists are available, in which the individual data fields are arranged below one another and otherwise distributed irregularly, these cannot be directly reused. In such cases, separate tools (such as MONARCH) are available that allow you to convert the unmanageable spool lists into a database format by setting up recognition patterns.

Offline data analyses: tax audit

What are the areas of use for offline data analysis tools in practice? Tax authorities worldwide use data extracts to perform tax audits. In Germany, for example, this procedure is regulated via the GDPdU regulation (principles regarding data access and the verifiability of digital documents, administration instruction in the form of a letter from the German Federal Ministry of Finance from July 16, 2001). GDPdU regulates the storage of digital documents and the obligation of the person subject to tax to co-operate. This person has to provide the data required for the external audit, including "transfer of data in various formats." From a content perspective, the objective of this type of audit is to check the accuracy of the taxes paid by the organization (sales tax, corporate tax, tax on wages, etc.) by analyzing the individual business transactions. For the offline analysis tools, the tax authorities use standard analysis scenarios that have been developed and that allow a check "at the push of a button."

Offline data analyses: external audit and internal audit

In addition to use by the tax authorities, offline analysis scenarios are increasingly being used in external and internal audit.

The audit focuses on individual business transactions, the detailed analysis of which can provide information about business processes.

[e.g.]

Document-Related Check in External and Internal Audit

A few examples of analysis scenarios are summarized below:
- *Accounts payable accounting:* detailed analysis of the ageing structure, evaluation of invoices entered twice, etc.
- *Accounts receivable accounting:* support for the selection of business transactions for the cut-off date check, detailed analysis of the ageing and country structure of the open items, plausibility checks in dunning (dunning blocks, dunning levels, etc.)
- *Asset accounting:* detailed analysis of the capitalizations, acquisitions and disposals, manual depreciation, etc.
- *General ledger:* analysis of manual postings, manual posting to accounts that are only supposed to be posted to automatically, etc.
- *Materials management:* inventory postings, plausibility checks for the material valuation, goods receipts without purchase orders, etc.

Segregation of duties check via documents

Amongst other things, the individual transactions can provide a reliable statement about the segregation of duties in business processes. If the analysis of the authorizations assigned deliver information about the *potential* for possible violations (for example, in the area of segregation of duties or tolerance limits), the individual documents themselves provide information about the *actual irregularities that have taken place*, as the user ID of the person entering the document is logged in the individual transactions.

> **Authorization-Related Data Analysis**   **[e.g.]**
>
> A typical segregation of duties scenario in purchasing, for example, is the check of the individual purchase orders, goods receipts, and invoice receipts, and the identification of related transactions entered by one and the same user.
>
> In the segregation of duties analysis of payment-relevant transactions, for example, a comparison of the person who enters the payment proposal list with the user who executed the payment run would be feasible. The payment process is seldom restricted to SAP, and thus similar evaluations can also be executed in downstream specialized payment systems (such as that provided by the Swiss software manufacturer Mammut) by, for example, comparing the person who enters a payment with the person who approved the payment.

In Chap. 12, "Fraud in an SAP System," we gave examples of data models that can contribute to uncovering fraud. Due to the special evaluation features, the offline data analysis tools enable some analysis scenarios that, for example, would be difficult to implement with SAP queries, such as the following: **Fraud**

- Postings by clerks that demonstrate a high ratio of reversals
- Postings at weekends or unusual times of the day
- Manual postings to accounts that have not been used for a long time
- Postings with high amounts close to the end of a period to customer accounts that have not been used for a long time
- Suppliers with similar master data (bank account etc.) to the employee
- Splitting of purchase orders to get around the maximum limit

However, there are no scenarios that can detect fraud with one hundred percent reliability. The aim of fraud-related evaluations is therefore more to identify the set of business transactions that show potential for fraud and that must subsequently be investigated in detail manually.

We primarily associate the acronym CAAT with audit and compliance issues, but if we look beyond this application and consider the functionality of CAAT, we soon discover that we can use CAAT tools not only to address audit-related ICS objectives, but also operational objectives in all possible IT-supported processes imaginable. If only the big disadvantage of offline data analyses did not exist: as the term implies, the evaluations are ex post.   **Disadvantage**

17.1.2 Online CAAT Reports and Evaluations

A further CAAT category is the various online evaluation options for the ICS-relevant data in ERP systems. In the SAP ERP environment, there is a whole range of options in this field, and they can generally be grouped into two areas: **Two types**

- **Reports in the SAP ERP system**
  In the user menu, which is structured according to the business processes, there is a separate information system in every section (for example: ACCOUNTING • FINANCIAL ACCOUNTING • ACCOUNTS PAYABLE • INFORMATION SYSTEM). The Audit

Information System (AIS) provides a summary of more than 600 audit-relevant ABAP reports in a clear structure. The AIS is available in every SAP ERP system as standard and all you have to do is configure it (see Sect. 4.3.8). SAP queries and SAP infosets also enable you to generate online evaluations quickly and easily. Numerous examples in Chap. 14, "Examples of Efficiency-Oriented and Profitability-Oriented Analysis Scenarios in SAP ERP," describe their use in detail.

- **Online monitoring tools and services that can be connected to the SAP ERP system**

  SAP Solution Manager (or its business process and SLA monitoring functionalities, see Sects. 4.4.1, "Direct ICS Content: What Controls Are Available in SAP?" and 6.2.5, "SAP Solution Manager"), the RSECNOTE tool, and SAP services such as SAP EarlyWatch Alert or the Security Optimization Service should be mentioned here. *SAP NetWeaver Business Warehouse* can also offer the option of developing ICS-relevant reports and queries.

Disadvantages of offline and online CAAT tools

In comparison to the offline data analysis tools, online evaluations offer a clear advantage, but the test and assessment results for both options are evaluated manually in an ICS process, and this is generally associated with a number of disadvantages:

- *The ICS-relevant documentation* for the respective evaluation option – the risk addressed, the control objective, the importance of the fields in the selection criteria, the assessment of the results, etc. – cannot be defined or cannot be defined sufficiently.
- The *evaluation results are generally assessed and logged* manually: The decision about whether the result is correct or not is always down to the discretion of one person – and with offline and online CAAT tools, this decision has to be retaken every time new evaluation results are available; the result of the assessment is generally also documented manually, for example, in Microsoft Excel.
- A differentiated *delivery of the evaluation results* to persons responsible (control or process owners), or printing out and filing an alert, or in the best case extracting it in file form and saving it, or sending it by e-mail, is suboptimal from a compliance perspective. A compliance process must be *compliant*. This means that the principle of traceability and the resulting logging requirements must be fulfilled, which is difficult to achieve with a manual process.
- The aggregation of monitoring and assessment results collated in Microsoft Excel, for example, makes *timely and centralized reporting* a resource-intensive challenge.

All in all, there are some disadvantages with both the offline and online CAAT tools, amongst other things because they are not integrated in an automated ICS process as a whole.

17.1.3 Compliance Management Software

Offline and online CAAT vs. compliance management software

Why have we distinguished compliance management software (CMS) as a separate option in this book – in addition to offline and online CAAT tools? Basically, similarly to online CAAT tools, CMS enables tests and monitoring "at the touch of a button." However, CMS also offers the option of overcoming the disadvantages mentioned in Sect. 17.1.2, "Online CAAT Reports and Evaluations."

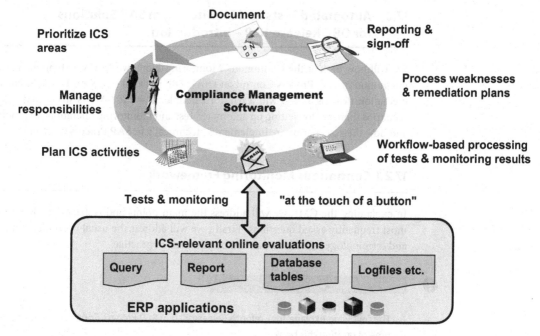

□ Figure 17.1 Test and monitoring automation using compliance management software

As you can see in Fig. 17.1, from an ICS perspective, automation means not only generating the results of test and monitoring options (for example, whether a control is effective or not) "at the touch of a button," but also including these results in the overall ICS process, including the documentation, right up to problem handling and reporting.

There are various ways for CMS to access the data in the target system:

- For example, the data can be the results of online CAAT tool-based evaluations (queries and reports in the target ERP system).
- The logic mapped in queries from CAAT tools can be reconstructed in CMS. However, there can be restrictions with regard to complex statistical functions, such as Benford's Law etc.

At this point you may also think of the *broadcasting features* within SAP NetWeaver BW that allow you to send the results of reports to users. However, this sending function does not allow more extensive functions that you would expect in an ICS process. The compliance management software in which test and monitoring results are broadcast (various tasks are sent to users via workflow) can therefore be considered as the next level of evolution of CAAT – a level at which the ICS process as a whole is automated to the maximum.

17.2   Automated Tests and Monitoring in SAP Solutions for GRC Release 10.0 – Introduction

We will now look at the Continuous Monitoring Framework (CMF) that enables the integration of SAP Process Control and SAP ERP in detail (see Sect. 16.4.4, "Issue Remediation Process"). You will learn, for example, how the CMF is structured, which scenarios there are for setting up automated test and monitoring operations in practice, and how these scenarios are implemented technically in SAP Process Control.

17.2.1 Continuous Monitoring Framework

In explaining the CMF, we will address the main points and restrict ourselves to the most frequently asked questions. Firstly, we will address the usual misunderstandings and terminology mutations that can be observed in practice.

> **❶ Note: Release Version**
>
> The following explanations refer to Release 10.0 of SAP Process Control current at the time of printing this book.

> **❶ Continuous Monitoring Framework – Terms**
>
> In practice, various names have become established for the Continuous Monitoring Framework (CMF), such as the following:
> - Automated Rules Framework (ARF)
> - Automated Controls Framework (ACF)
> - Automated Monitoring Framework (AMF)
> - Continuous Control Monitoring (CCM)
> - Continuous Monitoring Framework (CMF)
>
> However, all names refer to the same principle: the integration of compliance management software with SAP ERP systems for the purpose of setting up test and monitoring scenarios. With reference to SAP Process Control, however, only two terms are used – Automated Rules Framework and Continuous Monitoring Framework. These terms correspond to two functional areas.

As Fig. 17.2 shows, there are two different and independent areas in SAP Process Control in which you can set up automated test and monitoring scenarios:

1. **Continuous Monitoring**
   This section represents the Continuous Monitoring Framework (CMF). This is the new and considerably enhanced functionality available from Release 10.0.

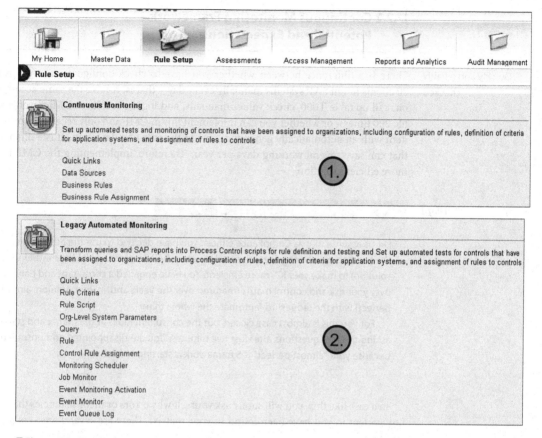

□ Figure 17.2 Two CM functionalities in SAP Process Control 10.0

2. **Legacy Automated Monitoring**
   This is where "old" versions are located, referred to as the Automated Rules Framework.

Unfortunately, SAP has not integrated the old functionality in the new version. This means that predefined scenarios that are available in the standard delivery scope of the SAP solutions for GRC are only available in the Automated Rules Framework, and not in the Continuous Monitoring Framework, and cannot always be used in the Continuous Monitoring Framework. In this book, we always refer to the Continuous Monitoring Framework (CMF) – the new functions in the SAP solutions for GRC 10.0. The example in Sect. 17.3.5, "Automation Using Predefined Best Practice Scenarios," is an exception that describes the structure of a predefined scenario from the older release.

17.2.2 Continuous Monitoring Framework – Potential and Expectations

Quickly and reliably checked

There is a difference between whether you have to check configuration settings for 20 clients in ten SAP systems manually every day – that is, receive the same access, log on, call up table T000, check values manually, and log the results in a Microsoft Excel file 200 times – or whether you can implement this in CMF and only receive a workflow item with an automatically generated issue in the case of a deviation. It is a difference that can save several working days per year. Therefore, implementing the CMF is the more efficient solution.

[e.g.]

Implementing the Control Matrix

Let us assume that as Compliance Officer, you have decided to use the advantages of the test and monitoring scenarios and to set up SAP Process Control (or another CMS solution) to make your ICS more efficient. You have engaged a consultant and handed over your risk and control matrix (matured over the years and, in your opinion, almost perfect) with the request to "automate the whole thing."

For you this is almost case closed, but the consultant looks at the matrix and starts asking the first questions after just five minutes. You are disappointed and unsettled because your "almost perfect" ICS framework is starting to falter.

In a case like this, you will surely ask yourself why errors or inconsistencies that were not evident to you have been found in your matrix. There are several answers to this question:·

- **Mixing of multiple controls**
  A documented control can often hide several possible control mechanisms, meaning that more specific information is required.
- **Descriptions are too general**
  The control descriptions are often too general – for example, no transactions are mentioned, meaning that it is not possible to connect the control to the underlying database tables/fields/objects, etc. without further effort. In practice, phrases such as *illustrative controls*, adopted from CobiT with copy & paste, are often used.

Note: CMF – the Devil Is in the Detail

Remind yourself of Chap. 14, "Examples of Efficiency-Oriented and Profitability-Oriented Analysis Scenarios in SAP ERP," in which you saw the level of detail of documentation required for setting up an automated test or monitoring scenario. This should give you a good impression of the initial effort and the skills required.

- **In-house developments in the system**
  The *in-house developments* in an ERP system are not always known as such. However, apart from the CMS functions, a consultant will be an expert (in an ideal case)

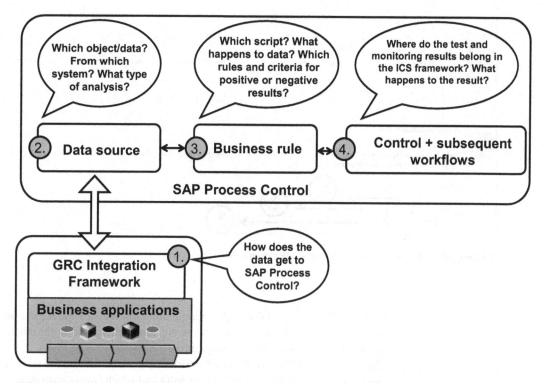

Figure 17.3   Main elements of the Automated Rules Framework in SAP Process Control

only in the compliance-relevant *standard processes* of an ERP system. Therefore, if the in-house developments are not documented precisely, mistaken assumptions or conclusions can be made.

There can be many other reasons for information from a risk and control matrix being insufficient for automating a control or risk assessment. A good consultant will certainly have the most common and efficient test and analysis scenarios in the SAP ERP environment to hand. However, the consultant's actual task is more about guiding the customer in analyzing what he wants, and helping the customer to create a documented specification – something that is required for every control.

Specifying controls

When working out the specifications, you will discover that it is not always necessary or possible to automate all mechanisms. Sometimes, a cost and benefits analysis will show simply and clearly that the risk to be covered or the information value gained is disproportionate to the implementation cost and effort that arises from automation.

Costs vs. benefits

Structure the CMF in SAP Process Control

If you had to summarize the structure of the Continuous Monitoring Framework in a few words, this would look as follows (see Fig. 17.3).

Let us take a closer look at Fig. 17.3.

Structure and main elements

- The *GRC Integration Framework* ❶ ensures that master data, control data, and trans-action data, as well as events, find their way from the target system to SAP Process

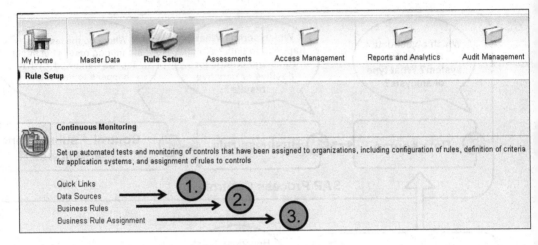

◻ Figure 17.4 Order for setting up the automated test and monitoring scenarios

Control. One part of the GRC Integration Framework is Real Time Agents: on one hand, they ensure the connection between different systems, and on the other, contain predefined analysis logic or programs.

— The *data sources* ❷ in SAP Process Control define which data is read from which system using the GRC Integration Framework and which type of analysis this data is subjected to. Here, there is a fundamental differentiation between the individual technical options for transferring data from an SAP ERP system to the GRC solutions.

— The *business rules* ❸ define selection criteria for the data to be analyzed and contain analysis rules and logic for applying and issuing the criteria. The analysis rules form the core of the CMF and they are used to determine whether as the result of a test, for example, an issue is to be generated with a specific status.

— The *control* ❹ forms the bridge between the technical structure (scripts and rules) as part of the CMF and the ICS framework. Test and assessment results are part of the ICS process (problem solving) that you will be familiar with from Sect. 16.4.3, "Planning Process, Tests, and Assessments."

When setting up test and monitoring scenarios, you bring the individual CMF elements together in the order shown in Fig. 17.4.

Firstly, in the work area RULE SETUP and then under CONTINUOUS MONITORING, you set up data sources ❶. You then create or adjust the rules ❷, whereby these build on the previously defined data sources. In the last step, you assign the rules to the individual controls ❸.

❶ Prerequisite for Setting Up Test and Monitoring Scenarios

The prerequisite for setting up test and monitoring scenarios is that the GRC Integration Framework, including the connection between SAP Process Control and the target system, is set up.

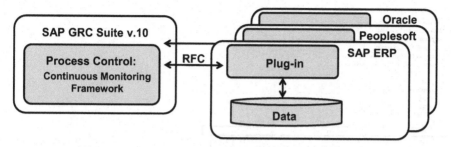

■ **Figure 17.5** Integration framework of SAP solutions for GRC 10.0 – simplified illustration

17.3 Setting up CMF Scenarios in SAP Process Control

Now that you have received a brief impression of the CMF structure in SAP Process Control Release 10.0, we will describe the individual steps for setting up CMF scenarios in SAP Process Control.

17.3.1 Connecting SAP Solutions for GRC with Business Applications

Before the CMF can work, integration is required between the SAP solutions for GRC and the business applications in SAP ERP. What do you need in the target system to connect it to SAP Process Control?

We have already stated that to do this, you need a CMF component – the GRC Integration Framework. This has primarily the following tasks/functions:

- It ensures a connection between the systems.
- It contains predefined analysis logic and programs.

To be more precise, it is the *plug-ins* within the GRC Integration Framework that fulfill these two tasks, as well as the connectors. The plug-ins have to be installed in a target system. The connectors are based, for example, on RFC technology (RFC = Remote Function Call) if the situation involves connecting SAP ERP systems. Figure 17.5 shows a simplified illustration of the GRC Integration Framework.

Plug-ins

In project practice, a question that is often asked is whether there are overlaps between the plug-ins for SAP Access Control and the plug-ins for SAP Process Control, and whether, for example, both plug-ins can be installed on the same system. The answer: from Release 10.0, both components use the same plug-ins; it was a different situation for the previous releases of the SAP solutions for GRC.

Plug-ins: SAP Process Control and SAP Access Control

Note: Installing Plug-Ins

The official information source for the installation of plug-ins is the Installation Guide available on SAP Service Marketplace (https://service.sap.com/instguides).

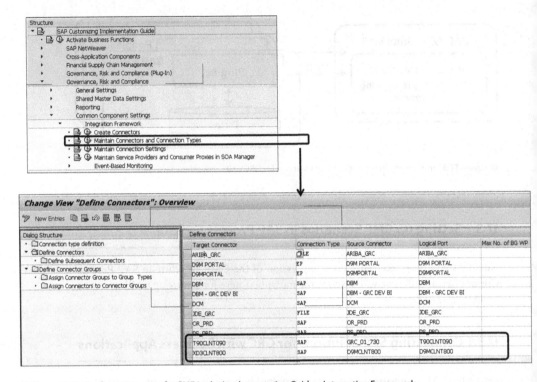

Figure 17.6   Configuration steps for CMF in the Implementation Guide – Integration Framework

> For SAP Process Control, installation file GRCPIERP is used – a file that is shared with SAP Access Control. For SAP Access Control, a further installation file is required, GRCPINW, but this is not relevant for SAP Process Control.

What configuration is required for the GRC Integration Framework in SAP Process Control? As you can see in Fig. 17.6, there are some menu items in the IMG under GRC • COMMON COMPONENT SETTINGS • INTEGRATION FRAMEWORK.

Setting up connectors   The first three menu items are mandatory and are processed in order from top to bottom.

1. **Create Connectors**
   Call up transaction SM59 and maintain the RFC connections.

2. **Maintain Connectors and Connection Types**
   In this configuration step you define connectors using the RFC connections previously created. Figure 17.6 shows two connectors used in the following sections for maintaining data sources and business rules.

3. **Maintain Connection Settings**
   You perform this action to complete the processing of the connectors for SAP Process Control. Select the integration scenario AM (Automated Monitoring). This

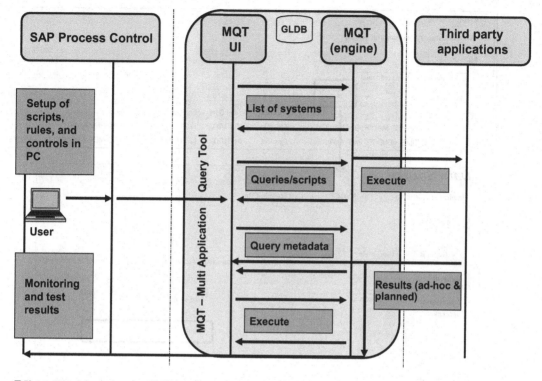

◻ Figure 17.7 Schematic setup of MQT

integration scenario is used for the CMF in SAP Process Control; further scenarios from SAP Access Control may be used.

4. In the subsequent step, you define permitted connectors for each subscenario (see Chap. 18, "Experiences from Practice and Projects").

What is the situation for non-SAP systems? You can use SAP NetWeaver Process Integration or individual web services to connect further systems. — Connecting non-SAP systems

There is also another option: together with the SAP partner Greenlight, SAP offers the Multi Application Query Tool (MQT, see Fig. 17.7).

The MQT can be used as an equivalent for the web service-based GRC Integration Framework and basically has the same tasks: it establishes a connection between two systems and delivers the programs for importing the required data from a third party application. MQT uses web services to establish the connection to SAP Process Control. The means for data extraction and analysis have to be developed on an application-specific basis. — Multi Application Query Tool

To find out what alternatives there are to MQT, see Sect. 17.4.1, "Use of SAP NetWeaver Business Warehouse for Continuous Monitoring." One of the options is to use SAP NetWeaver BW as an "agent" between third party applications and SAP Process Control. SAP NetWeaver BW has a very flexible ETL function (ETL = extract, transform, load). It allows you to extract data from almost any source and provide it in a form required for the analysis with BW. — Alternatives to MQT

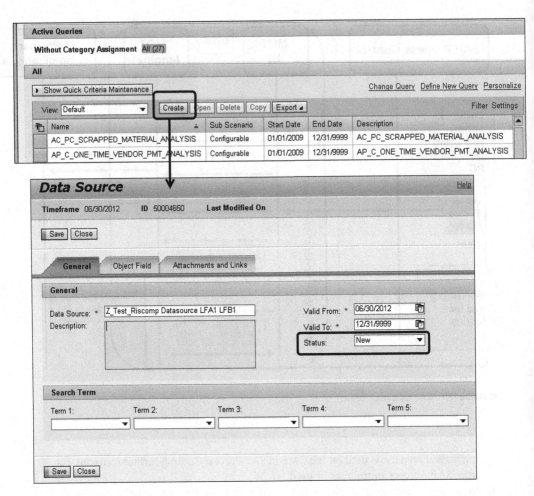

■ **Figure 17.8**   Creating a new data source

In practice, workarounds in which data is written to a Z* table in an SAP system from a third party system via web services using an ABAP program are also used. This data can then be applied using configurable rules. This procedure can only be recommended if the data model remains stable, as adjustments (such as adding new fields) can be very time-consuming.

17.3.2 Data Sources in SAP Process Control

A data source is the key element between the test and monitoring rules in SAP Process Control and the GRC Integration Framework. Figure 17.8 shows how to create a new data source.

On the initial entry screen – the header of the data source – you define the name, as well as the general description, validity period, and the status. The aim of the status

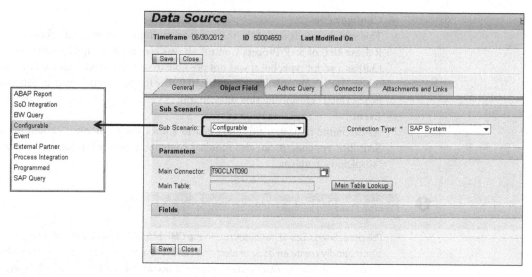

Figure 17.9 Available subscenarios for the CMF in SAP Process Control

control is to prevent data sources that have not been completely configured from being used in a subsequent maintenance step. You can also assign further search terms (configurable in the IMG) to the data source.

The next step is to define the details of a data source. This is one of the most important steps: you have to define whether the data source can address programs, queries, and database tables directly in the ERP target system. As Fig. 17.9 shows, this can take place in various ways; a data source can use various technical means to access the data in an SAP ERP target system.

These means are categorized as *subscenarios*; in detail, the following subscenarios are possible:

Subscenarios

— **ABAP Report**

This subscenario uses the standard ABAP programs for test and monitoring purposes. If you consider, for example, that AIS (Audit Information System) in SAP is a collection of approximately 600 SAP standard reports, the potential that integrating AIS in the GRC-supported compliance management process offers becomes clear. Further reports can also be integrated.

The prerequisite for this is that the report only reads and does not change data. To do this, in the target ERP system, it must be released for connection to the SAP solutions for GRC.

— **SoD Integration**

This subscenario enables the integration of SAP Access Control with SAP Process Control. The aim is to forward the risk analysis results for authorizations from SAP Access Control to SAP Process Control.

— **BW Query**

The name is self-explanatory – this subscenario can be used to integrate BW queries in the CMF of SAP Process Control.

▬ **Configurable**

This subscenario is one of the most important improvements and enhancements in Release 10.0 of SAP Process Control. It was also available in the previous release (3.0) as a script type, but it was not possible to connect several tables with one another. This is now possible in Release 10.0. The further maintenance of data sources is described below using this subscenario.

▬ **Event**

As the name indicates, this subscenario allows you to monitor certain events in SAP ERP systems. It can also monitor contents in network patterns, for example, "suspicious" patterns.

❶ Note: Event-Based Control Monitoring

The predefined *Cisco SONA check rule* in the CMF of SAP Process Control can be used to automatically create an issue or alert and send it to a person responsible via workflow if a pattern similar to social security numbers occurs in the network data flow (in the USA, details of social security numbers are handled very strictly).

▬ **External Partner**

This subscenario enables the use of various web services of CMF.

▬ **Process Integration (PI)**

If an organization uses SAP NetWeaver PI, Process Integration can be connected to the CMF of SAP Process Control. In practice, Process Integration is used to manage web services between individual applications in a distributed system landscape.

▬ **Programmed**

If a more complex logic is required in connection with CMF, you can use ABAP structures developed specifically for the SAP solutions for GRC to generate new programs. As already explained, some of the predefined rules are present in the "old" framework in SAP Process Control and belong to the subscenario "Programmed" or in ARF language to the script type with the same name.

▬ **SAP Query**

This subscenario enables the use of SAP queries or SAP Quick Views. Many of the implementation examples described in Chap. 14, "Examples of Efficiency-Oriented and Profitability-Oriented Analysis Scenarios in SAP ERP," are based on these SAP functions (SAP Query and SAP Quick Views).

Advantages of SAP queries

SAP queries have two advantages: on one hand, you can use them to implement more complex data models than with configurable scripts. On the other hand, you can avoid the development of the more complex ABAP check logic associated with the often time-consuming change management process.

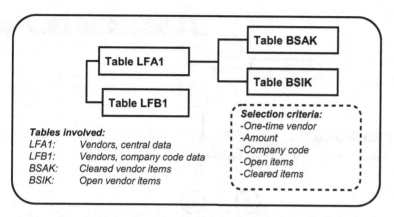

◻ Figure 17.10 Example data model of an SAP query

Example: Monitoring of Payments to One-Time Vendors   **[e.g.]**

In the following example, you could use SAP queries for automation.

— **Risk**
  Since it is possible to maintain the bank details when entering invoices for one-time vendors, this violates the segregation of duties principle. This bears a risk of fraud.

— **Control objective**
  The observance of the permitted maximum amount for the entry of incoming invoices must be checked regularly.

— **Implementation**
  In SAP Process Control, you have to set up an automated control. Using this control, when an invoice is entered for a one-time vendor, an issue is created and a person responsible is informed about this issue.

To map this control as an SAP query-based test scenario in SAP Process Control, in the SAP target system you have to create a query based on the data model described in Fig. 17.10.

You can use an SAP query created in the target system in the data source in SAP Process Control.

Once you have selected the subscenario and the main target system by defining the main connector, you have to create the object to be addressed in the target system in the data source. As described, the object depends on the subscenario selected.

If you have decided on the subscenario CONFIGURABLE, the result is as shown in Fig. 17.11.

By clicking MAIN TABLE LOOKUP ❶, you navigate to a search screen from which you can search for a table from the target system. Then, where necessary, you can add further tables and connect them to the main table ❷. This option represents a considerable increase in flexibility compared to the previous release (3.0) of SAP Process Control.

Data source: helpful additional options

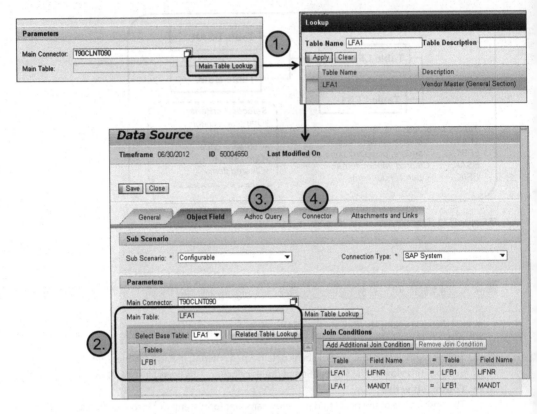

❑ Figure 17.11   Creating a data source, subscenario "Configurable"

Another function is also very useful: on the ADHOC QUERY tab ❸, you can check whether the connection from the data source to the target system works and whether data is displayed.

On the CONNECTOR tab ❹ you can add further target systems where necessary. This enables you to set up scenarios in which the same test and monitoring logic is used for multiple systems simultaneously.

Do not forget status maintenance!

When creating a data source, you cannot bypass the status REVIEW. To complete the creation of the data source and execute the next step – creation of a business rule – you have to reopen the data source, set the status to ACTIVE and save.

17.3.3 Creating Business Rules in CMF

The business rules are the core of the CMF. As the name states, a rule defines, for example, whether as test result, an issue is generated with priority high, medium, or low, or whether the test is positive. Figure 17.12 shows the creation of a business rule.

As part of "Guided Procedures," the user has to execute several steps that the system guides him through. The number and content of the steps can vary depending on which scenario type was defined in the underlying data source. In this example, we work

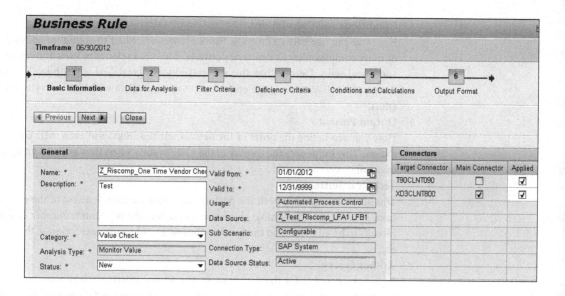

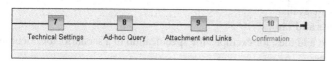

with the following maximum definition of individual steps that applies for scenario type CONFIGURABLE:

1. **Basic Information**
   In this step you enter the header data. As you can see in Fig. 17.12, in this example, when creating the business rule, the data source displayed in Sect. 17.3.2, "Data Sources in SAP Process Control," was selected. Here, in the CONNECTORS area, you have the option of defining whether one or more systems are to be addressed. With regard to the CMF, the CATEGORY field is particularly important: here you differentiate whether values or changes are checked (see Sect. 17.3.4, "Monitoring Data Changes in CMF").

2. **Data for Analysis**
   Here you have to adopt fields that you use later when defining filter criteria or analysis logic. You previously defined these fields in the data source.

3. **Filter Criteria**
   In this step, you can restrict data and only use relevant data records in the analysis.

4. **Deficiency Criteria**
   The heart of a business rule are the criteria that define whether a test or monitoring scenario delivers results. You have to define at least one deficiency criterion.

5. **Conditions and Calculations**
   Here you can use BRF+ (Business Rules Framework Plus) to configure additional or more complex filter or deficiency criteria. BRF+ is a science in itself and requires additional skills. Despite that, this step introduces a great deal of flexibility into the design of CMF scenarios, as it enables you to potentially avoid ABAP development effort.

6. **Output Format**
   Here you can define the order of the fields, their headings, and even their consolidation. This influences the display of the CMF results when they are later analyzed in detail.

7. **Technical Settings**
   This area can influence both the performance and the completeness of the evaluation, as amongst other things, here you can define the maximum number of data records to be analyzed and the synchronous or asynchronous execution of the logic etc.

8. **Ad-hoc Query**
   In the same way as for the data sources, the ad-hoc queries in business rules offer a very convenient option of executing tests to see whether the defined logic is correct and results are available.

9. **Attachments and Links**
   Here you can add files, for example, the specification of a scenario, for documentation purposes.

10. **Confirmation**
    This is the final step. Once you have performed this step, the business rule is saved with status DRAFT.

Figure 17.13 shows the contents of steps 3 and 4.

In the maintenance of filter and deficiency criteria (see Fig. 17.13), the following two settings are the most important maintenance steps:

— In the filter criteria, the selection was restricted to client 800 ❶.
— In the DEFICIENCY CRITERIA area, you can see the actual logic ❷ of the CMF rule: if, in the SAP target system, the *Is the account a one-time account?* field in the vendor master data (table LFA1) has the value X, this is an indication that the account is a one-time vendor. The rule set up would trigger an issue or an exception with priority high.

17.3.4 Monitoring Data Changes in CMF

As you saw in Sect. 17.3.3, "Creating Business Rules in CMF," when you create a business rule you have to make a basic decision: is it a value analysis or a change analysis? As you can see in Fig. 17.14, in this example, change-based monitoring is to be set up rather than value-based monitoring, and therefore the option CHANGE LOG CHECK must be entered in the CATEGORY field.

You then have to enter variants of analysis types – the variety of options has been considerably enhanced in Release 10.0. For example, you can monitor any change in the data, only changes that correspond to a specific pattern, or the number of changes.

The change analysis can analyze the changes themselves as well as the number of changes to specific field content.

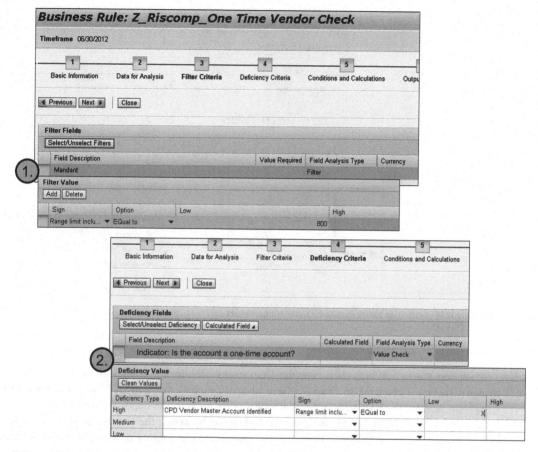

Figure 17.13 Important maintenance steps when creating a business rule

---

Monitoring changes could be useful in the following cases:

- For financial accounting, some settings in the G/L account master record are critical from an ICS perspective. This concerns, for example, the content of the Automated Postings Only field. If the content of this field is changed without authorization, under some circumstances, this can impair the ability to reconcile the general ledger with the subledgers. In this case, an automated control that triggers an alarm with every change is useful.

- Some changes only indicate irregularities if they occur frequently. It could be useful if several one-time vendors are created, for example, for each country. This can be detected by an automated control that sends a notification to the person responsible in the event of more than five changes to one-time vendors.

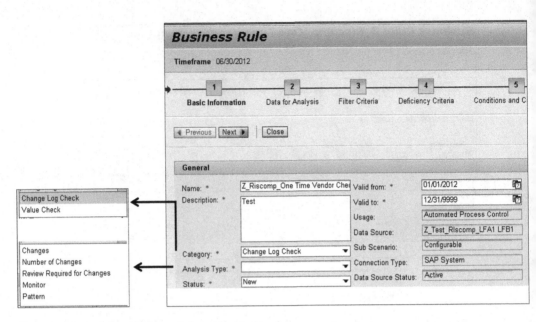

Figure 17.14   Setting up a business rule for monitoring changes

Where does the
change data come
from?
Which data does the Continuous Monitoring Framework access to analyze the changes? In Chap. 7, "General Application Controls in SAP ERP," you learned that in the SAP environment, amongst other options, the important basic principle of traceability can be implemented technically by saving the change documents and logging table changes. The CMF can apply these two logging options that are each based on different data models.

Change log tool
In practice, sometimes compliance-relevant objects are not included in the logging options. In order to enable monitoring of changes to these objects, or to be more precise, changes to the field contents in SAP Process Control, a snapshot-based logging function has been established in the CMF. Within this *change log tool*, the program GRCPCRTA_CHANGELOGGRC saves the snapshots on an object basis so that the rules in the CMF can evaluate the difference between the individual snapshots.

Limits
The obvious limitation of the change log tool, which can be traced back to the snapshot principle, is that the last change is always logged in a period that has expired since the last time program GRCPCRTA_CHANGELOGGRC was run. Under some circumstances, this can mean that not all changes are captured. Therefore, the frequency of the execution of this program has to be adapted to the expected change frequency as far as possible.

Advantage
The advantage of the change log tool in the CMF is that you can ensure the logging of compliance-relevant objects at short notice and easily, for example, as a reaction to findings from the external or internal audit.

Let us assume that as part of an SAP system audit, it was discovered that the important in-house developed Z* table that controls the implementation of the posting logic in an interface is not logged. In this case, you can activate the SAP Process Control change log specifically for this table. In comparison to the standard logging functions, this can lead to results much more quickly, as a change to the central Basis settings usually involves a time-consuming change management process. From a long-term perspective, you should of course ensure that logging is executed with the SAP standard functions as far as possible (see Sect. 7.2, "Controls for Data-Related Traceability").

17.3.5 Automation Using Predefined Best Practice Scenarios

The easiest way to automate controls is to use the predefined analysis rules in SAP Process Control. This option of finding the appropriate scenarios according to the plug & play principle was mentioned in Sect. 17.2.1, "Continuous Monitoring Framework," and you know that for predefined rules, SAP has brought together best practice experiences (for SAP and non-SAP systems). Unfortunately, the new Continuous Monitoring Framework (Release 10.0) does not contain any predefined scenarios; they are only available in the older Automated Rules Framework that originates from Release 3.0 of SAP Process Control and that is still available in Release 10.0 (see Sect. 17.2.1).

Plug & play

Note: Relevant SAP Notes

The following SAP Notes are recommended with regard to predefined scenarios within ARF:
- SAP Note 1314345 – SAP Delivered Rules Documentation
- SAP Note 1320737 – SAP Delivered Controls Documentation

In total, in SAP Process Control Release 3.0, there are more than 130 scripts for SAP applications, and at least as many rules that are based on these scripts (one script can be used in different rules).

Available scripts and rules

The range of predefined test and monitoring rules for SAP contains master data controls, configuration controls, and controls that focus on transaction data. From a content perspective, they are IT general controls (security-relevant parameters, change management controls, etc.), controls in financial accounting, in purchasing, sales and distribution, human resources, treasury, etc. Figure 17.15 shows an example. This is a predefined check rule `FIMPRCH_05T1_01_A` in CMF that helps you to monitor material price changes in financial accounting.

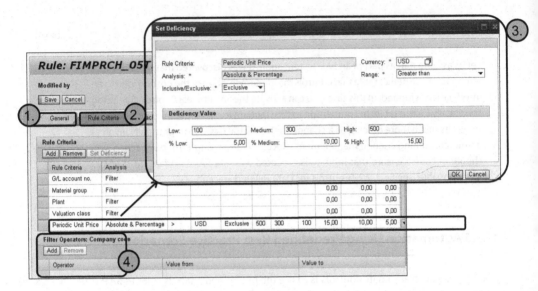

◻ Figure 17.15 Predefined rule for monitoring material price changes

[e.g.]   Example: Rule FIMPRCH_05T1_01_A – Analysis of Material Price Changes

Rule `FIMPRCH_05T1_01_A` identifies material price changes that exceed a predefined threshold value. It is a *semi-automated control*: the issue is not created automatically – it is only created once the changes detected have been analyzed. The analysis
is sent to a predefined user via workflow. As far as further ICS-relevant attributes are
concerned, this control is a detective control; the relevant assertions are rights (rights
& obligation) and valuation (valuation or allocation).

This rule is located under RULE SETUP • LEGACY AUTOMATED MONITORING • RULE.
As you can see in Fig. 17.15, the structure of the rule is much simpler in the old framework (just a few tabs and fields) than in the new Continuous Monitoring Framework.

The GENERAL area ❶ contains general header data; you actually maintain the rule
on the RULE CRITERIA tab ❷. You can define criteria and analysis logic for each field ❸
to identify issues. You can also maintain (optional) filter criteria ❹.

Use   How do you use the predefined rules in practice? You copy a rule, and once you have
adjusted the rule criteria and selected the required connectors, the rule is assigned to
a control. The advantage of predefined rules is primarily the low effort for setting them
up; this allows you to get first experience with the CMF quickly and easily.

However, as is often the case with a "one size fits all" approach, in some circumstances there can be a lack of flexibility, particularly with regard to the script type "GRC
programmed." For example, you cannot adjust the underlying analysis logic or use
additional fields. In such cases, you cannot avoid using further technical options in
CMF.

[e.g.]

Logic of the Script FIMPRCH_05T1_01_A

Let us take rule FIMPRCH_05T1 mentioned above. The script used in this rule, FIMPRCH_05T1_01_A, is the basis for the rule with the same name described.

- This script is based on a program from the GRC Integration Framework that was generated using the GRC-CMF-ABAP development framework (therefore script type "GRC-programmed"). The program reads content from database table MLHD (Material Ledger Document Header) and passes it on to SAP Process Control for analysis.
- The data extraction is based on the following selection criteria: company code, plant, G/L account number, valuation class, material group, price control, and user ID; the rule criteria use the Price field
- In SAP ERP, you can use various transactions to adjust the material price:
  CK24 – Price Update with Cost Estimate
  CK40 N – Edit Costing Run
  CKME – Activation of Planned Prices
  CKMLPC – Price Change
  MR21 – Price Change

  Therefore, it is obvious to ignore "safe" transactions in the analysis and to consider only the relevant transactions, such as MR21. However, as this field is not defined as a *filter* or *deficiency* in the script, this is not possible.

17.3.6 Connecting Controls with Rules

In the CMF context, automating test and monitoring operations means, for example, that the decisions about whether a control is effective, whether it is designed correctly (for the test scenarios), or whether there are deviations to predefined criteria (for the monitoring scenarios) are taken without involvement of a human being. You already know how the CMF is structured. The last step in setting up automated test and monitoring scenarios is connecting the ICS framework to the CMF. You do this by assigning business rules to controls (see Fig. 17.16).

You can only select a control ❶ if it has been defined as an automated control via selection of a corresponding attribute. You then assign the required business rules ❷ and in the last step, select the frequency of the test and monitoring operations ❸.

If, as part of an automated control, different systems (SAP and non-SAP systems) are addressed, or different analyses are to be executed in the same or in multiple systems (such as the analysis of changes and values), you would select the option of assigning multiple rules to one control.

Assigning multiple rules to one control

[e.g.]

Example: Assigning Multiple Rules to One Control

Let us assume that in your SAP system, you want to check the segregation of duties with regard to entering incoming invoices and entering purchase orders. In this case, you would think of both an authorization-based evaluation (preventive control)

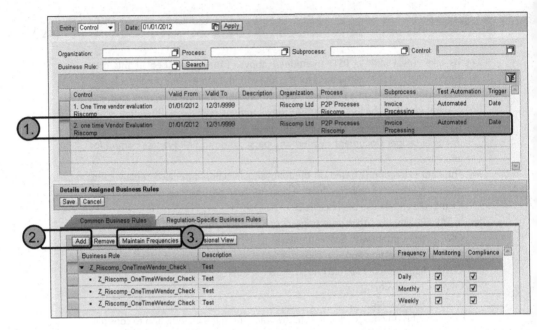

Figure 17.16   Assigning rules to a control

and a document-based evaluation (detective control). Both evaluations can be implemented by different rules in the CMF, and both rules can be assigned to the same control.

17.3.7 And off You Go!

Centralizing the selection criteria using organization-level system parameters (OLSP)

You now know how the CMF is structured and how to set up automated test and monitoring scenarios. But how do you handle these scenarios in an ICS process? In Sect. 16.4.4, "Problem-Solving Process," you learned that, from the view of a business user, there are virtually no differences between the treatment of manual or automated controls in SAP Process Control: all ICS activities have to be processed as tasks or workflow tasks in the inbox. To plan these tasks, as shown in Fig. 17.17, amongst other things you schedule effectiveness tests of the controls in the Planner ❶. You can apply this workflow-supported activity to both manual and automated controls.

Compliance vs. monitoring

Once you have entered the effectiveness test for an automated control – that is, a control to which one or more business rules are assigned – and the start date for this test has been reached, SAP Process Control triggers the logic defined in the CMF. If the test results are negative, they are sent to the person responsible by workflow. The result can be an issue or a review task with the option of creating an issue. We therefore associate the planner with a compliance-supporting role of SAP Process Control.

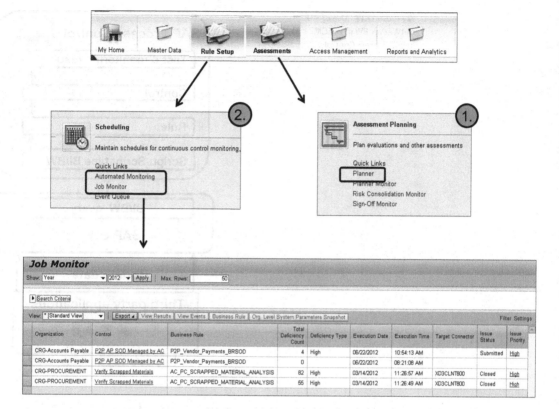

❏ **Figure 17.17** Use of automated test and monitoring scenarios in SAP Process Control

In addition to the Planner there is a further option: you can use the Job Monitor ❷ to implement the monitoring concept. This gives you an overview of all results of the active CMF scenarios. The prerequisite for this is that you have executed periodic scheduling using the AUTOMATED MONITORING option: you can use this option to create monitoring jobs with a required frequency.

The difference to the compliance-oriented use of CMF scenarios via the Planner is that with this option, the results are issued as exceptions by SAP Process Control rather than issues. Therefore, we associate the Job Monitor with the monitoring-supporting role of SAP Process Control.

17.4 Potential of CMF Scenarios in SAP Process Control

We will now give you an outlook to the as yet unused, or in practice rarely implemented potential of the Continuous Monitoring Framework in SAP Process Control: the use of Business Warehouse (also known as BI (Business Intelligence)) and the connection of SAP solutions for GRC to data from SAP BusinessObjects.

□ Figure 17.18 Use of SAP
NetWeaver BW in the CMF scenario
in SAP Process Control

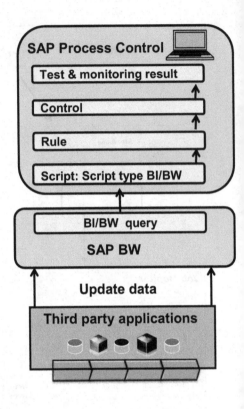

17.4.1 Use of SAP NetWeaver Business Warehouse for Continuous Monitoring

The use of BW queries in the CMF is similar to the use of SAP queries: a script of the type "Business Information Warehouse" uses a query in SAP NetWeaver BW to extract the data required and to apply it within the CMF.

Usage scenarios for
BW queries as part
of CMF

The use of BW queries can be an appropriate solution in particular for setting up the following two scenarios:

- **Key figure-based analyses**
  Many SAP customers use SAP NetWeaver BW for mapping various key figure-based analyses or reports. The individual BW-based key figures (key performance indicators, key risk indicators, etc.) can be used as triggers for workflows when criteria (threshold values etc.) defined in a rule are fulfilled.

- **SAP NetWeaver BW as agent for value analyses**
  There is great potential for the use of BW queries in their role as *link* or *agent* for the connection of third party applications to SAP Process Control. As stated in Sect. 17.3.1, "Connecting SAP Solutions for GRC with Business Applications," thanks to the high flexibility of the ETL engine (extract, transform, and load functions), the use of SAP NetWeaver BW is an alternative to the connection of third party systems to SAP Process Control based on MQT, SAP NetWeaver PI, or web services.

Figure 17.18 shows the second option: data from non-SAP applications arrives in SAP Process Control via SAP NetWeaver BW. In SAP NetWeaver BW, a BW script can

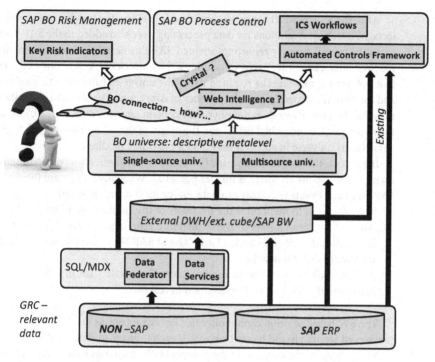

□ Figure 17.19 Existing and missing CMF integration options in SAP Process Control

query the data from the target system in real time (the info provider must be configured accordingly). Alternatively, the data has to be imported or updated in SAP NetWeaver BW periodically.

In an SAP system in which only BW scripts are used, no plug-ins are necessary as part of the integration framework. This special feature also applies to SAP queries.

The use of SAP NetWeaver BW as part of the CMF must be distinguished from the use of SAP NetWeaver BW as part of reporting. For use in customer-specific reporting, SAP NetWeaver BW contains predefined extractors for exporting the data from SAP Process Control (results of tests and assessments). For the use of BW queries as part of the CMF, the data comes from an ERP system.

Business Warehouse for GRC – reporting

17.4.2 Thoughts About SAP BusinessObjects

In Sect. 17.3, "Setting up CMF Scenarios in SAP Process Control," you learned about various options for using data from ERP systems in SAP Process Control to automate the test and monitoring scenarios. Figure 17.19 summarizes the possible routes for relevant data (at the bottom of the image) to the GRC applications. They are indicated with the word "Existing." The data from SAP systems and non-SAP systems can be used *directly* in SAP Process Control and SAP Risk Management, for example, via the PI infrastructure or web services, and via SAP NetWeaver BW.

After the SAP product range was enriched in 2008 by the purchase of BusinessObjects, new technical solutions for data processing were also added to the SAP portfolio.

In the overall strongly reporting-oriented SAP BusinessObjects environment (e. g., the SAP BusinessObjects Explorer solution), the *universes* represent one of the important options for merging the required data. The universes (divided into single-source and multisource depending on the number of data sources used) form a metalayer for the data. This *metalayer* does not physically contain any own data; instead, it describes the structure (the individual fields) and the origin of the data. Therefore, an SAP BusinessObjects universe in action is only a data-providing medium.

In practice, this data is mostly used for reporting purposes. However, in the environment of GRC solutions, there is further potential. What advantages are there in using SAP BusinessObjects universes as a data source for test and monitoring scenarios?

- The first point to mention is the *flexibility* of the connection of non-SAP systems. An SAP BusinessObjects universe therefore represents an agent, similarly to the BW option described in Sect. 17.4.1, "Use of SAP NetWeaver Business Warehouse for Continuous Monitoring."
- *No data redundancy:* The data is not "stored" separately (as in a BW system) but read from the relevant ERP application in real time.

The BW-based solution cannot offer this last advantage, as in a BW system, the data is reserved separately and has to be updated each time up-to-date results are required.

Future outlook   With regard to the contents of the potential GRC scenarios based on universes: due to the strong orientation of SAP BusinessObjects on reporting, as already mentioned, it is not analyses based on transaction data, master data, or configuration data that are desired, but aggregating KPI and KRI analyses. For the utilization options for the data from universes that can currently be implemented technically via SAP Crystal Reports or Web Intelligence, unfortunately the subscenarios necessary for integrating this data in the Continuous Monitoring Framework are missing. The options of SAP Crystal Reports in SAP Process Control are currently sufficient to represent data from universes graphically, but not to integrate the data in the CMF and thus directly in the workflow-based ICS or in risk management processes.

It would be feasible to imagine that the in-memory technology (SAP HANA) would not only have a positive effect on the analysis performance in continuous monitoring scenarios, but could also favor the integration of flexible and high-quality SAP BusinessObjects dashboards in the GRC suite, in particular an interactive drilldown of aggregated key figures or KPIs to the level of individual business transactions.

17.5   Summary

In this chapter, you have learned how to automatically monitor ICS-relevant ERP-supported processes and how to integrate this type of monitoring in the SAP Process Control-supported ICS process. In this context, it is important to understand the following: all types of data mentioned in Sect. 5.1.1, "Data in an SAP System," can be analyzed using offline or online CAATs, but also as part of the Continuous Monitoring Framework, to enable test and monitoring scenarios. The option of mapping such test and monitoring scenarios in a compliance management application such as SAP Process Control offers many advantages compared to offline and online CAAT tools.

Experiences from Practice and Projects

Theory without practice is of little benefit. Therefore, this chapter summarizes practical experiences from real projects.

In this chapter we present findings about project management for the implementation of SAP Process Control, as well as examples from practice of how SAP customers have automated their own ICS and compliance management processes.

18.1 Practical Experiences: Projects for ICS and Compliance Automation

The implementation of SAP Process Control is less complex than that of SAP ERP. With certain prerequisites, which we will address in this chapter, an organization can execute an implementation project with only a moderate amount of external support. In this chapter, you will learn which tools make the implementation easier, and which topics to focus on when creating a blueprint. You will also learn which project structure has established itself as best practice and which factors influence the effort involved in and success of a project.

18.1.1 Tools for Implementation

The technology is not one of the challenges when implementing SAP Process Control: the complexity of the application can be categorized as medium. We have already addressed some of the details of the implementation of SAP Process Control in Chap. 16, "ICS Automation Using SAP Process Control": in brief, SAP Process Control consists of workflows that are applied to master data objects, and authorization roles that connect objects, workflows, and people to form an ICS process. *(Low technical complexity)*

The greatest challenges consultants face is in the issue of "automated test and monitoring scenarios" through the integration with ERP systems (see Chap. 17, "Implementation of Automated Test and Monitoring Scenarios in the SAP ERP Environment"). Again, the reason for this is not the technology used in this special area (Automated Rules Framework (ARF)), but the process-specific, ERP-specific, and compliance-specific know-how that a consultant must have in order to be able to suggest and implement the ARF scenarios. This know-how represents a considerable success factor in a project (see Sect. 18.1.6). *(High know-how demands)*

At this point we will restrict ourselves to the technology: some points make the implementation process much easier.

The mere mention of the necessity of setting up workflows makes SAP customers who know the complexity of this topic shudder. As far as Process Control is concerned, *(Preconfigured workflows)* you can relax: the workflows in Process Control are preconfigured and all you have to do is activate them as part of the post-installation activities (see Sect. 16.2.1, "Technical Architecture and Installation"). What are sometimes adapted in practice are the roles that control the workflow-supported ICS process (see Sect. 18.1.3, "Business Blueprint").

Workflows are not the only thing that SAP has preconfigured: for all main Process Control (PC) elements, default values for the configuration are available in Business Configuration (BC) Sets. Again, all you have to do is activate these BC Sets.

BC Sets

BC Sets are available in Process Control in the following areas:
- **Roles**
  The authorization roles in BC Sets correspond to the SOX-driven and FDA-driven best practice ICS process.
- **Attributes**
  The attributes (required for the documentation of an ICS framework) are based on the COSO study.
- **Compliance initiatives**
  Two compliance initiatives are preconfigured – SOX and FDA.

The procedure model *Accelerated SAP* (ASAP) can also be applied to the implementation of SAP Process Control.

ASAP Roadmap content

SAP Process Control-specific content is available for the ASAP Roadmap tool. This content primarily consists of checklists, guidelines, and examples for a project plan. The level of detail of the ASAP approach for SAP Process Control corresponds to the relatively low complexity of the application.

Further tools and documentation sources

The following tools and documentation sources are also helpful:
- **Handling master data**
  For a mass upload of master data to SAP Process Control and Risk Management, the Master Data Upload Generator (MDUG, see Sect. 16.4.1, "ICS Documentation Process") is available, and since Release 10.0, Content Lifecycle Management.
  Consultancy companies offer a range of solutions for overcoming some disadvantages of standard tools: for example, the GRC Upload Tool from Riscomp can upload local data, that is, organization-specific controls (the MDUG tool cannot do this).
- **Documentation**
  In addition to the extensive documentation in the Implementation Guide, SAP Service Marketplace offers useful guidelines; the SAP Community Network and the standard training course GRC330 are a must for an SAP Process Control consultant.

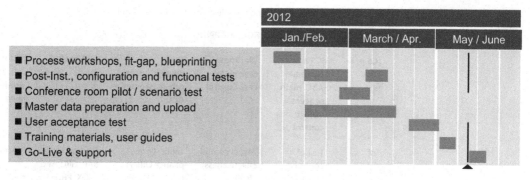

☐ Figure 18.1   High-level project structure for the implementation of SAP Process Control

18.1.2 Best Practice Project Structure for ICS Implementation

Figure 18.1 shows a compressed presentation of a project plan for implementing SAP Process Control. In this presentation, the individual work packages have been summarized at the level of project phases.

The structure of the high-level project plan, which comes from a project at a medium-sized organization, is easy to record – assuming that the processes to be implemented do not deviate greatly from the SAP standard functions and roles. Note the following special features:

- Conference room pilot phase
- Relatively large proportion of master data preparation in the overall project

The conference room pilot approach has established itself as a best practice. It involves a simulation of the ICS process to be implemented with the participation of key persons in the project (for example, project sponsor, ICS and compliance owners, internal audit, process owners, etc.). The documented ICS process is very abstract, and the joint simulation of this process allows the project participants to develop a better understanding of the aims of the project. In an ideal case, here, the participants experience their first (joint) success in the project.

Conference room pilot

The implementation of automated test and monitoring scenarios can have a considerable influence on the project structure. How strong this influence is depends on the number and complexity of the scenarios to be implemented. Here, the documentation and the test phase are important – see Sect. 18.2.2, "Integrated GRC Approach at Tecan."

18.1.3 Business Blueprint

A blueprint document records the process to be implemented and the technical details of the implementation. Based on experience, what makes up the core of the blueprint for the PC-based ICS automation?

From a content view, the document can be divided into the "manual" ICS process and the specifications for individual automated test and monitoring scenarios. In the

Manual and automatic

□ Table 18.1 Procedure for deriving the roles for SAP Process Control

PROCESS MAPPING		ROLE MAPPING			
ICS pro-cess	ICS activity, customer ABC, main process object: control	Workflow task in Process Control	Task owner/business role, customer ABC	ABAP role	ABAP role assignment level
ToC	Test of control (ToC)	Test of control effectiveness (TOE)	Group Compliance Officer ICS	Standard role SAP_GRC_SPC _SOX_PRC_ TESTER	Process
ToC	Issue handling for ToC	Issue TOE	Local Compliance Officer ICS	Custom, to be created	Organization
ToC	Issue handling for ToC	Remediation plan TOE	Process owner	Custom, to be created	Process
ToC	Review remediation results	Review remediation plan TOE	Local Compliance Officer ICS	Custom, to be created	Organization

manual ICS process, the focus is on the role-based presentation of the ICS process and the handling of ICS master data.

Roles as key to the ICS process
The key to the definition of an ICS process in SAP Process Control is the matrix of ICS activities and objects (for information about ICS modeling, see Sect. 15.1.2, "Concept of ICS Automation," and 17.1.1). The *roles* required can be derived from this matrix.

When defining the required roles, analyze the options for using or adjusting standard roles contained in BC Sets.

ToC requirements of authorization roles
Table 18.1 shows an example of a section of such a matrix:

1. As you can see, here, the ToC (test of control) process is mapped to the standard workflow *Test of control effectiveness* (effectiveness test) and this enables requirements of the authorization roles to be derived.
2. Once all relevant ICS activities (see Sect. 16.4.1, "ICS Documentation Process") have been covered by such overviews, the demand for each role and assignment level is consolidated to obtain the final list of required roles and the high-level definitions of their content.
3. The required roles are then mapped against the standard roles to determine the adjustment requirement where applicable.

The ARF is also considered in the role definition, as the automatically generated test and monitoring results are issued to the person responsible by workflow on a role-specific basis.

Master data
In addition to roles, the blueprint creation also focuses on the master data. The following is usually defined:

- The deviation of the individual attributes from the BC Set values
- List and specification of any required custom fields (object concerned, field type, length, etc.) as well as a list of all reports to which these custom fields have to be added
- With regard to the maintenance of the ICS framework, in particular, the procedure for the initial upload of the master data and, where applicable, further uploads as part of rollouts must be considered. There are various technical means available for doing this, for example, MDUG and, since Release 10.0, Content Lifecycle Management.
- As already stated, some consultancy companies offer their own solutions that allow you to overcome a range of disadvantages of standard tools: for example, the GRC Upload Tool from Riscomp can upload local data, that is, organization-specific controls.

If, in an implementation project, further customizing is required beyond adjusting the roles and creating custom fields, for example, setting up new compliance initiatives or even modifications or development (for example, customer-specific reports etc.), this must also be taken into account in the documentation.

Setting up automated test and monitoring scenarios requires special consideration in the blueprint phase. Whilst under some circumstances, you can set up and expand content for the individual scenarios later in live operation, you have to consider process-related and role-related issues within the ARF – that is, who the results have to be sent to by workflow – in the blueprint phase.

During the blueprint: planning control automation

The same applies to the GRC Integration Framework: setting up a connection between SAP Process Control and an SAP ERP system via RFC can take very little time, but connecting third party systems can require extensive technical specification.

18.1.4 ICS Content

The effort and expense involved in setting up an ICS framework that contains all major risks in all relevant processes and the corresponding controls can be enormous. Anyone who experienced the great SOX implementation wave will know what that means. The quality and degree of maturity of an ICS framework should be very high when SAP Process Control is implemented – even if when introducing compliance management software, we can assume that the ICS framework does not remain fixed but is developed further.

Content more expensive than software

Project Experiences   **[e.g.]**

Experience shows that a Process Control implementation project can also become an ICS redesign project. This is true, for example, if, at the start of the project, the internal control system (ICS) is only partially documented and initial ICS basic research has to be performed and investments made in content development. However, there are also customers (usually with a SOX background) whose standardized risk and control matrices can be converted into an uploadable template within a few days.

It is not only the effort required for the initial development of the ICS framework that makes the content so important: from the previous chapters, you know that an ICS framework is made up of many objects that co-determine the functions and the ICS process as a whole. Therefore, for SAP Process Control implementation, even perfect content has to be brought into a structure that enables the desired ICS process.

Functions   The following functions can also have a great influence on the ICS structure:

- **Shared services concept**
  In particular, this function can influence the structure of the IT general controls (see Sect. 16.4.1, "ICS Documentation Process").

- **Authorizations**
  In SAP Process Control, the assignment of rights for certain ICS activities is connected to authorization objects and their hierarchies – remember the concept of object-related security (see Sect. 16.5.2, "Object-Related Security in Action").

- **Reports**
  Hierarchical levels in the ICS master data are both selection levels and aggregation levels for the results.

- **Scoping**
  Remember the three options in the data model for linking risks with controls and subprocesses (directly, using control objectives, and using account groups): it is obvious that the data model has to be considered as one of the scoping options for the risk assessment.

ICS content and   The most important moments regarding handling of ICS content during a Process
Process Control   Control implementation project can be summarized as follows:

- **Initial upload of ICS master data**
  Up to Release 3.0, you can use the MDUG for this. From Release 10.0, the Content Lifecycle Management-supported functionality is also available.

- **Post-upload setup**
  Once the data has been uploaded to the system, only a few steps are required to ensure ongoing maintenance and traceability of the changes:

  - *Ongoing maintenance*
    You can set up workflows for this (see the "Segregation of duties principle for the maintenance of the ICS framework" section in Sect. 16.4.1). Mass uploads of new ICS content may also be necessary.

  - *Traceability of changes*
    Here, some technical prerequisites have to be fulfilled, such as the activation of table logging and the profile parameter `rec/client`.

ARF as ICS content   The ICS content in SAP Process Control includes scripts and analysis rules, including their assignment to the individual controls in the ARF (see Sect. 17.2.1, "Continuous Monitoring Framework"). However, in an implementation project, the road to this content is long and requires the right expectations. The importance of the documentation of the automated test and monitoring scenarios must not be neglected: every test and monitoring scenario requires its own specification. Therefore, the ARF content is one of the important product-specific contents of SAP Process Control that you have to develop first in an implementation project.

18.1.5 Factors that Influence the Project Expense

The expense involved in implementing SAP Process Control depends on many factors. The most important cost drivers are:

Cost drivers

- **Project approach**
  When you are deciding whether to adopt a pilot approach or a big bang approach, the first option is clearly recommended. In a pilot approach, you can use the know-how obtained in the project to execute later rollouts with internal resources as far as possible. Process adjustments may also cause lower costs if only a few units in the organization are affected.
- **Adjusting the authorization roles**
  The existing standard roles link the ICS objects to the ICS activities to form a best practice ICS process in SAP Process Control. If the desired procedure deviates from this standard process, you have to adjust ABAP authorization roles or create new ones; you often have to adjust the standard portal roles as well.
- **Custom fields**
  Where necessary you have to create additional fields and make them available in reporting.
- **Master data preparation**
  You have to reserve enough time for filling out the upload template (see Sect. 16.4.1, "ICS Documentation Process"). The effort required depends on the format and the quality of the risk and control matrix.

From this list, you can see that if you want a lean approach for the implementation, you have to base the implementation on the standard functions and the standard ICS process of SAP Process Control and have a mature and well-documented ICS framework. Keeping to the standard functions only in the GRC environment for cost reasons, without analyzing the improvement potential, would be an incorrect approach (with regard to the success factors, see Sect. 18.1.6).

The use of *automated test and monitoring scenarios* delivers the greatest added value for the ICS process, but is also associated with an effort that is not to be underestimated:

Continuous Monitoring Framework

- The risk-oriented analysis of the existing ICS framework to identify the potential for automation – including a cost/benefit analysis
- Tasks such as designing the selection criteria (system parameters at organizational level vs. rules) and connecting target systems to SAP Process Control technically represent a one-time effort.

When you implement any CMF scenario, you have to perform the following steps:

Implementing a CMF scenario

1. Every scenario requires a separate document that records the following:
   - Risk addressed
   - Control objective
   - Frequency
   - Underlying data model
   - Target systems
   - Type of analysis
   - Script type or subscenario in the data source

- Where applicable, technical implementation of the data selection
- Selection criteria
- Where applicable, maintenance of the report variants
- Rules for the analysis

2. You should also consider an estimation of the data volume, particularly for transactional controls. (Caution: you must consider system performance here.)
3. With the exception of the use of predefined rules, standard reports, or configurable scripts for which tables can be included in an analysis directly, for all other technical solutions, in the target ERP system, you have to establish either an SAP query or a program for extracting the data.
4. As you already know, the subsequent implementation in SAP Process Control involves the creation of the scripts and analysis rules, maintenance of the same, and subsequent linking of the rules with controls.

You have to reserve sufficient time for testing the CMF scenarios.

> **Approximate Estimation of the Efforts in the CMF Area for Each Control**
>
> The following is a graduated overview of the efforts in the CMF area:
> - **Low**
>   The effort for setting up automated test and monitoring scenarios for SAP ERP can be classified as relatively low when configurable scripts or data sources, predefined rules, and SAP standard reports are used.
> - **Medium**
>   The effort for SAP query-based automation and for more complex configurable scripts or data sources can be classified as medium.
> - **High**
>   This category generally includes non-SAP systems, as well as the development of specialized ABAP programs for SAP systems based on the GRC development framework.

18.1.6 Success Factors

The recipe for a successful implementation of SAP Process Control can be summarized in just a few points.

Start with a Proof of Concept or Pilot Project

Clear project scope
A clear project scope at the very beginning is the key to success.

- Begin with a proof of concept (PoC) or by building a prototype – with no "Go live" (optional). For the implementation, aim for a pilot approach ("Go live" with one or a few reporting units with subsequent rollouts).
- If you are using automated test and monitoring scenarios, as far as possible, include all types of technical implementation options (script types). The overall number of these scenarios in a pilot project should be manageable.

Do not Economize on Your GRC Processes

A successful project primarily means that the added value for your organization is noticeable. Many organizations see this added value amongst other things in saving on the implementation in the short term by, for example, restricting the implementation to standard roles of SAP Process Control and to the BC Set-based standard configuration. A one size fits all approach is rarely suitable for automating business processes. The situation is similar for automating your GRC management processes. The survival of your organization is not at risk in the event of a short-term failure of the SOX compliance process – it would still work using Microsoft Office. However, efficient design of your ICS can help your organization to fully exhaust the potential of your business processes. Therefore we recommend the following:

- Take time in the design phase. There is a lot to think about, particularly for integration scenarios: it is not just about the ICS process and your ERP systems, but also about embedding the ICS in performance, strategy, and risk management.
- The flexibility that the software introduces, for example, via the adjustment of roles, attributes, or configuration of compliance initiatives etc., should be fully exhausted where necessary.

ICS Content

Be open to suggestions from your consultant about risks and controls in your ERP-supported business processes. You may know your processes inside and out, and you will have improved and refined your ICS framework over the years, but due to the complexity of the ERP systems, numerous system risks and some good control mechanisms in the ERP environment remain hidden to everyone except for process experts from operative business or from the ICS compliance area. To successfully automate test and monitoring scenarios, you will often have to make changes or additions to your ICS framework for the following reasons:

Adjusting the existing ICS

- Not all possible control mechanisms have been identified for the risks you have detected.
- A control covers multiple possible control mechanisms.
- Not all relevant risks in your ERP-supported business processes are recognized.

Correct Know-How

The installation and post-installation of SAP Process Control requires the standard SAP Basis proficiencies in the SAP NetWeaver environment that are sufficiently available on the market.

In contrast, designing and mapping the GRC processes requires a range of skills from various disciplines. You will need a wide range of support in various work packages:

Support required

- To map the compliance management processes, you will need input from contact persons from risk management, ICS officers, the SOX compliance team, internal audit, etc.
- When automating test, monitoring, and risk analysis scenarios in the ERP environment, you will need access to the knowledge on process configuration in SAP Application Support and, where applicable, the knowledge of business analysts, particularly if ERP standard processes have been modified or adjusted.
- Last but not least: for the technical implementation of some scenarios you will need to develop ABAP reports or queries.

Requirements of
a consultant
During the implementation of SAP Process Control, high demands are placed above all on consultants:

- Knowledge of the implementation as well as process know-how of the GRC products of SAP is required.
- A compliance and ERP auditing background is essential.
- Furthermore, knowledge of the compliance-relevant SAP ERP standard processes, the underlying data models, and in particular, the most important application controls is a must: even if other specialists perform the technical part of the implementation (for example, the SAP infoset-based or ABAP-based test and monitoring scenarios), it is the consultant who has to create the technical specification.

18.2   Project Examples for ICS and Compliance Automation

We now present some organizations that have automated their ICS compliance processes with our support. You will learn how organizations of various sizes satisfy the ICS compliance requirements, what experiences were gained from implementation projects, and what benefits have already been achieved from the ICS automation.

18.2.1 Coverage of Swiss Compliance Requirements at KUONI

KUONI is one of the leading travel agencies in Europe. It has made a name for itself particularly in the premium segment and as a specialist for themed trips. The main branch of the company is in Zürich, Switzerland. KUONI has branches in more than 40 countries and employs just over 9000 employees.

General Conditions

KUONI is registered on the Swiss Stock Exchange and therefore has to fulfill the requirements of the Swiss Obligations Code, which requires the existence of an ICS (see Sect. 1.3.3 for details of Swiss compliance requirements).

ICS structure at
KUONI
To satisfy these requirements, KUONI has introduced an ICS based on the COSO study. Using a risk-based top-down approach, significant risks as well as relevant processes and related control mechanisms in external reporting were identified.

The controls were divided into three large groups:

- **Entity level controls (ELC)**
  KUONI considers some IT controls to belong to the entity level controls that also contain ICS basic concepts (behavior code, descriptions of workplaces, guidelines, and procedure instructions). In turn, these basic concepts represent the basis for an efficient ICS.
- **Process level controls**
  This group contains control mechanisms in the processes of financial accounting, sales and distribution, accounts payable accounting and accounts receivable accounting, purchasing, as well as payroll accounting.
- **General information technology controls**
  This group classically (see Sect. 3.2.2, "CobiT") represents three areas: program development and configuration, access to programs, data, and the computer center operation.

General Information Technology Controls		

This is a KUONI-specific term that was retained for the implementation. In this book, these controls are referred to as *IT general controls*.

The existence and effectiveness of approximately 1500 key controls is monitored in 23 reporting units. A total of approximately 250 people are involved in the ICS process. The process contains mainly the planning, execution, processing of measures, and reporting as part of the following ICS activities:

- The *assessment* of the design and the *monitoring* of the execution of controls are based on the documentation of the self-assessment that has to be performed by the control owner.
- The Group Compliance Officer at KUONI performs the *test* of the effectiveness of controls.
- As part of the *audit*, the internal audit department at KUONI and the external auditors document their independent assessment of the ICS set up.

ICS activities of KUONI

Motivation

What motivated KUONI to look for ICS software solutions? As you can imagine, an ICS process that is to a large extent manual is not the most efficient:

- **Documentation**
  Risk and control matrices were documented in Microsoft Excel, process descriptions in Microsoft PowerPoint, and the Extranet was used for document storage.
- **ICS activities**
  The test and assessment results were documented in Microsoft Excel-based and Word-based survey lists and sign-off documents. Any issues found and measures for rectifying them were documented in the same way.
- **Monitoring and reporting**
  In these circumstances, efficient and timely monitoring of the ICS environment and real-time reporting were not possible.

After a selection procedure, in which ten software providers participated, SAP Process Control was the winner. The main criteria for the selection were the high level of user-friendliness, the results of the cost-benefit analysis, and the high degree of coverage of the ICS process at KUONI by the best practice scenario of SAP Process Control.

Implementation

The complexity of the implementation project at KUONI can be classified as low; the facts can be summarized as follows:

- Overall, the project sequence corresponded to the structure presented in Sect. 18.1.2, "Best Practice Project Structure for ICS Implementation."
- The implementation was performed by an external consultant (the author of this book) and the Group Compliance Officer ICS at KUONI, with support from the KUONI IT department.

- The core of the KUONI ICS process supported by SAP Process Control is represented by workflow-based tests and assessments and the processing of issues and remediation plans.
- Four main roles were set up to map the KUONI-specific ICS process:
  - Control Performer
  - Local Compliance Officer ICS
  - Group Compliance Officer ICS
  - KUONI Auditor

  Review steps were activated based on four preconfigured workflows.
- The entire ICS framework of KUONI was transferred to SAP Process Control in a template-based master data upload (via MDUG).
- As part of a pilot project, two reporting units in Switzerland went live initially. For the selected implementation approach, in which both functions and master data were already set up for the whole of KUONI (the workflows followed the same structure for all units and were uploaded via MDUG at the beginning of the project), the further rollouts required only the setting up and assigning of new users.

Project Experiences and Next Steps

Efficient and intuitive process in action

KUONI's objective of establishing an efficient ICS compliance process was achieved, even without the use of automated test and monitoring scenarios:

- The intuitive usability of SAP Process Control, which required a minimum training effort, was particularly highlighted: the distribution of role-based training material with just a few pages for the process description was sufficient.
- The ICS documentation became much easier to handle. Furthermore, the logging functions in SAP Process Control ensured the traceability of all changes – something that was impossible in a manual, Microsoft Office-based ICS process.
- The administrative effort was reduced considerably: reminders via e-mail, centralized planning of tests and assessments, as well as a report-based monitoring of ICS activities save time.
- The real-time view of the status of the ICS compliance using standard reports has replaced the time-consuming Microsoft Excel-based ex post procedure in which results of tests and assessments had to be brought together manually and with great effort.

Harmonization, control awareness, transparency

Overall, according to statements from the company, through this strongly centralized approach in the ICS that was mapped in SAP Process Control, KUONI "has achieved greater harmonization of the ICS and process documentation. Control awareness and transparency have also increased generally."

What are KUONI's plans now? After a successful rollout of SAP Process Control 3.0 and two years of positive experience with this application, KUONI is planning to upgrade to the latest GRC Release, 10.0. The company is also thinking of enhancing SAP Process Control by adding another GRC component that is fully integrated with SAP Process Control: SAP Risk Management. This will enable an integrated compliance and risk management process. With the aim of connecting non-SAP applications to SAP Process Control 10.0, KUONI will also be looking more closely at the automated test and monitoring scenarios in the ERP environment.

18.2.2 Integrated GRC Approach at Tecan

Tecan is a leading global provider of laboratory instruments and solutions in biopharmaceuticals, forensics, and clinical diagnostics. The company specializes in the development, production, and distribution of automated workflow solutions for laboratories in the life sciences sector. Its clients include pharmaceutical and biotechnology companies, university research departments, and forensic and diagnostic laboratories. Founded in Switzerland in 1980 by engineers and enthusiasts, the company now has manufacturing, research, and development sites in both Europe and North America and maintains a sales and service network in 52 countries.

The word *innovation* is a key priority at Tecan – not only in the core business but also in the compliance area. In the author's opinion, Tecan was the first company worldwide to successfully implement a fully integrated risk-oriented approach in its own compliance management processes based on the SAP solutions for GRC 10.0. The author of this book executed and led the implementation in ramp-up mode in spring 2011.

General Conditions

Just like KUONI (see Sect. 18.2.1, "Coverage of Swiss Compliance Requirements at KUONI"), Tecan is registered on the Swiss Stock Exchange and therefore has to fulfill the requirements of the Swiss Obligations Code. It is therefore important to stress here that the driving factor behind the ICS automation was a correspondingly high prioritization by the management at Tecan and not the strict SOX regulations of the Securities and Exchange Commission with regard to an ICS.

Contents and handling of the ICS framework

Before automation was considered, the ICS at Tecan was handled manually. It consisted mainly of:

- Process controls from the areas of information technology, closing and consolidation, general ledger, asset accounting, accounts receivable and accounts payable accounting, treasury
- Segregation of duties rules for the processes mentioned

Motivation

Manual ICS processes are known for taking up a lot of time and resources. The effects are as follows:

- Although Tecan succeeded in implementing a centralized approach (depending on the scope, certain controls are applied in an organizational unit), a standardized manual maintenance of controls in Microsoft Excel is a challenge.
- Manual interpretation and collation of the survey results, the sample execution and documentation of tests, and the consolidation of results and creation of reports are also time-consuming activities.
- The segregation of duties rules, for which manual observance in the maintenance, and in particular, in the assignment of roles in the SAP environment is almost impossible.
- The effort for recurring manual evaluations in SAP systems (the IT landscape at Tecan is dominated by SAP applications) builds up over the year.

⌃ **Timeline and approach**

- **End 2010:** content & process definition phase
- **February 2011:** ramp-up implementation
- **May 2011:** pilot go-live (Swiss entities)

⌃ **Key facts:**

- **Continuous Monitoring (CM) in focus**
- **Custom roles in Process Control, custom risk rules in Access Control**

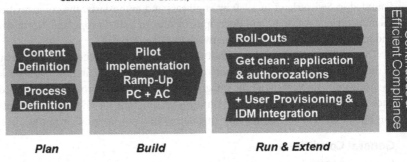

❑ **Figure 18.2** High-level overview of important project phases

Project

Pioneer with GRC 10.0

To automate the ICS compliance process and make it as efficient as possible, above all integrated in the SAP ERP landscape, the company decided on Release 10.0 of SAP Process Control and SAP Access Control. Before the ramp-up implementation phase of the project began in January 2011, the planning phase (content and process definition) had been running since October 2010. In this phase, the main objectives detailed below were achieved.

The existing ICS framework was updated: in particular, treasury processes that were set up (also SAP-supported) in the year before the GRC implementation and that were not sufficiently mapped in the ICS framework were affected. These included both process controls and segregation of duties rules.

CMF scenarios

Another important point was the identification of potential CMF scenarios (ARFS, Automated Rules Framework Scenarios: internal project name for continuous monitoring scenarios). To do this, documented risks in Tecan's ICS framework were investigated and approximately 35 relevant RAMS (Riscomp Automated Monitoring Scenarios) and five relevant predefined automated controls in the SAP solutions for GRC 10.0 were identified. In order to avoid endangering the tight time targets for a ramp-up project, 20 ARFS were selected for implementation based on the principle of "highest risk covered and lowest effort incurred."

The content and process definition phase was completed with the creation of a business blueprint containing the GRC processes to be implemented.

Figure 18.2 shows the overview of the most important project phases and objectives. With a complete revision of the standard role concept, the introduction of customer-specific segregation of duties rules and 20 ARFS, and the integration of SAP Access Control and SAP Process Control, the Tecan implementation project for the SAP solutions for GRC 10.0 can be classified as medium-sized.

☑ **20 automated test & monitoring scenarios are implemented**

- **ITGC: Change Management, Security**
- **General Ledger, Assets Accounting, P2P, O2C, Treasury**

☑ **Wide variety of technical options in GRC 10 was used**

- **Data Source types used: Programmable self-developed, Programmable pre-delivered, Configurable, SoD integration Access Control, ABAP reports**
- **Deployment models: timeframe vs. point in time; value vs. change log check etc.**

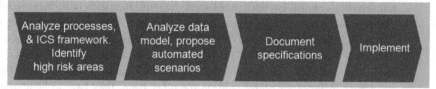

Analyze processes, & ICS framework. Identify high risk areas → Analyze data model, propose automated scenarios → Document specifications → Implement

Continuous Control Monitoring – implementation steps

☐ **Figure 18.3** Implementation of CM scenarios at Tecan

The implementation of ARF scenarios was one of the central highlights of the project. The following findings are worthy of mention:

Continuous Control Monitoring

- The new CM Framework (Continuous Monitoring) in Release 10.0 of Process Control offers considerable improvements and more flexibility. In particular, configurable scenarios have proven very beneficial: the majority of scenarios were implemented using this technical option.
- With a complex logic, particularly when change documents occur in combination with an evaluation, ABAP development can no longer be avoided. However, here too the structured ABAP Development Framework for GRC is beneficial.
- The implemented ARF scenarios were centralized in Process Control.
- The implementation of each scenario can be viewed as an independent implementation project – with all usual phases and steps. Figure 18.3 shows which phases the implementation of an automated scenario in Process Control runs through.

The following short-term and medium-term objectives were achieved in the SAP Process Control implementation project:

- The workflow-based processing of surveys and tests reduced the administrative effort and enabled a real-time view of the status of ICS compliance using report functions.
- As the internal auditor at Tecan stated, the reduction of the administrative effort led "to the possibility of using the time saved for more demanding tasks."
- At the beginning, the automatic scenarios set up uncovered a few "surprises." No serious violations or fraud cases were discovered, but the processes still had to be adjusted, particularly in the area of change management and the authorization concept.
- Thanks to the logging functions in the SAP solutions for GRC 10.0, the ICS compliance management process as a whole now demonstrates audit-compliant traceability.

- Overall, the implementation of the SAP solutions for GRC 10.0 at Tecan led to more reliable controls and thus to a stronger ICS.

The low level of training required was also highlighted as one of the positive project experiences: the processing of the workflow-based tasks proved to be very intuitive, even for users who otherwise rarely work with SAP Process Control.

What are the further objectives of Tecan in relation to the SAP solutions for GRC 10.0? While the rollouts of Process Control continue and a new (cleaned up) authorization concept has been established, the implementation of further modules of SAP Access Control is being planned: Compliant User Provisioning, Superuser Privilege Management, Integration of GRC with Identity Management. In parallel, a further function of the Risk Analysis & Remediation component already implemented is being introduced: mitigating controls. On one hand, these controls will be part of the ICS framework in Process Control, and on the other hand, they have to be assigned to mitigate risks in the event of violations of segregation of duties.

Operational compliance as objective

As already stated, the implementation of the *continuous compliance and monitoring concept* was part of the big vision of the customer that was successfully realized. One of the most important project findings is that at Tecan, the implementation of ARF scenarios for specialist departments demonstrated a clear potential, not only in the direction of compliance, but also for monitoring business process efficiency. At present, ideas are being gathered and the proposal for setting up new scenarios prepared. This makes the systemization of the topic of "operational compliance in the SAP environment" undertaken in this book even more significant (see Sect. 3.1.5, "Structure of Efficiency-Oriented and Profitability-Oriented Controls in the ERP Environment," and Chap. 14, "Examples of Efficiency-Oriented and Profitability-Oriented Analysis Scenarios in SAP ERP").

18.3   SOX at Ericsson

The name Ericsson does not require much explanation. With headquarters in Stockholm, Sweden, Ericsson is one of the largest global providers of technologies and services for operators of telecommunications networks. The facts: more than 1000 networks in 176 countries use technical systems from Ericsson, and 40 % of all calls on cell phones worldwide use Ericsson systems. Ericsson has been present on the telecommunications market for 134 years, and in this period, has registered approximately 25,000 patents: the company's product range includes mobile and fixed network-based infrastructures, telecommunications services, software, and broadband and multimedia solutions for network operators, organizations, and the media industry.

Ericsson's spirit of innovation is not reserved only for products and services – internal processes can also be termed "state of the art." This also applies to the SOX compliance process: according to Ericsson, PricewaterhouseCoopers rates it as one of the best of its kind. At present, this process ensures high transparency and reliability with regard to external financial reporting. In this report, you will learn what this process consists of and which steps Ericsson has undertaken to make the SOX compliance and ICS management processes more efficient.

18.3.1 ICS Framework at Ericsson

Ericsson is subject to the US SOX requirements as described in Sect. 1.2.1, "SOX in the USA." In order to satisfy these requirements, Ericsson has established an ICS framework that is divided into four areas: | Four areas

- Entity level controls
- Key controls relevant for financial reporting (or process controls)
- Segregation of duties controls
- General IT controls

You will see that the structure is somewhat different to the structure recommended in Sect. 3.1.4, "Structure of a Classic ICS Framework in the ERP Environment": the segregation of duties controls have been separated as an independent control area and general application controls are part of general IT controls. Let us look firstly at the Ericsson-specific definitions of the individual control areas. | Specific structure

Entity level controls have an overarching effect on Ericsson's ICS and relate generally to the environment of internal controls. This environment is the ICS framework; it influences the control awareness of the employees and represents the foundation for all other ICS components – provided the required measure of discipline and correct structures are in place in the organization. The control environment, and thus the ICS framework, is made up of three elements: integrity, ethical values, and the competence of the employee; leadership philosophy and leadership style; distribution of managerial authority and responsibilities and advancement of employees by management.

Key controls relevant for financial reporting are part of the business processes at Ericsson, as shown in Fig. 18.4.

The key controls are intended to minimize risks within a specific business process that could have a direct influence on external financial reporting. These key controls are documented in the form of a flowchart to make their integration in the general processes clear and to describe them in separate documents, as shown in Fig. 18.5. | Key controls

Segregation of duties controls are intended to ensure that transactions and business processes are handled correctly overall by individual employees in order to avoid error and fraud risks. | Segregation of duties controls

At Ericsson, the following activities must generally not be combined:

- Administration of property values: access to and control over cash, checks, assets, stocks, and products
- Authorization: approval process for business transactions
- Recording: entry of postings, maintenance of master data, and maintenance of various data in Human Resources
- Control activities: checking the accuracy, approval, and timeliness of business transactions recorded

Ericsson differentiates between two types of segregation of duties controls: | Two types

- **System-based segregation of duties**
  Limitation of access and access combinations for relevant transactions in Ericsson's ERP systems

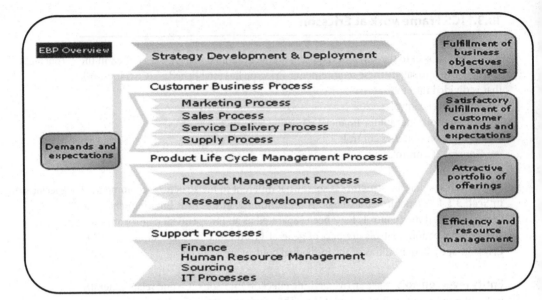

□ **Figure 18.4** Overview of the business processes at Ericsson (source: Ericsson)

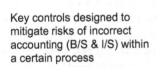

Key controls designed to mitigate risks of incorrect accounting (B/S & I/S) within a certain process

Key controls are mapped into the process charts – in accordance with the process flow

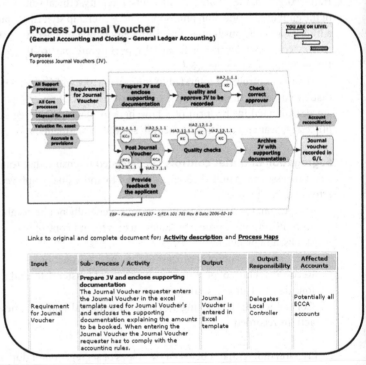

□ **Figure 18.5** Example of process documentation (source: Ericsson)

- **Manual segregation of duties**
  Here the aim is to ensure (for example, from an organizational perspective) that critical activities in processes relevant for financial reporting are not concentrated on one person.

IT key controls are mandatory for applications that support processes relevant to financial reporting. The aim of these controls is to guarantee an IT environment in which the reliability of financial figures is ensured. In the IT world at Ericsson, which is heavily oriented around outsourcing, these controls are primarily performed by external IT service providers. Despite this, Ericsson assumes responsibility for the effectiveness of controls, which are structured as follows:

IT key controls

- **IT change management controls**
  The aim of these controls is to ensure that all changes in the IT infrastructure and in the IT applications are requested, authorized, tested, and approved correctly before they are implemented. This should guarantee the accuracy and an appropriate quality of the intended functions.
- **Access controls**
  The aim of these controls is to ensure that only authorized persons have access to master and transaction data, and that these persons can only use those functions intended for them.
- **Controls in the computer center operation**
  These controls are intended to ensure the correctness of procedures such as monitoring, scheduling, backup, and recovery.
- **Network controls**
  These controls are aimed primarily at the security of systems relevant for financial reporting that can be accessed via the Ericsson Corporate Network (ECN). The aim is to exclude unauthorized use, disclosures, manipulation, or loss of data.

18.3.2 SOX Compliance Process at Ericsson

The SOX compliance process established at Ericsson is based on a risk-oriented top-down approach (see Sect. 2.2.1, "The Auditor's Focus") that consists primarily of three steps:

Risk-oriented top-down approach

- Identification of risks that can impair the reliability of financial reporting
- Analysis of the processes with regard to the presence of controls that can cover the risks identified
- Check of supporting documents for control execution

In order to fulfill the requirements of SOX 404 (see Sect. 1.2.1, "SOX in the USA"), all Ericsson companies have to demonstrate efficient entity level controls. Furthermore, the compliance of the process controls has to be proven at 52 Ericsson companies that, in total, make up 85 % of sales. In this context, manual segregation of duties controls are considered part of entity level controls. Segregation of duties controls implemented as part of the IT-supported authorization concept affect all companies at Ericsson that use SAP.

In 2004, Ericsson started the SOX implementation initiative for all companies. To support the compliance process, Ericsson implemented Risk Navigator and Access

Start of implementation

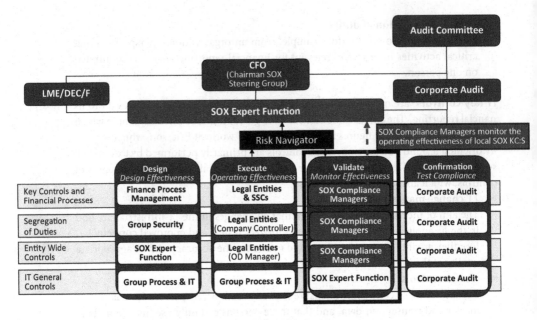

☐ **Figure 18.6**   Roles and steps in the compliance process (source: Ericsson)

Control. The decision to implement Risk Navigator was taken by the Finance Process Board in 2004. This is a web-based tool that – combined with the SNAP reporting tool – represents a very simple and user-friendly software solution used at Ericsson for documenting, tracking, assessing, and signing off controls.

Process participants   Who is involved in the SOX process at Ericsson? As you can see in Fig. 18.6, numerous experts from IT, compliance, and business departments are involved in this process, both at central and corporate level and at the level of local companies.

The central team, consisting of SOX experts, monitors the SOX compliance process at corporate level. The SOX experts (four persons) are supported in this task by local SOX compliance managers (18 persons).

According to its own statement about the effectiveness of the ICS, the management at Ericsson relies on several sources, as you can see in Fig. 18.7. The sign-off process required is triggered on a quarterly basis.

Executing and testing controls   The monitoring of the fulfillment of SOX compliance requirements has been established as a permanent process. All Ericsson companies have to regularly confirm the execution of controls (in self-assessments). The issues identified and the measures for rectifying these risks are documented in Risk Navigator. At some Ericsson companies, the controls are also subject to an independent internal and external assessment by an auditor whose primary aim is to check the effectiveness and design of the controls (in independent tests or tests of effectiveness).

A sign-off process is also triggered quarterly across the entire Ericsson organization. In this process, the management of all Ericsson companies has to acknowledge the current status of control execution and any issues present and confirm the effectiveness of the ICS. You can see the details in Fig. 18.8.

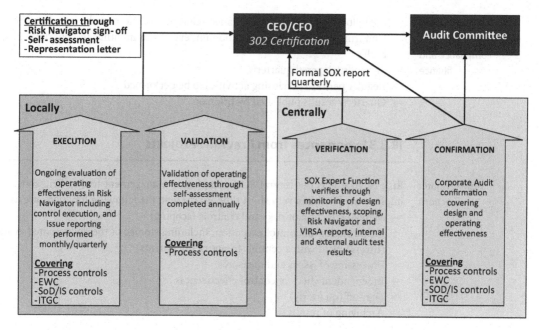

◘ Figure 18.7 Four ICS assurance sources for management (source: Ericsson)

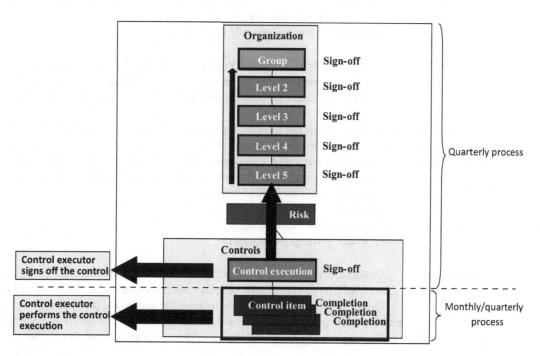

◘ Figure 18.8 Sign-off process at Ericsson

Connection
between
compliance and
finance

The following important compliance-relevant cycles are synchronized at Ericsson:
- Confirmations of control execution undertaken in monthly and quarterly planned cycles
- Sign-offs triggered quarterly
- Regular period-end closing activities to be performed
- Quarterly results published by Ericsson

18.3.3 Experiences from Previous Projects

Risk Navigator
functions

Risk Navigator is the central SOX compliance management tool at Ericsson. It was implemented within a very short time. At present, the following functions are used:
- Manual selection of risks and controls (scoping)
- Confirmation of control execution, including storage of the documented evidence (this is linked with a central storage of documents)
- Processing of issues and measures
- Independent check of control effectiveness
- Sign-off (quarterly)
- Archiving of results

Standardized
processes at
Ericsson

The smooth implementation of the tool-supported SOX process can be traced back to the fact that the business processes at Ericsson are very homogeneous:
- All companies use the same chart of accounts and the same ERP system (SAP ERP).
- The role-based authorization concept is centralized.
- Business processes are generally standardized.

The ICS framework defined on this basis is comprised of centrally documented key controls that are implemented for all relevant Ericsson companies. The centrally controlled SOX compliance process, consisting of the steps described, can be categorized as very efficient.

Tools for
authorization risks
and controls

Risk Navigator is not the only application with compliance relevance that Ericsson uses. To cover ICS issues regarding authorization, Ericsson uses SAP Access Control. This application was implemented globally from January 2005 to December 2007, and was categorized as the largest implementation worldwide (source: SAP AG 2007). Ericsson uses three Access Control components:
- Risk Analysis & Remediation
- Compliant User Provisioning
- Superuser Privilege Management

Balance sheet
reconciliation

Another application with direct compliance relevance (operative control execution) is AssureNET. It is a web-based application that is used for balance sheet reconciliation.

The aim of this reconciliation is to increase the quality and transparency of external financial reporting. Since 2008, AssureNET has been used at all Ericsson companies that are supported by an internal shared service center and that use an SAP ERP system.

18.3.4 Optimization Potential

Ericsson is interested in a permanent improvement in its own processes, and this also applies to the SOX compliance process. One of the possible means for improvement is the automation of manual test and monitoring scenarios. The potential is obvious – automation can save costs without impairing compliance. What is more, this automation can potentially increase the reliability of test results, simplify tests and assessments, avoid unnecessary activities thanks to the risk-oriented approach, and possibly reduce the cost of the external audit.

Good, better, automated

A further improvement potential option would be lower management workload due to the exception-based monitoring approach: an activity (for example, processing an issue or a remediation plan) only becomes necessary when there is an actual problem case.

Ericsson would also like to analyze further improvement potentials that offer risk-based scoping. The workflow technology also promises an increase in efficiency for tests, assessments, and sign-off activities. Workflows themselves can be seen as an automation of ICS activities.

In addition to the objective of satisfying the SOX articles, the important thing is to establish a stronger ICS. The shift of focus from detective controls to preventive controls that can be achieved, amongst other things, through automated test and monitoring scenarios, would not only strengthen the ICS on paper, but also where these controls are actually settled: in the business processes of Ericsson.

Strengthening the ICS

18.3.5 Steps Towards Optimization

Ericsson has consistently undertaken the concrete steps towards optimization of the SOX compliance management process over the last years. Last but not least, Ericsson performed a proof of concept (PoC) with SAP Process Control, with support from SAP AG and in particular, the author of this book.

Proof of concept

The aim of this PoC was to demonstrate that the existing compliance process can be mapped in Process Control to identify improvement potential.

The PoC was performed in two steps. In the first step, the current process, which is supported by Risk Navigator, was analyzed and recreated in a Process Control application. According to the results of the first PoC, the following functions in Process Control can effectuate improvements and increases in efficiency:

PoC: Step 1

- Materiality-based and risk-based scoping process
- Workflows and approval process for changes in the ICS framework documentation
- Centralized and flexible planning for compliance activities
- Workflow-based compliance activities
- Offline processing of workflow tasks (in Release 3.0 of Process Control, modification was required here)
- Aggregation of deficiencies functions
- Policy management function (since Release 10.0 of Process Control)
- Traceability and evaluation capability for all changes in the ICS framework documentation
- Flexible handling of local deviations in the ICS framework

PoC: Step 2   The second PoC step focused on the potential of automated test and monitoring scenarios and analyzed the content of the ICS framework (all key controls of Ericsson). The following was documented:

- SAP Process Control can be integrated with the Ericsson SAP ERP systems to analyze configuration data, master data, and transaction data in the ARF.
- Test and monitoring scenarios set up in this way can support or even replace a number of existing key controls.
- The integration with Ericsson's SAP NetWeaver BW could enable automated KPI monitoring, particularly as part of Ericsson's quality control framework (the Financial Quality Index is primarily relevant here).
- The Audit Information System in the Ericsson SAP ERP system, which is currently not used to the full extent, could be integrated in the ARF.
- SAP Process Control can be integrated with SAP Access Control, which Ericsson already uses – in particular, Risk Analysis & Remediation and mitigating controls (integrated since release 10.0). This would finally give a standardized view of the ICS (processes and authorizations) in Process Control.

The absolute majority of potential test and monitoring scenarios identified refer to the Ericsson SAP systems (currently ECC 6.0). A few scenarios would also be possible in non-SAP systems to cover ICS areas associated with high risks from a SOX compliance perspective.

The two basic options for implementing test and monitoring scenarios in Process Control can be divided into two models:

- **Replacement**
  This is the option of implementing a control in Process Control such that it is fully automated; the criteria for automatic generation of an issue are clearly defined. This issue is assigned to the person responsible for control execution or effectiveness tests.
- **Facilitation**
  This relates to semi-automated controls. Here, Process Control assigns a task rather than an issue to a person responsible. The task is to analyze the result of an automated evaluation and introduce follow-up measures where applicable.

As a result of a PoC performed, in which the author of this book supported Ericsson, and after weighing up the *total cost of ownership* (TCO) vs. identified improvement potential and increases in efficiency, Ericsson took the decision to implement SAP Process Control.

18.4   Review of the Stages of Evolution of the ICS and Conclusion

Content vs. process in an ICS   Literature and studies describe different development levels of the ICS, covering primarily categorizations that refer to the quality and reliability of an ICS (with regard to the content). Figure 18.9 shows an illustration that can be found on the official website of the IT Governance Institute.

According to this illustration, the status characterized as *Optimized* is the status that should be aimed for. Many organizations that categorize their own ICS as *optimized*

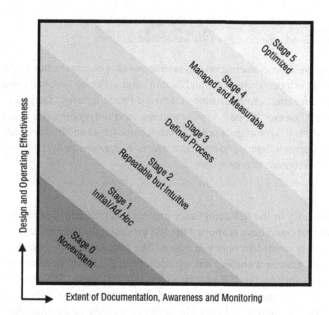

Design and Operating Effectiveness

Stage 5 Optimized

Stage 4 Managed and Measurable

Stage 3 Defined Process

Stage 2 Repeatable but Intuitive

Stage 1 Initial/Ad Hoc

Stage 0 Nonexistent

Extent of Documentation, Awareness and Monitoring

◻ Figure 18.9 Quality and reliability of controls (source: IT Governance Institute, IT Control Objectives for Sarbanes-Oxley)

are referring to the quality and reliability of their own controls. They often do not consider the efficiency of the activities around these controls (from a *process view*): even if a compliance process is primarily based on documentation in Microsoft Excel and Word, and communication takes place via e-mail, due to the perfect content of the ICS framework the ICS as a whole is also deemed perfect.

Here, therefore, we would like to highlight a further characteristic that is often forgotten and that, according to the *IT Governance Institute*, is required to fulfill "optimized ICS" prerequisites. The characteristic in question is the automation of the ICS and the compliance management processes:

> Technology is leveraged to its fullest extent to document processes, control objectives and activities, identify gaps, and evaluate the effectiveness of controls (Source: IT Governance Institute).

As a procedure for viewing the ICS primarily as a *process*, the different stages of evolution in the ICS process are presented below.

Anyone who remembers the great "SOX wave" and was involved in the implementation or checking of the ICS compliance processes knows what is meant by the first ICS evolution stage.

First Evolution Stage – Handmade Compliance

In the first stage, the ICS implementation was seen above all as documentation of the ICS. The end result of a documented risk and control framework may have had some undisputedly positive effects, such as harmonization and clear structuring of processes in an organization; however, the path to this result was long and winding, and at the end, compared to the ICS compliance process implemented based on Microsoft Excel and e-mail, was a rather inflexible and inefficient structure – however perfect the content, that is, the ICS content, may have been.

The lack of efficiency in the ICS compliance process was primarily due to missing software solutions that could have supported the ICS process – the software market reflects needs, and these needs had only just arisen. The first versions, for example, of Aris Audit Manager, may have enabled amongst other things control documentation, but they still did not support the ICS process as a whole efficiently. The experiences from the first phase, the expansion of existing and the creation of new software solutions, including Process Control and Risk Management, introduced another phase in the development of the ICS.

Phase Two – Efficient ICS Processes and the Birth of GRC

Organizations that have not got stuck in the Microsoft Excel phase have recognized the potential of ICS automation and have used either commercial or in-house developed compliance management software to make the ICS process more efficient and enable real-time reporting about the status of compliance.

The direct participation of process and control owners in the ICS process, for example, in the form of confirming control execution, is a further characteristic of this phase.

Seen from the legally prescribed compliance side, organizations started to expand the content of the ICS framework with operative objectives and risks.

The GRC vision was born: ICS compliance is no longer a stand-alone topic, but rather an element of corporate governance that is closely connected to risk management.

During the time in which the second edition of this book was being prepared, from winter of 2011/2012 to printing in September 2012, some pilot and PoC projects ran that focused on the automation of test and monitoring scenarios in SAP Process Control. SAP and other software manufacturers have recognized the potential of *continuous compliance and monitoring*, and the next stage of evolution was introduced. Some software manufacturers started to implement this vision much earlier (before 2007), but the offline approach of CAAT (see Sect. 17.1.1), which was implemented technically in products such as Approva BizRights, was associated with many disadvantages.

The Beginning of the Present – Continuous Compliance and Monitoring ❗

The automation of control tests and assessments, and the monitoring of key performance indicators and key risk indicators are parts of the integrated ICS and risk management process that marks the current breaking phase. Within the scope of the recognized reference models, the topics of GRC and business performance management are getting closer.

What will the future bring? Without wanting to look too deeply into the crystal ball, we refer again to the "merging of GRC, strategy, and performance topics" already described in Sect. 16.6.4 and that is the subject of current work: compliance, controls, risk, performance, and strategy are coming together in a software-supported process.

References

References

Behera, R.: Cross-Enterprise Integration with SAP GRC Access Control. Boston (2009)

Biskie, S.: Surviving an SAP Audit. Boston (2010)

Buchner, R.: Wirtschaftliches Prüfungswesen, 2nd edn. Munich (1997) (Available in German language only)

Däubler, W., Klebe, T., Wedde, P., Weichert, T.: Bundesdatenschutzgesetz – Kompaktkommentar, 3rd edn. Frankfurt am Main (2010) (Available in German language only)

Gola, P., Klug, C., Körffer, B., Schomerus, R.: BDSG. Bundesdatenschutzgesetz, 10th edn. Munich (2010) (Available in German language only)

Hartke, L., Hohnhorst, G., Sattler, G.: SAP-Handbuch Sicherheit und Prüfung, 4th edn. (2010) (Available in German language only)

Helfen, M., Trauthwein, H.M.: Testing SAP Solutions, 2nd edn. SAP PRESS (2010)

Hellberg, T.: Einkauf mit SAP MM, 2nd edn. Bonn (2009) (Available in German language only)

Horwath, P., Schäfer, H.-T.: Prüfung bei automatisierter Datenverarbeitung, 2nd edn. Berlin (1983) (Available in German language only)

Leffson, U.: Wirtschaftsprüfung, 4th edn. Wiesbaden (1980) (Available in German language only)

Lehnert, V., Bonitz, K.: Authorizations in SAP Software: Design and Configuration. SAP PRESS (2010)

Linkes, M., Karin, H.: SAP Security and Risk Management, 2nd edn. SAP PRESS (2010)

Maurer-Lambrou, U., Vogt, N.P.: Basler Kommentar Datenschutzgesetz, 2nd edn. Zurich (2010) (Available in German language only)

Minz, G., Zepf, G.: Computergestützte Jahresabschlussprüfung. Erfordernis, Möglichkeiten und Voraussetzungen. Betriebswirtschaftliche Forschung und Praxis **36**(5) (1984) (Available in German language only)

Minz, G.: Ansätze einer Prüfungstheorie für computergestützte Buchführungssysteme. Wirtschaftsprüfung **36**(18) (1983) (Available in German language only)

Montgomery, R.H.: Auditing Theory and Practice. New York (1912)

Oberhofer, B.: Datenschutz und Arbeitsrecht (Vol. Handbuch Datenschutzrecht) (2009) (Available in German language only)

Schäfer, M., Melich, M.: SAP Solution Manager Enterprise Edition, 2nd edn. Bonn (2009)

Schuppenhauer, R.: Grundsätze für eine ordnungsmäßige Datenverarbeitung (GoDV). Handbuch der DV-Revision, 5th edn. Düsseldorf (2005) (Available in German language only)

Siebert, J.: The SAP General Ledger, 2nd edn. SAP PRESS (2010)

Tinnefeld, M.-T., Ehmann, E., Gerling, R.W.: Einführung in das Datenschutzrecht, 4th edn. Munich (2004) (Available in German language only)

Wiegenstein, A., Schumacher, M., Schnizel, S., Weidemann, F.: Sichere ABAP-Programmierung. Bonn (2009) (Available in German language only)

Withus, K.-H.: Internes Kontrollsystem und Risikomanagementsystem – Neue Anforderungen an die Wirtschaftsprüfer durch das BilMoG. Die Wirtschaftsprüfung. Institut der Wirtschaftsprüfer in Deutschland e.V., (Ed.), Issue 17/2009 (Available in German language only)

Legislation and Directives Referenced

Loi de Sécurité Financière [Financial Security Act], France

Financial Statements Act, Denmark

Auditors' Act, Denmark

Aktiengesetz (AktG) [Stock Corporation Act], Germany

Bilanzrechtsmodernisierungsgesetz (BilMoG) [Accounting Law Modernization Act], Germany

Handelsgesetzbuch (HGB) [Commercial Code], Germany

Strafgesetzbuch (STGB) [Penal Code], Germany

Obligationsrecht (OR) [Obligations Code], Switzerland

Aktiengesetz (AktG) [Stock Corporation Act], Austria

GmbH-Gesetz (GmbHG) [Limited Liability Companies Act], Austria

Public Company Accounting Reform and Investor Protection Act (US SOX), USA

Gesetz zur Kontrolle und Transparenz im Unternehmensbereich (KonTraG) [Control and Transparency in Business Act], Germany

National Instruments (NI), Canada

Financial Instruments and Exchange (J-SOX), Japan

Basic Standard for Enterprise Internal Control, China

Foreign Practice Act, USA

Health Insurance Portability and Accountability Act (HIPAA), USA

Code of Federal Regulations (CFR), Title 21, USA

Bundesdatenschutzgesetz (BDSG) [Data Protection Act], Germany 2009

Datenschutzgesetz (DSG) [Data Protection Act], Austria 2000

European Union: Directive 95/46/EC of the European Parliament and of the Council of 24 October 1995 on the protection of individuals with regard to the processing of personal data and on the free movement of such data, Official Journal L 281, 11/23/1995

Council of Europe, COE: Convention for the Protection of Individuals with regard to Automatic Processing of Personal Data, 01/28/1981

Organisation for Economic Co-operation and Development, OECD: Recommendation of the Council Concerning Guidelines Governing the Protection of Privacy and Transborder Flows of Personal Data, September 23, 1980

UN General Assembly: Guidelines for the Regulation of Computerized Personal Data Files, December 14, 1990

US Department of Commerce: Safe Harbor Principles – Privacy Policy, 2000

Verordnung zur Durchführung des Datenschutzgesetzes (VDSG), Switzerland 1993

Internet Sources

German Federal Office for Information Security: IT-Grundschutz Catalogues, available at: www.bsi.bund.de/EN

German-speaking SAP user group (DSAG) SAP audit guides, data protection guides, etc., available at: http://www.sap.com/germany/about/company/revis/infomaterial/index.epx

SAP AG: Users and roles (BC-SEC-USR), available at: http://help.sap.com/

SAP AG: Security Guides, available at: http://service.sap.com/securityguide

The Author of this Book

Your GRC experts.

Maxim Chuprunov completed his studies in business administration, including various research projects, as a scholarship student of the German Academic Exchange Service in 2001 with his thesis on the topic "Auditing in the SAP Environment." Since then, he has remained loyal to this topic and is consistently expanding it in the GRC (governance, risk, and compliance) field. His specialist area includes connecting the specialist and compliance-specific views of business processes with technical solution know-how.

Before Maxim Chuprunov founded RISCOMP GmbH (Switzerland) at the end of 2010, he was employed at KPMG DTG in Munich, Germany and KPMG LLP in Boston, USA, as well as at SCHENKER AG in Essen, Germany, and SAP AG in Zürich, Switzerland.

At KPMG, he worked in the Information Risk Management and IT Advisory areas. In parallel to numerous projects at international groups of companies, he successfully completed professional exams to become a CPA (Certified Public Accountant) and CISA (Certified Information Systems Auditor), as well as acquiring certification as FI/CO consultant for SAP. At SCHENKER AG (Essen), he was responsible, within the scope of global rollouts, for the implementation of the FI and CO processes with SAP, including reporting to SEM.

In 2007, Maxim Chuprunov joined the Center of Expertise Financials & Compliance at SAP Switzerland. In his function as Senior Consultant, he has performed pioneering work in implementation projects and proofs of concept for SAP solutions for GRC with a focus on ICS automation. He is known in SAP Solution Management circles as an expert and creative force in tests and software design for SAP Process Control, and holds training courses for SAP Education.

Contributors to this Book

Reto Bachmann is a project manager in the Operational Excellence area at Mettler-Toledo International, Switzerland. From his time as an SAP consultant, he has around seven years of project experience in logistics-related topics, mainly in the consumer electronics, pharmaceuticals, and food industries (FMCG). He subsequently moved to the internal audit team of a Swiss chemical company, where over a period of four years, he developed and implemented data analyses for assessing the efficiency of the controls and the correctness of SAP processes effectively and with a view to cost optimization. He has since been active in similar roles at a Swiss pharmaceuticals company and for Mettler-Toledo International.

Reto Bachmann actively contributed to Chap. 14 of this book.

In SAP Business Development, **Günther Emmenegger** is responsible for the life sciences industry in the EMEA economic zone and India. After studying mathematics and applied physics in Freiburg im Breisgau, Germany, he worked in German space research and for 19 years, for a French chemical and pharmaceutical group. After four years as a validation consultant at an SAP implementation partner, since 2001 Günther has been active in various roles for life sciences customers of SAP.

Günther Emmenegger actively contributed to Chap. 13 of this book.

Jan Laurijsen studied business sciences, with a focus on business administration and engineering as well as information management. Since 1987 he has been working at Ericsson, and in this time, has gathered extensive experience in the areas of controlling, process management, and project management. He is responsible for the efficient design of the SOX compliance processes at Ericsson.

Jan Laurijsen provided considerable support with regard to the Ericsson practical report from Chap. 18.

Since 2000, **Volker Lehnert** has been active in various roles around compliance and security at SAP. Since 2012, he has been working for SAP AG Installed Base Maintenance and Support (IMS) as project manager for data protection. Volker Lehnert is the co-author of the data protection guide produced by DSAG, co-author of the SAP PRESS bestseller "Authorizations in SAP Software: Design and Configuration," and co-author of the book "Datenschutz in SAP Systemen" [Data Protection in SAP Systems].

Chapter 11 of this book was written in cooperation with Volker Lehnert (except Sect. 11.2).

For many years, **Marc Michely** has been involved with the optimization of process flows and controls in organizations in an international environment. As an auditor and consultant, he gathered experience in these areas and at PricewaterhouseCoopers Switzerland, in the System and Process Assurance department, focused on the area of central monitoring of organizational processes at shared service centers in international companies.

Chapter 12 of this book was written with support from Marc Michely.

Reviewer of this Book

Annett Nowatzki is an auditor and tax consultant and has worked at both Coopers & Lybrand and KPMG during her career. She has been active in various management positions, and in 2005, became a partner at KPMG. In 2010, she moved to the executive board of DSJ Revision und Treuhand AG. In addition to creating and auditing year-end and group financial statements in accordance with the German Commercial Code (HGB) and IFRS, she has extensive experience in auditing IT systems (particularly SAP). She has accompanied SAP implementations in numerous large and medium-sized organizations in Germany and other European countries from an audit perspective.

Index

Printed in the United States
By Bookmasters